T&T CLARK HANDBOOK OF CHRISTIAN ETHICS

Forthcoming titles in this series include:

T&T Clark Handbook of Analytic Theology, edited by James M. Arcadi and James T. Turner, Jr.
T&T Clark Handbook of Colin Gunton, edited by Myk Habets, Andrew Picard, and Murray Rae
T&T Clark Handbook of Theological Anthropology, edited by Mary Ann Hinsdale and Stephen Okey
T&T Clark Handbook of Christology, edited by Darren O. Sumner and Chris Tilling
T&T Clark Handbook of Christian Prayer, edited by Ashley Cocksworth and John C. McDowell

Titles already published include:

T&T Clark Handbook of Pneumatology, edited by Daniel Castelo and Kenneth M. Loyer
T&T Clark Handbook of Ecclesiology, edited by Kimlyn J. Bender and D. Stephen Long
T&T Clark Handbook of Christian Theology and the Modern Sciences, edited by John P. Slattery
T&T Clark Handbook of Thomas. F. Torrance, edited by Paul D. Molnar and Myk Habets
T&T Clark Handbook of Christian Theology and Climate Change, edited by Ernst M. Conradie and Hilda P. Koster
T&T Clark Handbook of Edward Schillebeeckx, edited by Stephan van Erp and Daniel Minch
T&T Clark Handbook of Political Theology, edited by Rubén Rosario Rodríguez
T&T Clark Companion to the Theology of Kierkegaard, edited by Aaron P. Edwards and David J. Gouwens
T&T Clark Handbook of African American Theology, edited by Antonia Michelle Daymond, Frederick L. Ware, and Eric Lewis Williams
T&T Clark Handbook of Asian American Biblical Hermeneutics, edited by Uriah Y. Kim and Seung Ai Yang
T&T Clark Handbook to Early Christian Meals in the Greco-Roman World, edited by Soham Al-Suadi and Peter-Ben Smit

T&T CLARK HANDBOOK OF CHRISTIAN ETHICS

Edited by

Tobias Winright

t&tclark

LONDON • NEW YORK • OXFORD • NEW DELHI • SYDNEY

T&T CLARK
Bloomsbury Publishing Plc
50 Bedford Square, London, WC1B 3DP, UK
1385 Broadway, New York, NY 10018, USA
29 Earlsfort Terrace, Dublin 2, Ireland

BLOOMSBURY, T&T CLARK, and the T&T Clark logo are trademarks of
Bloomsbury Publishing Plc

First published in Great Britain 2021
This paperback edition published in 2022

Cover design: Terry Woodley
Cover image © RapidEye/Getty

A catalogue record for this book is available from the British Library.

A catalog record for this book is available from the Library of Congress.

ISBN: HB: 978-0-5676-7717-4
PB: 978-0-5677-0026-1
ePDF: 978-0-5676-7719-8
eBook: 978-0-5676-7718-1

Series: T&T Clark Handbooks

Typeset by Newgen KnowledgeWorks Pvt. Ltd., Chennai, India

To find out more about our authors and books visit www.bloomsbury.com
and sign up for our newsletters.

Dedicated to Harmon L. Smith who three decades ago first taught me Christian ethics and health care ethics at Duke Divinity School.

CONTENTS

ACKNOWLEDGMENTS

I am grateful to each author for their contribution to this volume. Their dedication to this project and their diligence with their chapters was phenomenal. It is worth noting that twenty women and twenty-seven men (not including me) contributed to this collection of chapters. Originally there were more women, especially women of color, who were involved; however, for very understandable and legitimate reasons, several dropped out along the way. I believe their chapters would have increased not only the pages of this already lengthy handbook but also its quality, importance, and value. That said, I am truly pleased with what we have got, which is definitely a lot.

I also wish to thank my graduate assistants, Sam Herbig, who read and commented on first drafts of the chapters, and Addison Tenorio, who read and gave feedback on two drafts of the chapters as well as assisted with formatting them and putting together an index. Finally, I am indebted to Anna Turton, Senior Commissioning Editor for Theology, of T&T Clark, for her enthusiasm and encouragement for undertaking this project, and to Veerle Van Steenhuyse, Editorial Assistant for Theology, T&T Clark, for her tremendous toil to edit and shepherd it to publication.

Introduction: Christian Ethics and the Four Sources

TOBIAS WINRIGHT

This is not the first Christian ethics handbook in T&T Clark's reputable repository of religious and theological books. Well over a century ago, in 1908, T&T Clark published *A Handbook of Christian Ethics* by Scottish philosopher John Clark Murray (1836–1917), who was Emeritus Professor of Philosophy at McGill University in Montreal, Canada.[1] Not quite two decades later, in 1925, T&T Clark published another *A Handbook of Christian Ethics*, this time by Scottish Presbyterian David Stow Adam (1859–1925), who was Professor of Systematic Theology and Church History at Ormond College, Melbourne, Australia. Each of these handbooks were monographs. Indeed, Adam's was a "manual" containing his lectures in Christian ethics for "theological students preparing for ministry."[2] The present *T&T Clark Handbook of Christian Ethics* is different from these authorial ancestors. It is instead an edited volume, containing contributions from forty-seven theological ethicists, not including myself.

A comparison of the topics addressed also reveals both similarities and differences between these earlier handbooks and this one. That this is the case should not be surprising. Although the anterior works, like the present effort, attended to the place of love in Christian ethics, as well as the development of virtues, other methodological questions, and issues pertaining to family, to the state, and to more, a century later there are moral issues—from mass incarceration to climate change, from neuroethics to cyber warfare, from the war on drugs to migration, and more—and new (although they were always there, even if wrongly excluded by the privileged and the academy) voices—from women, people of color, and persons with genders and sexual orientations that are not the same as mine—that expand the scope of the field. Even so, this new Christian ethics handbook, while exhausting to edit, does not purport to be exhaustive.[3] Hopefully it will nevertheless serve to inspire, and be a springboard for, further contributions by scholars and students of Christian ethics.

Admittedly, during the interim between those earlier handbooks and this one, other reference volumes, more like the present edition, appeared and proved very useful, at

---

[1]John Clark Murray, *A Handbook of Christian Ethics* (Edinburgh: T&T Clark, 1908).

[2]David Stow Adam, *A Handbook of Christian Ethics* (Edinburgh: T&T Clark, 1925), vii.

[3]Obviously, this handbook cannot possibly cover every moral issue. Just a note about one that readers may expect to be included in it, but is not—namely, abortion: I originally recruited an ethicist to write a chapter on it, but he later withdrew from the project, and then I recruited another ethicist to do so, but she too dropped out.

least for me over the last quarter century in both my research and teaching as a Christian ethicist.[4] I continue to rely on them, too. Although these texts obviously are not as dated as the two aforementioned handbooks, they are more or less two decades old, and even those available as revised, second editions were published around ten years ago. Again, I still make use of these volumes; they have, and should have, a long shelf life, if only because many prominent Christian ethicists contributed to them. Still, as we embark on the third decade of the twenty-first century, this seems to be an appropriate time for a new Christian ethics handbook. Yet, even this one could not keep up to date, for as I write this introduction, well after the final drafts of these chapters were submitted for publication, the COVID-19 pandemic has impacted our lives and our work. Had this deadly crisis happened earlier, I am sure another chapter would have been included on the many moral questions that have arisen with it, and some of the contributors to this volume would have given attention to how it has affected the topics of their respective chapters. To paraphrase a proverb from Geoffrey Chaucer, time and tide wait for no Christian ethicist.

Another way that this present volume *may* differ from these others is that its contributors do not represent one school or approach within the discipline of Christian ethics. Hauerwas's and Wells's *The Blackwell Companion to Christian Ethics* aims "to stretch, inspire, and develop the reader's conception of Christian worship in order to challenge, enrich, and transform the reader's notion of the form and content of Christian ethics,"[5] and its contributors share this method and goal in their chapters. Indeed, because Hauerwas (and Harmon Smith, to whom I have dedicated this volume) taught me this approach to Christian ethics, I too have employed it.[6] Nevertheless, this is not the only way I do Christian ethics; it is a part of my toolbox, and I tend to rely on it when my audience is specifically Christian. Hence, unlike that volume, I did not solicit contributors based on their agreement with me on what Christian ethics should be or how it ought to be done. Indeed, I hope that readers will study and analyze the differences, which sometimes are subtle and at other times more pronounced, between these authors' chapters.

Although I am a Roman Catholic moral theologian, I envisioned this handbook as an ecumenical effort, with multiple denominational traditions and perspectives, including Orthodox, Catholic, and a variety of Protestant contributors. The authors are all from the United States and the United Kingdom. If I had more time and space, there would be contributors, too, from continental Europe and from other continents, especially in the global South.[7] I believe that we Christian ethicists in North America

---

[4]I have in mind not only "handbooks" but also a "dictionary" and some "companions," including James F. Childress and John Macquarrie, eds., *The Westminster Dictionary of Christian Ethics* (Philadelphia: Westminster John Knox, 1986); Robin Gill, *The Cambridge Companion to Christian Ethics*, 2nd ed. (Cambridge: Cambridge University Press, 2012; the first edition was published in 2001); Stanley Hauerwas and Samuel Wells, eds., *The Blackwell Companion to Christian Ethics*, 2nd ed. (Oxford: Wiley-Blackwell, 2011; the first edition was published in 2004); William Schweiker, ed., *The Blackwell Companion to Religious Ethics* (Oxford: Wiley-Blackwell, 2005); Gilbert Meilaender and William Werpehowski, eds., *The Oxford Handbook of Theological Ethics* (Oxford: Oxford University Press, 2007).

[5]Hauerwas and Wells, *Blackwell Companion to Christian Ethics*, 3.

[6]My most recent effort along these lines is Tobias Winright, "Conscience and the Military," in *Voting and Faithfulness: Catholic Perspectives on Politics*, ed. Nicholas P. Cafardi (Mahwah: Paulist, 2020), 204–24.

[7]For a recent, intentional attempt to bridge North American, British, and German theological ethics, see Maureen Junker-Kenny, *Approaches to Theological Ethics: Sources, Traditions, Visions* (London: T&T Clark, 2019). For a global network that has conducted international and regional conferences, as well as published volumes containing contributions from nearly everywhere around the world, see Catholic Theological Ethics in the World Church (CTEWC), which was founded by James F. Keenan, SJ, https://catholicethics.com/. A recent volume of essays by

and Europe should be more engaged with—listening to, learning from, being informed by—our colleagues from other continents around the world.[8] Perhaps a subsequent handbook composed of their work will foster such constructive dialogue among Christian ethicists as we forge forward during a century when climate change and other existential threats, from pandemics to nuclear proliferation and war, remind us that we are in this together.

The only framework that I asked contributors to try to employ—whether appreciatively or critically, or both—is known as the "Wesleyan Quadrilateral" of four sources for Christian ethics. Named after Methodist founder John Wesley (1703–1791), although he never used the phrase himself, the Quadrilateral refers to "four fonts," as Patrick T. McCormick and Russell B. Connors Jr. put it, from which Christian ethicists have drawn for moral guidance: scripture, tradition, reason, and experience.[9] I confess that my request that contributors try to keep this Quadrilateral, or at least some facet of it, in their sight as they write their chapters reflected some self-interest on my part. Indeed, throughout my teaching career, my basic undergraduate Christian ethics course has been organized around it. McCormick and Connors's book, which uses "some version of this method,"[10] has been one of my regular go-to texts, supplemented with articles and book chapters by other authors who also rely on one or more, or some combination, of these four sources. The chapters in this present Christian ethics handbook, therefore, will correlate usefully with that and other such textbooks.

Still, that the contributors to this volume were invited to work in some way with these four sources for their chapters is not to say that they all did so, at least explicitly, or that they drew from all four. Nor does it mean that they understood the fonts in the same exact way. And it does not presuppose a settled consensus on how to relate and integrate them. In her recent *Approaches to Theological Ethics: Sources, Traditions, Vision*, Maureen Junker-Kenny writes, "Theological ethics is thus a *res mixta*; it draws on and relates divine revelation and human reason to each other."[11] By her account, the Bible (scripture) and tradition have to do with revelation, and philosophical accounts of the human and the individual human sciences correlate "with reason in its different forms and capacities to examine human experience."[12] Similarly, senior Catholic moral theologian Charles E. Curran observes, "A catholic approach will be open to both divine and human sources of knowledge."[13] By the small-"c" in "catholic" Curran means a broad and inclusive Christian ethics that is ecumenical and not solely Roman Catholic, and he too associates scripture and tradition with divine revelation, and reason and experience with human

some of its members, spanning five continents, addresses the moral issue of homelessness; see James F. Keenan and Mark McGreevy, eds., *Street Homelessness and Catholic Theological Ethics* (Maryknoll: Orbis, 2019).

[8]See, e.g., Tobias Winright, "Review of *Doing Asian Theological Ethics in a Cross-Cultural and an Interreligious Context*, eds. Yiu Sing Lúcás Chan, James F. Keenan, and Shaji George Kochuthara," *Horizons* 44, no. 1 (June 2017): 262–4.

[9]Patrick T. McCormick and Russell B. Connors Jr., *Facing Ethical Issues: Dimensions of Character, Choices & Community* (Mahwah: Paulist, 2002), 18. The phrase "Wesleyan Quadrilateral" is attributed to twentieth-century Methodist theologian Albert C. Outler; see Ted A. Campbell, "'The Wesleyan Quadrilateral': A Modern Methodist Myth," in *Theology in the United Methodist Church*, ed. Thomas G. Langford (Nashville: Kingswood, 1990), 154–61.

[10]McCormick and Connors, *Facing Ethical Issues*, 19.

[11]Junker-Kenny, *Approaches to Theological Ethics*, 5.

[12]Ibid., 6.

[13]Charles E. Curran, *The Church and Morality: An Ecumenical and Catholic Approach* (Minneapolis: Augsburg Fortress, 1993), 29. Also, Charles E. Curran, *The Catholic Moral Tradition Today: A Synthesis* (Washington, DC: Georgetown University Press, 1999), 48.

sources of moral knowledge. Another senior Catholic moral theologian, Margaret Farley, likewise relies on this "map" consisting of scripture, tradition, "secular disciplines of knowledge," and "contemporary experience."[14] Already, it should be evident that even these reputable ethicists, who share much in common on these four sources, deviate somewhat from each other on them, too. As Curran highlights, "Great differences exist about the meaning of human reason and experience, and how they relate to Scripture and tradition."[15] McCormick and Connors, for instance, regard reason really not as a distinct source but "the way we interpret and integrate the insights and perspectives of the other three voices, the way we pull together the wisdom of experience, Scripture, and tradition to fashion a genuinely Christian response to the question at hand."[16] Although I referred each of the contributors to this present volume to these works by Farley, Curran, and McCormick and Connors to serve as a sort of a baseline for understanding the four sources, I left it to them to determine whether and how to incorporate the Quadrilateral into their respective chapters. Indeed, a few of the contributors to this volume forthrightly identify problems and limits with this Quadrilateral approach for Christian ethics—and rightly so, in my view.

Even the first four chapters within the volume's first part, "Fonts, Grounds, and Sources of Christian Ethics," which endeavor to explicate how scripture, tradition, experience, and reason inform Christian ethics, do not merely regurgitate what these other theologians have provided. The individual chapters within the two subsequent parts of this handbook—"Approaches, Methods, and Voices in Christian Ethics" and "Issues, Applications, and Twenty-First Century Agenda for Christian Ethics"—likewise do not necessarily concur completely with the ones in the first part or with those by Farley, Curran, and McCormick and Connors. In particular, more than one interpretation of what is constituted by either reason or experience will be evident. For the most part, though, it may be safe to say that most, if not all, of the contributors agree that each of the four sources is necessary if insufficient. Where disagreement surfaces most is in regards to questions such as: How do the four sources relate? Is one source primary? How do we adjudicate tensions and even contradictions among them? While I agree with Curran that we should "not allow any one of them to be the final arbiter"[17] and that we should take care to avoid any sort of "fundamentalism"[18] and "prooftexting"[19] (not only with scripture but also with any source of moral knowledge), I think that students and scholars will especially note the greater significance of experience in many of these chapters.

As Kathryn Lilla Cox observes in her chapter on "Christian Ethics and Reason," the Wesleyan Quadrilateral entails thinking with others, sharing experiences, studying scripture, and engaging various traditions. She adds, "Used well, this multipronged method enables a more multidimensional, deeply rooted, and interwoven foundation more representative of our lives and suited to creatively address and solve ethical questions and injustices." I sincerely hope that this is the case with this *T&T Clark Handbook of Christian Ethics*.

---

[14]Margaret Farley, *Just Love: A Framework for Christian Sexual Ethics* (New York: Continuum, 2006), 182–96.
[15]Curran, *Church and Morality*, 35.
[16]McCormick and Connors, *Facing Ethical Issues*, 19. Importantly, they do not reduce reason to logic and the intellect, and they broaden it to encompass imagination, affections, emotions, conscience, and the "heart."
[17]Curran, *Catholic Moral Tradition Today*, 55.
[18]Curran, *Church and Morality*, 30.
[19]Curran, *Catholic Moral Tradition Today*, 49.

PART ONE

Fonts, Grounds, Sources of Christian Ethics

CHAPTER ONE

Christian Ethics and Scripture: Ongoing Interpretation in Good Faith

KATHRYN D. BLANCHARD

Martin Luther is perhaps most (in)famous for his insistence that Christians learn salvific truth through *sola scriptura*—scripture alone—rather than through any other source. The Protestant Reformations of sixteenth-century Europe were about many things (economics and politics, among others), but in the churches the battle could be boiled down to authority: Who could know and speak for God? If Catholics placed authority in the Roman hierarchy and its traditions, Luther placed authority in the Christian Bible. Since the Bible itself contained everything necessary for faith, he reasoned, its message should be immediately accessible to individual readers of all kinds.

This was not as simple as it seemed. The Bible, as it turns out, is quite slippery. Not everyone finds the "plain meaning of scripture" quite so plain. Within his own lifetime, Luther already found himself disagreeing vehemently with other "Bible-believing" Christians—Zwinglians, Calvinists, and Anabaptists—over what the scriptures meant with regard to things like communion, free will, military service, and other contentious topics of early modern life. Ironically, Luther himself fell back on church tradition against some of his overly zealous (in his opinion) peers, such as those who noted that scripture speaks only of adult believers, not infants, being baptized, or who believed Jesus's example of eschewing violence was binding on all of his followers, unlike Luther's proverbial hangman.[1]

But even if he was looking through a glass darkly, Luther was onto something. While there has never been a time when Christians did not also depend on tradition, experience, and reason as sources for knowing who to be and how to live, *Christian* scripture has always made the difference between *Christian* ethics and other kinds of ethics. How then does that difference work? This chapter will highlight some of the challenges to relying on "scripture alone," while still affirming that there can be no genuinely Christian ethics without the witness of Christian scripture.

[1]Martin Luther, *The Works of Martin Luther*, ed. H. E. Jacobs and A. Spaeth (Philadelphia: Muhlenberg Press, 1943), LW 54:179–80.

DEFINING SCRIPTURE

In the summer of 2018, US attorney general Jeff Sessions cited Paul's letter to the Romans in order to bolster President Trump's policy of forcibly separating immigrant children from their parents when they crossed the US border. "I would cite you to the Apostle Paul and his clear and wise command in Romans 13," he said, "to obey the laws of the government because God has ordained them for the purpose of order."[2] This reading of scripture immediately brought forth a wave of protests from other Christians, who offered either alternate proof-texts or alternate readings of Romans 13. Most notably, more than six hundred clergy members of Sessions's own denomination, the United Methodist Church, lodged (and later dropped) a formal complaint against him for child abuse, immorality, racial discrimination, and false doctrine—as evidenced by "the misuse of Romans 13 to indicate the necessity of obedience to secular law, which is in stark contrast to Disciplinary [*sic*] commitments to supporting freedom of conscience and resistance to unjust laws."[3] The entire nation watched as Christians argued among themselves over who was using or abusing scripture, over whether the Bible demanded or forbade the continued detention of migrating minors.

It is common for Christians of all stripes to refer to "the Bible" as if it were relatively self-explanatory, but the term hides a long and complicated history. Although Jesus and all of his disciples were Jews, and although the gospels and epistles draw heavily from Jewish scriptures, there were some gentile Christians in the early church who were unconvinced that Christians should be reading Jewish scriptures at all. (And the "Old Testament" itself was still a work-in-progress at the time of Jesus.[4]) In 140 CE, a bishop's son named Marcion proposed a Christian canon that excluded Jewish scriptures altogether, along with the more Jewish-sounding parts of the gospels. Against Marcion, Irenaeus of Lyons (d. 202) insisted that Christianity relied upon exactly four gospels as well as the inclusion of the Old Testament scriptures, which "do everywhere make mention of the Son of God, and foretell his Advent and Passion. From this fact it follows that they were inspired by one and the same God."[5] With Irenaeus, a majority of Christian leaders continued to look to Jewish scriptures as key to understanding (what would become) the New Testament. This was not a simple matter of theological argument but of life and death, since Christians in the Roman empire were sometimes killed for possessing Christian scriptures—and no one wanted to die for the sake of a false gospel.[6]

"The Bible" became somewhat more stable in the mid-fourth century after Constantine made Christianity the official religion of his empire. Following the first universal council

---

[2]William Barber and Liz Theoharis, "Jeff Sessions Got the Bible Wrong. We Care for Strangers, Not Rob Their Rights," *Guardian*, June 19, 2018, https://www.theguardian.com/commentisfree/2018/jun/19/jeff-sessions-biblical-heresy-immigration.

[3]Sam Hodges, "Clergy, Laity File Complaint against Sessions," *United Methodist Church News*, June 18, 2018, http://s3.amazonaws.com/Website_Properties/news-media/documents/A_Complaint_regarding_Jefferson_Sessions.pdf. The charges were later dropped, drawing a line between "political" and "personal" behavior; Tara Isabella Burton, "Methodists Drop Church Charges against Jeff Sessions over Family Separation Policy," *Vox*, August 10, 2018, https://www.vox.com/2018/8/10/17675316/methodists-jeff-sessions-church-charges-ums-dropped.

[4]See Timothy H. Lim, *The Formation of the Jewish Canon*, Anchor Yale Bible Reference Library (New Haven: Yale University Press, 2013).

[5]Irenaeus of Lyons, *Against Heresies*, ed. Alexander Roberts, James Donaldson, and A. Cleveland Coxe (Buffalo: Christian Literature, 1885), 4:10.

[6]For a helpful overview of the process by which gospels were canonized, see *The Gospel of Judas* (National Geographic Video, 2006), DVD and online: https://www.youtube.com/watch?v=eRfUJYCko24. It should be

of church bishops at Nicaea in 325, Constantine commissioned fifty Bibles from Eusebius, bishop of Caesarea, "for the instruction of the church."[7] Along with the Old Testament (which for most readers at the time meant the *Septuagint*, the ancient Greek translation of the Hebrew scriptures from which most New Testament writers drew their scriptural references), Constantine and Eusebius's Bible included the four gospels we have today (according to Matthew, Mark, Luke, and John), Acts of the Apostles, the unnamed "epistles of Paul," and possibly John's Revelation.[8] This moment marked Christian history's earliest known example of a book called the Bible, but it would not be the last time Christians tried to determine what would count as official sacred scripture.

At the turn of the fifth century, Jerome (d. 420) translated both Hebrew and Greek testaments into Latin—a language that, at the time, was more accessible to educated people in the Western empire. His translation came to be called the *Vulgate* or "common" version. Jerome began with a list of texts established by Pope Damasus in 382; he called those texts from the Septuagint that were not also found among the thirty-nine books of Hebrew scripture *apocrypha* (hidden), though many Christians still recognized them as canonical. Jerome's Vulgate essentially served as the Bible for Western Christianity through the sixteenth century, and even Protestant Reformers working on new vernacular translations still relied on it for scholarly purposes. At the Council of Trent (beginning in 1545), Roman Catholics reaffirmed their commitment to Jerome's text as the word of God for the church. They soon authorized limited translations of vernacular versions, but for centuries they continued to discourage Bible reading by everyday Christians, reserving the power to read and interpret scripture for only those with the appropriate education.[9]

In Germany, Martin Luther recognized the need for a Bible that was readable and accessible to everyday people; like Constantine, he perceived that a budding nation would need its own book and its own church. But he struggled with what to include in his new translation—not the first ever German Bible, but the first to be translated from the original Hebrew and Greek rather than from the Vulgate or Septuagint. He balked but ended up including certain books that he did not find particularly edifying such as Esther, James, and Revelation. The intertestamental writings he relegated to a separate section (the Apocrypha) that was seen as less authoritative than the Old and New Testaments between which it stood.

---

noted that this documentary's interpretation of the Gospel of Judas is disputed by other scholars; see Elaine Pagels and Karen L. King, *Reading Judas: The Gospel of Judas and the Shaping of Christianity* (New York: Penguin, 2007).

[7]Eusebius, *Life of Constantine*, trans. Cameron Averil and Stuart Hall (Oxford: Clarendon, 1999), IV.36–7.

[8]While a table of contents of Eusebius's text is no longer extant, he elsewhere wrote in a manner revealing of the complexities of the canonization process,

> Paul's fourteen epistles are well known and undisputed. It is not indeed right to overlook the fact that some have rejected the Epistle to the Hebrews, saying that it is disputed by the church of Rome, on the ground that it was not written by Paul ... But as the same apostle, in the salutations at the end of the Epistle to the Romans, has made mention among others of Hermas, to whom the book called The Shepherd is ascribed, it should be observed that this too has been disputed by some, and on their account cannot be placed among the acknowledged books; while by others it is considered quite indispensable, especially to those who need instruction in the elements of the faith. Hence, as we know, it has been publicly read in churches, and I have found that some of the most ancient writers used it. This will serve to show the divine writings that are undisputed as well as those that are not universally acknowledged. (Eusebius, "Church History," in *Nicene and Post-Nicene Fathers, Second Series*, vol. 1, trans. Arthur Cushman McGiffert, ed. Philip Schaff and Henry Wace (Buffalo: Christian Literature, 1890), 3.3.5–7, http://www.newadvent.org/fathers/2501.htm)

[9]This policy changed with Pope Leo XIII's encyclical, *Providentissimus Deus* (Vatican City: Libreria Editrice Vaticana, 1893).

Protestants have generally followed Luther down the path of two canonical testaments, one Hebrew and one Greek, perhaps with an Apocrypha in between, translated into common language and cheaply printed, the better to spread quickly. The Authorized or King James Version (KJV) of 1611, containing thirty-nine Old Testament, fourteen apocryphal, and twenty-seven New Testament books, is English's most revered example. This text was translated and edited by committee, in large part for the sake of correcting interpretive "mistakes" facilitated by earlier, more Puritanical translations. When the early twentieth century saw multiple new English translations, some Christians held fast to the elegant KJV while others welcomed even more colloquial versions. In the twenty-first century there are hundreds of English translations available; the New International Version, preferably with a study guide, is generally the best selling, due to its "mix of firm authority and breezy accessibility," which "seems to be key to the commercial success."[10]

All this is to say, defining "scripture" is far from simple, making it that much more difficult to discuss the ways scripture might relate to Christian ethics. The late Allan Verhey, a theologian dedicated to scriptural ethics, declared that there is a "fundamental unity" in biblical ethics: "there is one God in Scripture, and it is that one God who calls for the creative reflection and faithful response of those who would be God's people." At the same time, there is "astonishing diversity" in the Bible, made up of "many books and more traditions, each addressed first to a particular community of God's people facing concrete questions of conduct in specific cultural and social contexts," and told in many different genres.[11] The beginning of wisdom, therefore, is to know that virtually any sentence beginning with "The Bible says ..." should come with an asterisk and a long disclaimer.

Nevertheless, despite the diversity of scripture and the contentious nature of biblical ethics, we forge onward undaunted, knowing that all language is provisional and sensible only within communities of shared designations. It is for this reason that Pope Leo XIII could rightly speak of what the Bible "owes to" tradition: "it is owing to the wisdom and exertions of the Church that there has always been continued from century to century that cultivation of Holy Scripture which has been so remarkable and has borne such ample fruit."[12] While Christian scripture does indeed distinguish Christian ethics from other ethics, such scripture would not exist without its formulation and promulgation by Christian churches—communities of embodied Christians who, across time and space, have seen fit to identify themselves according to (some version of) the Bible.

(HOW) DO CHRISTIANS DERIVE ETHICS FROM SCRIPTURE?

Granting that "scripture" is not any more self-explanatory than "tradition," "reason," or "experience," we may nevertheless inquire into how scripture and Christian ethics are practically connected. Among the earliest Christians, Jesus himself was "the chief model and authority for ethics"; he taught by both word and example.[13] In his absence they looked to other sources of practical wisdom, including civic and household authorities,

[10]Daniel Silliman, "The Most Popular Bible of the Year Is Probably Not What You Think It Is," *Washington Post*, August 28, 2015.

[11]Allan Verhey, "Ethics in Scripture," in *The New Testament and Ethics*, ed. Joel B. Green (Grand Rapids: Baker Academic, 2013), 1.

[12]Leo XIII, *Providentissimus Deus*, 6.

[13]Charles H. Cosgrove, "Scripture in Christian Ethics," in *The New Testament and Ethics*, ed. Joel B. Green (Grand Rapids: Baker Academic, 2013), 11.

church leaders, and common sense, as well as to Jewish scripture—with significant allowances made for Gentile Christians.[14] By the late ancient period, Christians seeking ethical advice could draw from both Old and New Testaments in a variety of ways; sometimes they found a straightforward and literal instruction, other times its lessons were allegorical. The main rule for knowing whether an ethic was authentically Christian was "guided by love of God and neighbor."[15]

Today, Christians still look to scripture for ethical help in a variety of ways. Some "Bible-believing" Christians at the conservative end of the spectrum are quick to claim that they pull their ethics directly from scripture, without undue departure from the literal meaning of its words; for example, the Bible teaches that marriage is between one man and one woman, like Adam and Eve (an extrapolation from an amalgamation of Genesis 1–2), so same-sex marriage is bad; or the Bible says, "I have come not to bring peace but a sword" (Mt. 10:34), thus authorizing the use of guns for self-defense. Such claims mask both the reader's interpretive lenses and the long traditions that forged them. As it happens, the Bible also teaches that marriage is between one man and several women (Abraham, Moses, David) or even hundreds of women (Solomon), and though the practice of polygyny had largely fallen out of favor by Jesus's time, it is nowhere forbidden in scripture. As for bringing swords, the Bible also says, "Whoever lives by the sword will die by the sword" (Mt. 26:52), which the earliest Christians generally took as a prohibition against political violence. For modern Christians to equate personal firearms or even nuclear weapons with swords is already an interpretive choice that reveals preexisting intuitive and cultural commitments.

Accepting the impossibility of drawing universal Christian ethics directly from scripture (even from apparently straightforward commands like the command not to kill), some readers at the liberal end of the spectrum appear to cast off scripture's authority nearly altogether, along with that of church tradition. Reason and experience convince such readers that sinful forces like sexism, ethnocentrism, and classism have corrupted not only the traditional *interpreters* of scripture but also *the scriptures themselves*; Paul is construed as a woman-hater, while the gospel writers are found to be anti-Semitic—to say nothing of the so-called Old Testament "God of Wrath." Sometimes it may seem, as one writer puts it, "that we need protection from the Bible, or at least from its interpreters."[16] Rather than dig deeply into the particularities of Christian scripture, then, liberals are wont to gloss over the distasteful biblical specifics and draw broad overarching themes from scripture, reason, and experience—themes of liberation, of Christ's identification with the poor and oppressed, or simply of being a good person and loving one's neighbor.

These disagreements among Christians would seem to validate the Catholic hierarchy's original objections to "those who, relying on private judgment and repudiating the divine traditions and teaching office of the Church, held the Scriptures to be the one source of revelation and the final appeal in matters of Faith."[17] The more scripture's authority is decentralized, the more it can be made personal to suit every reader. With no limits on interpretation, what kind of robust meaning can the term "Christian ethics" have? However, two millennia of Roman hierarchy suggest that centralized authority is no sure

[14]Ibid., 11. See also Amy-Jill Levine, "From Jewish Sect to Gentile Church," in *The Misunderstood Jew* (New York: HarperOne, 2006), 53–86.
[15]Cosgrove, "Scripture in Christian Ethics," 16.
[16]Joel B. Green, ed., *The New Testament and Ethics* (Grand Rapids: Baker Academic, 2013), xiii.
[17]Leo XIII, *Providentissimus Deus*, 13.

path to edifying interpretations. Persecution, crusades, burnings of Jews and "witches," and inquisitions are among the most popular medieval examples of the Catholic Church's failure to read the Bible humanely; more recently, widespread cover-ups of child sexual abuse by priests have shaken many Catholics' faith in their institution. Sexual abuse, fraud, and corruption plague the Eastern churches as well.[18] Vice is not unique to any particular group of Christians; Protestants, Orthodox, and Catholics alike seem eager to prove that "there is no one who is righteous, not even one; there is no one who has understanding, there is no one who seeks God."[19]

While Christian scripture is notoriously difficult to interpret, many battles over its ethics are almost certainly a matter of bad faith. In the case of American chattel slavery, there were white Americans who claimed to find justification in their scriptures. While Paul condoned slavery (1 Cor. 7:21), the Jesus of the gospels never mentioned it: "Neither the Bible, nor the Apostles, nor Jesus Christ ever condemned the institution of slavery as a sin," so anyone who did denounce it could be accused of "politicizing" the gospel without warrant.[20] African Americans and abolitionists, meanwhile, were quick to see the political import of obvious parallels between the "suffering servant" of scripture, despised and rejected despite his innocence (Isa. 53:3), and the suffering slaves of the United States. How could two such opposing interpretations arise from the same book?

Frederick Douglass, who escaped slavery as a young man in 1838, wrote pointedly about those Christians who used scripture to support the peculiar institution. "I should regard being the slave of a religious master the greatest calamity that could befall me," he wrote; "religious slaveholders are the worst."[21] In a foreshadowing of postmodern critiques, he asserted, "most unhesitatingly, that the religion of the south is a mere covering for the most horrid crimes."[22] But despite the wretched example of these slaveholding Christians, Douglass continued to find something in scripture that made him want to identify with Christian faith. "I love the pure, peaceable, and impartial Christianity of Christ," whom he elsewhere calls "the meek and lowly Jesus"; "I therefore hate the corrupt, slaveholding, women-whipping, cradle-plundering, partial and hypocritical Christianity of this land."[23] White Americans may go to church and quote the Bible, he argued, but they lack the mercy and neighbor love that Douglass took to be the essence of Jesus's good news. Though we today might wish that reason and experience had persuaded enslavers of the utter evil they perpetrated, even if the Bible or the church did not, their shared humanity with the enslaved seems not to have been obvious to all of them.[24]

That humans can be so blind to supposedly "common sense" meanings of scripture may be partly physical. Neuroscience challenges the very notion that we get our ethics *from* scripture; to the contrary, it concurs with historical evidence to suggest that we

---

[18]See, e.g., Orthodox Church in America, "Report of the Special Investigating Committee," November 8, 2008, http://orthodoxleader.paradosis.com/documents/sic-and-sc-reports/.

[19]Rom. 3:10-11, citing Psalms 14, 53.

[20]Edward J. Blum and Paul Harvey, *The Color of Christ: The Son of God and the Saga of Race in America* (Chapel Hill: University of North Carolina, 2012), 108.

[21]Frederick Douglass, "Slaveholding Religion and the Christianity of Christ," in *African American Religious History: A Documentary Witness*, ed. Milton C. Sernett (Durham: Duke University Press, 1999), 103. First published in *Narrative of the Life of Frederick Douglass* (1845).

[22]Ibid.

[23]Ibid., 106.

[24]Blum and Harvey note that some white Christians went to great lengths to discount those teachings of Jesus that would have likely led them to an abolitionist conviction, even finding the Golden Rule impractical and unseemly; *The Color of Christ*, 108.

bring our ethical gut feelings *to* scripture to find whatever we need.[25] But the fact that we bring ourselves to scripture can also be a great strength. Fresh readings of the Bible have flourished as scholarship has become more inclusive of people with all different types of baggage. The late theologian James Cone, who wore the lenses of an African American man born and raised in the Jim Crow South, was able to pair "the cross and the lynching tree" in a way that no white Christian had thought to do.[26] The biblical scholar Amy-Jill Levine, who wears the lenses of a Jewish woman, has made a career of reading New Testament texts in ways that enhance understanding of their Jewish contexts and content.[27] While it is essential to be self-aware and self-critical, Christian readers of the Bible need not pretend objectivity. It is not shameful to live in particular bodies in particular times and spaces; it is not wrong to have gut intuitions; our needs for survival and belonging are not inherently sinful. Where we do get into trouble with scripture is in not acknowledging the earthly facts of life that shape our readings.

CHRISTIANS AND SCRIPTURE, CHRISTIANS AND ETHICS

Christian ethics is that which proclaims the good news of Christ that is found in scripture. But as we have seen, what constitutes this good news has never been obvious. As Walter Brueggemann writes, scripture's witness is "bound to remain unsettled and therefore perpetually disputatious. It cannot be otherwise."[28] Shall we then conclude that any individual, anywhere, can use any text, anytime, to make it say anything they want? By no means! As social creatures, Christians interpret scripture through relationship—with God, with one another, and with scripture itself; the good news cannot be apprehended except by "long-term pastoral attentiveness to one another in good faith."[29] Relationships, like ethics, take time to develop, effort to maintain, and space to grow and change.

Despite the unsettled and unsettling nature of scripture, Brueggemann offers a few "facets of biblical interpretation" that can help draw a minimal boundary around it. First, he says that "the Bible is forceful and consistent in its main theological claim … the conviction that the God who created the universe in love redeems the world in suffering and will consummate the world in joyous well-being."[30] This claim is not undermined by the complex history of canonical development, nor by the variety of lenses people bring to scripture; on the contrary, it sheds light on the centuries-long process of love, suffering, and redemption through which individuals and groups circulated oral traditions, wrote them down, edited them, collected them, translated them, called them sacred, and tried to work out what it meant in their daily lives. Meanwhile, he says, "there is much in the text that is 'lesser,'" that is, not essential to the main claims.[31] The good news is bigger than any particular snippet or rule or circumstance and must thus be allowed to surprise or

[25]Jonathan Haidt, *The Righteous Mind: Why Good People Are Divided by Politics and Religion* (New York: Vintage, 2012), 367. He says this is especially true for professional ethicists, who specialize in offering "post hoc justification" for their positions and actions.
[26]James Cone, *The Cross and the Lynching Tree* (New York: Orbis, 2011).
[27]E.g., see again Levine, "Jewish Sect to Gentile Church."
[28]Walter Brueggemann, "Biblical Authority," in *Doing Right and Being Good*, ed. David Oki Ahearn and Peter J. Gathje (Collegeville: Liturgical, 2005), 39–40.
[29]Ibid., 40.
[30]Ibid.
[31]Ibid., 41.

even offend us with its weirdness. We must bring "faithful imagination" to it as we read, lest we reduce scripture with "a cold, reiterative objectivity" devoid of life-giving power.[32]

Another important facet for Brueggemann is ideology, especially our own. As history and neuroscience demonstrate, each one of us—both "experts" and lay readers—ineluctably brings a multitude of commitments and assumptions to our readings of scripture:

> Historical criticism is no innocent practice, for it intends to fend off church authority and protect the freedom of the autonomous interpreter. Canonical criticism is no innocent practice, for it intends to maintain old coherences against the perceived threat of more recent fragmentation. High moralism is no innocent practice, even if it sounds disciplined and noble, for much of it grows out of fear and is a strategy to fend off anxiety. Communitarian inclusiveness is no innocent practice, because it reflects a reaction against exclusivism and so is readily given to a kind of reactive carelessness.[33]

Though any one of these approaches can and surely does see some truths, none can claim to be the definitive way to read scripture. It is therefore incumbent upon Christians, if we seek to forge a deliberate relationship between ethics and scripture, to remain in dialogue with a variety of others who can help us avoid groupthink and unmask our "vested interests."

Above all, Brueggemann says, we must be on guard against trivializing the Bible. Our capitalist, technological, and militarized society is "sorely tempted to reduce the human project to commodity."[34] Under such conditions, the Bible can be treated as another bit of technology, a way to relieve stress, eliminate ambiguity, and control unwanted forces, personal or political. True scripture is on an urgent mission to shine a light in the darkness, to share the news of the redemption of God's beloved creation. The main threats to scripture's authority are therefore existential: the notion that creation is not good, that God is not love, that there is no hope for the future. Regardless of where ideology lands us on particular matters about sex or money, guns or meat, baptism or ordination, Christians who "attend to one another in good faith" can find agreement on the big picture. "The issues before God's creation (of which we are stewards) are immense; those issues shame us when our energy is deployed only to settle our anxieties."[35] While Christians must be extra careful about discerning where one person's trivial anxiety is another person's core identity—as in cases of race, ethnicity, ability, gender, and sexual orientation—there can be a broadly shared conviction that the light entrusted to us in scripture "is for walking boldly, faithfully in a darkness we do not and cannot control."[36]

Engaging Christian scripture is what makes Christian ethics Christian, just as engagement with the Torah and Talmud distinguishes Jewish ethics, or engagement with the Buddha's teachings distinguishes Buddhist ethics. All of humanity has access to reason, so the Bible is not necessary to having ethics, or even to having *good* ethics. But only ethics that develops in conversation with the Christian Bible is distinctively Christian. Furthermore, as even Luther knew, there could be no engagement with the Bible apart from engagement with the church. Scripture was brought to life and kept alive through church traditions, through embodied human beings devoted to "walking boldly" with Christ according to their best

---

[32]Ibid., 43.
[33]Ibid., 44.
[34]Ibid., 46.
[35]Ibid.
[36]Ibid., 47.

lights—with all the pros and cons that entails. Christian scripture is not a bludgeon, a self-help book, or a policy manual; it cannot tell us, in any precise way, how to live in the twenty-first century. It is rather a witness from faithful friends in the past who found themselves changed by good news and who were inspired to share that good news with us. Christian ethics is therefore a matter of having ears to hear the good news and eyes to see what it looks like when the good news takes hold of human beings and transforms them.

SUGGESTED READINGS

Birch, Bruce C., Jacqueline E. Lapsley, Cynthia D. Moe-Lobeda, and Larry L. Rasmussen. *Bible and Ethics in the Christian Life: A New Conversation*. Minneapolis: Fortress, 2018.

Green, Joel B., Jacqueline Lapsley, Rebekah Miles, and Allen Verhey, eds. *Dictionary of Scripture and Ethics*. Grand Rapids: Baker Academic, 2011.

Krueger, Michael J. *Canon Revisited: Establishing the Origins and Authority of the New Testament Books*. Wheaton: Crossway, 2012.

Pagels, Elaine. *The Gnostic Gospels*. New York: Vintage, 1989.

Pinckaers, Servais, OP. *The Sources of Christian Ethics*, 3rd ed., trans. Mary Thomas Noble. Washington, DC: Catholic University of America Press, 1995.

CHAPTER TWO

Christian Ethics and Tradition

D. STEPHEN LONG

Is tradition a source for Christian ethics, and if so, how? Addressing this question brings together three contested terms—tradition, Christianity, and ethics. Although a formal account could be given for each of them, their material content is often disputed both by those who affirm, and those who question, their viability. "Tradition" can signify nothing more than a process of handing over or passing along. It has a negative connotation when something is handed over that should not have been. The word "traitor" comes from the same Latin word from which the term "tradition" comes—*tradere*. It also has a positive connotation when what is handed over is something worthy of being passed along. In the latter sense, "tradition" can be a source for learning and wisdom. A mentor passes along her or his wisdom to an apprentice, who in turn passes it along to another. "Tradition" can also be authoritative teaching such as rabbinic teaching in Judaism, the sayings of the church fathers and doctors in Christianity, and hadith in Islam. Some Protestant churches, however, do not hold tradition as a source of authority; only scripture is authoritative.[1]

Tradition is a source, albeit a contested one, in nearly all religious traditions.[2] It is less so in ethics, especially philosophical ethics. There are, of course, ethical traditions such as virtue, Kantian, or consequentialist ethics. Each has sources that originated them and others who passed them along, repeating, correcting, modifying, and/or expanding the original ideas. Yet ethics does not have authoritative traditions in the same way that Judaism, Christianity, and Islam do. There is no Rabbinic Court (Beit Din), Catholic Magisterium, or Islamic Ulama among philosophical ethicists that oversees the application of authoritative tradition(s). This is not to suggest that tradition is irrelevant to ethics as a philosophical discipline, but its relevance differs from that of theological or religious inquiry.

As a scholarly discipline, ethics is older than Christianity and Islam but not than Judaism. Ethics originates in the west with the Greeks, especially Plato (427–347 BCE)

[1]The Protestant *sola scriptura* does not reject tradition; it claims to stand with the early church's understanding of it. It does reject the need for the Roman Catholic magisterium and apostolic succession as the institutional structure necessary for tradition. For a contemporary defense of the Protestant *Solas* that affirms tradition, see Kevin J. Vanhoozer, *Biblical Authority after Babel: Retrieving the* Solas *in the Spirit of Mere Protestant Christianity* (Grand Rapids: Brazos, 2016), 127–43.

[2]For a good discussion of its complexity, see A. N. Williams, "Tradition," in *The Oxford Handbook of Systematic Theology*, ed. John Webster, Kathryn Tanner, and Iain Torrance (Oxford: Oxford University Press, 2007), 362–78.

and Aristotle (384–322 BCE). There are other traditions of ethics such as that found in Confucius (551–479 BCE) that have had some influence on Christian ethics (an influence that is growing more and more), but two main sources of influence on Christian ethics have been Judaism and Greek philosophy, especially virtue ethics and the Stoic natural law tradition. These are not the only traditional sources; nearly every culture or nation has moral practices that provided, or can provide, sources of ethical wisdom, and Christian ethics draws on many of them. Some Christian ethics has also allied with modern traditions of philosophical ethics, and that poses more of a problem for the role "tradition" might play in Christian ethics because of the "moral point of view" that much of modern ethics adopts.

This brief introduction to the problems associated with bringing the terms tradition, Christian, and ethics together suggests that any adequate response to the original question posed requires attention to at least these three relations: (1) tradition and ethics; (2) Christianity and ethics; and (3) Christian ethics and tradition, including rival accounts of tradition within Christianity. Each of them will be explained in turn before presenting an answer to the question how tradition is, or can be, a source for Christian ethics.

THE RELATION BETWEEN TRADITION AND ETHICS

Tradition is seldom a source of authority among philosophical ethicists. "Reason" is more central. "Experience" also has an established place, but "tradition" has little to none. The 1967 multivolume *The Encyclopedia of Philosophy* has entries on "reason," "reasons and causes," and "experience" but no corresponding entry on "tradition."[3] There is one on "traditionalism," describing the counterrevolutionary movement in France. Likewise, the *Stanford Encyclopedia of Philosophy* has multiple entries associated with reason such as "public reason," "private reason," "practical reason," and "reasons for action" that includes subsets for entries on reason: "agent neutral vs. agent relative," "justification, motivation, explanation," and "internal vs. external."[4] It too has entries on experience, but it has no entry on "tradition" per se, only "the natural law tradition in ethics." If these two influential encyclopedias are any indication, "tradition" does not garner much attention from philosophical ethicists. Given their commitment to logical analysis and their claim for scientific rigor, ethicists working in analytic philosophy have little place for tradition. Analytic philosophy often approaches ethics through a complete, hierarchical method.[5] Because of its emphasis on history and hermeneutics, continental philosophical ethics has more of a place for tradition than analytic. Virtue ethicists are generally more open to tradition as a source of moral wisdom than most other modern ethicists. The latter tend to present ethics as an action-guiding method that generates an external state of affairs that can be described independently of the agents involved because the method adopts the "moral point of view."

William Frankena (1908–1994) presented the "moral point of view" in his meta-ethical theory of justification of moral concepts by drawing on the previous work of David Hume (1711–1776). Ethical judgments are justified when they arise from a consensus by agents who are "free, impartial, willing to universalize, conceptually clear, and informed about all

[3]Paul Edwards, ed., *The Encyclopedia of Philosophy*, 7 vols. (New York: Macmillan, 1967).
[4]The Metaphysics Research Lab, Center for the Study of Language and Information (CSLI), *The Stanford Encyclopedia of Philosophy* (Stanford: Stanford University, 2019), https://plato.stanford.edu.
[5]See Julia Annas, *The Morality of Happiness* (New York: Oxford University Press, 1993), 7–9.

possible facts." This consensus is, he notes, "ideal" and not "actual." It also assumes that morality is independent of any religious or philosophical tradition.[6] Tradition, then, could have at most a minimal role in the sense that the moral point of view is passed on from Hume in the eighteenth century through many others to Frankena and beyond, but the passing on, the tradition, is not and cannot be a source of authority for the moral point of view; it stands on its own as an independent, objective, universal feature that justifies ethics.

Not all philosophical ethicists find "the moral point of view" and its rejection of tradition to be rationally defensible. Alasdair MacIntyre has argued that the practical reasoning intrinsic to ethics requires a tradition-dependent rationality. His claim is not that this kind of rationality is one option among many, as if one freely chooses either to adopt a moral point of view that abstracts from tradition or to plant a foot in a tradition without any rational justification for so doing. Nor does he argue that every tradition embodies rationality. Some do not, and to that extent, a modern philosophical ethics that rejects tradition was "in some instances right."[7] Yet MacIntyre finds that much of modern philosophical ethics, because it is inattentive to history and tradition, ignores the conditions of its own possibility. Tradition is not unthinking obedience to unjustified authorities but rather the acknowledgment that "rational justification" is "essentially historical." An ethical teaching or judgment is "advanced," as MacIntyre puts it, through "the linguistic particularities of its formulation, of what in that time and place had to be denied if it was to be asserted, of what was at that time and place presupposed by its assertion, and so on."[8] Normative ethical judgments have histories, and MacIntyre calls philosophers to be attentive to those histories.

Take, for instance, the "moral point of view." It was not developed in a neutral, scientific laboratory by scientist-philosophers wearing lab coats unsullied from historical contingencies; it too has a history, and any justification of its central concepts would have to explain why this history with its particular linguistic formations is preferable to others, including those it displaced. Why did Hume advance it? Did he?[9] What was he reacting against? Was its adoption by philosophers reasonable, or have they ignored its history? Without such a historical account, then adopting the moral point of view lacks rational justification. It becomes a philosophical dogma accepted on blind faith, and tradition is not constituted through such means. MacIntyre's analysis leads him to conclude that only "from within some one particular tradition in conversation, cooperation and conflict with those who inhabit the same tradition" can the "formulation, elaboration, rational justification and criticism of accounts of practical rationality and justice" occur.[10] This could lead to a relativism where every person can simply assert the truth of her or his tradition as self-justifying, but MacIntyre rejects this implication. His argument is that tradition is inevitable but not self-justifying. There is no place to which philosophers or theologians could step outside of a tradition or traditions, set forth a neutral method, and use it to avoid a tradition-constituted reason for normative ethical judgments, but traditions are neither impermeable nor static. They develop through the inevitable

---

[6]William K. Frankena, *Ethics*, 2nd ed. (Englewood Cliffs: Prentice-Hall, 1973), 112.

[7]Alasdair MacIntyre, *Which Justice? Whose Rationality?* (Notre Dame: University of Notre Dame Press, 1988), 7.

[8]Ibid., 9.

[9]Geoffrey Sayre-McCord questions the interpretation of Hume that advances something like the moral point of view in "On Why Hume's 'General Point of View' Isn't Ideal—and Shouldn't Be," *Social Philosophy & Policy* 11, no. 1 (1994): 202–28. I'm grateful to Robert Miner for bringing this essay to my attention.

[10]MacIntyre, *Which Justice? Whose Rationality?* 350.

encounters with other traditions, and when two "rival standpoints," each claiming its own truth, confront one another, each can progress through a two-stage process. First, a tradition "characterizes the contentions of its rivals in its own terms." The point here is simple but significant. Take as an example two theological traditions that believe it is an obligation of justice to worship God, yet in one tradition there are multiple deities and the other only a single God.[11] If the latter is Judaism or Christianity, then when it encounters the other tradition it first must explain the conflict in terms of its own convictions. The multiple gods might be viewed as principalities or powers that should not be served. Neither Judaism nor Christianity could worship the multiple gods without ceasing to be the tradition that it is. It would not then become neutral or pluralistic; it would either become something else or possibly convert to the other tradition's conceptions. Traditions may reach dead ends and need to become something other, but before doing so they will first interpret the rival claims in their own terms. According to MacIntyre, this act of interpretation is only the first stage.

If in encountering another tradition, one finds it impossible to advance its enquiries, or flounders upon "insoluble antinomies," then it may have to revise itself using the resources of the other tradition, convert, or come to an end, especially if it finds the other tradition capable of advancing and resolving what it cannot. One tradition may find "resources to characterize and explain the failings and defects of their own tradition" in the resources of the other, but this, MacIntyre states, requires "a rare gift of empathy as well as of intellectual insight."[12] What is impossible is to assume a standpoint independent of all traditions that could adjudicate the rival claims as if moral, human agents were uninvolved referees. MacIntyre fears that this standpoint is what much of modern ethics claims to be. He refers to it as "liberalism," and one of his most important claims is that liberalism is also a tradition and should defend its moral claims, such as the "moral point of view," as a tradition, but because it lacks this awareness it cannot do so.

The philosopher Jeffrey Stout is both for and against MacIntyre's tradition-dependent rationality as a philosophical resource. He states, "Traditionalists are right ... to argue that ethical and political reasonings are creatures of tradition and crucially depend on the acquisition of such virtues as practical wisdom and justice."[13] Unlike most philosophers, Stout affirms tradition as a source for ethics. He disagrees with MacIntyre that "liberalism," which gives rise to modern democracy, either refuses or neglects to recognize itself as a tradition. He critiques MacIntyre and others who dismiss liberalism because it cannot account for itself as a tradition. He writes, "They are wrong, however, when they imagine modern democracy as the antithesis of tradition, as an inherently destructive, atomizing force."[14] Stout argues that MacIntyre failed on his own terms in the second stage of encountering a rival tradition. He has not had sufficient "empathy" and "intellectual insight" into liberalism as a tradition.[15] It too has a tradition-dependent view of practical reasoning and a place for the cultivation of virtues. MacIntyre's "traditionalism" wrongly demarcates tradition from modernity calling for an either-or. It overlooks why the tradition of liberalism emerged in the first place; it "was simply to

[11]The example is not the same as, but is inspired by, MacIntyre's discussion of interpreting the Roman gods in terms of Judaism and the Hebrew language: *Which Justice? Whose Rationality?* 380.

[12]MacIntyre, *Which Justice? Whose Rationality?* 167.

[13]Jeffrey Stout, *Democracy & Tradition* (Princeton: Princeton University Press, 2004), 11.

[14]Ibid., 11.

[15]Ibid., 128.

tailor the political institutions and moral discourse of modern societies to the facts of pluralism."[16]

Stout agrees with the feminist philosopher Susan Moller Okin that MacIntyre has two versions of tradition working in his philosophy. The first is tradition as ongoing debate about the goods that constitute the tradition that leaves it essentially incomplete. The second is "deferential submission to authoritative texts and authoritative interpreters of texts."[17] If the first version defines tradition, then it fits with liberalism as a tradition, but if it is the second then it does not. For the second assumes a "hierarchic institutional structure" that liberalism lacks. Stout dismisses tradition as a hierarchical authority, referring to it as "traditionalism." Democracy, he argues, is a more compelling tradition because it incorporates plural accounts of the good life without hierarchy.

Two important questions follow from Stout's observation. First, is a logical correlate of a hierarchic institutional structure that it fails to leave a tradition incomplete? This first question will be addressed in the final section below on rival traditions within Christianity, and the answer suggested will be mixed. Second, is modern democracy as immune to a hierarchical structure as Stout suggests? For MacIntyre, liberalism as a tradition includes economic arrangements founded upon capital and its rate of return. The radical income disparities that now rival what was once present in the *ancien régime*, and the ability of those differences to be passed down and self-replicating, call into question liberalism's opposition to hierarchy.[18]

CHRISTIANITY AND ETHICS

To this point, the discussion of tradition has been concerned with philosophical ethics. Christianity is a tradition, so if tradition has no role in ethics then the term "Christian ethics" would make little sense. If the moral point of view justifies ethical judgments, then *Christian* ethics is at most a contradiction, or ethics provides an independent theory of justification of moral norms to which Christianity must appeal for its justification, eliminating all aspects of its ethics which do not arise from a free, impartial agent who is willing to universalize his or her actions by abstracting them from the Christian tradition that renders them intelligible (the same would be true of Judaism, Islam, and any other religious or secular tradition). It should come as no surprise that many Christian ethicists find more possibility justifying a *Christian* ethics through the work of philosophers like MacIntyre or Stout. Yet, nothing in MacIntyre or Stout suggests that ethics requires Christianity for its viability. For both, ethics is a secular discipline in that it does not require a specific religious tradition for its intelligibility. MacIntyre and Stout differ over the secular nature of ethics as a discipline. MacIntyre's ethics finds theism indispensable for ethics. Stout's does not. He places his hope in "the people."[19] Yet both view philosophical ethics as a discipline distinct from Christian theology. Before discussing the place of tradition in Christian ethics, then, a brief discussion of bringing the terms "Christian" and "ethics" together is necessary. For if "Christian ethics" makes no sense, then asking the question that began this chapter is irrelevant.

[16]Ibid., 129.

[17]Ibid., 135–6.

[18]See Thomas Piketty, *Capital in the Twenty-First Century*, trans. Arthur Goldhammer (Cambridge: Belknap/Harvard, 2014), 335.

[19]Stout, *Democracy & Tradition*, 57.

Ethics is a practical discipline that seeks to pursue what is good and avoid what is evil. Christianity is a way of life that finds Jesus to be the manifestation of God's goodness present in the world, mediated through his body the church by the Holy Spirit. While most Christian ethicists would affirm the previous sentence, its significance for ethics differs among them. On the one hand, some ethicists, especially those working from a strong doctrine of natural law, develop ethics with little direct orientation to the central teachings of Christianity. This position, found among some Aristotelian-Thomists, assumes two basic axioms from Aristotle: (1) "a natural passive potency in a genus never expends beyond the active power of that genus"; and (2) "natural desire is never in vain."[20] The first axiom states that a potency will have an end proportionate to its nature. Someone may have a potential to run a mile under four minutes; accomplishing this feat is possible for human nature. But there can be no potency to run faster than the speed of light for that would "expend beyond the active power of the genus." The second axiom follows. A natural desire to achieve a natural end cannot be in vain.

If these axioms are accepted, then ethics will have a two-tiered structure. The first will be natural. Human beings have a natural passive potency to pursue good and avoid evil and within that natural potency are the means proportionate to their natural end to achieve it. Not everyone will do so any more than everyone will run a sub-four-minute mile, but the desire to do so is not in vain. Laid on top of this natural ethic that is available to all is a supernatural or Christian ethic available only to the baptized. It cannot be the fulfillment of a natural potency because its end—friendship with God—is not intrinsic to human nature. It requires something more than nature, something supernatural. Grace elevates nature to achieve this end not from a natural potency but from an obediential one. There is, then, a twofold end that requires a twofold ethic. The first is completely natural and available to all. The second is completely supernatural and comes as a gift mediated through the church's sacraments. This approach to Christian ethics could find common cause with something like ethical naturalism while it also generates a parallel Christian ethics.

On the other hand, some ethicists, especially those working in Augustinian or Protestant traditions, are more suspicious that we have access to a true knowledge of human nature as an easily accessible source for Christian ethics. Our nature is a good gift from the Good Creator, but identifying its goodness is marred by sin. In his posthumously published *Ethics*, Dietrich Bonhoeffer indicated this approach to Christian ethics when he wrote, "The knowledge of good and evil seems to be the aim of all ethical reflection. The first task of Christian ethics is to invalidate this knowledge." This is its first task because "the knowledge of good and evil shows that [the moral agent] is no longer at one with [his or her] origin."[21] The origin is God. Knowledge of good and evil without the knowledge of God is the temptation that befell Adam and Eve in Genesis 3. Ethics is a temptation because it assumes that we can have the good without God. Ethics is not a philosophical endeavor separate from theology; to know the good and to know God are one and the same.

These two positions represent ends on a continuum within which Christian ethics is pursued today. At one end, ethics can be a discipline independent of theology. A role for Christian ethics remains, but it will be limited to those whom grace elevates, perfecting

[20]Lawrence Feingold, *The Natural Desire to See God According to St. Thomas Aquinas and His Interpreters* (Ave Maria: Sapientia, 2010), 129–30.
[21]Dietrich Bonhoeffer, *Ethics* (New York: MacMillan, 1965), 17.

their nature. At the other end, ethics requires theology. The knowledge of God and the knowledge of the good are a single pursuit. There are mediating positions between these two ends, and the two ends are on a continuum. They are not opposites. Yet they will give rise to different evaluations of philosophy, and therefore ethics. The Aristotelian will view philosophy as a necessary foundation for ethical judgments, both natural and supernatural, if it is not to be fideistic. The Augustinian/Protestant will not make as sharp a distinction between philosophy and theology. These differences give rise to different views of tradition as a source.

CHRISTIAN ETHICS AND TRADITION

The first section of this chapter indicated that ethics requires practical reasoning as a tradition-dependent inquiry. This inquiry is philosophical and open-ended. There are no infallible judgments or magisterial overseers. Yet a second view of tradition was also identified, one that Stout refers to as "traditionalism." It has a hierarchical structure that can make infallible judgments on matters of faith and morals. Stout, like Okin, finds both accounts of tradition in MacIntyre and views them as competing, perhaps incompatible. If, however, we adopt the Aristotelian-Thomist approach to Christian ethics, then the two accounts of tradition are not competing. The first is tradition as philosophical inquiry, and the second is tradition as theological transmission.

In the Roman Catholic *Catechism*, tradition is a central source for "the transmission of divine revelation." The *Catechism* states that the Gospel was passed on in two ways. One was orally "by the apostles who handed on, by the spoken word of their preaching, by the example they gave, by the institutions they established, what they themselves had received—whether from the lips of Christ, from his way of life and his works, or whether they had learned it at the prompting of the Holy Spirit," and the other "by those apostles and other men associated with the apostles who, under the inspiration of the same Holy Spirit, committed the message of salvation to writing." The apostolic succession of bishops is a necessary institutional structure for the oral transmission of the Gospel. The *Catechism* states, "This living transmission, accomplished in the Holy Spirit, is called Tradition, since it is distinct from Sacred Scripture, though closely connected to it."[22]

Protestants expressed concern about tradition as a second source of authority alongside scripture, especially one that only a magisterial authority oversaw. At Vatican II, Roman Catholics responded to this concern by emphasizing that scripture and tradition are not two sources, but a single source. The Vatican II document *Dei Verbum* states,

> Hence there exists a close connection and communication between sacred tradition and Sacred Scripture. For both of them, flowing from the same divine wellspring, in a certain way merge into a unity and tend toward the same end. For Sacred Scripture is the word of God inasmuch as it is consigned to writing under the inspiration of the divine Spirit while sacred tradition takes the word of God entrusted by Christ the Lord and the Holy Spirit to the Apostles, and hands it on to their successors, in its full purity, so that led by the light of the Spirit of truth, they may in proclaiming it preserve this word of God faithfully.[23]

---

[22]Catholic Church, *Catechism of the Catholic Church* (Mahwah: Paulist, 1994), 24–5.

[23]Pope Paul VI, *Dei Verbum* (Vatican City: Libreria Editrice Vaticana, 1965), chap. 2.9.

It is still the case that a hierarchical structure, the institution of the episcopacy, proclaims and preserves the word of God, and it is possible for it to be done infallibly, but there is no reason why this understanding of tradition must be viewed as opposed to the incompleteness that concerns Stout and Okin. The fact that you need a teaching authority to preserve and interpret is a sign that the written text cannot be closed off from ongoing interpretation.

A similar view of tradition is found among the Orthodox who do not have a magisterium as the Catholics do. According to Georges Florovsky, the Orthodox Church views tradition as broader than the oral testimony of the Apostles preserved by apostolic succession. Tradition and scripture are sources that only have their intelligibility within the church. Florovsky writes,

> It is quite false to limit the "sources of teaching" to Scripture and tradition, and to separate tradition from Scripture as only an oral testimony or teaching of the Apostles. In the first place, both Scripture and tradition were given only within the Church. Only in the Church have they been received in the fullness of their sacred value and meaning. In them is contained the truth of Divine Revelation, a truth which lives in the Church. This experience of the Church has not been exhausted either in Scripture or in tradition; it is only reflected in them. Therefore, only within the Church does Scripture live and become vivified, only within the Church is it revealed as a whole and not broken up into separate texts, commandments, and aphorisms.[24]

Here too, the church preserves tradition not as something already complete and merely passed down but as something inexhaustible.

Both the Anglican and the United Methodist Churches affirm tradition as a "source of authority." The Anglican Church incorporates it as part of its "three-legged stool," and the Methodists as the Wesleyan Quadrilateral of scripture, reason, tradition and experience. Take for instance, the Episcopal Church's official statement on its "Sources of Authority." It states that the Anglican Church balances authority by way of a "three-legged stool" of tradition, scripture, and reason. Richard Hooker (1554–1600) is often credited with the three-legged stool, but just as Wesley never referred to the Wesleyan Quadrilateral, Hooker never used the term. Both are modern interpretations of emphases present in the earlier theologians. Hooker balanced the relationship between scripture and tradition between the Roman Catholic emphasis on a perceived "insufficiency" to scripture to which "traditions were added." For Hooker, scripture is sufficient for what it intends—human salvation—and here tradition adds nothing to scripture. But he also rejected an account of scripture's sufficiency that he found among Puritans. They rightly condemn the Catholic view but fall into another "dangerous extremity, as if scripture did not only contain all things in that kind necessary [for salvation], but all things simply, and in such sort that to do anything according to any other law were not only unnecessary but even opposite unto salvation, unlawful and sinful."[25] Reason and tradition offer wisdom on matters beyond salvation; for salvation, scripture suffices. Tradition has a more limited

[24]Georges Florovsky, *Bible, Church, Tradition: An Eastern Orthodox View* (Belmont: Nordland, 1972), 47. See also Stanley Hauerwas, *Unleashing the Scripture* (Nashville: Abingdon, 1993), 24.

[25]Richard Hooker, "Of the Laws of Ecclesiastical Polity," The Second Book, in *The Words of Mr. Richard Hooker*, arranged by John Keble (Oxford: Clarendon, 1888), 335–6. For a discussion on Hooker and his sources, see Paul Avis, "Exploring Issues of Authority in the Spirit of Richard Hooker," *Centre for the Study of the Christian Church & St George's House, Windsor Castle*, https://centres.exeter.ac.uk/CSCC/Interpreting%20Authority%20%20Paul%20Avis.htm.

role as a source than it does in Catholicism, but the Anglicans, like the Reformers, were committed to the authority of the patristic era and the early ecumenical councils. Tradition provides a "tacit dimension," including "silence," as a context to hear the word of God. The Orthodox theologian Andrew Louth writes, "If Scripture is the word, the voice, the utterance, then tradition is, in contrast, silence."[26] That silence is best discovered in the liturgy. Louth finds deep resonances between Hooker's understanding of tradition and the Orthodox Church.[27]

Methodists have been debating the "Wesleyan Quadrilateral" since it was first presented in its 1972 *Book of Discipline* as "Our Theological Task." Tradition has been interpreted as everything from one source among equals to its current status as the "process and form" of passing on the Gospel so that each generation does not imagine it must create Christianity anew. It is the "common story" grounded in a "consensus" that unites Christians. But tradition can go awry and must be normed by scripture. The United Methodist Church states, "Tradition acts as a measure of validity and propriety for a community's faith insofar as it represents a consensus of faith. The various traditions that presently make claims upon us may contain conflicting images and insights of truth and validity. We examine such conflicts in light of Scripture, reflecting critically upon the doctrinal stance of our Church."[28]

CONCLUSION

Nearly all Christian churches affirm tradition as a source, but they do so with rival claims—from the Roman Catholic institutional structure of apostolic succession to the liturgical silence of the Orthodox and common consensus of the early church among Protestants. No one would suggest that tradition should be the sole source for Christian ethics, nor should it be disregarded. If tradition becomes a completed, normative judgment incapable of historical development, overseen by an authoritarian rule, then it is traditionalism and should be questioned. But at its best, tradition serves to keep the present open to wisdom from the past for the sake of the future. Perhaps the best account of it remains G. K. Chesterton's memorable statement:

> I have never been able to understand where people get the idea that democracy was in some way opposed to tradition. It is obvious that tradition is only democracy extended through time. It is trusting to a consensus of common human voices rather than to some isolated or arbitrary record. … Tradition means giving votes to the most obscure of all classes, our ancestors. It is the democracy of the dead.[29]

Tradition is about listening and finding wisdom from voices in the past, voices that might have been silenced in their own day but can still speak,[30] or voices that have been

[26]Andrew Louth, "Tradition and the Tacit," in *Discerning the Mystery: An Essay on the Nature of Theology* (Oxford: Clarendon, 1985), 91.

[27]Ibid., 74, 90.

[28]United Methodist Church, "Theological Guidelines: Tradition," in *Book of Discipline* (Nashville: United Methodist, 2016), http://www.umc.org/what-we-believe/theological-guidelines-tradition.

[29]G. K. Chesterton, *Orthodoxy* (Charleston: Bibliobazaar, 2007), 47–8.

[30]For a powerful account that extends MacIntyre's tradition-dependent rationality by reminding us that sometimes we are in an epistemological crisis but have not yet recognized it because we have not heard silenced voices, see Willie J. Jennings, "Acosta's Laugh," in *The Christian Imagination: Theology and the Origins of Race* (New Haven: Yale University Press, 2010).

forgotten and need to be remembered. Tradition is also about forgetting the authority of some voices whose memory, we now can see clearly, directed us to evil and away from the good. Tradition keeps us open to the past in the present for the sake of the future.

SUGGESTED READINGS

Florovsky, Georges. *Bible, Church, Tradition: An Eastern Orthodox View*. Belmont: Nordland, 1972.

Hauerwas, Stanley. *Unleashing the Scripture*. Nashville: Abingdon, 1993.

Jennings, Willie James. *The Christian Imagination: Theology and the Origins of Race*. Yale University Press, 2010.

Louth, Andrew. *Discerning the Mystery: An Essay on the Nature of Theology*. Oxford: Clarendon, 1985.

MacIntyre, Alasdair. *Which Justice? Whose Rationality?* Notre Dame: University of Notre Dame Press, 1988.

Okin, Susan Moller. *Justice, Gender and the Family*. New York: Basic Books, 1998.

Stout, Jeffrey. *Democracy & Tradition*. Princeton: Princeton University Press, 2004.

Vanhoozer, Kevin J. *Biblical Authority after Babel: Retrieving the* Solas *in the Spirit of Mere Protestant Christianity*. Grand Rapids: Brazos, 2016.

CHAPTER THREE

Christian Ethics and Experience

LAURIE JOHNSTON

"Experience," one Christian ethicist writes, "is perhaps both the most-cited factor and wildest variable in debates over methods and questions in ethics."[1] What do we mean when we refer to "experience" as a source for ethical discernment? Whose experiences matter, what kinds of experience matter, and what sort of authority do these experiences hold? All of these questions remain topics of frequent and ongoing debate.

The content of human experience is complex and diverse, unique to each individual and yet profoundly shaped by social and cultural contexts. Experiences can be deeply communal and shared, but there is also an aspect of experience that is deeply interior and cannot be shared. Experience overlaps with the other sources of Christian ethics: the Bible and tradition are, in part, the record of the human experience of God and the life of the church. Using one's reason and apprehending the natural law draw upon our experiences and are themselves types of experience. Experience is both internal and external, spiritual and embodied, positive and negative. It includes events, relationships, history, art, emotions, and actions. And it is progressive, accumulating as we move through time. Aristotle thought it was important to accumulate sufficient life experience if one was to develop the ability to think ethically, suggesting that a young man may not be a "proper hearer" of lectures on ethics, because "he is inexperienced in the actions that occur in life."[2] Thomas Aquinas echoed this, saying that experience, accumulated over time, is vital for development of the virtue of prudence.[3] Others, however, suggest that "material for experience is lacking to no one."[4] Whether our experiences are few or many, we all face the challenge of discerning whether and how they can serve as forms of ethical guidance.

[1]Cristina Traina, "Papal Ideals, Marital Realities: One View from the Ground," in *Sexual Diversity and Catholicism toward the Development of Moral Theology*, ed. Patricia Beattie Jung and Joseph A. Coray (Collegeville: Liturgical, 2001), 270.

[2]Aristotle, *Nicomachean Ethics*, trans. W. D. Ross, 1.3, http://classics.mit.edu/Aristotle/nicomachaen.1.i.html.

[3]Thomas Aquinas, *Summa Theologiae*, trans. Fathers of the English Dominican Province (2nd ed., 1920), II–II.47.14, reply to objection 3. Online at http://www.newadvent.org/summa/index.html.

[4]Servais Pinckaers, OP, *The Sources of Christian Ethics*, 3rd ed. (Washington, DC: Catholic University of America Press, 1995), 94. Originally published as *Les sources de la morale chrétienne* (Fribourg: University Press Fribourg, 1985).

CHRISTIAN EXPERIENCE

What kind of experience matters? For many Christians who have considered experience as a source for ethics, the focus is on specifically Christian religious experience. This type of experience is what John Wesley had in mind when he first described what came to be known as the "Wesleyan Quadrilateral" (a term that was only coined much later, by American Methodist scholar Albert C. Outler). Wesley added the category of "experience" to the three sources that he inherited from Anglican theologians (scripture, tradition, and reason), because he had a particular kind of experience in mind. This particular experience was his famous moment of spiritual transformation, which occurred as he visited a meeting of a Moravian Brethren community in London, and "felt my heart strangely warmed."[5] This watershed moment shaped Wesley and the future of Methodism profoundly, and has left its mark on other strands of Christian tradition, such as Pentecostalism, that share Wesley's emphasis on personal spiritual experience in shaping Christian life and ethics.

Ecclesial experience need not be individualistic, though, and Wesley acknowledged the importance of communal reflection upon experience. He explained that it was important to engage in "conference"—that is, deep spiritual conversation—with fellow Christians as a way of testing one's insights about doctrinal and spiritual matters. Such "conference" would ensure that believers interpreted their religious experiences in the light of the Bible and tradition.[6] Another approach to communal discernment of experience, but in the Catholic tradition, might be found in the notion of the *sensus fidei*, or "sense of the faithful." This is the idea that communal Christian experience (including that of laypeople) plays an important role in the church's growth in understanding doctrine and morals. According to the document of the Second Vatican Council *Dei Verbum*, the apostolic tradition "develops in the Church with the help of the Holy Spirit. For there is a growth in the understanding of the realities and the words which have been handed down. This happens through the contemplation and study made by believers, [and] through a penetrating understanding of the spiritual realities which they experience."[7] Therefore, the spiritual experiences of the faithful represent a form of ongoing revelation. Consequently, if a moral teaching proposed by the hierarchy is rejected by many of the faithful, "it may indicate that certain decisions have been taken by those in authority without due consideration of the experience and the *sensus fidei* of the faithful."[8]

Christian religious experience can, of course, take many forms. One important form of communal ecclesial experience that has recently received increased attention as a source for Christian ethics is liturgy. As M. Therese Lysaught puts it, "The first question … in our study of Christian ethics is: Who or what do we worship?"[9] Reflecting upon the liturgy as a source of experience serves as a reminder, too, that we should not think of experience as only something that happens to us but as something in which we actively participate. A number of Orthodox Christian writers have particularly emphasized the

---

[5]*Journal of John Wesley*, vi.ii.xvi, May 24, 1738, https://www.ccel.org/ccel/wesley/journal.vi.ii.xvi.html.

[6]See Randy Maddox, "The Enriching Role of Experience," in *Wesley and the Quadrilateral: Renewing the Conversation*, ed. W. Stephen Gunter et al. (Nashville: Abingdon, 1997), 116.

[7]Paul VI, *Dei Verbum* (Vatican City: Libreria Editrice Vaticana, 1965), § 8.

[8]International Theological Commission, *Sensus Fidei in the Life of the Church* (Vatican City: Libreria Editrice Vaticana, 2014).

[9]M. Therese Lysaught, "Love and Liturgy," in *Gathered for the Journey: Moral Theology in Catholic Perspective*, ed. David Matzko McCarthy and M. Therese Lysaught (Grand Rapids: Eerdmans, 2007), 26.

connection between liturgy and ethics. For Alexander Schmemann, "the experience of joy as a result of participation in the liturgy is ... essential for the effective transformation of both persons and communities."[10] John Zizioulas goes so far as to argue that "the gathered community is the only setting from which we can extrapolate ethical actions."[11] And Vigen Guroian explains, "Christians must derive their ethics from the experience of God's Kingdom and truth which is found in the Church's worship."[12] He describes how the sacraments of baptism and Eucharist shape Christian identity—and therefore Christian ethics—in profound ways. Still, like other forms of experience, liturgical experience requires interpretation. For example, in churches where the priesthood is exclusively male, one must ask about the ethical implications of such liturgies for gender relations.[13] Guroian acknowledges the possibility that liturgy may even cause moral *deformation* at times, citing a case in which a Serbian Orthodox liturgical procession included an icon of former president and war criminal Slobodan Milosevic.[14] Thus, even the liturgy, that most Christian of experiences, requires a critical hermeneutic.

HUMAN EXPERIENCE

Beyond Christian religious experience, however, there remains the question of how to consider broader forms of human experience. How should Christian ethics draw upon what is sometimes called "general revelation"—that is, experiences of the world and of God active in the world that exist beyond just the Christian community? Wesley himself noted that experiences in the world shifted his perspective: his "frequent immersion in the lives of the poor ... led him to see economic matters in a new light. He remarked for example that he had 'lately had more experience' concerning instances of wronging widows and orphans that caused him to reconsider his initial assumption that the majority of English merchants were honest."[15] For a more dramatic example of experience shaping ethics, one could consider Bartolomé de Las Casas, a Spanish Dominican missionary in Mexico. In the Valladolid debate of 1550–1, he drew upon his experiences with native populations in the New World to argue for their protection against the abuses he had observed. In his *Short Account of the Destruction of the Indies*, he bluntly wrote, "The Spaniards have shown not the slightest consideration for these people, treating them (and I speak from first-hand experience, having been there from the outset) not as brute animals—indeed, I would to God they had done and had shown them the consideration they afford their animals—so much as piles of dung in the middle of the road."[16] In the contemporary era, the experiences of the victims of clerical sexual abuse in many churches have led many Christian communities and their leaders to a new understanding of the

---

[10]Maria Gwyn McDowell, "Seeing Gender: Orthodox Liturgy, Orthodox Personhood, Unorthodox Exclusion," *Journal of the Society of Christian Ethics* 33, no. 2 (2013): 80, citing Alexander Schmemann, *For the Life of the World: Sacraments and Orthodoxy* (Crestwood: St. Vladimir's Seminary Press, 1988).

[11]John Zizioulas, "Action and Icon: Messianic Sacramentality and Sacramental Ethics," in *Whither Ecumenism: A Dialogue in the Transit Lounge of the Ecumenical Movement*, ed. Thomas Wieser (Geneva: World Council of Churches, 1986), 68.

[12]Vigen Guroian, *Incarnate Love* (Notre Dame: University of Notre Dame Press, 1987), 73.

[13]See, e.g., McDowell, "Seeing Gender."

[14]Vigen Guroian, "Moral Formation and Christian Worship," *Ecumenical Review* 49, no. 3 (1997): 372.

[15]Maddox, "The Enriching Role," 125.

[16]Bartolomé de Las Casas, *A Short Account of the Destruction of the Indies*, trans. Nigel Griffin (London: Penguin, 1992), 13. See also Gustavo Gutiérrez, *Las Casas: In Search of the Poor of Jesus* (Maryknoll: Orbis, 1993).

importance of protecting the vulnerable and cultivating transparency and accountability in church authority structures.

One can find many other examples of Christians drawing upon their experiences in order to critique injustice. Recently, though, ethicists have given more explicit attention to human experience as a source. In Catholic theological ethics, an important shift toward considering human experience in general occurs in the document of the Second Vatican Council, *Gaudium et spes*: "There are a number of particularly urgent needs characterizing the present age ... To a consideration of these in the light of the Gospel and of *human experience*, the council would now direct the attention of all."[17] Echoing this insight, Edward Schillebeekcx argues that human experiences of suffering are a crucial starting point for all of Christian ethics and praxis. Such "negative contrast experiences" are an attack on "that which is worthy of human beings—which ... leads to indignation and is therefore a specifically ethical challenge and an ethical imperative."[18] Thus, attention to the various forms of suffering in the world today represents an essential component of ethical discernment.

On the other hand, positive experiences of human flourishing also hold key insights for ethics, inasmuch as they can teach us about the nature of the human person and our *telos* or purpose. In a world where there is often little agreement on what constitutes the "good life," many Christian ethicists have turned to virtue ethics and human flourishing as meaningful ways to articulate a Christian vision of human life and vocation. Servais Pinckaers writes that "the most fruitful experience is that of a morally virtuous act springing from the choice of truth and goodness."[19] Virtue ethicists often note the importance of moral exemplars for helping us recognize what constitutes human excellence and thereby develop virtuous character as well. For example, exposure to the lives of the saints provides an opportunity for us to learn vicariously from their experiences.

FEMINIST AND LIBERATIONIST APPROACHES TO EXPERIENCE

In recent decades, the most significant and sustained reflection upon human experience as a source for ethics comes from feminist and liberationist ethicists. These thinkers have argued that many forms of traditional theology arose from the experiences of white men who did not acknowledge how their social and cultural locations were shaping their theology. This led to "a situation in which men (male human beings) reflected upon the whole of life on behalf of the whole community of men and women, young and old."[20] While presuming to speak in universals, these forms of theology unwittingly imposed their own particular experiential categories, thereby doing violence to the experiences and theological insights of others.

In response, feminist and liberationist theologians have called for explicit attention to those forms of experience that have not been adequately represented in the tradition, including the experiences of women, the oppressed, and the poor. Giving particular

---

[17]Second Vatican Council, *Gaudium et spes* (Vatican City: Libreria Editrice Vaticana, 1965), § 46, emphasis added.
[18]Edward Schillebeeckx, OP, *Church: The Human Story of God*, trans. John Bowden (New York: Crossroad, 1991), 29.
[19]Pinckaers, *Sources of Christian Ethics*, 91.
[20]Mercy Oduyoye, "Doing Theology from Third World Women's Perspective," in *Feminist Theology from the Third World: A Reader*, ed. Ursula King (Eugene: Wipf and Stock, 1994), 29.

attention to these experiences is not merely a way to try to compensate for past neglect; many liberation theologians argue that the experiences of the oppressed are, in fact, a privileged locus for understanding God, humanity, and Christian discipleship. Gustavo Gutiérrez calls for Christians to make a "preferential option for the poor" in part as an *epistemological* stance. Similarly, James Cone argues for a profound epistemological priority for Black experience:

> The black theologian must reject any conception of God which stifles black self-determination by picturing God as a God of all peoples. Either God is identified with the oppressed to the point that their experience becomes God's experience, or God is a God of racism ... The blackness of God means that God has made the oppressed condition God's own condition. This is the essence of the Biblical revelation. By electing Israelite slaves as the people of God and by becoming the Oppressed One in Jesus Christ, the human race is made to understand that God is known where human beings experience humiliation and suffering.[21]

Cone's argument that God is known precisely through a particular form of experience is thus the key to his theology—and a challenge to Christians to reject an idolatry of white experience. Another critique arises from womanist and postcolonial theologians, who have called attention to the ways that white feminist theologians based in the United States and Europe have depicted "women's experience" in ways that are biased and incomplete.[22] Attending to experience is thus a task that is complex, ongoing, and requires deep critical analysis. As Kelly Brotzman cautions, "When we turn to experience as a source of moral knowledge, we must understand what we are dealing with: something heavy with received meanings, something irreducibly particular. To make experience central in our moral lives therefore does not make ethical discernment simpler; in fact, it makes it extraordinarily more complex."[23]

THE CHALLENGES OF USING EXPERIENCE AS A SOURCE FOR ETHICS

Given that the universe of human experience is vast, and there are many differences between humans' experiences, one might be tempted to make the solipsistic assumption that one can never truly understand others' experiences. As Margaret Farley asks, "Is experience so particular that it cannot be shared?"[24] Certain powerful human experiences seem to be so transformative and reshape a person's approach to the world so profoundly that it is difficult for those who have not shared this experience to understand. Racism, grinding poverty, torture, and other forms of trauma can fall into this category. More positively, falling in love or becoming a parent might also create a dramatic "before" and "after" in a person's life. The difficulty in explaining such experiences to those who have not experienced them for themselves raises epistemological questions: if experience is

---

[21]James Cone, *A Black Theology of Liberation* (Maryknoll: Orbis, 1970), 63–4.

[22]For an attempt to address this critique, see Gloria L. Schaab, "Feminist Theological Methodology: Toward a Kaleidoscopic Model," *Theological Studies* 62 (2001): 34–65.

[23]Kelly Brotzman, "Experience and Theological Ethics: A Schleiermacherian Investigation and Proposal" (PhD diss., University of Chicago, 2013), 222.

[24]Margaret Farley, "The Role of Experience in Moral Discernment," in *Christian Ethics: Problems and Prospects*, ed. Lisa Sowle Cahill and James F. Childress (Cleveland: Pilgrim, 1996), 143.

basically incommunicable, how can it be useful for ethics? And given our own finitude, bias, and propensity for sinful self-deception, how can we possibly expect that our own very partial version of experience might have anything to teach anyone else? How can we possibly learn from the experiences of others if we cannot ever really share them? Ultimately, attempting to learn from experience—our own as well as others'—requires a measure of faith. As H. Richard Niebuhr writes, "The acceptance of the reality of what we see in psychological and historically conditioned experience is always something of an act of faith; but such faith is inevitable and justifies itself or is justified by its fruits."[25] One might say further that this act of faith is justified by Christians' belief in the reality of a God who makes himself known within human history, within concrete human experience. It is grounded on faith in the Holy Spirit who is present in the world as a continuing source of revelation.

Nevertheless, experience requires cautious reflection and interpretation in order to yield its value for ethics. Experience itself does not automatically lead to insight, and it must be put into dialogue with the other ethical sources. Both John Wesley and *Gaudium et spes* reveal an expectation that human experience will, when accurately interpreted, be in harmony with scripture and tradition. Wesley's "expectation of such consensus was based on the assumption that it is the same self-revealing God being encountered through Scripture, tradition, and experience—when each of these is rightly and rationally utilized."[26] He was confident that even if individuals' experiences were quite different, together, the Christian community would be able to arrive at such a consensus.

In practice, though, conflicts between experience and the other sources of Christian ethics frequently appear. Ethicists disagree about how to weigh the various sources when there does not appear to be a consensus. For many Protestant ethicists, it has been particularly challenging to consider whether human experience might ever be weighted more heavily than scripture. For example, how should we weigh the experiences of gay Christians in life-giving, committed relationships against the scriptural prohibitions against homosexual activity?[27] For Catholic ethicists, the point of tension has often been between human experience as a source versus what are held to be absolute moral norms, drawn either from magisterial teaching or appeals to the natural law—or, often, both.

As an example of this latter type of conflict, one could consider Germain Grisez's work, *The Way of the Lord Jesus*. Grisez acknowledges, "Experience of certain sorts … not only contributes to moral insight but even is presupposed by knowledge of moral truth."[28] However, he also claims, "Christian experience reveals no new moral truths." He is particularly skeptical of any claims that experience could provide "a ground for criticizing the Church's moral teaching, including even certain moral norms asserted in Scripture and/or taught constantly and most firmly by the Church." In order to illustrate what he sees as the inability of experience to teach us about moral truth, he cites the example of slaveholders in the United States, whose experience of slaveholding failed to teach them that slavery was wrong. Grisez holds it to be a moral truth that slavery is always wrong, but for children growing up in slaveholding societies, "that essential

---

[25]H. Richard Niebuhr, *The Meaning of Revelation* (New York: Macmillan, 1941), 14.

[26]Maddox, "The Enriching Role," 122.

[27]For an interesting reflection upon the authority of scripture versus experience in relation to homosexuality, see Luke Timothy Johnson, "Homosexuality & the Church: Scripture & Experience," *Commonweal* 134, no. 12 (2007): 14–17.

[28]Germain Grisez, *The Way of the Lord Jesus*, vol. 2 (Chicago: Franciscan Herald Press, 1983), chap. 5, question C, no. 2, http://www.twotlj.org/G-2-5-C.html.

insight ... was one which children could not gain from experience."[29] Indeed, Grisez is correct that there is no guarantee that any particular form of experience will lead to ethical understanding or behavior. Nevertheless, Grisez's example unwittingly reveals that very importance of taking experience seriously in ethics. Grisez's own life experiences lead him to identify with the slaveholders, and he accurately notes their moral failure. However, he has failed to consider the experiences of the enslaved persons themselves. It is entirely likely that many of them, precisely because of their experience of slavery, came to an accurate conclusion that what they were suffering was morally wrong. As for the slaveholders, one might argue that it was precisely because of their failure to consider the slaves' experiences as important sources of moral insight that these slaveholders erred. Thus, Grisez's example inadvertently shows the importance of giving epistemological priority to the experiences of the oppressed—precisely what liberation theologians have been arguing, as we saw earlier.

Grisez's mistake, though, reveals how difficult it can be for us to take others' experiences into consideration. Even when we do attempt to take others' experiences seriously, we often filter them through our own experiences in ways that can be profoundly distorting. Human finitude and human sinfulness make experience risky as an ethical source. Still, as Niebuhr says, "It is not evident that the man who is forced to confess that his view of things is conditioned by the standpoint he occupies must doubt the reality of what he sees."[30] And experience is a source we cannot reject, lest we ignore the Holy Spirit and allow ethics to become irrelevant to the concrete lives of the humans whom theology should serve. Thus, it is important to find forms of communal discernment that will allow us to overcome our blind spots and limitations and arrive at a shared understanding of how experience should shape morality. As Lisa Cahill explains, this does not require relinquishing the authority of scripture or moral norms; rather, "the essential point to emphasize for an ethics which begins with, and remains respectful of, differences in experience, while not giving up the possibility of normative ethics, is that [what is] 'shared' is not achieved beyond or over against [experience], but rather in and through it."[31]

ENCOUNTERING THE EXPERIENCES OF OTHERS

What are some ways that we can move toward "shared experience" that are morally illuminating? First, it is very important to seek out experiences that may differ from our own, and from our own community's experiences. Not everyone agrees about this; Servais Pinckaers writes, "To know the human, it is not necessary to indulge in an unlimited number of experiences. In fact, too many would scatter our attention, exhaust our capacities, and risk confusing us. It is enough to sound the depths of the human experiences that come our way."[32] But surely this is insufficient; what if the only experiences that come his way are those of other men, or other Europeans? Even if we sound the depths of those experiences, we risk merely perpetuating our blind spots. Our finitude is not an excuse for laziness in moral inquiry.

---

[29]That insight might not have been gained from other sources of Christian ethics either, though. The Bible is ambiguous, and the teaching of the Catholic Church was historically quite ambiguous as well. See John Noonan, *A Church That Can and Cannot Change* (Notre Dame: Notre Dame University Press, 2005).

[30]Niebuhr, *The Meaning of Revelation*, 13.

[31]Lisa Sowle Cahill, *Sex, Gender, and Christian Ethics* (Cambridge: Cambridge University Press, 1996), 55.

[32]Pinckaers, *Sources of Christian Ethics*, 94.

How, then, can we apprehend experience that moves beyond our individual limitations? One way is the use of social science data, which can allow us to draw upon a large number of individual experiences.[33] However, social science is also vulnerable to assumptions and blind spots. Furthermore, data are not always compelling in any way that engages our affective capacities. Another arena of experience that better engages the affections, but is too often overlooked, is that of aesthetic experience. Literature, art, and music are often means of communicating and sharing the most powerful and important kinds of human experience. They deserve more attention from Christian ethicists.

That aesthetic experience and ethics might be related is not a new idea, nor is it unique to Christian ethics. Thinkers from Aristotle to Elaine Scarry have suggested that beauty has something to teach us about both truth and justice—perhaps because both beauty and justice have a sort of symmetry. In the theological tradition, Jonathan Edwards suggests that experiences of beauty allow us "to see more clearly and to be more receptive to what the material world communicates about the nature of God's beauty."[34] And because beauty is something that evokes a response from us, it creates a type of forward momentum that can lead us to wonder what such beauty—and what its author—might require from us. For Hans Urs von Balthasar, aesthetic experience is the best analogy for understanding our encounter with God, and the concern of ethics is how we should play our roles as actors in the "Theo-drama" that results.[35]

Part of the power of art as a source of ethical reflection is that it can distill the communal experience of generations into a communicable form. M. Shawn Copeland writes that "the blues" are an important source for theology and ethics, because "the blues narrate and authenticate human feeling, desire, and hope ... The blues rise from the musings and moaning of enslaved Africans in response to their 'peculiar experience' in the new world." The blues are such a powerful distillation of human experience that listening to them has "profound ramifications ... for *all* human life, especially whenever life is threatened by force, coercion and cynicism."[36] Similarly, Maureen O'Connell provides an excellent model of the use of aesthetic experience in ethics, as she reflects upon the insights about justice and injustice, violence and reconciliation that emerge from community-created murals throughout the city of Philadelphia.[37]

CONCLUSION: CHRISTIANITY AS THE FRUIT OF EXPERIENCE

In its earliest days, Christianity was described as simply "the way." It has always been rooted in the experience of Christ—an experience that, for Jesus's contemporaries, raised many questions about their religious traditions and scriptures. Jesus often pointed to

---

[33]See, e.g., Daniel Finn, ed., *Empirical Foundations of the Common Good: What Theology Can Learn from Social Science* (Oxford: Oxford University Press, 2017).

[34]Ki Joo Choi, "The Deliberative Practices of Aesthetic Experience: Reconsidering the Moral Functionality of Art," *Journal of the Society of Christian Ethics* 29, no. 1 (Spring/Summer 2009): 204–5.

[35]Hans Urs Von Balthasar, *The Glory of the Lord: A Theological Aesthetics*, ed. Joseph Fessio, Brian McNeil, and John Riches (San Francisco: Ignatius Press, 1983). See especially vol. 1, *Seeing the Form*.

[36]M. Shawn Copeland, "Theology at the Crossroads: A Meditation on the Blues," in *Uncommon Faithfulness: The Black Catholic Experience*, ed. M. Shawn Copeland with LaReine-Marie Mosely and Albert J. Raboteau (Maryknoll: Orbis, 2009), 104, emphasis in original.

[37]Maureen O'Connell, *If These Walls Could Talk: Community Muralism and the Beauty of Justice* (Collegeville: Liturgical, 2012).

experiences, rather than words, to convey his message. When the disciples of John the Baptist came to inquire if he was the Messiah, Jesus responded by asking them what they had experienced in his presence: "Go and tell John what you have seen and heard: the blind receive their sight, the lame walk, the lepers are cleansed, the deaf hear, the dead are raised, the poor have good news brought to them" (Lk. 7:22). Christian ethics begins first and foremost with this movement, to go and tell what we have seen and heard about Jesus. But along the way back to tell John, surely his disciples were wondering, "What does this experience really mean? And what should we do now?" Perhaps it was similar to the later conversation between Jesus's disciples along the road to Emmaus, who were "talking with each other about all these things that had happened" (Lk. 24:14). This is a way to describe the task of Christian ethics, in the end: talking together about the things that have happened—not just to us but to all of humanity and all of creation. As we walk together, wondering what to do next, we walk in the faith and hope that Christ will appear along the road to help us make sense of all that we have experienced.

SUGGESTED READINGS

Brown, Neil. "Experience and Development in Catholic Moral Theology." *Pacifica* 14 (October 2001): 295–312.

Choi, Ki Joo. "The Deliberative Practices of Aesthetic Experience: Reconsidering the Moral Functionality of Art." *Journal of the Society of Christian Ethics* 29, no. 1 (Spring/Summer 2009): 193–218.

De La Torre, Miguel A. *Ethics: A Liberative Approach*. Minneapolis: Fortress, 2013.

Farley, Margaret. "The Role of Experience in Moral Discernment." In *Christian Ethics: Problems and Prospects*, ed. Lisa Sowle Cahill and James F. Childress, 134–51. Cleveland: Pilgrim, 1996.

Maddox, Randy. "The Enriching Role of Experience." In *Wesley and the Quadrilateral: Renewing the Conversation*, ed. W. Stephen Gunter, Scott J. Jones, Ted A. Campbell, Rebekah L. Miles, and Randy L. Maddox, 108–27. Nashville: Abingdon, 1997.

Pinckaers, Servais, OP. *The Sources of Christian Ethics*. 3rd ed. Washington, DC: Catholic University of America Press, 1995.

Saiving, Valerie. "The Human Situation: A Feminine View." *Journal of Religion* 40 (1960): 100–12.

CHAPTER FOUR

Christian Ethics and Reason

KATHRYN LILLA COX

Theologian Richard Gula argues that we often lack imagination when making ethical decisions, leading to moral impoverishment.[1] Our lack of imagination has many causes, including a reliance on a preferred type of reasoning. For example, the Roman Catholic moral manuals prior to the Second Vatican Council (1962–5) primarily used deductive reasoning, which begins with a norm or principle like "be just." One then reasons from a principle or norm to a solution. This approach has many merits, including providing a standard universal starting point for ethics. Deductive reasoning from principles can, however, ignore contextual facts, a moral agent's history and experience, or insights from other disciplines. Using only deductive reasoning can lead to a moral minimalism and a narrowing of the ethical life to only avoiding sin. When this happens, deductive reasoning hinders (1) imagining other possible alternatives for acting well, (2) using multiple approaches for addressing the same ethical concern, and (3) considering where conversion can occur. Additionally, it deleteriously prioritizes individual sin while neglecting social, structural sin. Therefore, developing moral decision-making skills means learning to employ a variety of reasoning types and sources that will help foster moral richness, not impoverishment.

The "Wesleyan Quadrilateral" of sources utilized by Christian ethicists of most denominations fosters a rigorous approach to theological decision making and subsequent action. When consistently applied, it helps dismantle a reliance on one type of reasoning, helps moral agents and communities develop a habit of intellectual rigor, and prevents an oversimplification of, or easy answers to, complicated questions and concerns. Distinctive sources require utilizing various methodologies and different forms of reasoning. Weaving together knowledge and insights into truth that emerges when considering an ethical question or concern from the angles of scripture, tradition, and experience into a convincing, feasible, and practical form of action requires the imaginative feature of reasoning that Gula called for.

Reasoning well develops intellectual habits that aid our search for truth, clarity, meaning, and a logical, consistent stance that can be justified and applied to the issue or concern at hand.[2] Reason aids in evaluating, using, and understanding the dynamic interplay between the other three sources of Christian ethics used to help us act and live well. As theologian Margaret Farley writes, "Reason, after all, is involved in addressing

[1]Richard M. Gula, *Moral Discernment* (Mahwah: Paulist, 1997), 83. Gula with this claim implicitly recognizes the existence of various reasoning types.

[2]Russell B. Connors Jr. and Patrick T. McCormick, *Character, Choices, and Community: The Three Faces of Christian Ethics* (Mahwah: Paulist, 2002), 21–2.

all of the sources."[3] Therefore, asking "What do we mean by reason?" makes sense. How is reason employed when we think about and make decisions about acting? What types of reason have been identified? To begin mapping the terrain that examines these questions, this chapter focuses on reasoning, the Quadrilateral's fourth source.

This chapter unfolds in the following manner. First, I discuss and define several philosophical types of reason with their implications for theological ethics: practical, scientific, and imaginative. These types were chosen because they help showcase needed facets of ethical reasoning. They also work well with aspects of Christian faith, specifically, the desire to live a good life grounded in principles. They moreover demonstrate the contemporary relevance of ancient scriptural texts describing God's saving work in history. Second, I examine how reason is exercised when making an ethical decision about acting well. Given that we act not within silos, but within communities, discerning and dialoguing with those communities throughout the reasoning process is important. Finally, I will argue that utilizing different types of reasoning in the theological endeavor provides a variety of tools for using scripture, tradition, and experience, which ultimately yields a rich tapestry of possible life-giving courses of action. We need the theoretical analysis provided by scientific reasoning, the skill of imaginative reasoning, along with the intellectual habit of practical reasoning. All reasoning types are crucial for relating scripture to experience and interpreting tradition appropriately in order to determine what the demands of radical transformative discipleship in service of all God's people require of us today.

PRACTICAL REASON

While many types of reasoning have been identified in the Aristotelian tradition—*epistêmê*, *technê*, and *phronesis*, for example—only *phronesis* (practical reasoning) will be discussed here since it connects reason with wisdom, character, and action, which are so centrally important for theology. *Phronesis* is not the reasoning that helps us make choices between apples and oranges, or shorts and slacks. Rather, according to Daniel C. Russell, *phronesis* is "a long-term attribute of deliberating well about acting for the sake of those things."[4] By "those things" he means right goals and right ideals. Russell thinks that through use of practical reasoning we can train our passions and become "good at living one's life."[5] The capacity to set aims, make choices, train passions, and pursue ends for a good meaningful ethical life develops with practice. Therefore, with practical reasoning one can be a beginner, a more accomplished practitioner, or somewhere in between.[6]

Phronesis is practical because "before one can decide just how to achieve what one has decided to do, one must first decide what to do, here and now, in a concrete way, given all the particulars."[7] This means that *phronesis* requires the ability to gather facts, information, and relevant data. Practical reason tries to determine what rules, norms, virtues, and other sources are most pertinent to the ethical question at hand. Attention to rules and norms acknowledges communal wisdom and provides an objective framework

---

[3]Margaret A. Farley, *Just Love: A Framework for Christian Sexual Ethics* (New York: Continuum, 2006), 188.
[4]Daniel C. Russell, "Aristotle on Cultivating Virtue," in *Cultivating Virtue: Perspectives from Philosophy, Theology, and Psychology*, ed. Nancy E. Snow (New York: Oxford University Press, 2015), 22.
[5]Ibid., 22, 23.
[6]Ibid., 27.
[7]Ibid., 28.

for our reasoning. Practical reasoning also has a subjective component because the subject (person or community of persons) must determine what is required of me/us right now, in this time and place, with the specific people with whom I/we are interacting, while considering specific constraints or freedoms on my/our action. Answering questions that begin with who, what, when, where, and why helps us understand the specificity of an ethical question or issue. Finally, we need the ability to project into the future, see the potential results of our decisions, and envision other possible directions when determining a course of ethical action.[8] Here we begin to see the intersection of different reasoning types, since the ability to project into the future requires a knowledge base from the past (scientific reasoning) as well as the capacity to imagine different options for and possible results of our acting (imaginative reasoning).

The interplay between individuals and a community is complicated. Richard J. Bernstein is one thinker who attends to the role of the individual and community in practical reasoning. He advocates for a "practical rationality" that takes seriously the need for community, one's historical context, and dialogue to assess the values that guide deliberation about behavior and action. The contours of this practical rationality include recognizing that reason remains imbedded in "its historical context and horizons."[9] As such, living traditions give reason power because traditions can provide empirical support to the reasoning process.

Emphasizing social, cultural, and historical contexts differs from the Kantian/ Habermasian view of reason accentuating decontextualized universal moral norms. Even as Jürgen Habermas recognizes that norms originally arise in communities, he argues that, while supplying structure and a source of meaning for communities, traditions should not be embraced uncritically. Traditions should be examined for what distorts or hinders genuine discourse and community.[10] For example, communitarianism should be critiqued for how it reinforces oppressive gender roles or racism. Naming and excising distortions and impediments within traditions remains vital since what a community values becomes its impetus for acting. Likewise, we must evaluate our values when making judgments and decisions, because values can lead us to form either ethical communal structures and habits of just actions or distorted communal structures and patterns of unjust actions.[11] Hence, the need to both draw on and critique traditions and values in our ethical decision making.

At its best, theological ethics attends to universal claims for acting, such as be just, be loving, be merciful, while understanding that social, cultural, and historical contexts will help determine how justice, love, and mercy appear. Theologian Margaret Farley demonstrates this in her work. She looks historically at how a topic has previously been addressed and the various ways it is currently being addressed. She then examines and studies other relevant fields for illumination into the human condition and mines both

---

[8]George Lakoff and Mark Johnson, *Metaphors We Live By* (Chicago: University of Chicago Press, 1980); Mark Johnson, *Moral Imagination: Implications of Cognitive Science for Ethics* (Chicago: University of Chicago Press, 1993).

[9]Richard Bernstein, *Beyond Objectivism and Relativism: Science, Hermeneutics, and Praxis* (Philadelphia: University of Philadelphia Press, 1983), 37.

[10]Jürgen Habermas, "A Review of Gadamer's *Truth and Method*," in *The Hermeneutic Tradition: From Ast to Ricoeur*, ed. Gayle L. Ormiston and Alan D. Schrift (Albany: State University of New York Press, 1990), 213–44. Habermas is one of many philosophers who critique Gadamer's emphasis on hermeneutics and interpretation when considering norms and traditions.

[11]Bernstein, *Beyond Objectivism and Relativism*, 40.

scripture and tradition for fresh insights into stale debates. This yields possible decisions attentive to past and contemporary experience, grounded in tradition while analyzing a tradition's flaws and errors, and innovatively making scriptural themes applicable to new situations.[12]

SCIENTIFIC REASON

Thomas S. Kuhn, philosopher of science, seeks to correct the misperception that scientific knowledge and research results develop only sequentially and deductively. Kuhn acknowledges that scientists build on accumulated knowledge, facts, theories, and methods that furnish frameworks for subsequent scientific research.[13]

Observations about the world or research results might not, however, fit within an existing framework. Scientists, when confronted with unexpected research results, may repeat the experiment to verify the results. They may try to explain how unexpected results do fit into existing paradigms. They may attempt to solve or explain anomalies or crises using different assumptions, perspectives, or new angles of analysis including alternative but less-noticed strands within a tradition. When a solution or theory explaining an anomaly can be found using different methods or concepts, changes in the scientific system occur. Additional methods are recognized as valid inquiry tools. New research fields may develop.[14] Some beliefs are changed or rejected.[15] This process of accepting and adopting different assumptions, methods, frameworks, and the resulting knowledge as part of the normal scientific practice usually takes about a generation.[16]

Given this reality of how science works, Kuhn argues that envisaging scientific growth in new knowledge as a process rather than linear, sequential knowledge building is more accurate. Understanding scientific reasoning as a process is more fluid and integrative because it acknowledges and appreciates the fits, starts, dead ends, and eureka moments within science. It also accounts for the interplay between scientists and their external societal and cultural factors, which influence new scientific insights.[17]

Like scientists, theological ethicists operate within a framework supported and reinforced by specific ethical traditions. Accepted ethical frameworks and methods usually function well. They do fail, however, to provide convincing arguments and solutions to a wide range of ethical questions and injustices. Theological ethicists might then retrieve and revive overlooked, underutilized, or forgotten strands in our traditions. Using insights from other disciplines and lived experience, theological ethicists develop alternative methodological approaches for employing sources as they seek to respond to ethical questions and injustices.

Therefore, as in science, methodological plurality and ways of reasoning among theological ethicists occurs. What might appear as a departure from tradition is really the field of theological ethics developing as practitioners deal with anomalies, crises, and new questions. While commonalities exist between those practicing "new" and

---

[12]See, e.g., her norms for sexual ethics steeped in the Catholic social tradition. Farley, *Just Love*, 207–44.

[13]Thomas S. Kuhn, *The Structure of Scientific Revolutions*, 3rd ed. (Chicago: University of Chicago Press, 1996), 10.

[14]Ibid., 82–91.

[15]For example, people used to think the earth was flat rather than round. In light of new evidence, this belief was corrected.

[16]Kuhn, *Structure of Scientific Revolutions*, 144–5, 150–2.

[17]Thomas S. Kuhn, *The Copernican Revolution* (Cambridge: Harvard University Press, 1957), 132–3, 141.

"old" theology, "new" theology often functions from different sets of assumptions and frameworks than does "old"-er theology. Yet "new" theology builds upon and draws from the tradition already in place, even as it will also undergo its own scrutiny and analysis. Some theologians function in both groups, laying the groundwork for subsequent developments in our understanding of the theological tradition.

Karl Rahner, SJ, is one such theologian whose definition of rationality showcases this rooted innovation. He argues that rationality is concerned with language, concepts, distinctions, and the connection between various propositions. Rationality builds "systems" and "frameworks" to support our propositions, poses "questions of verification," and critically examines the presuppositions operating behind propositional statements.[18] Rahner contends, however, that we do not always use deductive or linear reasoning to arrive at understanding and insight. He argues that our starting points for reasoning are "unavoidably arbitrary." Therefore, the act of reasoning, which should include feedback, influences and changes the original starting point of reflection and its underlying assumptions.[19] We must assess, at times, both reason's conclusions and the presuppositions behind our conclusions.

Premised on his belief that words and conceptual knowledge fail to fully express or grasp the depth of an experience of God or humans, Rahner argues we only asymptotically approach total understanding.[20] We never fully capture all aspects of knowing, the truth, or the good. Given this reality, we must continually challenge ourselves to seek spaces for conversion, new ways of living, and better alternatives for answering ethical questions. Newness should not be confused with a lack of appreciation for the old or tradition. Rather, newness indicates the required ongoing conversion as we develop our ability to live the gospel. We are constantly called to conversion and asked to stretch in order to more fully integrate ourselves and live the gospel message. This perspective on rationality and understanding leaves room for reassessment and reformulation of principles, ethical norms, and actions because of new insights, experiences, or questions. A nonlinear and discursive reasoning style requires human feedback and engagement with others. It also provides a framework to consider the other sources (scripture, experience, and tradition) of theological ethics.

IMAGINATIVE REASON

Cognitive philosopher Mark Johnson observes that, theoretically, a deductive application of norms, laws, and rules to situations (with no consideration of context) works in the abstract. But people consider their relationships and affections (whether consciously or unconsciously) in addition to rules, laws, and principles when discerning and concretely acting. Thus, while deductive reasoning theoretically works, Johnson finds it unhelpful in daily life. Daily life requires grappling with situations where the "right" thing to do is not clear and we need additional acuity beyond what the rules, laws, and principles at hand provide.[21] These ambiguous times necessitating additional insight require what he

---

[18]Karl Rahner, "Faith between Rationality and Emotion," in *Theological Investigations*, vol. 16, trans. David Morland (London: Darton, Longman & Todd, 1979), 61.

[19]Ibid.

[20]Ibid.

[21]Johnson, *Moral Imagination*, 75. For a look at how imagination can function in moral theology, see Richard Gula, "Let the Mind of Christ Be in You: Moral Formation and the Imagination," *Theology Digest* 51, no. 4 (2004): 315–26; Philip S. Keane, *Christian Ethics and Imagination* (Ramsey: Paulist, 1984), 79–109.

calls the imaginative feature of our rationality. He defines this imaginative feature as "that [which] is at once insightful, critical, exploratory, and transformative."[22] Imaginative rationality teaches the ability to perceive alternative goods and values that might be at stake or to envision how certain courses of action would affect one's relationships and ability to form a meaningful life. For example, we exhort children "to imagine how you would feel if 'x' was done to you," hoping that this imaginative task helps them learn empathy and compassion for others, leading to changed behavior.

Theologian William Dych, SJ, discusses imaginative rationality in a different way from Johnson with his attention to embodied knowing. Dych questions the "Cartesian ideal," arguing that "it is not the 'mind' which thinks, but *people* think, and think from out of the totality of themselves."[23] This totality of the self includes the history of our experiences, which provides the interpretive framework for future encounters with the world and others. Dych argues that we school our reasoning capacities when we engage the world not only with our conceptual minds but with our bodies. These embodied relationships begin with our time in the womb and its preverbal, embodied form of knowledge. Our bodies provide the locus and means for interacting with each other, and these experiences can be stored as smells, emotions, and bodily responses as well as ideas and thoughts.[24] Therefore, when discerning ethical actions, we need to pay attention not only to what reason tells us but also to what our bodies and affections indicate about ethical courses of action. Attention to preverbal and embodied knowledge also requires self-knowledge since preverbal and bodily knowledge appears differently to different people. With attention to embodied knowledge, Dych reminds Christians of the theological truth of the Incarnation: God became flesh.

The Incarnation points out the importance for theological ethics of thinking and knowing both conceptually and experientially because the Christian faith "is not in the first instance a body of abstract, eternal truths."[25] Christian faith is about the ongoing relationship between God and humanity taking place in time and history. We experience, live, and think about relationships. Jesus of Nazareth, who is the Christ, is central to Christian faith—past, present, and future. Therefore, while preserving continuity with the past, the gospel comes alive in the present, enabling us to imagine the possibilities for living the gospel today.[26] Stated differently, the gospel message does not require choosing creativity (imagination) over intellectual articulation of the faith, mind knowledge over body knowledge, or deductive over inductive reasoning. Rather, living the gospel message well involves creativity, conceptualization of the faith, and plural forms of knowledge and reasoning.

EMPLOYING REASON IN A THEOLOGICAL DISCERNMENT OF MORAL ACTION

Why talk about different types of reasoning when considering moral action? Some actions we pre-consider, other actions require in the moment thinking, and past actions get

---

[22]Johnson, *Moral Imagination*, 187.

[23]William Dych, "Theology and Imagination," *Thought* 57 (March 1982): 118.

[24]Bessel van der Kolk, *The Body Keeps the Score: Mind, Brain and Body in the Transformation of Trauma* (New York: Penguin, 2015).

[25]Dych, "Theology and Imagination," 124.

[26]Ibid., 127.

reviewed. In each instance some form of reasoning occurs, and, depending on the type of action, the reasoning used differs.

During the pre-action stage the individual or community ideally engages practical reasoning as described earlier. This stage also requires scientific reasoning (facts, prior data, method) as well as imaginative reasoning. Imaginative reasoning helps determine relevant knowledge and its application from scripture, tradition, and experience. Ideally for Christians, judgments and determinations are grounded in the question of what is asked of us here and now to build the kingdom of God. Discernment and moving toward a decision about how to act demands dialogue with each other, with the tradition, and with God.

The action stage occurs when we enact the decision made during our pre-action stage. Thought or reasoning still happens when we act. For example, when trying to soothe a crying infant, if our first attempt to calm the child fails, the moment requires thinking about another course of action. This type of reasoning happens fast, requiring both practical reasoning—drawing on experience—and imaginative reasoning to determine what might work for this infant.

Reflecting on, explaining, and/or justifying to other people a past action or precluded actions requires the work of reasoning. This work could confirm the action, require acknowledging that the action taken was incorrect, prompt a nuanced assessment that some portions of the action could have been done differently, and set groundwork and foundations for future actions. Reflecting on prior actions could and often does include an analysis or determination about their effects, consequences, and reverberations. Questions needing answers may arise, such as: Why did we act differently than we planned to act? Why is our logical, reasonable, and consistent stance not enough to move us or others to act? Why is it that narratives, parables in scripture, poetry, or metaphors grab our attention and often compel us to action when reasoned positions often do not? Was our action sufficient or are next steps needed?

Recall a decision, either individual or communal, that you made based on false assumptions, poor logic, incomplete data, or some combination of these factors. These decisions showcase why dialogue with others is necessary both before and after acting. First, our reasoning can be flawed. We can be illogical in our thinking or can reason poorly. Second, our context, whether social, geographical, cultural, and so on, affects what we know, notice, value, or even ignore or fail to notice. Third, neuroscience and brain studies have demonstrated and continue to show how we often act without thinking, at least, not without full input from the neocortex.[27] When under threat, individuals can enter fight, flight, or freeze mode. If we are in fight, flight, or freeze mode, propelled into irrational thinking, others can help return us to rational thinking through dialogue. Communities or groups of people can end up in group hysteria, groupthink, or tribal thinking because of fear, uncertainty, or nostalgia. This reality that we all participate in group or tribal thinking means that to understand each other we must engage others. Dialogue requires epistemological openness because when we learn from others we might need to change our position or conclusion pertaining to an ethical course of action. Dialogue at its best

[27]Neuroscientific research is helping us understand more deeply what structures and informs our thinking processes. See, e.g., Van der Kolk, *Body Keeps the Score*; Daniel Siegel, *The Developing Mind: How Relationships and the Brain Interact to Shape Who We Are*, 2nd ed. (New York: Guilford, 2012); and Daniel Kahneman, *Thinking Fast and Slow* (New York: Farrar, Straus and Giroux, 2011).

will be mutually corrective, expanding our understanding and insights as we seek greater comprehension of truth and goodness.

Finally, our temptation to think in either/or categories truncates the deep-thinking reflection and discernment necessary for responding to today's complex ethical questions. While sometimes helpful, either/or categories can obliterate the complexity and subtly of considerations for moral action. Additionally, we often want efficient, fast, and quick thinking about our past and future actions. While fast thinking is required at times, the work of addressing complex, interrelated ethical questions, which includes thinking about our own biases or gaps in comprehension and engaging in more study and research, takes time and requires slower thinking. Slower thinking fosters a capacity to think more deeply, clearly, reflectively, and imaginatively to address complex ethical questions and concerns.

Therefore, while not perfect, the Wesleyan Quadrilateral necessitates that we (1) think with others, (2) share experiences, (3) study scripture, and (4) engage various traditions. Used well, this multipronged method enables a more multidimensional, deeply rooted, and interwoven foundation more representative of our lives and suited to creatively address and solve ethical questions and injustices.

CONCLUSION

This chapter briefly explored the fourth resource for Christian ethics: reason. The chapter did not analyze a natural law, inductive, or deductive approach. Instead, practical, scientific, and imaginative reasoning were described. These different reasoning approaches provide possibilities for new visions of our reasoning to emerge. Practical, scientific, and imaginative reasoning together account for objective criteria, human experience in all its dimensions, and historical development of ideas, along with new insights and different perspectives from various fields. Taken together rather than independently, these types of reason provide a complex understanding of human reasoning that can meet the needs of a multidimensional, interconnected world requiring practical responses that honor the rich, nuanced, and diverse environments in which we live, move, and act.

Scientific reasoning helps us see the importance of principles, theoretical frameworks, concepts, facts, and data. Scientific reasoning reveals the necessity of testing theories and hypotheses and changing our understanding of the world. Yet, scientific reasoning requires imagination. One must be able to consider and reflect on why answers to ethical questions or solutions for injustice are not working, while considering other possible explanations and answers. As noted earlier, new questions, new experiences, and applications of principles and values in different cultures require imagination. Here scripture, forgotten aspects of traditions, another community's or individual's knowledge and wisdom based on experience can shape and inform our imagining of different possibilities for future action. Practical reasoning, which aims at living well, applies both scientific and imaginative reasoning when considering the needs in a given situation. Applying practical reasoning to arrive at ethical decisions and actions involves attending to the relational, incarnational, dialogical, and embodied features of our reasoning and knowing.

Nevertheless, there remains a provisional character to the judgments and conclusions of our reason. Our reason functions only as well as: the information we are given; the wisdom we have; the feasibility and accuracy of our communal norms, standards, and cultures; and the integrated features of our complex, magnificent brains connected to our complex, magnificent bodies. This insight should give us hope in a world awash with ethical concerns. It means that, when all works well, we influence our individual behavior and communal decisions and shape future generations through interpretations of scripture, tradition building, and experience. We can foster enriching, life-giving relationships that contribute to meaningful lives. Likewise, when we fail, err, and cause harm, or do not anticipate unintended, unwanted consequences, that is not the end. The provisional character of our reasoning means we can go back, reevaluate decisions, reconsider other options, and/or reformulate norms. We can arrive at new conclusions, new judgments, and new courses of action grounded in a framework that supplies rationales for our new proposals.

David Tracy calls this feature of our reasoning "relative adequacy." By this he means our judgments stand grounded in the best information, understanding, and interpretation we have now; yet judgments are subject to change or reaffirmation in light of new information, understanding, or experience.[28] Recognizing the relative adequacy of our judgments and actions requires intellectual humility and the cultivation of reasoning as an intellectual habit where we remain mindful of our own successes and shortcomings when reasoning toward just actions.

Relatively adequate judgments necessitate seeking not perfect but better solutions than ones currently employed. Methodologically, this means returning again and again to the Quadrilateral of sources to revisit questions of how we define ourselves, understand the world, and interpret the meaning and coherence in our lives as we strive to live just, loving, and good lives. Practical reasoning helps us see that when considering how to act referencing sacred scripture, tradition, and experience, it is not only to arrive at objective, abstract truths but also to make sure the gospel message of life, salvation, redemption, and the kingdom of God is made relevant and applicable in today's world. The scientific, imaginative, and practical dimensions of reasoning remain crucial to theological ethics as we seek to live a life of dialogical, relational, and embodied discipleship. In other words, as we strive to live an incarnational and not a theoretical ethical life, seeking wisdom in love.

SUGGESTED READINGS

Bushlack, Thomas. "Shadows of Divine Virtue: St. John of the Cross, Implicit Memory, and the Transformation Theory of Infused Cardinal Virtues." *Theological Studies* 81, no. 1 (March 2020): 88–110.

Dych, William. "Theology and Imagination." *Thought* 57 (March 1982): 116–27.

Spohn, William C. *Go and Do Likewise: Jesus and Ethics*. New York: Continuum, 1999.

Traina, Cristina L. H. *Feminist Ethics and Natural Law: The End of the Anathemas*. Washington, DC: Georgetown University Press, 1999.

Vogt, Christopher P. "Virtue: Personal Formation and Social Transformation." *Theological Studies* 77, no. 1 (March 2016): 181–96.

[28]David Tracy, *Plurality and Ambiguity* (Chicago: University of Chicago Press, 1987), 22–6.

PART TWO

Approaches, Methods, and Voices in Christian Ethics

CHAPTER FIVE

Christian Ethics, Norms, and the Moral Evaluation of an Act

JAMES T. BRETZKE, SJ

The present always has a past and so we begin in addressing the themes of how, first, "ethics" can be "Christian," second, what is generally understood by the category of moral "norms," and third, what then is involved in the ethical judgment of a moral action, by briefly summarizing how these questions would be treated in the Roman Catholic moral scholastic manualist tradition. The manualists predominated in the period from the seventeenth to the mid-twentieth century. The Second Vatican Council (1962–5) began a methodological paradigm shift in the understanding of these categories, as well as the whole discipline of Christian ethics. Finally, in bringing us to the present status of the question, this chapter looks at how tensions arose in differing approaches to the question following the close of the Council, which have a great bearing on the different contemporary understandings of the moral evaluation of human acts.

THE SCHOLASTIC MORAL MANUALIST TRADITION

While there were a few different approaches to the organizing structure of the various pre-Vatican II moral manuals, they paid almost no attention to the explicitly "Christian" nature of ethics as might be found among Protestant counterparts.[1] Both the authors and the professors were priests; laypeople were not involved apart from serving as subjects in the confessional "cases" studied. The audience for the most part was seminarians and priests, and the overall purpose of the texts centered on helping priests in the confessional to judge as accurately as possible the "species" (i.e., "moral nature") of the sins being confessed. The confessor gauged the penitent's overall individual culpability by considering his or her awareness, freedom, and key circumstances. Part of this assessment also considered other factors such as age, interior freedom, level of education, and so on. Finally, the confessor then assigned an appropriate penance as "satisfaction" for the sins committed.

[1]For an overview of the range of moral manuals published, as well as many other topics treated in moral theology, see James T. Bretzke, SJ, *A Research Bibliography in Christian Ethics and Catholic Moral Theology* (Lewiston: Edwin Mellen, 2006).

Therefore, the approach followed usually stressed a strong deontological normativity that focused on rules and duties, often structured around the Ten Commandments. Canon law also added to the template for the application of the moral principles, especially in relation to the fulfillment of the Precepts of the Church (such as the duty to attend Sunday Mass and keep the required Lenten fasts) and finally the proper administration of the Catholic sacraments. The focus was primarily on an abstract, philosophical presentation of a scholastic theory of natural law and how human acts fit within that category. The primary paradigm utilized was that of law, interpreted in a classicist, static mode. Whatever was an immoral act in the seventeenth century would likely be the same in the eighteenth, nineteenth, and twentieth centuries, though some nonmorally determinative features such as local customs might be superficially considered. Larger theological themes that would be found in Protestant ethics (which did not consider Confession a sacrament), as well as most of the New Testament, the Sermon on the Mount, and even "Jesus" himself, likely were not mentioned at all in these Latin tomes, beyond offering a brief proof text to confirm a rule or principle established on other grounds.

One major reason for these surprising lacunae revolves around the major purpose of these manuals, which was, as noted above, to aid the priest in the sacrament of Penance. The larger spiritual dimension of the Christian life was not treated in any organic sense of discipleship and/or moral formation and growth. Rather, the focus clearly was on evaluation of individual moral actions as interpreted through a scholastic philosophical and theological framework, often expressed in short Latin aphorisms.

For example, the classic saying *agere sequitur esse* (action follows being) was a foundational metaphysical principle in scholasticism that grounded moral action and one's moral duties and ethical possibilities in one's nature as a human being.[2] Here the moral "ought" or normative duty is founded on the "is," found in the physical reality of the individual. In terms of evaluation of the moral act, several other traditional concepts were employed. The tradition spoke of two kinds of actions performed by humans, but only one of these, the *actus humanus* (human act) denoted moral acts. The other kind of human action was called an *actus hominis* (an act of "man"), such as respiration, which was certainly "done" by humans but generally without a moral valence. It is quite difficult to translate these terms into inclusive language *and* still maintain their key distinction. *Actus humanus* remains translated in Church documents, like the *Catechism of the Catholic Church*, as "human act," while *actus hominis* is rendered as "act of man."

Full moral evaluation of an individual human act, *actus humanus* as distinguished from an *actus hominis*, required sufficient attention to the so-called three "fonts of morality" (*fontes moralitatis*). First, the action itself (*in se*) with its corresponding moral object (*finis operis*). Next would be the particular and concrete set of circumstances in which the moral agent made the decision to undertake this particular action. Finally, and most importantly, is the subjective intention(s) (*finis operantis*) the moral agent had in choosing and performing the action *in se*. A genuine human moral act required, therefore, both freedom to act in this particular way and the corresponding knowledge of what that particular choice involved.

If any of these requisite elements is missing, then the action itself would not be a true moral action, even if done by a human person. If one or more of these requisite elements were diminished (e.g., freedom, or knowledge, or extenuating circumstances), then the

[2]For a translation and brief explanation of Latin theological terms such as this, see James T. Bretzke, SJ, *Consecrated Phrases: A Latin Dictionary of Theological Terms*, 3rd ed. (Collegeville: Liturgical, [1998] 2013).

individual's moral culpability for the moral choice would be diminished but not removed entirely. Here is where the corresponding notion of *intrinsece malum in se* (intrinsically evil acts in themselves) entered into the discussion.[3] Such actions termed "intrinsic evils" already presume consideration of intention and circumstances. No further additional motives nor other mitigating circumstances would turn a morally evil object into a morally good one. For example, murder is defined as the unjustified taking of innocent human life and thus according to a reading of the three fonts of morality could be judged to be intrinsically evil and always wrong. Even if the murder victim were a sexual offender or had done some other heinous acts that may have provoked homicidal rage on the part of the murderer, the action itself still would be considered to be always morally wrong. Often this last point is misunderstood, such that a claim is advanced that the species "intrinsically evil" acts have no consideration whatsoever of intention and circumstances, and thus the mere commission of these acts by an individual is always and everywhere a serious moral evil. While a common misperception, this view is not in fact in accord with Thomas Aquinas nor the Catholic tradition.

Application of the manualist mode of moral analysis was done through a type of deductive casuistry that started with the concrete case at hand, often termed a *casus conscientiae* (case of conscience). Relatively little attention was given over to a thorough consideration of all the morally relevant features of the individual(s) involved. Instead, after arriving at a judgment of the key aspects of a person's state of life (e.g., married, single, in religious vows, etc.), the casuistry turned fairly quickly in a deductive analysis and application of what were considered to be the relevant moral principles involved. Thus, if the case involved the decision of a married couple whether or not to try to limit further offspring, the moral answer would allow only for the practice of abstinence—whether total, or periodic (at the time called the rhythm method). Even this periodic abstinence was held as morally suspect by some moralists up to Pius XI's 1930 encyclical *Casti connubii* (On Chaste Wedlock), which opened up the moral possibility of this practice. However, any and every form of artificial contraception was judged "an offense against the law of God and of nature, and those who indulge in such are branded with the guilt of a grave sin as a most grievous sin."[4]

There was a very high level of confidence in moral judgments pronounced on a wide array of both simple and complex ethical issues. One probable reason for this confidence was the long-standing success of the manualist tradition itself. For example, a widely used pre-Vatican II *Dictionary of Moral Theology* edited by Cardinal Francesco Roberti (Italian edition 1957; English translation 1962) offered in its 1,350 pages definitive pronouncements on everything from "Abandonment to God" to "Worldliness," giving the clear impression that the Catholic discipline had a clear answer to virtually any, and every, ethical issue and was far superior to all other ethical systems. Another reason for this moral confidence was the strong belief in the quasi-supernatural quality of the role of the Magisterium of the Catholic Church, which held that this office enjoyed *ex officio* the special assistance of the Holy Spirit in the exercise of its charism of authority.[5] Thus, when

[3]For a helpful series of recent essays on this topic, see Nenad Polgar and Joseph A. Selling, eds., *The Concept of Intrinsic Evil and Catholic Theological Ethics* (Lanham: Lexington, 2019).

[4]Pope Pius XI, *Casti connubii* (Vatican City: Libreria Editrice Vaticana, 1930), § 56.

[5]The special assistance of the Holy Spirit to the Magisterium has long been regarded as a mark of the True Church. See Vatican II's Dogmatic Constitution on the Church (*Lumen gentium*), § 25, and the *Catechism of the Catholic Church*, nos. 74–100.

the official Church spoke in one of its organs or pronouncements the faithful could trust that this was the nearest thing to the very voice of God speaking here and now.

THE PARADIGM SHIFT WITH VATICAN II

Both this method and this confidence began to shift in the late 1950s and early 1960s. While Vatican II is often portrayed as a major turning point in the development of contemporary Christian ethics in the Catholic tradition, some important groundwork had been laid in the decade before the Council began. Two innovative approaches to the traditional moral manuals emerged in 1954: Bernard Häring, CSsR's *Das Gesetz Christi* (1963 translation as the *Law of Christ*) and Gérard Gilleman, SJ's *Le primat de la charité en théologie morale* (1959 translation as *The Primacy of Charity in Moral Theology*). Both of these watershed works proposed a single key biblical theme as the organizing metaphor for the construction of Christian ethics. Häring went on to serve as a very important *peritus* (expert) at the Council. He was instrumental in the drafting of some key documents that influenced how the discipline of moral theology was revised, such as the Pastoral Constitution on the Church in the Modern World (*Gaudium et spes*), and the Decree on Priestly Training (*Optatam totius*). The latter document stated explicitly that scripture ought to be the "soul" of all theology, and in particular moral theology's "scientific exposition, nourished more on the teaching of the Bible, should shed light on the loftiness of the calling of the faithful in Christ and the obligation that is theirs of bearing fruit in charity for the life of the world."[6] While several Roman Catholic moralists sought to integrate scripture into the framework of moral theology, this biblical mandate was *not* universally and warmly received.[7]

In the two decades that followed the close of the Council, an ongoing debate raged over the so-called *proprium* or distinctiveness of Christian ethics. Two schools of thought emerged from moral theologians writing after the Council. One was the "Moral Autonomy" School (Josef Fuchs et al.) that emphasized universal moral norms discovered and applied through individual conscience, and which saw the Bible essentially as confirming the ethical content that could (and should) be arrived at without recourse to the sacred claim of scripture. Scripture could help with intention and moral motivation, but the content would be accessible to all via what Aquinas called *recta ratio* or "right reason." The other school, often termed the *Glaubensethik* or Faith Ethics School, held that scripture was indispensable for coming to a proper, and fuller, grasp of Christian ethics, with the added special assistance of the Holy Spirit given to the Magisterium as the authentic (i.e., authoritative) interpreter of scripture itself, though it "is not above the word of God, but serves it, teaching only what has been handed on, listening to it devoutly, guarding it scrupulously and explaining it faithfully in accord with a divine commission and with the help of the Holy Spirit."[8] This explicit attention to the ongoing action in the Church of the Holy Spirit was promised by Jesus in his Farewell Discourse (cf. Jn 14:16-17, 26, and 16:13-14). Here he speaks of the divine gift of the Paraclete (παράκλητος, Latin *Paracletus*) who will serve as Advocate (counselor, helper, comforter), teacher,

[6]Second Vatican Council, *Optatam totius* (Vatican City: Libreria Editrice Vaticana, 1965), § 16.
[7]One theologian, though, who did much to bring scripture into Christian ethics was William C. Spohn. See his *Go and Do Likewise: Jesus and Ethics* (New York: Continuum, 1999) and *What Are They Saying about Scripture and Ethics?*, rev. ed. (New York: Paulist, [1984] 1995).
[8]Cf. Second Vatican Council, *Dei Verbum* (Vatican City: Libreria Editrice Vaticana, 1965), § 10.

and progressive revealer. This crucial pneumatological dimension marks a significant development in the understanding of the traditional discipline of moral theology as well as its unfolding application through a deeper practice of spiritual discernment in concrete situations.

CONFLICTING PARADIGMS IN POST-VATICAN II MORAL THEOLOGY

One key insight from Thomas Kuhn's 1962 seminal work on paradigm theory, *The Structure of Scientific Revolutions*, borne out in many of the post-Vatican II developments in several areas of theology and church practice, is that established structures, thought patterns, core concepts, and academic constructions do not change easily or quickly—even in the face of compelling data and reasons to support the necessity of such changes.[9] The areas of moral norms and the corresponding analysis of the layers of meaning in human moral acts give us two contested arenas of tension that revolve in large extent on the grounding paradigms one brings to their consideration.

Semper Idem (Always the Same) was the episcopal motto of Cardinal Alfredo Ottaviani (1890–1979), who served as the head of the Supreme Sacred Congregation of the Roman and Universal Inquisition (a.k.a. the Holy Office, and today the Congregation for the Doctrine of the Faith). He was one of the staunchest conservatives at Vatican II, and, though the president of the Pontifical Birth Control Commission (1963–6), he did not join the sixty-four members voting to accept the so-called Majority Report,[10] which accepted the possibility of the legitimacy of a conscience-based decision by married couples to use artificial birth control for sufficiently serious reasons. Instead, he sided with the four-person minority who opposed the Majority Report and prepared their own Minority Report, which held that any change in Catholic Church teaching should be impossible and that each and every use of artificial means to block procreation was *contra naturam* (against nature) and therefore intrinsically evil. The Minority Report[11] ultimately carried the day as it furnished the basis for Pope Paul VI's highly controversial 1968 encyclical, *Humanae vitae*, which left largely unchanged the key teaching on the illicitness of artificial contraception. This still unresolved debate marks many of the differences in contemporary disagreements over the precise meaning and evaluations of moral acts.

This *Humanae vitae* debate illustrates quite well the clash of paradigms in normative Christian ethics. Philosopher-theologian, Bernard Lonergan, SJ, in a 1967 seminal article outlined two contrasting worldviews as being Classicist or Historicist.[12] The former views the world, human nature, and core human institutions as essentially static and unchanging, whereas the Historicist perspective sees human reality as more dynamic and developing, even though a core understanding of human nature could be traced

---

[9]Thomas S. Kuhn, *The Structure of Scientific Revolutions* (Chicago: University of Chicago Press, 1962).

[10]This report was leaked to a number of English-language periodicals and can be found as an appendix to Robert Blair Kaiser's well-researched account of the Pontifical Birth Control Commission in his *The Encyclical That Never Was: The Story of the Pontifical Commission on Population, Family and Birth, 1964–1966* (London: Sheed & Ward, [1985] 1987): 1–18.

[11]Like the "Majority Report" this too was "leaked" to sympathetic press organs and can still be found online in a variety of websites, such as "Minority Report of the Papal Commission for the Study of Problems of the Family, Population, and Birth Rate," http://www.bostonleadershipbuilders.com/0church/birth-control-minority.htm.

[12]Bernard Lonergan, SJ, "The Transition from a Classicist World-View to Historical-Mindedness," in *Law for Liberty: The Role of Law in the Church Today*, ed. James E. Biechler (Baltimore: Helicon, 1967).

throughout history. For the Classicist perspective, though, whatever was morally true in the thirteenth century should be equally valid in the twenty-first century in every essential aspect. The Classicist worldview interpreted the natural law through an abstract, deductive mode of moral analysis, beginning with the enunciation of a formal principle, such as absolute prohibition against lying. Lying was judged *contra naturam* to the true "nature" of the faculty of human speech, being the communication of truth. This abstract prohibition then was applied to concrete situations by forbidding any speech that was *locutio contra mentem* (speech contrary to what one was actually thinking), because this would represent a frustration of the natural end of that given faculty. Similarly, the "faculty" of sexuality was viewed as essentially ordered to procreation (in the context of marriage), and thus anything done physically to block the completion of that end was judged to be a sin *contra naturam* against the proper use of the sexual faculty.

God, of course, created all of nature and instilled in all human beings the natural law, as well as the faculty of *recta ratio* or right reason, to discover this natural law and apply it throughout human moral life. However, in the Classicist paradigm, the natural law was primarily identified with the "order of nature" rather than "order of reason," and so whatever emerged for a deductive moral analysis of the biological nature of human faculties provided the corresponding moral obligation. Thus, the moral principle of *agere sequitur esse* (action follows being) was decoded through the reading of the "is" of human biology which in turn largely produced the "ought" of normative morality. The Classicist versus Historicist worldviews were often cast methodologically as approaching morality either through a Physicalist or Personalist framework.[13]

The contrasting approach to moral theology that gained popularity during and after Vatican II is often called either Revisionism or Personalism. While there is a difference between these two terms, both reject the Classicist Paradigm in favor of a more nuanced and open-ended Historicist Paradigm. In a seminal article[14] the influential Louvain moral theologian Louis Janssens proposed that the fundamental moral criterion should be the human person "integrally and adequately considered," which he then outlined as incorporating eight dimensions discernible in an inductive manner more in tune with the historical world view: (1) subject; (2) embodied subject; (3) part of the material world; (4) inter-relational with other persons; (5) an interdependent social being; (6) historical; (7) equal but unique; (8) called to know and worship God. Much of the teaching of the Magisterium since Vatican II, including John Paul II's "Theology of the Body,"[15] utilizes personalist vocabulary, even if there is tension over the integration of Personalist categories with Physicalist deontological moral norms. While Personalism is better at lifting up the morally relevant features in a thicker description of both the moral act and the agent, this paradigm too has significant weaknesses. It often is rather vague and indeterminate, especially when trying to concretize or specify material norms, the real

[13]Much has been written on this topic and still very helpful is Brian V. Johnstone, CSsR, "From Physicalism to Personalism," *Studia Moralia* 30, no. 1 (1992): 71–96.

[14]Louis Janssens, "Artificial Insemination: Ethical Considerations," *Louvain Studies* 5, no. 1 (1980): 3–29.

[15]In his weekly audiences between 1979 and 1984, Pope John Paul II gave a number of addresses on the theme of theological anthropology and human sexuality. This so-called Theology of the Body was picked up by many commentators, such as Christopher West, as breaking significant new ground, though it likewise has been critiqued by others as presenting an "essentialist" reading of human sexuality with insufficient attention paid to the concrete features of many difficult situations in which individuals and couples find themselves. See Christopher West, *Theology of the Body Explained: A Commentary on John Paul II's Man and Woman He Created Them*, rev. ed. (Boston: Pauline Books and Media, 2007); and Charles Curran, *The Moral Theology of Pope John Paul II* (Washington, DC: Georgetown University Press, 2005).

"do's and don'ts" of the moral life. It can be more easily "abused" and is perhaps more open to the deceptive processes of human rationalization: "My conscience says it's okay" or "No one is being hurt by this." Thus, many authors have begun to suggest that while Personalism is clearly important for fundamental moral theology, by itself it is insufficient to ground a full and complete consideration of the natural law and moral norms.

One major influence of this paradigm shift, though, is a major methodological revision in the process of casuistry used to mediate moral norms with concrete persons in their particular contexts. This is casuistry with the accent on the human face. It begins with an inductive investigation of as many morally relevant features as possible and then turns to integrating the corresponding moral principles, with the accent on the personal discernment and appropriation of conscience. While Personalism is a major development in Christian ethics, it is *not* a rupture with the past. Rather, it builds on the deeply personal understanding of conscience outlined in *Gaudium et spes* (§ 16) and on Aquinas's notion of *lex indita non scripta* (the law is "inscribed" in human nature, rather than "written" or given from an external source). Moral norms remain absolute, but only in the abstract. When it comes to interpreting and applying natural law grounded moral norms in the concrete, it is difficult (if not impossible) to achieve the same universality and certainty. Helpful here is the Thomistic principle of *lex valet ut in pluribus* (the moral law binds in most [but not all] cases), which he outlined in his treatise of the natural law.[16]

ONGOING INTERWOVEN TENSIONS IN CHRISTIAN ETHICS

Before Vatican II, there was something of a chasm between Protestant and Roman Catholic ethicists that for centuries suggested two sharply demarcated and often hostile camps. However, from the 1960s onward there have been significant developments that James Gustafson outlined in his 1978 *Protestant and Roman Catholic Ethics: Prospects for Rapprochement*.[17] A good deal of academic cross-fertilization ensued, with influential Catholic moralists such as William C. Spohn and Lisa Sowle Cahill studying under Protestants such as Gustafson, and the influential Methodist theologian Stanley Hauerwas teaching for a dozen years at the Catholic University of Notre Dame. Catholics became familiarized with Protestant thinkers such as H. R. Niebuhr's responsibility ethics, while Aquinas, virtue ethics, and even natural law thinking found their way into Protestant reflections. These, and other emerging scholars, sought to make Christian ethics more biblical, spiritual, and ecumenically collaborative.

In 1966, the Episcopalian theologian Joseph Fletcher published his controversial *Situation Ethics: The New Morality*, which proposed that "all laws and rules and principles and ideals and norms, are only *contingent*, only valid *if they happen* to serve love" in a given situation which by its nature would be unique.[18] Several cases were included to illustrate how a particular set of circumstances might transform the application of what was usually considered an absolute moral norm. One case entitled "Sacrificial Adultery?" concerned Frau Bergmeier, a German woman picked up and imprisoned in a Russian

[16]Thomas Aquinas's treatise on the natural law comes in the middle of his larger discussion on law and the types of law in the *Summa Theologiae*. The *ut in pluribus* principle referenced here is discussed in *ST*, I–II.94.2. Fundación Tomás de Aquino, https://www.corpusthomisticum.org/sth1090.html.

[17]James M. Gustafson, *Protestant and Roman Catholic Ethics: Prospects for Rapprochement* (Chicago: University of Chicago, 1978).

[18]Joseph F. Fletcher, *Situation Ethics: The New Morality* (Philadelphia: Westminster, 1966), 30, emphasis in original.

work camp. She eventually sought to get herself impregnated by a friendly guard in order that she might win early release as a medical liability and thus return to gather her family together in the ruins of postwar Germany. Whether the case itself was actually historical remains unknown, but ensuing academic debate remains pronounced. In 1968, Gene H. Outka and Paul Ramsey edited *Norm and Context in Christian Ethics* on this divisive topic.[19] Included were essays by leading Protestant and Catholic theologians, in addition to the editors themselves, such as Charles Curran, Fletcher, Gustafson, Häring, and several others. Ten years later in response to Catholic Richard McCormick, SJ's, seminal work on the moral theory of proportionalism in double-effect cases, he, along with Paul Ramsey, released a series of essays under the title *Doing Evil to Achieve Good: Moral Choice in Conflict Situations*.[20] Proportionalism makes a distinction between moral evil (which is never allowed) and ontic or nonmoral evil (which may be chosen for serious proportionate reasons). For example, most surgeries involve ontic evils of pain, scarring, and so on, and we accept these as necessary, nonmoral evils to achieve the good of the surgery performed. In this same vein, terminating a tubal (ectopic) pregnancy, which has no chance of a viable birth, to safeguard the mother's health represents an allowable ontic evil and does not correspond to the intrinsic evil of elective abortion.[21]

At the same time as these casuistical debates, increasing attention was given to the discipleship dynamics of Christian moral character, the life of the virtues, and the corresponding ethical imagination that put these into concrete practice. Häring in his 1978 three-volume manual of moral theology, *Free and Faithful in Christ*, termed this dynamic as the necessary "creative fidelity" to the Spirit of God's Word in our world.[22] This moral discernment theme of creative fidelity captures well the dynamic tension that will always legitimately exist in mediating moral norms and the corresponding ethical evaluations of human action in Christian ethics. John Paul II began his 1993 *Veritatis splendor* encyclical on fundamental moral theology with a commentary of Jesus's encounter with the Rich Young Man (cf. Matthew 19; Mark 10; Luke 18). This exchange also shows that for Christian disciples, merely keeping the Commandments is not enough. Jesus's love encourages and empowers the emptying of oneself both to enrich others and to join in the community of disciples to follow him.

Pope John Paul II was succeeded in 2005 by Joseph Ratzinger, who took the name Benedict XVI. He had been the Prefect of the Congregation for the Doctrine of Faith (1980–2005) and had the reputation of being a strict watchdog for moral orthodoxy. Many of John Paul II's key teachings on moral theology may have had a Ratzinger ring to them, but Benedict XVI himself did not continue this focus on a rigorous interpretation of fundamental moral theology. Instead, he published three encyclicals on the theological virtues of love and hope, and the last of these, "On Charity and Truth" (*Caritas in veritate*), focused on the problems of social justice and especially the common good associated with the dynamics of globalization. A fourth encyclical, "The Light of Faith" (*Lumen fidei*), was in the works when Benedict decided to resign in February 2013.

---

[19]Gene Outka and Paul Ramsey, *Norm and Context in Christian Ethics* (New York: Scribners, 1968).

[20]Richard A. McCormick, SJ, and Paul Ramsey, *Doing Evil to Achieve Good: Moral Choice in Conflict Situations* (Chicago: Loyola University Press, 1978).

[21]While this sort of case is often associated with proportionalism, even conservative non-proportionalists accept this basic point. See Martin Rhonheimer, *Vital Conflicts in Medical Ethics: A Virtue Approach to Craniotomy and Tubal Pregnancies*, ed. William F. Murphy Jr. (Washington, DC: Catholic University Press of America, 2009).

[22]Bernard Häring, *Free and Faithful in Christ*, 3 vols. (Slough, UK: St. Paul, 1978).

His successor, Pope Francis (2013–present), published *Lumen fidei* in 2013 and explicitly acknowledged Benedict's role in the earlier draft of the encyclical. The encyclical was the capstone of Benedict's treatment of the theological virtues and spoke of faith as the guiding light for all Christian life and action in the world. Francis's papacy itself illustrates further development in the paradigm shift begun at Vatican II. Francis's emphases on mercy, forgiveness, outreach to the marginalized, a reluctance to condemn individuals from on high, and pastoral accompaniment in a lived moral discernment all represent more than a shift in tone. The recovery of mercy as a key biblical theme requires a corresponding need for better and wider practice in the interpretation and application of moral norms. Pope Francis's Apostolic Exhortations *Evangelii gaudium* ("The Joy of the Gospel," 2013), *Amoris laetitia* ("The Joy of Love in the Family," 2016), and *Gaudete et exsultate* ("Rejoice and Be Glad [Mt. 5:12] on the Universal Call to Holiness," 2018) are all good examples of these new pastoral responses to contemporary challenges on both the global and individual levels. However, indifference and even outright strong pushback from conservative culture warriors give further testimony to the earlier observations made on the difficulty of achieving true paradigm shifts.

SUGGESTED READINGS

Bretzke, James T., SJ. *Handbook of Roman Catholic Moral Terms*. Washington, DC: Georgetown University Press, 2013.

Curran, Charles E., and A. McCormick Richard, SJ, eds. *Readings in Moral Theology, No. 1: Moral Norms and Catholic Tradition*. New York: Paulist, 1979.

Fuchs, Josef, SJ. *Christian Morality: The Word Became Flesh*, trans. Brian McNeil. Washington, DC: Georgetown University Press; Dublin: Gill and Macmillan, 1987.

Noonan, John T., Jr. *A Church That Can and Cannot Change: The Development of Catholic Moral Teaching*. Notre Dame: University of Notre Dame Press, 2005.

Selling, Joseph A. *Reframing Catholic Theological Ethics*. Oxford: Oxford University Press, 2016.

CHAPTER SIX

Virtue Ethics

DANIEL DALY

Virtue ethics is a normative approach that focuses on the cultivation and practice of virtues. A virtue is an admirable character trait that enables a person to consistently do what is good and right with ease and joy. After a hiatus of approximately seven hundred years, virtue has regained a central place in Christian ethics. Since the 1970s, Catholics and Protestants alike have turned to virtue ethics to discern the shape of the Christian life.

Unlike in other ethical methodologies, the person's moral character is primary in virtue ethics. Crucially, moral character is a relevant moral reality *in addition* to action, not instead of it. Virtue ethicists contend that a person's moral character and her actions exist in a dialectical relationship and that neither is sufficiently understood in the absence of the other. Actions emerge from and form moral character. While virtue ethics is an academic approach, many non-academicians utilize virtue reasoning in their ethics. Parents, for instance, often employ a virtue approach regarding the moral development of their children. They are concerned both with what their children do *and* who their children become.

This chapter has three goals. First, it endeavors to introduce the basic meaning and approach of virtue ethics. Second, it argues for a distinct account of virtue ethics based in a personalist theological anthropology. Third, it identifies undertheorized areas within virtue ethics and so concludes with a "call for papers."

Before beginning, a note on the difference between virtue ethics and virtue theory is needed. In virtue ethics, the virtues, such as justice and charity, serve to organize other normative concepts, such as rules, principles, and duties. These concepts gain their normative power in relation to the virtues that they reflect and help to cultivate. A virtue ethic relies on a virtue theory, which seeks to explain what a virtue is, how virtues are acquired or accepted, and why virtue is a relevant moral category. This chapter is an exercise in both virtue ethics and virtue theory.

VIRTUE AND THE FOUR SOURCES

The thread that binds this volume, John Wesley's Quadrilateral, recognizes that theological ethics is a practice that accounts for both *fides et ratio*. Scripture and tradition are the revelatory sources in the Quadrilateral, while reason and experience codify the need to account for human insights when asking questions concerning goodness and rightness. However, my approach to the sources of theological ethics differs slightly from Wesley's. Here I offer a further explanation of one source and modification of another.[1]

[1]This section is influenced by Margaret Farley's account of the Quadrilateral in her book *Just Love: A Framework for Christian Sexual Ethics* (New York: Continuum, 2008), 182–96.

The revival and continued development of virtue ethics have drawn on all four sources. In William Spohn's view, "Virtue ethics and spirituality are best ways to appropriate the moral vision of Jesus witnessed in the New Testament."[2] Stanley Hauerwas, Allen Verhey, James Keenan, Lucas Chan, and others have agreed with this assessment. St. Thomas Aquinas is mainly responsible for the prominence of virtue in the theological tradition, and in turning to his work, moralists have retrieved a long-neglected and essential part of the moral tradition. For Aquinas, the virtues supplied the organizing principles for his normative ethics. As he wrote in the prologue to the *Secunda Secundae* in the *Summa Theologiae*, "Accordingly we may reduce the whole of moral matters to the consideration of the virtues" because "in this way no matter pertaining to morals will be overlooked."[3]

It is important to emphasize that experience is a communal, not individualistic, source. "Though a crucial part of my experience is my self-experience, 'my experience' alone is never a source at all."[4] Experience is not "raw," idiosyncratic, and unreflective. "Raw experience carries with it no evaluation."[5] The moment a person reflects on and makes sense of experience she does so using socially established language and concepts. The category of experience involves each and every person in the community but is never reduced to any one person in the community. Turning to virtue, human experience indicates that people possess moral character and that their actions emerge from it. We sometimes remark that a typically patient friend "acted out of character" when he lost his temper. Like actors on a stage, people "stay in character" by consistently exercising their moral character traits.

The fourth source is secular science, not reason. The secular sciences, such as psychology, sociology, and economics, are sources containing distinct sets of data and conclusions. Ethicists must account for secular science to address reality. Consider medical ethics. The Christian medical ethicist will need to know the science of fetal development and pregnancy if he is to make cogent ethical claims regarding abortion.

The existence of moral character has been the subject of significant debate in various secular sciences. The field of psychology, in particular, has taken an interest in the notion of character and durable character traits. Some psychologists ascribe the "situationist challenge" to the existence of virtue. These scholars reject the idea that settled character traits exist and instead insist that social situations cause and explain human action.[6] However, at the turn of the millennium, other studies in psychology refuted the situationist challenge and argued that traits are relatively stable throughout adulthood.[7] Such debates illumine and refine what the virtues are, how they are formed,

---

[2]William Spohn, *Go and Do Likewise: Jesus and Ethics* (New York: Continuum, 2000), 27.

[3]Thomas Aquinas, *Summa Theologiae*, II–II, Prologue. All citations of the *Summa* are drawn from: Saint Thomas Aquinas, *Summa Theologiae*, 5 vols., trans. Fathers of the English Dominican Province, reprint (Allen: Christian Classics, 1981).

[4]Todd Salzman and Michael Lawler, *Virtue and Theological Ethics: Toward a Renewed Ethical Method* (Maryknoll: Orbis, 2018), 101.

[5]John T. Noonan, "Development in Moral Doctrine," in *Change in Official Catholic Moral Teachings: Readings in Moral Theology No. 13*, ed. Charles Curran (New York: Paulist, 2003), 297.

[6]Tom Bates and Pauline Kleingeld, "Virtue, Vice, and Situationism," in *The Oxford Handbook of Virtue*, ed. Nancy E. Snow (New York: Oxford University Press, 2018).

[7]William Fleeson, R. Michael Furr, Eranda Jayawickreme, Erik G. Helzer, Anselma G. Hartley, and Peter Meindl, "Personality Science and the Foundations of Character," in *Character: New Directions from Philosophy, Psychology, and Theology*, ed. Christian Miller, R. Michael Furr, Angela Knobel, and William Fleeson (New York: Oxford University Press, 2015), 51–7.

and how they guide action. Below I show how virtue ethics profits from an engagement with social theory.

Reason is a human capacity, not a source. Following Aquinas, I understand reason as the umbrella term for two distinct cognitive capacities: *ratio* and *intellectus*. *Ratio* is discursive reason. Ratiocination is probing, testing, investigative, and integrative in the attempt to discover truth. *Intellectus* is the contemplative reception of truths regarding things transcendent. It is intuitive and insightful.[8] These capacities are engaged in all four of the sources.

CONTEMPORARY CHRISTIAN VIRTUE ETHICS

We begin with the most influential non-Christian and Christian accounts of virtue, produced by Aristotle and Aquinas, respectively. Aristotle's *Nicomachean Ethics* defined a moral virtue as a "state of character which makes a man good and which makes him do his work well."[9] This will involve acting in a way in which one follows the mean between the vicious extremes to the "right extent, at the right time, with the right motive, and in the right way."[10] Drawing on Aristotle, "the Philosopher," Aquinas argued that a virtue is a good habit, residing in a power of the soul, by which the person consistently does the good with ease and joy.[11]

In the last quarter of the twentieth century, new accounts of virtue emerged. Methodist theologian Hauerwas distanced himself from Aquinas by arguing that virtues are the traits the enable a person to be faithful to the Christian story.[12] Philosopher Alasdair MacIntyre profoundly influenced Christian virtue ethics with his book, *After Virtue*.[13] There MacIntyre argued that the virtues reflected and sustained a community's notion of the moral good. It is only through the virtues and virtuous practices that people have a sense of the morally excellent life as a whole. Echoing Aquinas, Mennonite theologian Josef Kotva wrote, "Virtues are those states of character or character traits acquired over time that contribute to the human good."[14] Catholic ethicist Spohn produced an Aristotelian definition when he wrote that a virtue is "a disposition to act, desire and feel that involves the exercise of judgment and leads to a recognizable human excellence, an instance of human flourishing."[15] One finds a consensus here. First, character is a moral reality. Virtue ethicists argue that ethics is not limited to the evaluation of actions alone but that character is morally essential as well. Second, virtue goes beyond moral minimums and the simple binaries of right and wrong. A virtue approach focuses on moral supererogation, moral excellence, and the emulation of moral exemplars. The virtue ethicist asks, "Which traits compose the life of moral excellence?" "What is the virtuous action in this situation?" and, crucially for Christians, "What would Jesus do?"

---

[8]Aquinas, *Summa Theologiae*, I.79.8–10.

[9]Aristotle, *Nicomachean Ethics*, trans. W. D. Ross, 1106a20. http://classics.mit.edu/Aristotle/nicomachaen.html.

[10]Ibid.

[11]Aquinas, *Summa Theologiae*, I–II.55, 56.

[12]Stanley Hauerwas, *A Community of Character: Toward a Constructive Christian Social Ethic* (Notre Dame: University of Notre Dame Press, 1991), 132.

[13]Alasdair MacIntyre, *After Virtue*, 2nd ed. (Notre Dame: University of Notre Dame Press, 1984).

[14]Josef Kotva, *The Christian Case for Virtue Ethics* (Washington, DC: Georgetown University Press, 1997), 38.

[15]Spohn, *Go and Do Likewise*, 28.

Reflecting on this diversity, Jennifer Herdt has argued that there are three distinct approaches to Christian virtue ethics: natural law, particularist, and analytic.[16] The first is typically Catholic, the second Protestant, and the third more philosophical than theological. She has claimed that the natural law draws primarily from the work of Aquinas, while the particularist has its historical roots in St. Augustine and has been deeply influenced by the work of Hauerwas. Philosophers compose the analytic school. The distinctive mark of analytic virtue ethics is its focus on systematizing, simplifying, and justifying virtue discourse. Analytic virtue ethics engages in metaethical questions regarding the nature of the good and how notions of the good and virtue can be used to construct a robust normative virtue ethics.

Herdt's typology warrants a three-point response. First, it is more accurate to claim that the Catholic approach to virtue is grounded in theological anthropology. The natural law constitutes one anthropological approach but does not exhaust the category. Below I show how Catholic virtue ethicists have developed a virtue ethic based on a personalist anthropology. Second, a coherent virtue theory should draw on insights from all three schools that Herdt has identified. Because virtue is an ethics of the person, an accurate theological portrait of the person is requisite. However, such a portrait is not sufficient. Hauerwas rightly argued that "our capacity to be virtuous depends on the existence of communities which have been formed by narratives faithful to the character of reality."[17] While there is an objective anthropological basis for what counts as a virtue, the virtues are mediated to agents only through a community.[18] Catholic virtue ethicists David Cloutier and William Mattison have suggested that the communal formation of personal character is the area in most need of development in Catholic virtue ethics.[19] Put differently, Catholic virtue ethicists should draw upon the particularist school to further explain the development of the virtues. Finally, all of this work should draw on a philosophical, analytic approach to virtue. As I show throughout the chapter, philosophers of virtue ethics such as Julia Annas, Rosiland Hursthouse, Lisa Tessman, and Linda Zagzebski all contribute to the development of Christian virtue theory.

PERSONALIST CHRISTIAN VIRTUE THEORY

The previous section argued that there are several accounts of virtue. The remainder of this chapter sketches the core aspects of a personalist account. A personalist approach begins with the existing person, not the abstract faculties of the person. The fathers of the Second Vatican Council called for a personalist approach to ethics: "Human activity must be judged insofar as it refers to the human person integrally and adequately considered."[20]

---

[16]Jennifer Herdt, "Varieties of Contemporary Christian Virtue Ethics," in *The Routledge Companion to Virtue Ethics*, ed. Lorraine Desser-Jones and Michael Slote (New York: Routledge, 2015).

[17]Hauerwas, *A Community of Character*, 116.

[18]Lawler and Salzman, *Virtue and Theological Ethics*, 63.

[19]David Cloutier and William C. Mattison III, "The Resurgence of Virtue in Recent Moral Theology," *Journal of Moral Theology* 3, no. 1 (2014): 231.

[20]This quotation comes from the official commentary on *Gaudium et spes* and refers to § 51. See Richard A. McCormick, SJ, *Corrective Vision: Explorations in Moral Theology* (Kansas City: Sheed & Ward, 1994), 14. For the commentary, see *Schema constitutionis pastoralis de ecclesia in mundo huius temporis: Expensio modorum partis secundae* (Vatican City: Vatican Press, 1965), 37–8. Indeed, even the wording within the commentary comes from the Belgian moral theologian Louis Janssens (1908–2001), who had proposed that the fundamental criterion for ethically evaluating human actions is "the human person integrally and adequately considered." For him, such "a personalist standpoint" entails consideration of any human action "as a whole means for

Gaudium et spes, in fact, presents an integral and adequate portrait of the person. There we find that the person possesses human dignity, moral freedom, and in "his [*sic*] innermost nature ... is a social being, and unless he relates himself to others he can neither live nor develop his potential."[21] This account suggests that Christian ethics should judge an action according to how it respects human dignity and promotes human relationships. The virtues, then, are traits such as love, mercy, and solidarity—traits by which a person freely affirms the value of, and loves, God, self, neighbor, and creation.

The virtues are excellences of relationality and relationship, not excellences of individual powers or faculties of the person. Virtue is non-reducible to any one aspect of the person, such as her appetites or external actions. Virtue resides in the whole person, engaging her cognitive, emotional, and executive capacities. Thus, the virtuous person feels, thinks, and acts in virtuous ways. For instance, the virtuous woman is emotionally moved by the suffering of others, discovers what she should do to alleviate that suffering, and can carry out the good that she knows she should do. In sum, virtue is about relationality and emerges from every capacity of the whole person.

Virtue as Operative Habits

As earlier definitions suggested, virtues are good habits. Contrary to a colloquial understanding, habits are not rote or routine. Habits do not produce mindless activities, but rather, the most intelligent and loving ways of acting. Philosopher Julia Annas claimed that habits are analogous to nonmoral skills, such as playing a musical instrument.[22] Just as the skillful jazz musician quickly and easily adapts to the band's change in tempo, so too does the merciful parent quickly and easily discern how to comfort his suffering child. Once the parent discovers the right way to respond to the suffering child, she can execute the action. These skilled ways of acting are second nature for the musician and parent. Virtues are a person's moral muscles, capacitating and enabling the agent to know *and* do what is virtuous.

All of this is to suggest that a virtue is an *operative* habit about how one relates to God, others, self, and creation. The virtues enable and facilitate the performance of good, virtuous actions. Virtue ethics is concerned with both being and doing. Returning to the skill analogy presented above: Does becoming a good fastball hitter make it easier to hit a fastball? Of course it does! The habit one has acquired (hitting a fastball well) facilitates certain operations (hitting *this* fastball, right now). Similarly, the person who acquired the virtue of justice will quickly, easily, and joyfully attempt to return a found wallet to its rightful owner.

Virtue and Happiness

Many virtue ethicists have argued that the virtues share an intrinsic relationship to happiness. The possession and practice of the virtues are essential to the happy life. Aquinas argued that happiness principally consists in virtue.[23] Following Aristotle, he wrote that to be happy in this life "external goods are necessary, not as belonging to the

---

the promotion of the human persons who are involved and for their relationships." Louis Janssens, "Artificial Insemination: Ethical Considerations," *Louvain Studies* 8 (1980): 24; also see Louis Janssens, "Particular Goods and Personalist Morals," *Perspectives* 6, no. 1 (1999): 55–9.

[21]Second Vatican Council, *Gaudium et spes* (Vatican City: Libreria Editrice Vaticana, 1965), § 12.

[22]Julia Annas, *Intelligent Virtue* (New York: Oxford University Press, 2011), chap. 1.

[23]Aquinas, *Summa Theologiae*, I–II.5.4.

essence of happiness, but by serving as instruments to happiness, which consists in an operation of virtue."[24] Here the happy life is co-existential with the virtuous life. In its fullness, the happy, virtuous life is characterized by friendship with the God revealed in the person of Jesus Christ. The virtues, then, are those traits that enable a person to grow in friendship with God and neighbor.

Cardinal Virtues

The Christian tradition has codified two sets of virtues: the cardinal virtues and the theological virtues. The cardinal, or acquired virtues, are proportioned to human nature. St. Ambrose of Milan first referred to prudence, justice, temperance, and fortitude as the cardinal virtues. These are the virtues from which all other acquired virtues "hinge" (*cardo* in Latin). Prudence enables the person to choose the action that rightly attains the intended end. All virtues rely on the rational direction of prudence in order to realize their specific ends. Justice pertains to human relations. The just person habitually renders to others their due. Temperance enables the person to control his appetites in order to promote his physical well-being. This virtue guides a person's actions regarding food, drink, and sex. Fortitude is the virtue that guides a person to pursue a good that is difficult to achieve. It enables a person to act virtuously even when she experiences fear.

The cardinal virtues are acquired through intentional, recurrent virtuous actions. This fact poses a logical problem: How does a person who lacks virtue perform virtuous actions and thereby acquire the virtues? While such a person could follow norms that promote virtuous behavior, the richest modes of virtue acquisition are through the emulation of exemplars and through what virtue ethicists call "practices." When one emulates an exemplar such as Jesus, she uses the exemplar's character to guide her prudential discernment of an action. She questions, "What would Jesus do in this situation?" Here the agent emulates the actions, emotions, and relationships of the virtuous figure. John Paul II gestured toward but did not develop an exemplarist virtue methodology in *Veritatis splendor* when he wrote that "Jesus' way of acting and his words, his deeds and his precepts constitute the moral rule of Christian life."[25] Drawing on John Paul, Patrick Clark has argued that Christian virtue ethicists should draw more deeply on exemplarism.[26]

Christian virtue ethicists have appropriated Alasdair MacIntyre's technical definition of practice, as a socially established activity through which goods internal to that activity are progressively realized.[27] Practices, for MacIntyre, are fields or disciplines within a society. Medicine, baseball, and the Christian life are all practices. Each of these practices is composed of sub-practices or exercises. For instance, fasting is a Christian sub-practice when it is done "in order that the mind may arise more freely to the contemplation of heavenly things."[28] A focus on God is the good internal to the practice of fasting. Such an exercise cultivates the acquired virtue of temperance, as well as the acceptance of the infused virtue of charity. Dieting, on the other hand, involves forgoing food for the sake of a good external to the action, namely, weight loss. The dieter fails to grow in either virtue because dieting is a technique ordained to an external end. The sacraments, the

---

[24]Ibid., 4.7.
[25]Pope John Paul II, *Veritatis splendor* (Vatican City: Libreria Editrice Vaticana, 1993), 20.
[26]Patrick Clark, "The Case for an Exemplarist Approach to Virtue in Catholic Moral Theology," *Journal of Moral Theology* 3, no. 1 (2014).
[27]MacIntyre, *After Virtue*, 187.
[28]Aquinas, *Summa Theologiae*, II–II.147.1.

works of mercy, and centering prayer are all Christian sub-practices that cultivate the virtues and the practice of Christianity.

While many virtue ethicists draw on the traditional cardinal virtues, other ethicists have reframed the cardinal virtues in light of contemporary theological anthropology. Recall that the cardinal virtues perfect the person in proportion to human nature. Keenan was the first to suggest that the virtues do not perfect powers or "things" inside of us, but rather, the ways that we are. We are, Keenan noted, "beings in relationship."[29] The virtues perfect our relationships. While prudence serves to guide practical reason, the virtues of self-care, fidelity, and justice perfect how a person respectively relates to self, friends, and distant others. Above, I drew on this promising approach to briefly sketch a personalist virtue theory, while Todd Salzman and Michael Lawler have appropriated Keenan's insight for their own virtue theory.[30] This is an area of virtue theory that is ripe for further development.

Theological Virtues

The human person has been created for a supernatural purpose: life with God. The cardinal virtues, which individuals acquire through their efforts, cannot attain such a life. Growth in one's relationship with God requires grace. The theological virtues name and conceptualize the activity of God's grace in a person's moral life. The theological virtues orient the person to the final, ultimate, and supernatural end of human existence, whereas the cardinal virtues orient the person to a proximate, penultimate, and natural end.

In 1 Thessalonians (1:3 and 5:8) and 1 Corinthians (13:13), St. Paul wrote of a triad of traits that the followers of Jesus should possess: faith, hope, and love. Aquinas rendered these as faith, hope, and charity. Faith is the virtue by which a person believes in the God that she cannot see. Faith is difficult to maintain and so is supported by hope, which is the trait that enables a person to persevere in her faith. Finally, charity is a particular form of love. Love is an affective affirmation of the good of the other, wills and promotes the well-being of the other, and ultimately desires union with the other. Charity enables an agent to love God and his neighbor for the sake of God who loves his neighbor.[31] Charity, as the greatest of the theological virtues, directs all of the virtues, including the cardinal virtues, to its end: friendship with God and neighbor. According to Gustavo Gutiérrez, "Charity is God's love in us and does not exist outside our human capabilities to love and build a just and friendly world."[32] The love of God spreads throughout one's life to all whom one encounters, even one's enemies. Just "as the power of a furnace is proved to be the stronger according as it throws its heat to more distant objects," so too is one's love of God stronger if it leads one to love all of one's neighbors.[33]

Unlike the cardinal virtues, the theological virtues cannot be acquired but must be infused by God. However, while "infused virtue is caused in us by God without any action on our part," Aquinas also emphasized that such infusion is "not without our consent."[34] The infusion of virtue does not subvert the person's free will.[35] The person can either

[29]James Keenan, "Proposing Cardinal Virtues," *Theological Studies* 56, no. 4 (1995): 718.
[30]Salzman and Lawler, *Virtue and Theological Ethics*, 84–5.
[31]Aquinas, *Summa Theologiae*, II–II.23.1.
[32]Gustavo Gutiérrez, *A Theology of Liberation* (Maryknoll: Orbis, 1988), 113.
[33]Aquinas, *Summa Theologiae*, II–II.27.7.
[34]Ibid., I–II.55.6.
[35]Ibid., II–II.24.10 ad 3.

accept or reject God's gracious gift. Acceptance or consent is required for the infused virtues to take root. Here Aquinas followed the meaning and logic of "gift." Gifts are unearned and thus freely given by the giver but must be freely accepted in order to be possessed by the recipient.

There are three primary modes of acceptance of the infused virtues. The first is through virtuous actions. Acts of charity "dispose man to receive the infusion of charity."[36] Here the practice of charity enables a fuller acceptance of God's gift of charity. Prayer is the second mode of acceptance. Aquinas wrote, "Our motive in praying is, not that we may change the Divine disposition, but that, by our prayers, we may obtain what God has appointed."[37] That is, prayer aids in accepting the grace that God has offered. Prayer opens the person to consent to God's infusion of faith, hope, and charity. Finally, the sacraments both confer the virtues and dispose a person to accept the infusion of the virtues.[38] Charity, in particular, is "kindled" by the Eucharist.[39]

VIRTUE ETHICS AND ACTION-GUIDANCE

Some have accused virtue ethics of lacking practical guidance.[40] Philosopher of virtue Rosiland Hursthouse has argued that the field has been more theoretical than applied.[41] Virtue ethics has, in the words of Catholic ethicist Josef Selling, "unsolved problems. Chief among these is the issue of how to translate a virtuous attitude into a concrete behavior."[42] These are merely apparent, not real, problems.

Virtue ethicists believe that the virtues, unlike other ethical methodologies, provide excellent action-guidance regarding what we might call "everyday" matters. For instance, the virtue of patience provides clear and substantive guidance for drivers. This virtue enables a person to endure hardships without resorting to anger or hatred of her neighbors.[43] Thus, the person who drives patiently drives in a way that promotes the common good, and will drive within the speed limit, courteously allowing other drivers to enter the roadway when it is reasonable. In doing so, she will cultivate the virtue of patience. While the moral matter at stake is mundane, the guidance the virtues provide is significant, as most of the traits of the person emerge from such mundane matters. This is one of the great insights of virtue; moral character is forged in the mundane.

The critique of virtue ethics primarily pertains to "quandary ethics" or the ethics of dilemma. The ethical stakes are higher in such cases. For example, moral quandaries include the bombing of military installations with human shields, and performing a hysterectomy on a pregnant woman with uterine cancer. To address these kinds of questions, many Christian ethicists continue to turn to manualist principles, such as double effect and cooperation. While the moral manuals that constituted Catholic ethics from the Council of Trent until Vatican II have died, manualist principles have enjoyed a robust afterlife.

---

[36]Ibid., II–II.24.2 ad 3.
[37]Ibid., II–II.83.3 ad 2.
[38]Ibid., III.62.2, 89.1.
[39]Ibid., III.79.4.
[40]Robert Louden, "On Some Vices of Virtue Ethics," *American Philosophical Quarterly* 21 (1984): 227–36.
[41]Rosiland Hursthouse, "Applying Virtue Ethics," in *Virtues and Reasons: Essays in Honor of Phillipa Foot*, ed. Rosiland Hursthouse, G. Lawrence, and W. Quinn (Oxford: Oxford University Press, 1995), 57.
[42]Joseph Selling, *Reframing Catholic Theological Ethics* (Oxford: Oxford University Press, 2016), 151.
[43]Aquinas, *Summa Theologiae*, II–II.136.

There are two reasons ethicists rarely turn to the virtues for moral quandaries. First, virtue ethics continues to be misunderstood as an ethics of being, not doing. As I have argued in this chapter, it is an ethics concerned with both because neither is sufficiently understood in the absence of the other. The second reason is that virtue lacks a formulaic decision procedure. Consider the principle of double effect. The principle of double effect contains four necessary conditions that an act must satisfy in order to be morally licit. The principle provides a clear formula with which to make moral judgments.

Morally discerning with the virtues is different. There is no "formula" to follow, but there is a method. Bernard Lonergan defined a method as a "normative pattern of recurrent and related operations yielding cumulative and progressive results."[44] Virtue ethics offers a method for moral discernment. Discerning with the virtues requires the agent to ask, "What is the virtuous action in these circumstances?" More concretely, the agent asks, "What is the courageous action? What would the courageous person, such as Servant of God Dorothy Day, do?" Virtue methodology invites the moral agent to use the virtues themselves, such as courage, to guide the agent's moral discernment, and turn to exemplars of the virtues, such as Day, for action-guidance. As noted above, the agent imagines what the exemplar would do if similarly situated. Here the virtues and their exemplars *guide* prudential discernment. When adequately employed, this method guides the agent to the goal of the Christian life: an ever-growing friendship with God and God's beloved.

Some object to the fact that virtue methodology relies heavily on prudential reasoning. However, all ethical methodologies rely on prudential reasoning. It is mistaken to believe the norms and principles obviate the need for prudence and moral discernment. Norms and principles are not self-applying; like the virtues, they guide prudential discernment. Principles and norms are *tools* for moral discernment and do not subvert such discernment.

Case: Harboring People Who Are Undocumented

A contemporary moral dilemma helps to demonstrate the action-guiding capability of virtue ethics.

Imagine a Good Samaritan has taken in a mother and her two young children, who have fled death threats in their Central American country. The family is undocumented. Deportation to their homeland will expose the family to grave danger. The Good Samaritan is aware that federal law currently "makes it an offense for any person who [knowingly] conceals, harbors, or shields from detection [an] alien in any place, including any building or any means of transportation."[45] People convicted of such a crime can be sentenced to "the basic statutory maximum term of imprisonment [which] is 5 years." In fact, in 2017, former attorney general Jeffery Sessions sent a memo urging all federal prosecutors to vigorously enforce the federal statutes on harboring "aliens."[46]

What should the Good Samaritan do when Immigration and Customs Enforcement (ICE) agents arrive at her house and ask if she is harboring undocumented persons? If she misinforms the agents, she risks arrest and prosecution for violating federal law. A truthful confession exposes the family to the likelihood of violence.

---

[44]Bernard Lonergan, *Method in Theology* (New York: Herder and Herder, 1972), 13–14.

[45]United States Department of Justice, "Justice Manual," 1907. Title 8, U.S.C. 1324(a) Offenses, https://www.justice.gov/jm/criminal-resource-manual-1907-title-8-usc-1324a-offenses.

[46]Jeffrey Sessions, "Renewed Commitment to Criminal Immigration Enforcement," *Politico*, April 11, 2017, https://www.politico.com/f/?id=0000015b-5e9a-da80-afdf-dfffab4b0001.

The Good Samaritan who uses a virtue approach would ask: What kind of person turns over such a vulnerable family? What is the merciful action in this case? What would Jesus, or St. Maximillian Kolbe, do? Under Nazi occupation in Poland, St. Maximillian Kolbe sheltered two thousand Jewish persons in his Franciscan friary before being arrested. He then volunteered to die in the place of a stranger in Auschwitz. As an exemplar of solidarity with the suffering, Kolbe's witness guides the Good Samaritan to misinform the ICE agents of the presence of undocumented immigrants. Here the virtues themselves, or the exemplars of the virtues, guide her moral discernment.

The virtues should have more than a supplemental role in action guidance. However, as Cloutier and Mattison argued, often "virtue is incorporated into already existing methodological frameworks rather than being truly foundational."[47] The full maturation of the discipline will be realized when ethical analyses are made based on the virtues, without immediate reference to other methods.

VIRTUE, MORAL AGENCY, AND SECULAR SCIENCES

While Christian accounts of virtue have affirmed the causal power of God's grace in shaping character, the tradition lacks a substantive explanation regarding if and how social structures influence agency, action, and moral character. There is a growing consensus that Christian ethics, in general, and virtue, in particular, require a better account of the relation of the community and personal moral agency. Earlier I cited Cloutier and Mattison on the need for virtue ethicists to better understand how communities shape the action and character of their members. Along similar lines, Lisa Cahill has argued that "in addition to the person, we need to consider traditions and communities 'integrally and adequately.' "[48]

Social theory helpfully addresses such critiques. The subject matter of social theory is the relationship of culture and social structures to human agency. Social theorists have identified the "structure-agency problem," which exists because the reciprocal causal relationship among personal moral agency and social structures is complex and challenging to explain.[49] A solution to the structure-agency problem will explain how people shape structures and how structures shape moral agency and character. While space does not permit a thoroughgoing evaluation of the many possible solutions to the problem, some Christian ethicists have argued that critical realist social theory provides the best understanding of the structure-agency relation.[50] Critical realist theory maintains that persons are free moral agents but are enabled and constrained by the cultural and structural realities that they encounter. Here a virtue ethicist finds that character remains freely acquired by the agent but that one's communal setting renders certain habits more or less easily acquired. For example, contemporary American structures facilitate the acquisition of the virtue of tolerance of human differences while also impeding the acquisition of the virtue of ecological justice. More work remains in this area, but essential inroads have been paved, and virtue ethicists would do well to turn to social theory to address the vexing structure-agency problem.

---

[47]Cloutier and Mattison, "Resurgence of Virtue," 229.

[48]Lisa Sowle Cahill, "Reframing Catholic Ethics: Is the Person and Integral and Adequate Starting Point?" *Religions* 8, no. 10 (2017): 17.

[49]Dave Elder-Vass, *The Causal Power of Social Structures* (New York: Cambridge University Press, 2001), 1.

[50]See Daniel Finn, ed., *Social Structures, Culture, and Moral Agency: A Primer on Critical Realism for Christian Ethics* (Washington, DC: Georgetown University Press, 2020).

SOCIAL OPPRESSION AND "REAL VIRTUE"

One of the most important developments in twenty-first-century virtue ethics is the critique of the idealized account of virtue present in Aristotelian-inspired virtue theories. Following Aristotle, many virtue ethicists have presumed the acting person possesses the material and social goods needed to cultivate the virtues. Aristotle's virtue ethics was for the Athenian gentleman, with the means, leisure, and social standing to develop his character. Led by philosopher Lisa Tessman, a group of scholars has drawn on social science, ethnography, liberationist, and feminist thought to argue that the opportunities to cultivate the classical virtues are constrained for the poor, women, ethnic and racial minorities, and other socially marginalized peoples. Tessman's solution is to argue that there are "burdened virtues." A burdened virtue is "a morally praiseworthy trait that is at the same time bad for its bearer, disconnected from its bearer's well-being."[51] "Oppositional anger" counts as such a virtue for Tessman, for it rightly rages at those who create and maintain oppressive social structures, and consistently attempts to transform/overthrow such structures. Sarah MacDonald and Nicole Symmonds have proposed rioting as such a virtue for its capacity to enable the weak to reclaim agency.[52] However, MacDonald and Symmonds recognize that such rage and rioting are detrimental to an agent's psychological health and well-being.

The virtue realism of Tessman et al. has significant implications for Christian virtue ethics. First, if virtue is to be an ethics for all Christians, and not just the privileged, then ethicists must critically examine what counts as a virtue. Is "rioting" a virtue for the oppressed? Second, ethicists should reconsider the complicated relationship between the virtues and human well-being and happiness. Must a virtue promote the well-being and happiness of its possessor? Third, does the work of Tessman et al. address the critiques of virtue ethics that have emerged from liberative and feminist ethicists? For example, Miguel de la Torre has argued that liberative ethics and virtue ethics are "fundamentally irreconcilable." He has claimed that unjust social and power relationships have defined what "Euroamericans consider virtuous," and that historically those virtues have been implemented to mask those very injustices.[53] Like de la Torre, Christian feminist scholar Laura Stivers has critiqued virtue ethics for its failure to present a sophisticated analysis of how social structures and systems of power contribute to oppression. Echoing Tessman, she chided the field for its failure to take the experience of those on the underside of history as the starting point for reflections of justice.[54] These critiques require responses from virtue ethicists. The work of Tessman, de la Torre, and Stivers highlight the need for virtue ethicists to draw on more robust accounts of what constitutes a social structure if virtue ethics is to be relevant to all Christians, not only those who enjoy social privilege.

[51]Lisa Tessman, *Burdened Virtues: Virtue Ethics for Liberatory Struggles* (Oxford: Oxford University Press, 2005), 124.

[52]Sarah MacDonald and Nicole Symmonds, "Rioting as Flourishing? Reconsidering Virtue Ethics in Times of Civil Unrest," *Journal of the Society of Christian Ethics* 38, no. 1 (2018): 25–42.

[53]Miguel de la Torre, "Virtue Ethics: A Libertarian Response," in *Christian Faith and Social Justice: Five Views*, ed. Vic McCracken (New York: Bloomsbury, 2014), 167.

[54]Laura Stivers, "Virtue Ethics: A Feminist Response," in *Christian Faith and Social Justice: Five Views*, ed. Vic McCracken (New York: Bloomsbury, 2014), 170–3.

CALL FOR PAPERS

This chapter has identified areas for development, but space prohibits such work here. I hope that the chapter serves as a "call for papers" of sorts. In particular, the chapter calls for scholarship:

1. Utilizing a personalist theological anthropology in virtue theory.
2. Integrating the social sciences, especially critical realist social theory, into an understanding of how social structures enable and constrain the practice and acquisition of the virtues.
3. Employing the virtues as tools for action-guidance, including regarding moral dilemmas.
4. Moving away from "ideal virtue" toward "real virtue." Ethicists should critically examine what constitutes a virtue in light of the reality of the social oppression and marginalization of peoples throughout the globe.

SUGGESTED READINGS

Annas, Julia. *Intelligent Virtue*. New York: Oxford University Press, 2011.

Hauerwas, Stanley. *A Community of Character: Toward a Constructive Christian Social Ethic*. Notre Dame: University of Notre Dame Press, 1991.

Salzman, Todd A., and Michael G. Lawler. *Virtue and Theological Ethics: Toward a Renewed Ethical Method*. Maryknoll: Orbis, 2018.

CHAPTER SEVEN

Conscience

ELIZABETH SWEENY BLOCK

Theologians and ethicists have been writing about conscience for many centuries, yet a univocal definition remains elusive. Richard Gula once wrote, "Trying to explain conscience is like trying to nail jello to the wall; just when you think you have it pinned down, part of it begins to slip away."[1] This is so because conceptions of conscience have developed and evolved over many centuries, but also because conscience holds together, or even holds in tension, opposite poles of the moral life. For instance, scholars often describe conscience as deeply private and personal, even as it is profoundly relational, formed and exercised in community. Conscience also mediates the tension between subjectivity and objectivity, between the self and the world. Additionally, conscience names a process that involves the interior life of a person and not simply her actions, and this is much more difficult to define with precision. Furthermore, conscience cannot be easily separated from other ambiguous concepts, including freedom, truth, authority, and church, which means conscience is necessarily representative of many theological debates. Statements about the nature of conscience always imply larger determinations about what the moral life entails and requires; therefore, much is at stake when theologians take up the topic of conscience today.

Perhaps more important than defining conscience is identifying what having a conscience or living as persons of conscience implies. James Bretzke, SJ, uses the phrase "conscience-based moral living," which rightly turns conscience into more of an action than an object. Conscience is not a thing that we possess, but a way of life.[2] This chapter provides a brief history of conscience, including traditional terminology and distinctions associated with conscience. I offer a brief section on Protestant and Orthodox conceptions of conscience, but the primary focus of this chapter is on conscience in Roman Catholic moral theology since the Second Vatican Council, after which scholarship on conscience exploded as theologians worked to situate conscience in the new personalist paradigm of morality. I focus on three features of the contemporary conscience: the holistic nature of conscience, shorthand for the moral self; the primacy of conscience, although its work involves integrating numerous moral sources; and the relationality and reciprocity of conscience. I conclude, all too briefly, with attention to two ongoing challenges to conscience: the constant tension between conscience as discernment versus obedience, which is a particular challenge for Catholics given the role of the magisterium in moral matters, and the more pressing, non-denominational matter of the impact of cultures of

[1]Richard Gula, SS, *Reason Informed by Faith: Foundations of Catholic Morality* (Mahwah: Paulist, 1989), 123.
[2]James T. Bretzke, SJ, *A Morally Complex World: Engaging Contemporary Moral Theology* (Collegeville: Liturgical, 2004), 138.

racism, misogyny, homophobia, and xenophobia on conscience. This short chapter cannot do justice to conscience, but my hope is that it at least provides a helpful introduction and indicates where there remains work to be done.

HISTORY AND TERMINOLOGY

The first use of the Greek word for conscience, *syneidesis*, is attributed to Democritus of Abdera in the fifth century BCE, who used it to mean a faculty of self-reflection. This term is absent from later Greeks, including Plato and Aristotle, but they used terms that are recognized as precursors to conscience and that reflect this moral self-awareness, including "wisdom" and "prudence." Linda Hogan observes that conscience in Greek, Latin, and Jewish texts can be used to mean awareness in a nonethical sense, and these instances can give a false impression of the frequency of the use of conscience in a moral sense. Additionally, she notes that the idea of conscience as self-reflection and as a guide were conveyed by other terminology, such as wisdom and heart, and this is important to include in the history of conscience, even if explicit references to *syneidesis* (Greek) or *conscientia* (Latin) are lacking.[3]

Conscience is virtually absent from the Hebrew Bible, save for two or three references, but here too scholars have identified references to the interior life, the need to interiorize the law, and to the "heart" as precursors to conscience. St. Paul in the New Testament is the first person to reference a guiding or future-oriented dimension of conscience, as opposed to conscience as only a judgment on past actions. These two dimensions of conscience—reflection on past actions and guidance on future actions—are referred to as the consequent and antecedent conscience or the judicial and legislative conscience. Conscience is said to look back at our actions, perhaps feeling remorse but possibly also affirming what one has done, and to legislate future actions.

In addition to the distinction between the judicial and legislative conscience, there is also a distinction made between the habitual and actual conscience, a distinction that is the result of an error of transcription that shaped all future discussions of conscience. Alongside the Greek word for conscience, *syneidesis*, we have another word to contend with: *synderesis*. It is believed that St. Jerome (*c.* 340–420) invented the word *synderesis* by scribal error in his *Commentary on Ezekiel* ("perhaps the monk had too much wine with dinner," jokes moral theologian Charles Curran[4]), yet it has become a mainstay in understandings of conscience. *Synderesis* is the "spark of conscience," the desire to discern and do good. Medieval theologians accepted both terms and sought to explain their coexistence. Thomas Aquinas understood *synderesis* to be the innate knowledge that human beings have to seek good and avoid evil. *Synderesis* has come to be known as the habitual conscience, knowledge that inclines us to act well, distinct from the actual conscience, which applies that knowledge. For Aquinas, *conscientia* or conscience is the act of applying knowledge to a particular situation, that is, acting on the knowledge of the habitual conscience. Contemporary moral theologian Hogan insists that although it would be easy to dismiss these distinctions as obsolete and insignificant, the presence of both the habitual and actual conscience

[3]Linda Hogan, *Confronting the Truth: Conscience in the Catholic Tradition* (Mahwah: Paulist, 2000), 37–8.
[4]Charles Curran, *The Catholic Moral Tradition Today: A Synthesis* (Washington, DC: Georgetown University Press, 1999), 175.

> allows us to make a distinction between the basic goodness of a person and the occasional lapses into bad judgment, of which we are all capable. In an important sense, it prefigures a very modern recognition that although individuals may make wrong decisions or act against what they know to be right, this does not mean that their basic or fundamental orientation is flawed.[5]

One signifies moral orientation, the other action.[6]

This leads to the third important distinction that has less to do with conscience itself and more to do with errors of conscience. Granting that one may have the knowledge and inclination to seek good and yet still err in action, we are now in the territory of the erroneous conscience. St. Paul famously admitted that he knew the good and yet did not necessarily do it.[7] The erroneous conscience is one that errs, but it may do so either vincibly or invincibly. Vincible ignorance indicates that the person should have known better and is therefore culpable for her erroneous action. Invincible ignorance recognizes that a person may have a certain conscience, meaning that she believes sincerely that her understanding and action are right and true, but still err. This distinction between vincible and invincible ignorance is, therefore, a distinction that determines culpability.

Invincible ignorance hinges on a well-formed and informed conscience. Different theologians have interpreted the erroneous conscience differently. Bernard of Clairvaux believed actions done through invincible ignorance are bad and not excused. Peter Abelard claimed that intention alone can make an action good. Aquinas stated that an erroneous act is objectively wrong but the person is not responsible for this wrong act. Alphonsus Ligouri went beyond Aquinas and claimed that invincibly wrong actions are not just excused but are good.[8] Aquinas's position is generally accepted today: if a person believes that something is a commandment of God, then to disobey one's conscience on this matter is to disobey God. This sentiment is echoed in Vatican II's *Pastoral Constitution on the Church in the Modern World*, which states, "Conscience frequently errs from invincible ignorance without losing its dignity. The same cannot be said for a man who cares but little for truth and goodness, or for a conscience which by degrees grows practically sightless as a result of habitual sin."[9] That an invincibly erroneous conscience retains its dignity further solidifies the sacredness of conscience, although the categories of vincible and invincible ignorance may no longer be adequate in the face of unconscious biases and implicit forms of discrimination pervasive in our culture, including racism, sexism, homophobia, and xenophobia. I return to this problem in the final section of this chapter.

PROTESTANT AND ORTHODOX CONCEPTIONS OF CONSCIENCE

It is perhaps not all that surprising that the author of an essay on Protestant conscience argues that "conscience, or at least *consciousness* of conscience, has been given a far more

---

[5]Hogan, *Confronting the Truth*, 67.

[6]This is a distinction and synthesis that moral theologians still grapple with today. What is the relationship between the person and her actions? In the twentieth century, the fundamental option theory placed greater emphasis on a person's orientation and less weight on actions, although a person's orientation is expressed in and through her actions. See Darlene Weaver, *The Acting Person and Christian Moral Life* (Washington, DC: Georgetown University Press, 2011).

[7]Rom. 7:19.

[8]This summary of different positions on error is the work of Curran, *Catholic Moral Tradition Today*, 88.

[9]Second Vatican Council, *Gaudium et spes* (Vatican City: Libreria Editrice Vaticana, 1965), § 16.

elevated role in Christian moral thinking than it actually deserves."[10] Dave Leal has a number of concerns about conscience, including its focus on conscious reasoning when moral agents are often not aware of willing most of the time and its misplaced confidence in humans as the source of their own good actions, neglecting the will of the divine. He asserts that "conscience is not ultimate, and we may hope beyond the experience of it to a fulfillment in the one who is Truth himself."[11] Still other Protestant theologians are more appreciative of conscience. In an essay on what he calls the "transmoral conscience," Paul Tillich sympathizes with theologians who argue that conscience's confusing and contradictory connotations warrant the elimination of the term from the study of ethics, yet he believes conscience is "a definite reality which ... can and must be described adequately."[12] For Tillich, the conscience should be "transmoral," that is, "it judges not in obedience to a moral law, but according to its participation in a reality that transcends the sphere of moral commands."[13] The transmoral conscience accepts our moral imperfection and the guilt that accompanies every decision we make and every act we perform; it rises above the moral realm, where we attain a joyful conscience as the result of justification by God's grace. In other words, the transmoral conscience transcends the realm of law by the acceptance of divine grace; it conquers "the bad, moral conscience" that dwells in absolute despair. This is one answer to Leal's concern that conscience is too human-centered. H. Richard Niebuhr also suggests that conscience is not individual and that moral agents cannot both be accused by and accuse themselves, meaning that the judgments of conscience must come from another if conscience "is to avoid self-contradiction."[14]

For this reason, Niebuhr is critical of the Anglican Bishop Joseph Butler and German philosopher Immanuel Kant, both of whom he reads as recognizing conscience as merely an inward judge of oneself and one's own actions. However, Jeffrey Morgan argues that it is a misunderstanding of Kant's conscience to believe that he "gives the modern moral subject a license to view herself as accountable not to a tradition, a community, a particular history, or to an objective moral order but to herself as her own lawgiver."[15] Rather, "Kant's theory of conscience stands in a line with figures like Augustine and Chrysostom and these depictions in the New Testament of the individual standing before God in conscience."[16] According to William Schweiker, "Conscience is a term for human transcendence in which the claims of the 'integrity' of life, one's own and that of others, is constitutive of the self. In the religions, this means that 'conscience' is a communication among and between worlds, including the divine world, without collapsing those worlds into one."[17] For Schweiker, conscience

---

[10]Dave Leal, "Against Conscience: A Protestant View," in *Conscience in World Religions*, ed. Jayne Hoose (Notre Dame: University of Notre Dame Press, 1999), 21.
[11]Ibid., 56.
[12]Paul Tillich, *Morality and Beyond*, Library of Theological Ethics, foreword by William Schweiker (Louisville: Westminster John Knox, [1963] 1995), 65.
[13]Ibid., 77.
[14]H. Richard Niebuhr, *The Responsible Self: An Essay in Christian Moral Philosophy* (New York: Harper & Row, 1963), 74.
[15]Jeffrey Morgan, "Self-Knowledge and the Approximation of Divine Judgment: Conscience in the Practical Philosophy and Moral Theology of Immanuel Kant," *Journal of the Society of Christian Ethics* 36, no. 1 (2016): 111.
[16]Ibid., 119.
[17]William Schweiker, "The Ethical Limits of Power: On the Perichoresis of Power," *Studies in Christian Ethics* 29, no. 1 (2015): 12.

is ethical awareness of the claim of the integrity of life on human existence before God.[18]

In the Orthodox tradition, "conscience is part of a conceptual system to describe ascesis, the spiritual struggle necessary for fellowship with God; it does not have ... the sense of a secular autonomous faculty by which justice may be discerned."[19] Conscience is inseparable from "the invitation to human beings to intimate communion with the Divine Trinity."[20] Conscience draws one into a living relationship with God and is part of the whole ascetical life, concerned with awareness and discernment. There is much to be learned from the humility of the Orthodox conscience. "There is no luminous, self-evident awareness of what is right and wrong in the spiritual life. The human being is, from the start, a mystery to him or herself."[21] Orthodox prayer books include prayers for forgiveness of sins that one may not even know he has committed. There is explicit recognition of the reality that conscience can be wrong because human beings are fallible.

CONSCIENCE SINCE VATICAN II

The earlier-cited excerpt from Vatican II's *Pastoral Constitution on the Church in the Modern World* is the conclusion of a longer passage that is the quintessential statement on conscience in the Roman Catholic Church:

> In the depths of his conscience, man detects a law which he does not impose upon himself, but which holds him to obedience. Always summoning him to love good and avoid evil, the voice of conscience when necessary speaks to his heart: do this, shun that. For man has in his heart a law written by God; to obey it is the very dignity of man; according to it he will be judged. Conscience is the most secret core and sanctuary of a man. There he is alone with God, Whose voice echoes in his depths. In a wonderful manner conscience reveals that law which is fulfilled by love of God and neighbor. In fidelity to conscience, Christians are joined with the rest of men in the search for truth, and for the genuine solution to the numerous problems which arise in the life of individuals from social relationships. Hence the more right conscience holds sway, the more persons and groups turn aside from blind choice and strive to be guided by the objective norms of morality.[22]

This statement on conscience is only the beginning of a flurry of activity around the term. Conscience entered a new phase post-Vatican II, wherein it became less of a mechanism for discrete decisions and more of a representation of a person's moral self, which includes but certainly is not limited to actions and concrete decisions. Widespread interest in conscience in the decades following the Council is the result of the working out of a new paradigm in morality, one that is person-centered or "personalist" as opposed to act-centered. That is, the Second Vatican Council marked a shift in moral theology from a focus on specific actions as right or wrong to a focus on the character and orientation of the person, although this shift was in the making prior to the Council and has continued

---

[18]William Schweiker, "Responsibility and the Attunement of Conscience," *Journal of Religion* 93, no. 4 (2013): 471.

[19]Stephen Thomas, "Conscience in Orthodox Thought," in *Conscience in World Religions*, ed. Jayne Hoose (Notre Dame: University of Notre Dame Press, 1999), 104.

[20]Ibid., 105.

[21]Ibid., 106.

[22]Second Vatican Council, *Gaudium et spes*, § 16.

to evolve since then. Conscience, understood traditionally as the faculty of moral decision making that determines how we act, was naturally implicated in this paradigm shift. If morality is not determined solely by actions, but is in fact also constituted by a person's character and relationship with God, then understandings of conscience must account for this change. Many scholars who have written about conscience in the past fifty years have done so in order to situate conscience in this personalist paradigm. What has been said about conscience has been in the service of accentuating the character, narrative, and history of a person and not only her actions. In what follows, I will highlight three significant features of conscience today: its holistic nature, its primacy, and its relationality.

THE HOLISTIC CONSCIENCE

Bernard Häring describes the experience of conscience as God's calling the whole person.[23] Richard Gula notes, "Whereas in the past we tried to restrict conscience to a function of the will or of the intellect, today we understand conscience as an expression of the whole person. Simply put, conscience is 'me coming to a decision.'"[24] Since the Second Vatican Council, many scholars have emphasized the holistic nature of conscience, but a concrete definition of conscience remains elusive, in part because conscience is not merely a "thing" to which we can point. Scholarship on conscience has retained the association of conscience with an inner sense of right and wrong but has also emphasized the roles of reason, grace, emotions, and intuition in conscience and situated conscience within the many dimensions of the person's experience, including cultural and religious background, education, emotions, past history, and future plans.[25] For Hogan, conscience is a term that indicates moral self-governance and highlights that moral activity is freely chosen.[26] Anne Patrick identifies conscience as an aspect of the self, a kind of personal moral awareness.[27] These contemporary examples equate conscience with the moral self and moral agency.

Gula describes conscience as a capacity, process, and judgment. This tripartite structure illustrates the fluid nature of conscience and indicates that conscience is not merely a faculty or a part of the body or the brain. As a capacity, conscience is "the fundamental characteristic of being human"[28] and "our general sense of value and ... responsibility which makes it possible for us to engage in moral discussions."[29] This capacity is often equated with *synderesis*, sometimes referred to as "the spark of conscience." As a process, conscience "searches for what is right through accurate perception"[30] and includes analysis and reflection. This is important because it implies that conscience is in constant motion, always searching, on an endless journey toward the truth. We are never finished; our story is always incomplete. Finally, Gula retains the more common understanding of conscience as a "concrete judgment of what I must do in a situation based on my personal perception

[23]Bernard Häring, *Free and Faithful in Christ: Moral Theology for Clergy and Laity, Vol. 1* (New York: Crossroad, 1978), 227.
[24]Gula, *Reason Informed by Faith*, 131.
[25]For these descriptions of conscience, I am indebted to Charles Curran and Linda Hogan. See Curran, *Catholic Moral Tradition Today*, 172, 186; and Hogan, *Confronting the Truth*, 9, 13.
[26]Hogan, *Confronting the Truth*.
[27]Anne E. Patrick, *Liberating Conscience: Feminist Explorations in Catholic Moral Theology* (New York: Continuum, 1996).
[28]Gula, *Reason Informed by Faith*, 10, 244.
[29]Ibid., 132.
[30]Ibid.

and grasp of values."[31] This is a discrete act of conscience, in a particular moment, introduced above as *syneidesis* or *conscientia*: the act of applying moral knowledge to a particular situation.

Bretzke builds on this holistic picture of conscience by identifying conscience as a "modality of being human," that is, a way of being human in the world and which gives us insight into the true nature of human morality.[32] Bretzke focuses on what he calls "the spiral of conscience-based moral living," which further implies that conscience is not merely a faculty or judgment but a way of life, our moral self always in progress.[33] "A spiral suggests both a certain circularity in the process of conscience development as well as an ongoing and upward progression as we grow in moral wisdom and skill in putting this wisdom into practice."[34] Bretzke's spiral begins with and returns to the formation of conscience, which requires paying attention to a multitude of sources of moral wisdom, especially to voices other than the ones we commonly, or want to, hear; we must escape our comfort zone and hear the voices of those from whom we differ. In between the forming and informing of our conscience comes reconsideration, reflection, discernment, decision, and action, finally returning to formation. Even as scholars such as Bretzke argue that conscience is not merely about decision making, often in our efforts to capture the meaning of conscience we end up right back at conscience as judgment. Bretzke himself notes the weakness of his spiral model: "It is still very intellectual and rationalistic and seems to suggest that conscience is mostly about coming to the right answer."[35] However, Bretzke is much more interested in identifying conscience as the process of "moral striving to seek out and do good and avoid or minimize evil." Here again it is evident that conscience names a process, the ongoing work of moral selves on a journey.[36]

THE PRIMACY OF CONSCIENCE AND INTEGRATING SOURCES OF MORAL WISDOM

The Second Vatican Council emphasized the primacy of conscience. The above excerpt from *The Pastoral Constitution on the Church in the Modern World* indicates that conscience is a sanctuary, a sacred space where we meet God but also a space that cannot be intruded upon by outside authorities. Earlier in the chapter, I noted that a conscience that errs invincibly retains its dignity, another indication of the sacredness of conscience. As a sacred space where we encounter God's voice, however, conscience is not radically autonomous. Following one's conscience is not the same as doing whatever strikes one as good and right, independent of any outside sources of moral wisdom. Rather, as Hogan has described it, conscience "is the individual's personal and self-conscious integration of collective moral wisdom with her/his own learned insight."[37] Not only do we again

---

[31]Ibid.

[32]Bretzke, *A Morally Complex World*, 130–1.

[33]Ibid., 138–44.

[34]Ibid., 138.

[35]Ibid., 142.

[36]It has been argued that conscience has become a means of being consistent with oneself rather than the means of judging ourselves as God judges us. The worry is that conscience loses touch with the transcendent and universally binding moral law against which we should judge ourselves. See Jeffrey Morgan, "A Loss of Judgment: The Dismissal of Judicial Conscience in Recent Christian Ethics," *Journal of Religious Ethics* 45, no. 3 (2017): 539–61.

[37]Hogan, *Confronting the Truth*, 15.

get the sense that conscience is a process or ongoing work, but we also see here that it requires attention to multiple sources of moral wisdom. "Since conscience is the source of free and responsible decision making, it is rightly regarded as the supreme authority in ethics. However, Christianity operates with a community-based model of ethics not with an individualistic one."[38] Conscience-based moral living must integrate sacred texts, the collective wisdom of Christians past and present, persons entrusted with preaching the Christian message, one's own experiences of the living God, and the knowledge we gain from other disciplines, including science, sociology, psychology, and history. The church plays a central role in formation of conscience, but the authority of the church vis-à-vis individual consciences remains a source of tension and debate to which I will turn below.

THE RELATIONALITY AND RECIPROCITY OF CONSCIENCES

Perhaps one of the most important developments with respect to conscience since the Second Vatican Council has been recognition of how profoundly communal and social it is. Bernard Häring used the phrase "the reciprocity of consciences" and argued that conscience is "the person's moral faculty, the inner core and sanctuary where one knows oneself in confrontation with God and with fellowmen." He claimed that we "can confront ourselves only to the extent that we genuinely encounter the Other and the others."[39] This is a critical reminder that if we think of conscience as profoundly individual and autonomous, we misunderstand not only conscience but also the meaning and purpose of the moral life.

Conscience is a social phenomenon. We are always and ought to be influenced by our social relationships. Moral reasoning takes place not in a vacuum but in context. The church can provide a community in which faithful moral reasoning can take place. Hogan continues this contextual, communal theme, observing that all moral truths are understood and lived out in particular situations and contexts. Recently theologians have emphasized the importance of respect not only for one's own conscience, but for the consciences and conscientious judgments of others. Hogan urges us to think about conscience not as a "conversation stopper," which it often can be when someone evokes the phrase "I followed my conscience" or "My conscience is clear." Rather, conscience is relational in that living as a person of conscience requires deliberate self-reflection and self-awareness as the foundation for dialogue.

> In justifying our ethical positions to one another we must explain why we believe we are correct in holding the view we do, for example, on the equality of men and women, or the goodness of same-sex relationships, but we should do so in a manner that conveys something about the moral framework out of which we are speaking and acting, and which we hope will be intelligible and convincing to the other.[40]

Legal scholar Robert Vischer similarly urges us to break conscience out of its "black box," wherein conscience is a law unto itself, accessible and accountable to no one. Conscience is "not some self-contained black box but comprises convictions about right and wrong

---

[38]Ibid., 14.
[39]Häring, *Free and Faithful in Christ*, 224.
[40]Linda Hogan, "Marriage Equality, Conscience, and the Catholic Tradition," in *Conscience and Catholicism: Rights, Responsibilities, and Institutional Responses*, ed. David E. DeCosse and Kristin E. Heyer (Maryknoll: Orbis, 2015), 91.

in the world of actions and is as likely to serve as path of dialogue as path of isolation."[41] Although the moral authority of conscience may be highly personal, the authority of conscience is made possible by claims that originate outside the person. Conscience is not merely the means for justifying whatever I believe to be right. Conscience exists and functions in relation to things outside itself, including objective moral norms and the needs and well-being of the surrounding community. Invoking conscience should not stop the conversation but open us to dialogue.

CHALLENGES OF CONSCIENCE

In 1874, John Henry Cardinal Newman wrote, "Conscience is the voice of God, whereas it is fashionable on all hands now to consider it in one way or another a creation of man."[42] The same could be said today. Because conscience is at least in part personal and private, there exists always this danger that conscience will be purely self-referential, nothing more than a source of self-justification for whatever we want to do, "a creation of man" with no connection to objective moral truths. If I declare that my conscience dictates that I act this way, or if I contend that "my conscience is clear," does that simply make it so? The short answer is "no," but this is tricky territory.

Scholars generally agree that conscience is the medium between subjectivity and objectivity, between the self and the world, including moral objectivity. As Curran puts it,

> The subject pole concerns the human person and involves one's basic orientation and the virtues or attitudes that characterize each one. The object pole considers the world, the communities, and the relationships in which people live and the values and principles that direct them in these areas. The church itself constitutes an important part of the object pole, but the primary importance of the church for Christian morality requires that the church be considered first in Catholic moral theology.[43]

The subject pole of the moral life encapsulates "who the person is as subject," while the object pole is constituted by "what the person does as agent."[44] The object pole of morality reminds us that morality is not solely about individual humans and our feelings, desires, wishes, and hopes. That there is an object pole of morality indicates not only that there is something true, irrespective of whether you or I recognize or concur with this truth, but also that we as subjects interact with objects, people, communities, and a world that are outside of us. The push and pull, give and take, between these poles is conscience at work. This is again why the formation of conscience with attention to a multitude of sources is critical; without this, conscience is in danger of being purely self-referential.

This is a perennial problem surrounding conscience: how to navigate the personal and sacred nature of conscience while also hearing, respecting, and living the truths of one's faith. Ideally, these components of the moral life are in harmony, but this is not always the case. In these situations, is the work of conscience obedience or discernment? Bretzke

---

[41]Robert Vischer, *Conscience and the Common Good: Reclaiming the Space between Person and State* (New York: Cambridge University Press, 2010), 22.
[42]John Henry Cardinal Newman, *Letter to the Duke of Norfolk*, 247. http://www.newmanreader.org/works/anglicans/volume2/gladstone/index.html#titlepage.
[43]Curran, *Catholic Moral Tradition Today*, 83.
[44]Ibid., 95.

has called this the next great *quaestio disputata* in the Catholic Church.[45] There are still those who identify a rightly formed conscience as one that is fully aligned with Church teaching, while others argue for respecting decisions made in conscience, even if those decisions appear to be "in objective non-compliance" with Church teaching. Unlike Pope John Paul II, who worried about the separation of freedom from truth and subsequently equated conscience with obedience in his 1993 encyclical *Veritatis splendor*, Pope Francis errs on the side of discernment. In *Amoris laetitia*, Francis writes of the difficulty that Church leaders have in "mak[ing] room for the consciences of the faithful, who very often respond as best they can to the Gospel amid their limitations, and are capable of carrying out their own discernment in complex situations. We have been called to form consciences, not to replace them."[46] This is a bold statement about the primacy of conscience in relation to the magisterium.

Perhaps the greatest challenge to conscience today is not how to balance discernment and obedience but how to form and inform our consciences in a world mired by structural sin, or what Bryan Massingale calls "culturally legitimated social evil."[47] Racism, sexism, homophobia, and xenophobia are daily realities, not only in explicit acts but also built into our systems, structures, and cultures, such that we are implicated in injustice simply by virtue of our participation in everyday life. Attending to conscience is a reminder to be deliberately self-reflective, aware of who we are, what we are doing, and how what we do impacts who we are. But we must also strive for a deep and honest awareness of our own context and culture, which define us and form our ways of life. We must remove the blinders that conceal our own involvement in sinful injustice. This problem reveals the inadequacy of invincible ignorance, which too easily renders people blameless and fails to account for implicit cultural evils.

At a gathering of Catholic theologians, Massingale spoke these words: "Our moral theology [is] becom[ing] conceptually complicit in structural injustice."[48] If we fail to understand conscience as the moral self, relational, navigating the tension between discernment and authority, accountable to the consciences of others, and wounded by unconscious biases and cultural evils, then conscience becomes an inadequate term at best, an instrument of injustice at worst. Conscience ought to unify, not divide.

SUGGESTED READINGS

Bretzke, James, SJ. "Conscience and the Synod: An Evolving Quaestio Disputata." *Journal of Moral Theology* 5, no. 2 (2016): 167–72.

Cox, Kathryn Lilla. *Water Shaping Stone: Faith, Relationships, and Conscience Formation.* Collegeville: Liturgical, 2015.

DeCosse, David E., and Kristin E. Heyer, eds. *Conscience and Catholicism: Rights, Responsibilities, and Institutional Responses.* Maryknoll: Orbis, 2015.

[45]James Bretzke, SJ, "Conscience and the Synod: An Evolving *Quaestio Disputata*," *Journal of Moral Theology* 5, no. 2 (2016): 167–72.

[46]Pope Francis, *Amoris laetitia* (Vatican City: Libreria Editrice Vaticana, 2016), § 37.

[47]Bryan Massingale, "Social Sin versus Cultural Evil: Insights from African American Socio-Political Analysis," paper delivered at the 73rd Annual Convention of the Catholic Theological Society of America, Indianapolis, June 8, 2018. See also, Bryan Massingale, "Conscience Formation and the Challenge of Unconscious Racial Bias," in *Conscience and Catholicism: Rights, Responsibilities, and Institutional Responses*, ed. David E. DeCosse and Kristin E. Heyer (Maryknoll: Orbis, 2015), 53–68.

[48]Ibid.

DeCosse, David E., and Thomas A. Nairn, OFM, eds. *Conscience and Catholic Health Care: From Clinical Contexts to Governmental Mandates*. Maryknoll: Orbis, 2017.
Hogan, Linda. *Confronting the Truth: Conscience in the Catholic Tradition*. Mahwah: Paulist, 2000.
Keenan, James, SJ. "Redeeming Conscience." *Theological Studies* 76, no. 1 (2015): 129–47.

CHAPTER EIGHT

Natural Law

ELIZABETH AGNEW COCHRAN

A commitment to natural law understands human beings as universally obligated to adhere to commonly shared moral norms, particularly norms of justice. Cicero offers an early definition of the natural law that highlights many of its paradigmatic characteristics: the natural law is given by God; it functions both universally (across geographic and cultural contexts) and eternally (so that it is continuous over time); and human beings are constructed in a manner that allows them to discern principles of the natural law.[1] Natural law is crucial for contemporary Christian ethics for at least two reasons. First, natural law grounds a philosophical framework that aligns with moral realism—that is, a worldview that affirms that objective accounts of goodness and truth exist—at a historical moment that many public intellectuals describe as a "post-truth" era.[2] As a universal standard of justice, the natural law holds accountable nations, governments, individuals, social groups, and other structures that fall short of this standard. Thus, natural law plays an important role in civil rights advocacy. Texts such as Martin Luther King Jr.'s "Letter from Birmingham Jail" illustrate how this role is realized. In this text, King directly invokes Thomas Aquinas's account of natural law to argue that laws can be deemed "just" only insofar as they cohere with the moral or natural law.[3]

In addition to supporting the notion of moral realism, natural law theories tend to align with accounts of human flourishing that take seriously embodied dimensions of human personhood. Aristotle's ethic, central to the natural law tradition, understands human flourishing in relation to the fulfillment of capacities rooted in our biological natures.[4] In both Aristotle and Aquinas, the coupling of law with theories of virtue leads to an account of law whose coherence is bound to the broader ends and purposes for which human beings exist. Natural law theory can thus accommodate the historical and material dimensions of human existence, even while maintaining a commitment to moral realism that guards against unfettered moral relativism. Edward Vacek contrasts this dimension of natural law ethics with approaches to ethics such as divine-command

---

[1]Cicero, *Treatise on the Commonwealth*, Bk 3, in *On the Commonwealth and On the Laws*, ed. James E. G. Zetzel (New York: Cambridge University Press, 1999), 71.

[2]The *Oxford English Dictionary* named "post-truth" the 2016 word of the year, and a *Washington Post* article links this decision to the increased use of the term following Brexit and the US Presidential election. See Amy B. Wang, "'Post-Truth' Named Word of the Year by Oxford Dictionaries," *Washington Post*, November 16, 2016. For additional uses of the term, see, e.g., William Davies, "The Age of Post-Truth Politics," *New York Times*, August 24, 2016; Jamie L. Vernon, "Science in the Post-Truth Era," *American Scientist* 105, no. 1 (2017): 2.

[3]Martin Luther King Jr., "Letter from Birmingham Jail," April 16, 1963.

[4]See Alasdair MacIntyre, *After Virtue: A Study in Moral Theory*, 3rd ed. (Notre Dame: University of Notre Dame Press, 2007), x–xi, 196–7.

theory, which focuses more exclusively on the dictates of laws as God's commands. Natural law theory, Vacek argues, allows us to think of right actions as including appropriate "emotions, attitudes, or desires" even as these are qualities of human activity that cannot logically be commanded.[5]

While these dimensions of natural law indicate its importance for contemporary Christian ethics, scholars debate the character of natural law and its interplay with other commitments central to Christian theology. I explore two of these scholarly conversations briefly here. The first centers on how one might reconcile a commitment to natural law theory with an acknowledgment of cultural and moral diversity. The second considers the extent to which natural law can be conceived and articulated in a manner that makes it a viable approach for Protestant ethics in particular. A consideration of these questions highlights a number of promising approaches to the natural law in recent scholarship and simultaneously clarifies certain contemporary debates.

MORAL REALISM AND CULTURAL DIVERSITY

One perennial question that arises in considering the natural law concerns its compatibility with cultural, moral, and religious diversity. The notion of natural law presumes the existence of certain kinds of objective goods or norms and provides philosophical grounding for challenging human rights violations. But a belief in natural law could also put one at risk for enacting a kind of colonialism that imposes norms of Western philosophical traditions in non-Western contexts. Martha Nussbaum explores this risk in an essay on female genital mutilation as a traditional cultural practice in select African contexts. Nussbaum stresses the importance of acknowledging and wrestling with our status as Western observers before imposing a judgment on a tradition outside one's own. But she ultimately argues against female genital mutilation on grounds that the practice opposes universal views of justice and human well-being.[6] Nussbaum's essay concretely recognizes the challenges of finding balance between a natural law ethic and efforts to allow for cultural difference. At the same time, Nussbaum's essay defends the importance of the natural law as a philosophical tool that promotes conditions that support human flourishing.

Christian theologians likewise explore this question through considering the nature and scope of universal moral norms, with particular focus on the degree to which specific goods and norms can be derived from Aquinas's account of the natural law. Both the personalism of John Paul II and the "new natural law theory" developed by Germain Grisez, John Finnis, and Robert George advocate views of the natural law as giving rise to precise and specific behavioral norms. John Paul II's 1993 encyclical *Veritatis splendor*, a text that argues heavily against moral and cultural relativism,[7] identifies a set of "intrinsically evil acts" that can be discerned through attending to "reason," as well as the magisterial tradition and scripture.[8] Intrinsically evil acts are those that "radically contradict the good of the person" made in God's image, thereby violating the

[5]Edward Collins Vacek, "Divine-Command, Natural-Law, and Mutual-Love Ethics," *Theological Studies* 57, no. 4 (1996): 643–4.
[6]Martha Nussbaum, "Judging Other Cultures: The Case of Genital Mutilation," in *Sex and Social Justice* (New York: Oxford University Press, 1999), 118–29.
[7]See, e.g., Pope John Paul II, *Veritatis splendor* (Vatican City: Libreria Editrice Vaticana, 1993), § 32–3, 53.
[8]Ibid., § 80–1. This list coincides with intrinsically evil acts enumerated in Pope Paul VI, *Gaudium et spes* (Vatican City: Libreria Editrice Vaticana, 1965), § 27.

"objective moral order" to which human beings are bound. In arguing for the existence of intrinsically evil acts, *Veritatis splendor* simultaneously affirms the goodness of moral norms that prohibit these evil acts and argues that humans are by their natures obligated to follow these norms "without any exception."[9]

Just as *Veritatis splendor* puts forth a view of the natural law as giving rise to a number of clearly defined moral norms, so do proponents of the "new natural law theory," associated with Grisez, Finnis, and George. Advocates of this position argue that one can derive specific, concrete, and objective goods from Aquinas's account of the natural law's precepts.[10] Aquinas affirms, as the first principle of practical reason, that good should be done and evil avoided. He further specifies three categories of human goods whose pursuit follows from this general principle: goods oriented toward self-preservation, goods shared with animals (such as procreation and care for children), and goods proper to our own rational nature (such as the pursuit of wisdom and the knowledge of God, and social relations with others).[11] Exemplifying a "new natural law" reading of Aquinas, Finnis builds on this position to maintain that a number of specific "basic goods," universal goods linked to human well-being, can be derived from, as he puts it, the "first principles of one's own practical reasoning."[12] He affirms that these goods have intrinsic value.[13] He identifies these goods as life, knowledge, play, "aesthetic experience," friendship, "practical reasonableness," and religion,[14] but he acknowledges possible variations in the precise enumeration of these goods.[15]

A number of other Catholic ethicists, however, interpret Aquinas's account of the precepts of natural law in more general terms that resist deriving overly specified norms from these precepts. Leaving moral discourse at the level of general precepts is a means of affirming certain goods that are shared across traditions while simultaneously more readily accommodating moral differences across cultural traditions. Robert J. Levine's analysis of the notion of "informed consent" in health care ethics supports the idea that more general moral norms can accommodate cultural variation more easily than overly determinate principles can. Levine argues that there are two broad approaches to thinking about standards for researching on human subjects. "Universalists" advocate the adoptions of "universally applicable standards" for guiding this research. "Pluralists," in turn, allow for some universal standards but argue that variations in cultural moral codes and practices require more flexibility in conceiving other norms. Levine ultimately upholds a universalist approach but clarifies that the notion of "informed consent," as adopted in the Declaration of Helsinki, is too precise to function effectively as a universal

---

[9]Pope John Paul II, *Veritatis splendor*, § 80–2. *Veritatis splendor* itself cites Augustine more heavily than Thomas Aquinas, but it is nonetheless appropriate to interpret the text, in part, as an explication of both personalism and natural law. For more discussion of John Paul II's development of personalism in relation to Thomistic natural law theory, see Janet E. Smith, "Natural Law and Personalism in *Veritatis Splendor*," in *Veritatis Splendor: American Responses*, ed. Michael E. Allsopp and John J. O'Keefe (Kansas City: Sheed and Ward, 1995), 194–207.

[10]John Finnis, *Natural Law and Natural Rights*, 2nd ed. (New York: Oxford University Press, 2011), 94–5; see also Finnis, *Aquinas: Moral, Political, and Legal Theory* (New York: Oxford University Press, 1998), 86–7. For a defense of new natural law theory that explores its implications for, and continuity with, later views of human rights, see Robert P. George, "Natural Law," *Harvard Journal of Law and Public Policy* 31, no. 1 (2008): 172–96.

[11]Thomas Aquinas, *Summa Theologiae*, trans. Fathers of the English Dominican Province (2nd ed., 1920), I–II.94.4. Online at http://www.newadvent.org/summa/index.html.

[12]Finnis, *Natural Law and Natural Rights*, 83–5.

[13]Ibid., 118–21.

[14]Ibid., 85–90.

[15]Ibid., 91–2. For a similar list, see Germain Grisez, *The Way of the Lord Jesus, Volume 1: Christian Moral Principles* (Chicago: Franciscan Herald, 1983), 124.

standard for research on human subjects; such an overly specified concept presumes a view of personhood specific to particular cultures (a Western, individualistic perspective) and excludes other feasible anthropologies.[16] Levine therefore argues that universal standards for ethical research are better preserved through adopting more general principles, such as Immanuel Kant's principle of "respect for persons," in the most abstract or "formal" sense of treating humans as ends in themselves rather than means to other ends.[17] As he explains, this principle "is universally applicable when stated at the level of formality employed by Immanuel Kant," but "when one goes beyond this level of formality or abstraction, the principle begins to lose its universality. When one restates the principle of respect for persons in a form that reflects a peculiarly Western view of the person, it begins to lose its relevance to some people in Central Africa, Japan, Central America, and so on."[18] For Levine, adopting abstract principles is a means of affirming universalism in a manner than supports pluralist concerns.

Lisa Cahill argues that post-Vatican II Roman Catholic feminist theological ethicists draw on Aquinas to support positions that are committed both to moral realism and to preserving an understanding of universal norms that is sensitive to cultural variation, a universalism that is "inductive, socially grounded, and revisable."[19] She contends that Thomistic natural law benefits from (and at least to some degree lends itself to) integration with a range of feminist approaches to ethics, which help to ensure that natural law attends sufficiently to human existence as embodied and informed by being situated in specific historical, social, and political contexts.[20] This influential strand of Catholic ethics aligns with the work of thinkers such as Nussbaum to support moral standards that are determinate enough that they meaningfully preserve commitments to justice and enable conditions that support human flourishing. At the same time, this strand of Catholic ethics allows for fluidity in expressing the general goods and norms upheld in a commitment to natural law, and, in doing so, offers positions more open to diversity of cultural expressions than positions associated with more determinate principles.

Jean Porter's account of the natural law provides a concrete example of a Catholic Thomistic approach to natural law that prioritizes human goods and ends over determinate moral principles. Porter presents her view as a "reformulation of scholastic natural law" that selectively retrieves a range of texts and authors, including Aquinas.[21] Her theory of natural law emphasizes happiness (*eudaimonia*)[22] and a teleological view of human nature[23] as providing a starting point for understanding the natural law. To some degree, this view of natural law gives rise to substantive and specific moral norms, but in contrast to "new natural law" theorists, Porter prioritizes the individual exercise of practical wisdom over advocating for a "fully determinate account of the (one and only one) happy way of life."[24] In doing so, she posits a conception of natural law that allows

[16]Robert J. Levine, "Informed Consent: Some Challenges to the Universal Validity of the Western Model," *Law, Medicine, and Health Care* 19, nos. 3–4 (1991): 210–11.

[17]Immanuel Kant, *Grounding for the Metaphysics of Morals*, 3rd ed., trans. James W. Ellington (Indianapolis: Hackett, [1785] 1993), 36.

[18]Levine, "Informed Consent," 212.

[19]Lisa Sowle Cahill, "Renegotiating Aquinas: Catholic Feminist Ethics, Postmodernism, Realism, and Faith," *Journal of Religious Ethics* 43, no. 2 (2015): 194–5.

[20]Ibid., 200–6.

[21]Jean Porter, *Nature as Reason: A Thomistic Theory of the Natural Law* (Grand Rapids: Eerdmans, 2005), 45–7.

[22]Ibid., 163–77.

[23]Ibid., 103–25.

[24]Ibid., 221.

for a range of practices through which characteristically human goods can be cultivated and embodied.

NATURAL LAW AND PROTESTANT MORAL THOUGHT

A second major question regarding the natural law concerns the degree to which Protestant theological and moral commitments stand in tension with the natural law. Through much of the twentieth century, many Protestant ethicists were suspicious of natural law for at least three reasons. First, natural law could be conceived in a manner that threatens divine sovereignty, insofar as it stands as a law to which all moral beings (including God) are subject.[25] Second, natural law is often conceived in a manner that would attribute a certain kind of authority or normativity to standards discernible in the natural world.[26] Some Protestant ethicists see this orientation to nature as problematic because it fails to recognize Jesus Christ as uniquely definitive of moral goodness and to affirm the life, death, and resurrection of Christ and the narrative of scripture as primary sources of moral knowledge. It is generally accepted that Karl Barth is a major influence on the widespread concern that natural law stands at odds with these Christian commitments. Stephen J. Grabill, for example, contends that the 1934 debates between Barth and Emil Brunner heavily influenced much of the negative view of natural law among twentieth-century Protestant ethicists, who followed Barth in seeing natural theology as antithetical to other Reformed convictions.[27] J. Daryl Charles likewise makes note of this debate and contends that the "suspicion and skepticism about natural-law theory" that is present among many Protestants is largely, "but not all," Barthian.[28] Third, natural law advocates commonly affirm that human nature is structured in a manner that provides us with intuitive knowledge, or capacities for obtaining knowledge, regarding objective moral standards. Such an anthropology would seem at odds with understandings of original sin upheld in strands of Protestant theology associated with particular forms of Calvinism, which conceive natural moral faculties as so fully corrupted by original sin that these faculties are necessarily unreliable as sources of moral knowledge and as motivators for moral action.

While these theological concerns about the natural law have led many Protestants to view it with wariness, some strands of Protestant ethics even in the twentieth century embraced a more positive account of the created world as a potential source of moral

---

[25]For more discussion, see Neil Arner, "Precedents and Prospects for Incorporating Natural Law in Protestant Ethics," *Scottish Journal of Theology* 69, no. 4 (2016): 381.

[26]For a helpful discussion of how various theologians incorporate insights from the sciences into their views of nature and natural law, see Stephen Pope, *Human Evolution and Christian Ethics* (New York: Cambridge University Press, 2007), 268–96.

[27]Stephen J. Grabill, *Rediscovering the Natural Law in Reformed Theological Ethics* (Grand Rapids: Eerdmans, 2006), 21–9.

[28]J. Daryl Charles, "Protestants and Natural Law," *First Things* 168 (2006): 36. At the same time, there is some recognition that Barth himself advocates a position more complex than portions of these debates might suggest. Grabill notes that Barth's heavy criticism of natural theology and natural law may have softened during his career, even as he argues that Barth retains even in his later work the essential "theological reasoning and biblical hermeneutics" that lead to a rejection of natural law (29). The nuances in Barth's thought merit further consideration; Arner helpfully makes note of a number of ethicists who are "reintegrating Barth in ways that qualify his opposition to natural law theory" (Arner, "Precedents and Prospects," 376–7). But it is broadly accepted that particular readings of Barth were an important influence on Protestant suspicions of natural law in subsequent decades.

knowledge, indicating that forms of natural law thinking remained part of this tradition.[29] One noteworthy example is the work of Dietrich Bonhoeffer, whose account of the created world shows the potential in Protestant theology to construct a view of the natural law distinctively rooted not in the doctrine of creation but in a theology of redemption. For Bonhoeffer, the natural world is a potential source for moral norms precisely because this world has been redeemed through the incarnation, death, and resurrection of Jesus Christ. Bonhoeffer stresses that Jesus Christ is the source of all existence and redemption.[30] Christ redeems creation, but this does not imply an endorsement of creation as it already is. Bonhoeffer rejects Luther's account of the "orders of creation"[31] and stresses that the church should not endorse created institutions of natural forms of justice independently of the restoration of these institutions in Christ.[32] To link his view of divine activity in the world closely to God's work of redemption, Bonhoeffer adopts the language of "mandates of creation," which function as tasks rather than forms of being.[33] These mandates arise from the divine command and are also grounded in both scripture and the revelation of Christ.[34] Bonhoeffer's view of the mandates of creation provides conceptual space for thinking of the natural world as a possible source of moral norms, and Bonhoeffer's conviction that no part of the world is unredeemed by Christ[35] grounds this account.[36]

More recently, increasing numbers of Protestant theological ethicists are showing interest in recovering accounts of the natural law, primarily through tracing forms of natural law thinking at work in Luther, Calvin, and their successors through the eighteenth century. The views of natural law retrieved here differ from the argument seen above in Bonhoeffer, that the created world is best interpreted through the theology of redemption. David VanDrunen contrasts sixteenth- and seventeenth-century Reformed views of the natural law with twentieth-century interpretations of the natural world rooted in the theology of redemption. He explains that through a commitment to natural law and the Augustinian conception of two cities or two kingdoms, "the older Reformed writers rooted political and cultural life in God's work of creation and

[29]While Bonhoeffer's perspective represents a tendency of twentieth-century Protestant ethics to highlight redemption, rather than creation, as a starting point for ethics, there are also other noteworthy exceptions to the argument that twentieth-century Protestant thinkers neglected the natural law (even in more traditional forms). For example, Vincent Lloyd in *Black Natural Law* (New York: Oxford University Press, 2016) puts forth an important study detailing how nineteenth- and twentieth-century thinkers W. E. B. Du Bois and Martin Luther King Jr. developed (building on earlier thinkers such as Frederick Douglass) a distinctive tradition of natural law thought that complements a number of contemporary perspectives. Likewise, select other twentieth-century Protestant theologians drew explicitly on traditional natural law language despite Barth's objections. Most prominent among these thinkers are Emil Brunner, *The Divine Imperative*, trans. Olive Wyon (Philadelphia: Westminster, 1947); James Gustafson, *Ethics from a Theocentric Perspective*, 2 vols. (Chicago: University of Chicago Press, 1981); and Paul Ramsey, *Basic Christian Ethics* (New York: Scribner, 1950).

[30]Dietrich Bonhoeffer, *Ethics* (Minneapolis: Fortress, 2005), 54–5.

[31]Ibid., 68–9.

[32]Ibid., 344.

[33]Ibid., 68–9.

[34]Ibid., 388–9.

[35]Ibid., 65–70.

[36]Oliver O'Donovan's *Resurrection and Moral Order* (Grand Rapids: Eerdmans, 1986) provides another strong example of such a perspective. For O'Donovan, the resurrection is the starting point for the work of Christian ethics, but he simultaneously criticizes perspectives that maintain a strong dichotomy between an "ethic of creation" and an "ethics of the kingdom," precisely because creation is restored through the resurrection (15). Resurrection provides a necessary framework through which one interprets the created world and discerns its order, even as O'Donovan complicates this position by arguing that the created world necessarily has a cosmic ordering and *telos* even prior to the resurrection (55, 87).

providence, not in his work of redemption and eschatological restoration through Jesus Christ."[37] Contemporary Protestant ethicists' interest in recovering more historical accounts of the natural law centers around at least two sets of concerns. First, recent work from Protestant scholars such as Jennifer A. Herdt and J. Daryl Charles suggests that adopting a form of natural law theory is a means of embracing the nuances and complexities of historical Protestant thought, particularly the Reformed tradition. Not only do scholars increasingly suggest that the Reformers themselves largely accept a view of natural law broadly continuous with Scholasticism,[38] but later generations of theologians in the Reformed tradition also continued to presume a framework for moral reflection shaped by natural law thinking.[39] Attention to the natural law thus facilitates a process of focused retrieval that brings insights from significant historical voices to bear on contemporary ethical reflection.

Second, the natural law provides a possible point of entry for conversations across traditions. Charles and Grabill argue that a resurgence of interest in natural law is a means of supporting ecumenical dialogue, particularly between Protestants and Catholics.[40] Philip Ziegler contends a number of contemporary Protestant retrievals of natural law theory are motivated by a desire to articulate Christian moral commitments in a manner that is persuasive and understandable for non-Christian or public audiences.[41] Likewise, VanDrunen affirms that theologians who wish to retrieve a Reformed account of the natural law must seriously consider "how, concretely, Christians can make natural law arguments in the public square with theological integrity and some degree of persuasiveness to a religiously mixed crowd."[42] In reflecting on such concerns, Herdt argues that historical developments in Calvinism suggest that contemporary theologians and ethicists should resist the temptation to attempt to derive overly concrete and specific moral norms from the natural law. Herdt explains that historically, when Reformed thinkers attempted to stretch Calvin's view of natural law too far in the direction of an action-guiding moral theory, the attempt resulted in the emergence of positions that were removed from Calvin's substantively rich theological convictions. She stresses that the natural law can support theologically rich contributions to "public moral discourse" designed to facilitate a "just civic order."[43] But her caution serves as a reminder to Protestants that it is worthwhile to be deliberate when engaging in historical retrievals of our tradition, especially insofar as significant contemporary thinkers see dimensions of modern Protestant thought as indirectly implicated in the emergence of secular morality.[44]

---

[37]David VanDrunen, *Natural Law and the Two Kingdoms* (Grand Rapids: Eerdmans, 2010), 2. VanDrunen's focus is primarily on Reformed Calvinist perspectives, and the contrast he sets up places Calvin at odds with "neoCalvinists" for whom Dutch theologian Abraham Kuyper is a primary interlocutor.

[38]Jennifer A. Herdt, "Calvin's Legacy for Contemporary Reformed Natural Law," *Scottish Journal of Theology* 67, no. 4 (2014): 418, n. 8; J. Daryl Charles, *Retrieving the Natural Law: A Return to Moral First Things* (Grand Rapids: Eerdmans, 2008), 114.

[39]For example, Grabill includes chapters on Johannes Althusius and Francis Turretin.

[40]Charles, "Protestants and Natural Law," 155. Grabill, *Rediscovering the Natural Law*, 7–8. Arner also stresses the potential of natural law to promote ecumenical dialogue.

[41]Philip G. Ziegler, "The Fate of Natural Law at the Turning of the Ages," *Theology Today* 67, no. 4 (2011): 419–20.

[42]VanDrunen, *Natural Law and the Two Kingdoms*, 432–3.

[43]Herdt, "Calvin's Legacy," 416–17.

[44]See, e.g., Alasdair MacIntyre, *A Short History of Ethics* (Notre Dame: University of Notre Dame Press, 1966), 121–6; MacIntyre, *After Virtue*, 52–4; and Charles Taylor, *A Secular Age* (Cambridge: Belknap Press of Harvard University Press, 2007), 74–99.

CONCLUSION

The natural law is an ancient notion with continued interest for Christian ethicists. It serves as a vehicle through which theological ethicists can engage historical perspectives and enrich our understanding of them. It also provides a framework for defending moral realism and for conceptualizing and defending notions of truth, goodness, and justice that stand beyond the immediate particulars of the Christian tradition. The promise of the natural law lies in its offering a language through which to reflect meaningfully on the moral life while simultaneously attending to particular theological convictions and more universal claims. The challenge for its adherents is to allow ourselves to continue to wrestle with tensions between universal and particular moral norms and commitments, and to avoid the temptation of setting these tensions aside too hastily.

SUGGESTED READINGS

Cunningham, Lawrence S., ed. *Intractable Debates about the Natural Law: Alasdair MacIntyre and Critics*. Notre Dame: University of Notre Dame Press, 2009.

Finnis, John. *Natural Law and Natural Rights*, 2nd ed. New York: Oxford University Press, 2011.

Grabill, Stephen J. *Rediscovering the Natural Law in Reformed Theological Ethics*. Grand Rapids: Eerdmans, 2006.

Porter, Jean. *Nature as Reason: A Thomistic Theory of the Natural Law*. Grand Rapids: Eerdmans, 2005.

Traina, Christina L. H. *Feminist Ethics and Natural Law*. Washington, DC: Georgetown University Press, 2002.

CHAPTER NINE

Emotions and Christian Ethics

MICHAEL P. JAYCOX

The purpose of this chapter is to offer conceptual clarity on the ethical significance of emotion, an account of the development of theological and philosophical reflection on emotion, and a critical eye toward a dominant culture that delegitimizes appropriate emotional responses to suffering and abuses of power.[1] In contrast to popular notions of emotion as a nonmoral, individualistic experience or as a raw impulse requiring careful control, historical and contemporary traditions of Christian ethical thought emphasize emotional integration and development as a normative ideal. Emotions provide a rich and highly relevant source of moral insight that should more robustly inform ethical analysis of, and practical Christian responses to, urgent social justice challenges. After a brief survey of experience, scripture, and tradition, I will propose a general ethical stance aligned with a cognitive view of emotion. To illustrate the practical applicability of such a view, I will also explore the complex dynamics of compassion and anger in response to suffering as a result of systemic oppression and injustice.

EXPERIENCE

As a way of recognizing the depth and complexity of human emotional experiences, I highlight in this section salient insights on emotion available from philosophy and underrepresented voices.

Ancient Greek and Roman philosophers have exerted, for better or for worse, a heavy influence on Christian theological and ethical thought about emotion. Aristotle understood the ethical significance of emotions teleologically, as inclinations that support human flourishing. Although he thought emotion is shared with nonhuman animals that lack reason, he understood human emotion to be already partially or potentially rational.[2] One will feel emotions, such as compassion or anger, for example, if one has the corresponding

[1]A parenthetical note: Several different terms have come to indicate "emotion" in common English usage, including feeling, desire, inclination, affection, passion, disposition, and so on. Some scholars make persuasive arguments for offering clear and distinct definitions for each of these terms, but I do not find this approach necessary here for the purpose of achieving conceptual clarity. Thus, I use the aforementioned terms interchangeably throughout this chapter. When there is a substantive difference in the way two authors use the same term, I will indicate this difference by use of adjectives.

[2]Aristotle, *On the Soul*, trans. Hippocrates Aristotle (Grinnell, IA: Peripatetic Press, 1981), 414a30–b15; Aristotle, *Nicomachean Ethics*, trans. Martin Ostwald (Upper Saddle River, NJ: Prentice Hall, 1999), 1102b10–3a1;

set of specific beliefs about the situation: that the suffering is serious, that harm was unjustly inflicted, and so on.[3] Such emotions are a potential cause of moral weakness, but an agent can habituate them, by way of an intermediate stage of continence, to become virtuous and fully integrated with reason.[4] Aristotle envisioned an organic synergy of desire and deliberation, not an opposition.[5] Virtuous agents by definition are moved toward the purpose of their action by their properly integrated emotions, which should be felt "at the right time, toward the right objects, toward the right people, for the right reason, and in the right manner."[6] This fairly demanding normative standard aside, Aristotle imagined that the number of emotionally integrated human beings is still likely to be a fairly small club, due to the fact that external goods (good childhood upbringing, good health, sufficient wealth, friendships) are also constitutive of flourishing in his account. A significant lack of access to any of these goods, which most people in the ancient world would have been relatively powerless to control, would cause misery for an otherwise virtuous agent or even stymie the possibility of virtuous development altogether.[7]

By contrast, the Stoics argued that to possess virtue is in itself to flourish, virtue being the self-sufficient good that an agent *can* control.[8] A life of virtue involves cultivating indifference toward external conditions that the agent *cannot* control, which is to say, freedom from behaving as if they had real value or importance.[9] Chrysippus and Seneca proposed that emotion is best understood as a false judgment that a particular external condition does have real value and importance, a judgment that results from the agent's free assent to a preliminary impulse suggesting that evaluation.[10] These Stoic authors generally recommended that we examine the course of all our evaluative judgments for their truth or falsity, especially the preliminary impulses that might give rise to emotion, the ultimate goal being to prevent and eliminate emotion altogether as an obstacle to virtue.[11] This apparently extreme position must be understood in the broader context of Stoic imperatives to show equal respect for the agency of all individuals possessing the capacity for reason and to prioritize the universal, impartial law of justice over the partial bonds of love.[12]

Martha C. Nussbaum, *The Therapy of Desire: Theory and Practice in Hellenistic Ethics* (Princeton: Princeton University Press, 1994), 80–3.

[3]Aristotle, *Rhetoric*, trans. John Henry Freese (Cambridge, MA: Harvard University Press, 1926), 1378a8–80b17, 1385b6–6b16.

[4]Aristotle, *Nicomachean Ethics*, 1105b15–6b20, 1147a10–52a35.

[5]Ibid., 1139a15–b5.

[6]Ibid., 1106b20.

[7]Ibid., 1099a30–101a20.

[8]Seneca, "On the Happy Life," in *Moral Essays*, vol. II, trans. John W. Basore (Cambridge, MA: Harvard University Press, 1951), 3.3–4, 4.4–5, 15.5–16.3.

[9]Richard Sorabji, *Emotion and Peace of Mind: From Stoic Agitation to Christian Temptation* (New York: Oxford University Press, 2000), 194–210. Note that good external conditions may be chosen as "preferred indifferents" if such a choice is not contrary to virtue; see Nussbaum, *Therapy of Desire*, 359–66; T. H. Irwin, "Stoic and Aristotelian Conceptions of Happiness," in *The Norms of Nature: Studies in Hellenistic Ethics*, ed. Malcolm Schofield and Gisela Striker (New York: Cambridge University Press, 1986), 205–44.

[10]Seneca, "On Anger," in *Moral and Political Essays*, ed. John M. Cooper and J. F. Procopé (New York: Cambridge University Press, 1995), 2.1.4–2.4.2; Seneca, "Epistle 75 On the Diseases of the Soul," in *Moral Epistles*, vol. II, trans. Richard M. Gummere (Cambridge, MA: Harvard University Press, 1953), § 11–14; Seneca, "Epistle 113 On the Vitality of the Soul and Its Attributes," in *Moral Epistles*, vol. III, trans. Richard M. Gummere (Cambridge, MA: Harvard University Press, 1953), § 17–20; Sorabji, *Emotion and Peace of Mind*, 33, 35, 70–1.

[11]Nussbaum, *Therapy of Desire*, 366–401.

[12]Martha C. Nussbaum, *Upheavals of Thought: The Intelligence of Emotions* (New York: Cambridge University Press, 2001), 12, 359; also, Nussbaum, *Therapy of Desire*, 324–5.

The Stoics argued that we will be unable to give all humans the equal and impartial respect they justly deserve if we allow false judgments about the seriousness of harm and suffering (e.g., compassion toward victims who share a special relation with us, or anger toward their perpetrators) to influence our actions.[13]

Enlightenment philosophers radically altered the descriptive understanding of emotion through shifts in epistemology and anthropology, as well as a shift away from teleological ethics. René Descartes analyzed the human being as a unified machine in which each part performs its distinctive function. Emotions begin as bodily movements of sense perception in response to external objects, which are transmitted through the nerves to the pineal gland, and from there to the soul, where the emotion becomes a self-reflexive experience of the subject.[14] While Descartes did offer classic Stoic remedies for managing excessive emotions, in themselves emotions "are all in their nature good," in that their function is to provide the self with sensory knowledge about the outside environment.[15] Thomas Hobbes presumes this Cartesian, mechanistic concept of emotion in his argument that individuals, being motivated by self-interest and fear in the state of nature, will seek the security of political society through contractual submission to an absolute ruler.[16] While the ruled may be able to experience individual contentment, provided they can reliably obtain what they desire and avoid that to which they are averse, these emotions ironically do not inform the imposed rational morality created by the laws of the ruler.[17]

Sensing a problem in treating emotions as morally irrelevant, David Hume claimed that emotion, not rationality, is the decisive factor underlying all moral choices, and he granted pride of place to sympathy as the crucial inclination that grounds human sociality and moderates self-interest.[18] Adam Smith similarly argued that the moderation of self-interest by sympathy allows capitalism to function without causing harm to society and to be justifiable as a moral economic system.[19] Hume and Smith both presumed that our emotions can be habituated by virtue or vice, but having abandoned a teleological framework, the actual moral content of Humean emotions remains utterly relative to the particular object preferences and valuations that happen to emerge as individual agents interact with one another in a social environment.[20] Thus, Hume and Smith's proposals stand as observations of typical human behavior rather than arguments for why emotional inclinations ought to be regarded as morally decisive. Despite the fact that Immanuel Kant attacked Hume's theory, arguing that actions of beneficence motivated by sympathy have "no true moral worth," because nonrational emotions are unreliable motivators by

[13]Seneca, "On Mercy," in *Moral and Political Essays*, ed. John M. Cooper and J. F. Procopé (New York: Cambridge University Press, 1995), § 1.17.1–3, 2.4.4, 2.5.1.

[14]René Descartes, *The Passions of the Soul*, trans. Stephen H. Voss (Indianapolis: Hackett, 1989), arts. 22, 23, 25, 27, 51.

[15]Ibid., arts. 40, 48, 49, 211.

[16]Thomas Hobbes, *Leviathan*, ed. J. C. A. Gaskin (New York: Oxford University Press, 1996), 1.13.3, 1.13.6–9, 1.13.14.

[17]Ibid., 1.6.2–4, 1.6.7, 1.6.58, 1.11.1, 1.13.10, 1.13.13, 1.17.2.

[18]David Hume, *A Treatise of Human Nature*, ed. L. A. Selby-Bigge and P. H. Nidditch (New York: Oxford University Press, 1978), 2.2.7, 2.3.3, 3.2.2.

[19]Adam Smith, *The Theory of Moral Sentiments*, ed. Ryan Patrick Hanley (New York: Penguin Books, 2009), 1.1.1–2, 4.2, 7.3.2; Amartya Sen, *The Idea of Justice* (Cambridge: Harvard University Press, 2009), 184–90; Amartya Sen, "Rational Fools: A Critique of the Behavioral Foundations of Economic Theory," *Philosophy & Public Affairs* 6, no. 4 (1977): 326–9.

[20]David Hume, *Essays, Moral, Political, and Literary*, ed. Eugene F. Miller (Indianapolis: Liberty Fund, 1987), § 1.18; J. B. Schneewind, "The Misfortunes of Virtue," *Ethics* 101, no. 1 (1990): 52–4.

comparison with rational obligation, the descriptive moral psychology he presumed was identical to Hume's.[21]

While Hume and Kant's racist views are already well known, the broader context of their views was the oppositional understanding of rationality and emotion in Enlightenment moral psychology. Early modern European scientists simply presumed this opposition as they constructed racial categories through the Cartesian "normative gaze," assigning emotional excess as an attribute of the non-European bodies they "observed" in order to position Europeans as morally superior.[22] This deployment of rationality and emotion as essentialized racial characteristics normalized (and still normalizes) white supremacist practices such as colonialism, enslavement, and disenfranchisement, making clear that Enlightenment ideals of freedom and equality were never intended to apply to everyone.[23] Frantz Fanon documented and analyzed the psychological effects of this pattern of cultural domination, arguing that the sense of "shame and self-contempt" felt by Black persons is grounded in a colonized desire to identify with whiteness and against the supposed attributes of blackness, which include immoderate emotional impulses and a lack of full rational capacities.[24] Reflecting on his own experience, Fanon noticed that he was himself hesitant to express anger toward whites, precisely for fear of fulfilling the racist stereotype of the violent Black male.[25]

Building upon these insights, a critical tradition focused on interrogating the distribution and use of social power emerged as a central aspect of Black American thought on emotion, given that "to be a Negro in this country and to be relatively conscious, is to be in a rage almost all the time."[26] Both James Baldwin and Malcolm X deconstructed white Christian norms prohibiting anger, political resistance, and the use of violence, exposing these as a white supremacist ruse designed to encourage Black persons to cooperate with their own oppression.[27] Audre Lorde argued that anger is the only reasonable response to racism, that it has the potential to raise critical consciousness in others if used with precision in interpersonal communication, and that it can unite Black and white feminists in pursuing common political goals.[28] Cornel West emphasizes that anger promotes appropriate self-love in the Black community by removing the psychic barriers to that love, while bell hooks argues that anger informs and enables a more radical Black subjectivity and, in so

---

[21]Immanuel Kant, *Grounding for the Metaphysics of Morals*, trans. James W. Ellington (Indianapolis: Hackett, 1993), 11; Rosalind Hursthouse, *On Virtue Ethics* (New York: Oxford University Press, 1999), 99–107. The later Kant did attempt to systematize the relationship between obligation and inclination, but inclinations such as sympathy play an auxiliary role in the circumscribed realm of supererogatory imperfect duties; see Immanuel Kant, *The Metaphysics of Morals*, trans. Mary Gregor (New York: Cambridge University Press, 1996), 145–62; Schneewind, "The Misfortunes of Virtue," 195–8.

[22]Cornel West, *Prophesy Deliverance! An Afro-American Revolutionary Christianity*, rev. ed. (Louisville: Westminster John Knox, 2002), 47–57.

[23]Richard H. Popkin, "Hume's Racism Reconsidered," in *The Third Force in Seventeenth-Century Thought* (Leiden: Brill, 1992), 64–75; J. Kameron Carter, *Race: A Theological Account* (New York: Oxford University Press, 2008), 79–121; Charles W. Mills, "Kant and Race, *Redux*," *Graduate Faculty Philosophy Journal* 35, nos. 1–2 (2014): 125–57; Charles W. Mills, *The Racial Contract* (Ithaca: Cornell University Press, 1997), 12–13, 16–19, 21–3, 44–5, 53–62.

[24]Frantz Fanon, *Black Skin, White Masks*, trans. Richard Philcox (New York: Grove, 2008), 91–6, 102, 106.

[25]Ibid., 113–19.

[26]James Baldwin, "The Negro in American Culture," *Cross Currents* 11, no. 3 (1961): 205.

[27]James Baldwin, *The Fire Next Time* (New York: Penguin, 1990), 27–8; Malcolm X, with the assistance of Alex Haley, *The Autobiography of Malcolm X* (New York: Penguin, 2001), 257, 349, 357–8, 361.

[28]Audre Lorde, *Sister Outsider* (Berkeley: Crossing, 1984), 124–33, 145–75.

doing, acts as a "catalyst" for political resistance to systemic injustice.[29] If ethical analysis is to take the role of social power seriously as an influence on emotional self-understanding and expression, then ethicists must reckon with the significance of social location as we attempt to understand and evaluate emotions: "The rage of the oppressed is never the same as the rage of the privileged. One group can change their lot only by changing the system; the other hopes to be rewarded within the system."[30]

SCRIPTURE

Unlike ancient philosophers, the authors of the Hebrew scriptures are not preoccupied with questions about the nature of emotions or their role in a flourishing life. Rather, emotions are simply presumed as indicators of the quality of a relationship between two parties. The biblical authors unapologetically portray the God of Israel as passible, as feeling emotions of compassion and anger toward human beings.[31] Salvation history provides the context for divine and human emotions, including God's promise of covenant fidelity (most significantly the Sinai covenant with an oppressed people), the people's breaking of covenant, and God's subsequent initiations and restorations of covenant. The covenant command to love God presumes and requires that the people feel an inclination of loyalty toward the God who liberates from oppression, just as the frequent commands to show compassion for vulnerable persons presume and require that the people "know the heart of an alien" (Exod. 23:9).[32] The prophets' alternating messages of comfort and wrathful denunciation inform the people about God's emotional responses to their suffering and their failures to keep the covenant by tolerating social injustice.[33] The Psalms encompass a broad range of human emotions in relation to God and society—joyful gratitude for God's fidelity, lament voiced by the victims of social injustice, and even the desire to seek revenge against perpetrators.[34] Given the covenantal context, justice and mercy become the background theological-ethical values in relation to which divine and human emotions function and become intelligible.[35]

Paul's approach to emotions is influenced not only by his experience of the risen Christ but also by his Judaism and the Stoic philosophical context prevalent at the time of his writing. Seneca's recommended process of bringing all thoughts into conformity with universal reason, eliminating false beliefs (emotions), and practicing indifference toward that which does not matter for attaining virtue, resonated greatly with the emerging Christian narrative of conversion, in which the self turns from the example of the world and brings one's life into conformity with the example of Christ in community.[36] Although

---

[29]Cornel West, *Race Matters*, 2nd ed. (New York: Vintage, 2001), 135–51; bell hooks, *Killing Rage: Ending Racism* (New York: Henry Holt, 1995), 8–30, 191–2.

[30]hooks, *Killing Rage*, 30. For an internal critique of Black traditions that promote a normative role for emotion in political life, see Vincent Lloyd, *Black Natural Law* (New York: Oxford University Press, 2016), 118–43.

[31]Abraham J. Heschel, *The Prophets* (New York: Harper & Row, 1962), 247–78.

[32]Jacqueline E. Lapsley, "Feeling Our Way: Love for God in Deuteronomy," *Catholic Biblical Quarterly* 65, no. 3 (2003): 350–69. All quotations from scripture are provided in the New Revised Standard Version.

[33]Heschel, *The Prophets*, 3–26, 216–31, 279–306.

[34]Patrick D. Miller, *They Cried to the Lord: The Form and Theology of Biblical Prayer* (Minneapolis: Fortress, 1994); Erich Zenger, *A God of Vengeance? Understanding the Psalms of Divine Wrath*, trans. Linda M. Maloney (Louisville: Westminster John Knox, 1996).

[35]Heschel, *The Prophets*, 195–220.

[36]Troels Engberg-Pedersen, *Paul and the Stoics* (Louisville: Westminster John Knox, 2000); Jan N. Sevenster, *Paul and Seneca* (Leiden: Brill, 1961); Wayne A. Meeks, *The Origins of Christian Morality: The First Two Centuries* (New Haven: Yale University Press, 1993), 23–32.

Paul expected the imminent return of Christ within a Jewish apocalyptic frame, his proposed ethic of sexual desire also reflects well-established social attitudes and cultural traditions. He exhorts the married and the celibate to subject their sexual desire to Stoic self-control in order that they would be "free from anxieties" (1 Cor. 7:32), his dualism of "flesh" and "spirit" reflects the supposed propensity of emotion to subvert choosing the good, and his lists of vices and virtues combine traditional Jewish sexual prohibitions and Stoic emotional prescriptions in a standard form of Hellenistic moral exhortation.[37] An enduring legacy, therefore, of Paul's writings is that the emotion of sexual desire takes on a highly morally ambivalent meaning, being perceived as a potential hindrance to the singleness of heart idealized in both Second Temple Judaism and early Christian communities.

It is impossible, however, to speak credibly about the actual emotional content appropriate for Christian life without examining the verb that the biblical authors reserved almost exclusively for the purpose of indicating Jesus's emotional response to human suffering, *splanchnizomai*, which is usually translated as "to have compassion" or "to be moved with compassion." Occurring twelve times in the Synoptic gospels (Mt. 9:36, 14:14, 15:32, 18:27, 20:34; Mk 1:41, 6:34, 8:2, 9:22; Lk. 7:13, 10:33, 15:20), it indicates that Jesus had this specific emotional disposition toward groups and individuals who were sick, hungry, poor, grieving, or otherwise made socially powerless and vulnerable in the context of Roman imperial institutions. In every instance, this compassion motivates his action to alleviate the suffering and to integrate the affected group or individual into a new institution: the social, political, and economic life of the Reign of God.[38] In the few instances in which the biblical authors do not use the verb in reference to Jesus himself, it occurs in parables to illustrate the kind of commitment to culturally transgressive, nonreciprocal action that is also expected of Jesus's followers, most notably in the Parable of the Good Samaritan (Lk. 10:25-37).[39] In this way, the emotional dispositions found in the encounter narratives and in the parables function to "tutor" those of the reader.[40] The implied ethical code is a radically exemplarist virtue ethic, for Jesus's disciples are meant to imitate his emotional disposition as the incarnation of the compassion of God: "Be merciful, just as your Father is merciful" (Lk. 6:36). Moreover, following the compassionate example of Jesus in a context of systemic oppression requires not only the alleviation of suffering but also taking the risk of political resistance that exposes and condemns the root causes of suffering. Jesus's own holy anger, for example, moved him to expel the money changers from the Second Temple as a prophetic denunciation of the corrupt Sadducean establishment, knowing that the cost of this action might be his life.[41]

---

[37]Peter Brown, *Late Antiquity* (Cambridge: Harvard University Press, 1987), 14–15, 24–7; Dale B. Martin, *The Corinthian Body* (New Haven: Yale University Press, 1995), 171–4, 198–228; Margaret A. Farley, *Just Love: A Framework for Christian Sexual Ethics* (New York: Continuum, 2006), 33–40.

[38]John H. Elliott, "Temple versus Household in Luke-Acts: A Contrast in Social Institutions," in *The Social World of Luke-Acts: Models for Interpretation*, ed. Jerome H. Neyrey (Peabody: Hendrickson, 1991), 224–30.

[39]Maureen H. O'Connell, *Compassion: Loving Our Neighbor in an Age of Globalization* (Maryknoll: Orbis, 2009), 68–70; John R. Donahue, *The Gospel in Parable: Metaphor, Narrative, and Theology in the Synoptic Gospels* (Philadelphia: Fortress, 1988), 131–4; William C. Spohn, *Go and Do Likewise: Jesus and Ethics* (New York: Continuum, 2000), 89–91; Jon Sobrino, *The Principle of Mercy: Taking the Crucified People from the Cross* (Maryknoll: Orbis, 1994), 15–26.

[40]Spohn, *Go and Do Likewise*, 134–6.

[41]Ibid., 79–81.

TRADITION

The perception that it was necessary for Christian disciples to take significant political risks by acting in accordance with the divine example of compassion and anger was largely lost in the subsequent development of mainstream Christian theological ethics. Augustine, however, retains and develops the crucial connection between emotional inclinations and political commitments as the basis of his political theology. Having redefined a commonwealth as "an assemblage of reasonable beings bound together by a common agreement as to the objects of their love," he provides a warrant for viewing the historically attainable versions of human society as valuable though imperfectly just, lying on a spectrum in relation to the ideal society of perfected love for God and for the neighbor in God.[42] If this reformulation of political justice in terms of divine love enables us to evaluate the quality of human societies, then it should also enable us to evaluate the quality of human emotions in relation to their implicit political outcomes. Despite the profound Pauline ambivalence with which Augustine views sexual desire, he ultimately departs from the Stoics, insisting that human emotions, which Christ possessed, are morally neutral in themselves. Their actual degree of goodness depends on the quality of justice in the political societies to which they point and how humans use their broken yet graced wills to direct and order these loves in action.[43] Thus, Augustine reframes the basic ethical question: While on pilgrimage in the earthly city, to what degree are we ordering our loves to sustain the common agreement about the goods that are essential to a flourishing human life?[44]

By way of some contrast, Thomas Aquinas argued that "every agent ... does every action from love of some kind," because agents always act for a purpose that is both rationally known and emotionally desired.[45] Emotions are indeed morally neutral in themselves, simply inclining us toward goods necessary to preserve our general animal nature. But to the extent that they are integrated with the rational will by which human animals are distinctively free and responsible, they are to that same extent morally good and presupposed in every action proceeding from virtue.[46] Even actions enabled by the theological virtue of charity, such as almsgiving, still presuppose a compassion in which two agents experience a union of their emotional responses to suffering.[47] However, the cost of emphasizing the rational integration of emotion is that Aquinas inadvertently renders emotions politically irrelevant. A rational will habituated by the virtue of justice is both necessary and sufficient for choosing right actions in regard to other agents, and in principle it makes this determination independently of emotions, which are generally referable to the common good but contribute no insight to determining what is just.[48] For

---

[42]Augustine, *The City of God*, trans. Marcus Dods (New York: Modern Library, 2000), XIX.14, XIX.24; Eugene TeSelle, "The Civic Vision in Augustine's *City of God*," *Thought* 62, no. 246 (1987): 268–80; David Hollenbach, *The Common Good and Christian Ethics* (New York: Cambridge University Press, 2002), 126–9; Peter J. Burnell, "The Status of Politics in St. Augustine's *City of God*," *History of Political Thought* 13, no. 1 (1992): 23–7.

[43]Augustine, *City of God*, XIV.6–9; Eric Gregory, *Politics and the Order of Love: An Augustinian Ethic of Democratic Citizenship* (Chicago: University of Chicago Press, 2008), 256–63, 274–80, 288–91.

[44]Augustine, *City of God*, XIX.17.

[45]Thomas Aquinas, *Summa Theologiae*, trans. Fathers of the English Dominican Province (New York: Benziger Brothers, 1948), I–II.28.6, 24.3.

[46]Ibid., I–II, 26.1, 56.4, 59.1–2; Diana Fritz Cates, *Aquinas on the Emotions: A Religious-Ethical Inquiry* (Washington, DC: Georgetown University Press, 2009), 185–6, 213–18, 226–37.

[47]Aquinas, *Summa Theologiae*, II–II.30.2; Diana Fritz Cates, *Choosing to Feel: Virtue, Friendship and Compassion for Friends* (Notre Dame: University of Notre Dame Press, 1997).

[48]Aquinas, *Summa Theologiae*, I–II.59.4–5, 64.2; II–II.58.2 ad 4, 58.4–5, 58.8–9.

instance, Aquinas defends anger as an aspect of human nature, observing that its cause "is always something considered in the light of an injustice" and that to draw such an inference "requires an act of reason."[49] Yet he confines anger's normative expression to the context of interpersonal grievances such that it is never directed to institutions, and he argues that public actions to protect the common good against threats should not proceed from anger, as it is prone to excess and not reliably integrated with reason.[50]

Although the sixteenth-century reformers said comparatively little about the significance of emotion per se for ethics, John Calvin called attention to our sense of awe at the glory of God the creator and the beauty of creation itself, which would have been "a school in which we might learn piety," had we not been totally corrupted by original sin.[51] In addition to reliance on scripture for accurate intellectual knowledge of God, Calvinist piety involved an emotional stance of Stoic indifference toward external conditions, particularly material "gifts," so as to use them in service to the poor and the common good.[52] Moreover, indicators of individual election by God, such as a sense of calling and the assurance of faith, relied practically on a considerable amount of emotional awareness, reflection, and verification.[53] Jonathan Edwards used a Humean moral psychology to explicate this Calvinist spirituality, arguing that since "it is our inclination that governs us in our actions" and enables us to respond to beauty, grace "removes the hindrances of reason" and "sanctifies the reason" by first making an aesthetic appeal to our emotional sense.[54] While he does distinguish between true religious affections and mere impulsive passions, it is clear that Edwards understands God as working through emotion, rather than the intellect, in order to free the human will for love, "the fountain of all the affections."[55]

PRACTICAL REASON

Reflecting critically on experience, scripture, and tradition, contemporary Christian ethicists should adopt a cognitive account of emotion in order to subvert structured abuses of power and address urgent social justice challenges. Critical traditions of thought about emotion, particularly Black American thought, emphasize that the abuse of power by privileged groups creates dominant cultural expectations regarding who is allowed to express which emotions in public, and these expectations are raced and gendered. This system virtually ensures that persons of color and women, despite occupying optimal structural positions for recognizing and critiquing systemic injustices, will likely be dismissed by white persons and men as "hysterical," "aggressive," "unstable,"

---

[49]Ibid., I–II 46.4, 47.2; Diana Fritz Cates, "Taking Women's Experience Seriously: Thomas Aquinas and Audre Lorde on Anger," in *Aquinas and Empowerment: Classical Ethics for Ordinary Lives*, ed. G. Simon Harak (Washington, DC: Georgetown University Press, 1996), 47–88; Bryan N. Massingale, "Black Catholic Theology: Anger for the Sake of Justice," *Proceedings of the Catholic Theological Society of America* 51 (1996): 263–5.

[50]Aquinas, *Summa Theologiae*, I–II.46.7 ad 3, 47.1–2; II–II.108.1, 157.1–3, 158.1–3, 158.5–8.

[51]John Calvin, *Institutes of the Christian Religion*, trans. Henry Beveridge (Grand Rapids: Eerdmans, 1989), I.5.1–3, 5.6, 5.9–10, 14.20–22; II.6.1.

[52]Ibid., III.7.5, 7.8–10, 9.3–4, 10.1–5, 19.7–8.

[53]Ibid., III.10.6; IV.1.3.

[54]Jonathan Edwards, "Religious Affections," in *Selected Writings of Jonathan Edwards*, ed. Harold P. Simonson (New York: Frederick Ungar, 1984), 161; Edwards, "A Divine and Supernatural Light," in *Selected Writings of Jonathan Edwards*, ed. Harold P. Simonson (New York: Frederick Ungar, 1984), 74.

[55]Edwards, "Religious Affections," 163, 165; James M. Gustafson, *Ethics from a Theocentric Perspective, vol. 1: Theology and Ethics* (Chicago: University of Chicago Press, 1981), 195–204.

"irrational," or generally clouded in their judgment. In the context of a society structured by oppression, these culturally produced, hegemonic discourses about emotion will function ideologically to preserve the status quo and serve the interests of the privileged.[56]

Lying behind these ideological discourses is a common presupposition that emotion behaves like a "hydraulic" surge of impulsive energy, and this presupposition finds its philosophical origin in the Enlightenment concept of emotion as a nonrational, mechanistic, bodily impulse toward or away from an object that an agent happens to want to pursue or avoid. If this were an accurate description of emotions, then Kant would have been right to argue that emotions are unreliable as a basis of moral judgment but have some limited utility as moral motivators, provided they are subjected to rational scrutiny and control so that they do not hijack moral judgment. Theologians and philosophers who mean to retrieve a more positive, normative role for emotion in ethics nevertheless retain on occasion this nonrational, hydraulic model.[57] Indeed, even John Courtney Murray presumed this model as he reconstructed a Thomistic public theology, advocating a form of civic friendship that protects the common good by means of an emotionally detached, natural law consensus.[58]

The hydraulic model not only is empirically unsustainable[59] but also renders the referential content of emotion unintelligible, for our emotions are always *about* someone or something in particular, even if the agent lacks full awareness of the referential content. At the end of the day, human beings are not bundles of animal impulses with an added layer of rational consciousness that operates as "morality." Emotions as they are found in human beings are qualitatively different, precisely because they are constitutive of how we experience and understand ourselves as agents.[60]

Martha Nussbaum's cognitive model frames emotion as an intelligent ascription of value to specific relationships and social conditions to which the agent is deeply attached, a judgment that these vulnerable and contingent "external goods" are constitutive elements of promoting flourishing for the self and for others.[61] This model allows us to recognize emotional judgments as already rational, though differently rational by comparison with deliberative, prudential judgment. Diana Fritz Cates, while also rejecting the hydraulic model, has criticized Nussbaum's cognitive account as excessively intellectual, as not able

[56]Emilie Townes, *Womanist Ethics and the Cultural Production of Evil* (New York: Palgrave Macmillan, 2006), 111–38.

[57]Authors who employ a hydraulic model while attempting to sketch a positive role for emotion include J. Giles Milhaven, *Good Anger* (Kansas City: Sheed & Ward, 1989); Beverly Wildung Harrison, "The Power of Anger in the Work of Love: Christian Ethics for Women and Other Strangers," in *Making the Connections: Essays in Feminist Social Ethics*, ed. Carol S. Robb (Boston: Beacon, 1985), 3–21. For critiques of the hydraulic model, see Robert Solomon, *The Passions: Emotions and the Meaning of Life*, 2nd ed. (Indianapolis: Hackett, 1993), 77–88; Nussbaum, *Upheavals of Thought*, 22–6, 96, 136–7.

[58]John Courtney Murray, *We Hold These Truths: Catholic Reflections on the American Proposition* (Garden City: Image, 1964), 19–20.

[59]Authors who provide empirical evidence against the hydraulic model by demonstrating the intentional and evaluative aspects of emotion include Stanley Schachter and Jerome E. Singer, "Cognitive, Social, and Physiological Determinants of Emotional State," *Psychological Review* 69, no. 5 (1962): 379–99; Richard Lazarus, *Emotion and Adaptation* (New York: Oxford University Press, 1991), 89–92, 149–50; Lazarus, "On the Primacy of Cognition," *American Psychologist* 39, no. 2 (1984): 124–9; Antonio Damasio, *Descartes' Error: Emotion, Reason, and the Human Brain* (New York: Putnam, 1994), 127–8, 136–9; Damasio, *Self Comes to Mind: Constructing the Conscious Brain* (New York: Vintage, 2012), 9–10, 115–38, 186.

[60]Mary Midgley, *Beast and Man: The Roots of Human Nature*, rev. ed. (New York: Routledge, 2002), 166, 180–7, 243–72, 309–38.

[61]Nussbaum, *Upheavals of Thought*, 22–33.

to account for the everyday experience of being drawn toward what we desire or the instances of real conflict between knowledge of the good and will to choose the good.[62]

However, a cognitive model can account for the conflictual aspects of emotional experience by reference to psychological development over the course of life, instead of the metaphysical categories of intellectual apprehension, intellectual appetite, and sensory appetite.[63] Nussbaum notes that the patterns of emotional judgment individuals intentionally choose as adults often come into conflict with other patterns of emotional judgment that originate in the specific relationships and institutional conditions that influenced them during early childhood socialization. These earlier emotional patterns might not affect adult functioning with a "hardwired" necessity, yet they might remain somewhat impervious to the sort of major modification that Aristotle and Aquinas envision in their accounts of virtuous habituation.[64] Stated in theological terms, sin infects and distorts human emotions because we are all socialized into, and continue to participate in, institutions and cultures that generate and reproduce structural evil. "Original" sin (understood in this institutional and cultural sense) preselects for those who benefit from this evil certain dominant or default patterns of emotional judgment that protect them from perceiving their moral complicity and responsibility. Thus, if theological ethicists are to understand emotions according to a cognitive model, then the normative ideal of emotional integration is not adequately described in metaphysical language, in which emotion is habituated by reason proper, but rather in developmental language of increasing one's awareness of conflicting patterns of emotional judgment and one's capacities for empathy with self and others even in the midst of an imperfectly just world.

Moreover, a cognitive model better accounts for the positive role of institutions and cultures that mediate grace, particularly the church for Christians, in shaping and educating emotional judgments regarding the vulnerable and contingent aspects of human flourishing, which in turn suggests a major role for emotions in contributing to public consensus about the social values to be safeguarded by institutional reform.[65] Although the emotional judgments needed to motivate long-term work in pursuit of institutional justice, such as anger, may become burdensome or toxic to their bearers, strategic expression and effective organizing can help to mitigate this damage.[66] A cognitive model also supports organized efforts to creatively subvert and interrupt the ideological stereotyping activities of privileged groups, so that they can acknowledge as fully cognitive the insight and agency that members of oppressed groups contribute to the public consensus.[67]

For the most intransigent varieties of systemic injustice, such as the local crisis of racial injustice in the United States and the global crisis of climate change and environmental injustice, a critical mass of persons with normatively integrated compassion and anger will be practically necessary to enact structural change ahead of the emotional culture of majorities. While it may be true that evolved traits such as kin altruism present a "natural" limit to the perception that justice and solidarity are due to persons outside

---

[62]Cates, *Aquinas on the Emotions*, 42–3, 50–7, 63–5, 70–4.

[63]Cates tends to prefer these metaphysical categories as a way of accounting for these experiences; see ibid., 65–74, 267.

[64]Nussbaum, *Upheavals of Thought*, 230–5; Nussbaum, *Therapy of Desire*, 424–30.

[65]Nussbaum, *Upheavals of Thought*, 401–54.

[66]Lisa Tessman, *Burdened Virtues: Virtue Ethics for Liberatory Struggles* (New York: Oxford University Press, 2005), 95, 107–31; Saul Alinsky, *Reveille for Radicals*, 2nd ed. (New York: Vintage, 1989), ix–x.

[67]Townes, *Womanist Ethics*, 19–22.

of one's own special relations, the solution to this problem is not simply to demand a higher ethical standard but to create institutional conditions that expand the boundaries of compassion, such that support for a universal ethic of human rights would become second nature, even for the privileged.[68] In other words, while there may yet be real moral limits to significant emotional change in persons and groups who have experienced heavy influence from ideological formation and oppressive institutions, ongoing work to reform political and economic structures can help to inculcate normative emotional judgments in a greater proportion of society's members, which in turn increases public support for further institutional reform.

Considered from this standpoint, scriptural narratives that sustain an ethic of compassion among and toward victims who suffer, as well as anger toward oppressors, are not merely analogous to the current ethical and political struggles of the contemporary world. For Christians, these narratives should also be considered the normative basis for evaluating the actual emotional judgments that guide action in this world, which while seemingly defined by injustice is also already being redeemed by God. At the end of salvation history, the church hopes that even the anger of victims toward their perpetrators, the righteous desire to hold them accountable, will be accompanied by an offer of compassion, for even the oppressor is dehumanized by their own participation in structural evil.[69] Ultimately, our humanizing emotions in the present are signs that point toward the eschatological fulfillment of love, to that society outside of history in which, at last, we will be able to see rightly, to rest in the beauty of God, and to live "in perfect charity with the world."[70]

SUGGESTED READINGS

Baldwin, James. *The Fire Next Time*. New York: Penguin, 1990.

Cates, Diana Fritz. *Aquinas on the Emotions: A Religious-Ethical Inquiry*. Washington, DC: Georgetown University Press, 2009.

Fanon, Frantz. *Black Skin, White Masks*, trans. Richard Philcox. New York: Grove Press, 2008.

Gregory, Eric. *Politics and the Order of Love: An Augustinian Ethic of Democratic Citizenship*. Chicago: University of Chicago Press, 2008.

Nussbaum, Martha C. *Upheavals of Thought: The Intelligence of Emotions*. New York: Cambridge University Press, 2001.

O'Connell, Maureen H. *Compassion: Loving Our Neighbor in an Age of Globalization*. Maryknoll: Orbis, 2009.

Sobrino, Jon. *The Principle of Mercy: Taking the Crucified People from the Cross*. Maryknoll: Orbis, 1994.

[68]Stephen J. Pope, *Human Evolution and Christian Ethics* (New York: Cambridge University Press, 2007), 214–49; O'Connell, *Compassion*, 110–19.

[69]Baldwin, *The Fire Next Time*, 16–17, 88–9.

[70]The Episcopal Church, *The Book of Common Prayer* (New York: Church Publishing, 1979), 504.

CHAPTER TEN

Narrative

DALLAS GINGLES

This chapter proceeds in three steps. In this first section, I briefly introduce the concept of narrative in Christian ethics by identifying influential figures whose work will serve as the paradigmatic narrative approach. In the second through fourth sections, I attend to the way the narrative approach relates to the four fonts of reason, experience, tradition, and scripture. Finally, in the fifth section, I offer a typology of narrative approaches that suggests a critical question for the narrative approach that remains unresolved. I conclude by posing that question.

The narrative approach to Christian ethics is a relatively recent disciplinary development. Theologians were attending to narrative by the mid-to-late twentieth century, as contemporary forms of hermeneutics and literary theory migrated from their native disciplinary homes into biblical studies, philosophy, and theology. By the early 1980s, narrative was on the ascent within Christian ethics, and it has remained important since that time. This ascent of narrative and its continued importance is due not least to the influence of its most vocal proponent: Stanley Hauerwas. In fact, by 1998 Hauerwas's "narrative turn" had already been so influential for over ten years that it was the subject of "a critical appraisal."[1] Because of its disciplinary influence, Hauerwas's approach will serve as the paradigm for narrative Christian ethics for current purposes.[2]

Perhaps one reason Hauerwas's project has attracted so many followers is that he draws together a range of diverse thinkers for whom the category of narrative is of central importance, especially Alasdair MacIntyre and John Howard Yoder.[3] For these

[1]Victor Anderson, "The Narrative Turn in Christian Ethics: A Critical Appraisal," *American Journal of Theology & Philosophy* 19, no. 3 (September 1998): 293–312. It might be more accurate to move the dating of Hauerwas's influence all the way to "the 1970s" as Jeffrey Stout does when he draws attention to Hauerwas's publications of *Vision and Virtue: Essays in Christian Ethical Reflection* (Notre Dame: Fides, 1974) and *Truthfulness and Tragedy: Further Investigations into Christian Ethics* (Notre Dame: University of Notre Dame Press, 1977). Jeffrey Stout, *Democracy and Tradition* (Princeton: Princeton University Press, 2004), 142–4.

[2]Of particular importance is Hauerwas's account of narrative in *The Peaceable Kingdom: A Primer in Christian Ethics* (Notre Dame: University of Notre Dame Press, 1983). This book remains a standard text in courses in Christian ethics in universities around (at least) the United States. See, e.g., Eric Gregory, "A Sample Syllabus for Christian Ethics and Modern Society" in the "Syllabus Project" of the Society of Christian Ethics, https://scethics.org/sites/default/files/ChristianEthicsSyllabusFall2014-1_0.pdf. More recent critical appraisals of Hauerwas's work are now ubiquitous; for a particularly informative appraisal see, Sean Larsen, "How I Think Hauerwas Thinks about Theology," *Scottish Journal of Theology* 69, no. 1 (2016): 20–38.

[3]Because I follow the contours of Hauerwas's account below in the second through fourth sections, in these sections I treat MacIntyre and Yoder synthetically with Hauerwas, before prizing them apart in the fifth section. Throughout, I signal in the footnotes which of these (and other) influences is bearing most of the conceptual weight for the topic at hand. Another important strand of narrative thinking that influences Hauerwas is the postliberalism of the so-called Yale school, which is also sometimes conflated with "narrative theology" (e.g.,

thinkers, the category of narrative refers to the importance of the storied structure of identifiable communities—especially the storied structure of Christianity.[4] More recently, ethicists have expanded the bounds of the discourse by attending to a wider range of narrative traditions within Christianity, and by calling for more rigorous engagement with ethnographic narratives.[5] Others have criticized an over-reliance on narrative in Christian ethics.[6]

While there are diverse approaches to narrative ethics, they all share in some way in an underlying criticism of approaches to Christian ethics that rely on modern moral philosophy's quest for universal (i.e., tradition-independent) ethical norms and reasons. The most compelling version of this criticism comes from MacIntyre's *After Virtue*, in which he critiques the fragmentation of modern moral discourse. On MacIntyre's telling, modern ethics lacks an account of the narrative shape of human life and thus necessarily lacks an intelligible account of morality in which the virtues serve to move humans along that narrative arc toward their proper end. Hauerwas borrows extensively from MacIntyre to launch a broadside attack on modern Christian ethics, calling into question—among other things—the traditional constellation of scripture, tradition, reason, and experience.[7] Narrative ethics is, in short, a fundamental challenge to traditional renderings of the four fonts, perhaps most substantively to the understanding of reason.

REASON

Where modern ethics sought to be universal—what Hauerwas calls "an unqualified ethics"—narrative ethics points out the qualified, tradition-dependent, nature of all ethics. In modern ethics, reason is a feature of general human nature that guides autonomous individuals in neutral settings to make decisions based on what Hauerwas calls "unchangeable principles" (i.e., quandary ethics). By contrast, in the narrative turn, reason is ordered less to decision making and more to the task of making moral questions,

---

George Lindbeck and Hans Frei). For current purposes I leave these to the side (though there is one citation to Lindbeck below). This is because I take it that while the postliberal approach provides a very helpful conceptual background, not least by providing a connection between narrative and language in *theology*, MacIntyre and Yoder bear more directly on the relationship between narrative and Christian *ethics*. I admit that this is a bit of a problem insofar as Hauerwasian narrativism seeks to close the gap between theology and ethics.

[4]On the importance of narrative as a necessary condition for the existence of a tradition of moral inquiry, see especially Alasdair MacIntyre, *After Virtue*, 3rd ed. (Notre Dame: University of Notre Dame Press, 2007).

[5]For important representative texts from ethnic minority traditions, see the bibliographies of the African American, Asian American, and Latino/a Ethics working groups of the Society of Christian Ethics (https://scethics.org/resources). For a representative account of the Pentecostal tradition, see Daniel Castelo, *Revisioning Pentecostal Ethics: The Epicletic Community* (Cleveland: Center for Pentecostal Theology, 2012). For a representative account of the turn to ethnography, see Michael Banner, *The Ethics of Everyday Life* (Oxford: Oxford University Press, 2014).

[6]See, e.g., Oliver O'Donovan, *Entering into Rest: Ethics as Theology*, vol. 3 (Grand Rapids: Eerdmans, 2017).

[7]"Modern ethics" is a cypher for the wide variety of moral philosophers and theologians within modernity. The dominant categories of modern ethics against which the narrative position is defined are deontology and utilitarianism. Thus, Hauerwas writes,

> Though these two positions are often depicted as antithetical, in fact they share some fundamental assumptions. Each assumes that moral philosophy gains its primary rationale from acknowledgment of some moral quandary, when, for example, there is a conflict between rules. Little attention is paid, therefore, to how or why a "situation" came to be described as a "moral" problem in the first place. Ethics, it seems, begins with questions such as "Should I or should I not have an abortion?" But then no account is given for why and how we have come to describe a certain set of circumstances as abortion, or adultery, or murder, and so on. (*The Peaceable Kingdom*, 23)

claims, and judgments intelligible. Without a narrative structure within which they can be located, individual and communal moral claims run the risk of, or succumb to, meaninglessness. Thus, in place of abstract modern reason we find a more locally attuned "narrative rationality." Narrative rationality proceeds not by ordering lower-level moral principles to higher but rather by attending closely to the controlling narrative within which one has learned to identify a moral question or topic at all.

The exercise of this kind of rationality further distinguishes the narrativist project from the modern moral tradition. Having freed itself from Kantian concerns about heteronomy and autonomy, narrativism prioritizes the identity of the community over the identity of the individual. This is because it is from a community that one receives one's existence and one's moral language. Moral character formation (i.e., that process in which one comes to see oneself as a character in a moral story) is the process of learning to integrate the narrative of one's life into the controlling narrative of the community—a narrative that is constitutive of the community and of communal identity. If rationality consists in the work of integrating one's story into the communal story, it is obviously necessary for one to be able to identify the constitutive features of the controlling communal narrative and to be able to retell it in such a way as to integrate one's story into it. One learns to tell the story (i.e., learns the proper exercise of reason) not by locking oneself in an ivory tower for an extended bout of abstract conceptual gymnastics but rather by engaging in the ongoing story of the community by participating in its constitutive practices.

EXPERIENCE AND TRADITION

Practices are the embodiments of the controlling narrative (we might say something like outward and visible signs of inward and invisible identity). It is within these practices that the narrative resides, as it were, implicitly and sometimes explicitly. This, then, brings us to the topics of experience and tradition. If in modern ethics experience is conceived of as a morally neutral and irreducible fact of existence (i.e., people just have experiences before they conceptualize them), narrativism sees all experiences as located within a "framework or medium that shapes the entirety of life and thought."[8] Because human lives have a narrative shape, there are no neutral or uninterpreted experiences. We can only experience within a context in which we have the language that makes experience possible: trees, for instance, do not have experiences even though they are acted upon. Experience is the privilege of linguistic creatures, and language is necessarily communal. Thus, while in some forms of modern ethics, experience is epistemic trumps, in a narrative framework, experience is of (at most) only secondary epistemic value.

Another way to put this is to say that experience is always conditioned by tradition. Tradition here is understood as the ongoing passing down of a set of practices that are themselves constitutive of a community. Contrary to much popular interpretation of the idea of tradition, then, tradition is not, by necessity, conservative. Indeed, "when a tradition is in good order it is always partially constituted by an argument about the goods the pursuit of which gives to that tradition its particular point and purpose."[9] The

---

[8]George A. Lindbeck, *The Nature of Doctrine: Religion and Theology in a Postliberal Age* (Louisville: John Knox, 1984), 33.

[9]MacIntyre, *After Virtue*, 222.

good the pursuit of which gives Christianity "its particular point and purpose" is the God made known in Jesus Christ. The debate over this God and the proper forms of that pursuit makes up the tradition, so that the debate is itself one of the practices that constitutes the tradition. Part of this ongoing debate is based on disagreement about the number and form of the practices that constitute the Christian tradition. Roman Catholic doctrine specifies the exact number of sacraments and the proper form each sacrament should take. Baptist doctrine rejects the idea of sacraments but specifies other versions of Christian practices that order the Christian's pursuit of God. If we take a wide view that encompasses both Catholics and Baptists within the Christian tradition, we can understand the tradition as an ensemble of practices that are themselves always under debate—but that remain identifiable as Christian practices insofar as their object of pursuit is the God made known in Jesus Christ.

What this account of tradition actually means for ethics is far from obvious. More traditional accounts of the way tradition functions in moral inquiry focus on the teaching role of the church. The church (or particular branches of the church, such as Catholics or Baptists) make judgments about moral questions, and the tradition thus functions as a moral authority that must be taken into account by a Christian tasked with making a moral decision. Among the most obvious (if fraught) examples are the church's teachings on issues of sexuality or abortion. In a case where a Christian is faced with a difficult decision about, say, whether to have an abortion, the church's (i.e., the tradition's) prohibition of abortion functions as a moral authority that, along with scripture and reason, must inform the decision. In a strong version of the role of tradition, the church's prohibition is understood as a final word, though it may seldom function as such. In a weak version, one may licitly disagree with the tradition based on one's own conscience in light of one's interpretation of scripture, but the teaching of the tradition functions as a guide against which one tests one's own beliefs. One's dissent, therefore, must actually dissent from the tradition, not simply ignore it.

By contrast, narrativist understandings of tradition are necessarily shaped by the local traditions of each individual narrativist. A narrativist from a tradition with a strong interpretation of the teaching role of the tradition will likely have to affirm the strong version of the teaching role of the church, and vice versa for a narrativist from a tradition with a weak version. The role of tradition is itself traditioned.

This means that the tradition informs a Christian's moral decision(s) less by its moral pronouncements—though these certainly remain important—and more by providing the set of practices, which, if practiced, will properly form the character of the Christian such that he or she will be capable of living well within the ongoing story of God's dealings with the church. Here the role of reason and tradition are held tightly together. Recall that the exercise of narrative rationality is the work of integrating one's own story into the story of the tradition. Because the story resides latently in the practices that are oriented to the good the pursuit of which gives the tradition its particular point and purpose, it is by engaging in the practices of the tradition that one reasons oneself into the tradition.

In a narrative approach, then, the role of the tradition in the moral life is primarily one in which, by its shared practices, it—the tradition—forms or inculcates in Christians the virtues necessary for the pursuit of the good that is the Christian God. The tradition shapes agents as much (or more) than it provides rules to them. This in turn means that the moral rules of the tradition—since, in fact, rules do remain part of the tradition's teaching—are themselves traditioned and subject to genealogical critique. This shows the close relation between narrativism and historicism, some versions of which conceive of tradition as little more than an exercise in power.[10]

SCRIPTURE

The Christian tradition, however, is not a story of simple will or domination. The fundamental narrative of the Christian community is not just a story of the Christian community—a self-substantiating story. Rather, the controlling narrative of the church is told in the irreducibly diverse set of texts called the Bible.[11] And since the Bible is a story of Israel's God, centered around the story of Jesus as the incarnation of that God, culminating in Jesus's divesture of divine power to the point of death on a cross, whatever moral pronouncements the church makes, it believes them to be in keeping with this fundamental story.

For Hauerwas, because this story of Jesus is the controlling narrative, Christian narrative ethics is an ethics of nonviolence. Jesus's clear teaching of enemy love, as well as his self-sacrifice are normative for Christians. The practices that are constitutive of the Christian community themselves bear witness to, and even embody, these same goods. Other narrativists disagree with Hauerwas on the issue of nonviolence, but they share with him an emphasis on the centrality of the biblical narrative, especially the teaching and example of Jesus.

That deep agreement among narrativists on the importance of Jesus's teaching and example undergirds fundamental disagreement about normative ethics. It also suggests that while, in the narrative turn, the Bible retains axiological primacy among the four sources, there are substantive differences within narrative approaches to ethics—and that these have to do more with scripture than with tradition, reason, or experience. To explain why this is so, I offer a typology of narrative Christian ethics that suggests a substantive division between the MacIntyrian and Yoderian approaches.

CHRISTIAN ETHICS AND NARRATIVE: A TYPOLOGY

Recall that a MacIntyrian account of practice is crucial in this paradigm of Christian narrative ethics. Because the practices of a community are the embodiment of the narrative rationality of the community, one betters one's character by engaging in these communal practices. The better one becomes at the practice, the more one is able to engage in the ongoing debate over the meaning of the practices themselves; thus, one becomes a full member of a living tradition. In the Christian community, these practices (assuming that the variety of practices from, for example, Catholics and Baptists are, in fact, practices the object the pursuit of which is the Christian God) relate to the central story of the Christian community: the story of Jesus. Indeed, in the practice of the Eucharist, the practice itself directly participates in, or depending on one's ecclesial tradition, immediately recalls, the

---

[10]In fact, Hauerwas has stated, "I'm a historicist all the way down." See Gary Dorrien, "Truth Claims: The Future of Postliberal Theology," *Christian Century* 118, no. 21 (July 18–25, 2001): 25. On a related note, Sean Larsen writes, "I once heard Stanley say, 'Ever since I read Foucault, I realized it's all power. I want power. I want to take over the world. I just want to do it nonviolently.'" See Larsen, "How I Think Hauerwas Thinks about Theology," 37.

[11]Though, as I will indicate in the next section, the relation between the narrative of the church and the biblical narrative is complicated.

central story of the controlling narrative. Not only does the narrative reside latently in the practice, but the practice also is intrinsically related to the narrative—we might even say it is an eternal repetition of the climax of the narrative itself.[12]

Crucially, though, while the relationship between practice and narrative is intimate, they are conceptually distinct. The typology I suggest here relates to the order between them. I take it that Hauerwas's account of practice is more MacIntyrian than Yoderian (though Yoder does have an account of practices) and that his emphasis on the narrative of scripture is more Yoderian than MacIntyrian.[13] While it is not clear to me which order Hauerwas uses—narrative before practice or practice before narrative—I suggest the following typology of post-Hauerwasian narrativists (including narrativists who are not directly in the Hauerwas genealogy). Let us call those who give priority to practice MacIntyrians and those who give priority to the biblical narrative Yoderians.

The ordering of narrative and practice that a narrativist uses is related to the tradition within which the narrativist is operating. That order, in turn, influences the narrativist's interpretation of the concept of tradition. So, while the order between practice and narrative can be reversed, in both cases one's interpretation of tradition will follow from one's preferred ordering between narrative and practice (but, again, the decision about how to order practice and narrative is itself already traditioned). MacIntyrians give priority to practice because the narrative of the tradition is enacted, and thus told most properly and formatively, in the practices themselves. Yoderians prioritize the biblical story because, as the controlling narrative of the tradition, it norms and judges the practices of the tradition.[14]

One crucial issue that distinguishes these types is the epistemological question of how we know what the constitutive practices of the Christian tradition are. For MacIntyrians, we know the practices of the tradition because we have received them from the tradition. That reception itself is the warrant for the legitimacy of the practice, exactly because whatever practices are handed down from the tradition are constitutive of the tradition. Any valid practice is by definition a practice that enables the pursuit of the good that is the point and purpose of the tradition. This means that while there are innumerable activities a tradition might undertake at any point in its history, these activities will only be practices if they necessarily enable the pursuit of the good that is the tradition's goal. The tradition serves as a kind of filter through which constitutive practices are passed down while historically contingent activities are not. Here the filter will almost certainly include the teaching role of the church. That is, an account of practices that are constitutive of the church requires something like a magisterium to differentiate between practices and activities.

By contrast, a Yoderian account conceives of practices less as constitutive of tradition and more as those activities that reflect the biblical narrative, especially the narrative of Jesus. MacIntyrians understand the controlling narrative as the narrative of the Christian tradition, the inception point of which is the story of Jesus. Yoderians understand the

[12]See, e.g., Paul J. Griffiths, *Decreation: The Last Things of All Creatures* (Waco: Baylor University Press, 2014).
[13]See John Howard Yoder, *Body Politics: Five Practices of the Christian Community before the Watching World* (Scottdale: Herald, 1992).
[14]There is an obvious correlation between the MacIntyrian/Yoderian types and the differences between Catholics and Protestants. For the former, the liturgy culminates in the practice of the Eucharist, whereas for the latter, the liturgy is ordered to the proclamation of the Word. In this distinction we can see how the Reformation understanding of the primacy of scripture substantively changed not only *a* practice, but indeed *the central* practice, of the church.

controlling narrative to be the story of Jesus, of which the tradition is an outworking. The distinction is subtle but important. For Yoderians, the story of Jesus, including the manifold diversity of the stories of Jesus in the Gospels, are morally formative because they display the character of God to which Christians are called to conform. The paradigmatic statement of this position is Yoder's *The Politics of Jesus*, in which Yoder interprets the Lukan portrayal of Jesus in a political key.[15] What comes first is not a community-constitutive practice of politics after which—or through which—we access the narrative of Jesus (though Yoder certainly admits that the historic peace church tradition informs his reading). Rather, the biblical narrative provides its own account of politics that stands aside the tradition to offer both a moral norm and a word of judgment on any current practice that falls short of that norm. In a MacIntyrian framework, the relation between practice and narrative is linear, with the practice offering a way into the narrative. In a Yoderian framework the relation between narrative and practice is asymmetrical. The narrative is axiologically—not linearly—prior.

We can extend and complicate the typology a bit further. If an essential part of Hauerwas's project is the attempt to hold together these two positions, he is not alone. While drawn from different conceptual wells, this is one way to interpret liberationist approaches that prioritize praxis.[16] Gustavo Gutiérrez articulated the paradigmatic version of this approach in his *A Theology of Liberation*.[17] Subsequent liberationist projects fit within this paradigm insofar as they hold together praxis and dogma by focusing on the moral practices of particular communities—especially communities that have historically been oppressed by, or excluded from, dominant political regimes. Like Yoderians, they draw heavily on readings of the biblical text in ways that do not always square with the dominant Christian tradition in which they find themselves—or at least with versions of the tradition from which they are explicitly dissenting. Like MacIntyrians, they prioritize the practices (often described as something like "liberative practices") of the communities from which they come. This tension within this approach is similar to the tension within the Hauerwasian approach as well. Indeed, for all the disagreement between many liberationists and Hauerwas, at the level of their approaches to the task of ethical reflection, there is a great deal in common between them.

CONCLUSION

There is probably little of great importance that hangs on the distinction I have drawn between MacIntyrians and Yoderians. Narrative ethicists of all stripes can do their work without locating themselves in one of these types. But it does seem to indicate a difference in disposition among those who follow some form of narrativist approach to Christian ethics. And that disposition is telling, for while there are many similarities between self-described narrativists—in the ways they approach the task, in their criticisms of the discipline of ethics and their criticisms of modernity writ large, in their ways of conceiving of reason as narrative rationality—the conclusions they draw are as varied as the modern (non-narrativist) ethicists they criticize. This suggests a question for the current state, and the future, of narrative ethics.

---

[15]John Howard Yoder, *The Politics of Jesus*, 2nd ed. (Grand Rapids: Eerdmans, 1994).
[16]I am indebted to Elisabeth Kincaid for pointing out this connection.
[17]Gustavo Gutiérrez, *A Theology of Liberation: History, Politics, and Salvation* (Maryknoll: Orbis, 1988).

Part of the narrative approach is to criticize the moral fragmentation of modernity. If that criticism and analysis is right, then what do we make of the deep moral disagreements between narrativists? Perhaps some narrativists simply have not given up the pretenses of modernity and are thus just not very good narrativists. Perhaps, though, the different dispositions and different judgments of narrativists suggests that moral fragmentation is not just a modern mistake but is instead part of a much longer narrative. Practitioners of narrative approaches to Christian ethics should reckon with this kind of deep disagreement among them as they continue to think critically about the ways the practices of the Christian tradition and the biblical narrative equip Christians to live within a world of competing narratives and difficult choices.

SUGGESTED READINGS

Hauerwas, Stanley. *The Peaceable Kingdom: A Primer in Christian Ethics*. Notre Dame: University of Notre Dame Press, 1983.

MacIntyre, Alasdair. *After Virtue*, 3rd ed. Notre Dame: University of Notre Dame Press, 2007.

O'Donovan, Oliver. *Entering into Rest: Ethics as Theology*, vol. 3. Grand Rapids: Eerdmans, 2017.

Stout, Jeffrey. *Democracy and Tradition*. Princeton: Princeton University Press, 2004.

CHAPTER ELEVEN

Responsibility

ESTHER D. REED

Christian ethics today is too focused on the individual as the locus of responsibility without adequate consideration of sinful social structures and how the meaning of responsibility might be conceived in societally relational terms. This chapter argues that Christian ethics needs a social connection model of responsibility (re)learned from Christ Jesus and biblical witness to the lived practices of the early church. It unfolds in four stages. First is an explication of responsibility as a (problematic) modern concept. Second is a Christologically learned invitation to reverse modern, Western philosophical ways of thinking about responsibility (from I-You-I to You-I-You). Third is the suggestion that this reversal of the meaning of responsibility must understand "You" to be not only my neighbor, near and far away, but also the natural environment, the land and all living organisms. Fourth is the challenge to link an ethic of responsibility to global citizenship.

RESPONSIBILITY AS A MODERN CONCEPT

Responsibility is a modern concept. As philosopher Richard Peter McKeon explained in his 1957 article, "The Development and the Significance of the Concept of Responsibility," the modern concept of responsibility is variously (1) an expression of personal freedom over against necessity, especially natural necessity; (2) individual autonomy before the law that holds everyone accountable for their actions; and (3) the individual's rationality as a member of society. The modern concept of responsibility takes shape amid debates about agency that are free from determination by natural forces and unconstrained by the will of the state or other political powers.[1]

Modern framings tend to conceive of responsibility as a problem that belongs to the individual. Like Immanuel Kant, F. D. E. Schleiermacher does not often use the term "responsibility" (*Verantwortung*), yet his influence shapes the discourse in significant ways. Schleiermacher was not an individualist, for whom the goal of enlightenment is for individuals to direct their own lives autonomously in accordance with the requirements of reason. To the contrary, he propounded an understanding of the individual self as relational and rooted in community. His commitment to ethical individuality is a

[1]There are occurrences in French of *responsabilité* and the Latin *responsabilis* as early as the fourteenth century, but these link to translations of the Greek *aitia* (in Latin, *causa*, meaning cause of imputation of praise or blame) and *amartia* (missing the mark or guilt or sin). See Richard Peter McKeon, "The Development and the Significance of the Concept of Responsibility," *Revue Internationale de Philosophie* 11, no. 39.1 (1957): 26. For a fuller explication of the ideas treated in this section, see Esther D. Reed, *The Limit of Responsibility: Dietrich Bonhoeffer's Ethics for a Globalizing Era* (London: Bloomsbury T&T Clark, 2018), chap. 2.

quintessentially modern expression of the meaning of duty, however, that feeds into later conceptions of responsibility. Schleiermacher lays the groundwork for modern liberal (theologico-ethical) thinking about personal duty not as a gift bestowed by God, and to be returned to God and neighbor on account of God, but an action with its source in the self to be exercised between persons. His particular challenge was to demonstrate the unity of the self as moral agent. With Schleiermacher, responsibility is set to become a problem integral to the individual's care of his or her own soul, a "lifelong inquiry" possessed by every individual capable of moral reflection: "the being which bears within it the source of movement, of deciding its being or nonbeing."[2] The problem of responsibility is a burden that belongs to the individual as an autonomous agent.

The idea of responsibility became bound up with the theory of capitalism in the writings of Max Weber. In his distinction between "the ethic of conviction" (*Gesinnungsethik*) and "the ethic of responsibility" (*Verantwortungsethik*), Weber's purpose was to understand why individuals act in what they deem to be a responsible manner. Hence, the focus on motivation in the opening chapter of *Economy and Society*, where basic sociological terms are established and explained: "A motive is a complex of subjective meaning which seems to the actor himself or to the observer an adequate ground for the conduct in question."[3] Weber's challenge is to arrive at causally adequate interpretations that relate motivation to the action in question, thereby attaining meaning.

Of interest for our purposes is Weber's diagnosis of a cleavage in how the modern person thinks about responsibility, and his suggestion that the meaning of responsibility may be expressed as the rational accumulation of wealth. What God demands, he says, according to the ordering of the moral life that Protestantism encourages, is not labor in itself but rather rational labor expressed as a personal calling such that the worldly asceticism of Protestantism—whether Calvinist, Pietist, Methodist, or Baptist—yields individuals committed to the performance of duty and who embody the ethos of rationally organized capital and labor necessary to the growth of modern capitalism: "Ascetic conduct meant a rational planning of the whole of one's life in accordance with God's will. And this asceticism was no longer an *opus supererogationis*, but something that could be required of everyone who would be certain of salvation."[4] Responsible Protestant living entails the accumulation of wealth in morally sanctioned ways. Responsibility is capitalism. Capitalism is responsibility.

---

[2]Jan Patočka and James Dodd, eds., *Heretical Essays in the Philosophy of History* (Chicago: Open Court, 1996), 82. See, for instance, how Schleiermacher's "Toward a Theory of Sociable Conduct" (1799) affirms that the self exists in contextualized, dialogic interdependence with others. Friedrich Schleiermacher, *Toward a Theory of Sociable Conduct and Essays on Its Intellectual-Cultural Context*, ed. Ruth Drucilla Richardson (Lewiston: Edwin Mellen, 1995), 23–4.

[3]Max Weber, *Economy and Society: An Outline of Interpretive Sociology*, ed. Günther Roth and Claus Wittich (Berkeley: University of California Press, 1978), 11. Scholars vary in their interpretations of what Weber means by "the ethic of responsibility." The *Gesinnungsethiker*, says Eric Voegelin, is an ideologue who lacks adequate guidelines for action, "who has transformed the conscience into an order-destroying form of deception"; whereas, the *Verantwortungsethiker* can be unprincipled and irresponsible, and lacking value-informed guidelines. Eric Voegelin, "Freedom and Responsibility in Economy and Democracy," in *Published Essays, 1953–1965*, of *The Collected Works of Eric Voegelin*, vol. 2, ed. Ellis Sandoz (Columbia: University of Missouri Press, 2000), 78–9. By contrast, Bradley Starr asks readers to be more sympathetic to Weber's confronting of value conflict in society and to his development of an ethic of responsibility that takes account of this. Bradley E. Starr, "The Structure of Max Weber's Ethic of Responsibility," *Journal of Religious Ethics* 27, no. 3 (1999): 416–17.

[4]Max Weber, *The Protestant Ethic and the Spirit of Capitalism*, trans. Talcott Parsons (New York: Routledge, 2001), 79.

Martin Buber challenged the egocentrism that could not understand the problem of responsibility from any perspective other than that of the individual "I." Buber's landmark work, *I and Thou*, redescribed human life, or its basic ontology, as essentially a movement in response to the Other, the eternal Thou. His fundamental conviction, learned from ancient Jewish traditions, is that every person is presented with two options in regard to their attitude to the world: *I-It* or *I-Thou*. *I-It* is an orientation or stance that objectifies the other person and expresses an attitude of separation and detachment. The *I* experiences the world as "Other" and encounters other people as "its." Such relationships are focused on the use that can be made of the Other. In contrast, *I-Thou* relationships are open to different kinds of encounter, in which each person is on a journey of discovery. The self becomes truly a self as an "I," in encounter: "Here is the cradle of the real life."[5]

For Emmanuel Levinas, encounter with the face of the Other means that the responsibility of self to the Other is immediately personal, concerned with basic material needs, and not reducible to calculation but, rather, potentially infinite.[6] Responsibility is not borne by the individual alone but is asymmetrical, in the sense that the person without immediate and basic material needs bears less responsibility than the person capable of responding to the demand inherent in the Other's experience of need. The problem, as Simone Drichel observes, is that ethics, and especially an ethic of responsibility, becomes a form of sacrificial masochism.[7] My responsibility to the Other never ends. Responsibility becomes a potentially unbearable burden.

RESPONSIBILITY IN CHRIST

In contrast to dominant modern philosophies of responsibility, Dietrich Bonhoeffer holds that responsibility learned in Christ has a *You-I-You* structure and not an *I-You-I* structure. Like Buber and Levinas, he has a relationally structured understanding of responsibility that begins in the Other. For the disciple, however, the potentially unbearable burden of responsibility is borne by Christ Jesus alone.

As becomes apparent in his dissertation *Sanctorum Communio*—completed by Bonhoeffer in 1927 at age 21—the real problem with all modern philosophies of responsibility is the self-divinizing of humanity. So, for instance, his complaint against Schleiermacher is that the latter's account of relationality is constructed individualistically and framed in terms of the satisfaction of a need: "The reason for the formation of religious community lies in the need of individuals to communicate. The church is the satisfaction of a need; it is constructed individualistically."[8] For Bonhoeffer, the concepts of personhood, relationality, and responsibility are learned in Christ. Societal existence does not originate in need but in God's gift of You to me: "When the concrete ethical barrier of the other person is acknowledged or, alternatively, when the person is compelled to acknowledge it, we have made a fundamental step that allows us to grasp the *social ontic-ethical basic-relations of persons*."[9] You stand before me as person. "This is a purely

[5]Martin Buber, *I and Thou*, trans. Ronald Gregor Smith (New York: Scribner, 1958), 24, 62.
[6]Emmanuel Levinas, *Ethics and Infinity*, trans. Richard A. Cohen (Pittsburgh: Duquesne University Press, 1985).
[7]Simone Drichel, "Face to Face with the Other Other: Levinas versus the Postcolonial," *Levinas Studies* 7, no. 1 (2012): 22.
[8]Dietrich Bonhoeffer, *Sanctorum Communio: A Theological Study of the Sociology of the Church*, trans. Reinhard Krauss and Nancy Lukens, ed. Clifford J. Green, *Dietrich Bonhoeffer Works*, vol. 1 (Minneapolis: Augsburg Fortress, 1998), 159.
[9]Ibid., 50, emphasis in original.

ethical transcendence, experienced only by those facing a decision."[10] And here is the point that matters for our purposes. Responsibility is located not in an ideal or abstract concept but in your address to me, at a particular time and place: "At the moment of being addressed, the person enters a state of responsibility or, in other words, of decision."[11] Every human being originates in relation to the Other: "The more clearly the barrier is perceived, the more deeply the person enters into the situation of responsibility."[12] "The I comes into being only in relation to You; only in response to a demand does *responsibility* arise."[13] "You" may be understood here as referring both to Christ Jesus and to the neighbor encountered in and through him. Bonhoeffer is clear about this toward the end of *Sanctorum Communio*, where he affirms that responsibility is Jesus Christ's vicarious representative action. Herein is the true meaning of responsibility.[14]

Reading Bonhoeffer today, the challenge for Christian ethics is to develop a You-I-You account of responsibility as vicarious representative action (*Stellvertretung*), which begins in Christ and is enacted by believers, with and for believers, both within the church community and as action taken by the church for the sake of the world. The challenges of such an ethic of responsibility are vast. What does it mean for those who have benefitted for centuries from sinful social structures that have destroyed natural environments, perpetuated the arms race, disrupted local barter economies, fueled corruption at every level and more, to take seriously that You, that is, the one most affected by these realities, hold the meaning of responsibility for *me*? What about the complex legacy of colonialism? What happens when a You-I-You-structured ethic of responsibility includes the land and everyone most vulnerable to pollution, soil erosion, and acid water? Very poor people in diverse countries around the world bear the brunt of the consequences of climate change, the targeted killing of terrorist suspects, downturns in the global economy, and more.

A You-I-You ethic means that those most vulnerable to these risks bear the meaning of responsibility for those who contribute most to pollution, who consume the most energy, and so on. The challenge is to realize that Christian ethics in the modern era has been too focused on the individual without adequately considering sinful social structures. With Bonhoeffer, this chapter affirms that Christ Jesus's vicarious representative action is the meaning of responsibility for the Christian church.[15] The meaning of responsibility is found in Christ Jesus and, because of the revelation of God's ways to humankind in him, is found in our neighbor too. In Christ, the modern, philosophical I-You-I structuring of the problem of responsibility is recast as a You-I-You relationship. The issue becomes how the meaning of responsibility might be better conceived in societally and environmentally relational terms.

RESPONSIBILITY AS RESPONSIVITY TO THE NATURAL ENVIRONMENT

As the environmental crisis seems to worsen every hour, Christian ethics must expand the You-I-You relationship to include the natural environment, the land, and all living

[10]Ibid., 52.
[11]Ibid., 48.
[12]Ibid., 49.
[13]Ibid., 54, emphasis in original.
[14]Ibid., 146–8.
[15]Ibid.

organisms. Bonhoeffer's reversal of the meaning of responsibility from I-You-I to You-I-You, wherein he treats responsibility as the mode of living to which every human being is called, must be understood to include responsiveness to the earth. "You," the land—from which oil is extracted, minerals and metals are mined, that takes our chemical waste and sewage sludge, microplastics, and more—hold the meaning of responsibility for me.

School children have grasped this reality. Since her solo protest in August 2018, Greta Thunberg has been joined in protests by striking from school by tens of thousands of school and university students in Australia, Belgium, Germany, the United States, Japan, and more than a dozen other countries.[16] The Fridays for Future movement is a powerful call for adults to listen to the cry of the earth. Pope Francis makes a similar point in his encyclical *Laudato Si'*, which calls upon every person to listen to the cry of the earth and the cry of the poor.[17] The basic problem goes deep, says Francis: "It is the way that humanity has taken up technology and its development according to an undifferentiated and one-dimensional paradigm. This paradigm exalts the concept of a subject who, using logical and rational procedures, progressively approaches and gains control over an external object."[18] Humanity attempts to extract everything possible from nature, works with the idea of unlimited growth, assumes falsely that there is an infinite supply of the earth's goods, and resorts rapidly to confrontational relationships with other human beings: "The precarious condition of our common home has been the result largely of a fallacious economic model that has been followed for too long. It is a voracious model, profit-oriented, shortsighted, and based on the misconception of unlimited economic growth."[19]

Listening to the cry of the earth must have a much higher priority in Christian ethics. A Christian ethic of responsibility must rediscover how the gospel of creation yields an ecology capable of remedying the damage we have done, in ways that will protect our common heritage, and seek sustainable and integral development.[20] Consider how the land has a relationship with YHWH that predates that of Israel and is variously active, capable of executing divine judgment, resting, and praising God (Lev. 18:28; Lk. 19:40). Biotic (relating to living organisms) and abiotic (physical rather than biological) creation alike were created by God. Biblical texts attribute agency to the land. All creation praises God. When some of the Pharisees told Jesus to rebuke his disciples for shouting with a loud voice as he entered Jerusalem, he replied, "I tell you, if these were silent, the very stones would cry out" (Lk. 19:40).

RESPONSIBILITY FOR GLOBAL CITIZENS

The environmental crisis is awakening Christian people and others to the realities of creaturely existence on our shared planet. Linked etymologically to the Latin *civitas* ("city") and associated with membership of a delimited political community and legal status accompanied by rights and duties, citizenship is increasingly used in connection with the idea of living in the world. Use of the word "citizenship" is shifting from the

---

[16]Matthew Taylor, Sandra Laville, Amy Walker, Poppy Noor, and Jon Henley, "School Pupils Call for Radical Climate Action in UK-Wide Strike," *Guardian*, February 15, 2019.
[17]Pope Francis, *Laudato Si'* (Vatican City: Librería Editrice Vaticana, 2015).
[18]Ibid., § 106.
[19]Pope Francis, "Address of His Holiness Pope Francis to Participants at the Meeting Promoted by the Dicastery for Promoting Integral Human Development on the Mining Industry," Consistory Hall Friday, May 3, 2019.
[20]Francis, *Laudato Si'*, § 63.

city and nation-state to include the global. The meaning of citizenship is changing. Thus, GlobeScan, an insights and strategy firm, reported in a 2016 report for the BBC World Service that, for the first time in fifteen years of tracking, nearly one in two people (49 percent) surveyed across fourteen tracking countries and among more than twenty thousand people see themselves more as global citizens than citizens of their country.[21]

The idea of global citizenship is supported at the highest political levels. In 2012, Ban Ki-Moon, then United Nations secretary general, launched a Global Education First Initiative with an aim of fostering global citizenship, that is, of developing a generation that shares the values of peace, human rights, respect, cultural diversity, justice, and a desire for the common good.[22] Campaigning organizations draw attention to our world as an increasingly complex web of connections and interdependencies, and help learners to become more skilled in evaluating the ethics and impact of their decisions.[23] Oxfam Education offers a range of study materials for assemblies and lesson plans, all of which encourage young people to develop the knowledge, skills, and values they need to engage with the world.[24] Who, then, is the global citizen? What are the responsibilities of global citizenship?

Christian ethicists and political theologians have written much about citizenship in recent years. Two types are prominent today: neo-Augustinian liberal theologies of citizenship and post-liberal theologies of liberation, or of the multitude, that reject the inherently capitalist logic of liberalism and look for different ways of being community. Questions must be asked about each type and the possibility faced that neither is adequate—at least as currently framed—to link a Christian ethics of responsibility to global citizenship.

Typically, in Christian ethics, questions about citizenship are approached with reference to Augustine's fifth-century text *City of God*. Is Augustine the figure with whom to engage questions of global citizenship today? As John M. Rist reminded readers in *Augustine Deformed: Love, Sin and Freedom in the Western Moral Tradition*, the figure of Augustine is unavoidable in present-day debates about citizenship, neighbor-love, free will, duty, civilization, and more:

> For better or worse, when in late antiquity much of that substructure disappeared from view—to be rediscovered piecemeal as the centuries passed—it was largely the Augustinian world-picture that remained in the West, and it was on the strengths and weaknesses of that world-picture (often handed down in more or less deformed versions) that subsequent discussion rested.[25]

Augustine's *City of God* is incontrovertibly the most significant theological work on citizenship in the mainstream Christian theological corpus. The most influential recent theologies of citizenship have been sustained engagements with Augustine's *City of God*

---

[21]"Global Citizenship a Growing Sentiment among Citizens of Emerging Economies: Global Poll," *Globescan*, April 27, 2016, https://globescan.com/global-citizenship-a-growing-sentiment-among-citizens-of-emerging-economies-global-poll/.

[22]"Global Education First Initiative," UNESCO, http://www.unesco.org/new/en/gefi/about/.

[23]"What Is Global Citizenship," IDEAS, http://www.ideas-forum.org.uk/about-us/global-citizenship.

[24]"What Is Global Citizenship," OXFAM, https://www.oxfam.org.uk/education/who-we-are/what-is-global-citizenship.

[25]John M. Rist, *Augustine Deformed: Love, Sin and Freedom in the Western Moral Tradition* (New York: Cambridge University Press, 2014), 6.

and associated theologico-political writings (Jean Bethke Elshtain, Oliver O'Donovan, Eric Gregory, Charles Mathewes, Timothy Jackson, etc.).

The problem for our purposes is not Augustine's language of *civitas terrena* ("city of this world") as equating to sin. Augustine as rhetor heaps scorn on the pretensions of the world's dominant ideologies and remains an invaluable dialogue provocateur when developing criteria against which to judge corruption and disordered loves including the *animus dominandi*, disorder and lawlessness. The more difficult challenge is reengaging his ethic of love in our globalizing era. Few of Augustine's contemporary commentators have, to date, engaged explicitly enough with how he might speak to global citizenship. Much is to be gained for an ethic of global citizenship, however, by revisiting Augustine's idea that citizenship is determined by that which is loved:

> A people we may say, is a gathered multitude of rational beings united by agreeing to share the things they love. There can be as many different kinds of people as there are different things for them to love. Whatever those things may be, there is no absurdity in calling it a people it is a gathered multitude, not of beasts but of rational creatures, united by agreeing to share what they love. The better the things, the better the people; the worse the things, the worse their agreement.[26]

While it is easier to read Augustine as speaking to the horizontal, person-to-person, and group-to-group interactions of societies that require and manifest themselves in structures of common action and just institutions at the local or national level, the challenge is to expand our conceptions of his meaning to the entire world and creaturely existence on our shared planet. Only a failure of moral imagination need stand in our way:

> Loving, like knowing, is something we do only with others. Together, not alone, we acquire our capacity to engage the world in cognitive affection. The goods that we love, created and uncreated, are goods common to all, and we love them properly as our own goods only as we understand that they are everybody else's.[27]

Christian ethics must develop better ways of linking responsibility to global citizenship; every resource in our traditions must be rethought and reused.

Different challenges arise when engaging post-liberal theologies of liberation or "the multitude" that derive energy from rejection of the inherently capitalist logic of liberalism. Consider Joerg Rieger and Kwok Pui-Lan's *Occupy Religion: Theology of the Multitude*, which adopts the wider Occupy movement's slogan, "We are the 99 Percent." They understand the 99 percent, or multitude, to include the working class, migrant and seasonal workers, unpaid domestic laborers, the unemployed and the underemployed, the poor and destitute, and all whom Michael Hardt and Antonio Negri dub "figures of social production."[28] Attention is drawn especially to the gross income inequality that separates the wealthiest people in the world from the 99 percent, thereby coloring everything else, and to Korean *minjung* theology that affirms God's option for those who are not the

---

[26]Augustine, *City of God*, bk. XIX, chap. 24, in *From Irenaeus to Grotius: A Sourcebook in Christian Political Thought*, trans. and ed. Oliver and Joan O'Donovan (Grand Rapids: Eerdmans, 1999), 162.

[27]Oliver O'Donovan, *Common Objects* (Grand Rapids: Eerdmans, 2002), 19.

[28]Michael Hardt and Antonio Negri, *Multitude: War and Democracy in the Age of Empire* (New York: Penguin, 2004), 15. Cited in Joerg Rieger and Kwok Pui-Lan, *Occupy Religion: Theology of the Multitude* (Lanham: Rowman & Littlefield, 2012), 6.

politically powerful or members of the social elite, but the majority poor, including those marginalized for a variety of socioeconomic reasons.[29]

Written to unite the different liberation movements, *Occupy Religion* reflects on the unity and difference of these movements rather than the unity and difference of all humanity. The 1 percent is the "Other" that uses racism as a tool to shore up dominant power as *Occupy Religion* talks about "the dichotomy of the 1 percent and the 99 percent" not strictly in economic terms but in ways that have broader implications and "can no longer be separated from other aspects of life."[30] At issue for a Christian ethic of responsibility in a globalizing era is whether an ethic of citizenship learned from inherently oppositional philosophies of consciousness is problematic, and whether neighborly love of, and solidarity with, the 99 percent is possible only via an identity framed against the 1 percent. Can post-liberal theologies of liberation avoid forms of relation in which the "other" is an alien necessity whose objectified existence becomes a means of the actualization of self-consciousness? Do post-liberal theologies of liberation or "the multitude" that derive energy from rejection of the 1 percent or, indeed, from resistance to the inherently capitalist logic of liberalism, remain caught in a logic of negation, opposition, and alienation?

It is helpful at this point to recall G. W. F. Hegel's Parable of the Lord and Bondsman. Few texts from nineteenth-century philosophy have had a greater impact on modern social theory.[31] In this parable, both "self" and "other" define themselves in terms of how they are seen by the Other. The "I" is reduced to a mirror image of himself as he appears to "the other," and *vice versa*. Both "I" and "Other" need to be recognized in the fullness of their individuality and personhood, but each becomes fearful that the Other might "consume" their identity by choosing to disregard them or misconstruing what they see. Neither can revert into immediate self-consciousness without mediation through the Other, because that equates to nonrecognition and death. For each, the way to a more fulfilled existence is for the "I" to gain some control over how "the other" perceives him, and the same is true for "the other" in reverse. Our question is whether any philosophy of consciousness that derives its energy from the opposition of one against an "other"—male versus female, Black versus white, 1 percent versus 99 percent, and so on—remains inadequate as a basis for a Christian ethic of citizenship.

RESPONSIBILITY RELEARNED AT PENTECOST

Prior to Pentecost, says Bonhoeffer, Jesus's disciples represented him as followers and those sent out to preach the kingdom of God and heal the sick (Mt. 10:1-24; Lk. 9:1-6). In Jesus's absence, they were timid and afraid. After Pentecost, the disciples are endowed

[29]Ahn Byung-Mu has argued convincingly that German historical-critical exegesis typically viewed the *ochlos* as similar to the "antique choir" or chorus "thereby failing to acknowledge its social and theological significance." Instead, he observes Jesus's consistent commitment to the *ochlos* and points out that Jesus's call to follow him is to the crowd as well as the disciples (Mk 8:34-38). Ahn Byung-Mu, "Jesus and the Ochlos," in *Minjung kwa Hankuk Shinhak* (Seoul: Korean Theological Study Institute, 1982), 87–8. Noted by In Sung Chi, *Holiness and Wholeness: Toward a Holistic Christian Spirituality in Korean Syncretic Context* (DTh diss., Toronto School of Theology, 1998), 233. See also Volker Küster, "Jesus and the Minjung Revisited: The Legacy of Ahn Bying-Mu (1922–1996)," *Biblical Interpretation* 19, no. 1 (2011): 5.

[30]Pui-Lan, *Occupy Religion*, 169, intro.

[31]For an account of this impact, see R. H. Roberts, "The Reception of Hegel's Parable of the Lord and Bondsman," *New Comparison: A Journal of Comparative and Literary Studies* 5 (1988): 23–39.

with his Spirit; his presence is theirs all the time. The community of disciples no longer merely represents Christ but shares in his very life:

> Formerly the disciple-community "represented" Christ; now it possesses him as revelation, as Spirit. *Thus the day of the founding of the actualized church remains Pentecost.* Since human community was formed only when it became a community of will and spirit, and since human spirit is operative only in sociality, *the church originates with the outpouring of the Holy Spirit, and so too the Holy Spirit is the spirit of the church-community of Christ.*[32]

The difference between representing Christ and possessing his life is encountered at Pentecost. Hence, the challenge to Christian ethics to rethink the meaning of responsibility from this event. Reencountering the scriptures is the only way forward in our strivings toward an ethic of global citizenship. Of course, the politics of Pentecost is not about what, today, we might term "party politics," nor aimed at any objective other than witness to Christ. It is clear, however, that Pentecost effects not only a public but also a political witness of the church for the following reasons:

1. The gospel of Christ has a universalizing claim of because the good news is *for all.*
2. The Pentecostal church is *open to new possibility.*
3. The mission and service of the church are *inherently public*, because the church has a body.
4. The Pentecost church is *inherently political* in at least three further respects:
   a. as a social event that is immediately and inherently universalizing, extending to the many multitudes of the globe;
   b. as a social event that is open to infinity and to new possibilities that might break with the current, dominant order;
   c. as a social event that marks a space for action into which the truth is spoken, concerns the situation(s) into which the procedures of truth are addressed, and empowers those hitherto relatively powerless because of exploitation or untruths not of their making.[33]
5. Further marks of the politics of Pentecost include public utterance, communicability, and empowerment of those previously too frightened to speak.

Framing an ethic of responsibility in a globalizing era will be difficult. All the resources of Christian traditions across the world will be required. For all Christian people, however, Pentecostal witness to the cross and resurrection of Christ Jesus is perhaps the place to start.

SUGGESTED READINGS

Bonhoeffer, Dietrich. *Sanctorum Communio: A Theological Study of the Sociology of the Church*, trans. Reinhard Krauss and Nancy Lukens, ed. Clifford J. Green. *Dietrich Bonhoeffer Works*, vol. 1. Minneapolis: Augsburg Fortress, 1998.

Buber, Martin. *I and Thou*, trans. Ronald Gregor Smith. New York: Scribner, 1958.

Reed, Esther D. *The Limit of Responsibility: Dietrich Bonhoeffer's Ethics for a Globalizing Era*. London: Bloomsbury T&T Clark, 2018.

[32]Bonhoeffer, *Sanctorum Communio*, 152, emphasis in original.

[33]Alain Badiou describes politics as a "truth procedure" in *Metapolitics*, trans. Jason Barker (London: Verso, 2011), 141.

CHAPTER TWELVE

Worship and Christian Ethics

STEPHEN B. WILSON

As a form of critical reflection, theology requires the use of reason. But it is a kind of deliberation that draws on sources that transcend the human intellect. As this volume demonstrates, those resources include scripture, tradition, and experience, especially the personal and communal experience of God. These three elements converge in corporate worship or liturgy. Reading the Bible constitutes a vital component of Christian worship. Liturgy is a continuous expression of the church's tradition. Worship is an activity in which people can experience communion with God, other human beings, and the rest of creation. Because of these factors, worship is essential for Christian existence. Since it is so important, one feature of contemporary theology has been an interest in liturgy's possible role in shaping what Christians believe and how they live. The purpose of this chapter is to highlight some of the key figures and prominent themes that have emerged in modern discussions of the relationship between worship and Christian ethics.

THE PIONEERS

Contemporary interest in this topic was sparked by efforts to bring about liturgical reform and renewal by the Liturgical Movement, which began as an effort to restore Roman Catholic monastic worship. It eventually spread beyond monastic and even Roman Catholic circles. Virgil Michel, OSB, was a key figure in this expansion. He was a founder of the Liturgical Press and the journal *Orate Fratres* (now *Worship*), which became prominent vehicles for liturgical scholarship in the English-speaking world. As for substance, Michel's primary contribution was sustained consideration of the connections between liturgy and Christian living.

When Michel discusses the possible impact of worship on the Christian life, he starts with the sacrament of Baptism.[1] Baptism brings one into conformity with Christ, a transformation made possible by the reception of the theological virtues via grace. This transformation continues in the sacrament of Confirmation when one receives the seven gifts of the Holy Spirit, which bring with them increased responsibility within the church, both morally and liturgically. In terms of the former, Confirmation should bring with it more faithful living in day-to-day life and participation in the church's social outreach. In terms of the latter, it

[1]Most of the following paragraph is a summary of Virgil Michel's *Our Life in Christ* (Collegeville: Liturgical, 1939), 89–136.

should issue forth in a fuller sharing in the priesthood of Christ, a priesthood centered on the Eucharist. Michel considers the Eucharist to be essential for the Christian life because it is the means by which Christ and his crucifixion become present. As Christians participate in Christ's self-offering, their own self-giving becomes an expression of charity "whereby one gives one's whole self in love to God."[2] Because it involves the giving of one's life, the Eucharist continues even after the rite itself has ended. Michel states that the reality of Christ's presence in the Eucharist "endures long after the species are dissolved" and even "grows with every Christ-like action of ours, which is the living Christ acting supernaturally in all our Christ-conformed and Christ-formed actions."[3]

Based on what has been said thus far, one of the ways liturgy is morally meaningful for Michel is how it cultivates virtues. The issue then is how it does so. Conventionally, Michel affirms that the sacraments are means of grace, the ordinary ways that Christians receive grace and thus the virtues. The key is in how the sacraments convey grace. One of his central ideas is the "sacramental principle." He describes it as the notion that God makes Godself present to humans "*through external visible things*, and *to act in human souls by means of material things, words, and actions.*"[4] In terms of the sacraments, the principle means that they do not serve as mere conduits for an otherwise distinct reality. Rather, they embody that which they convey. For example, the Eucharist, the sacrament of charity, is itself an embodiment of God's love and our love of God. As Michel put it, "The liturgy is ... the primary and indispensable source of the true Christian spirit: it not only teaches us what this spirit is but also has us live this spirit in all its enactments. In the liturgy the teaching is inseparable from the putting into practice."[5] In developing the point, he highlights how participation in the liturgy was the way members of the early church acquired the virtue of solidarity: "Such was the sublime lesson of Christian solidarity that was brought home to the early Christians increasingly by their active participation in the liturgy. It was brought home to them not only as a truth learned, but as a principle put into regular practice, which repetition formed a permanent attitude and habit of mind."[6]

The previous two quotes come from an article that is about what many people would consider to be social ethics. Yet, in contrast to such a demarcation, Michel exemplified a holistic approach, linking liturgy and life, encompassing both personal morality and social ethics. Because Baptism makes one a member of the church, the Christian life and the liturgy that shapes it are essentially social. The primary way in which the social nature of both comes to expression is the parish, "the cell of Christian life."[7] The Eucharist is the center of parish life, yet the social dynamic it creates continues beyond the liturgy to include actions like the works of mercy. Michel also supported movements that extended beyond the parish (the Catholic Worker and cooperative movements, for example) as ways of living out the social logic of the liturgy. Additionally, he used the dynamics of the liturgy as the basis for critiquing other social arrangements, especially economic liberalism, individualism, and totalitarianism.

Michel was not the only person in the early twentieth century who was thinking about the broader implications of Christian worship. Anglican authors also took up this topic

---

[2]Ibid., 97.
[3]Virgil Michel, "The Effects of Communion," *Orate Fratres* 11, no. 4 (1937): 161.
[4]Michel, *Our Life in Christ*, 77, emphasis in original.
[5]Virgil Michel, "The Liturgy the Basis of Social Regeneration," *Orate Fratres* 9, no. 12 (1935): 542.
[6]Ibid., 543.
[7]Virgil Michel, "The Parish, Cell of the Christian Life," *Orate Fratres* 11, no. 10 (1937): 438–40.

in ways that paralleled Michel's work. A prominent example would be A. G. Hebert, especially his *Liturgy and Society*. The concern of this text is the possible impact the church and its liturgy may have on society. He specifically seeks to address the issues presented by Western, industrialized society. The Industrial Revolution led to people being viewed as things, proverbial cogs in a machine. Although he does not use the terminology, Hebert indicates that society had lost sight of the importance of both the common good and the dignity of the human person. What might the church contribute to such a society? He contends that the fundamental social task of the church is to make itself visible through its worship and thus show the wider society what a true society is: "the deepest contribution which the Church can make to society must spring out of her life as the Church of God—that is, the life which finds its expression in the structure of the Church and in her liturgy."[8]

RECENT TRENDS

After the era of Michel and Hebert there was an extended period in which discussions of liturgy and ethics were on the wane. That began to change in the late 1970s. In 1979 the *Journal of Religious Ethics* devoted a special issue to the subject.[9] Since then, interest in the topic has increased tremendously as scholars from a variety of traditions and approaches have broached the topic from multiple angles. Given the proliferation of literature in this area, it is impossible to summarize it here. Instead, we will discuss five major developments in recent writings on the relationship between liturgy and ethics.

The first tendency is an insistence on the connection between liturgy and ethics being understood in terms of the former's relationship with (social) justice. In the 1980s and 1990s, it was common to view the moral importance of liturgy almost exclusively in these terms. Looking at texts from this period, one finds a preponderance of titles like *Liturgy and Social Justice*,[10] *Liturgy, Justice and the Reign of God*,[11] and *The Liturgy That Does Justice*.[12] Although scholars took different approaches to treating the nature of the relationship, one common tactic was to define the nature of justice and then to show how liturgy promotes justice or fails to do so. In some of those accounts, the depictions were rather brief,[13] while in others they were more developed.[14] Another characteristic of these pieces was discussing justice as if it were merely a principle or idea that must then be applied to specific circumstances. Here it must be remembered that justice is also a virtue, a habit that predisposes a person to act justly, which leads to our next topic.

---

[8]Arthur G. Hebert, *Liturgy and Society: The Function of the Church in the Modern World* (London: Faber and Faber, 1935), 202.

[9]See *Journal of Religious Ethics* 7, no. 2 (1979); this special issue was edited by Frederick Carney.

[10]Edward M. Grosz, ed., *Liturgy and Social Justice: Celebrating Rites—Proclaiming Rights* (Collegeville: Liturgical, 1989).

[11]J. Frank Henderson, Stephen Larson, and Kathleen Quinn, *Liturgy, Justice and the Reign of God: Integrating Vision and Practice* (Mahwah: Paulist, 1989).

[12]James L. Empereur and Christopher G. Kiesling, *The Liturgy That Does Justice* (Collegeville: Liturgical, 1990).

[13]See, e.g., James F. White, "The Eucharist and Justice," in *Eucharist and Ecumenical Life: A Conference on Theological and Pastoral Developments*, ed. Ronald P. Byars (Lexington: Kentucky Council of Churches, 1985), 42–51.

[14]See, for instance, Mark Searle, "Serving the Lord with Justice," in *Liturgy and Social Justice*, ed. Mark Searle (Collegeville: Liturgical, 1980), 13–35; R. Kevin Seasoltz, "Justice and the Eucharist," *Worship* 58, no. 6 (1984): 507–25.

Another recent trend has been a focus on how worship can provide a context in which participants can gain the knowledge and skills necessary for being Christian. This emphasis traces its recent origin back to Don Saliers's article, "Liturgy and Ethics: Some New Beginnings," which appeared in the aforementioned issue of the *Journal of Religious Ethics*.[15] In this essay, he states that the "Christian moral life can be characterized as a set of affections and virtues" formed in response to Christ.[16] Liturgy helps cultivate those affections and virtues, doing so in two ways. On the one hand, the textual portions of worship provide a vision of life derived from scripture that informs the moral imagination of Christians. On the other hand, the performative aspects of worship enact that vision of life. By performing those actions, Christians can learn to live the Christian story. As Saliers puts it in a later work, "Patterns of prayer, reading, proclamation, and sacramental action are precisely the practices of communal rehearsal of the affections and virtues befitting 'life in Christ'."[17]

The timing of Saliers's 1979 article was prescient because in the coming years there would be a groundswell of interest in virtue and character in moral philosophy and theology. Given the increased attention to these topics, there have been numerous works on how liturgy may play a role in shaping Christian character. As one surveys the literature, certain tendencies can be seen. As with Saliers, other theologians tend to concentrate on two aspects of the liturgy: ritual actions and liturgical texts, with the former understood as practices that habituate people and the latter orienting people in the world.[18] Another common feature is that scholars from various churches often work within their specific liturgical traditions. For example, Vigen Guroian highlights how the Eastern Orthodox rites of initiation help form virtues such as humility,[19] while Irma Fast Dueck discusses how the Mennonite hymnbook, *Hymnal: A Worship Book*, provides a framework for worship that can cultivate a community whose members are linked by gratitude and peaceableness.[20]

One of the possible pitfalls in describing liturgy as a means of moral formation is that it could suggest that liturgy is only preparatory for morality. This possibility brings us to a third emphasis in contemporary discussions of liturgy and ethics, namely, the idea that the liturgy itself enacts a set of social relations that are already moral. Put differently, corporate worship is a kind of political action that is constitutive of the specific community known as church. Although this idea goes back to Michel and Hebert, contemporary authors like William T. Cavanaugh and Bernd Wannenwetsch have made it a focus of their work.

Cavanaugh has laid out his position in multiple works, including *Torture and Eucharist* and *Theopolitical Imagination*.[21] For Cavanaugh, politics is an act of imagination that

---

[15]Don E. Saliers, "Liturgy and Ethics: Some New Beginnings," *Journal of Religious Ethics* 7, no. 2 (1979): 173–89. This essay was reprinted in his Festschrift, *Liturgy and the Moral Self: Humanity at Full Stretch before God*, ed. E. Byron Anderson and Bruce T. Morrill (Collegeville: Liturgical, 1998), 15–35.

[16]Saliers, "Liturgy and Ethics," in *Liturgy and the Moral Self*, 22.

[17]Don E. Saliers, *Worship as Theology: Foretaste of Glory Divine* (Nashville: Abingdon, 1994), 176.

[18]See, e.g., E. Byron Anderson, *Worship and Christian Identity: Practicing Ourselves* (Collegeville: Liturgical, 2003); M. Therese Lysaught, "Eucharist as Basic Training: The Body as Nexus of Basic Training," in *Theology and Lived Christianity*, ed. David M. Hammond (Mystic: Twenty-Third Publications, 2000), 257–86.

[19]Vigen Guroian, *Incarnate Love: Essays in Orthodox Ethics* (Notre Dame: University of Notre Dame Press, 1987), 51–78.

[20]Irma Fast Dueck, "The Performance of Worship and the Ordering of Our Lives: Liturgy and Ethics in the Mennonite Tradition," *Mennonite Quarterly Review* 79, no. 1 (2005): 51–67.

[21]William T. Cavanaugh, *Torture and Eucharist: Theology, Politics, and the Body of Christ* (Malden: Blackwell, 1998), and Cavanaugh, *Theopolitical Imagination* (New York: T&T Clark, 2002).

involves how bodies are situated in time and space by different practices. As an act of imagination, politics has a mythic quality to it, whether the underlying story is Hobbes's *Leviathan* or the Christian scriptures. Insofar as politics involves organizing bodies, it also always involves ritual, be it ones focused on violence or those centered on peaceful coexistence. Thus, both the church and the nation-state are political, though with their own defining stories and rites. Moreover, they are both religious in that they make claims about what—be it God or one's nation—is worthy of one's *crucial* commitment, of "the ultimate sacrifice." Also, they do not inhabit different spaces, one sacred and one secular. Instead, they occupy the same space—creation—though with different ways of imagining that space. In this context, the moral significance of the liturgy lies in the liturgy itself being a set of political and thus moral actions that stand in contrast with those of the modern nation-state. Does that mean that the church has no social role beyond the celebration of the liturgy itself? Not so for Cavanaugh. He argues that the politics embodied in the Eucharist are focused on *kenosis* and that self-giving should continue after the rite itself. He points to the Catholic Worker movement and Focolare communities as examples of what a "church in the streets" might look like.[22]

Wannenwetsch's fullest contribution to the topic is his book, *Political Worship.*[23] Like Cavanaugh, he maintains that the church is constituted by a set of practices: the proclamation of the Word and the administration of the sacraments. Drawing on Ludwig Wittgenstein, he depicts worship as a "form of life." When discussing its importance, he emphasizes its relationship to scripture. The Canon serves as the grammar to worship as a form of life such that, strictly speaking, the Bible is the standard for the Christian life and worship is the first expression of that life. The form of life that is shared "among Christian citizens [in worship] spills over, so to speak, into the secular *polis*."[24] How so? In answering this question, Wannenwetsch talks about different "publics," of which the church is one. He holds that all publics are equal. That insistence, though, renders the church socially compromised. Even though he argues that the church is "the model of a true public," he also says that it confronts other groups as merely another public, an aggregate of like-minded individuals.[25] It would seem that, for Wannenwetsch, it is individual Christians, not the church, that have a direct role in social life outside of worship. The contrast with Cavanaugh is stark. For Cavanaugh, the Eucharist forms the body of Christ, a true public that endures even after the celebration with a church in the streets performing actions like the works of mercy. For Wannenwetsch the church seems to have no enduring presence: the body of Christ as social phantasm.

There is one critical way that Cavanaugh and Wannenwetsch's ideas coincide. This commonality focuses on how the liturgy is socially significant. They agree that the liturgy does not express some principle—say, justice—that must be distilled from worship and subsequently applied to so-called real life. Rather, both insist that the celebration of liturgy is itself social and ethical. Yet the Christian life is not reducible to what happens in liturgical rites because life involves actions in addition to those celebrations. This point brings us to a fourth characteristic of contemporary accounts of worship and Christian

---

[22]William T. Cavanaugh, "The Church in the Streets: Eucharist and Politics," *Modern Theology* 30, no. 2 (2014): 394, 401.

[23]Bernd Wannenwetsch, *Political Worship: Ethics for Christian Citizens*, trans. Margaret Kohl (New York: Oxford University Press, 2004).

[24]Ibid., 11.

[25]Ibid., 241.

ethics, namely, how the liturgy may help Christians understand and respond to particular moral concerns.

Monika K. Hellwig's *The Eucharist and the Hunger of the World* was a relatively early example of a work that examines how the liturgy might inform a response to a crucial moral concern, in this case, hunger.[26] She notes that the Eucharist is a celebration of divine hospitality such that Christians are called to extend that hospitality to meet hunger in the world. Since the historical basis and symbolic focus of the Eucharist is a meal, it is unsurprising that other theologians have also used it as the liturgical starting point to address issues related to food.[27] The sacraments generally, and the Eucharist specifically, have also proved helpful bases for broaching ecological concerns.[28] In addition to topics that seem "natural" for being analyzed from a liturgical perspective, scholars have also looked at subjects that at first might seem ill-suited for such an approach, including issues of war and peace[29] and criminal justice.[30] Since these pieces are focused on very specific topics, these issues are usually addressed in short works like articles and essays, which means they are disconnected from each other. A notable exception is *The Blackwell Companion to Christian Ethics*.[31] Although this work is a collection of essays from different authors, it is given coherence by being organized around the basic structure of the Eucharist as it is celebrated by most churches. The volume focuses on the possible impact Eucharistic celebration may have for the Christian life in general and in response to specific concerns. Regarding the latter, contributors highlight how various aspects of the rite may shape how Christians respond to multiple issues related to race, gender, criminal justice, abortion, war and peace, health care, and so on.

The final focal point in recent conversations about liturgy and ethics is the flipside of the first. If liturgy can be a source of justice, then it can also perpetuate injustice. In analyses of this topic, there have been two basic approaches. Some scholars are concerned with the relationship in general terms.[32] Most theologians, however, are interested in how liturgy might extend injustice toward groups that have historically been subject to oppression. For example, feminist theologians have noted how the language, roles, and gestures of worship can perpetuate patterns of patriarchy and even encourage violence against women.[33] Similarly, liberation theologians have argued that the Eucharist has been

---

[26]Monika K. Hellwig, *The Eucharist and the Hunger of the World*, 2nd rev. exp. ed. (Kansas City: Sheed & Ward, 1992). The original version was published by Paulist Press in 1976.

[27]David N. Power, "The Eucharistic Table: In Communion with the Hungry," *Worship* 83, no. 5 (2009): 386–98; Laura M. Hartman, "Consuming Christ: The Role of Jesus in Christian Food Ethics," *Journal of the Society of Christian Ethics* 30, no. 1 (2010): 45–62.

[28]See, for instance, Kevin W. Irvin, "The Sacramentality of Creation and the Role of Creation in Liturgy and Sacraments," in *Preserving the Creation: Environmental Theology and Ethics*, ed. Kevin W. Irwin and Edmund D. Pellegrino (Washington, DC: Georgetown University Press, 1994), 67–111; Gordon W. Lathrop, *Holy Ground: A Liturgical Cosmology* (Minneapolis: Fortress, 2003), 125–52.

[29]Timothy F. Sedgwick, "In Times of War and Rumors of War," *Anglican Theological Review* 85, no. 3 (2003): 421–7; Tobias L. Winright, "The Liturgy as a Basis for Catholic Identity, Just War Theory, and the Presumption against War," in *Catholic Identity and the Laity*, ed. Timothy P. Muldoon (Maryknoll: Orbis, 2009), 134–51.

[30]Amy Levad, "'I Was in Prison and You Visited Me': A Sacramental Approach to Rehabilitative and Restorative Criminal Justice," *Journal of the Society of Christian Ethics* 31, no. 2 (2011): 93–112; Tobias L. Winright, "Liturgy and (God's) Justice for All: The Eucharist as Theological Basis for Translating Recent Catholic Teaching on Capital Punishment," in *Translating Religion*, ed. Anita Houck and Mary Doak (Maryknoll: Orbis, 2013), 118–36.

[31]Stanley Hauerwas and Samuel Wells, eds., *The Blackwell Companion to Christian Ethics* (Malden: Blackwell, 2006).

[32]See, e.g., James F. White, "Worship as a Source of Injustice," *Reformed Liturgy and Music* 19 (1985): 72–6; Nicholas Wolterstorff, "Justice as a Condition of Authentic Liturgy," *Theology Today* 48, no. 1 (1991): 6–21.

[33]See, for instance, Marjorie Procter-Smith, "'Reorganizing Victimization': The Intersection between Liturgy and Domestic Violence," in *Christian Perspectives on Sexuality and Gender*, ed. Elizabeth Stuart and Adrian

domesticated to the point that it at once reflects and reinforces the division between rich and poor.[34] But there are other liberation theologians who allow for a more positive role for liturgy. For instance, James H. Cone has argued that the worship of the Black church in the United States has empowered African Americans in their struggle for freedom.[35] Even when theologians highlight the ways liturgy can express injustice, they still affirm a relationship: worship might involve malformation, but it is nonetheless formation.

CONCLUSION

The praise of God in both liturgy and life is at the center of Christian existence. As such, there is a necessary link between Christian worship and the Christian life. As Vatican II's *Sacrosanctum concilium* affirms, the liturgy is the source and summit for all that the church does.[36] But it should also be noted that liturgy is not magic. Simply attending a worship service is not necessarily going to impact the "participants" in a manner that extends beyond the service itself. If liturgy is going to make a greater impression on the lives of Christians, then at least two things are required. First, churches need to provide more catechesis on the nature and significance of worship. Second, when people do worship, they should be present as more than mere spectators. What is needed is "full, conscious, and active participation"[37] that allows the community to be informed by the celebration in order to be transformed by it. Both points were stressed by Virgil Michel in the early twentieth century, showing that in many ways the church is still trying to catch up to him.

SUGGESTED READINGS

Chauvet, Louis-Marie. *Symbol and Sacrament: A Sacramental Reinterpretation of Christian Existence*, trans. Patrick Madigan and Madeleine Beaumont. Collegeville: Liturgical, 1995.

Laytham, D. Brent, and David D. Bjorlin. "Worship and Ethics: A Selected Bibliography." *Studia Liturgica* 43, no. 2 (2013): 169–88.

Phillips, L. Edward. "Liturgy and Ethics." In *Liturgy in Dialogue: Essays in Memory of Ronald Jasper*, ed. Paul Bradshaw and Bryan Spinks, 88–101. Collegeville: Liturgical, 1993.

Searle, Mark. "Liturgy and Social Ethics: An Annotated Bibliography." *Studia Liturgica* 21, no. 1 (1991): 220–33.

Wainwright, Geoffrey. *Doxology: The Praise of God in Worship, Doctrine, and Life.* New York: Oxford University Press, 1980.

Thatcher (Grand Rapids: Eerdmans, 1996), 380–95; Janet Walton, *Feminist Liturgy: A Matter of Justice* (Collegeville: Liturgical, 2000).

[34]See, e.g., Rafael Avila, *Worship and Politics*, trans. Alan Neely (Maryknoll: Orbis, 1981); Tissa Balasuriya, *The Eucharist and Human Liberation* (Maryknoll: Orbis, 1977).

[35]James H. Cone, "Sanctification, Liberation, and Black Worship," *Theology Today* 35, no. 2 (1978): 139–52.

[36]Second Vatican Council, "*Sacrosanctum concilium*," in *Vatican Council II: The Conciliar and Post Conciliar Documents*, vol. 1, rev. ed., ed. Austin Flannery (Northport: Costello, 1996), § 10.

[37]Ibid., § 14.

CHAPTER THIRTEEN

Autonomy and Heteronomy in Eastern Christian Thought and Post-Enlightenment Moral Paradigms

DEMETRIOS HARPER

It would be inaccurate to claim that Eastern Christian confessions possess something that could be characterized as an independent or coherent "system" of ethics according to the modern understanding thereof. A century ago, this lack of distinct ethical systematicity could perhaps have been attributed to the geopolitical circumstances of the Eastern Churches and, in the case of the Greek Orthodox Church, the insularity brought on by centuries of Turkish rule.[1] However, in the case of Russian religious intellectuals of the nineteenth and early twentieth centuries, this "argument from insularity" does not stand. Well-educated Russians were fluent in the Western intellectual canon and well aware of the ethical *aporiai* posed by the philosophical tradition, especially German Idealism.[2]

Beginning with the theologians and philosophers of the Russian Emigré in the twentieth century, Eastern Christianity added its voice to the chorus of religious dialogue and has been granted a seat at the table of interconfessional discourse. Though a substantial body of work now exists that seeks to define and distinguish Orthodox positions on topics ranging from anthropology to Triadology, few books on ethics have been produced by Eastern Christian authors that differentiate Orthodox views from normative Western views,[3] and there are virtually no magisterial treatises aspiring to provide the outline of a moral "system."[4] There are arguably two reasons for this. First, it seems evident that many

[1]Christos Yannaras, *Orthodoxy and the West*, trans. Peter Chamberas and Norman Russell (Brookline: Holy Cross Orthodox Press, 2006).

[2]Paul Gavrilyuk, *Georges Florovsky and the Russian Religious Renaissance* (Oxford: Oxford University Press, 2014); Georges Florovksy, *Ways of Russian Theology*, part 2, in *The Collected Works of Georges Florovsky*, vol. 6 (Belmont: Büchervertriebsanstalt, 1987).

[3]Notable exceptions are Christos Yannaras, *The Freedom of Morality*, trans. Elizabeth Briere (Crestwood: SVS Press, 1996); Joseph Woodill, *The Fellowship of Life: Virtue Ethics and Orthodox Christianity* (Washington, DC: Georgetown University Press, 1998).

[4]Though not providing what could be termed a "system," Georgios Mantzarides's two-volume work (in Greek) on Christian ethics comes close to being magisterial in scope. It aspires to give a basic outline of what constitutes

contemporary thinkers from the Eastern tradition have, consciously or unconsciously, received the presuppositions of normative philosophical ethics uncritically, not regarding them as being significantly different in character from the practical moral expressions of the faith. The second and rather more obvious reason for this dearth of contemporary Orthodox ethical theory lies in the fact that the Eastern Church still relies very heavily upon the unmediated use of ascetic literature from Late Antiquity and the Middle Ages for ethical guidelines.[5] These spiritual treatises, as is typical of the approach of the era, are not intended to be systematic works of philosophy and do not treat moral issues as distinct questions. Rather, they are regarded as integral aspects of spiritual anthropology and theology. Though significant work is clearly needed in order to properly interpret these works and apply the principles therein to the lives of typical Orthodox laypeople, this traditional "integrated" approach would be regarded by many, both East and West, as a strength, representing in practice a living rendition of a Christian virtue-based ethic in the contemporary era.[6]

Nevertheless, due to the limited effort to bring the principles of Eastern Christian morals into dialogue with Western philosophical assumptions and their voluntary or involuntary reception by the majority of modern subjects, this traditional mindset is manifested in the typical Orthodox Christian alongside conflicting axioms that originate in post-Enlightenment thought and culture, effectively creating a moral schizophrenia. This tension is particularly acute when it comes to the beloved modern conception of autonomy and its associated characteristics,[7] and it arguably creates agents who possess an internal awareness of the traditional claims of moral authority but who externally reflect the embedded mechanisms of autonomous moral judgment when interfacing with other members of the "*polis*." It is obviously beyond the scope of this brief chapter to provide a thoroughgoing analysis of the dynamics that give rise to this tension. In keeping, therefore, with the more modest aspirations of an introduction to the problematic, this chapter shall seek to briefly outline the post-Enlightenment views of autonomy and heteronomy, contrasting them with the principles reflected in the treasuries of Eastern spirituality and theology. While the sources for the Orthodox views of autonomy and heteronomy are regarded as authoritative by Eastern confessions, many of them also stand as common sources for Western confessions as well, especially the Catholic tradition. As such, this effort to set in relief the rather different way the Eastern Christians of Late Antiquity and the Middle Ages approached the question of human autonomy is intended to be of ecumenical import.

THE GENEALOGY OF AUTONOMY

The intellectual dynamics that laid the groundwork for the modern conception of moral autonomy in Western philosophical thought began to take clear shape in the thought of Dutch philosopher Hugo Grotius (1583–1645), whose work on natural law constitutes a clear shift from the prevailing views of the Medieval Scholastics and lays the groundwork

---

Eastern Orthodox ethical criteria and seeks to provide Orthodox answers to an array of contemporary problems. See his *Χριστιανική Ηθική*, 3rd ed., 2 vols. (Άγιον Όρος: Ι. Μ. Μονή Βατοπαιδίου, 2015).

[5]An excellent example is John Climacus's *The Ladder of Divine Ascent*, which is traditionally read by monastics and non-monastics alike during Great Lent.

[6]Cf., among others, Perry Hamalis and Aristotle Papanikolaou, "Toward a Godly Mode of Being," *Studies in Christian Ethics* 26, no. 3 (2013): 271–80.

[7]Georgios Mantzarides also juxtaposes the traditional Eastern Christian view of self-determination and the post-Kantian notion of autonomy. See his *Χριστιανική Ηθική*, vol. 1, 131–40.

for the moral theories of the Enlightenment.[8] Though Grotius may rightly be regarded as the concrete exemplar of this shift toward the Enlightenment, Michel de Montaigne (1533–1592) also presages this trend by rejecting the traditional conception of "morality as obedience,"[9] which conflicts with the theologically oriented views of morals and natural law put forth by later Medieval Scholastic thinkers like Francisco Suárez (1548–1617).[10] In any case, as J. B. Schneewind argues in his *tour de force*, *The Invention of Autonomy*, Grotius represents a clear shift from morality that is grounded in and inextricably connected to a Christian confession, a move that was clearly motivated by the plethora of religious wars and conflicts of his era.[11] A "minimal" or generic Christianity became the normative baseline used to sustain a belief in moral principles, thereby disconnecting moral theology from natural law and transferring ethical authority from the theologian to the philosopher.[12] This Grotian thread would be appropriated and thoroughly developed by Thomas Hobbes (1588–1679), whose views of natural law are grounded in what could be described as scientific empiricism and constitute another significant milestone in the genealogy of moral autonomy. In Hobbes's view, moral laws are not derived from divine commands manifested through revelation or disclosed through contemplation of the natural world, but rather through a pragmatic and philosophical assessment of the natural world and human interaction therein, through a study of cause and effect.[13] Though Hobbes portrays an exceedingly pessimistic view of the natural world, he persistently refuses to follow the traditional Christian theological pattern and identify it as "fallen."[14] Rather, Hobbes bases his natural law and social contract theories upon the belief that we simply need to achieve a proper awareness of the realities of the human condition, the prerequisite for which is proper and rigorous scientific knowledge. While the nature of Hobbes's theism remains a matter of debate, and God's relationship to morality remains ambiguous in the Hobbsean scheme,[15] it is evident that he believes a proper use of reason provides human agents with all that they need in order to determine moral obligations;[16] humanity no longer requires direct commandments by divine ordinance as God merely mandates what reason discloses as obligatory.[17] This autonomy of practical reason is a view that, to a greater or lesser degree, would essentially define the moral spirit of the Enlightenment. Voltaire (1694–1778), following in the wake of this natural law voluntarism and the subsequent gulf between the divine and the function of human reason, ascribes a similarly autonomous state of moral determination to humanity—or

[8]See especially Grotius's *Commentary on the Law of Prize and Booty*, trans. Gwladys L. Williams and Walter H. Zeydel (Oxford: Clarendon, 1950), and *On the Law of War and Peace*, trans. Francis W. Kelsey (Oxford: Clarendon, 1925). This section on the development of autonomy is heavily reliant upon the analysis of J. B. Schneewind in his book, *The Invention of Autonomy* (Cambridge: Cambridge University Press, 1998).

[9]Schneewind, *The Invention of Autonomy*, 50–2. Cf. *The Complete Essays of Montaigne*, trans. Donald M. Frame (Stanford: Stanford University Press, 1958), especially Book III.1–13, 784–858.

[10]Cf. Terence Irwin, *The Development of Ethics*, vol. 2 (Oxford: Oxford University Press, 2008), 28–69.

[11]Ibid., 67–9.

[12]Ibid. The reader should note that Terence Irwin downplays to some extent Grotius's contribution. See *The Development of Ethics*, 88–99.

[13]Thomas Hobbes, *Leviathan* (Oxford: Clarendon, 1965), 23–9; Alasdair MacIntyre, *A Short History of Ethics* (Abingdon: Routledge, 2002), 127–31.

[14]Kinch Hoekstra, "Hobbes on the Natural Condition of Mankind," in *The Cambridge Companion to Hobbes's Leviathan*, ed. Patricia Springborg (Cambridge: Cambridge University Press, 2007), 109–27.

[15]For an example of this ambiguity, see Hobbes, *Leviathan*, 15, 71–9. See also Schneewind, *The Invention of Autonomy*, 96–7.

[16]Cf. Hobbes, *Leviathan*, 15, 16, 71–84.

[17]Schneewind, *The Invention of Autonomy*, 96–7.

to the "enlightened" members thereof, in any case.[18] Julien Offray de La Mettrie (1709–1751) and Denis Diderot (1713–1784), also rigorous naturalists, ultimately dispense with the divine altogether, taking the step of excising what had essentially become superfluous to the moral considerations of human nature and its material circumstances.[19]

The thought of Jean-Jacques Rousseau (1712–1778) marks another significant shift and constitutes an important step toward the crystallization of the modern concept of autonomy. Rejecting the naturalism of his predecessors and departing particularly from Hobbes's lugubrious naturalism, Rousseau argues that humanity's natural state is one of innocence, but it is also too primitive for the formation of morals.[20] Rather, it is the passage from "natural" to "social," from individual to collective, which creates the impetus for the formation of ethics, insofar as natural instincts and their self-serving character are unable to serve the interests of the human being qua social being. The functionality of this moral system is achieved through the ideal of the *volonté générale* or "general will," which displaces private or "natural" desire.[21] Despite the collectivist language, Rousseau shows himself to be a true forerunner of Immanuel Kant by suggesting that this "general will" ought to be self-prescribed. Indeed, a human agent's willing of the general is "freedom" while, conversely, volitional movements arising from private desires and natural impulses are slavery.[22] Perhaps most significant, however, is Rousseau's rejection of the philosophical elitism supported by other members of the Enlightenment, arguing that the increase in knowledge does not in itself lead to the moral improvement of humanity. His argument for a general will is grounded in what many take to be a moral egalitarianism and a form of popular sovereignty,[23] views that Kant would critically appropriate.[24]

Although the initial groundwork for the modern notion of autonomy was established by the post-Grotian natural law voluntarists, and some of the fundamental currents that contribute to it are already present in the works of Rousseau, it is in the *oeuvre* of Kant (1724–1804) that it is truly concretized; in the *oeuvre* of the German transcendental idealist autonomy becomes an indelible feature not only of Western philosophical thought but also of the moral psychology of the typical modern Westerner or, for that matter, any individual influenced by Western thought and culture.[25] Contributing directly to Kantian notions of autonomous morality is Rousseau's moral egalitarianism, which manifests itself *inter alia* in Kant's hatred of servility and his repudiation of all kinds of class hierarchy, including ecclesiastical authority.[26] In ontological terms, Kant's moral theory rests on a rigorous anthropocentricity and the human subject's attempt to legislate himself in the

[18]Ibid., 458–60. Cf. MacIntyre, *Short History of Ethics*, 176–7.

[19]Schneewind, *The Invention of Autonomy*, 462–5, 466–70.

[20]See Rousseau's "*Second Discourse*," in *The Discourses and Other Political Writings*, trans. and ed. Victor Gourevitch (Cambridge: Cambridge University Press, 1997), 111–88; Schneewind, *The Invention of Autonomy*, 470–1; MacIntyre, *Short History of Ethics*, 179–82.

[21]See Rousseau's Notes, in *The Discourses and Other Political Writings*, trans. and ed. Victor Gourevitch (Cambridge: Cambridge University Press, 1997), 213; Irwin, *The Development of Ethics*, 866–77.

[22]Jean-Jacques Rousseau, "Of the Social Contract I," in *The Social Contract and Other Later Political Writings*, trans. and ed. Victor Gourevitch (Cambridge: Cambridge University Press, 1997), 41–56.

[23]Irwin, *The Development of Ethics*, 865, 867, 868.

[24]Ibid., 874.

[25]Cf. Bernard Williams, *Ethics and the Limits of Philosophy* (Abingdon: Routledge, 2011), 193–6; Schneewind, *The Invention of Autonomy*, 483.

[26]See Immanuel Kant, *Religion within the Boundaries of Mere Reason*, in *Religion and Rational Theology: The Cambridge Edition of the Works of Immanuel Kant*, trans. Allen Wood and George Di Giovanni (Cambridge: Cambridge University Press, 1996), 6: 98, 121–2, 327; Schneewind, *The Invention of Autonomy*, 489–90.

phenomenal world, free of the necessity of natural causation.[27] This latter aspect of his thought is directed at the natural law voluntarists who preceded him and constitutes a direct repudiation of their thought. His formulation of the famous categorical imperative presupposes that a human being is only free and, therefore, only truly moral to the extent that she autonomously determines the rightness of a volitional movement, unrestrained and uncompelled by all external causes.[28] While natural impulses are one of the prominent challenges to human autonomy, Kant also regards the external influence of other rational beings as constituting a violation of a moral agent's autonomy. In short, all exoteric influences—including those who "speak in the name of God"—constitute a heteronomous source for volitional evaluation and therefore an intrusion upon an agent's properly derived moral determination. In effect, this approach to autonomy and the rejection of all heteronomous dictates places humanity on an equal footing with God in terms of our own dignity to self-govern.[29] As Kant affirms in his *Groundwork*, "Even the Holy One of the gospel must first be compared with our ideal of moral perfection before we can recognize him to be such."[30] Put another way, we recognize the moral perfection of Christ to the extent that we properly and autonomously evaluate his actions, free of the external pressures of natural movement and influence of the other. In terms of our autonomy, then, we are identical to Christ; he is merely better at self-legislating due to the perfection of his will and his capacity to resist heteronomous realities.

ANCIENT CHRISTIANITY AND SELF-DETERMINATION

Though diverging with regards to detail, most historians of intellectual history would readily acknowledge that the advent of the Christian era coincided with a new concept of moral self-governance and, consequently, culpability.[31] Though many of the pagan philosophical traditions posited versions of self-determination that resembled or even influenced Christian formulations, the Biblically derived notion that all human beings regardless of social class are created according to the image and likeness of God introduced the theological supposition of a basic ontological equality between human beings hitherto unknown in the ancient world, even if it has been ignored or conveniently overlooked at times by its adherents.[32] The immediate consequences of this view in terms of ethical

---

[27]For an excellent example of Kantian anthropocentricity, see Immanuel Kant, *Critique of Pure Reason*, trans. Norman Kemp Smith (London: Macmillan, 1929), A822/B850 and A213/B260. For his views of self-legislation, see *Groundwork of the Metaphysic of Morals*, trans. H. J. Paton (New York: Harper Perennial, 1964), 4: 387, 400–3, 431–3. Cf. Paul Guyer, *Kant's System of Nature and Freedom* (Oxford: Oxford University Press, 2005), 116; Robert Hanna, *Kant, Science, and Human Nature* (Oxford: Oxford University Press, 2006), 15–20.

[28]Kant, *Groundwork*, 4: 421–2; Kant, *The Metaphysics of Morals*, trans. Mary J. Gregor (Cambridge: Cambridge University Press, 1996), 6: 216–17.

[29]Schneewind, *The Invention of Autonomy*, 509–12.

[30]Kant, *Groundwork*, 4: 408.

[31]This is strongly reaffirmed by Kyle Harper, *From Shame to Sin: The Christian Transformation of Sexual Morality in Late Antiquity* (Cambridge: Harvard University Press, 2013), 80–133; Harper objects to Michael Frede's assertions that the concept of free will is not unique to the Christian tradition but can, in fact, be attributed to Epictetus. See Frede's *A Free Will: Origins of the Notion in Ancient Thought*, Sather Classical Lectures 68, ed. A. A. Long (Berkeley: University of California Press, 2011), 66–88.

[32]For an array of informed opinions on the development of the concept of will, most of whom acknowledge the significant role that Christian thinkers and their presuppositions played in its development, see the following authors: Albrecht Dihle, *The Theory of Will in Classical Antiquity*, Sather Classical Lectures 48 (Berkeley: University of California Press, 1982), 99–144; René Antoine Gauthier, *Aristote: Léthique à Nicomaque*, vol. 1 (Louvain: Édition Peeters, 2002), 255–66; Charles Kahn, "Discovering Will from Aristotle to

thought is the repudiation of what is now termed "moral luck," namely, the tacit assertion on the part of ancient philosophers that the potential for proper moral development is contingent upon the right sort of external circumstances.[33] The hapless recipients of bad "moral luck" in the form of underprivileged upbringings, improper moral training, and so on had little or no hope of achieving a proper character. Conversely, the ancient and medieval Christian thinkers who cultivate in their works the universally applied notion of ethical self-determination affirm that, regardless of one's starting point, all possess an inherent capacity for the recognition and pursuit of the good regardless of one's social upbringing as well as an unnecessitated volitional faculty. The cultivation of classical notions of virtue remains a significant feature in these perspectives, but it is conditioned by an evangelical and universal call to repentance and salvation. A *prima facie* examination of these ancient and medieval Christian notions might seem to suggest many common features with the post-Enlightenment and, especially, Kantian conceptions of autonomy. In a broad sense, it would not be incorrect to suggest that modern autonomy owes its existence to the formation of Christian moral principles. Nevertheless, a more careful examination of the older sources, still beloved and regarded as authoritative by many contemporary practicing Eastern Christians, discloses a mindset that explicitly and implicitly contradicts the criteria for truly autonomous moral determination.

MORAL SELF-DETERMINATION AND OBEDIENCE IN THE GREEK PATRISTIC TRADITION

In turning to ancient sources—which, in scholarly terms, belong to what many would term the "Greek Patristic Tradition"—perhaps the most striking conceptual contradiction of autonomy comes in the form of "obedience" (*hypakoē*) to a spiritual guide or *gerondas*.[34] This practice was established early on as an indispensable aspect of spiritual life in the monastic communities that coalesced in the fourth and fifth centuries, and it has remained a venerated feature of Eastern Orthodox spirituality until our present era. Though not a central motif in his spiritual writings, Evagrius of Pontus (345–399), a pioneer of eastern monasticism, is careful to exhort both male and female monastics living in community to attend to the words of their spiritual guides.[35] One of the most well-known literary sources providing an exposition of obedience is *The Ladder of Divine Ascent*, authored by John of Sinai (*c.* 579–659)[36] or, as he is more commonly known, John Climacus. In the fourth chapter or "step," John addresses the practice, defining it thus: "Obedience is absolute renunciation of our own life, clearly expressed in our bodily actions ... obedience

Augustine," in *The Question of "Eclecticism": Studies in Later Greek Philosophy*, ed. John Dillon and A. A. Long (Berkeley: University of California Press, 1988), 235–58.

[33]Cf. Bernard Williams, "Moral Luck," in *Moral Luck: Philosophical Papers 1973–1980* (Cambridge: Cambridge University Press, 1981), 20–39.

[34]This emphasis on obedience was a feature of what we would now refer to as "Macarian spirituality," named for the influential monastic writings attributed to Macarius of Egypt (*c.* 300–391). See Marcus Plested, *The Macarian Legacy: The Place of Macarius-Symeon in the Eastern Christian Tradition* (Oxford: Oxford University Press, 2004).

[35]See Robert Sinkewicz, "The Two Treatises: To Monks in Monasteries, and Exhortation to a Virgin," in *Evagrius of Pontus: The Greek Ascetic Corpus*, trans. Robert Sinkewicz (Oxford: Oxford University Press, 2003), 127–8, 131.

[36]These dates are based on what still remains tentative conjecture. See Alexis Torrance, *Repentance in Late Antiquity: Eastern Christian Asceticism and the Framing of the Christian Life c. 400–650 CE* (Oxford: Oxford University Press, 2013), 158–60.

is the tomb of the will and the resurrection of humility."[37] Later in the same chapter, John uses stronger language, suggesting not only that the "exile of the will" precedes the acquisition of true obedience but that its maintenance depends on the ongoing "killing" of all willful manifestations.[38] John further suggests that it is not only our "will" that we offer up to our spiritual superior but also our private "discernment" (*diakrēsis*) and opinions.[39] Climacus's endorsement of the renunciation of "will" may sound odd to many readers, especially given the primordial Christian emphasis upon self-governance and volitional freedom. Despite its initial appearance here, Climacus is speaking in what could be described as a "monastic idiom," which reappears elsewhere and is recorded in *The Philokalia*, the celebrated anthology of Eastern monastic literature compiled by Nicodemus of the Holy Mountain.[40] Climacus is not denying the concept of free will as such, nor is he necessarily suggesting that the volitional faculty in an anthropological sense must atrophy into nonexistence. Indeed, scholarly evidence suggests that the term he uses here, *thelēma* or *thelēsis*, comes to be associated with the volitional faculty in a philosophical sense in the writings of Maximus the Confessor, whose engagement with the Christological controversies of the seventh century provided the impetus for standardization of the expression.[41] When, therefore, Climacus speaks of "will" and its denial, he is arguably referring to what Maximus and his theological progeny would later call *gnōmē*, which in the idiom of the time refers to a private or particular disposition of will, or even to a private opinion.[42] Consequently, though the idiomatic suggestion of a "cutting-off" of the will would continue to survive as a literary device in some monastic writings, its intention is generally—at least in the case of pro-Chalcedonian writers—not meant to express the complete abrogation of the volitional faculty.

If obedience is not a rejection of free will or the complete effacing of moral self-governance, then what is Climacus's purpose in using such rigorous, anti-individualistic language? The first clue to his underlying intention comes via his comment regarding discernment: "Obedience is an abandonment of discernment in a wealth of discernment."[43] This comment is clarified later on in the same chapter when John suggests that a monk's

---

[37]John Climacus, *The Ladder of Divine Ascent*, 4.3, trans. Lazarus Moore (Boston: Holy Transfiguration Monastery, 1991), 21. For the original text, I consulted the *Κλίμαξ*, in *Ἰωάννου τοῦ Σιναΐτου ἅπαντα τὰ ἔργα*, Φιλοκαλία τῶν νηπτικῶν καὶ ἀσκητικῶν πατέρων 16, ΕΠΕ, Ἐλευθέριος Μερετάκη (Θεσσαλονίκη: Πατερικαὶ Ἐκδόσεις Γρηγόριος ὁ Παλαμᾶς, 1996).

[38]Climacus, *The Ladder of Divine Ascent*, 4.4 and 44.4, 21, 38.

[39]Ibid., 4.3, 21.

[40]See, e.g., the comment of St. Hesychios, the priest, *On Watchfulness and Holiness*, in *The Philokalia*, vol. 1, trans. and ed. Kallistos Ware et al. (London: Faber and Faber, 1979), 167, who says that the monk must "cut off his will" to the abbot.

[41]John D. Madden is among the first to argue for the originality of Maximus's contribution to the genealogy of the concept of will. See his "The Authenticity of Early Definitions of Will (*thelēsis*)" in *Maximus Confessor: Actes du Symposium sur Maxime le Confesseur, Fribourg (2–5 Septembre 1980)*, ed. Felix Heinzer and Christoph Schönborn (Fribourg: Éditions Universitaire Fribourg, 1982), 61–82. Madden's "originality thesis" is defended by David Bradshaw, "St Maximus the Confessor on the Will," in *Knowing the Purpose of Creation Resurrection*, Proceedings of the Symposium on St Maximus the Confessor, ed. Maxim Vasiljević (Alhambra: Sebastian Press, 2013), 143–58. For an up-to-date and comprehensive overview of Maximus's view, see Ian McFarland, "The Theology of Will," in *The Oxford Handbook of Maximus the Confessor*, ed. Pauline Allen and Bronwen Neil (Oxford: Oxford University Press, 2015), 516–32.

[42]McFarland, "The Theology of Will," 520–2. For the context and background of "will" and its correlative expressions in Maximus, see Paul Blowers, *Maximus the Confessor: Jesus Christ and the Transfiguration of the World* (Oxford: Oxford University Press, 2016), 156–65.

[43]Climacus, *The Ladder of Divine Ascent*, 4.3, 21.

acquisition of obedience requires him to offer up his private discernment and, in effect, to sacrifice *voluntarily* personal distinctiveness not only to the spiritual superior but also to the brotherhood as a whole.[44] For, as John argues, one of the greatest dangers to spiritual life is *idiorythmia*, literally "self-reliance" or "following one's own devices."[45] In offering up personal distinctiveness to a spiritual superior, a monk is offering up his private dispositions to all the members of his spiritual community, which is itself a free volitional act. Climacus's monk is not so much denying his own intrinsic freedom of will as he is seeking the co-governance and insight of those who are more advanced in virtue, and, through them, struggling to direct his volitional disposition such that it harmonizes with the other members of the community. In this vein, the spiritual superior functions as an embodiment of the rest of the community, enabling the younger monk gradually to excise his private concerns and live for the sake of others.

However, this relationship of superior to novice, which echoes to some extent the role of the Stoic sage, is one of reciprocity. The reciprocal core of this reality is disclosed in Climacus's admonitions directed to the spiritual guides and superiors, which argue that though the novice must offer obedience to the superior, it is incumbent upon the superior to bear and even repent for the faults and falls of others.[46] In addressing this relationship in the *Ladder*, Alexis Torrance defines this role of the spiritual father as constituting "Christ-like repentance," causing the superior to existentially imitate the intercessory and expiatory character of Jesus Christ and his earthly dispensation.[47] As Torrance argues elsewhere, Climacus's view presupposes what could be described as a "personal interrelatedness of repentance,"[48] and therefore, in ethical terms, a cooperative exchange whereby those who are more advanced in virtue and in the art of ethical self-governance function as the moral compass of those who are not, guiding them but also voluntarily taking upon themselves the existential wounds inflicted by their infractions. We might punctuate this by noting yet another passage from Climacus's chapter on obedience, where he praises the monastics who are willing to bear the blame and responsibility for actions of their erring brothers, even going so far as to supplicate the spiritual superior to punish them in the stead of the true offenders.[49] Put in ethical terms, the cultivation of character and the diachronic habituation of virtue are achieved via volitional collaboration and the willingness to embrace the "law of the other" and his or her heteronomous influence, but it is also attained through the voluntary assumption of co-culpability in the face of moral wrongs and co-suffering of the consequences.

This communal approach to moral governance is, to some extent, rendered more evident in the writings of John Cassian (*c.* 360–435), a figure whose influences truly transcend the boundaries of East and West and who, among other things, constitutes one of the primary sources for Benedict of Nursia's monastic rule.[50] Like Climacus, Cassian tacitly warns of the dangers of *idiorythmia* and reliance upon one's private and unregulated judgment.[51] In discussing the disastrous spiritual demise of an experienced

[44]Ibid., 4.2–5, 21–2.
[45]*Κλίμαξ ς΄*, 80; Climacus, *The Ladder of Divine Ascent*, 4.5, 22.
[46]Torrance, *Repentance in Late Antiquity*, 172.
[47]Ibid., 171.
[48]Ibid., 162–3.
[49]Climacus, *The Ladder of Divine Ascent*, 4.18, 26.
[50]See A. M. C. Casiday, *Tradition and Theology in John Cassian* (Oxford: Oxford University Press, 2007), 119–60.
[51]John Cassian, *On the Holy Fathers of Sketis and on Discrimination*, in *The Philokalia*, vol. 1, trans. and ed. Kallistos Ware et al. (London: Faber and Faber, 1979), 100.

monk, he asserts, "This would not have happened to him had he been armed with the virtue of discrimination, which would have taught him to trust, not his own judgment, but rather the advice of his fathers and brethren."[52] In the same treatise, Cassian implores the reader to consider the examples of the arts and sciences. Just as it is impossible to acquire a proper and complete knowledge of these disciplines without the instruction and oversight of experienced and learned teachers, so it is also impossible to acquire a working capacity in the spiritual arts and their accompanying aptitude for moral self-governance.[53] The proper use of our volition and practical reason depend upon the "heteronomous" oversight of our fellow spiritual travelers. Following Cassian's implication here, we could say that, insofar as human agents are organically bound one to another, the autonomous and exclusive reliance upon one's private moral conscience ultimately constitutes a violation of one's community. This is why, in Cassian's view, it always ends in moral and spiritual disaster.

LOVE AND *MIMESIS*

These currents of the Eastern monastic tradition also flow into the *oeuvre* of the aforementioned Maximus the Confessor (*c.* 580–662), though they are philosophically developed and manifested in a far more rigorously intellectual framework. Central to Maximus's moral theology and ascetic teaching is "love" or *agapē*, which figures prominently in his philosophical and dogmatic treatises as well as his ascetic writings.[54] Yet *agapē* is no mere private sentiment but constitutes the impetus and ground for moral practice as a whole, thereby suggesting that all moral judgment and orientation presuppose an awareness of one's community and the persistent presence of a real, tangible "other." In this way, Maximus retools the older Aristotelian paradigm, exchanging justice for love as the central and all-defining virtue.[55] Insofar as *agapē* is the chief virtue, narcissistic self-love, or *filautia*, is its inverse and the progenitor of all vice. As he demonstrates in one of his earliest works, *The Ascetic Life*, ascetic discipline should not be considered a private enterprise intended primarily for the sake of internal moral perfection.[56] Rather, its purpose is the effacement of *filautia* and the diachronic restoration of temporal and eternal relationships with the Creator and our fellow creatures. To quote the Confessor directly, "He who is unable to separate himself from the passionate yearning for material things shall neither love God nor his neighbor authentically."[57] Defining this activity in ontological terms, Maximus argues that divine love will eschatologically gather together the fragmented portions of human nature into a functional unity, existing as a single mode in solidarity of will and disposition.[58] If love is the metaphysical impetus for the pursuit

[52]Ibid.

[53]Ibid., 104.

[54]See Maximus's *Four Hundred Texts on Love*, in *The Philokalia*, vol. 2, trans. and ed. Kallistos Ware et al. (London: Faber and Faber, 1981), 48–113 and *Letter 2: On Love*, in *Maximus the Confessor*, The Early Church Fathers, trans. Andrew Louth (Abingdon: Routledge, 1996), 84–93. For a systematic account of Maximus's aretology and its foundations, see Demetrios Harper, *The Analogy of Love: St. Maximus the Confessor and the Foundations of Ethics* (Yonkers: St. Vladimir's Seminary, 2019), chap. 4.

[55]See Maximus's *Quaestiones ad Thalassium I* 40.60–70, *Corpus Christianorum, Series Graeca* 7, ed. C. Laga and C. Steele (Turnhout: Brepols, 1980), 269–71.

[56]*Liber asceticus*, 100–15, *Corpus Christianorum, Series Graeca* 40, ed. P. Van Deun (Turnhout: Brepols, 2000), 17. See also the introduction to the *Quaestiones ad Thalassium I* 380–90, 39–41.

[57]*Liber asceticus*, 100–110, 17. The translation is mine.

[58]Maximus, *Letter 2: On Love*, 88.

of virtue and the ground of morals, *mimēsis* or "imitation" is the pedagogical means by which it is recognized and acquired. Creatively appropriating and redeploying principles from the Areopagitic corpus, the Confessor establishes the *imitatio Christi*, the existential imitation of Christ and his virtues, as the epistemological core of his moral theology.[59] True followers of Christ imitate his mode of existence, disclosing through their lives and examples divine virtue. The lives and modes of these "exact imitators" are in turn imitated and imparted unto the morally immature.[60] When viewed through a contemporary lens, we might say that Maximus's view entails the recognition of autonomy as a point of departure for human agency. However, the ideal of *agapē* calls for the voluntary sacrifice of autonomy and private moral space for the sake of moral co-governance and a reciprocal unity of wills, which depends upon the concrete examples of the Incarnate Logos and his "exact imitators."

CONCLUSION

To reiterate the introduction to this chapter, the typical Orthodox Christian, insofar as he or she is informed by both ancient and contemporary paradigms, tends to hold moral views that are mutually contradictory. While this brief chapter has focused on sources that are particularly venerable from an Eastern Christian standpoint, this moral schizophrenia is at least potentially an embedded psychological feature of anyone who participates in a confession strongly informed by the Patristic writings of the late antique and medieval periods. As such, the foregoing aspires to encourage all, regardless of confessional affiliation, to reconsider their ethical presuppositions and to further facilitate a reflexive evaluation of their views of ethical governance and its relationship to the "other." This may indeed encourage some to abandon the last vestiges of traditional conceptions in favor of a consistent post-Enlightenment viewpoint. However, some may be encouraged to follow the likes of Greek Orthodox philosopher Christos Yannaras and repudiate contemporary notions of autonomy in favor of what he terms a "Eucharistic ethos."[61] Either way, it is an evaluation that goes beyond the purview of a few intellectual specialists, possessing real import for all moral agents who would regard themselves as Christian.

SUGGESTED READINGS

Bingaman, Brock, and Bradley Nassif, eds. *The Philokalia: A Classic Text of Orthodox Spirituality*. Oxford: Oxford University Press, 2012.

Harper, Demetrios. *The Analogy of Love: St. Maximus the Confessor and the Foundations of Ethics*. Scholarly Monographs Series 3. Yonkers: St. Vladimir's Seminary, 2019.

---

[59]See *St. Maximus the Confessor's Questions and Doubts* III, 1, trans. Despina Prassas (DeKalb: Northern Illinois Press, 2010), 156–7; *Ambiguum*, 48.6, in *On Difficulties in the Church Fathers II*, Dumbarton Oaks Medieval Library 29, trans. and ed. Nicholas Constas (Cambridge: Harvard University Press, 2014), 218–20.

[60]*Liber asceticus*, 635–65, 73–4.

[61]Yannaras, *The Freedom of Morality*, 89–106. Neil Messer discusses Yannaras's repudiation of moral autonomy in his chapter, "Christos Yannaras's *The Freedom of Morality* and Western Christian Ethics," in *Christos Yannaras: Philosophy, Theology, Culture*, ed. Andreas Andreopoulos and Demetrios Harper (Abingdon: Routledge, 2018), 77–88. In the same volume, see Demetrios Harper, "The Purpose of Morality in the Theological Schema of Christos Yannaras," 56–74, for a critique of Yannaras's notion of a "Eucharistic ethos."

Torrance, Alexis. *Repentance in Late Antiquity: Eastern Asceticism and the Framing of the Christian Life c. 400–650 CE*. Oxford: Oxford University Press, 2013.

Woodill, Joseph. *The Fellowship of Life: Virtue Ethics and Orthodox Christianity*. Washington, DC: Georgetown University Press, 1998.

Yannaras, Christos. *The Freedom of Morality*, trans. Elizabeth Briere. Crestwood: St. Vladimir's Seminary, 1984.

CHAPTER FOURTEEN

Christian Ethics and Other Religions

DAVID A. CLAIRMONT

The language of "other" or "otherness" appears prominently in nearly every academic field in the modern academy, from psychology and philosophy to anthropology and political science.[1] Classifying a person, an idea, a practice, or a community as "other" means that one is making a judgment about what is different from oneself or one's own community. At the same time, consciously labeling an "other" is also making a claim about what one calls one's "own" and therefore is saying something about oneself and how one understands one's commitments and community. Speaking of "others" can be put to good or evil political purposes (one can, e.g., claim a responsibility to care for "others," but one can also shun that responsibility or even claim that what does not appear like oneself "does not belong"). Yet the reality of negotiating what is "self" and what is "other" is also a natural process, as in the case of personal differentiation in human child development.

In religious terms, the language of "other" or "otherness" has been used historically in two related ways. The most frequent use designates as "other" what is different from the religion one claims as one's own (one's "home tradition" as some have called it).[2] A less frequent but no less significant use of "other" language is directed at the religious and ethical life itself, wherein "other" or "otherness" is taken to be a feature of all talk about God and of the human quest to live a good life in right relation with God and other people. Each religion in its own way has dealt with this twofold perplexity of otherness: to see what is different than oneself as other while at the same time seeing the unknown or even the unknowable in oneself.

[1]For example, on the topic of "otherness" in psychology and psychoanalysis, see Jean Laplanche, *Essays on Otherness* (New York: Routledge, 1992); and Dominique Scarfone, "A Brief Introduction to the Work of Jean Laplanche," *International Journal of Psychoanalysis* 94, no. 3 (2013): 545–66; in philosophy, see Emmanuel Levinas, *Totality and Infinity: An Essay on Exteriority*, 2nd ed., trans. Alphonso Lingis (Pittsburgh: Duquesne University Press, 1991); and Paul Ricoeur, *Oneself as Another*, trans. Kathleen Blamey (Chicago: University of Chicago Press, 1992); in anthropology, see Nigel Rapport, "Anthropology through Levinas: Knowing the Uniqueness of Ego and the Mystery of Otherness," *Current Anthropology* 56, no. 2 (2015): 256–64; in political science, see Louiza Odysseos, *The Subject of Coexistence: Otherness in International Relations* (Minneapolis: University of Minnesota Press, 2007); and Odysseos, "Prolegomena to Any Future Decolonial Ethics: Coloniality, Poetics and 'Being Human as Praxis'," *Millennium: Journal of International Studies* 45, no. 3 (2017): 447–72; and in theology, see Miroslav Volf, *Exclusion and Embrace: A Theological Exploration of Identity, Otherness, and Reconciliation* (Nashville: Abingdon, 1996).

[2]See, e.g., Francis X. Clooney, SJ, "Thomas Merton's Deep Christian Learning across Religious Borders," *Buddhist-Christian Studies* 37 (2017): 49–64.

If one were to give a summary statement of what Christianity is, we might consider the following as a rough approximation: Christianity is a community of sinners who seek the mercy of God as the root of loving relations that give birth to justice. Similarly, if one were to say in short what ethics is, we might begin with the following preliminary definition: Ethics is the critical reflection on one's own life and the lives of others.[3] To qualify ethics as Christian (the title of this volume refers to "Christian ethics") emphasizes either that the critique originates from the Christian community, in its sources and its aspirations, or that it is carried out by the Christian community, in its arguments and activities.

A helpful way to begin thinking about Christian ethics and other religions is to consider how the sources of Christian ethical thinking—frequently enumerated as scripture, reason, experience, and tradition—help us to understand the similarities and differences between Christian ethics and the forms of ethics in other religious traditions.[4] In what follows, I examine one typology of interreligious interactions that comes from the Roman Catholic tradition and then explore how each of the four sources of Christian ethics just mentioned helps us better to understand these different kinds of interaction.

In its 1991 document *Dialogue and Proclamation*, the Pontifical Council for Interreligious Dialogue (PCID) described four forms of interreligious dialogue:

1. The *dialogue of life*, where people strive to live in an open and neighborly spirit, sharing their joys and sorrows, their human problems and preoccupations.
2. The *dialogue of action*, in which Christians and others collaborate for the integral development and liberation of people.
3. The *dialogue of theological exchange*, where specialists seek to deepen their understanding of their respective religious heritages, and to appreciate each other's spiritual values.
4. The *dialogue of religious experience*, where persons, rooted in their own religious traditions, share their spiritual riches, for instance with regard to prayer and contemplation, faith and ways of searching for God or the Absolute.[5]

The PCID articulated a rationale for dialogue shared by many Christians that values the truth, goodness, and beauty of other religions.

> These traditions are to be approached with great sensitivity, on account of the spiritual and human values enshrined in them. They command our respect because over the centuries they have borne witness to the efforts to find answers "to those profound mysteries of the human condition" ... and have given expression to the religious experience and they continue to do so today.[6]

---

[3]For a more extensive discussion of this understanding of ethics and of the perplexity of otherness, see William Schweiker and David A. Clairmont, *Religious Ethics: Meaning and Method* (Malden: Wiley-Blackwell, 2020).

[4]These sources are generally recognized across a range of Christian denominations as significant and worth engaging despite sometimes serious debate about the meaning and relative priority of each source and the relationship among them. Among the sources consulted by all the contributors to this volume, see Charles E. Curran, *The Catholic Moral Tradition Today: A Synthesis* (Washington, DC: Georgetown University Press, 1999), 48–55; Curran, *The Church and Morality: An Ecumenical and Catholic Approach* (Minneapolis: Augsburg Fortress, 1993), 29–39; Margaret Farley, *Just Love: A Framework for Christian Sexual Ethics* (New York: Continuum, 2006), 182–206.

[5]Pontifical Council for Interreligious Dialogue, *Dialogue and Proclamation* (Vatican City: Libreria Editrice Vaticana, 1991), § 42. This document references earlier Catholic discussions of these same forms of dialogue.

[6]Ibid., § 14.

Each religion articulates its own way of confronting the "mysteries of the human condition" and thereby provides an opening to think about religious others while acknowledging the "otherness" involved in the human struggle to live well within a search for the fullness of religious truth. Pairing the four forms of dialogue with the four sources of ethics yields the following chart:

	Scripture	*Tradition*	*Reason*	*Experience*
Dialogue of Life				
Dialogue of Action				
Dialogue of Theological Exchange				
Dialogue of Religious Experience				

In the remainder of this chapter, I develop four examples, each of which illustrates a Christian encounter with another tradition (Buddhism, Native American/First Nations, Islam, and Daoism) to examine each of the four forms of dialogue listed above. In each case, I will highlight one of the sources while also referring to the other three sources, noting how that particular form of dialogue and the source in question illuminate the similarities and differences between Christianity and other religions on ethical matters.[7]

DIALOGUE OF LIFE—A BUDDHIST-CHRISTIAN ENCOUNTER

The dialogue of life is the most basic form of dialogue, present in everyday conversations about human experience and about the joys and sorrows that characterize the human condition. Ethics, we said earlier, is a critical reflection on the ways of living found in one's own community and in other communities concerning what people ought to seek (the good) and how they ought to seek it (the right). This critical reflection may be understood as an exchange between reason and experience, and both of these sources are central to Buddhist and Christian examinations of the good life, although how these sources relate to each other and to the other two sources—scripture and tradition—are decidedly different in these two traditions.

As Christianity takes its name from the relationship of the followers of Jesus as Christ ("anointed") to the person and his teachings, so Buddhism takes its name from the relationship of the followers of Siddhartha Gautama as Buddha ("enlightened") to the person and his teachings. Buddhism no less than Christianity is a religion of experience, yet each employs reason in different ways to consider and critique experience. The heart of the Buddha's teaching focuses on the experience of the world as a place of constant change and on the mental states that occur as one seeks either attachment to or detachment from the things of this world. Many Buddhist texts focus on the Buddha's

[7]Each form of dialogue is illustrated with a comparison between Christianity and one other religious tradition. It is certainly true that each form of dialogue could be illustrated by pairing Christianity with one of the other traditions examined here or another tradition not invoked in these comparisons could also be used. These comparisons are intended to illustrate certain similarities and differences between Christianity and other traditions and also to accentuate certain aspects of the four forms of dialogue. In this short chapter, not every source will be given equal space in each example. There are important differences in how each tradition understands the four sources, although I maintain that there are rough analogues to each of the sources in the traditions examined here. The first example will be somewhat longer than the rest but only to offer a clearer picture of how the sources work together in each form of dialogue.

own attempt to see deeply the nature of reality and to formulate practical guidance to help other people attain that same insight. The Buddha emphasized that religious insight has a deeply experiential component and that it is the experience of life that leads one to seek a higher wisdom about its ultimate meaning.[8] For the Buddha, religious insight begins with questions about the nature of human experience, in particular its quality of being fundamentally subject to change, beset by desire, and ultimately unsatisfactory. One should, the Buddha advocated, scrutinize any wisdom received from one's teachers and especially from religious authorities. Yet the Buddha did believe that he was a reliable teacher because what he taught (the *Dharma* ["truth" or "law"]), which culminated in the path leading to enlightenment and the elimination of suffering, could be verified by anyone who followed the path he discovered. He also taught that the monastic community he formed which would carry on his teachings was itself also a reliable source of deep wisdom and practical guidance. These "three jewels" of Buddhist veneration—the person of the *Buddha*, his teaching (*Dharma*), and the monastic community (*Saṅgha*)—are the central objects of Buddhist belief and may be said to constitute a kind of Buddhist tradition. To become a Buddhist, one must at minimum "take refuge" in these three jewels and, in so doing, combine one's reason and experience with tradition.[9]

Both Christianity and Buddhism, we might say, are experiential religions but in different ways. Whereas Christianity foregrounds the Christian's *experience of the person of Jesus* as central to faith in Jesus as Christ, Buddhism foregrounds the Buddhist's *experience of what the person of the Buddha experienced* as central to committing oneself to Buddhist teachings. Reason interacts with each kind of experience, but in each case differently. In the Christian case, the content of Christian faith includes beliefs about God and that the world depends on God for its existence. It also includes beliefs about human beings—what they are at their deepest level and what is their purpose as creations of a loving God. The content of these beliefs is not contrary to reason and many have argued, both within and outside the Christian community, that belief in some kind of divine being and the basis for and content of morality can be rationally demonstrated. Christians hold that God revealed to humanity additional knowledge about the divine nature (e.g., that God is best expressed as a Trinity of persons in loving relation with each other), which, many Christians hold, does not contradict reason but goes beyond what reason can know without divine assistance. In this sense, scripture as communicating what has been revealed about the divine nature and divine activity has been passed down to the human community but depends on experience and reason for its interpretation. It contains something of the experience of the early community as it struggled to formulate what it had learned about God through revelation. In this way, scripture forms a tradition of experience and of reasoning about God.

In the Buddhist case, we have rough structural equivalents to each of the four sources, but each source differs markedly in its content. Many Buddhists believe in divine beings, although the Buddha himself did not claim to be a god but rather sought the alleviation of the unsatisfactoriness of life through his own efforts. While it would not be proper to speak

[8]The relationship between faith and wisdom is complex in any religious tradition. In the Buddhist-Christian comparison, while we do find a useful comparison in the search for a wisdom rooted in experience, we do not find the same confidence in faith outside of trust in personal experience.

[9]The formulation of the "three jewels" is a canonical reference. See, for example, the Kālāma Sutta in the Aṅguttara Nikāya 65. *Numerical Discourses of the Buddha: A Translation of the Aṅguttara Nikāya*, trans. Bhikkhu Bodhi (Somerville: Wisdom, 2012).

of revelation in the Christian sense when speaking of the Buddha, there are texts which the Buddhist community has handed down to subsequent generations and which are revered as sacred because of the depth of insight they contain about what the Buddha understood to be the most profound human questions and the path he discovered for answering them. So we have a rough correlate in Buddhism to *scripture* in the Christian context.[10] We may speak of a Buddhist *tradition* as a commitment by Buddhists to the teaching preserved by the monastic community and applied for the benefit of each subsequent generation.

The basic shape of a Buddhist and Christian dialogue of life would begin with the shared human recognition that life in all its forms contains some element of struggle, both external (to survive and thrive in community with other people) and internal (since one's immediate desires, if fulfilled, do not always seem to be in a person's best interest). These struggles are the stuff of daily life, from the mundane challenges of daily labor to facing life-changing events and global catastrophes. Both Buddhists and Christians believe that scrutinizing small decisions and momentary states of mind with which we approach those decisions are foundational to living a good life.

DIALOGUE OF ACTION—A FIRST NATIONS-CHRISTIAN ENCOUNTER

Because Christians approach ethics as a constructive activity of doing what is good and not simply as an exercise in avoiding what is evil, they are necessarily involved in cooperative actions with other people who also seek the good. Yet often Christians have worked against the good of others, their liberation and authentic development, rather than cooperating with them to cultivate the true human flourishing of all. The first encounters between Christians and the indigenous peoples of the Americas were driven by commercial, political, and religious ambitions. European nations that sought economic and political advantage through exploration and commerce across the Atlantic also brought their Christian cultures with them. Often commercial explorations were given religious justification, so that commercial and military expansions were undertaken for putatively religious reasons: to preach Christianity, its beliefs and ways of life, to those who had not previously encountered it. Christian culture was often destructive to indigenous ways of life and did not include any real dialogue between the culture of the conqueror and the culture of the conquered, or if dialogue occurred it was for the purpose of understanding just enough about indigenous beliefs to try to counter them with Christian ones. The history of Christian presence among First Nations/Native Americans and the conversion of many to Christianity made it more difficult to preserve

[10]Across the various Buddhist traditions, there are a number of texts recording the words of the Buddha and the forms of life of the early Buddhist communities. Of the three main branches of Buddhism recognized today—the *Theravāda* (the "way of the elders"), the *Mahāyāna* (the "great vehicle"), and the *Vajrayāna* (the "diamond" or "thunderbolt" vehicle)—the earliest is the *Theravāda*, which is that form of Buddhism commonly practiced in the South and Southeast Asian countries of Sri Lanka, Burma/Myanmar, Thailand, Cambodia, and Laos. In terms of sacred writings, there are three main collections of writings (*Tipiṭaka* or "three baskets") which constitute the heart of the *Theravāda*: the *Suttapiṭaka*, which contains stories of the many events in the life of the Buddha and the discourses the Buddha gave to his early monastic community; the *Vinayapiṭaka*, which contains the code of conduct for the early monastic community and the stories of how those regulations came to be; and the *Abhidhammapiṭaka*, which is a detailed philosophical analysis of the nature of the Buddha's insight and a highly complex enumeration and categorization of the mental states arising on the way to the attainment of the highest insight wisdom.

indigenous cultures, including First Nation languages, stories, religious customs, and the integrity of the ways of life of indigenous communities on which indigenous thought and practice were based. Even so, there have been important historical examples and more recent developments of a real dialogue of action between Christianity and the religious ethics of many First Nations of the Americas.

The first example comes from the period of sixteenth-century colonization and settlement in the Americas. Two interrelated ethical issues arose during this period: the enslavement of native peoples by European colonizers and conversion of native peoples by colonial missionaries. As David Lantigua has documented, although the project of European colonialism had strong religious foundations from the time of its inception, Christian theologians were also strongly divided on the proper response to indigenous religious practices.[11] Some such as Juan Ginés de Sepúlveda (1490–1573 CE) argued that systems of servitude and enslavement could be justified through an argument that appealed to the responsibility of so-called higher cultures. Others, such as Bartolomé de Las Casas (1484–1566 CE), argued that the rights of indigenous peoples were rooted in the ability of all people to make free choices about the proper way to worship God, which was itself the basis of the natural right to be free from forced conversion and to have one's home and property respected. Tradition was invoked both in terms of theological precedent in how to interpret difficult cases (e.g., Augustine and Thomas Aquinas on appropriate means of conversion and the defensibility of servitude) but so too were claims about the natural law and whether reason apart from faith could offer a sufficient defense of the actions proposed. The experience on the part of some theologians, such as Las Casas, of the suffering endured by the indigenous people as a result of the *encomienda*-forced servitude system of which he was himself once a part, prompted a reevaluation of the tradition in light of new events and interpretations of scripture. As Lantigua explains, "For the theologians, the human capacity for God—expressed in the use of reason and receptivity to the faith—set the parameter for affirming the possessions and political sovereignty of Amerindian peoples."[12]

A second example comes from the somewhat more recent context of nineteenth- and early-twentieth-century educational initiatives for Native American/First Nation children by Christian missionaries in North America. From the 1850s onward, missionaries operated schools for Native American children, and in 1860, the Bureau of Indian Affairs began a series of government funded schools, beginning with the transformation of the military post Fort Simcoe in Yakima, Washington to an educational institution.[13] The first boarding school for Native American children was the Carlisle Indian School established in 1879 in Pennsylvania.[14] In many cases, from Carlisle onward, Native American children were removed from their homes and sent away to regional boarding schools, the purpose of which was to "Americanize" them through a Christian program of education. It was

---

[11]David M. Lantigua, "The Freedom of the Gospel: Aquinas, Subversive Natural Law, and the Spanish Wars of Religion," *Modern Theology* 31, no. 2 (2015): 312–37. See also David M. Lantigua, "The Image of God, Christian Rights Talk, and the School of Salamanca," *Journal of Law and Religion* 31, no. 1 (2016): 19–41; David M. Lantigua and David A. Clairmont, "Between Inculturation and Natural Law: Comparative Method in Catholic Moral Theology," *Journal of Moral Theology* 2, no. 2 (2013): 60–88.

[12]Lantigua, "The Image of God," 30.

[13]Albert Culverwell, "Stronghold in the Yakima Country: Fort Simcoe and the Indian War, 1856–59," *Pacific Northwest Quarterly* 46, no. 2 (1955): 46–51. See also Carolyn J. Marr, "Assimilation through Education: Indian Boarding Schools in the Pacific Northwest," unpublished paper, https://content.lib.washington.edu/aipnw/marr.html.

[14]Jessica Ruggieri Matthews, "Killing a Culture to Save a Race: Writing and Resisting the Discourse of the Carlisle Indian School" (PhD diss., George Washington University, 2005).

not until the passage of the Indian Child Welfare Act in 1978 that parents of Native American children could legally resist, without penalty, the removal of their children from their reservation homes and placement in non-reservation schools many miles away.[15]

Many of these early schools were focused on the removal of indigenous cultural influences from children for the sake of their assimilation into the expanding US culture which, as Roger Iron Cloud and Raymond Bucko observe, depended on a deeply ingrained belief in "cultural evolution" that ranked cultures according to the relative likeness to a European norm.[16] Yet there were some interesting exceptions that point to a dialogue of action across religious traditions. Donna Peterson has examined the legacies of three Catholic mission schools: St. Paul's Mission in Hays, Montana (with students from the Gros Ventre and Assiniboine tribes), St. Labre Indian School in Ashland, Montana (with students from the Northern Cheyenne and Crow), and St. Stephens Indian School in St. Stephens, Wyoming (with students from the Northern Arapaho and Eastern Shoshone tribes).[17] In some cases, worship at the mission churches changed and the construction of new churches reflected architectural and artistic elements of native culture. In other cases, Native American culture and especially language study appeared in revised curricula. At the St. Stephens Indian Mission School in the 1970s, to address growing financial need at the school, administrators, parents, and the wider community at the Wind River Reservation turned over control of the school from the church to the reservation community. While "the new owners are some 120 residents of the Wind River Reservation,"[18] as Peterson explains, the new directors of the school voluntarily retained Catholic religious instruction after 90 percent of surveyed families responded that they would like to see the religious instruction of the old mission school retained. Ninety-eight percent of registered families requested that the now-optional religious instruction under the new system be provided for their children because "the maintenance of a religiously centered value system is seen as far more favorable to Indian ways than the more 'modern' and secular system of the public schools."[19] A dialogue of action that acknowledged past injustice but also recognized shared values allowed the community to envision a new form of education for the next generation of Native American students.

DIALOGUE OF THEOLOGICAL EXCHANGE—A MUSLIM-CHRISTIAN ENCOUNTER

Dialogue among religions also occurs through more formal discussions among theologians, religious leaders, and other religious persons. A focus on scripture and tradition as sources

[15]A law passed by the Fifty-Second Congress of the United States in 1893 had established penalties, including withholding financial support, to parents who did not send their children to off-reservation schools when no equivalent education was available on the reservation. For more information, see *The Indian Child Welfare Act*, https://www.tribal-institute.org/lists/icwa.htm. For specific details of the law, see "USC 283: Regulations for Withholding Rations for Nonattendance at Schools," http://uscode.house.gov/view.xhtml?req=granuleid:USC-prelim-title25-section283&num=0&edition=prelim.

[16]Raymond A. Bucko, "Father Eugene Buechel, S.J. and the Lakota—Images and Imagination," *American Catholic Studies* 116, no. 3 (2005): 83–8. See also Roger Iron Cloud and Raymond Bucko, "Native American Children and Religion," in *Children and Childhood in American Religions*, ed. Don S. Browning and Bonnie J. Miller-McLemore (Piscataway: Rutgers University Press, 2009), 119–32.

[17]Donna Patricia Peterson, "Conflict, Tension, Strength: The History of St. Paul's Mission, St. Labre Indian School, and St. Stephens Indian School, 1884–Present" (PhD diss., University of New Mexico, 2015).

[18]Ibid., 185.

[19]Ibid., 187.

for ethical thinking is a useful example to understand how a dialogue of theological exchange happens. For example, both Islam and Christianity profess belief in one God, and both traditions base that belief on revelation preserved in the sacred texts of the Qur'ān and the Bible. However, as Ebrahim Moosa describes, the competing theological schools of medieval Islam model different ways of relating reason and revelation:

> The Mu'tazila promoted a doctrine of ethical objectivism in which reason and revelation were coeval. The Ash'arīs accepted discursive reason, but for them reason was always subject to the authority of revelation. Their position can be described as ethical subjectivism. For the Mu'tazila, reason is capable of deciding if something is good or detestable; the Ash'arīs believe that something is good or bad because the divine discourse declares it to be so.[20]

The preferred way of relating these sources has implications for Islamic religious ethics.

Among the most difficult topics raised in a Muslim-Christian dialogue of theological exchange are the Christian doctrine of the Trinity and status of Jesus and Muḥammad. On the former, as Oddbjørn Leirvik argues,

> Islamic orthodoxy seems to rule out any induction from human experience to theology. The basis of theology is the divine, revealed Word of the Qur'ān, considered to be un-created in the theological orthodoxy that came to be victorious in the formative period of Islam. In this orthodox perspective, then, Christ as the uncreated, living Word of God in Christian tradition is the religious equivalent not to Muḥammad, but to the divine revelation of the Qur'ān.[21]

On the latter, the centrality of God's oneness (*tawḥīd*) is difficult to reconcile with the Christian formulation of the Trinity as the truth of the inner life of God; yet, as David Burrell argues,

> the difficulties which the early Christians had in formulating anything like a "trinitarian doctrine" all turned on respecting the *shema*: "God our God is one!" So what Christians really claim is that God's revelation in the person of Jesus opened his followers to a view of the inner life of the one God, a view which challenges theologians to a proper articulation.[22]

In both examples, we see a dynamic relationship between scripture—both what it says and the kind of source it is taken to be—and the tradition of interpretation of those texts that views indeterminate meanings in the textual tradition as a prompt for creative theological and ethical thinking. The dialogue of theological exchange may produce areas of agreement and clarify theological disagreements, but it may also have important consequences for ethical matters. For example, in Christian ethical debates about the proper relationship between natural law and divine command ethics, the Muslim-Christian dialogue may produce important insights into the relationship between faith and reason in the ethical dialogue between these two traditions. It also may caution

---

[20]Ebrahim Moosa, "Islamic Ethics?," in *The Blackwell Companion to Religious Ethics*, ed. William Schweiker (Malden: Blackwell, 2005), 239–40. As Moosa notes, "Muslims affiliated to the Sunnī branch follow the Ash'arī school or other analogous ones, while those affiliated to the Shī'a branch developed their own type of rationality, also borrowing some ideas from the Mu'tazila doctrine," 240.

[21]Oddbjørn Leirvik, *Images of Jesus Christ in Islam*, 2nd ed. (New York: Continuum, 2010), 5.

[22]David B. Burrell, "Trinity in Judaism and Islam," in *The Cambridge Companion to the Trinity*, ed. Peter C. Phan (Cambridge: Cambridge University Press, 2011), 358.

against judgments about controversial moral issues drawn from textual traditions that are still the subject of much debate.

DIALOGUE OF RELIGIOUS EXPERIENCE— A DAOIST-CHRISTIAN ENCOUNTERS

As the PCID noted above, a "dialogue of religious experience" happens "where persons, rooted in their own religious traditions, share their spiritual riches, for instance with regard to prayer and contemplation, faith and ways of searching for God or the Absolute."[23] Yet understanding what religious experience is, or even experience more generally, is one of the most complex topics in the study of religion. For example, we might ask whether experience is the kind of thing we ever access apart from our linguistic and cultural frameworks. If experience is something that is always to some extent linguistically mediated, then our experience would be so radically particular that we could not connect with others on the level of experience, whether we are speaking of everyday or religious experience.[24] Can there be such a thing as a dialogue of religious experience if the cultural and linguistic features of religions are so drastically different? A good place to see this difficulty is through a comparison between Christianity and the traditional Chinese religion of Daoism.

Along with Buddhism, Confucianism, and "traditional patriarchal religion" focusing on propitiation of deities and veneration of ancestors, Daoism is held as one of the main religious traditions of China.[25] As Roger Ames and Henry Rosemont explain, early Chinese religions focused on family reverence (*xiào*), the centrality of which qualifies other virtues that were also held to be central to the Confucian way such as proper conduct (*rén*), appropriateness (*yì*), ritual propriety (*lǐ*) and wisdom (*zhì*).[26] The origin of these virtues came in the more explicitly religious discourse of the pre-Confucian period (i.e., in the dynasties prior to 550 BCE), wherein "[a] good king sought to serve and gain the favor of Heaven in order to control important events in the human realm."[27] The mandate of heaven (*tianming*) had a complex relationship to the "way" (*dao*) that governed heaven and earth. Early Daoist texts such as the *Daodejing* and the *Zhuangzi* (fourth to third centuries BCE) also focused on cultivating forms of virtue (*de*) but responded to the natural world and also the social order as it reflected the mandate of heaven. However, these Daoist texts also reacted against the Confucian focus on social norms and ritual piety, which were not seen always to mirror the *dao* in their conceptualization or execution. As Philip J. Ivanhoe describes, the stories of sagacious people in the *Zhuangzi*

---

[23]Pontifical Council for Interreligious Dialogue, *Dialogue and Proclamation*, § 42.

[24]This discussion of experience roughly parallels the debates between George Lindbeck and David Tracy on the nature of religious experience, as in Lindbeck's contrast between the experiential-expressive model (Bernard Lonergan and Tracy) and the cultural-linguistic model (Lindbeck's preferred model). See David Tracy, *Blessed Rage for Order: The New Pluralism in Theology* (Chicago: University of Chicago Press, 1996); and George A. Lindbeck, *The Nature of Doctrine: Religion and Theology in a Postliberal Age* (Louisville: Westminster John Knox, 1984), esp. 30–40.

[25]Zhongjian Mou, "A Study of Chinese Traditional Patriarchal Religion," *Studies in Chinese Religions* 2, no. 4 (2016): 331–65.

[26]Roger T. Ames and Henry Rosemont Jr., "Were the Early Confucians Virtuous?," in *Ethics in Early China: An Anthology*, ed. Chris Fraser, Dan Robins, and Timothy O'Leary (Hong Kong: Hong Kong University Press, 2011), 21.

[27]Philip J. Ivanhoe, "Origins of Chinese Ethics," in *The Blackwell Companion to Religious Ethics*, ed. William Schweiker (Malden: Blackwell, 2005), 376.

> follow the hidden seams deep in the pattern of nature and by so doing are able to lead highly effective yet frictionless lives. Such individuals accord with rather than collide with the things and events they encounter in life and manage to pass through them all without incurring or causing harm ... Following Heaven, according with the natural, is the overriding criterion for determining which actions are appropriate. There is a pattern in Nature and the Daoist sage follows it.[28]

How might a Christian and a follower of traditional Daoism be in dialogue about religious experience in light of the four sources of ethics? Living virtuously by conforming one's life to the impersonal *dao* does not sound like an experience of "prayer and contemplation, faith and ways of searching for God or the Absolute," although a search for the appropriate way to conform one's actions to the *dao* does seem to provide an initial analogue. Experience as a religious source for moral reasoning is a bit more difficult to discern here since conformity of earthly rule to heaven's mandate seems to focus more on the human exemplars rather than divine action. Moreover, the *dao* is not, as it is for the Confucian tradition, clearly transparent and controllable through rule and ritual action. The *Daodejing* reveals that "the Dao is eternal and without a name. It is [In its] original state it is inconspicuous. Still the world cannot subdue it. If princes and kings could keep up with it, all things would come on their own to obey them."[29] An experience of it depends on reason (virtue is found in knowledge of the *dao* and living according to that knowledge) but moves beyond reason, and its tradition is not that of the Confucian sage but of the contemplative enigma. The Christian experience of God is neither of these and there is no easy equivalence between *dao* and Christian views of God, although the virtuous life in both cases requires reflection on the experience of the world and proving the source of that experience. Returning to our earlier point, religious experience has the quality of otherness, both when comparing across traditions but even within a single tradition.

CONCLUSION: INTEGRATING LIFE, ACTION, THEOLOGICAL EXCHANGE, AND EXPERIENCE

Each form of dialogue introduced above calls upon the four sources of theological and ethical reflection in different ways, depending on which of the sources is foregrounded in each particular interreligious exchange. Some might prioritize scripture and tradition as sources in an ethical dialogue that leads with theological exchange, while others might prioritize experience and reason where the forms of dialogue move from a dialogue of life to a dialogue of experience. In each case, Christian encounters with other religions provide occasions whereby each participant in dialogue may examine anew the meaning of these sources in their tradition and the ways the tradition has integrated these ethical sources in response to new challenges. Since interreligious encounter is seldom if ever scripted, such dialogue often introduces the humbling recollections of history. Perhaps one of the greatest promises of Christian ethical engagement with other religions is its

[28]Cited in Yong Huang, "Respecting Different Ways of Life: A Daoist Ethics of Virtue in the Zhuangzi," *Journal of Asian Studies* 69, no. 4 (2010): 1052–3.

[29]*Daodejing* 32, trans. Horst J. Helle, *China: Promise or Threat? A Comparison of Cultures* (Boston: Brill, 2017), 74.

ability to help religions come to terms with the "other" elements of their theological and ethical histories—a frequently opaque but vitally necessary dialogue across time.

SUGGESTED READINGS

Ames, Roger T., and Henry Rosemont Jr. "Were the Early Confucians Virtuous?" In *Ethics in Early China: An Anthology*, ed. Chris Fraser, Dan Robins, and Timothy O'Leary. Hong Kong: Hong Kong University Press, 2011.

Clooney, Francis X., SJ. "Thomas Merton's Deep Christian Learning across Religious Borders." *Buddhist-Christian Studies* 37 (2017): 49–64.

Ivanhoe, Philip J. "Origins of Chinese Ethics." In *The Blackwell Companion to Religious Ethics*, ed. William Schweiker. Malden: Blackwell, 2005.

Lindbeck, George A. *The Nature of Doctrine: Religion and Theology in a Postliberal Age*. Louisville: Westminster John Knox, 1984.

Moosa, Ebrahim. "Islamic Ethics?" In *The Blackwell Companion to Religious Ethics*, ed. William Schweiker. Malden: Blackwell, 2005.

Tracy, David. *Blessed Rage for Order: The New Pluralism in Theology*. Chicago: University of Chicago Press, [1975] 1996.

PART THREE

Issues, Applications, and Twenty-First-Century Agenda for Christian Ethics

Section A: Politics and Society

CHAPTER FIFTEEN

Politics and Political Theology

ELIZABETH PHILLIPS

This chapter finds itself in a section with the title "Christian Ethics and Political Issues." Like most syllabi and textbooks in Christian ethics, this volume is divided into methodological sections and "issues" sections, with "political" as one type of issue alongside medical/bioethical, sexual, economic, justice, and environmental issues. Nothing is wrong with this way of organizing subjects in Christian ethics, *per se*, and I have often written and taught within similar frameworks. Done well, it can be clarifying. However, it can also be argued that situating the political as a type of "issue" in ethics is not without its problems—problems that bring into relief some of the differences between the frameworks of Christian ethics and Christian political theology.

Framing of the political as an ethical issue bears the distinct marks of (1) modern academic divisions of disciplines based on the sciences, where theology is the "pure" work of "theory" and politics is one among several areas where "social ethicists" do the work of "application," and (2) modern decisionistic and quandary-based approaches to ethics in which the horizon for consideration of politics is a set of problems that need solutions. I will take each of these in turn.

POLITICS AS APPLICATION

The volumes of St. Thomas Aquinas's *Summa Theologiae* are neatly divided into three parts. For contemporary learners and practitioners of Christian ethics or systematic theology, the order of these three sections may seem strange. First comes his treatment of theology proper: the Trinity and the doctrine of Creation. Second comes his moral theology. And third is Christology, the church, and the sacraments. Why are the doctrinal or dogmatic topics straddling the moral or ethical topics in this way? This was an intentional assertion by Aquinas that moral theology is not separate from doctrine. As D. Stephen Long has noted, "His discussion of Christian morality in the second part of his *Summa Theologiae* both depends upon the first part, where he sets forth the doctrines of the Trinity and creation, and requires the third part on Christology, church and sacraments for its completion."[1] Many scholars of Aquinas have commented upon the irony and inaccuracy of the practice of studying the second part in isolation from the others, as if

[1]Duane Stephen Long, "Moral Theology," in *The Oxford Handbook of Systematic Theology*, ed. John Webster, Kathryn Tanner, and Iain Torrance (New York: Oxford University Press, 2007), 457.

he wrote the second part for the ethicists and the other two parts for the theologians. Aquinas, obviously, knew no such distinction, and he intentionally positioned his work against the medieval precursors of such distinctions.

Interestingly, even if we do pursue the inevitably detrimental and anachronistic attempts to divide his work into dogmatic and moral theology, if we then further attempt to isolate his political work, we find it stretches across the parts of the *Summa*.[2] The political is not a topic or issue isolated to the second part. As with the classical philosophers and the early theologians before him, in the work of Aquinas any consideration of what is good and ultimate will necessarily be infused with considerations of the political. An attempt to isolate the political thought of most patristic authors would be equally detrimental and anachronistic. The political is a thread woven throughout the letters, apologies, sermons, and treatises of early Christianity.

Sharp distinctions between ethics and systematic theology arose in the modern era, and most prominently in Protestant theology. Even the idea of "moral theology" would become associated with Catholicism as opposed to the "Christian ethics" of Protestantism. Protestant ethics would eventually be further divided into theological ethics and social ethics, in which the Bible and Christian tradition remained valid sources for the former but the social sciences became the guide for the latter. By the end of the twentieth century, Protestants (particularly in America) who were studying or teaching Christian approaches to the political were most likely doing so under the heading of "social ethics" and with methods informed substantively by social science. Joining with social science in applying frameworks (and philosophical assumptions) from the modern scientific method, Christian ethics too was divided into its pure or fundamental pursuits (theological ethics) and its applied pursuits (social ethics). The social ethicist's work was to identify social problems, understand them through social-scientific methods, and offer remedies to them through the application of Christian principals and norms derived from pure theology. Critics of this pure/applied division note how not only subject matter but also source material was wrenched apart in such disciplinary separation; so-called theological ethics has often neglected experience as a source and so-called social ethics has often neglected both scripture and tradition.

Protestants were not entirely alone in drawing such distinctions. From the Council of Trent until the present, there has been an official distinction in Catholicism between dogmatic or fundamental theology and moral theology. However, these were framed in relation to Aristotelian distinctions between intellectual and moral virtues instead of pure and applied scientific methods. The sources of reason, scripture, and tradition were equally important for both discourses, and experience would come to be recognized as a source in more recent versions of both. From the late nineteenth century there also developed a distinct tradition of Catholic Social Teaching (encyclicals as well as other official teaching and conciliar documents and statements), Catholic Social Thought (wider treatment of the issues of social teaching by theologians and lay people), and Catholic Social Tradition (diverse forms of activism, organizing and policy-making related to social teaching). Whereas politics became the purview of the social ethicist in Protestantism, Catholic learners and teachers of Christian approaches to the political might do so under any one of this wide variety of headings, or a combination thereof.

---

[2]See, e.g., the excerpts in *Aquinas: Political Writings*, trans. and ed. R. W. Dyson (Cambridge: Cambridge University Press, 2002).

One consequence of these disciplinary and methodological divisions, most prominently in Protestant social ethics, but doubtless too in some forms of moral theology and Catholic Social Thought/Tradition, was that the political largely ceased to be a category for constructive, systematic, or doctrinal work—the kind of work done in pure or fundamental disciplines. Practitioners became far less concerned—if at all—with theologies of the political or politics of the theological and focused instead on political "issues" in ethics and the moral life. Questions of the meaning and nature of human sovereignty and its relation to the sovereignty of God, and questions of the place of the political in creation, for examples, become eclipsed by the pursuit of identifying and addressing social problems.

POLITICS AS PROBLEM

Christian ethicists very rightly should, of course, seek to identify and address social problems. This is not in question. However, a good deal of the game of moral theology has already been given away if the political is always already perceived in terms of problems to be solved. Conceptualizing the political as an issue to be addressed by practitioners of methods of application not only divides social ethics from theology, splitting the four sources of Christian ethics between its pure and applied forms instead of holding them in conversation with one another, but also sets the parameters of the discourse as one of social problems that need moral solutions. These social problems may be correctly identified and meaningfully addressed, and they may be exactly the sorts of problems to which Christian ethicists' attention should be turned; my argument here is not to question the *validity* of the social-problem-solving-discourse but to question its *sufficiency*. Focusing *solely* on the status quo of readily identifiable problems and seeking to come to decisions about their status and/or remedies can prevent the Christian ethicist from understanding the subject theologically, removing from access crucial theological resourcing for the entirely valid task of addressing problems.

Both the identification of politics as a problematic issue and the agenda of making decisions about the quandaries it poses constrain the moral imagination as well as praxis. One aspect of retrievals of the virtue tradition in recent Christian ethics has been an awareness of the limitations of quandary-based frameworks, which have largely been determined by approaches that assume that there is a clear set of quandaries facing the ethicist, and the task is employing either deontological or consequentialist methods for making these difficult decisions. Advocates of virtue ethics not only critique deontology and consequentialism on their own terms but also note how the employment of the two methods in late modern Christian ethics results in ethical enquiry being overdetermined by the difficult/exceptional instead of the everyday, the quest for the best method of reasoning instead of the best way of life, the focus on doing and not being, and the removal of teleology and other wider questions of meaning and ultimacy from moral reasoning. The possible subjects of enquiry into the political as well as methods, sources, and horizons for political enquiry are limited in all these ways when the political is reduced to quandaries.

The same can be said of any number of topics that are likewise treated as the "issues" (read: problems to be addressed by "applied ethics"). Two examples will illustrate the insufficiency of the issues-and-problems framework. Consider the framing of medical ethics. There is a conventional set of issues that Christian ethicists consider: reproduction, contraception, and abortion; euthanasia, assisted suicide, and end-of-life; medical resources and access; and new medical technologies. The vast majority of the conversation is framed as: here is a professional medical practice; should Christians be for it or against it? And what method will you employ in order to decide? Theological questions about the meaning of health and suffering, life and death, interdependence and the common good, sexuality and procreation are marginalized. Not only should such questions be pursued in their own right, apart from the ethical, but attention to them is also crucial for good moral reasoning in medical ethics.

Consider, as another example, the female body in Christian ethics. In light of feminist and womanist insight it becomes clear that the female body only ever enters into most Christian ethics in relation to problems to be solved; women's bodies become "issues" in sexuality, reproduction, contraception, and biotechnology. Both the agency of women and the wonder and dignity of the female body are eclipsed. Our moral horizon, limited by the social-problem-solving discourse has only furthered the objectification of women, making our bodies sites of debate instead of agency and sites of concern instead of awe.

Situating politics as a set of issues—problems to be addressed through applied or social ethics—is equally detrimental to our theological understandings and praxis of the political as it has been in these two examples. One of the ways in which this has come to light in recent decades, and I argue one important way to recover some of what has been lost in our disciplinary silos and decisionistic methods, is through the work of political theology.

THE RISE OF POLITICAL THEOLOGY

Critiques of social ethics as an applied social science and of ethics as quandary-based decisionism are by no means new. Both critiques have been central to the work of prominent theologians on both sides of the Atlantic since at least the 1980s. Importantly, during these decades social science theory and practice have also taken post-structuralist turns, giving rise to internal critiques of the positivism in which these disciplines arose and first influenced Christian ethics. Perhaps it should come as no surprise, then, that interest in political theology as a discipline has become so prominent in the wake of the ascendency of critiques of the positivism and structuralism of early social science, and of the limitations of ethics-as-quandary. More scholars and students are crossing previously strict disciplinary boundaries and coming to political theology from both theology and ethics (not to mention philosophy of religion and religious studies, or the many versions of political theology outside the theological disciplines).

Political theology, broadly defined, has always been part of Christian theology. Using this sense of the phrase, Cavanaugh and Scott offer a good guiding definition:

> Theology is broadly understood as discourse about God, and human persons as they relate to God. The political is broadly understood as the use of structural power to organize a society or community of people ... Political theology is, then, the analysis and criticism of political arrangements ... from the perspective of differing interpretations of God's way with the world.[3]

Throughout scripture and the traditions of Christian theology, political theology has been a consistently central task. It emerged as a distinct discourse in the twentieth century,

---

[3]Peter Scott and William T. Cavanaugh, eds., *The Blackwell Companion to Political Theology* (Oxford: Blackwell, 2007), 2.

by the name "political theology" in Germany as theologians grappled with Christian complicity in the Third Reich and its Holocaust, but also in Latin America as theologian-priests faced down the church's complicity in poverty and political oppression, and in North America as Black and women theologians began to bring their voices to the fore. Emerging as distinct movements across the West in the mid-twentieth century, these discourses eventually converged and inspired later discourses (such as public theology, various liberative and contextual theologies, and various postliberal theologies) which came to be studied and practiced under the umbrella title, "political theology." Around the turn of the twenty-first century, new courses, textbooks, academic journals, and professional groups began to appear, more firmly establishing political theology as a distinct academic discipline.

But is political theology the answer? Can political theology open up the restricted horizons of politics as an issue in Christian ethics? Or, perhaps the first question is whether the diagnosis offered here should be answered by pointing to better ways of doing ethics. Do we need political theology or do we just need better moral theology? My answer is yes. We need, and many Christian ethicists and moral theologians currently do, better ethics than I have described above (as is surely evident in this volume). And I join with many proponents of virtue ethics who would argue that the critical and constructive retrieval of virtue employed through the use of all four sources of Christian ethics goes a long way toward overcoming the limitations of approaching politics as a set of problematic issues. However, I also argue that political theology is something distinct from politics in Christian ethics and that both political theology and Christian ethics are needed disciplines and tasks.

Ted Smith has argued that ethics is limited to a horizon of "moral obligations that play out within immanent networks of cause and effect."[4] He argues that although the "immanent frame" of ethics may be able to "accommodate many kinds of moral reasoning"—including deontology, consequentialism, and virtue—it cannot readily imagine, recognize, or accommodate that which exceeds the frame and/or is exceptional to it.[5] Ethicists are often caught within this immanent frame, arguing about whether or not this or that action or practice can be justified within it—seeming to be on opposite sides of something but actually arguing two sides of the same frame.

Political theology is not a remedy in that somehow we will agree more about politics if we do political theology instead of ethics. Rather, political theology can, and indeed must, exceed the ethical frame and can therefore reveal what is being missed within it, what it cannot account for, and what questions are worthy of enquiry beyond moral justification. However, although political theology may exceed the ethical, it cannot erase the ethical. Remember, as we have already established in this chapter, early and medieval Christian theology did not divide the two tasks or understand them to have differing practitioners. Contemporary constructs of academic discipline and specialization may separate Christian ethics and political theology, and we must understand them as distinct tasks, but we must not conceive of them as tasks to be chosen between. Both ethical work in politics by moral theologians and the work of political theology are needed. Consider, as an example, the specific case of violence: how it can be, is, and should be treated in Christian ethics and political theology.

---

[4]Ted A. Smith, *Weird John Brown: Divine Violence and the Limits of Ethics* (Stanford: Stanford University Press, 2015), 4.
[5]Ibid., 5.

VIOLENCE IN CHRISTIAN ETHICS AND POLITICAL THEOLOGY

The vast preponderance of Christian ethicists' thinking, writing, and teaching on the subject of violence focuses on a single question (and subsidiary questions thereof): whether or not Christians can justifiably employ violent means. Thus, courses and textbooks in Christian ethics focus primarily on debates concerning just war and pacifism and perhaps (in the American context especially) capital punishment. There is a quandary to be solved: Christians have a duty to apply both the norms of love and justice, but we do not agree on whether the application of these norms rules out the use of violence, or sometimes tragically requires violence as a last resort, or positively commands violence for preservation of the social order. The ethicist and the student of ethics are meant to choose a side, to determine their own solutions to the violence quandary.

Much influential work has already been done on how the debate between just war and pacifism has obscured the common theological ground of peace and taken focus away from practices of peacemaking.[6] This is one—and a particularly crucial—way of opening up the moral imagination beyond the binary options of just war and pacifism, and to my mind it is one of the most important topics in teaching Christian ethics. This is one example of how better practice of ethics goes a long way toward answering the limitations I have described. However, the introduction of peacemaking theories does not necessarily move us beyond the ethical quandary; it *may* only add another option for addressing it.

By contrast, entirely different questions are on the table in political theology. For example, why is it that virtually all Christian theology has assumed that the state can and indeed must employ violent means? Whether this assumption is framed as a pre-lapsarian intention for human government or a post-lapsarian requirement of sin, and whether it is argued that Christians can or cannot themselves be the executioners of state violence, state violence *per se* was virtually unquestioned in Christian tradition until the late twentieth century. Political theologians question state violence and ask why Christian tradition (including its traditional pacifist strands) has not questioned this deep-seated assumption.

For some political theologians, this work begins with the politics of doctrines of creation, eschatology, and anthropology. Is violent conflict part of our natural state, due to original sin? Is violence a consequence of the fall which is overcome in Christ, and if so, what does that mean this side of the eschaton? Some political theory, both explicitly theological and not, situates itself in a trajectory of thought from St. Augustine through Luther then Hobbes and Machiavelli. This trajectory sees the basic condition of the world and humanity as violence that government must control in order to minimize. John Milbank famously argued in *Theology and Social Theory* for an "ontology of peace" in Augustine, which insists that the world and humanity were created in, and move toward a future of, peace.[7] In Milbank's argument, this is a theopolitical conclusion, not an ethical conclusion; it is an argument about the character of human sociality, not about just war versus pacifism.

---

[6]Especially Glen Stassen, *Just Peacemaking: Transforming Initiatives for Justice and Peace* (Louisville: Westminster John Knox, 1992); Glen Stassen, ed., *Just Peacemaking: Ten Practices for Abolishing War* (Cleveland: Pilgrim, 2004); Walter Wink, *Engaging the Powers: Discernment and Resistance in a World of Domination* (Minneapolis: Fortress, 1992).

[7]John Milbank, *Theology and Social Theory: Beyond Secular Reason* (Oxford: Blackwell, 1990 and 2006).

A different theopolitical enquiry can be seen in the work of William Cavanaugh, whose political theology has been particularly influential in opening up questions about state violence apart from questions of just war versus pacifism. In *Theopolitical Imagination*, Cavanaugh argued against the idea that the modern, secular state rescued Western civilization from the inherent violence of religion, questioning both the historical accuracy of this narrative as well as identifying its alternative soteriology—a false theology in which the state is seen as the savior of the people.[8] In *The Myth of Religious Violence*, Cavanaugh extended this argument significantly, identifying and arguing against the myth that religion is a transhistorical and transcultural feature of human life, essentially distinct from "secular" features such as politics and economics, which is peculiarly dangerous and inclined to violence and therefore must be controlled by restricting religious access to public power.

The myth, Cavanaugh argues, depends on three assertions (or assumptions): (1) that there is something called "religion" that has existed across time in all human cultures and is separable from other facets of human life such as politics, (2) that "religion" is peculiarly prone to violence and/or that the preponderance of human violence has its genesis in "religious" impulses, and (3) that the modern, secular state is the antidote to "religious violence" (asserted either in terms of the rise of the secular nation-state saving the West from the chaos of religious wars, or in more recent terms of the spread of Western, liberal secularism as able to save the West from the religious violence of Islam).

The problem with this narrative is not that it ascribes violent behavior to "religious" people, groups, and movements—Cavanaugh does not by any means deny that Christians, among others, do indeed act violently. According to Cavanaugh, however, "The problem with the myth of religious violence is not that it condemns certain kinds of violence, but that it diverts moral scrutiny from other kinds of violence. Violence labeled religious is always reprehensible; violence labeled secular is often necessary and sometimes praiseworthy."[9]

The issues at stake are, resolutely, always and already both theological and political. The myth enshrines a counter-soteriology, giving the secular state savior status; and the myth authorizes violence instead of reducing it.

> In foreign policy, the myth of religious violence serves to cast nonsecular social orders, especially Muslim societies, in the role of villain. They have not yet learned to remove the dangerous influence of religion from political life. Their violence is therefore irrational and fanatical. Our violence, being secular, is rational, peace making, and sometimes regrettably necessary to contain their violence. We find ourselves obliged to bomb them into liberal democracy.[10]

M. Shawn Copeland's work in political theology demonstrates how questions and discourses outside the ethical frame help us look beyond the state in our political considerations of violence. As Maureen O'Connell has noted, "Copeland clearly stands in the tradition of post-Holocaust German political theology" so that for her, "[f]aith is not merely a private experience, but a profoundly political one animated by the dangerous memory of Christ." Yet she " 'troubles' the Euro-centric waters of political theology from

---

[8]William T. Cavanaugh, *Theopolitical Imagination* (New York: T&T Clark, 2002).

[9]William T. Cavanaugh, *The Myth of Religious Violence: Secular Ideology and the Roots of Modern Conflict* (New York: Oxford University Press, 2009), 121.

[10]Ibid., 4.

her location at the crossroads of sexism and racism," realities that have "marked her own body in a way that the Holocaust never marked the German Christian bodies of Metz or Moltmann or Soelle."[11]

In *Enfleshing Freedom*, Copeland considers the "wounding, then, terrorizing of the Black body through commodification, abuse, and lynching," relating these experiences to the "dangerous memory" of the crucifixion and our formation in the Eucharist to see clearly and to transform the violence of the world.[12] Copeland names the violence of the slave trade's removal of Black subjectivity through the erasure of social and familial bonds, objectification of persons-as-commodities, high expectations of both performance and morality (without the resources of decent nutrition and living conditions, much less the dignities of education or freedom), as well as the obvious physical violence of the transport, selling, raping, and beating on which the trade depended. She goes on to describe, in devastating historical narratives, the continued terrorizing of Black bodies after slavery in the era of lynching. The demand of this history of violence, Copeland insists, is solidarity—not a vague, liberal feeling of empathy, but a specifically Eucharistic solidarity:

> Our daily living out, and out of, the dangerous memory of the torture and abuse, death and resurrection of Jesus Christ constitutes us as his own body raised up and made visible in the world … Eucharist is a countersign to the devaluation and violence directed toward the exploited, despised black body … In spatial inclusion, authentic recognition, and humble embrace of different bodies, Eucharistic celebration forms our social imagination, transvalues our values, and transforms the meaning of our being human, of embodying Christ.[13]

Key to Copeland's argument is that the Eucharist is not thereby reduced to the ethical. She reminds us that "the crucial social consequences of Eucharist can never overtake the real presence the Eucharist effects." The heart of Eucharistic solidarity and resistance to racist violence is not located in human action, but in divine action. "In our presence, the Son of Man gathers up the remnants of our memories, the broken fragments of our histories, and judges, blesses, and transforms them. His Eucharistic banquet re-orders us, re-members us, restores us, and makes us one."[14] Eucharist is *the* performative liturgy; the slave traders and the lynch mobs performed idolatrous anti-liturgies.

Lest the ethicists begin to worry that such political-theologizing detracts from or discourages concrete political praxis, we only need to consider Copeland's enactment of solidarity in relation to the Black Lives Matter movement. In a call to action to her fellow political theologians, urging us to take concrete actions in relation to racism, she wrote,

> We do political theology because we want to collaborate in a most fundamental way in healing and creating relations in history and society. We want to coax forward a different sociality. Our contribution is to think and rethink, in light of the divine promise of an eschatological future, the manner and effects of the fragile yet resilient webs of relations that constitute the reality in which we live. Our work is to open that sociality to the desire, hope, and loving expectation of something (even Someone) transcendent.[15]

---

[11]Maureen O'Connell, "Disturbing the Aesthetics of Race," in *Enfleshing Theology: Embodiment, Discipleship, and Politics in the Work of M. Shawn Copeland* (Lanham: Fortress Academic, 2018), 234.
[12]M. Shawn Copeland, *Enfleshing Freedom: Body, Race, and Being* (Minneapolis: Fortress, 2010), 110.
[13]Ibid., 127.
[14]Ibid., 128.
[15]M. Shawn Copeland, "Memory, #BlackLivesMatter, and Theologians," *Political Theology* 17, no. 1 (2016): 2.

Perhaps we would not articulate our reasons for doing Christian ethics much differently. My argument is not that as Christian ethicists and political theologians we are doing unrelated tasks for opposing reasons, rather that we can perform these two discourses within related yet differing frameworks, drawing on related but differing sources, aiming toward related yet differing horizons. Christian theology continues to need the immanently normative frames of the ethicists as well as to be opened to that which exceeds them in the practices of theopolitics.

SUGGESTED READINGS

Cavanaugh, William T. *Theopolitical Imagination*. New York: T&T Clark, 2002.

Cavanaugh, William T. *The Myth of Religious Violence: Secular Ideology and the Roots of Modern Conflict*. New York: Oxford University Press, 2009.

Cavanaugh, William T. *Migrations of the Holy: God, State, and the Political Meaning of the Church*. Grand Rapids: Eerdmans, 2011.

Copeland, M. Shawn. *Enfleshing Freedom: Body, Race, and Being*. Minneapolis: Fortress, 2010.

Copeland, M. Shawn, and Elisabeth Schüssler Fiorenza, eds. "Violence against Women," *Concilium*. Maryknoll: Orbis, 1994.

Hovey, Craig, and Elizabeth Phillips, eds. *The Cambridge Companion to Christian Political Theology*. New York: Cambridge University Press, 2012.

CHAPTER SIXTEEN

Human Rights

WILLIAM O'NEILL, SJ

In the wake of the Holocaust, human rights emerged as a *cri de coeur* against what the Universal Declaration of Human Rights (UDHR, 1948) called "barbarous acts which have outraged the conscience of [hu]mankind."[1] Enshrined in the Universal Declaration, subsequent covenants, conventions, and regional charters, human rights have become, says Elie Wiesel, the "worldwide secular religion" of modern, pluralist polities.[2] Yet modern "rights talk" remains deeply contested. For many communitarian and postmodern critics, natural or human rights are merely the dubious heritage of bourgeois liberalism, the stepchild of Enlightenment rationalism. Apologists for a divine right order dismiss such rights as the coin of a secular realm;[3] while for others, the very idea of rights is "ineliminably religious."[4] In this chapter, I will explore the differing uses of rights rhetoric, considering (1) the characteristic features of modern human rights discourse, (2) the complex genealogy of rights, with particular attention to Christian sources, and (3) several of the salient criticisms of our rights talk in light of contemporary Christian interpretations that temper appeals to reason with scripture, tradition, and the concrete experience of victims and their advocates.

THE SENSE OF RIGHTS

As we shall see, the genealogy of human rights precludes any rigid definition. Yet, certain characteristic features of modern usage reveal a family resemblance. Thus, in general, we may understand rights as one's entitlement (as the subject of rights) to a social good (the object of rights), which we may enjoy, assert, or enforce (the nature of rights) with respect to some individual or group (the bearer of the correlative duty or respondent of rights), in virtue of generally recognized warrants and backing (justification). Human rights appear, then, to be a species of moral *claim*-rights, as opposed to mere privileges, entitling moral agents to certain social goods by virtue of their common humanity.[5] Such rights

[1]"Preamble," in *Universal Declaration of Human Rights*, 1948, http://www.un.org/en/universal-declaration-human-rights/index.html.
[2]Elie Wiesel, "A Tribute to Human Rights," in *The Universal Declaration of Human Rights: Fifty Years and Beyond*, ed. Yael Daniele et al. (New York: Routledge, 1999), 3.
[3]Nicholas Wolterstorff, "Modern Protestant Developments in Human Rights," in *Christianity and Human Rights: An Introduction*, ed. John Witte Jr. and Frank S. Alexander (Cambridge: Cambridge University Press, 2010), 156.
[4]See Michael J. Perry, *The Idea of Human Rights: Four Inquiries* (Oxford: Oxford University Press, 1998), 11–41.
[5]Alan Gewirth, *The Community of Rights* (Chicago: University of Chicago Press, 1996), 8–13.

are logically prior to legislative enactment or juridical decision, even as they generate systemic imperatives for positive legal recognition.

Theoretical treatments of human rights vary with their interpretation of the subject—what properties or powers underwrite subjective rights claims—and the nature or comparative force of the rights claimed. We must, that is, determine which rights are accorded relative priority or deemed to be of paramount importance in cases of conflict with not only other rights but also customary practice or collective social aims. Certain rights may be inalienable or imprescriptible; but even in theories admitting exceptions, human rights are typically, in Ronald Dworkin's felicitous terms, regarded as "trumps" such that they bear a certain threshold weight against competing claims.[6]

The relative force or urgency of rights claims is, in turn, a function of their respective objects or the particular social goods claimed (e.g., whether civil-political liberties take precedence over rights to nutritional well-being or health care). Broadly speaking, "negative" rights elaborated in the International Covenant on Civil and Political Rights (ICCPR) comprise liberties from coercion, such as religious liberty, freedoms of speech and assembly, and so on; while "positive" rights in the International Covenant on Economic, Social, and Cultural Rights (ICESCR) specify entitlements to social goods such as nutrition, potable water, health care, education, employment, and so on. Theorists will sometimes speak of generations of rights, where civil political liberties constitute the first generation; economic, social, and cultural rights, the second generation; and collective or group rights (e.g., of indigenous peoples), the third. As claim-rights, moreover, human rights differ from mere juridical immunities inasmuch as they impose correlative duties, which may themselves be parsed as negative or positive. Thus, human rights claims generally obtain *in rem* in imposing negative duties of forbearance or noninterference upon all recipients whether persons or corporate entities (e.g., governments or institutions of civil society). Yet correlative duties may also enjoin positive measures of protection, provision, or aid which fall primarily upon social institutions.[7]

Finally, multiple variations are wrung on the backing of human rights, ranging from the secular, a priori grounding of Kantian morality to distinctively religious justifications of human dignity (our creation in the *imago dei*). Non-foundationalist warrants are likewise offered in pragmatic appeals to an overlapping consensus of cultural systems, customary convention, or political regimes. In international jurisprudence, the Universal Declaration affirms our common "faith in fundamental human rights," yet allows for differing, particular justifications of such rights in distinctive religious or philosophical traditions. Criticisms of human rights, as we shall see in the third section, question the cultural hegemony of liberal rights theory, the putative metaphysical foundations of rights, and the reductive secularism of modern rights talk.

A WESTERN GENEALOGY OF HUMAN RIGHTS

No moral injunction in the Hebrew Bible is more significant than that of "doing the right" in Covenant fidelity. The Decalogue, for instance, admonishes us to provide for the substance of many human rights as an expression of divinely sanctioned *sĕdāqāh* (justice) and *mišpāt* (righteousness). In a similar vein, other religious traditions enjoin comparable

[6]Ronald Dworkin, *Taking Rights Seriously* (Cambridge: Harvard University, 1978), xi.

[7]See Henry Shue, *Basic Rights: Subsistence, Affluence, and U.S. Foreign Policy*, 2nd ed. (Princeton: Princeton University Press, 1996), 35–64; Gewirth, *The Community of Rights*, 31–70.

responsibilities, even if what is believed to be objectively right is not explicitly parsed in terms of the jural relationships (claimant/respondent) implied by subjective right (*jus subjectivum*).[8] Recent historiography traces the origins of such subjective rights ("*jura* in the law of persons, of things, and of actions") to the corpus of classical Roman law (100 BCE to 250 CE).[9] With the recovery of Roman law in the late eleventh and early twelfth centuries, later jurists grounded subjective right in natural law (*jus naturale*), bequeathing us the concept of subjective natural right.

The developing *corpus juris* of medieval cannon law followed suit. *Jus subjectivum*, writes R. H. Helmholz, signified that "a lawful power could inhere in an individual, even a basic human right," albeit in a limited sense. Thus, in canon law, backed by the laws of nature, "the *jus sustentationis* meant that in times of extreme dearth, the poor could take from the available stock of property. They had a right to take enough to sustain themselves without being guilty of theft."[10] Further variations are worked on role of subjective rights with the elaboration of concordats, treaties, and charters from the eleventh to the sixteenth centuries, like the *Magna Carta* (1215), controversies regarding the natural right of property and Franciscan poverty, and the rise of nominalism in the fourteenth century. Still, further variations appear in Muslim and Jewish jurisprudence, informed by Roman law, from the eighth to the twelfth centuries. By the Renaissance, a new, secular note is sounded as poets and philosophers like Pico della Mirandola exalt the dignity and autonomy of the "new Adam."[11]

In his magisterial treatise, Brian Tierney contends that premodern uses of subjective natural rights betrayed little of the "atomic individualism" of the "more egotistical impulses of early modern capitalism." The use of subjective rights was not "necessarily opposed to the communitarian values of traditional societies. Nor was the idea dependent on any particular version of Western philosophy; rather it coexisted with a variety of philosophies, including the religiously oriented systems of the medieval era and the secularized doctrines of the Enlightenment."[12] Indeed, the myth of secular origins is belied by the distinctive religious uses of rights, not only in the major tributaries of the Protestant Reformation in the writings of Martin Luther, John Calvin, Thomas Cranmer, and Menno Simons but also in the neo-scholastic treatises of Bartolomé de Las Casas, Francisco de Vitoria, Fernando Vázquez, and Francisco Suárez.[13] Notable, especially in this novel inflection of Thomism, was Vitoria's defense of the natural rights of indigenous peoples in his *Relectio de Indis* and Las Casas's impassioned denunciation of the suppression of indigenous rights under the Spanish imperial rule. Yet for many a partisan and critic alike, it is a commonplace that natural or human rights are the currency of modernity—the coin of a "disenchanted" realm. Before considering distinctive religious

---

[8]See Wesley Hohfeld, "Some Fundamental Legal Conceptions as Applied in Judicial Reasoning," in *Fundamental Legal Conceptions as Applied in Judicial Reasoning: Essays by Wesley Newcomb Hohfeld*, ed. Walter Wheeler Cook (New Haven: Yale University Press, 1923), 35–64.

[9]Charles Donahue, "*Jus* in Roman law," in *Christianity and Human Rights: An Introduction*, ed. John Witte Jr. and Frank S. Alexander (Cambridge: Cambridge University Press, 2010), 67.

[10]R. H. Helmholz, "Human Rights in the Canon Law," in *Christianity and Human Rights: An Introduction*, ed. John Witte Jr. and Frank S. Alexander (Cambridge: Cambridge University Press, 2010), 101, 106.

[11]Giovanni Pico della Mirandola, *On the Dignity of Man; On Being and the One; Heptaplus*, trans. Charles Wallis, Paul Miller, and Douglas Carmichael (Indianapolis: Bobbs-Merrill, 1965).

[12]Brian Tierney, *The Idea of Natural Rights: Studies on Natural Rights, Natural Law and Church Law 1150–1625* (Atlanta: Scholars Press, 1997), 347.

[13]See Wolterstorff, "Modern Protestant Developments," 156.

contributions to contemporary human rights discourse, let us briefly consider what for many theorists remains the regnant paradigm.

With the eclipse of the divinely inspired common good in early modernity, the modern natural lawyers of the seventeenth and eighteenth centuries looked less to the finality (*telos*) of natural law, than to the natural convergence of rational (prudential) wills.[14] Indeed, natural law itself succumbs to the secularized doctrines of the Enlightenment. Adumbrated in Grotius, the disenchantment of modern natural law theory emerges clearly in the writings of Hobbes and Pufendorf.[15] In a nominalist vein, Hobbes opposes liberty as the "Right of Nature" (*jus naturale*) "to use [one's] power, as he will himself, for the preservation of his own nature," to the "Law of Nature (*lex naturalis*)," which "determineth, and bindeth." For stripped of Grotius's "natural sociability," it is "the foresight of their own preservation" that leads "men who naturally love liberty, and dominion over others," to submit to "that restraint upon themselves, in which we see them live in Commonwealths." Society is itself a grand artifice, "an artificial man" created by our mundane *fiat*.[16]

The Lockean strain of liberal rights theory, by contrast, envisions a more peaceable kingdom in our natural state. Locke grounds the civility of mores in our natural equality, from which springs "the obligation to mutual love." Yet the "law of nature" regulating our natural "state of liberty" turns less on Aquinas's (or Richard Hooker's) *common good* than the domain of individual, pre-political rights.[17] Indeed, private property becomes the regnant metaphor of rights, the *raison d'être* of the social contract. Rousseau, too, appeals to the social contract; yet, where the Hobbesian *pactum subjectionis* resolves the will of all into the will of one, Rousseau depicts the social bond (*lien social*) as the will's self-limitation. For it is only "with civil society" that we acquire "moral freedom, which alone makes man the master of himself."[18]

For Kant, the formal generality or "universal voice" of will is entirely *sui generis*: the will's transcendental freedom is itself the *ratio essendi* of the moral law. Freedom of the choice is internally limited by the autonomous "self-legislation" of *the rational will* so that rights are defined independently of scripture and tradition.[19] For critics, like Hegel, Kantian morality, arising from the "pure unconditioned self-determination of the will,"

[14]The "minimalist core of universal moral principles" of the modern school of natural law, writes Richard Tuck, rests not in the metaphysical *telos* of the common good but in the empirically demonstrable "desire for self-preservation." Richard Tuck, "The Modern Theory of Natural Law," in *The Languages of Political Theory in Early-Modern Europe*, ed. Anthony Pagden (Cambridge: Cambridge University Press, 1987), 117. Tierney, however, denies Tuck's contention that "Grotius had … converted the skeptical humanists' language of self-preservation into a language of *natural rights*" (Tierney, *Idea of Natural Rights*, 320–4).

[15]Cf. A. P. d'Entrèves assertion that the doctrine of natural law as "set forth in the great treatises of the seventeen and eighteenth centuries," from Pufendorf's *De Jure Naturae et Gentium* (1672) to Burlamaqui's *Principes du Droit Naturel* (1747) and to Vattel's *Droit des Gens ou Principes de la Loi Naturelle* (1758), "has nothing to do with theology … The self-evidence of natural law has made the existence of God perfectly superfluous." A. P. d'Entrèves, *Natural Law: An Introduction to Legal Philosophy*, 2nd ed. (London: Hutchinson, 1970), 55.

[16]Thomas Hobbes, *Leviathan*, in *British Moralists: 1650–1800*, vol. 1, ed. D. D. Raphael (Oxford: Clarendon, 1969), 38–9, 52.

[17]John Locke, *The Second Treatise of Government*, ed. Thomas P. Peardon (Indianapolis: Bobbs-Merrill, 1952), 4–6.

[18]Jean-Jacques Rousseau, *The Social Contract: Or, the Principles of Political Rights*, trans. Maurice Cranston (New York: Penguin, 1968), bk. 2, chap. 7, 84.

[19]Immanuel Kant, *Critique of Practical Reason*, trans. Lewis White Beck (Indianapolis: Bobbs-Merrill, 1956), 5 (pagination is that of the Prussian Academy Edition, vol. 5). See Immanuel Kant, *The Metaphysical Elements of Justice: Part I of the Metaphysics of Morals*, trans. John Ladd (Indianapolis: Bobbs-Merrill, 1965), 315–16 (pagination is that of the Prussian Academy Edition, vol. 6).

is but an "an empty formalism."[20] Once derived from the ethical ideal of the common good, concrete social bonds must now be constructed through the exercise of individual will. Kant's Romantic critics, such as Herder, thus bid us return to the concrete ethical life. The "rights of man," wrote Edmund Burke, were a "monstrous fiction," spawning anarchy, "false ideas and vain expectations," bringing "ruin" in their wake.[21] Jeremy Bentham, too, regarded rights as "anarchical fallacies" and as "simple nonsense: natural and imprescriptible rights, rhetorical nonsense,—nonsense upon stilts."[22] For Marx, the modern doctrine of rights merely enshrined the proprietary interests of the bourgeoisie.[23]

Recent historiography, noted above, reveals the complex genealogy of rights. Rights have not descended from Kant's empyrean, or even the "semantic revolution" Michel Villay discerned in Ockham's nominalist epistemology.[24] Yet the history of rights is also one of what Nicholas Wolterstorff calls "historical amnesia." When twentieth-century Protestant writers "refer or allude to a narrative of origins, that narrative is always the common secular-origins narrative," framed "as a story of decline."[25] Natural rights, that is, inevitably fall prey to the atomistic and agonistic political philosophies that emerged in the Enlightenment. In the wake of the French Revolution, a similar declensionist narrative underwrote papal rejection of rights. Pope Gregory XVI (1831–46) railed against modern liberties, and his successor, Pius IX (1846–78), proscribed religious liberty as a "crazed absurdity" (*deliramentum*). Strains of anti-modernism persisted in the pontificate of Leo XIII (1878–1903) and his successors, Pius X and Pius XI, even as their social encyclicals betrayed an emerging acceptance of natural or human socioeconomic rights.

Doctrine develops, even in the absence of explicit theoretical legitimation. The new and postwar world political order marked by the triumph of liberal democracies and the rise of state Communism led Pius XII (1939–1958), in J. Bryan Hehir's words, to take "the first steps to bring the church's teaching on political-civil rights in line with the socio-economic teaching" of his predecessors' encyclicals.[26] The pope's Christmas Addresses offered an initial rapprochement with liberal regimes in affirming a limited set of civil and political rights in a constitutional state. Progressively, modern rights were grafted onto the traditional stock of natural law until the full range of civil, political, and socioeconomic rights recognized in the Universal Declaration was incorporated into magisterial teaching in John XXIII's encyclical, *Pacem in terris*, in 1963. The sea change in Catholic social teaching, grounded in the seminal writings of John Courtney Murray, Pietro Pavan, and Jacques Maritain, comes to fruition with the critical recognition of a right to religious liberty in the Conciliar Declaration, *Dignitatis Humanae*, two years later.

In a characteristically irenic turn, Pope John XXIII and his successors resolve the seeming antinomy of personal rights and the common good: *Pacem in terris* glosses the

---

[20]G. W. F. Hegel, *Hegel's Philosophy of Right*, trans. T. M. Knox (Oxford: Oxford University Press, 1952), para. 135.

[21]Edmund Burke, *Reflections on the Revolution in France*, 1700, in *Works*, vol. 2 (London: Bohn's British Classics, 1872), 305–6, 412; cf. Burleigh Taylor Wilkins, *The Problem of Burke's Political Philosophy* (Oxford: Clarendon, 1967), 59–60, 109–10.

[22]Jeremy Bentham, *Anarchical Fallacies*, in *Works*, vol. 2 (Edinburgh: William Tait, 1843), 523.

[23]Karl Marx, "On the Jewish Question," in *The Marx-Engels Reader*, ed. Robert Tucker (New York: W. W. Norton, 1978), 43.

[24]Tierney, *Idea of Natural Rights*, 13–42.

[25]Wolterstorff, "Modern Protestant Developments," 156.

[26]J. Brian Hehir, "The Modern Catholic Church and Human Rights: The Impact of the Second Vatican Council," in *Christianity and Human Rights: An Introduction*, ed. John Witte Jr. and Frank S. Alexander (Cambridge: Cambridge University Press, 2010), 117.

premodern, perfectionist teleology of *Mater et Magistra* (depicting the common good as "the sum total of those conditions of social living, whereby [we] are enabled to achieve [our] own integral perfection"[27]) in deontological terms of the "rights and obligations" implied by the "natural dignity" of conscience. "It is agreed that in our time," says Pope John, "the common good is chiefly guaranteed when personal rights and duties are maintained."[28] Where earlier human dignity was circumscribed in the metaphysical teleology of a hierarchically stratified, sacral state, dignity now emerges as the very hermeneutical touchstone of political legitimacy. We have, in a sense, come full circle as the Catholic Church embraces the modern discourse of human rights proclaimed in the Universal Declaration, which drew upon the *Bogota Declaration of the Rights and Duties of Man* from less than a year before (1948), which was itself informed by the earlier encyclical tradition. Neither was the rapprochement merely notional. John Paul II and his successors, Benedict XVI and Francis, proved to be ardent defenders of human rights, in the heritage of Las Casas.[29]

Faith in dignity, deriving from creation in the *imago dei*, is no less a leitmotif of mid-to-late twentieth-century Protestant rights discourse—even if, as Wolterstorff observes, a fully developed theological rationale was wanting. Thus, the inaugural Assembly of the World Council of Churches in Amsterdam (1948) affirmed, "We are profoundly concerned by evidence from many parts of the world of flagrant violations of human rights ... [T]he churches ... must work for an ever wider and deeper understanding of what are the essential human rights if men are to be free to do the will of God."[30] Recent Protestant theological appropriations of "rights talk" have gone far to remedy our "historical amnesia," including, notably, Wolterstorff's own agapist justification and David Gushee's appeal to the sacredness of life. Further contributions by Desmond Mpilo Tutu, Arthur J. Dyck, Jürgen Moltmann, Max Stackhouse, and so on join an ecumenical litany, including Catholic interpretations by J. Brian Hehir, David Hollenbach, Linda Hogan, Ignacio Ellacuría, Bénézt Bujo, Aquiline Tarimo, and so on.

CRITICISMS

Much more might be said, and such a brief treatment as this is necessarily limited. It would be remiss, however, not to address several salient criticisms of our modern lingua franca. For what Jack Donnelly describes as the hegemonic discourse of human rights remains problematic.[31] Indeed, pretensions to an integral and comprehensive dispensation of rights were quickly banished by the Cold War's separation of what the Universal Declaration had united: civil political liberties in the ICCPR vied now with social, economic, and cultural rights in the ICESCR. Postmodern and decolonial criticism recalls Marx's earlier critique of individual rights abstracted from the ensemble of social relations. Makau Mutua objects

[27]Pope John XXIII, *Mater et Magistra* (Vatican City: Libreria Editrice Vaticana, 1961), § 65.
[28]Pope John XXIII, *Pacem en terris* (Vatican City: Libreria Editrice Vaticana, 1963), § 60.
[29]See Mary Ann Glendon, "Catholicism and Human Rights," Marianist Award Lecture, University of Dayton, 2001, https://ecommons.udayton.edu/uscc_marianist_award/7/.
[30]*Report of the Church and the Disorder of Society*, WCC First Assembly, Amsterdam, 1948. Quoted in Robert Traer, *Faith in Human Rights: Support in Religious Traditions for a Global Struggle* (Washington, DC: Georgetown University Press, 1991), 21.
[31]See Jack Donnelly, *Universal Human Rights in Theory and Practice*, 3rd ed. (Ithaca: Cornell University Press, 2013), 55–7.

to the UDHR's "bias and exclusivity,"[32] while critics like Jean-François Lyotard regard the very "demand for [universal] legitimation" as itself a symptom "of cultural imperialism." The discourse of rights is finally revealed as but one of many local narratives, *petits recits*, whose justification rests only in the "pragmatics of their own transmission."[33] And so, says Richard Rorty, the "emergence of the human rights culture" owes "nothing to increased moral knowledge, and everything to hearing sad and sentimental stories."[34]

Directed principally against the secular, Enlightenment paradigm, such criticisms are telling, yet not decisive. To be sure, only a cursory response can be offered here, but the genealogy of rights rehearsed above belies the cultural hegemony of secular liberal theory. Indeed, the richer dignitarian strain of rights in the Universal Declaration recalls the complex origin of modern subjective rights in "a variety of philosophies, including ... religiously oriented systems."[35] Rights talk, to be sure, may betray exclusivity and bias—neglecting both pre-modern and postmodern, non-Western uses. And yet, to follow Rorty in fixing the sense of rights by the "hyperindividualism" of bourgeois liberal use[36] is tacitly to concede its hegemony—denying the fecundity of non-Western translations. Might we not rather learn from the pragmatics of actual discourse? For a richer, more communitarian use of rights "from below" emerges in the US civil rights movement, *Las Madres de la Plaza de Mayo* in Argentina, and in victims' testimony in the South African Truth and Reconciliation Commission (TRC). In their struggles, victims invoke human rights in a Gramscian vein—venturing, in Edward Said's words, "interpretations of those rights in the same place and with the same language employed by the dominant power," disputing "its hierarchy and methods," elucidating "what it has hidden," and pronouncing "what it has silenced or rendered unpronounceable."[37]

Here, rights do not so much suppress our native tongues in a grand metanarrative, as let victims speak. Rights, we may say, function as a deep grammar, not only of dissent against crimes that outrage the conscience of humanity but also of weaving social narratives anew.[38] Testimony evokes what was systemically effaced. "Now through the Truth and Reconciliation Commission," writes Tutu, victims "would be empowered to tell their stories, allowed to remember and in this public recounting their individuality and inalienable humanity would be acknowledged." Preserving the conditions or capabilities of such discursive agency, the use of rights in the TRC, says Tutu, exhibited the "dignity and humanity of those who were cruelly silenced for so long."[39]

---

[32]Makau Mutua, as quoted in Mary Ann Glendon, *A World Made New: Eleanor Roosevelt and the Universal Declaration of Human Rights* (New York: Random House, 2001), 224. Mutua's address was given at the Human Rights Policy Conference, sponsored by the Belfer Center of the Kennedy School of Government of Harvard University, November 4, 1998; see also Makau Mutua, *Human Rights: A Political and Cultural Critique* (Philadelphia: University of Pennsylvania Press, 2002).

[33]Jean-François Lyotard, *The Postmodern Condition: A Report on Knowledge*, trans. G. Bennington and B. Massouri (Minneapolis: University of Minnesota Press, 1984), 27.

[34]Richard Rorty, "Human Rights, Rationality and Sentimentality," in *The Politics of Human Rights*, ed. Obrad Savić (New York: Verso, 1999), 71, 78.

[35]Tierney, *Idea of Natural Rights*, 347.

[36]Mary Ann Glendon, *Rights Talk: The Impoverishment of Political Discourse* (New York: Free Press, 1991), x, xii, 171–83.

[37]Edward Said, "Nationalism, Human Rights, and Interpretation," *Raritan: A Quarterly Review* 12, no. 3 (1993): 26–51, 45–6. Cf. Antonio Gramsci, *Selections from the Prison Notebooks*, trans. Quentin Hoare and Geoffrey Nowell Smith (New York: International Publishers, 1971).

[38]See Ludwig Wittgenstein, *Philosophical Investigations*, 3rd ed., trans. G. E. M. Anscombe (New York: Macmillan, 1968), pt. 1, paras. 111, 373, 496–7, 664.

[39]Desmond Mpilo Tutu, *No Future without Forgiveness* (London: Rider, 1999), 32–3.

Now such a performative use of rights need not be justified apodictically, by pure reason alone. Neither are rights prediscursive properties of sovereign selves, squatting outside history. In a Habermasian vein, it suffices that *we* recognize, pragmatically, the implicit "grammatical" conditions of discourse in testimony, aiming at persuasion rather than coercion. Such a pragmatic use of rights is a clearing for distinctively religious appropriations. For we do not speak a grammar, but grammatically, so that basic human rights must be narratively embodied, configuring our particular narrative traditions, many of which are ineliminably religious. Indeed, Christians, Buddhists, Hindus, Confucians, Muslims, Jews, indigenous believers, and other religious persons and communities *have* embraced human rights rhetoric, inscribing the grammar of rights in their distinctive traditions and scriptures. Such meditating traditions, in turn, provide not only ultimate justification for our "faith in fundamental human rights" but also rich interpretative repertories (narratives, parables, tropes, etc.) inspiring social mobilization.[40] In the words of Jon Sobrino,

> All through history, humanity has felt itself to be in the presence of something called the holy, or the sacred. It may have been religious or it may have been secular, and it has varied with time and place, although we could indicate elements of a common substrate. In our own age, there can be little doubt that the defense of human rights represents for many of us something sacred—something that makes ultimate demands on us and holds out the promise of salvation.[41]

SUGGESTED READINGS

Donnelly, Jack. *Universal Human Rights in Theory and Practice*, 3rd ed. Ithaca: Cornell University Press, 2013.

Gewirth, Alan. *The Community of Rights*. Chicago: University of Chicago Press, 1996.

Hogan, Linda. *Keeping Faith with Human Rights*. Washington, DC: Georgetown University Press, 2015.

Tierney, Brian. *The Idea of Natural Rights: Studies on Natural Rights, Natural Law and Church Law, 1150–1625*. Atlanta: Scholars, 1997.

Witte, John, Jr., and Frank S. Alexander, eds. *Christianity and Human Rights: An Introduction*. Cambridge: Cambridge University Press, 2010.

Wolterstorff, Nicholas. *Justice: Rights and Wrongs*. Princeton: Princeton University Press, 2008.

---

[40]For such a pragmatic justification, see my *The Ethics of Our Climate: Hermeneutics and Ethical Theory* (Washington, DC: Georgetown University Press, 1994).

[41]Jon Sobrino, *Spirituality of Liberation: Toward Political Holiness*, trans. Robert R. Barr (Maryknoll: Orbis, 1988), 105.

CHAPTER SEVENTEEN

Migration

ELIZABETH COLLIER

While there have always been people "on the move," the phenomena of migration are some of the most critical areas of human concern at this time in history. Tens of millions of people are displaced from their homes and *hundreds of millions* are living in a location other than the place of their birth, due to circumstances outside of their control.[1] Current global crises that contribute to migration flows are projected to worsen and the numbers of displaced people only to increase in the coming years. These will be the result of everything from political instability to climate change, aging populations with low replacement birth rates but high standards of living, and continued globalization of business without consistent flows of labor.[2] The push and pull factors of migration can be difficult to fully comprehend because they are a result of the complex interplay of economic, political, historical, environmental, religious, and other factors. Complicating this is the milieu within which migration is encountered: the deep-seeded biases, lack of understanding and fears of those in the pass-through or receiving communities, as well as the immigration laws, border enforcement, and rhetoric of all of the communities from, through, and to which people move.

With these complexities, limitations, and challenges in mind, there is much work for Christian ethicists to do. In keeping with the format of this volume, this entry briefly describes where the field of Christian migration ethics currently is in the areas of scripture, tradition, reason, and experience, and suggests directions for future work.

SCRIPTURE

There are extensive resources in scripture for ethical reflection on migration. Being on the move or in exile is a central motif throughout the Hebrew Bible and is also important in key events in Jesus's life. The injunctions regarding how to treat those on the move or resettling are consistent and numerous. The push/pull factors for why different figures, families, and groups were on the move throughout scripture (God's command, famine, exile, brutal dictator, regional conflict, enslavement, etc.) often correlate in varying degrees to the phenomena experienced by many people today. The experience of being a migrant is a central element of salvation history.

---

[1]International Organization for Migration, *Global Migration Indicators Report 2018*, https://www.iom.int/global-migration-trends.

[2]From climate change alone, by 2050 there are projected to be between 25 million and 1 billion displaced people. International Organization for Migration, *Migration, Climate Change and the Environment*, https://www.iom.int/complex-nexus#estimates.

Generally speaking, when Christians appeal to scripture for guidance on migration-related issues, more often than not they recount a well-known story of an important figure who is either "on the move" or encountering someone who is, along with the corresponding command or "obvious" message regarding the requirement for people to welcome the stranger. The Hebrew Scriptures contain many of the most prominently referred to stories or passages. For instance, although Cain's punishment requires wandering, he is protected. For Abraham and Sarah, they heed God's call to move, encounter famine and foreign powers in their travels, and they offer hospitality to the three strangers who visit them. Isaac, Jacob, Ruth, and Naomi are all on the move for different reasons and various parts of their stories are often referred to. The Exodus is an obvious, predominant narrative with many themes to be explored, and the experience of the Israelites in Egypt is highlighted repeatedly. There is the important Leviticus command to "love thy neighbor as yourself" (9:18), and the oft-cited directive: "When an alien resides with you in your land, you shall not oppress the alien. The alien who resides with you shall be to you as the citizen among you; you shall love the alien as yourself, for you were aliens in the land of Egypt: I am the Lord your God" (Lev. 19:33-34). There is also the prominent mantra of "the widow, the orphan, and the alien" cited to indicate the care needed for those who are without the necessary relationships in the social structures of the time (e.g., Deut. 10:17-19).

The commands relating to how to treat the foreigner or stranger are repeated more often in scripture than commands on any other issue, except those regarding the supremacy of God. One scholar argues that this repetition was because people needed to be constantly reminded that the "other" in their midst was not a danger to the homogenous community.[3]

In the New Testament, the focus for migration-related guidance is on two sets of citations. First is the important motif of the Holy Family as the paradigmatic migrant family. They are "on the move" at the time of Jesus's birth for the census. After his birth they flee to Egypt to avoid Herod's slaughter and, as a result of fear of returning to where they came from, they ultimately settle in Nazareth. Matthew 25 is also central, particularly in light of the serious ramifications for one's salvation if one is going to hear, "I was a stranger and you did not welcome me" (v. 43).

Scriptural citations are often used in one of two ways. First, people use them to validate the rationale of some people's need to migrate today, by showing the extent to which some of the central figures in Jewish and Christian history had to move for similar reasons. Second, people use the citations to explain how people who are migrating should be treated in light of what is gleaned from the scriptural references. It is unusual for anything outside of scholarly writings to go beyond a simple recounting or quoting of these stories. For instance, the United States Conference of Catholic Bishops (USCCB) has a well-run, up-to-date website for immigration issues called justiceforimmigrants.org. There are church documents, educational resources, public policy statements, photo galleries, advocacy information, and detailed resources for migrants on a variety of important issues. On the "Bible" tab, however, there are four brief scriptural citations, where only a line from the Bible is listed, with no exegesis, commentary, or thematic exploration.[4]

---

[3]W. Gunther Plaut, "Jewish Ethics and International Migrations," *International Migration Review* 30, no. 1 (1996): 20.

[4]United States Conference of Catholic Bishops, *Justice for Immigrants: We Are One Family under God*, https://justiceforimmigrants.org/home/news/community-engagement-resources/about-us/catholic-social-teaching/bible/.

There is much work to be done by Christian ethicists for considering what scripture reveals to us about how to respond to the complex factors associated with the phenomenon of migration today in light of our faith commitments. For instance, exegetical and pastoral writings by Jewish scholars and rabbis are an important source for delving into the original language, contexts, and possible interpretations of the citations mentioned so far. The Hebrew word *ger* (often translated as "foreigner") appears sixty times, with six different uses.[5] What are the contexts of these uses? How to do they relate to the migration issues faced today? What do these uses call individuals and the community to understand or do? More Christian ethicists are including such exegetical and interpretive work in their scholarship on migration, but this is a relatively recent development and is ripe for further exploration.

Recently, scholars have been proposing ways of understanding what scripture reveals about what it means to be in right relationship with different types of "others." They ask questions such as: Do people have responsibilities to various categories of Others?[6] How are the concepts of hospitality,[7] kinship,[8] or the neighbor to be understood in a Christian context in light of revelation? These proposals warrant further exploration and additional contributions.

Further work also needs to be done on the frameworks available for interpreting scripture for guidance on ethical issues today. Relatively recent work on migration and scripture through the lens of virtue has advanced biblical ethics in the Catholic tradition and provided an example of how other hermeneutical tools are important for migration ethics, including the voices of those whose hermeneutic is formed by the experience of being on the move.[9] There is no overarching "migrant" experience. How one reads, interprets, and understands the Bible and its relevance for today will be impacted by one's comprehensive social location before, during, and after migrating, as well as one's experiences of the forces that led to the need to migrate, the transit experience, and all that met them where they landed. A multitude of voices from and with a diverse set of experiences brings an unparalleled depth to what is revealed to all of us by scripture. Miguel De La Torre explains that the biblical hermeneutics of those on the margins "reveal a God who is the liberator, the seeker of justice, the doer, and the subverter."[10] These images come from the reflections primarily of those who have migrated from different regions and contexts or those who advocate for migrants.

The convergence of exegesis, methodological frameworks, and diverse hermeneutical lenses is necessary for a more complete understanding of how scripture speaks to a proper Christian response to migration today. A final crucial element in this pursuit is a translation of these tools into resources for Christians and their communities. People in some communities can recite chapter and verse of the Bible, but believe that the "stranger" or the "alien" is the one who crossed the border with a valid visa or the neighbor who is

[5]Stuart Krauss, "The Word *Ger* in the Bible and Its Implications," *Jewish Bible Quarterly* 34, no. 4 (2006): fn. 1.
[6]Tisha Rajendra, *Immigrants and Citizens: Justice and Responsibility in the Ethics of Immigration* (Grand Rapids: Eerdmans, 2017).
[7]Alain Thomasset, SJ, "The Virtue of Hospitality According to the Bible and the Challenge of Migration," *The Bible and Catholic Theological Ethics*, ed. Yiu Sing Lucas Chan, James F. Keenan, and Ronaldo Zacharias (Maryknoll: Orbis, 2017).
[8]Kristin Heyer, *Kinship across Borders: A Christian Ethic of Immigration* (Washington, DC: Georgetown University Press, 2012).
[9]Thomasset, "Virtue of Hospitality."
[10]Miguel A. De La Torre, *Reading the Bible from the Margins* (Maryknoll: Orbis, 2002).

legally here. Others are not familiar with the centrality of migration in scripture. There is a need for resources for catechists, preachers, and others in churches and religious education sectors.[11]

EARLY CHRISTIANITY

Just as migration is an integral element of salvation history, it is also central to understanding human history. As a result of the migrations that began occurring within a few decades of Jesus's death, the Christian tradition has reflected upon, responded to, accompanied, accommodated, and spread as a result.

A dizzying array of migrations occurred throughout the Patristic era for political, religious, and economic pursuits. According to Peter Phan, migration was central to the experience of many early Christians, with some initial migration of Greek-speaking Jewish Christians around the time of Stephen's martyrdom and the killing of James, the brother of John, with Christians preaching to Jews who had migrated, and also to Gentiles in Judea, Samaria, Phoenicia, Cyprus, and Antioch.[12] A much more extensive migration occurred after the destruction of the Temple, with Christians going to five general areas that Peter Phan describes: Mesopotamia and Syria, where we get some of the originating documents such as the *Didache* and the *Gospel of Thomas*; Greece and Asia Minor, resulting in some of Paul's letters and Acts; the western Mediterranean, including Rome and Carthage, where important church leaders and theologians arose and many were martyred; Egypt, where theologians such as Clement and Origen were; and finally East Asia and India, of which not much is known.[13] A third migration occurred during the Patristic era involving the Germanic tribes between the third and sixth centuries, including the Vandals, the Goths, the Anglos, and the Saxons.[14]

According to Phan, the early Christian migrations involved some of the same push/pull factors experienced by people migrating today: religious persecution, land being conquered, trade, rural-to-urban migration, and evangelization. Christians who migrated had to decide how much to culturally and linguistically assimilate, how to establish their unsanctioned religious communities within the larger foreign community, and how to maintain their religious and ethical practices in spite of those in place where they settled.[15] Christian theology was simultaneously developing in the midst of these extensive migrations and resettlement questions. As a result, the *self-understanding* of Christians, practically, sociologically, spiritually, and theologically, was that of the stranger, the foreigner, the sojourner.[16] Phan explains that in light of the social location of the early Christians, their understanding of the realities of migration, and the injunctions

---

[11]An example of such a resource is Catholic Relief Services' "CRS University" initiative. On migration, CRS partnered with Elizabeth Collier, Charles Strain, and Anselm Academic to create a primer on migration and Christian ethics (*Global Migration: What's Happening, Why and a Just Response*) and complementary online modules for high school, university, and parish education on basic migration facts, migration narratives, and ethical teaching.

[12]Peter Phan, "Migration in the Patristic Era," in *A Promised Land, a Perilous Journey: Theological Perspectives on Migration*, ed. Daniel G. Groody and Gioacchino Campese (Notre Dame: University of Notre Dame Press, 2008), 43.

[13]Ibid., 43–4.

[14]Ibid., 45–6.

[15]Ibid., 47.

[16]Phan goes through the Hebrew, Greek, and Latin constructions of these (biblical) terms and how early Christian writings integrated and combined them into similar or even new meanings. Ibid., 48–9, 54.

to welcome the stranger permeating the Hebrew Scriptures and Jesus's life and teaching, "the virtue most highly recommended to the community was *philoxenia*, literally, love of strangers or hospitality."[17] This resulted in hospitality being central theologically and in practice.

TRADITION

Having briefly explained how Christians should understand migration in light of the Hebrew Scriptures, the New Testament, and early Christianity, we now move to some of the developments within the Christian tradition that occurred from the mid-nineteenth century to present. It is appropriate to include the foundational category of experience, in conjunction with the exploration of tradition at this point.

There were significant migrations of people during the late nineteenth and twentieth centuries from Europe to North America and during the twentieth and twenty-first centuries from many regions south to north. In the Western European migrations of the nineteenth and twentieth centuries, the Catholic Church developed institutionalized ministries for "people on the move." Priests would accompany groups of people from their homeland to where they were seeking to settle. Parishes and dioceses in the receiving countries developed extensive social services to help immigrants navigate their new situations and to provide rituals and spiritual resources from their homelands. The experiences of the church communities being themselves recent migrants and ministering to those who just arrived gave insight for the development of the contemporary tradition of how and why people should be welcomed and what the expectations of those migrating and those receiving them should be. Over time ministries developed for almost everyone "on the move": the Roma, migrant farmworkers, tourists, circus workers, military personnel, refugees, and so forth. This is a recognition that being away from one's home, temporarily or permanently, voluntarily or forcibly, continues to be a central human experience for so many people, riddled with individual, communal, and theological challenges.

In terms of institutional teaching, the Roman Catholic Church has an "official" documentary tradition on migration that began in 1952 with *Exsul familia*, promulgated by Pius XII.[18] This apostolic constitution begins with the image of the Holy Family and goes on to recount some of the institutionally specific ministries, activities, and resources set up by the church or church-affiliated institutions throughout the centuries. While this apostolic constitution is typical of its time and genre, its emphasis on the role of migration-related needs and ministries historically is an important connection to the earlier material highlighted above and illustrates the dialectical relationship between the development of the tradition and the migration experiences of Christians. At Vatican II and during the next few decades, many Vatican documents and papal addresses include familiar injunctions regarding how immigrants and refugees should be treated.[19]

A significant development in church teaching occurred in the first decade of the new millennium as the US Catholic bishops published a pastoral statement, *Welcoming the Stranger among Us: Unity in Diversity*, in 2000, and their subsequent collaboration

---

[17]Ibid., 50, emphasis in original.

[18]Pope Pius XII, *Exsul familia nazarenthana* (Vatican City: Libreria Editrice Vaticana, 1952).

[19]United States Conference of Catholic Bishops (USCCB), "Quotes from Church Teachings on the Rights of Migrants and Refugees," http://www.usccb.org/issues-and-action/human-life-and-dignity/migrants-refugees-and-travelers/quotes-rights-migrants-refugees.cfm.

in 2003 with the Mexican bishops' conference on the pastoral letter, "Strangers No Longer: Together on the Journey of Hope," which addressed migration in Latin and North America, from the perspectives of sending, pass-through, and receiving countries. The bishops were unusually self-critical of the ways that the institutional church has not always served newcomers well, and they were blunt about the ignorance, fear, and competition that often characterize the responses of people of faith to immigrants. There is a call to *conversion*, *communion*, and *solidarity* in both documents: conversion of mind and heart, which the bishops believe will lead to a communion where those in receiving countries show hospitality and the migrants are welcomed and feel a sense of belonging. Conversion will then lead to a building of community and actual solidarity between people in the communities and those who continue to migrate.[20] What is also interesting about these documents is the integration of vignettes of migrants' lives and even the stories of particular deaths along the border.[21] Nowhere else in official Catholic teaching are such narratives included and this is an important new development in theological ethics to be further explored and integrated.

Another significant development within theological ethics is the impact that the integration of the voices of scholars with the life experience of being a migrant, the work of those with direct experience serving and advocating for migrants, and networks of scholars from around the globe collaborating on the theological reflection and scholarship on migration. While the *academic* literature is beginning to include more diverse voices and their insights, a pressing issue is the lack of pedagogical resources that include diverse hermeneutical frameworks and also facilitate the communion/experiential learning required for conversion and solidarity, at all levels of education, for homiletics and parish education/formation, in religiously affiliated schools, and for pastoral ministries. For instance, there is not widespread knowledge of the Pope's annual message on the World Day of Migrants and Refugees, in spite of the fact that this day has been highlighted every year for well over a hundred years. The US Catholic bishops celebrate National Migration Week every January, with toolkits, resources, and activities to bring attention to migration issues, but these materials are not disseminated widely or integrated into the life of most parishes, schools, or campus ministries. The Archdiocese of Chicago's Immigration Ministry has developed innovative, comprehensive, lay-led legal, social service, and spiritual programs, for immigrant families, those in detention, those being deported, as well as educational materials for parishes without an immigrant presence. They also organize vigils and large events to promote understanding of migration issues. Their focus is primarily on accompaniment of migrants in their social and legal journeys and promoting *communio* between immigrant and nonimmigrant communities.[22] The ministries of the office are finally beginning to be replicated in a few other locations nationally, but few people outside of immigrant communities know of the work the office is doing. Finally, only some in the Catholic hierarchy (often immigrants themselves) are very vocal about public policies and specific legislative proposals and even fewer participate in public demonstrations, such as *Posada* processions at Advent or masses

---

[20]USCCB and Conferencia del Episcopado Mexicano, "Strangers No Longer: Together on the Journey of Hope," January 22, 2003, § 40–4, http://www.usccb.org/issues-and-action/human-life-and-dignity/immigration/strangers-no-longer-together-on-the-journey-of-hope.cfm.

[21]Ibid., § 87.

[22]Archdiocese of Chicago's Office of Human Dignity and Solidarity Immigration Ministry, www.catholicsandimmigrants.org/about-us-2/mission-and-vision/.

celebrated at the border with people on both sides participating.[23] There are many types of research opportunities for people to examine the theological, pastoral, spiritual, and impact/effectiveness of the newly implemented initiatives, responses, and accompaniment on all of those involved.

REASON

Due to the complex web of factors related to why, how, and where people migrate from and to, as well as the biases and assumptions of those in receiving regions, many other sources of knowledge are required for understanding migration and reflecting on ethical responses. Migration ethics is an interdisciplinary field requiring scholars from vastly different areas of expertise to collaborate. Migration flows are often treated as unexpected emergencies that need to be swiftly stopped. In reality, there are usually historical, political, environmental, and economic elements understood by specialists who study it, but not the general public. An example of this is the "migrant caravan" of people from Central America intending on applying for political asylum in the United States covered by the media in fall 2018. The violence that Salvadorans in the group fled was rooted, in part, in US economic and military interventions in the 1980s. The result of the United States supporting, supplying, and training the Salvadoran military, along with denying asylum claims in the United States and incarcerating, then deporting, others who developed gang affiliations in the prison, contributed to the confluence of factors that made El Salvador one of the most dangerous countries in which to live. The roles of public policy, the Catholic Church in El Salvador, the development of liberation theology, the role of activism, and legal support by Christian churches in the United States, along with economic policy, military science, political science, and the history of power in the El Salvador, are only a few of the research areas that contribute to an understanding of the causes of the caravan and what the proper responses are for Christians in receiving countries.

Another example is the circular migration in agriculture that developed in the mid-twentieth century between US farming communities and various regions in Mexico. These long-standing employment-based relationships, along with more recent US agricultural subsidies (of corn in particular) and increased US border enforcement, resulted in Mexicans needing to permanently settle in the United States and bring their families, rather than the previous practice of working different harvest seasons in the United States and then returning to family and community in Mexico during the off-seasons.[24] This particular "Case of Corn" illustrates how one industry's successful lobbying efforts and subsequent subsidy, amidst other complex and seemingly unrelated forces, can result in citizens of one country being forced to move in order to support themselves. Analyses from agricultural economics, political science in the United States and Mexico, and immigration law are required for ethical reflection on this issue.

Due to the wide-ranging reasons for migration flows, the combination of interdisciplinary partners is endless. The main categories of interlocutors for the purposes of this discussion are economics, business ethics, political philosophy, environmental

---

[23]See the USCCB-created website, www.justiceforimmigrants.org, and the Archdiocese of Chicago's Office for Human Dignity and Solidarity: Immigration Ministry, www.catholicsandimmigrants.org/.

[24]For concise explanation of "The Case of Corn," see Elizabeth Collier and Charles Strain, *Global Migration: What's Happening, Why and a Just Response* (Winona: Anselm Academic, 2017), 59–62.

science, law, sociology, and agricultural sciences. These areas of research have similar challenges to those of theological ethics. There is a need not only for the voices of those who have migrated from many different regions of the world for myriad reasons but also for the voices of those who have worked with and on behalf of people who migrate. There is also the challenge of tackling the ubiquitous use of binary categories (benefit/ burden, legal/illegal, citizen/foreigner, closed/open borders, us/them) so that our language, arguments, and proposals can be more relevant to the reality on the ground in terms of both problems and solutions.

While there is an extensive network of research and university centers, scholars, and advocacy groups globally, there needs to be more attention paid to effectively disseminating the findings broadly. What can the disciplines of communications, behavioral economics, and neuropsychology tell us about how storytelling, the arts, or video production can overcome things like the singularity effect and psychic numbing? It is known that humans will respond to the needs of one person whose story, photo, or need is presented, but as one more person and another and another are added to the list of people who need help, the human brain becomes overwhelmed and care for the other quickly dissipates. What other academic disciplines can help with the continued development of theological ethics and the more effective dissemination of facts and teaching so that solidarity between God's creation more adequately reflects what scripture reveals about how to react to the phenomena of migration? Interfaith collaboration on academic, institutional, and pastoral resources and programs is also an area ripe for Christian ethicists to explore in order to move beyond the very limited ad hoc and localized work being done so far.

Because of the complexity and variety of the factors that result in migration itself, as well as all that contributes to the reactions that people have to those who migrate, there is much for Christian ethicists to engage and contribute to research, teaching, ecclesiology, pastoral ministries, and all that leads Christians to consider what they do and what they fail to do in their daily life and faith journey. With the numbers of people "on the move" predicted to only increase in the coming decades, this is a critical area for Christian ethicists to work.

SUGGESTED READINGS

Brazal, Agnes, and Maria Teresa Davila, eds. *Living with(out) Borders*. Maryknoll: Orbis, 2016.

Collier, Elizabeth, and Charles Strain. *Religious and Ethical Perspectives on Global Migration*. Lanham: Lexington, 2014.

Heyer, Kristin. *Kinship across Borders: A Christian Ethic of Immigration*. Washington, DC: Georgetown University Press, 2012.

Rajendra, Tisha. *Migrants and Citizens: Justice and Responsibility in the Ethics of Immigration*. Grand Rapids: Eerdmans, 2017.

CHAPTER EIGHTEEN

Feminist Ethics and Age-Based Policy

SARAH MOSES

Any effort to map an agenda for Christian ethics in the twenty-first century must address the topic of aging and the elderly. Undergirding my approach is the vision of the 1965 Vatican II document, *Gaudium et spes*, which called for "reading the signs of the times": "We must be aware of and understand the aspirations, the yearnings, and the often dramatic features of the world in which we live."[1] Trends that arose in the last century now continue into the twenty-first century, and commentators observe that both individually and societally we are in a new moment in human history as regards aging. Though once considered the privileged concern of wealthier European and North American nations, the historic demographics of contemporary aging have become a global reality. At the Second World Assembly on Ageing in 2002, a United Nations official stated, "If the demographic focus of the 20th century was on education and employment for the young, then the theme for the 21st century will be the elderly."[2]

From a demographic perspective, population aging and increased longevity are well-established trends with global reach. While differing in degree, the process of population aging (whereby the proportion of older people within a population increases and the proportion of younger ages decreases) is a reality reaching beyond countries in Europe and North America to countries in Asia and South America, and will also reach areas within Africa by the middle of this century. While there is variation between countries, general global trends are clear: the percentage of world population 65 and older will continue to grow dramatically through the first half of the twenty-first century, while the youth population (20 and younger) and the working-age population will remain flat or grow only slightly.[3] It is not an exaggeration to say that these trends are new in human experience: for instance, for the first time in human history, globally the number of persons 65 and older will exceed children under age 5 before the year 2050.[4]

---

[1]Second Vatican Council, *Gaudium et spes* ("Pastoral Constitution on the Church in the Modern World"), in *Vatican Council II: Constitutions, Decrees, Declarations*, ed. Austin Flannery (Northport: Costello, 1996), 162–82.

[2]Reuters, "UN Offers Action Plan for a World Aging Rapidly," *New York Times*, April 14, 2002, A4.

[3]Wan He, Daniel Goodkind, and Paul Kowal, "An Aging World: 2015" (Washington, DC: United States Census Bureau, International Population Reports, 2016), 3.

[4]Ibid.

Aging populations pose new questions for international programs and policies, such as the particular needs of elderly refugees or global health needs related to illnesses such as Alzheimer's. But aging populations also pose enormous challenges at the national level where some countries are growing old before they establish even basic pension and social insurance programs. Population aging has developed hand in hand with another trend: enormous gains in human longevity that marked the second half of the twentieth century. For instance, in the United States, life expectancy went from forty-five years in 1900 to almost eighty years by 2000.[5] Persons reaching age 65 in the United States can now expect to live an additional 19.4 years, and the fastest growing segment of the elderly population is those aged 85 and older. In fact, in the United States, the population 85 and older is expected to more than double from 6.4 million in 2016 to 14.6 million in 2040.[6] Globally, life expectancy at birth stood at 68.6 years in 2015 and is expected to increase to 76.2 years by 2050. While life expectancy rates vary by region, with North America having the highest life expectancy overall, the trend toward longer life is expected to continue increasing: for instance, Africa is projected to increase from a current average life expectancy of 59.2 years to 71 years by 2050.[7]

Global increased life expectancy reflects significant success in public health, lower mortality rates, and healthier populations. However, these gains in life expectancy also pose new challenges for age-based social security and retirement systems as well as social expectations of and attitudes toward older workers. Furthermore, increasing numbers of people are now living to ages in which certain forms of disease and disability become more common. While research shows that modifications in health and lifestyle at earlier ages produce benefits in old age, and medical technology in areas such as cardiovascular disease has advanced, it is also true that the likelihood of concurrent conditions increases with age ("multimorbidity"). Increased longevity also means people are living longer with conditions such as dementia and diabetes and, thus, producing significant strains on health care resources and systems.[8] This brief overview of contemporary aging at the macro and global level is meant to illustrate why aging and the elderly are one of the pressing "signs" of our time demanding serious engagement from Christian ethics. Aging cannot be approached exclusively as an individual, subjective reality, but must be understood as a social and common question for us all, as a primary social-ethical issue this century. For the experiences of individual elderly and their families, and the individual choices available to shape one's old age, are profoundly influenced and limited by the political, economic, and health care systems in which persons are embedded. As a contribution to Christian ethics in the twenty-first century, this chapter offers perspectives and insights in response to ethical challenges arising from contemporary aging, drawing upon four classic sources: experience, scripture, tradition, and reason. My analysis will also demonstrate the particular contribution of feminist methodologies to Christian ethics, especially in the category of experience.

---

[5]Paul B. Baltes and Jacqui Smith, "New Frontiers in the Future of Aging: From Successful Aging of the Young Old to the Dilemmas of the Fourth Age," *Gerontology* 49, no. 2 (2003): 33.

[6]"2017 Profile of Older Americans" (Washington, DC: Administration for Community Living, US Department of Health and Human Services, 2018), 1–2.

[7]He, Goodkind, and Kowal, "An Aging World: 2015," 33.

[8]Ibid., 45.

EXPERIENCE

As a primary source of Christian ethics, experience provides the starting point for ethical reflection on aging. Like other contributors to this volume, I understand experience to include the subjective, personal experiences of individuals and groups as well as more objective, macro-level accounts of human experience provided by disciplines such as the social and natural sciences. As William Schweiker observes, such resources enable religious ethical traditions to fulfill the "descriptive task" of ethics, which is to accurately and broadly explain what is actually occurring, and to identify the ethical issues presented.[9] In the introduction I provided a brief macro-level account of the aging experience today by drawing upon demographic and social science resources. Such "big picture" experience is crucial for understanding ethical challenges at the societal and public policy level, but it also nuances one's grasp of individual experience by placing it within larger dynamics it represents. As a source for moral reflection, experience also demonstrates that a religious ethical tradition such as Christianity does not depend solely on internal sacred sources but draws on knowledge and insight from shared human realities and from other fields of intellectual inquiry such as psychology, sociology, and the natural sciences.

On the topic of aging, as with other topics, a feminist perspective on experience proves invaluable to a Christian ethical analysis. I use the term *feminist* first in its most general sense: as the broad social and intellectual movement that prioritizes the perspectives and voices of women and seeks to make visible women's experiences. As a social movement and a method of intellectual inquiry, feminism also demands particular attention to the impact of human actions and policies on the well-being of women in an effort to achieve equality. In her comprehensive history and overview of feminism, Rosemarie Tong traces the development of a variety of "feminisms," as the movement came to encompass a vast diversity of women's perspectives such as womanist, postcolonial, and global feminism.[10] Likewise, scholars such as Rita Gross, Elisabeth Schüssler Fiorenza, and Katie Cannon reflect the history of feminist Christian theology and ethics and the diversity of perspectives now represented in the field.

As regards contemporary aging, a feminist lens is crucial for highlighting the distinctive experiences women face in old age. For one, in all countries women's life expectancy on average exceeds that of men, with the gender gap in life expectancy differing in size depending upon the country. Longevity in and of itself is not a problem, but it is significant in relation to other aspects of women's experience of old age. Data from around the world shows that older women are more likely to live alone. For instance, in the United States, a larger percentage of older men are married (70 percent) as compared with older women (46 percent), and almost half of women 75 and older live alone.[11] In addition, the poverty rate for older women is higher than for older men worldwide. As one UN report observes, lower income for older women globally is tied to gender-biased features of pension and social security schemes, lower rates of participation in the formal labor force, higher rates of self-employment among women, and interruptions to work and career due to childbearing and rearing.[12] In the United States, older women

---

[9]William Schweiker, "On Religious Ethics," in *The Blackwell Companion to Religious Ethics*, ed. William Schweiker (Malden: Blackwell, 2004), 6.

[10]Rosemarie Tong, *Feminist Thought: A More Comprehensive Introduction*, 3rd ed. (Boulder: Westview, 2009), 200.

[11]"2017 Profile of Older Americans," 1.

[12]This report makes notes that old age is a risk factor for poverty for men and women, but with greater impact for elderly women due to differences in lifetime income and pension benefits. United Nations, *Income*

have a higher poverty rate than older men, and a higher percentage of elderly living alone are poor in comparison with persons living with spouses or other family members, which is noteworthy since older women are more likely to live alone.[13] Deepening our understanding further, later movements within feminism such as womanist, global, and postcolonial approaches help bring attention to the differences *among* older women based on race/ethnicity, socioeconomic status, and geographic location. For instance, in the United States, minority elderly such as African Americans and Hispanics have higher rates of poverty than older white Americans, with the highest rate of poverty experienced by older Hispanic women living alone.[14] Higher rates of poverty among elderly women of color impact a wide range of factors including adequate housing, access to health care, and quality of long-term care options. Global and postcolonial feminist perspectives call attention to the vulnerability of older women in countries without developed pension and social security systems. In addition, a UN report identified the risk of abuse and violence against older women in parts of the world with discriminatory views of widows and negative stereotypes of older women as "witches."[15] Given the enormous variation globally of national legal systems, the United Nations has responded by devoting specific attention and resources to strengthening the legal rights of older persons around the world.[16]

In addition to the insights a feminist perspective reveals about the diverse experiences of older women themselves, it also focuses attention on the reality of women as caregivers. As noted above, while it is generally true to say that in the twenty-first century people are living longer in good health, it is also true that we live longer in late old age, a stage in which chronic disease and disability are more likely. The care needs generated in late old age impact women in distinct ways. According to the Family Caregiving Alliance, 65 percent of older Americans rely exclusively on family and friends for their long-term care needs, and in the United States, roughly 66 percent of informal caregivers are women, with the average caregiver a woman of 49 years old who also works outside the home.[17] One way in which eldercare impacts female caregivers is through decreased work hours and income, lower wages and benefits, and reduced retirement income.[18] Furthermore, if women are more likely to take time off for caregiving and try to reenter the workforce later in life, continued evidence of ageism in hiring is particularly troubling for women.[19] Given lost wages and benefits, female caregivers are at a higher risk for poverty in their own old age. In addition to the financial consequences, the well-documented negative health impacts of long-term caregiving disproportionately affect wives and daughters

Poverty in Old Age: An Emerging Development Priority 2016, http://www.un.org/esa/socdev/ageing/documents/PovertyIssuePaperAgeing.pdf.

[13]"2017 Profile of Older Americans," 10.

[14]Ibid.

[15]United Nations, "Neglect, Abuse and Violence against Older Women" (New York: Division for Social Policy and Development, Department of Economic and Social Affairs, 2013), 43.

[16]Office of the High Commissioner, "Human Rights of Older Persons," United Nations Human Rights, June 14, 2019, https://www.ohchr.org/EN/Issues/OlderPersons/Pages/OlderPersonsIndex.aspx.

[17]"Women and Caregiving: Facts and Figures," Family Caregiving Alliance, National Center on Caregiving, 2003, https://www.caregiver.org/women-and-caregiving-facts-and-figures.

[18]The MetLife Mature Market Institute, National Alliance for Caregiving, Center for Long Term Care Research and Policy, "The MetLife Study of Caregiving Costs to Working Caregivers: Double Jeopardy for Baby Boomers Caring for their Parents," June 2011, 10–12.

[19]David Neumark, Ian Burn, and Patrick Button, "Is It Harder for Older Workers to Find Jobs? New and Improved Evidence from a Field Experiment," *Journal of Political Economy* 127, no. 2 (2019): 922.

since they bear the majority of the caregiving burden.[20] A similar picture exists in other countries where caregiving is a highly gendered activity, and even more in countries lacking sufficient social security programs for women as they age. As one article suggests, caregiving should be viewed as a "women's health issue globally" given that more women than men engage in informal caregiving.[21]

Not only is eldercare an ethical concern for informal caregivers but also for paid long-term care workers. For instance, at the beginning of the twenty-first century the vast majority of home care aides are women, and are more likely to be women of color and immigrants, with a median income of about $13,000 per year.[22] The percentage of direct elder care workers in the home and in institutions who are women is 90 percent, which is higher than any other health care occupation.[23] This overwhelmingly female eldercare workforce has very little job security or benefits, and home care workers often lack adequate protection under labor laws.[24] Furthermore, data shows that many countries face a current and future lack of paid eldercare workers; this combined with unattractive work conditions has fueled a reliance on foreign-born, immigrant workers in both the formal and informal sectors.[25] For example, in the United States one study reported that one in four direct care workers in nursing homes, assisted living facilities, and home care agencies is foreign born.[26] The US pattern of immigrant long-term care workers is similar in many developed nations around the world.[27] Thus, womanist, global, and postcolonial feminist perspectives help focus attention on the conditions of long-term eldercare workers and demonstrate the connection between labor and immigration policies and quality care for older people, particularly in the poorer countries these workers leave. Bringing a feminist lens to experience demonstrates that any adequate Christian ethical response to contemporary aging must take seriously both the benefits and the challenges of the new old age, with nuanced attention to the way those challenges impact women and minorities in particular ways.

SCRIPTURE

We move now to consideration of scripture as a source for the Christian moral tradition as it seeks to respond to the ethical challenges of contemporary aging. As in any attempt to place biblical texts in dialogue with contemporary moral questions, one must acknowledge at the outset the different cultural and historical contexts within the biblical canon itself, and between the biblical world and the contemporary. This is clearly true in relation to aging and old age if one considers the vast demographic differences between the ancient Near East and today's societies. As biblical scholar J. Gordon Harris insists

---

[20]"Women and Caregiving."

[21]Judith Berg and Nancy Fugate Woods, "Global Women's Health: A Spotlight on Caregiving," *Nursing Clinics of North America* 44, no. 3 (2009): 375.

[22]David Rolf, "Life on the Homecare Front," *Generations* 40, no. 1 (2016): 82.

[23]Paul Osterman, *Who Will Care for Us? Long-Term Care and the Long-Term Care Workforce* (New York: Russell Sage Foundation, 2017), 5.

[24]Ibid., 33, 40.

[25]Susan Reinhard, Donald Redfoot, and Brenda Cleary, "Health and Long-Term Care: Are Immigrant Workers Indispensable?," *Generations* 32, no. 4 (2008/2009): 25.

[26]Robert Espinoza, "Immigrants and the Direct Care Workforce" (Bronx: PHI Research Brief, 2017), 3, https://phinational.org/resource/immigrants-and-the-direct-care-workforce/; Osterman, *Who Will Care for Us?*, 5.

[27]Colette V. Browne and Kathryn L. Braun, "Globalization, Women's Migration, and the Long-Term-Care Workforce," *Gerontologist* 48, no. 1 (2008): 16.

in his exhaustive study of aging in the Bible, there is no simple correspondence between old age in the biblical world and contemporary old age.[28] Nonetheless, it is possible to identify general patterns in the experience of aging and old age, which provide points of correspondence between ancient experience recorded in biblical texts and contemporary experience. For instance, as today, the Bible identifies a distinct life stage associated with growing older, and transitions in communal identity and role which accompany it. Scripture is also realistic in identifying the changes and difficulties that often occur in the aging process, such as physical decline and financial insecurity. Thus, as the Christian moral tradition has long affirmed, scripture can provide a vital source for ethical reflection and analysis. As James Gustafson wrote, "One need not appeal to strict analogies between events recorded and interpreted in Scripture and events of the present, but rather one can appeal to theological affirmations that are informed and governed by the biblical witness."[29] In this chapter I am particularly interested in scripture as a source that helps Christian ethics respond to the distinct challenges older women face. While there are a variety of feminist approaches to scripture within contemporary biblical studies, they share a goal of reading the Bible to "empower women," and to highlight biblical themes of liberation for oppressed and marginalized groups.[30]

One clear element of the biblical witness is the insistence upon care for the elderly as a moral obligation of family and society and as a key measure of a just society. This is evident in the familiar commandment to honor one's father and mother found in the Decalogue (Exod. 20:12; Deut. 5:16), and the Hebrew legal code contains texts prohibiting elder abuse and neglect.[31] In addition to legal texts, admonitions to respect and honor the elderly are found throughout the Wisdom literature, particularly Proverbs. Particularly relevant to the problem of poverty for older women, biblical scholars argue that the honor and respect enjoined by the Bible extended to material support, including food, clothing, and housing.[32] The concern for respect and care of the elderly found in the Hebrew Bible has parallels in the writings of the early church found in the New Testament. For example, Jesus criticizes the Pharisees for teaching that a religious commitment to make offerings to God ("the vow of Corban") absolves one of the responsibility to provide material care for aging parents (Mk 7:5-13). Furthermore, when a wealthy man asks what he must do to be righteous, Jesus includes honoring of father and mother in the list of moral commandments he emphasizes (Mk 10:19). The epistles echo Jesus's teachings and first-century Jewish culture in affirming the requirement to honor father and mother and also to care for aging widows within the church (Eph. 6:1-3; Col. 3:20; 1 Tim. 5:4, 8). Within the biblical witness, the moral imperative to respect and care for the elderly was not only based on a vision of a healthy society but also upon the theological understanding of God's special concern for the poor and weak. The God of Exodus who acts on behalf of a group of oppressed slaves demands justice for the weak and vulnerable in society. This is evident in prophetic texts such as Micah, which condemn a breach in just relations between the generations in Israelite society (Mic. 7:6). Thus, while in ancient societies the

[28]J. Gordon Harris, *God and the Elderly: Biblical Perspectives on Aging* (Philadelphia: Fortress, 1987), 11.

[29]James F. Gustafson, "The Place of Scripture in Christian Ethics: A Methodological Study," *Interpretation* 24 (1970): 449–50.

[30]Elisabeth Schüssler Fiorenza, *But She Said* (Boston: Beacon, 1992), 7.

[31]Harris, *God and the Elderly*, 30, 57.

[32]Rolf Knierim, "Age and Aging in the Old Testament," in *Ministry with the Aging*, ed. William Clements (San Francisco: Harper & Row, 1981), 29; Robert Martin-Achard, "Biblical Perspective on Aging: 'Abraham Was Old ... and the Lord Had Blessed Him' (Gen. 24:1)," *Concilium* 3 (1991): 37.

initial and primary location for care of the elderly was the family, the biblical concern for the poor and weak enjoined a general social obligation upon all members of a community in protecting the well-being of its aged members.

A second important ethical insight from the biblical witness is the insistence upon ongoing purpose in old age and the community's responsibility to enable purpose through the meaningful social participation of the elderly. The Bible's insistence on purpose and participation in old age is not based upon the false, rosy view of aging often reflected in contemporary versions of "successful aging," but is strikingly realistic about the physical and cognitive changes that may accompany aging such as blindness, weakness, and infertility.[33] The biblical witness insists that older persons continue to be called to purpose and participation *within* these realities of age-related disability. Crucial to this ethical insight is the narrative literature of the Bible where we find a rich collection of stories of older people.[34] For example, in the Gospel of Luke, Simeon and Anna are both identified as being in late life (Luke 2). An important detail of the story is that these elderly figures continue meaningful participation in the community through service in the Temple. Additionally, when Mary and Joseph bring the baby Jesus to the Temple, Simeon and Anna play a prophetic role in declaring the good news of what God is doing through this child. As scholars Richard and Judith Hays comment, "These two aged figures also suggest that radical openness to the redeeming power of God may be found among elders—perhaps particularly there."[35] The vision of old age found in these stories is reinforced in New Testament epistles that insist upon the ongoing importance and responsibilities of older members of the Christian community. Harris argues that elderly members are "key to the success of the Christian movement. Old age brings some transitions but decreasing responsibility is not one of them."[36] Significant for our contemporary period, older women and widows are explicitly included in that vision. For instance, in addition to insisting on material support for older widows, 1 Timothy also asks older women to continue in prayer, hospitality, service to the sick, and "doing good in every way" (1 Tim. 5:10). As Stephen Sapp observes, the epistles depict older women as having "important work to do" in the community beyond their roles as wives and mothers.[37] While differences exist between the ancient world and our own, a contemporary Christian ethical response to aging should be informed by scripture's dual affirmations: financial and physical care of the elderly as a fundamental measure of a just society and the elderly as retaining purpose and responsibility within the community.

TRADITION

A third source for Christian ethics is tradition. Charles Curran describes tradition as the "beliefs, doctrines, practices, rituals, and church life" that have shaped and been

---

[33]Anthropologist Sarah Lamb's work provides insightful critique of the concept of "successful aging" in North America, which excludes poor elderly and elderly with disease and disability. See Sarah Lamb, "Permanent Personhood or Meaningful Decline? Toward a Critical Anthropology of Successful Aging," *Journal of Aging Studies* 29 (2014): 41–52.

[34]For a more extensive survey of this material, see Sarah Moses, *Ethics and the Elderly: The Challenge of Long-Term Care* (Maryknoll: Orbis, 2015), 93–108.

[35]Richard B. Hays and Judith C. Hays, "The Christian Practice of Growing Old: The Witness of Scripture," in *Growing Old in Christ*, ed. Stanley Hauerwas et al. (Grand Rapids: Eerdmans, 2003), 7.

[36]Harris, *God and the Elderly*, 89.

[37]Stephen Sapp, *Full of Years: Aging and the Elderly in the Bible and Today* (Nashville: Abington, 1987), 107.

handed on by the church as a living community in different times and places.[38] Given that definition, I understand tradition as encompassing both "official" teachings of church hierarchies and the "unofficial" writings and practices of lay people and theologians. Church is used here in the broadest sense, not limited to any one branch of Christianity. A goal in this section is to present an ecumenical picture of tradition, drawing from contemporary Catholic and Protestant writings, and to ask how those writings can inform a Christian ethical response to aging for the twenty-first century.[39]

One central theme that can be traced through contemporary tradition is a theology of discipleship in which the agency and dignity of older people is affirmed through a vision of persons as called to purpose and service throughout their lives. For example, two official Catholic documents written in response to the United Nations' declaration of 1999 as the "International Year of the Older Person" drew on the theme of discipleship in connection with old age. In "The Dignity of Older People and Their Mission in the Church and in the World," the Pontifical Council for the Laity argued for a revision of the church's understanding of the elderly: "Far from being passive recipients of the Church's pastoral care, older people are irreplaceable apostles."[40] Likewise, in "Blessings of Age," the US Conference of Catholic Bishops stated their goal "to form a fresh perspective, one that sees older persons as active participants in contributing to the Church's life and mission."[41] In these documents the concept of discipleship critiques wider cultural views of old age as lacking roles and meaningful purpose. Lifelong identity as a disciple suggests the church has the responsibility to be the kind of community that fosters and enables true forms of contribution and participation by older members. The Pontifical Council affirms this responsibility by demanding revision of the church's approach to pastoral care, "helping [the elderly] to derive particular spiritual enrichment from their active participation in the life of the ecclesial community."[42] Furthermore, echoing the Bible's recognition of age-related weakness and disability, the US Catholic bishops urge the church to honor God's call to older people even with changed physical and cognitive abilities: "Even those who obviously need pastoral care—the homebound, the disabled, the seriously ill—are also able to give pastoral care, for example, by praying for their families, caregivers, and others, by sharing their own faith lives, or even through the simple yet powerful ministry of presence."[43]

In recent writings from Protestant thinkers, one can see a similar emphasis on the dignity of the elderly as lifelong disciples, and on the mutuality of friendship as defining of Christian community. For example, theologian Freda Gardner argues that central to the vocation of Christians is the concept of discipleship, and critiques the church's existing view of older people: "What I am suggesting here is that the church, like the culture, thinks of the elderly as a different species of human being, maybe an obsolete

[38]Charles E. Curran, *The Catholic Moral Tradition: A Synthesis* (Washington, DC: Georgetown University Press, 1999), 52.

[39]For analysis of older Christian traditions, see David Aers, "The Christian Practice of Growing Old in the Middle Ages," in *Growing Old in Christ*, ed. Stanley Hauerwas et al. (Grand Rapids: Eerdmans, 2003), 38–59.

[40]Pontifical Council for the Laity, "The Dignity of Older People and Their Mission in the Church and in the World" (Vatican City: Libreria Editrice Vaticana, 1998), 11.

[41]United States Conference of Catholic Bishops (USCCB), "Blessings of Age: A Pastoral Message on Growing Older within the Faith Community" (Washington, DC: USCCB, 1999), http://www.usccb.org/issues-and-action/marriage-and-family/blessings-of-age-english.cfm.

[42]Pontifical Council for the Laity, "Dignity of Older People," 3.

[43]USCCB, "Blessings of Age."

human being."[44] Similarly, D. Stephen Long affirms the lifelong purpose indicated by the rituals of church tradition: "Baptism, like ordination, brings with it lifelong tasks. The goal of the Christian life is not leisure, forced or voluntary, at the end of life, but faithful service."[45] From the perspective of Christian tradition, a person's old age is not a passive stage of life, or a static stage in which change and development is no longer possible. In this regard, Anglican theologian Rowan Williams has argued: "It is not an exaggeration to say that ... growing old will make the greatest creative demands of your life."[46] The vision of older people as lifelong disciples called to growth and purpose is powerful in contemporary societies that often infantilize older people. As ethicists Stanley Hauerwas and Laura Yordy write, "That the elderly are freed from such [moral] obligations in our society correlates with the view that human development ends in early adulthood, or at least in middle age. Many dominant images in American culture portray old people as set in their ways, that is, as not capable of learning anything significant, much less growing in virtue."[47]

A robust theology of discipleship also promotes a vision of community based upon mutuality and equality between all members. The fundamental equality of discipleship then promotes an approach to older people as subjects with agency and not merely as objects of the aid of others. Within this vision, there are not two classes of persons: those who are dependent and needy and those who are independent and giving. Rather, though expressed in different ways, there is an equality in the mutual give-and-take of Christian fellowship made possible by the shared call to discipleship at every age. Hauerwas and Yordy draw on the image of friendship to capture this reality: "This Christological basis of friendship calls friends to be Christlike to one another in particular ways: to give and receive service from one another, to offer correction when appropriate, to be patient, and so forth."[48] The equality and mutuality of Christian community does not require the church to ignore the challenges and difficulties many elderly experience. Instead, it challenges the church to recognize and enable genuine forms of participation and contribution from all its members. While the contemporary theological sources sketched here do not focus explicitly on women, the central themes of discipleship and friendship are relevant to elderly women in the twenty-first century. The emphasis on friendship and fellowship is crucial for the many elderly women who live alone, and discipleship is a way to expand one's sense of dignity and purpose beyond the gendered roles of wife and mother.

REASON

In the concluding section of this chapter we turn to the fourth major source for Christian ethics—reason. Reason has been understood in a variety of ways throughout Christian history, but can be described as the universal human capacity for reflection on

[44]Freda Gardner, "Another Look at the Elderly," in *The Treasure of Earthen Vessels*, ed. Brian Childs and David Waanders (Louisville: Westminster John Knox, 1994), 184.
[45]D. Stephen Long, "The Language of Death: Theology and Economics in Conflict," in *Growing Old in Christ*, ed. Stanley Hauerwas et al. (Grand Rapids: Eerdmans, 2003), 149.
[46]Rowan Williams, "The Gifts Reserved for Age: Perceptions of the Elderly," in *Faith in the Public Square*, ed. Rowan Williams (New York: Bloomsbury, 2012), 245.
[47]Stanley Hauerwas and Laura Yordy, "Captured in Time: Friendship and Aging," in *Growing Old in Christ*, ed. Stanley Hauerwas et al. (Grand Rapids: Eerdmans, 2003), 173.
[48]Ibid., 178.

and practical application of human experience and shared values such as equality and dignity. While traditions within Christianity have historically differed in their appraisal of reason (from suspicion to affirmation of human capacity), it is accurate to say that the anthropology of major Christian thinkers has widely affirmed some role for natural human reason. As regards contemporary aging, I will focus on reason as creating the possibility for shared public deliberation—understood as the space in which all members of a society, operating from their particular traditions, come together to constructively engage challenges common to all. In this regard, reason is crucial for the possibility of church-world engagement, in which Christians can engage non-Christians in the public sphere. This vision was affirmed by *Gaudium et spes* in its insistence that the church has something to offer the world and, in turn, the church has something to learn from the world. Ethicist David Hollenbach wrote of Vatican II's vision, "The relation of Church to society is neither oppositional nor one of identity; it is a relation of mutual interaction and dialogue."[49] Thus, I will highlight priority areas for Christian ethics to engage in public deliberation about the challenges of aging in the twenty-first century, with special attention to women.

First, we need robust deliberation about what it means to achieve a just society for *all* ages. In that regard, the public policies of countries must address the material poverty that exists within the older population, with particular concern for the ways in which gender inequity throughout life produces distinct burdens for older women. Older women globally experience greater income insecurity than men, and this inequality should be addressed. Solutions such as crediting contributory pension schemes during maternity leave and family care leave are one way in which some countries have sought to lessen the financial inequality between genders in old age.[50] Furthermore, the concept of justice includes consideration of whether societies hinder or enable meaningful social participation for all their members. In the Christian theological tradition, discipleship teaches that persons of all ages and abilities are called and empowered for various forms of service. This theological vision shares values with voices in the public sphere urging societies to welcome the new old age and value the contribution of their elderly citizens. For example, the 1991 United Nations' General Assembly resolution "Principles for Older Persons" identified "participation" as one of five principles needed to create a just society for the elderly: "Older persons should remain integrated in society ... Older persons should be able to seek and develop opportunities for service to the community and to serve as volunteers in positions appropriate to their interests and capabilities."[51] A commitment to justice as participation demands attention to concrete policies such as long-term care structures since lack of access to home and community-based care contributes to the isolation and marginalization of many poor elderly. Because older women live longer, and are more likely to live alone and have less financial resources, they are particularly vulnerable to such marginalization. The crisis in long-term care availability and access globally is an area of ethical concern, which Christian ethics should prioritize

[49]David Hollenbach, *The Common Good and Christian Social Ethics* (New York: Cambridge University Press, 2002), 275.

[50]United Nations Department of Economic and Social Affairs, "Economic Inequalities in Old Age," United Nations, June 5, 2017, https://www.un.org/development/desa/ageing/wp-content/uploads/sites/24/2016/08/Briefing-Paper_Economic-Inequalities_Final.pdf.

[51]United Nations Human Rights Office of the High Commissioner, "United Nations Principles for Older Persons," United Nations, December 16, 1991, https://www.ohchr.org/EN/ProfessionalInterest/Pages/OlderPersons.aspx.

and contribute to public deliberation about just solutions.[52] For example, policies such as universal long-term care insurance need to be considered as a means of enabling more elderly to purchase quality long-term care.[53]

A second priority area for Christian ethics should be caregivers, both informal and formal. Globally, elder caregiving is still an overwhelmingly gendered reality, and thus policies affecting caregivers have a huge impact on the well-being of women worldwide. As gerontologist Nancy R. Hooyman observes, "Despite greater attention by policy makers, caregiving remains undervalued in [US] society, partly because of intersecting inequities experienced by women as caregivers and care recipients."[54] Within the public sphere, Christian ethicists can find common ground with advocates for family and paid caregivers. A major challenge for unpaid family caregivers is the loss of income and pension contributions that result from interruptions to career and part-time work. In the United States, states have begun to experiment with programs that allow the elderly to use long-term care benefits to pay family caregivers, which provides income for caregivers and provides the elderly with more personalized care.[55] In addition, increasing the availability of formal community-based long-term care services can be seen as complementing family caregiving. Not only do community-based services honor the wishes of older people to continue living at home, but they also lessen the emotional and physical toll family caregivers experience.[56] While family still provides a significant amount of elder care globally and is often preferred by the elderly, smaller family sizes and other economic and social trends indicate that in the twenty-first century all societies must take steps to enhance formal long-term care services.[57] Toward that end societies need to acknowledge the current and projected shortage of direct care workers as an issue of urgent social ethical concern.[58] Moreover, given the migration of long-term care workers from poorer to richer countries, national solutions to this challenge require global perspective and cooperation. Within countries like the United States, low wages and a lack of fringe benefits are major barriers to the recruitment of direct care workers. Thus, public deliberation concerning long-term care must consider what justice requires as regards the working conditions of direct care workers.[59] From a global perspective, wealthy nations must honestly assess the negative impact on poorer countries from the migration of direct care workers and commit to more fair practices such as those proposed by the World Health Organization's "Global Code of Practice on the International Recruitment of Health Personnel," adopted by the World Health Assembly in 2010. Global health initiatives should also prioritize funding for training and recruiting local long-term care workers in poorer countries.

[52]The United Nations reported that in 2015, 48 percent of elderly persons globally receive no formal provision of long-term care services, and only 5.6 percent of older persons are covered by national legislation that provides formal long-term care services for all; United Nations Department of Economic and Social Affairs, "The Growing Need for Long-Term Care: Assumptions and Realities," September 12, 2016, https://www.un.org/esa/socdev/ageing/documents/un-ageing_briefing-paper_Long-term-care.pdf.

[53]Mark R. Meiners, "Partnership Long-Term Care Insurance: Lessons for CLASS Program Development," *Journal of Aging & Social Work* 24, no. 2 (2012): 152.

[54]Nancy R. Hooyman, "Social and Health Disparities in Aging: Gender Inequities in Long-Term Care," *Generations* 38, no. 4 (Winter 2014–15): 25.

[55]Osterman, *Who Will Care for Us?*, 53, 59.

[56]Hooyman, "Social and Health Disparities in Aging," 27–8.

[57]United Nations Department of Economic and Social Affairs, "Growing Need for Long-Term Care," 3.

[58]Osterman, *Who Will Care for Us?*, 16–25; Moses, *Ethics and the Elderly*, 28–9; Browne and Braun, "Globalization, Women's Migration," 19.

[59]"Understanding Direct Care Workers: A Snapshot of Two of America's Most Important Jobs" (Washington, DC: US Department of Health and Human Services, 2011), 25; Osterman, *Who Will Care for Us?*, 145–54.

This chapter represents an effort to place aging and the elderly on the agenda of Christian ethics in the twenty-first century. Furthermore, the chapter has demonstrated the enduring value of the four classic sources of moral reflection in our own context: experience, scripture, tradition, and reason. While not limited to this topic, contemporary aging also demonstrates the important insights provided by a feminist perspective. Feminist approaches do not replace the four classic sources, but rather transform them by bringing explicit attention to women's experiences and voices. Unlike many topics in applied ethics, aging is a reality with global reach and potentially confronts every person. As such, Christian ethics must attend to public deliberation on this topic in contemporary societies.

SUGGESTED READINGS

De Lange, Frits. *Loving Later Life: An Ethics of Aging*. Grand Rapids: Eerdmans, 2015.
Gawande, Atul. *Being Mortal: Medicine and What Matters in the End*. New York: Metropolitan, 2014.
Moses, Sarah. *Ethics and the Elderly: The Challenge of Long-Term Care*. Maryknoll: Orbis, 2015.
Ridenour, Autumn. *Sabbath Rest as Vocation: Aging toward Death*. London: T&T Clark, 2018.
Swinton, John. *Dementia: Living in the Memories of God*. Grand Rapids: Eerdmans, 2012.

CHAPTER NINETEEN

Focal Practices, Virtuality, Authenticity, and Public Space

TREVOR GEORGE HUNSBERGER BECHTEL

The relationship between information, dissemination, and public space has been of ethical concern for Christians since at least the advent of the printing press. Each new advance in information technology—print, radio, television, computers, the internet, cell phones, social media—has been lauded and pilloried inside and outside the church, and the argumentation sounds similar from epoch to epoch. Much theological and Christian reflection on technology follows down one of two paths. On one hand, technology is often demonized as a distraction or addiction and online identity eschewed as less authentic than concrete local relationships. The other path is one of encouraging saintly, if not heroic, use of technology, typically for the purpose of winning souls to Christ. Sociological and philosophical reflection sometimes has more nuance and depth but is equally bifurcated. A characteristic example is the debate between more pessimistic Nicholas Carr and optimistic Clay Shirky as written in their respective books *The Shallows* and *Cognitive Surplus*.[1]

Carr sees the internet as an interruption machine diminishing our ability to converse in robust ways. We might go on the internet to read about something, say the fall of the Tunisian government accomplished as one of the first Twitter revolutions in 2011, or the continued gun-control advocacy of the Parkland Youth in 2018, but the CNN homepage has an article about Caspar the smartest dog ever passing away and then you watch some cat videos and NBA highlights and soon you do not know where you are. This pattern of interruption leads to reduced attention spans, especially for long linear arguments like the ones found in books. The internet is good at holding our attention but Carr's key point is that it holds our attention in order to then diffuse it rather than to encourage focus and sustained engagement. His arguments are based on neurological and social scientific studies, and with the rise of the cell phone as the way more and more people navigate the internet, Carr's approach only becomes more compelling. It may be that the time of the long linear focused argument is gone and that we will need to build the new society on

[1]Nicholas Carr, *The Shallows: What the Internet Is Doing to Our Brains* (New York: W. W. Norton, 2011); Clay Shirky, *Cognitive Surplus: How Technology Makes Consumers into Collaborators* (New York: Penguin, 2010).

differently formed patterns of attention. This isn't necessarily bad, although Carr mourns its passing, but it is really unpredictable.

Shirky, on the other hand, argues that this is a time of cognitive surplus. He makes a compelling comparison between the industrial revolution and the information revolution. In London in the industrial revolution the increase in free time from factory work led to a sharp increase in the consumption of gin. People didn't know what to do with themselves and so they dulled their freedom through drink. But in the era after the gin cart craze people built public libraries and museums and laid the foundation for the contemporary public square. The next large burst of free time has been dulled by television where we sit transfixed by a passive medium that occupies our attention. Shirky sees the sharing and collaboration inherent in the internet and social media as the turning point into a new era of great public creativity and society creation. We cannot predict the shape of this new human interaction through information but Shirky's books and articles are replete with stories of people doing great things with new information technologies to benefit themselves, each other, and society.

Writing several years later, Zeynep Tufekci, herself active both personally and academically in engaging Twitter to effect political change, suggests a third factor shaping the relationship between the internet and public space: the dynamic between increased access to mass discourse and the increasingly fractured nature of that discourse.[2] Social platforms like Facebook and Twitter pull people together in old and new ways and often seem like places where large groups of people encounter each other together. They seem public, but as Eli Pariser notes in *The Filter Bubble*, people actually experience these platforms in personalized segments.[3] Tufekci poetically notes, "Today's phantom public sphere has been fragmented and submerged into billions of individual capillaries."[4] It is easier for anyone to participate in mass discourse, but that discourse has also become more and more private, happening behind everyone's backs. The 2016 US presidential election is a powerful example of this point; when Donald Trump became president everyone was surprised, and the United States as a whole began to realize just how fractured civil discourse had become.

In the remainder of this chapter I want to propose one way forward in public spaces for the Christian ethicist faced with a world increasingly dominated by these three arguments—distraction and interruption, creativity and collaboration, and access and fragmentation. How can people with an interest in the shape of a life lived according to Christ's witness be guided by the echoes of this witness in reason, experience, scripture, and tradition? There are several assumptions that guide my approach here that will become clear over the next paragraphs. While the shape of public space in an era increasingly shaped by the tools and methods of the virtual is unpredictable, the shape of our response need not be novel. Likewise, the virtual is not space to ignore but rather should be inhabited by the same bodily practices that have shaped Christian engagements in concrete spaces. The account I develop begins with Albert Borgmann's focal practices and a consideration of the cell phone as a focal tool of the virtual. The cell phone is a useful illustration because the focal practices and burdens it encourages show the coming

---

[2]Zeynep Tufekci, *Twitter and Tear Gas: The Power and Fragility of Networked Protest* (New Haven: Yale University Press, 2017).

[3]Eli Pariser, *The Filter Bubble: How the New Personalized Web Is Changing What We Read and How We Think* (New York: Penguin Books, 2011).

[4]Zeynep Tufekci, "The {Divisive, Corrosive, Democracy Poisoning} Golden Age of Free Speech," *Wired* 26, no. 2 (February 2018): 50.

together of people in virtual spaces. I then develop an account of the virtual and end with a discussion of authenticity.

FOCAL PRACTICES

Generally, philosophers of technology are either some kind of instrumentalists or determinists. Determinists believe that technologies have inherent values. Our tools shape our use of them for good or ill, perhaps more than our intention. Determinists believe that the fast pace of our society is because our tools promote speed. Determinists believe that guns kill people. Phones that constantly demand our attention are going to promote a culture of inattention. Determinism is especially compelling in a context like I have described so far. When people don't think about how they use technology, they aren't going to be able to control it. It will control them. The most compelling determinist when it comes to technology is the philosopher Albert Borgmann. Borgmann is not a strict determinist, but he does believe that our technologies shape our interaction. He makes a really important distinction between "focal practices" and "technological devices."[5]

Simply, a focal practice is something that requires our attention and in so burdening us creates a variety of good results. A cooking stove in a pioneer house could be an example of a focal practice. Maintaining one is a burden but everyone gathers around it and also works on being a family while they labor at the stove. A device, on the other hand, unburdens us and becomes nearly invisible so that we no longer need to worry about it. A microwave oven is a good example of a device. It requires no maintenance, and if we eat prepackaged food (and are then separated even from the process of cooking), no preparation in order to deliver the same service that the cooking stove did. However, the microwave oven does not bind us together as a family; it allows us to separate our lives based on individual interest and occupation.

To make the point more precise, our society's use of Amazon.com to not only buy but also read books unburdens us from needing to go to bookstores or libraries to read Borgmann. (It also weakens bookstores and libraries.) However, we lose out on a whole world of social interaction when unburdened in this way. Borgmann argues that technology is freeing us from burdens that we should not want to be rid of.[6] This argument is compelling because it considers technology in a pervasive way and considers the kind of people we become when we use certain technologies in certain ways. People immersed in computers and cell phones and the internet are for Borgmann unlikely to become virtuous in the same ways that people who are focused on worthwhile tasks that build family and strengthen the bonds of Christian friendship. Their lives are disappearing into their technology. I disagree slightly with Borgmann—not that his account of focal practices and technological devices is not compelling. It is always going to be better for a family to work together to cook a meal on a stove than to use a microwave to heat up individual portions at individually convenient times. It is always going to be better for a society to patronize bookstores and libraries than to make more individualized decisions about books. My chief departure from Borgmann is in thinking that new technologies can in fact become compelling focal practices. I am the other kind of technological philosopher—an instrumentalist.

---

[5]Albert Borgmann, *Technology and the Character of Contemporary Life: A Philosophical Inquiry* (Chicago: University of Chicago Press, 1987).

[6]Ibid., 134–41.

A strict instrumentalist believes that technologies have no inherent value. How we use the instrument shapes the morality of its use. Guns don't kill people. People kill people. Cell phones aren't irritating; people who use cell phones are irritating. We can choose the goods of safety, politeness, and attention when we choose the cell phone and therefore become virtuous users of technology. I think that the best thinking about technology is modified instrumentalism. I definitely believe, with the determinists, that some tools shape their users. The difference between the gun and the cell phone is important. Guns are only good at killing people or at least injuring people. When guns are used for protection, defense, or safety, they do so by killing or threatening to kill people. Guns have determined uses. Cell phones are less determined. Cell phones are actually more open to becoming focal practices than landlines used to be. I have four arguments for why this is the case based on my own experience of using cell phones.

First, there is the consideration of safety. Cell phones keep me and those around me safe. Wherever I am I can call 911 (the telephone number to dial in the United States for emergencies) or take a picture and bring people who are paid to keep us safe to the situation. If I were a woman walking at night I could be on the phone the whole time. I could have a virtual protector. I began to insist that my parents buy a cell phone when my father had a bad bicycle accident. My phone has the ability to tell me where in the world I am through GPS, and through apps like Find my Friends, enables me to track the location of those who let me. This is particularly useful when my partner drives to meet a new client. I can calmly and quietly check where she is and that she has left at the right time. I can also get an accurate read on when she will get home and prepare supper accordingly.

Second, there is politeness. Cell phones let me text people if I need to be late for a meeting. Cell phones let people text me if they need to be late for a meeting. The extra connectivity can be freeing. Texts can be the politest of communications. I have already been in a meeting and received a text that a colleague will be late. This happens without much interruption. Later when the colleague's voice was needed to address a problem I could note they had been held up.

Third, cell phones perfectly replace the technology that they supplant. Almost everything that my landline did my cell phone does better. There are two exceptions that I can think of. It is nearly impossible to lose a phone that is wired into the wall. I have misplaced my cell phone on numerous occasions. Landlines did not store impressively long lists of other people's contacts. This meant that I used to have all my friends' phone numbers memorized. If I do not have my cell phone for whatever reason, I can no longer recall even very close friends' phone numbers. It would not need to be this way. Computers did not perfectly replace the typewriter or the pen but we decided they were better at writing and messaging most of the time. We lost something though when we stopped sending handwritten letters to each other. The burden of writing in pen and ink conveys something importantly different than anything I produce on my computer.

Fourth, regarding attention, cell phones let me control when I am reachable. They can be turned off. This is a great advantage cell phones have over landlines. If I want to spend an hour with my partner in our home I can choose to be solely focused on her for that time. Cell phones can allow for me to be more virtuous than landlines. It is not a wonder that the Amish use cell phones. The Amish provide some very interesting examples of technological discernment and experimentation that is based in decisions that consistently place the religious community first. Some technologies, like the car or television, they reject. Some are adapted like a variety of tools made to run on pneumatics powered by gas generators rather than electricity. Cell phones are also permitted for business purposes but never inside the home. Others, like roller blades or gas barbeques, are easily accepted.[7] This community-focused discernment seems extreme from the outside, but this is partly because we so rarely engage in discernment around technology.

The ability of a cell phone to browse the internet also means that many people now have access to the internet with its employment and social service opportunities without the need to own a computer or to buy internet access. The excellent A.L.I.C.E. material hardship measures created by the United Way include cell phones as a necessity, not a luxury. Cell phones stand to greatly reduce the digital divide giving significantly more low-income people internet access.

Now, of course, there are many things to hate about cell phones, stemming from bad etiquette, bad driving, bad practices of resource extraction, and bad habits of use. I have not focused on these, but I am open to arguments that suggest that the use of cell phones is problematic because of their ubiquity. One of the burdens of the landline was that it didn't move. This was purely a disadvantage in terms of having a conversation on the telephone, but it did restrict the space in which people could have telephone conversations to the area around their phones. Now there are very few places that are not technically capable of hosting a telephone conversation.

The other thing that I have not focused on in this account of the replacement of landline telephones is all of the other things that cell phones have also replaced. I no longer own a metronome, a guitar tuner, a voice recorder, an answering machine, a calendar. I still own a level, a camera, a bible, a radio, an outside thermometer, and a calculator, but I don't really ever use them. This is one of the ways in which cell phones are great examples of environmental stewardship as they make obsolete many items we might otherwise need to buy.

I also own a few maps, and I do look at them occasionally, because I really like maps, but when I travel to a destination that I have not been to before I depend on my phone. The use of GPS to navigate is an interesting further example of replacement and burdenedness. In most ways GPS is a great improvement over a paper map. It shows us where we are on the map, it can plot the best route accounting for traffic conditions and construction, and the maps can be updated so that my phone is always more accurate than a paper map would be. GPS is so good at removing the burden of a map that we sometimes trust them too much. When we used a paper map we always knew that we needed to pay attention to what we were doing or we would end up lost. It is a bit too easy to just let our phones take over and then on those rare occasions that we should have been paying attention and the GPS is wrong we end up lost or worse in danger. GPS is a great replacement for maps, but of course it is not a perfect representation of the world. It is virtual.

The associated burdens of the focal practices of cell phone use are in many ways associated with our coming together in virtual spaces. Christian ethics needs a robust account of the virtual in order to navigate the space outlined at the beginning of this chapter. The virtual is connected not just to the internet and computer-generated worlds but also to potential and to change and to virtue.

---

[7]Donald B. Kraybill, *On the Backroad to Heaven: Old Order Hutterites, Mennonites, Amish, and Brethren* (Baltimore: Johns Hopkins, 2002).

VIRTUALITY

The field of meaning for the word "virtual" is large and diverse, and much of our thinking about it is shaped by Marcel Proust who defines the virtual as that which is real but not actual, ideal but not abstract.[8] Most simply something is virtual when it is not quite concrete: the paper I am not quite finished or the meal I have almost finished preparing. These things are real, they exist, but they are not yet actual. This gives virtuality a pastness, which is relative to the finished paper or the meal that is ready to eat; the virtual is in the past. Here we also find the slightly used car that is virtually new. In the contemporary imagination, the virtual stands for digitally mediated representations of aspects of the world, like virtual banking. This usage makes sense, when I pay my credit card online I don't need to duplicate the transaction at the bank; it is real but not concrete. When I use my computer to enter a virtual world, say to play a game, or view an architectural model, or visit a place I have not been, the buildings I see are not actually in my computer, but I can interact with them and my interaction can have real-world effects. Virtual reality can be used for safety training, or to cure phobias, or to practice for dangerous situations. The virtual is generative in this sense embracing multiple potentials. In Brian Massumi's words, "The virtual is the mode of reality implicated in the emergence of new potentials. In other words, its reality is the reality of change: the event."[9] Virtuality is a useful concept in helping us identify the movement between categories when events or action become present, or become concrete.

The words *virtue* and *virtual* derive from the Latin "virtus" or strength. An older meaning of virtue is as the embodiment of divine power. Angels used to be called virtues in this sense. In Reformation debates about the presence of Christ's actual body and blood in the bread and wine of the Eucharist, virtuality allowed someone like Thomas Cranmer to tread a middle ground between Luther and Rome. These examples illustrate the "ideal but not abstract" part of the Proust quote and suggest an openness to moral categories and an ontology of becoming and embodiment in the concept of the virtual. The virtual loosens the boundaries between the categories it mediates. Karen Franck connects this set of meanings to computer-generated worlds in a profound way:

> I am ... fascinated with the body and the "non-body" in cyberspace. I anticipate entering a virtual world someday soon. Will I leave my body behind? What kind of body might I wish to leave, or keep, and why? Virtual reality is very physical. I won't just see changing images on a flat screen; I will have the feeling of occupying those images with my entire body. ... If the virtual is so physical, what body will I leave behind? Not my physical body. Without it, I am in no world at all. It is physical bodies that give us access to any world.[10]

This insight—that it is only through our physical bodies that we access the world—is key. When a cell phone connects me to other people—through a telephone conversation, through Twitter, through knowing where my partner is on the map, or most decisively through augmented reality games and applications that overlay new layers on the concrete

---

[8]Marcel Proust, quoted in Gilles Deleuze, *Bergsonism*, trans. Hugh Tomlinson and Barbara Habberiam (New York: Zone Books, 1988), 96.

[9]Brian Massumi, "Sensing the Virtual, Building the Insensible," in *Hypersurface Architecture*, ed. Stephen Perrella, *Architectural Design* (Profile no. 133) 68 (May–June 1998).

[10]Karen A. Franck, "When I Enter Virtual Reality, What Body Will I Leave Behind," *Architectural Design* 65 (November–December 1995), 20–3.

world like Pokémon Go or Snapchat—it is bringing us together as virtual bodies in a virtual world.

VIRTUAL BODIES

I want to explore the possibility of virtual bodies as both full of potential and openness to divine embodiment by considering for a moment the writing of the apostle Paul. Paul certainly had a rich sense of his and other's individual bodies and the ways in which they are bound in relationship and grace one to another. Perhaps this is seen nowhere more clearly than in the letter to Philemon where Paul focuses on his own individual reputation in an attempt to persuade Philemon to release the slave Onesimus. Paul has a rich sense of the importance of individual bodies but by no means is he limited to thinking of bodies as individual.

In fact, we owe to Paul our use of "body" to refer to social groups (e.g., 1 Cor. 12:12-27). After Paul, it is not just the "body of Christ" as a word for the church that makes sense but also a whole host of uses of the body to mark political, economic, and social entities. The social body is not only a grouping of individual bodies but also its own creation as an extension of the body of Christ. Paul also details a commitment to what I would name *virtual bodies* in 2 Cor. 3:1b-3:

> Surely we do not need, as some do, letters of recommendation to you or from you, do we? You yourselves are our letter, written on our hearts, to be known and read by all; and you show that you are a letter of Christ, prepared by us, written not with ink but with the Spirit of the living God, not on tablets of stone but on tablets of human hearts.

The language of this exhortation, which we know because it is a text of words, an unnecessary letter, names the Corinthians as the body by which people can come to know Christ. This body occurs simultaneously in three ways: individually, socially, and virtually. The individual Corinthians shape the relationships of both division and unity that together form the social body which Paul here addresses as a letter of Christ. Christ's body is extended virtually by the Corinthians in body and by Paul in letter. Most importantly, Paul asserts that these amount to the same thing. The body of the Corinthians becomes a virtual letter of Christ, just as Paul's letter to the Corinthians becomes a virtual body. The exchange of encouragement occurs in the passing of letters from Paul to his congregations, but the logic of these interstices is a bodily one. These letters form a virtual body. And Christians believe, in important ways, that Paul's body and certainly Christ's body are also available to us now. These bodies are in the past but are virtually also bodies in the present.

There are ways too in which virtual space also extends the bodily interaction of the living with the recently dead through the persistence of Facebook profiles and provides an opportunity for last engagements by providing an address to which messages can be sent. This is part of the blurring of boundaries encouraged by the virtual.

AUTHENTICITY

This raises questions of authenticity. Authenticity is an important concept for us; when we are truly ourselves (a theologian is going to say who God created us to be), we are authentic. When we present a version of ourselves that is deliberately false, we are engaging in some kind of lying. There is an important difference between authenticity and illusion in terms of how we present ourselves to others. Paul reflects on this difference a great deal, and questions of deception and authenticity are present in the biblical narrative from the beginning. Space does not allow an exegesis of the deception stories in Genesis, but even a cursory read of the Esau's blessing or Abraham's attempts to pass off his wife as his sister reveals that deception in political and public space is not novel. Perhaps the most decisive account of authenticity in the biblical text is the one given by A. K. M. Adam in relationship to Paul's signature in his essay, "Deconstruction: On making a difference." Adam argues for a differential account of authenticity, which would allow us to "recuperate from our captivity to undecidable questions,"[11] encouraging us to recognize that interpretation and deconstruction can never be guaranteed by recourse to a single foundation like the identity of an author, patterns of speech, or a signature. Adam wants us to pursue our retrieval of the biblical text, and in other writings also our retrieval of those we meet in virtual spaces through charitable interpretation and a valuing of different approaches to interpretation.

In a recent study four close friends of a person were asked to describe that person's personality.[12] Then, four strangers were asked to describe that same person's personality, but only based on what they observed about that person on Facebook. The study showed a high level of agreement between the two groups of describers. The Facebook profile was an authentic version—authentic enough that the strangers could describe the person as accurately as the close friends. Jeff Hancock, who ran the study, suggests that technologically mediated communication is often more honest than face-to-face communication. This is because humankind began to communicate by speaking at around 50,000 BCE, but didn't begin to communicate by writing until approximately 3000 BCE. That is roughly 47,000 years of communication with no traces of that communication left behind for later review. Humankind has therefore evolved to speak in a way in which our words disappear, in which lying is easy, but we are living in an environment where everything is recorded.

Negotiating a world characterized by distraction and interruption, creativity and collaboration, and access and fragmentation is never going to be a simple task. As Hancock suggests, the challenges of attending to deception and authenticity are something we have been struggling with since the advent of writing. As Christians, potentially open to Paul's suggestions about how to follow Jesus, we might want to consider that our communities—primarily but not only the church—already have the resources to help us negotiate this terrain in both virtual and concrete space. Even as the tools themselves morph to support different modes of participation (as Facebook has done from its original ongoing yearbook style format to its new democracy-defying misinformation-machine algorithm), we have what we need to both project ourselves into public spaces and hold each other accountable to Christ's way, in the regular practices of our communities. If we do this well enough we may even be able to participate in the rehabilitation of public spaces.

What I have tried to suggest in this chapter is that virtuality, when understood carefully as a bodily space that can be inhabited authentically, can allow for the exercise of focal practices. We are faced with new challenges but as Christians we do not necessarily need

[11]A. K. M. Adam, *Postmodern Biblical Criticism* (Philadelphia: Fortress, 1995), 41.
[12]Jeff Hancock, "The Future of Lying," *Ted.com*, September 2012, https://www.ted.com/talks/jeff_hancock_the_future_of_lying/.

new solutions, even if we will constantly need to incorporate new practices to realize our goals.

SUGGESTED READINGS

Bennett, Jana. *Aquinas on the Web? Doing Theology in an Internet Age*. London: Bloomsbury, 2012.

Gaillardetz, Richard. *Transforming Our Days: Spirituality, Community and Liturgy in a Technological Culture*. New York: Crossroad, 2000.

Kallenberg, Brad. *God and Gadgets: Following Jesus in a Technological Age*. Eugene: Wipf and Stock, 2010.

Shields, Rob. *The Virtual*. New York: Routledge, 2002.

Weinberger, David. *Everyday Chaos: Technology, Complexity, and How We're Thriving in a New World of Possibility*. Boston: Harvard Business Review Press, 2019.

Issues, Applications, and Twenty-First-Century Agenda for Christian Ethics

Section B: Conflict, War, and Peace

CHAPTER TWENTY

Terrorism and the Responsibility to Protect

BRIAN STILTNER

In Christian ethics, terrorism and the protection of populations fall under the subfield of political and social ethics, where they are commonly examined in light of human rights theories or the ethics of war and peace. This chapter takes the latter vantage point. Within this frame, analysis of terrorism includes investigating why such violence occurs, whether it can and should be stopped by militaristic actions, and what postwar and preventative strategies will forestall terrorism. Analysis of protecting populations includes the practicality and morality of military intervention before and during a humanitarian crisis, and how to build systems of national and international justice to prevent atrocities.

CHRISTIAN ETHICAL POSITIONS ON WAR AND PEACE

Many of the above issues turn on the enduring question of whether and when war can be justified. The debate among Christians over the moral permissibility of war, at both the popular and the scholarly levels, has continued in one form or another for the entirety of Christian history. The debate will never be fully resolved because the sources that guide Christian ethics are not univocal. In scripture can be found texts that describe God as fighting battles on the side of God's people (Deut. 9:30; Exod. 15:3-6; 2 Chron. 32:20-22), others that counsel forgiving one's enemies (Lk. 6:27-28) and not living by the sword (Mt. 26:52), and others that support political rulers' martial power (Rom. 13:1-5). Following the diverse options presented in the Bible, the tradition has developed and taken varied forms. In the early centuries, Christian leaders forbade Christians to serve in the military, but later, this profession became acceptable. By the end of the Patristic era, church leaders supported the option of a just war waged by the state, but during the Reformation, new Christian communities became thoroughly pacifist. Over the centuries, five ethical positions took shape as possible options for Christians.

Pacifism renounces deadly violence in fidelity to the teaching and actions of Jesus, who taught his disciples to "turn the other cheek" (Mt. 5:39), that is, not to respond to violence with violence,[1] and who preached an inclusive, nonviolent Kingdom of God, drawing upon peaceable imagery from the Book of Isaiah (e.g., 2:4, 11:6). Most significantly, Jesus accepted his violent execution at the hands of the state, instead of

[1]For an interpretation of "turn the other cheek" as a counsel of resistance, not passivity, see Walter Wink, *Jesus and Nonviolence: A Third Way* (Minneapolis: Augsburg Fortress, 2003), 9–16.

calling upon twelve legions of angels to fight for him (Mt. 26:53-54). Christian pacifists understand churches as communities whose members try to live peacefully as disciples of Jesus and to act as peacemakers, as he counseled (Mt. 5:8). Not all Christian pacifists hold to absolute nonviolence: some accept personal self-defense, and many accept modest force by domestic police, among other exceptions.[2]

Just-war theory ("theory" may be replaced with "thought" or "tradition," all of which may be abbreviated as JWT) has its roots in ancient Roman legal thought and has been developed over two millennia by philosophers, theologians, and international lawyers. The biblical bases for this position include the example of the early Hebrews fighting to defend themselves in the Holy Land (see the above citations from Deuteronomy and Exodus, yet note the following discussion of holy war), the existence of armies and military leaders during the Jewish kingdoms, and St. Paul's teaching that "there is no authority except from God, and those authorities that exist have been instituted by God" (Rom. 13:1). In the Christian tradition, St. Augustine (354–430) is one of the earliest and most important architects of a set of criteria that came to constitute JWT. Combining Greek and Roman legal concepts, particularly from Cicero, with biblical insights, Augustine articulated the first three of several just-war criteria: that a war be (1) declared by a legitimate ruler who possesses (2) a right intention (3) for a just cause.[3] In the medieval and early modern periods, just-war theorists further stipulated that a just war must be undertaken (4) as a last resort with (5) a reasonable hope of military success and (6) an expected good outcome that is proportionate to the death and destruction to be caused. These six criteria for going to war came to be known as the *jus ad bellum* criteria, distinguished from two criteria for justice in the conduct of war (*jus in bello*): (1) that war be fought by proportionate methods and (2) that all attacks discriminate between combatants and noncombatants.[4]

According to most contemporary just-war theorists, all of the criteria in both sets must be satisfied—there must be a reasonable case for each standard that is more probable than the objections to it—for the war to be considered ethically justified, although this is one of many methodological issues that just-war theorists and Christian ethicists continue to debate.[5] Recently, just-war theorists have proposed a third category of justice after war (*jus post bellum*), in which the country or coalition that wins a war has the moral duty to make up for the damage it has caused by facilitating the restoration of the civic order and encouraging restorative justice instead of harsh punishment.[6] Even more recent

---

[2]For a delineation of versions of Christian pacifism across several spectrums, see David L. Clough and Brian Stiltner, *Faith and Force: A Christian Debate about War* (Washington, DC: Georgetown University Press, 2007): 44–50; also, Tobias Winright, "From Police Officers to Peace Officers," in *The Wisdom of the Cross: Essays in Honor of John Howard Yoder*, ed. Stanley Hauerwas et al. (Grand Rapids: Eerdmans, 1999), 84–114.

[3]Augustine expresses his views of ideas about just war in *The City of God* and in some sermons and letters. Key passages can be found in Arthur F. Holmes, ed., *War and Christian Ethics: Classic and Contemporary Readings on the Morality of War*, 2nd ed. (Grand Rapids: Baker Academic, 2005), Ernest L. Fortin and Douglas Kries, eds., *Augustine: Political Writings* (Indianapolis: Hackett, 1994), and similar anthologies.

[4]The *in bello* criterion of discrimination is often described as the principle of noncombatant immunity. Notably, the US Catholic Bishops proposed an additional *ad bellum* criterion of comparative justice, which means asking, "Which side is sufficiently 'right' in a dispute, and are the values at stake critical enough to override the presumption against war?" (National Conference of Catholic Bishops, *The Challenge of Peace*, 1983, no. 92).

[5]The question of whether JWT presumes a "presumption against war" has been particularly debated; on this and other methodological debates, see Clough and Stiltner, *Faith and Force*, 64–7.

[6]See Mark J. Allman and Tobias L. Winright, *After the Smoke Clears: The Just War Tradition and Post War Justice* (Maryknoll: Orbis, 2010).

are proposals for justice before war (*jus ante bellum*) that emphasize the importance of avoiding war through proactive steps.[7]

Pacifism and JWT are usually considered the main contenders for a Christian theory of war and peace, but three other positions have been influential. The holy war position, also known as the "Crusade mentality," has been an influential attitude in Christian history, especially during the era of the Crusades from the late ninth to the late fifteenth centuries, when various popes encouraged Christians to fight Muslims and take back the Holy Land, and even, at times, to kill Muslims, Jews, or other Christians. This view states that God can command believers to fight offensive battles in God's name, as happened when God commanded the Hebrews to completely destroy the men of Canaan and enslave the women and children, if they did not surrender (Deut. 20:10-18). No Christian ethicist adopts this position now, yet it remains important for understanding the mindset of violent extremists in Christianity and other religions who do truly adopt holy war as an ethical principle, or who describe themselves as just warriors but who must be denounced as the holy warriors they are.[8]

Christian political realism takes just-war insights about the necessity of force in an imperfect world to stronger or—its advocates would say—more consistent conclusions. Generally speaking, political realists have a pessimistic view of human nature, especially as expressed in group contexts. Realists are therefore prepared to act outside the bounds of standard morality in order to protect the self-interests of a nation or other group. The American Protestant theologian Reinhold Niebuhr (1892–1972) is identified as the progenitor of contemporary Christian realism, and he in turn credited St. Augustine with being "the first great 'realist' in Western history."[9] In contrast to JWT, Christian realism does not see war as a reasonable action for the sake of the common good but as a tragic yet necessary use of imperfect methods. Christian realists typically consider military action as one option from the toolbox of coercive measures that governments must use to establish a modicum of justice.

Over the last one hundred years or so, Christian leaders and ethicists have criticized warfare in increasingly strong terms, such that even those still holding to a just-war position tend to espouse a nonbelligerent version that sees war as almost always a mistake. This is the fifth, and most recent, Christian ethical position on war—just peacemaking. Baptist ethicist Glen Stassen (1936–2014) championed this approach, which he developed in collaboration with twenty-two scholars who held a range of ethical positions on war. Stassen proposed that pacifists, realists, and just-war thinkers support the following practices for preventing war, and should further agree that these activities deserve the full attention of governments, NGOs, churches, scholars, and activists:[10]

[7]See Rachel Hart Winter, "Justice in War Preparations: A Just War Application to Testing in the Marshall Islands," in *Can War Be Just in the 21st Century? Ethicists Engage the Tradition*, ed. Tobias Winright and Laurie Johnston (Maryknoll: Orbis, 2015), 112–28.

[8]See Mark Juergensmeyer, *Terror in the Mind of God: The Global Rise of Religious Violence*, 4th ed. (Oakland: University of California Press, 2017) and the six volumes in the University of Chicago Press's Fundamentalism Project, edited by Martin E. Marty and R. Scott Appleby and published from 1994 to 2004.

[9]Reinhold Niebuhr, "Augustine's Political Realism" (orig. pub. 1953) in *The Essential Reinhold Niebuhr*, ed. Robert McAfee Brown (New Haven: Yale University Press, 1986), 124.

[10]Glenn H. Stassen, ed., *Just Peacemaking: The New Paradigm for the Ethics of Peace and War*, 3rd ed. (Cleveland: Pilgrim, 2008). See also a contribution to the framework by interreligious scholars: *Interfaith Just Peacemaking: Jewish, Christian, and Muslim Perspectives on the New Paradigm of Peace and War*, ed. Susan Brooks Thistlethwaite (New York: Palgrave Macmillan, 2012).

1. Support nonviolent direct action.
2. Take independent initiatives to reduce threats.
3. Use cooperative conflict resolution.
4. Acknowledge responsibility for conflict; seek forgiveness.
5. Advance democracy, human rights, and religious liberty.
6. Foster just and sustainable development.
7. Work with emerging cooperative forces in the international system.
8. Strengthen the UN and international efforts for cooperation and human rights.
9. Reduce offensive weapons and the weapons trade.
10. Encourage grassroots peacemaking groups and voluntary associations.

Christians supporting these practices[11] have been highly influenced by reflecting on humanity's experience of war in the twentieth century and by rational study of the causes and consequences of modern warfare. Reflecting these developments, for example, is Pope Francis, who said in a 2018 address, "I emphasize again that the use of violence never leads to peace. War begets war; violence begets violence."[12]

Four of these Christian positions (excepting holy war, because of its uncritical endorsement of violence) are legitimate normative options for responding to ethical problems of war. Next, these positions will be tested out on terrorism and mass atrocities. Although every student and scholar eventually identifies with a theory that they think is truest to the four sources of Christian ethics, they can and should continue to learn from the perspectives of the other normative theories.

ARE THERE ETHICAL AND EFFECTIVE STRATEGIES FOR ENDING TERRORISM?

To properly grasp the challenge of terrorism, one should have a sense of its history, current expressions, and political and psychological causes. By learning from experts on terrorism, Christian ethicists use the fonts of experience and reason in developing their responses. Terrorism is massively destructive and tragic.[13] From 2006 to 2016, the number of terrorist incidents ranged from 10,000 to over 14,000 annually, with a dip in the year 2012 to 6,771 incidents. The average annual death toll from those incidents was just under 20,000 per year, with a dip to 11,098 in 2012, followed two years later by a high of 32,763 deaths. No country is immune from the possibility of a terrorist strike, yet most of the recent carnage is concentrated in the Middle East, the Indian subcontinent, and central Africa. The country that saw the most terrorism in 2016 by far was Iraq (2,956 attacks), followed by Afghanistan (1,340), India (927), Pakistan (734), the Philippines (482), and Nigeria (466).

One of the leading experts on terrorism, Bruce Hoffman, defines it as "the deliberate creation and exploitation of fear through violence or the threat of violence in the

[11]A very similar approach is "peacebuilding," a set of proactive practices developed through a long-standing collaboration between Catholic and Mennonite scholars and activists. See Robert J. Schreiter et al., eds., *Peacebuilding* (Maryknoll: Orbis, 2010).

[12]Pope Francis, "General Audience," May 16, 2018, https://w2.vatican.va/content/francesco/en/audiences/2018/documents/papa-francesco_20180516_udienza-generale.html.

[13]The data that follow are from Statista Research Department, "Terrorism—Statistics & Facts," Statista: The Statistics Portal, July 4, 2019, https://www.statista.com/topics/2267/terrorism/. See also the National Consortium for the Study of Terrorism and Responses to Terrorism, http://www.start.umd.edu/.

pursuit of political change," which is "ineluctably political in aims and motives" and "perpetrated by a subnational group or nonstate entity."[14] This account pulls together all of the necessary elements that experts find essential for understanding what terrorism is and how it differs from crime, random violence, and warfare.[15] In what sense, then, is terrorism a religious phenomenon? Theorists stake out a range of positions: some see religious fundamentalism as central to terrorism, others as incidental.[16] A sensible middle ground is offered by the sociologist Mark Juergensmeyer, who interprets religious ideology as a ramping-up force—like ideological gasoline poured on fires already lit by political injustice and economic dislocation. He suggests that "religious violence is on the rise because religion provides persons and groups threatened and humiliated by modernity and globalism with the resources to recast their struggle for identity and dignity as a 'cosmic war.'"[17] Juergensmeyer calls terrorist acts instances of "performative violence," which means that "like religious ritual or street theater, they are dramas designed to have an impact on the several audiences that they affect."[18] The perpetrators of such violence try to reclaim, in their own eyes, a sense of dignity by making the public take notice of their sensational attacks.[19] In sum, Hoffman, Juergensmeyer, and many other experts affirm that terrorism is typically a matter of both ideology and tactics.

Christian ethicists ask: In light of what we know about terrorism, what is the morally proper way to respond to it? Edward Long has described three basic approaches: war intensified, law enforcement, and just peacemaking.[20] The first approach, "war intensified," reflects the thinking of some in the just-war camp and many in the realist camp; it favors military attacks against terrorist groups. Long identifies this as the paradigm for the American and British governments' responses to the September 11 attacks. After initially targeting al Qaeda strongholds in the hills of Afghanistan in the fall of 2001, the United States proceeded to oust the Taliban government and take over administration of the nation. A little over a year later, the United States invaded Iraq on the grounds that it, too, was a sponsor of terror. Nearly two decades later, both countries are highly unstable. Tens of thousands of people still die annually in these countries and their regions as a result of the wars—largely from terrorism that arose in the wake of the post-invasion instability. The Costs of War Project at Brown University estimates the cumulative total death toll from these two wars as nearly 800,000 people, including 19,000 American and allied military personnel.[21] Expecting these kinds of results, Long and many Christians ethicists opposed the wars, especially the Iraq War, at their outset. The ethical criticism of "war intensified" is that, no matter how just it may feel to seek military retribution

[14]Bruce Hoffman, *Inside Terrorism*, 3rd ed. (New York: Columbia University Press, 2017), 43–4.

[15]Clough and Stiltner offer ways to distinguish terrorism from these other forms of violence; see *Faith and Force*, 154–9.

[16]Patrick McCormick provides a helpful survey of the representative literature on this topic as of the mid-2000s, in "Violence: Religion, Terror, War," *Theological Studies* 67, no. 1 (2006): 143–62.

[17]Ibid., 145.

[18]Juergensmeyer, *Terror in the Mind of God*, 155.

[19]McCormick, "Violence: Religion, Terror, War," 145; Juergensmeyer, *Terror in the Mind of God*, 157.

[20]Edward LeRoy Long Jr., *Facing Terrorism: Responding as Christians* (Louisville: Westminster John Knox, 2004), chaps. 3 and 5.

[21]In figures last updated on its website in November 2019, over 770,000 people have died due to direct violence from these wars, Watson Institute of International and Public Affairs, "Costs of War," Brown University, https://watson.brown.edu/costsofwar/papers/summary. See also http://www.iCasualties.org for an ongoing accounting of military deaths in these conflicts.

for a terrorist attack, it is all too easy for the responding nation to lose its sense of proportionality and to violate many other just-war criteria.

The second approach, law enforcement, considers terrorist attacks, in most cases, not as acts of war, but as criminal actions. This approach emphasizes such tactics as the surveillance of terrorist groups, the preemptive arrests of those planning attacks, and putting attackers on trial. Addressing terrorism as crime rather than as war leads to measured responses. A law enforcement approach is less likely to cause the death of bystanders; it is less likely to result in a decades-long military quagmire. It appears that the law enforcement approach can be supported by advocates of all four Christian ethical positions on war, as long as the enforcement is conducted with legal and ethical constraints that are typically expected of policing.[22] Therefore, one enforcement tactic that has been roundly condemned by Christians ethicists and by the churches is any use of torture to extract information from suspects.[23] Another controversial counterterrorist tactic—supported by some Christian ethicists and condemned by others—is the use of drone strikes.[24]

Moving to the third approach, Long specifically cites Stassen's just peacemaking practices. Long believes this should be the leading approach to terrorism (though he does not deny the need for law enforcement as well) because just peacemaking is more proactive than law enforcement alone and more likely to make for lasting security. The ten practices listed earlier help redirect negative social energies away from the frustrated expression of terrorism. When pursued steadily over time by many stakeholders, including religious groups and grassroots civic organizations, peacemaking practices can lead to substantial social reconciliation, such as the 1997 Good Friday Peace Accords in Northern Ireland and the Columbian peace process, which came to fruition in 2016.[25]

As international lawyers and political scientists wrestle with the legitimacy of counterterrorist militarism under the state sovereignty system, some Christian leaders have proposed that the system itself needs to be rethought. In the 1960s, Pope John XXIII wrote, "Today the universal common good poses problems of world-wide dimensions, which cannot be adequately tackled or solved except by the efforts of public authority endowed with a wideness of powers, structure and means of the same proportions."[26] The pope's claim is affirmed by the majority of contemporary Christian ethicists, who believe that most problems of modern warfare can be effectively addressed only with international cooperation.[27]

[22]See Tobias Winright, "Just Cause and Preemptive Strikes in the War on Terrorism: Insights from a Just-Policing Perspective," *Journal of the Society of Christian Ethics* 26, no. 2 (Fall/Winter 2006): 157–81.

[23]See Anna Floeke Scheid, "Torture, Terror, and Just War," in *Can War Be Just in the 21st Century? Ethicists Engage the Tradition*, ed. Tobias Winright and Laurie Johnston (Maryknoll: Orbis, 2015), 83–95. See also the National Religious Campaign against Torture website, http://www.nrcat.org/.

[24]Brian Stiltner, "A Taste of Armageddon: When Warring Is Done by Drones and Robots," in *Can War Be Just in the 21st Century? Ethicists Engage the Tradition*, ed. Tobias Winright and Laurie Johnston (Maryknoll: Orbis, 2015), 14–28; Kenneth R. Himes, OFM, *Drones and the Ethics of Targeted Killing* (Lanham: Rowman & Littlefield, 2016).

[25]See, e.g., John D. Brewer, Gareth I. Higgins, and Francis Teeney, *Religion, Civil Society, and Peace in Northern Ireland* (New York: Oxford University Press, 2011); Cécile Mouly, María Blen Garrido, and Annette Idler, "How Peace Takes Shape Locally: The Experience of Civil Resistance in Samaniego, Colombia," *Peace & Change* 41, no. 2 (2016): 129–66.

[26]Pope John XXIII, *Pacem in terris* (Vatican City: Libreria Editrice Vaticana, 1963), § 137.

[27]For an example of a sanguine versus a skeptical account of the international legal system, see Mary Ellen O'Connell, "The Just War Tradition and International Law against War: The Myth of Discordant Doctrines," *Journal of the Society of Christian Ethics* 35, no. 2 (2015): 33–51, and, in the same journal and issue, Nigel Biggar, "Just War and International Law: A Response to Mary Ellen O'Connell," 52–62.

WHO IS THE GOOD SAMARITAN WHEN MASS ATROCITIES OCCUR?

Mass atrocities are another problem requiring international cooperation while also demonstrating the limitations of the nation-state system, particularly when they occur within the boundaries of a sovereign state. According to the UN, there are three types of atrocities defined as crimes in international law: genocide, crimes against humanity, and war crimes.[28] The ethical issue of war prompted by these crimes is the propriety of "humanitarian intervention," encompassing several tricky questions: Legally, *may* outside countries militarily intervene in a country where atrocities are occurring? Ethically, *must* they intervene? *Who* should intervene, and *when*? And *how* should they intervene—is it right to use military force that might kill some of the citizens in need of protection, and should outside countries put their own soldiers at risk?

Many Christian theorists have challenged the term itself: intervention with the use of weapons is hardly humanitarian, say pacifists and peacemakers, while realists believe it is naive to get embroiled in another nation's conflict for merely humanitarian reasons.[29] Just-war theorists are the most likely to support such intervention, on the basis of such teachings as the Old Testament injunction to defend the vulnerable (e.g., Isa. 1:17 and Ps. 82:3-4) and the New Testament parable of the Good Samaritan (Lk. 10:25-37), wherein Jesus mandates his listeners to help a neighbor in need even when such action would put one at risk. Of course, care must be taken when applying a first-century biblical story to modern sociopolitical realities, but it is a source from which these ethicists draw inspiration. Protestant ethicist Paul Ramsey (1913–1988), an influential just-war theorist with a realist bent, famously posed this question, "What do you think Jesus would have made the Samaritan do if he had come upon the scene while the robbers were still at their fell work?"[30] His rhetorical implication is that the Christian's loving duty is to intervene to help a neighbor whose life is at risk, whether it is an individual or a large group of neighbors. Ramsey interprets Augustine as following this line of thinking when he laid out his JWT: war should not be based on claims of self-defense but on obligations to love and protect neighbors.[31] Ramsey joins humanitarian (or better, loving) motives to militarist actions when it comes to intervention. To be conceptually candid, then, Christian just-war theorists should identify the matter as one of "military intervention for humanitarian purposes" or "militarized intervention" instead of the softer "humanitarian intervention."

Since international law is built on the foundation of the nation-state system, the presumption has been that nations should not intervene in each other's domestic disputes. The theologian and jurist Hugo Grotius (1583–1645) and subsequent scholars enshrined this principle in international law, even as they recognized some rare exceptions. At the end of the twentieth century, the international community, after witnessing mass atrocities

---

[28]UN Office of the Special Advisers on the Prevention of Genocide and the Responsibility to Protect, *Framework of Analysis for Atrocity Crimes: A Tool for Prevention* (United Nations, 2014), 1, http://www.un.org/en/genocideprevention/prevention.html.

[29]Christian realists often diverge from purely political realists on this matter. The latter are wont to say that intervention is ridiculous without a strong strategic interest, while the former are concerned that rule of law be followed and that interventions actually make a crisis better. See H. David Baer, *Recovering Christian Realism* (Lanham: Lexington, 2014), 61–7.

[30]Paul Ramsey, *Basic Christian Ethics*, reprint ed. (Louisville: Westminster John Knox, 1993), 169.

[31]For an incisive account of Ramsey on this score, along with a pacifist response, see Stanley Hauerwas, "On Being a Church Capable of Addressing a World at War," in *The Hauerwas Reader*, ed. John Berkman and Michael Cartwright (London: Duke University Press, 2001), 426–58.

in Somalia, Rwanda, and the Balkans, more explicitly recognized the need of citizens to be protected within the boundaries of their sovereign states. UN Secretary General Kofi Annan challenged the international community to develop a new consensus on how to address the challenges of mass atrocities. In response, the government of Canada and a group of foundations established the International Commission on Intervention and State Sovereignty (ICISS), which issued in September 2001 a report titled *The Responsibility to Protect*.[32] This term, often abbreviated R2P, has garnered substantial support from the United Nations, international law experts, human rights organizations, and religious institutions. The R2P proposal—which is now often labeled a "doctrine" and a "norm"—was discussed at the 2005 UN World Summit where the participating heads of government affirmed that "each individual State has the responsibility to protect its citizens from genocide, war crimes, ethnic cleansing and crimes against humanity" and that the international community, through the UN, should use "appropriate diplomatic, humanitarian and other peaceful means" to protect populations and to build nations' capacity to prevent crises from breaking out.[33]

Just-war theorists use their criteria to determine when and how a militarized intervention could be ethical, and thinkers from the other normative Christian positions are willing to join the debate on those grounds.[34] Take the example of Syria's civil war, which has been raging since 2011 and is intertwined with a fight against the terrorist organization, the Islamic State in Iraq and the Levant (ISIL). The war has displaced over seven million people internally and prompted over five million refugees to flee the country. Massacres of civilians have abounded. Syrian military forces under the control of President Bashir al-Assad have used chemical weapons against civilians. Assad has proven completely unwilling to protect his own citizens, favoring only those who are loyal to his regime. These features constitute a just cause for the international community to intervene to protect civilians. But whether any of the remaining JWT criteria can be satisfied is contested. Given the criteria of last resort and probability of success, and citing the endless wars in Afghanistan and Iraq, pacifists and just peacemakers believe that military interventions almost always cause more harm than good. In addition, these critics cite evidence that the bombing campaigns against ISIL by Russia and by a US-led coalition have killed thousands of civilians.[35] Most religious commentators, both scholars and clerics, condemn bombing interventions, such as the Trump administration's retaliation against Syria for the use of chemical weapons.[36]

Legitimate authority is another highly contested criterion. As with terrorism, the question of military intervention for humanitarian purposes raises questions about global order in the nation-state system. When the majority of the world's heads of state approved the R2P doctrine in their 2005 summit, they affirmed that the Security Council can mandate coercive action in the interests of peace and justice, as provided for by the UN Charter.[37]

---

[32]Available at the website of the International Coalition for the Responsibility to Protect, http://responsibilitytoprotect.org/. The brief history recounted here draws from the foreword of this report.

[33]UN General Assembly, *2005 World Summit Outcome*, 60th session, October 24, 2005, nos. 138–9, https://www.un.org/ruleoflaw/blog/document/2005-world-summit-outcome/.

[34]See the application of the criteria to R2P by Kenneth R. Himes, OFM, "Humanitarian Intervention and the Just War Tradition," in *Can War Be Just in the 21st Century? Ethicists Engage the Tradition*, ed. Tobias Winright and Laurie Johnston (Maryknoll: Orbis, 2015), 50–64.

[35]E.g., Stephanie Nebehay, "Russia and U.S. Air Strikes Caused Mass Civilian Deaths in Syria: U.N.," Reuters, March 6, 2018.

[36]See, e.g., Maryann Cusimano Love, "More U.S. Bombs in Syria Will Help No One," *America*, April 9, 2018.

[37]UN General Assembly, *2005 World Summit Outcome*, no. 79.

However, the permanent members of the Council, each of whom has veto power, can rarely agree on any military action. Throughout the Syrian conflict, for instance, Russia's president Putin was a staunch supporter of Assad's regime, while the Obama and Trump administrations maintained that Assad should leave power. Yet the US administrations never pushed to make Assad leave power, which would have provoked a conflict with Putin. Since it is usually in one or more powerful nations' selfish interests *not* to have a humanitarian crisis resolved (in the case of Syria, Putin's likely interest was to become a global power broker[38]), it's very difficult to get the permanent members of the Council to support an intervention or to conduct an intervention for truly humanitarian aims. Pacifists, while aware of the flaws of the Security Council, believe that international agreement remains crucial to prevent abuse. In the current context, militarized humanitarian intervention that lacks official UN approval amounts to vigilante action, they argue.[39] Some just-war thinkers agree with that view, while others want to retain more than one route to militarized humanitarian intervention,[40] even if future UN reforms make it possible for the Security Council to render less politicized decisions over interventions.

Given all of these difficulties, it appears that militarized humanitarian interventions are only rarely both ethically justified and practically effective. Perhaps the only major case that met the test *and* turned out relatively well was the 1999 NATO bombing intervention in Kosovo to stop Serbia's ethnic cleansing of the Kosovar Albanians. A strong case can be made from a Christian JWT perspective that the bombing was necessary and just, despite the lack of official sanction from the United Nations. But not all just-war theorists—and ever fewer pacifists, peacemakers, and realists—agree.[41]

What everyone can agree on is that cases calling for intervention are always messy, and it would always be preferable to employ preventative strategies. The architects of the Responsibility to Protect doctrine present it as a comprehensive toolkit that should be employed before, during, and after humanitarian crises. As ICISS cochair Gareth Evans writes, "It is unfortunate that so much of the R2P discussion should have focused on [military force], because this has led many, particularly in the global South, to misunderstand R2P as being *only* about the use of force," when, in fact, the framework is about "prevention at least as much as, if not more than, reaction, and about many much less extreme kinds of reaction."[42] Very much like the just peacemaking practices, the R2P approach affirms that economic development, democratization, and the proactive involvement of international institutions help societies avoid the path to crisis. In this work, religious organizations at the local, national, and international levels have valuable contributions to make.[43]

---

[38]Dmitriy Frolovskiy, "What Putin Really Wants in Syria," *Foreign Policy*, February 1, 2019, https://foreignpolicy.com/2019/02/01/what-putin-really-wants-in-syria-russia-assad-strategy-kremlin/.

[39]Clough and Stiltner, *Faith and Force*, 98–9.

[40]For the latter view, see Michael Walzer, *Arguing about War* (New Haven: Yale University Press, 2004), 103.

[41]For the range of the Christian debate on this case, see William Joseph Buckley, ed., *Kosovo: Contending Voices on Balkan Interventions* (Grand Rapids: Eerdmans, 2000). See also Clough and Stiltner, *Faith and Force*, 88–100.

[42]Gareth Evans, *The Responsibility to Protect* (Washington, DC: Brookings Institution Press, 2008), 128. Appendix B of this book sorts forty-four strategies under one of three "toolboxes"—prevention, reaction, rebuilding. Only one of these strategies is the threat and use of military force.

[43]The UN's genocide prevention office worked with religious leaders to create in 2017 a *Plan of Action for Religious Leaders and Actors to Prevent Incitement to Violence That Could Lead to Atrocity Crimes*, https://www.un.org/en/genocideprevention/documents/Plan_of_Action_Religious_Prevent_Incite.pdf.

CONCLUSION

This chapter has surveyed the approach of Christian ethics to two contemporary injustices—terrorism and mass atrocities. These two issues are large and complex, each with their own dynamics, but, as seen in this chapter, some illuminating commonalities and connections can be drawn between them. They both reflect the horrible violence that people can do to others. They both arise when civil societies and political systems have broken down. Addressing both issues raises challenges for the authoritative role of nation-states in the international system. While both evils should be stopped, it is often unclear on whom that responsibility falls if a national government is unable or unwilling to stop terrorism or atrocities within its borders, or if the government itself is the perpetrator. Last, it is hotly debated whether military actions are moral *and* effective means to stop these horrors.

The four normative ethical positions take varying approaches to these matters, but in light of the contemporary realities of war, there seems to be more joining these positions than dividing them. All the positions understand that people can do great harm to each other when civil order breaks down. Therefore, all of the positions support taking proactive, preventative approaches to avert humanitarian crises and to make terrorism less likely. Just peacemaking has much to offer because it develops sensible solutions that the other positions can likewise support. However, the positions differ on such matters as the wisdom of using military force when a terrorist group such as ISIL is gaining territory, or what to do when the UN Security Council is stalemated over a humanitarian crisis. At times like these, some realists and just warriors just want to stop debating and see some kind of action taken, while pacifists find such "shoot from the hip" attitudes alarming. Just peacemakers have again pointed the way beyond a stale debate, by reminding us that Christians should not wait upon the great political powers to act, but should rather take their own initiatives at the grassroots. "Nonviolent direct action is a strategy that lances the festering boil of violence and produces healing without resort to war."[44]

By listening to the experience of those who suffer from violence, by learning from the successes of those participating in grassroots peacemaking movements, and by dialoguing with experts in the analysis of the root causes of violence, Christian ethics as a field has developed a more cautious approach to commending military action as the solution to problems and has more deeply embraced Jesus's invitation to his disciples, "Blessed are the peacemakers, for they will be called children of God" (Mt. 5:9).

SUGGESTED READINGS

Clough, David, and Brian Stiltner. *Faith and Force: A Christian Debate about War*. Washington, DC: Georgetown University Press, 2007.

Evans, Gareth. *The Responsibility to Protect: Ending Mass Atrocity Crimes Once and for All*. Washington, DC: Brookings Institution, 2008.

Stassen, Glenn H., ed. *Just Peacemaking: The New Paradigm for the Ethics of Peace and War*, 3rd ed. Cleveland: Pilgrim, 2008.

Winright, Tobias, and Laurie Johnson, eds. *Can War Be Just in the 21st Century? Ethicists Engage the Tradition*. Maryknoll: Orbis, 2015.

[44]John Cartwright and Susan Brooks Thistlethwaite, "Support Nonviolent Direct Action," in *Just Peacemaking: The New Paradigm for the Ethics of Peace and War*, 3rd ed., ed. Glenn H. Stassen (Cleveland: Pilgrim, 2008), 41.

CHAPTER TWENTY-ONE

Killer Robots and Cyber Warfare: Technology and War in the Twenty-First Century

MATTHEW A. SHADLE

Modern militaries utilize computers and digital communications to exercise command and control and achieve warfighting aims. As stated in the movie *Sneakers*, "The world isn't run by weapons anymore, or energy, or money. It's run by little ones and zeroes, little bits of data. It's all just electrons."[1] This has made possible a range of new weapon technologies. Computers themselves have become a potential weapon of war, used to disrupt or damage the computer systems of opponents. If, as most Christians have believed over the centuries, military service can be a form of discipleship when carried out ethically,[2] then it behooves Christians to think through the ethical implications of these new military technologies.

This chapter seeks to serve as a guide for Christians engaged in this ethical reflection. It is divided into three sections. The first section introduces how the four sources of Christian ethical reflection—scripture, tradition, reason, and experience—might inform a discussion of military technology in the twenty-first century. The second section examines the ethical implications of robotic warfare, including both remote-controlled drones and autonomous robots. The third section explores the issue of cyber warfare.

SOURCES

All Christians believe that scripture is the definitive written record of God's revelation, and therefore the normative source for Christian ethical reflection. Nevertheless, it is not at all obvious what relevance the ancient texts of the Bible have in a world of artificial intelligence, botnets, and zero-day exploits. Is there too much distance between the world of the Bible and our digital age?

[1]Phil Alan Robinson, dir., *Sneakers* (Universal City: Universal Pictures, 1992).

[2]Daniel M. Bell Jr., *Just War as Christian Discipleship: Recentering the Tradition in the Church Rather Than the State* (Grand Rapids: Brazos, 2009).

Although the authors of the Bible could not have anticipated contemporary robotic and cyber warfare, they offer a vision of the human person that ought to guide Christians as they consider these issues. The Bible affirms that the human person is a bodily creature, and that the human body is good (Gen. 1:31, 2:7). God came to dwell among humankind by taking on flesh (Jn. 1:14). The human person is also not an abstraction, but a concrete being who lives in history. God entered into human history, marked by division and domination, through making a covenant with Israel and through the Incarnation of the Son. Additionally, the human person is a moral agent, capable of making free choices and freely responding to God's grace. This biblical anthropology is important to keep in mind when considering the seemingly disembodied, virtual experience of cyberspace and the possibility of lethal machines with artificial intelligence.

The Bible also provides Christians with a foundational way of thinking about violence. Jesus teaches that Christians should not seek out conflict and violence, but rather should pursue reconciliation (Mt. 5:24) and strive to be peacemakers (Mt. 5:9). Christians are called to love their neighbors (Mt. 22:39) and their enemies (Mt. 5:44). The follower of Jesus ought to be skeptical about the moral rectitude of violence and war. Nevertheless, the Bible's teaching on war remains ambiguous. In the Old Testament, God calls on the people of Israel to engage in war with their neighbors.[3] The Apostle Paul writes that governing authorities bear the sword as agents of God (Rom. 13:4). The ambiguities in the Bible's views on violence and war were left to be worked out in the Christian tradition.

Finally, although God calls on humankind to exercise dominion over the earth by means of technology, scripture also warns of the potential for technology to become a form of idolatry. This is particularly true when it comes to military technology. When the Israelites flee Egypt, Moses exhorts the Israelites to trust in God rather than fear "all Pharaoh's horses and chariots, his chariot drivers and his army" (Exod. 14:9). God, through the prophets, also warns the Israelites against putting undue trust in their own weapons: "Because you have trusted in your power and in the multitude of your warriors, therefore the tumult of war shall rise against your people" (Hos. 10:13-14). Similarly, Jesus calls on Peter to put his trust in God rather than the sword at the moment when the former is to be put to death (Mt. 26:52-54). As these examples suggest, the idolatry of weaponry is very closely related to relationships of domination and oppression, a notion that will be important to keep in mind when considering contemporary military technology.

With biblical teaching as its foundation, over the centuries the Christian tradition has continued to ponder the ethics of violence and war. This has taken place most prominently in the just-war tradition, which proposes that Christians can be morally permitted to participate in military combat. Over time, this tradition developed a set of ethical criteria for assessing the justice of war, divided into the *jus ad bellum* criteria governing the decision to go to war and the *jus in bello* criteria governing the conduct of war. These just-war criteria have proved adaptable to changing technologies and warfighting strategies, and therefore they provide a helpful starting point for thinking through the implications of robotic and cyber warfare. Although this chapter approaches these issues from the perspective of the just-war tradition, it is important to point out that there is also

[3]The Old Testament presents a number of distinct, inconsistent moral and theological perspectives on war. See John A. Wood, *Perspectives on War in the Bible* (Macon: Mercer University Press, 1998).

a significant tradition of pacifism and nonviolence within Christianity that might provide a different perspective on robotic and cyber warfare.

Christian ethical reflection on war has always appealed to both reason and experience. The just-war criteria are themselves principles of practical reasoning, and the just-war tradition draws on more foundational forms of moral reasoning, most prominently theories of natural law, but also rights-based theories of morality. Experience has also played an important role in the development of the just-war tradition. For example, the experience of total war during the First and Second World Wars made clear the devastating impact of modern military technology and caused just-war theorists to become more skeptical of the causes that could justify war. In a similar way, the experience of the US military with using armed drones must inform moral reasoning about robotic warfare. Data about known cyberattacks over the past three decades provides a helpful starting point for ethical reflection on cyber warfare.

ROBOTIC WARFARE

While the term "robot" may conjure up futuristic images of C-3PO or RoboCop, in reality, robots are already a part of our everyday lives. Robots operate in manufacturing plants, and Roombas clean people's homes. The US military, and a number of other militaries around the world, also make use of robots. These include not only drones, or unmanned aerial vehicles (UAVs), but also land-based robots (unmanned ground vehicles, or UGVs), and robots that operate on or in the water (unmanned surface vehicles, or USVs, and unmanned underwater vehicles, or UUVs). These robots perform a variety of functions such as reconnaissance, targeting enemy combatants, and detecting and removing bombs and mines.[4]

An ethical evaluation of robotic warfare requires a more precise definition of the terms "robot" and "autonomy." Armin Krishnan defines a robot as "a machine, which is able to sense its environment, which is programmed and which is able to manipulate or interact with its environment."[5] Robots therefore exercise at least a limited autonomy to make decisions in response to sensory perceptions, even if that decision-making power is the result of programming by humans. There are degrees of robot autonomy, however, and completely autonomous robots remain only a future possibility. Krishnan distinguishes three types of autonomy: (1) preprogrammed autonomy, in which robots follow a single set of predetermined instructions, or follow one of a number of sets of instructions based on sensory data; (2) supervised autonomy, in which robots make complex decisions from a variety of options, but human operators can intervene in the decision-making process and exercise control over other, more complex functions of the robot; and (3) complete autonomy, in which robots can function on their own, without human input, and can potentially learn and modify their behavior.[6]

Advocates for military robots make a number of moral arguments in their favor. Bradley Jay Strawser argues that there is a moral imperative to reduce the risk to human soldiers by replacing them with robots on the battlefield.[7] Robots can also more easily

---

[4]Armin Krishnan, *Killer Robots: Legality and Ethicality of Autonomous Weapons* (Burlington: Ashgate, 2009), 10–13.
[5]Ibid., 9.
[6]Ibid., 43–4.
[7]Bradley Jay Strawser, "Moral Predators: The Duty to Employ Uninhabited Aerial Vehicles," *Journal of Military Ethics* 9, no. 4 (2010): 342–68.

access difficult locations and more precisely identify targets than human soldiers, waging war more effectively and discriminately, and robots do not become tired or afraid.[8] Many Christian ethicists have likewise argued that there is nothing inherently wrong with the use of armed drones, if the traditional just-war criteria are followed.[9] The use of military robots nevertheless raises a number of important ethical questions.

Armed UAVs, or drones, are robots with very limited autonomy, operated by humans through remote control. Some drones, such as the Reaper, can exercise a great deal of autonomy in navigating to their destination, but currently all drones depend on human operators located at distant military bases to make targeting decisions. Drones enable militaries to find and attack adversaries in terrain difficult for human soldiers to traverse. Therefore, although armed drones have been used alongside human soldiers on the battlefield, they are more commonly used on their own to carry out two distinct types of strikes: targeted killings and signature strikes.

A targeted killing involves taking the life of a particular individual based on evidence that he or she is an enemy combatant. A targeted killing need not be a drone strike; it could be carried out by special operations forces or a bombing, for example. Nevertheless, because of their mobility and efficiency, drones have increasingly been used by the United States to carry out targeted killings in the global war on terrorism.[10] Targeted killings must be carefully distinguished from assassinations. Assassinations are a type of targeted killing carried out against civilian leaders during peacetime, and are prohibited by international law; targeted killings of members of the enemy's chain of command during wartime, however, are not assassinations and may be permitted by international law, depending on the circumstances.[11] That being said, targeted killings raise a host of ethical issues.

One important question is how a potential target is identified as an enemy combatant. On an active battlefield, combatants can typically be distinguished from civilians by the former's participation in armed combat. Many targeted drone strikes, however, take place far from the active battlefield. Since the September 11 terrorist attacks, the United States has argued that terrorist organizations, even though they are not active participants in battle, should always be considered imminent threats, because their members plan in secret.[12] This doctrine has been used to justify targeted killings in countries such as Pakistan, Yemen, and Somalia. Mary Ellen O'Connell argues that this interpretation strains traditional interpretations of self-defense.[13] Even if one accepts the US government's position, it requires a level of transparency and accountability concerning how targets are chosen that has been lacking under the Bush, Obama, and Trump administrations. The executive branch of government should provide the public with a clear description of the criteria used to determine if someone is an imminent threat, and Congress or the courts should have some oversight over how those criteria are applied.

Signature strikes are aimed at targets whose identity is not known, but who exhibit a certain "signature" of characteristics identifying them as enemy combatants. They raise

[8]Jai Galliott, *Military Robots: Mapping the Moral Landscape* (Burlington: Ashgate, 2015), 42–3.
[9]Tobias L. Winright and Mark J. Allman, "Obama's Drone Wars: A Case to Answer," *The Tablet*, August 18, 2012, 6–7; Brian Stiltner, "A Taste of Armageddon: When Warring Is Done by Drones and Robots," in *Can War Be Just in the 21st Century?*, ed. Tobias Winright and Laurie Johnston (Maryknoll: Orbis, 2015), 14–18.
[10]Kenneth R. Himes, OFM, *Drones and the Ethics of Targeted Killing* (Lanham: Rowman & Littlefield, 2016), 1–2.
[11]Ibid., 3–6.
[12]Ibid., 129–35.
[13]Mary Ellen O'Connell, "Flying Blind: U.S. Combat Drones Operate outside International Law," *America*, March 15, 2010, https://www.americamagazine.org/issue/729/article/flying-blind.

ethical issues distinct from those posed by targeted killings. Signature strikes require drone operators to make targeting decisions based on visuals picked up by the drone's cameras and human intelligence gathered on the ground. Although signature strikes could be carried out by missiles fired from a distance or even by troops on the ground, aerial drones are particularly well-suited for carrying out this form of attack because of their capability of surveilling targets and firing upon them simultaneously. In carrying out such strikes, drone operators are required to apply the traditional just-war criterion of discrimination, identifying combatants while minimizing harm to civilians. Unfortunately, the United States has not consistently applied this principle, in some cases identifying all "military-age males" in a combat zone as combatants. As with targeted killings, it is hard to evaluate US adherence to the principle of discrimination since targeting policies are shrouded in secrecy, and therefore greater transparency is needed.[14]

Critics of armed drones have argued that drone strikes have led to a disproportionate number of civilian casualties, even when combatants are the target.[15] Although a handful of early reports suggested that US drone strikes were killing a disproportionate number of civilians, more recent studies have shown that these strikes have led to limited civilian casualties relative to combatant deaths.[16] Even so, civilian deaths and the destruction of homes and civilian infrastructure must always be proportionate to the military aims accomplished by such strikes.

A number of ethicists have also raised concerns about the effects of drone warfare on the human operators themselves. Some argue that the use of drones and other military technologies risks diminishing the "warrior ethos" of soldiers by immunizing them from risk,[17] or that it is harmful to "martial virtues" such as courage, loyalty, honor, and mercy.[18] Others claim that drone technology encourages operators to take a callous, dehumanizing attitude toward their targets, as if playing a video game.[19] David Grossman's groundbreaking work showed that technologies that distance soldiers from their targets such as artillery, bombers, and missiles diminish their resistance to killing.[20] As Kenneth R. Himes points out, however, this distancing effect is partially mitigated by the fact that drone operators see their targets and witness the damage their actions cause, in some cases more vividly than soldiers on the ground.[21] More nuanced studies are needed to understand the interplay between technological systems and human decision-making.[22]

Some ethicists argue that human frailty, rather than technology, is the greatest obstacle to ethical warfighting, and therefore advocate for the development of fully autonomous robots or lethal autonomous weapons. For example, Ronald C. Arkin argues that

---

[14]Himes, *Drones*, 125–8.

[15]E.g., see Robert Wright, "The Price of Assassination," *New York Times*, April 13, 2010, https://opinionator.blogs.nytimes.com/2010/04/13/title-2/.

[16]Himes, *Drones*, 135–42; Avery Plaw, "Counting the Dead: The Proportionality of Predation in Pakistan," in *Killing by Remote Control: The Ethics of an Unmanned Military*, ed. Bradley Jay Strawser (New York: Oxford University Press, 2013), 126–53.

[17]M. Shane Riza, *Killing without Heart: Limits on Robotic Warfare in an Age of Persistent Conflict* (Washington, DC: Potomac Books, 2013).

[18]Robert Sparrow, "War without Virtue?," in *Killing by Remote Control: The Ethics of an Unmanned Military*, ed. Bradley Jay Strawser (New York: Oxford University Press, 2013), 84–105.

[19]Peter W. Singer, *Wired for War: The Robotics Revolution and Conflict in the 21st Century* (New York: Penguin, 2009).

[20]David Grossman, *On Killing: The Psychological Cost of Learning to Kill in War and Society* (Boston: Little, Brown, 1995).

[21]Himes, *Drones*, 13–14.

[22]Galliott, *Military Robots*, 149–51.

robots with sufficient intelligence could be programmed to distinguish combatants from noncombatants while eliminating those human factors that lead to poor decision-making in combat situations, such as fatigue, fear, and other emotions.[23] Although artificial intelligence of this sophistication is currently beyond the grasp of engineers, we must grapple with the ethical implications of this technology before it emerges.

Arguments in favor of lethal autonomous weapons are based on a misunderstanding of moral decision-making. Moral decision-making is qualitatively different from the form of reasoning required to identify and disarm an underwater mine, for example. The ability to distinguish combatants and noncombatants on the battlefield requires an ability to interpret motivations, which in turn requires self-consciousness and the ability to empathize with others. Absent developments in artificial intelligence beyond what is on the horizon, only human beings are capable of this type of moral reasoning, and therefore only humans should be trusted with decisions over life and death. The potential use of lethal autonomous weapons also raises the question of accountability for the accidental killing of civilians by an autonomous robot. The robot itself could not be held responsible, and human responsibility would be so diffuse that no one in particular would be held accountable.[24]

The use of the remote-controlled robots of today and the autonomous robots of tomorrow also raises important strategic and political questions. In our current geopolitical context, robotic warfare is a weapon of the powerful against the weak. Armed drones and other military robots allow powerful nations to exercise domination over less powerful nations across vast distances, protecting their own citizens from harm while exposing the citizens of weaker nations to death and destruction. Even if a particular military engagement is morally justified, powerful nations must consider the strategic and political risks of deploying robots in ways that encourage resentment and resistance.[25] Likewise, the increased use of military robots in place of human soldiers could allow governments to take military action without democratic input, since the populace would hardly be affected by the decision. Without democratic accountability, governments could be emboldened to engage in military action that violates the just-war criteria because the general public will be more sensitive to concerns about whether war is being used as a last resort or whether it is proportionate when the lives of their fellow citizens are on the line.[26]

CYBER WARFARE

Whereas robotic warfare raises the possibility of applying artificial intelligence to the realm of kinetic combat, cyber warfare involves the application of human intelligence to conflict through cyberspace. Joseph S. Nye Jr. defines cyberspace as "the Internet of networked computers but also intranets, cellular technologies, fiber-optic cables, and space-based communications."[27] Although cyberspace enables us to communicate and interact with one another seemingly unconstrained by space or physical bodies, it is

[23]Ronald C. Arkin, "The Case for Ethical Autonomy in Unmanned Systems," *Journal of Military Ethics* 9, no. 4 (2010): 332–41.
[24]Galliott, *Military Robots*, 211–28.
[25]Daniel M. Bell Jr., "The Drone Wars and Just War," *Journal of Lutheran Ethics* 14, no. 6 (2014): 12–14; Himes, *Drones*, 145–51.
[26]Himes, *Drones*, 159–65.
[27]Joseph S. Nye Jr., "Nuclear Lessons for Cyber Security?," *Strategic Studies Quarterly* 5, no. 4 (2011): 19.

important to remember that cyberspace remains an embodied phenomenon. We interact with machines through our physical bodies, and online networking depends on the physical infrastructure of computer systems and communication conduits.[28] Cyberspace likewise has a political dimension, since its physical layer exists within the world of sovereign territorial states; computer servers, smartphones, and so on exist within the physical boundaries of states and therefore fall under their political jurisdiction, and cyberspace is governed by international institutions such as the International Corporations for Assigned Names and Numbers (ICANN).[29]

This political dimension of cyberspace is essential for understanding cyber warfare. Political motivations are one factor that distinguish cyber warfare from other types of cyberattacks, such as cybercrime. Likewise, even though cyberspace makes it possible to carry out attacks on vulnerable computer systems anywhere in the world, the majority of state-sponsored cyber conflicts take place between neighboring states and are linked to traditional political conflicts.[30]

An ethical analysis of cyber warfare depends on properly defining what we mean by "cyber warfare" and several other related terms. This is particularly true because these terms are increasingly used in the popular media in careless ways that may increase the likelihood of conflict between states. Before defining cyber warfare, it is important to define the broader term "cyberattack." Martin C. Libicki understands a cyberattack as "an operation that uses digital information (strings of zeroes and ones) to interfere with an information system's operations and thereby produce bad information and, in some cases, bad decisions."[31] A cyberattack can cause the corruption of information, the disruption of system functioning, or even the damaging or destruction of a physical system.

A cyberattack can be distinguished from two other kinds of cyber actions: exploitation or cyber espionage and cyber defense. Cyber espionage refers to the penetration of a system to gain information about the system or to get access to the data stored on the system; it can be carried out for its own sake or as preparation for a cyberattack. Cyber defense refers to the effort to detect and prevent cyber espionage and cyberattacks aimed at one's own systems. Cyber espionage or cyberattacks can be carried out for criminal purposes, for example if hackers steal the credit card numbers of a retail franchise's customers or install a ransomware virus that shuts down a hospital's network until they pay a ransom. Valeriano and Maness distinguish cybercrime from cyber conflict by highlighting the latter's political motivations, defining it as cyberattacks carried out "in order to impact, change, or modify diplomatic and military interactions between entities [i.e., states and non-state actors]."[32] This distinction, however, is not always black and white; for example, was the hack of the Sony Corporation by North Korean hackers to preempt the release of a film portraying the assassination of Korean leader Kim Jong Un a cybercrime or a politically motivated cyber conflict?

The key question that remains is to determine which forms of cyber conflict merit the name "cyber warfare." Cyberattacks carried out in conjunction with kinetic warfare, what Libicki calls "operational cyber warfare," certainly do.[33] For example, militaries can

[28]Martin C. Libicki, *Cyberspace in Peace and War* (Annapolis: Naval Institute, 2016), 21–2.

[29]Brandon Valeriano and Ryan C. Maness, *Cyber War versus Cyber Realities: Cyber Conflict in the International System* (New York: Oxford University Press, 2015), 23.

[30]Ibid., 9.

[31]Libicki, *Cyberspace*, 19.

[32]Valeriano and Maness, *Cyber War*, 32.

[33]Libicki, *Cyberspace*, 19.

disrupt enemies' weapons networks, insert false messages into enemy communication systems, or feed false information to tracking systems. What Libicki calls "strategic cyber warfare," which is carried out separately from kinetic warfare, is more difficult to define. A distributed denial of service (DDoS) attack, for example, in which an individual harnesses a number of computers together into a "botnet" to overwhelm a target site with traffic and temporarily disable the site, should not be considered an act of cyber warfare since it does no lasting damage to the victim's system. Some definitions of cyber warfare limit it to those cyberattacks that can potentially lead to the death of enemies;[34] such definitions, however, seem overly restrictive. The *Tallinn Manual*, a document produced by a group of scholars sponsored by the NATO Cooperative Cyber Defence Centre of Excellence in Estonia, attempts to define cyber warfare by means of an analogy with kinetic warfare; a cyberattack should be considered cyber warfare if it causes physical damage comparable to a kinetic attack.[35] For example, a cyberattack capable of doing significant damage to a nation's electrical grid could be classified as an act of war since a kinetic attack with similar effects would likewise be an act of war.

The just-war tradition provides insights into how cyber warfare might be waged ethically, but the possibilities raised by cyber warfare also pose intriguing questions to the just-war tradition. Some of the most important considerations pertain to the *jus ad bellum* criteria of just cause and proportionality. For one, when can a cyberattack by one state against another be justified? If an act of cyber warfare is considered analogous to kinetic warfare in its destructive potential, then it makes sense that such a cyberattack could be justified under conditions similar to those that would justify kinetic warfare. Most contemporary just-war theorists agree that war can only be justified in response to the aggression of one state against another or of a state against its people, and therefore an act of cyber warfare could be justified if it helped to hinder such aggression. Because some forms of cyberattack could be characterized as acts short of war, however, it is possible that they might be justified in retaliation for a broader range of offenses as an alternative to more destructive forms of kinetic violence.[36] A second important question is what kinds of responses to a cyberattack are morally justified. In 2011, the Obama administration took the position that an act of cyber warfare could merit a kinetic response,[37] a position later taken up by the *Tallinn Manual*.[38] Libicki, however, advocates for what he calls the "Las Vegas Rules": "what starts in cyberspace stays in cyberspace." He argues that even though cyberattacks can reach the destructive potential of kinetic weapons, to resort to the retaliatory use of kinetic force risks escalating the conflict to levels of destruction far beyond the capacities of cyber war. Conflict would be more restrained if cyberattacks are met with retaliatory cyberattacks.[39]

Cyber warfare poses real quandaries on the question of legitimate authority.[40] The just-war tradition claims that, except in rare cases of revolution or civil war, only states can justly wage war. In cyberspace, however, there is nothing analogous to the state's

[34]Valeriano and Maness, *Cyber War*, 29.

[35]International Group of Experts at the Invitation of the NATO Cooperative Cyber Defence Centre of Excellence, *Tallinn Manual on the International Law Applicable to Cyber Warfare*, ed. Michael N. Schmitt (New York: Cambridge University Press, 2013), 52–3.

[36]Thomas Rid, *Cyber War Will Not Take Place* (London: Hurst, 2013), 142.

[37]Valeriano and Maness, *Cyber War*, 5.

[38]International Group of Experts, *Tallinn Manual*, 52–3.

[39]Libicki, *Cyberspace*, 324–9.

[40]John Arquilla, "Twenty Years of Cyberwar," *Journal of Military Ethics* 12, no. 1 (2013): 84.

"monopoly on violence." State agencies, criminal organizations, and lone wolf hackers all have the potential to carry out dangerous cyberattacks. Cyberspace is not a lawless, virtual space, but rather exists in the physical world governed by sovereign states, however, and states have the responsibility to investigate and prosecute cybercriminals. This can be difficult, though, and indeed some states such as Russia actively support cybercriminals. Similarly, states are incapable of defending their citizens against cyberattacks in the same way they can provide military defense. To do so would require the surveillance of the private networks of businesses and private citizens. Therefore, the private sector has the primary responsibility for providing for its own cyber defense, even if in many cases they do not have the capability of defending against a sophisticated attack. In 2011, a private commission of luminaries in the United States called the Blair-Huntsman commission proposed that private entities might even be authorized to carry out a retaliatory cyberattack if breached,[41] but this is an unwise judgment. Most private entities do not have the same ability to correctly attribute the source of an attack as do state agencies, and more importantly, private cyberattacks could easily escalate into an unmanageable cyber conflict.

The just-war tradition's *jus in bello* criteria stipulate that soldiers must discriminate between combatants and civilians, and that inadvertent civilian casualties and the destruction of civilian infrastructure must be proportionate to the military objectives achieved. These criteria have important implications for cyber warfare. No act of cyber warfare, for example, can be aimed at an exclusively civilian target, for example a power plant serving a purely civilian population. As with kinetic warfare, however, many potential targets serve both civilian and military populations. Therefore, any attacks against these targets must be carefully weighed against the standard of proportionality. One potential risk of cyberattacks is that worms and other cyber weapons can easily spread beyond their intended targets, making their effects unpredictable. This can make calculations of proportionality difficult, if not impossible. For example, the Stuxnet virus, a sophisticated cyber weapon likely developed jointly by the United States and Israel, was successfully used to disable Iranian nuclear centrifuges at the Natanz reactor in 2009. Despite being designed specifically for the reactor's computer system, by 2010 the virus had spread to computers throughout the world.[42]

The secrecy and deception involved in cyber warfare also raise ethical dilemmas. Many cyber weapons avoid defenses by mimicking the appearance of normal network traffic, and most hackers avoid revealing their identities. Ruses and ambushes have always been part of warfare, and the medieval theologian Thomas Aquinas argued that these tactics are morally acceptable.[43] The Third Geneva Convention of 1949, however, requires soldiers to carry their arms openly and wear uniforms or some other identifying insignia, preventing soldiers from disguising themselves as civilians, a tactic in some ways similar to stealth hacking. This prohibition, however, is intended to prevent danger to civilians, and therefore does not seem relevant to the case of cyber warfare. On the other hand, hiding one's identity in cyber warfare does seem to undermine the justice of one's cause. The just-war criterion of right intention requires one to clearly state the cause for which one is fighting so that others can evaluate the claim and so that the claimant can be held

[41]Valeriano and Maness, *Cyber War*, 6.

[42]Fred Kaplan, *Dark Territory: The Secret History of Cyber War* (New York: Simon & Schuster, 2016), 203–11.

[43]Thomas Aquinas, *Summa Theologiae*, trans. Fathers of the English Dominican Province (New York: Benziger Brothers, 1947–8), II–II.40.3.

accountable for their actions. Concealing one's identity makes this impossible. Perhaps a secret cyberattack could be justified if the responsible state identified itself and its claims soon after the strike is carried out.

CONCLUSION

The explosion in computing, digital, and networking technologies over the past several decades has radically transformed warfare and created several new ethical challenges. Both armed drones and cyber warfare, in different ways, allow combatants to strike enemies over vast distances, but raise questions about how humans interact with technology and how this affects ethical decision-making in warfare. The future development of lethal autonomous weapons challenges our very understanding of what ethical decision-making on the battlefield means, and the reality of cyber warfare requires us to revise our understanding of the nature of war. Nevertheless, the Christian ethical tradition—guided by scripture, tradition, reason, and experience—is well-equipped to address these challenges, while also expanding its own horizons.

SUGGESTED READINGS

Galliott, Jai. *Military Robots: Mapping the Moral Landscape*. Burlington: Ashgate, 2015.

Himes, Kenneth R., OFM. *Drones and the Ethics of Targeted Killing*. Lanham: Rowman & Littlefield, 2016.

Kaplan, Fred. *Dark Territory: The Secret History of Cyber War*. New York: Simon & Schuster, 2016.

Krishnan, Armin. *Killer Robots: Legality and Ethicality of Autonomous Weapons*. Burlington: Ashgate, 2009.

Libicki, Martin C. *Cyberspace in Peace and War*. Annapolis: Naval Institute, 2016.

Strawser, Bradley Jay, ed. *Killing by Remote Control: The Ethics of an Unmanned Military*. New York: Oxford University Press, 2013.

Valeriano, Brandon, and Ryan C. Maness. *Cyber War versus Cyber Realities: Cyber Conflict in the International System*. New York: Oxford University Press, 2015.

CHAPTER TWENTY-TWO

Holy Disobedience: Political Resistance and Christian Ethics

ANNA FLOERKE SCHEID

Many citizens in the United States view practices of political resistance as, at best, mere nuisances and, at worst, criminal thuggery. Rallies, marches, civil disobedience, and other forms of political resistance are met with a great deal of suspicion, derision, and even hostility. Commenters on social media say things like:

> Interesting how these individuals have plenty of time to protest, but no time to get a job, go to work, and be productive responsible members of society.
> Pants up, don't loot! Get a job! All lives matter! Just do what you're told and you won't have a problem.
> Marching is easier than thinking ... Hilarious. Hard to stop giggling.[1]

Political resistance has advanced civil rights in the United States and continues to advance human rights around the world. The activities that colonists used to found the United States were forms of political resistance: those opposed to British rule boarded a private ship and destroyed private property, tossing cargo crates full of tea into Boston Harbor; they declared themselves independent of the British Empire and began to disobey the British laws that governed the colonies long before the first shots of the Revolutionary War were fired. Practices of political resistance, like rallies and civil disobedience, won American women the right to vote and American people of color the right to swim in public pools, play in city parks, sit in restaurants, go to schools, and demand equal justice under the law alongside white Americans. Political resistance has made vital contributions to our national heritage in the United States, and represents aspects of US history of which Americans are rightly proud. And yet, so often today, Americans dismiss acts of political resistance as evidence of laziness, stupidity, or immorality. This chapter will counter those perceptions, by illustrating how practices of political resistance can be understood in the light of Christian ethics, with special attention to its four sources: scripture, tradition, reason, and experience.

[1]These three remarks appeared in the comments section of the *Washington Post*, the *St. Louis Post-Dispatch*, and the *New York Times* in response to mass protests.

SCRIPTURE

When faced with moral questions, or with more general considerations of how to live a good and happy life, Christian ethics seeks "relevant moral wisdom or insights ... revealed to us in the Bible."[2] Here, I ask two questions of scripture related to the topic of political resistance. First, how is peace understood in the Judeo-Christian tradition, and what does it have to do with justice and injustice? Second, what does the life of Jesus, as depicted in the gospels, reveal about Christian discipleship and political resistance?

In the Hebrew Scriptures—also called the Old Testament by Christians—peace is the fruit of justice. The Hebrew word *shalom* means "just peace" and it involves the establishment of right relationships among God, humanity, and the rest of creation. Where human relationships are rent asunder, where tyrants deny human rights, where the basic needs of human communities go unmet, there is no justice and, therefore, no peace. This same understanding of true peace led Pope Paul VI to write that "peace is not simply the absence of warfare, based on a precarious balance of power; it is fashioned by efforts directed day after day toward the establishment of the ordered universe willed by God, with a more perfect form of justice."[3] The suppression of violence may indicate a false peace, but a true peace is built on justice. This is why Pope Paul VI exhorted Christians: "If you want peace, work for justice."[4] This relationship between peace and justice resounds in the shouts of protesters across the country who cry out: "No justice, no peace!" Likewise, Martin Luther King Jr. echoed this idea in his "Letter from Birmingham Jail," when he described "negative peace" as the absence of overt conflict, but positive peace as the presence of justice.[5] Based on the idea that justice is a prerequisite for peace, King argued that only laws that confirm the moral law of God are true laws. King concluded that an unjust law is no law at all and therefore need not be obeyed. As we will see in the sections on tradition and experience below, throughout the history of Christianity subversive voices—often those belonging to women and people of color—have consistently demonstrated that the false peace must be disrupted, and resisted, and that sometimes disobedience is holy.

The four gospels in the Christian Bible depict Jesus as a person who, from a young age, was intent on obedience to God before any human authority. When he perceived that the commandments of God conflicted with those of human beings or institutions, Jesus aligned himself with the commands of his faith. At the age of 12, the gospel of Luke tells us that Jesus secretly remained behind in Jerusalem following his family's annual pilgrimage to the temple there. After three days of searching, his parents found him in the temple "sitting in the midst of the teachers, listening to them and asking them questions" (Lk. 2:46).[6] His parents were "astonished": "Son," his mother asked, "why have you done this to us? Your father and I have been looking for you with great anxiety!" (Lk. 2:48). With considerably less sympathy for his parents' feelings than we might expect, Jesus replied, "Why were you looking for me? Didn't you know I would be in my Father's house?" Jesus did not hesitate to resist even his parental authorities when they conflicted with his

[2]Russell B. Connors Jr. and Patrick T. McCormick, *Character, Choices, and Community: The Three Faces of Christian Ethics* (Mahwah: Paulist, 1998), 20.

[3]Pope Paul VI, *Populorum Progressio* (Vatican City: Libreria Editrice Vaticana, 1967), § 76.

[4]Pope Paul VI, *If You Want Peace Work for Justice* (Vatican City: Libreria Editrice Vaticana, 1972).

[5]Martin Luther King Jr., "Letter from Birmingham Jail," *Christian Century*, June 12, 1963, 767–73, https://www.christiancentury.org/article/first-person/letter-birmingham-jail.

[6]All biblical quotes use the New American Bible, Catholic Bible Press, 2012.

relationship with God. And Jesus's convictions only strengthened as he grew older and carried out a ministry dedicated to disrupting false peace, and ushering in *shalom*.

Jesus often did not get along with authoritative religious figures because he viewed them as encumbering the people rather than liberating them. The synoptic gospels tell us that Jesus and his disciples once walked through a grain field on the Sabbath, picked the heads of grain off the stalks, and ate them. While picking and eating wheat berries probably does not sound like "holy disobedience" to our twenty-first-century ears, in Jesus's context it surfaced serious tensions. Work is forbidden for Jews on the Sabbath, and harvesting grain like Jesus and his followers did was considered a form of work. The scandalized Pharisees—who function as the epitome of legal authority in the gospel accounts—confronted Jesus about allowing his disciples to break laws: "Why are you doing what is unlawful on the Sabbath?" (Lk. 6:1-12). The Gospel of Mark suggests that Jesus responded that the Sabbath, the day for rest, was made for humankind, not the other way around (Mk 2:27). In Luke, Jesus responded by doubling down, doing more work on the Sabbath: he stood before the Pharisees and healed a man with a withered hand. The Pharisees were aghast and insulted. They "became enraged and discussed together what they might do to Jesus" to punish his lawless disobedience.

These confrontations between Jesus and the religious elite of his day occurred throughout Jesus's ministry. At one point in the Lukan account, Jesus accepts a dinner invitation from a Pharisee only to spend the meal berating him at length for all the ways that the Pharisees upheld laws that burdened ordinary people (Lk. 7:36-50). Moreover, Jesus accused the religious leaders of a half dozen forms of hypocrisy, and no fewer than six times in four sentences does Jesus declare "woe" upon them. He also calls the Pharisees ignorant fools, and accuses them of obstructing the way to salvation. Finally, he calls them inheritors of their ancestors' penchant for murdering prophets (Lk. 11:37-54). Again, this occurs in the context of a dinner party at which Jesus is a guest! Jesus makes it quite clear that he does not countenance laws, institutions, or systems that burden the poor and vulnerable; he resists these unjust structures even when it puts him in danger.

Finally, and of the utmost significance, having disobeyed his parents and his religious leaders, Jesus engages in political resistance, disrupting the imperial powers of his day: the authorities of the Roman Empire. It is this last form of holy disobedience that results in Jesus's execution by crucifixion on the charge of treason ("He declared he was the King of the Jews" [Jn 19:21]) at the hands of the Roman governor, Pontius Pilate.

A critical turning point in Jesus's ministry, and one which many biblical scholars agree brought him to the attention of Roman authorities, was the event that Christians refer to as "the cleansing of the temple." South African theologian, Albert Nolan, calls the incident "the missing link explaining how Jesus suddenly became so famous and indeed notorious."[7] Scholars and archeologists think that the marketplace occupied the area of the Temple Mount known as the "Court of Gentiles"—an area around 1,000 feet long and 700 feet wide. Like any marketplace it would have been filled with booths where people were selling food, sacrificial animals, and other items that Jews who had traveled from long distances on pilgrimage to the temple would need to purchase to participate in the temple rituals and to replenish their supplies before their journeys home. The only coinage accepted in the temple was the Tyre—hence there were currency exchanges available for those who needed to change their money. Much like in our own day, the

[7]Albert Nolan, *Jesus before Christianity*, 25th anniversary ed. (Maryknoll: Orbis, 2001), 124.

currency exchanges would charge a hefty fee for their service, and the cost of the goods sold would be driven up high to increase profits (like the price of popcorn and soda at a movie theater). The activities around the temple amounted to economic exploitation of those who had made pilgrimages to the temple in order to participate in the religious rituals prescribed by their faith. The sellers and money changers were taking economic advantage of the people in the shadow of the house of God.

All four gospels depict how Jesus reacted to this exploitative marketplace. He drove out the livestock, the sellers, and the bankers. He upended their booths and scattered money and goods all over the place. No one would have an easy time figuring out whose goods or cash were whose after the disruption. In the Gospel of John, Jesus makes a whip out of cords to drive people out by force. In Mark's Gospel, Jesus "does not permit anyone to carry anything through the temple," which was likely being used as throughway for the traffic of goods. After the "cleansing" Jesus sits down in the former marketplace and begins to teach and heal people, restoring the temple area to "a house of prayer" rather than "a den of thieves." Nolan suggests that Jesus must have "placed guards" around the area and at the courtyard gateway "to prevent angry traders from returning." The cleansing of the temple was no less than a massive act of civil disobedience, led by Jesus himself and carried out by him and his followers. Jesus saw injustice in the temple marketplace, and he, in words familiar to today's activists, *shut it down.*

TRADITION

Tradition attends to "the lives and examples of saints,"[8] the teachings of the church, and the wisdom that has been passed down about the "lived faith" from the "people of God" for generations.[9] In thinking about political resistance from the perspective of tradition, I want to explore the witness of the early Christian martyrs and content from Catholic social teaching (CST).

The earliest Christians often found themselves living in a religiopolitical climate hostile to their faith. While it is true that Rome was often tolerant of a diversity of religious beliefs, the institution of the Imperial Cult under the Emperor Augustus involved the deification of the emperor and required making sacrifices to Rome's civic gods. This resulted in waves of persecution against those whose religious beliefs prevented them from worshiping Rome's gods, including Christians who, drawing on their Jewish heritage, professed monotheism. Christians who refused to cooperate with, or who resisted, the Imperial Cult could be imprisoned or put to death, and many were. These were the days of the gladiatorial "games," of the public killing of prisoners for sport, and even of the marching of Christian children dressed like lambs into arenas of hungry lions. Note that political oppressors almost always find ways to mock their victims' beliefs or ideologies as part of their torture. Dressing Christian children like lambs as they marched them to their slaughter was, of course, a way of mocking their faith in the Good Shepherd.

During one wave of persecution, two Christian women, Perpetua and Felicity, were arrested along with several others as part of a Roman raid. Perpetua, Felicity, and their companions are among the most well-known of the early Christian martyrs because they wrote down their experiences while in prison awaiting their execution, and somehow

[8]Connors and McCormick, *Character, Choices, and Community*, 21.

[9]Charles Curran, *The Catholic Moral Tradition Today: A Synthesis* (Washington, DC: Georgetown University Press, 1999), 52.

managed to smuggle the accounts out to be preserved. In an effort to mock their beliefs the Romans attempted to force them to wear pagan ceremonial garb to their own executions.

> When they were brought to the gate, and were constrained to put on the clothing—the men, that of the priests of Saturn, and the women, that of those who were consecrated to Ceres—that noble-minded woman [Perpetua] *resisted* even to the end with constancy. For she said, "We have come thus far of our own accord, for this reason, *that our liberty might not be restrained* ... that we might not do any such thing as [wear the garb of those dedicated to pagan gods]."[10]

The Roman authorities relented and the martyrs were permitted to wear their own clothes to their execution. Reflecting on this, Tertullian wrote, "Injustice acknowledged the justice."[11] Perpetua and Felicity, for refusing to obey laws requiring them to worship the Roman Empire and its gods, endured prison, state-sanctioned torture and public flogging, state-orchestrated attacks by wild animals for the purposes of other people's entertainment, and eventually death by sword. Their holy disobedience resulted ultimately in their canonization to the sainthood in the Roman Catholic tradition.

While the tradition of CST rarely explicitly remarks on political resistance, several concepts from CST cooperate easily with a variety of forms of political resistance. Perhaps the most pertinent of these is the common good, which includes the role of good governance. One way of thinking about the common good is that it is the end goal of justice, considered broadly. And while all individuals, groups, and institutions have a role to play in promoting the common good, the government is directed toward the common good as its entire purpose. In his social encyclical, *Mater et Magistra*, Pope John XXIII called the common good "the whole *raison d'être*" of the nation-state and the "duty" of "public authority."[12] In accordance with the common good, the government is called upon to protect the human rights of individual citizens, to promote the well-being of the community itself (through just taxation to support things like schools, roads, parks, and health care, as well as through laws that oppose discrimination, fraud, etc.), and finally to promote peace and security. But what if the state is not promoting the common good? What if it is directed to the private interests of the ruler, or the ruling class? John XXIII did not discuss in an explicit way what remedies individuals or groups within a nation-state might avail themselves of if the government is not fulfilling its duty to protect the common good. However, David Hollenbach and Meghan Clark, two theological ethicists studying the common good, agree that participation is key to holding government accountable to the common good.[13] Here participation is understood broadly as practices that enable persons and groups to shape the social structures that affect their lives. Since political resistance is a form of participation that aims to hold government accountable, and to shape the structures that affect our lives, we can confidently state that the Christian tradition supports political resistance as a remedy against injustice and toward the promotion of the common good.

---

[10]"Passion of Perpetua and Felicitas," in *Voices of Early Christianity: Documents from the Origins of Christianity*, ed. Kevin W. Kaatz (Santa Barbara: Greenwood, 2013), 120, emphasis added. Perpetua herself wrote most of the account while Tertullian is widely accepted as a secondary author/editor.

[11]Ibid.

[12]Pope John XXIII, *Mater et Magistra* (Vatican City: Libreria Editrice Vaticana, 1961), § 20 and 37.

[13]See David Hollenbach, *The Global Face of Public Faith: Politics, Human Rights, and Christian Ethics* (Washington, DC: Georgetown University Press, 2003); Meghan J. Clark, *The Vision of Catholic Social Thought: The Virtue of Solidarity and the Praxis of Human Rights* (Minneapolis: Fortress, 2014).

REASON

Reason as a source of Christian ethics points both to the contribution of "secular disciplines"[14] and to the way human beings use our intellectual gifts to analyze the insights that emerge from the other three sources. In this section, I will first discuss how social science has confirmed the effectiveness of nonviolent political resistance. Next, I will discuss civil disobedience as a crucial but misunderstood form of nonviolent political resistance.

Erica Chenoweth and Maria Stephan are two social scientists who have analyzed thousands of cases of nonviolent and armed political resistance over the course of the twentieth century. Examining the evidence, they found that nonviolent political resistance is effective at producing social change, "even under conditions in which most people would expect nonviolent resistance to be futile, including situations in which dissent is typically met with harsh regime repression."[15] Political resistance can be rather effective, because it has the power to mobilize vast numbers of people in a way that armed resistance cannot do.[16] Only a small slice of society—those who are relatively strong and healthy, those with the capacity to reason and think clearly—can become soldiers in armed revolutions. However, everyone, old and young alike, grandparents, mothers with their small children, teenagers, and the disabled can all participate in forms of nonviolent political resistance like protests and boycotts. This insight harkens back to the point about participation made in the section on CST above: the more people who can participate in political resistance, the more it is likely to be effective.

One effective, but often misunderstood, tactic of political resistance is civil disobedience. Civil disobedience is planned, peaceful, intentional violation of a law in order to draw attention to an injustice, often, but not always, an injustice embodied by the law itself. The primary purpose of civil disobedience (and other forms of nonviolent direct action like marches and rallies) is not to create tension, but rather to publicly expose and directly confront injustice, so as to transform unjust social structures. That is why Martin Luther King Jr., when accused of causing a ruckus in Birmingham, pushed back: "We who engage in nonviolent direct action are not the creators of tension. We merely bring to the surface the hidden tension that is already alive. We bring it out in the open, where it can be seen and dealt with."[17] When activists peacefully and intentionally break laws, they disrupt the false peace with clear purposes in mind. Specifically, civil disobedience seeks attention: activists *want the world to watch them*. They often choose to commit civil disobedience in as *large* numbers as possible and as *many* places as possible because this draws more attention to their concerns. Those who commit civil disobedience *really* want the attention of the people who have the *power* to fix the injustice they have surfaced.

The list of civil disobedients is long, and the consequences can be serious. Those who have committed civil disobedience include the colonists who threw tea into Boston Harbor, Henry David Thoreau, Harriet Tubman, Mahatma Gandhi, Martin Luther King Jr., Rosa Parks, Nelson Mandela, Archbishop Desmond Tutu, Steve Biko, Malala Yousafzai, and thousands of others. Those who choose to commit civil disobedience are, just like Jesus when he cleansed the temple, courting arrest and jail, risking prison sentences and large

[14]Margaret Farley, *Just Love: A Framework for Christian Sexual Ethics* (New York: Continuum, 2006), 189.
[15]Erica Chenowith and Maria Stephan, *Why Civil Resistance Works: The Strategic Logic of Nonviolent Conflict* (New York: Columbia University Press, 2011), 220.
[16]Ibid., 220.
[17]King, "Letter from Birmingham Jail."

fines, and in extreme cases even physical injury or death. These are the degrading and humiliating consequences of civil disobedience, so it is worth asking what it takes to make people believe that breaking laws is the best way they have of making their voices heard.

EXPERIENCE

Experience is perhaps the most powerful source we can bring to bear on the topic of political resistance. The lived reality of Christians who, motivated by their faith, engage in nonviolent direct action, in the form of marches, protests, boycotts, and civil disobedience, constitutes a vast heritage. It can be traced back to Jesus's own cleansing of the temple; through the early Christian martyrs like Perpetua and Felicity; through the Protestant reformation (after all, note that the root of the word "Protestant" is "protest") whose leaders objected to Papal abuses of power among other things; into the Second World War wherein heroes of the Christian faith like Sophie Scholl and Dietrich Bonhoeffer gave their lives resisting Nazism; and all the way into the present day. Indeed, the record of Christian experience of political resistance looms large in global history. Here I discuss three more recent examples of political resistance that, to varying degrees, were motivated by faith in Jesus the Disruptor.

Around the same time that King led African Americans and white allies in the United States to use nonviolent resistance to claim their civil and human rights, Black South Africans were doing the same in struggle against apartheid in their nation. Apartheid was a system of government instituted by South Africa's white minority that secured economic and social privileges for whites in South Africa through an elaborate system of racial segregation that affected Black South Africans' freedom of movement, education, and employment, and guaranteed that there would be a permanently impoverished Black South African underclass. For decades thousands of South Africans worked to disrupt apartheid, through both nonviolent and armed measures. They refused to follow unjust laws, and endured severe consequences for their rebellion. Christians were among those who participated directly as individuals in political resistance, and Christian churches banded together in support of the revolutionary movement.

The South African Council of Churches (SACC) brought together dozens of Christian denominations "to teach, prophesy, rebuke and correct the wrongs that seek to define society."[18] SACC built solidarity among a number of South African Christian communities, and supported nonviolent political resistance against apartheid as a core aspect of Christian faith in the South African context. "Our belief is that a relevant and authentic spirituality cannot but constrain us to be involved, as we are involved, in the socio-political realm," declared Archbishop Desmond Tutu, Secretary General of SACC from 1978 to 1985.[19] "It is precisely our encounters with Jesus in worship and the sacraments, in Bible reading and meditation, that force us to be concerned about the hungry, about the poor, about the homeless, about the banned and detained, about the voiceless whose voice we seek to be."[20]

As witness to the ways in which the four sources of Christian ethics can sometimes overlap and intertwine, it is notable that SACC's experience of political resistance

---

[18]See South African Council of Churches at http://www.sacc.org.za/pages/about.html.

[19]Desmond Tutu, "Address to the Provincial Synod of the Anglican Church in Southern Africa," in *The Rainbow People of God: The Making of a Peaceful Revolution*, ed. John Allen (New York: Image Doubleday, 1994), 30.

[20]Ibid., 30–1.

emerged from a reading of scripture. Archbishop Tutu promoted interpretations of the Bible that emphasized liberation from oppression, with special attention to the Exodus account of God emancipating the Hebrews from slavery in Egypt. In the light of scripture, Tutu proclaimed that SACC had a "definite bias in favor of the oppressed and exploited in our society."[21]

SACC activities of political resistance against apartheid were comprehensive. The organization supported individuals under banning orders (a robust version of house arrest), and their families as well as political prisoners and their children and spouses. They also arranged and paid for legal services for those arrested and detained in the course of political protest.[22] In short, SACC was committed to encouraging and supporting political resistance in opposition to the injustice of apartheid. They viewed the Christian church in South Africa as having a duty not to cooperate with the unjust government.

Christian political resistance also brought down the dictatorial regime of Ferdinand Marcos in what has come to be called the Philippines' Bloodless Revolution. Marcos was a Filipino dictator in the 1980s, who ran a corrupt and nepotistic administration, defrauding the public, and placing his family members in key positions of power. In response to Marcos's electoral fraud, students across the Philippines began to organize protests, and Marcos used these protests as a pretext to suspend civil rights. He instituted a stronger security state, characterized by martial law, suppression of the press and media, and the arrest of hundreds of protesters as "enemies of the state."[23]

As is often the case, the people's political resistance led to government repression. Marcos grew the military and increased economic benefits for soldiers in an attempt to win their loyalty. He began to use torture and intimidation to quash dissent. Finally, Marcos orchestrated the assassination of a political rival and claimed victory in two rigged elections.

These atrocities motivated the Filipino people to build a massive campaign of holy disobedience. Led by Cardinal Jaime Sin, the largely Catholic population marched and rallied in the streets, boycotted government-controlled facilities, refused to pay utility bills, and carried out a nationwide general strike. Their political resistance culminated in a public rally in which over a million Filipinos occupied the area surrounding the headquarters of the armed forces.

The resistance teemed with Christian language and imagery. Members of religious orders, priests, and nuns participated in massive numbers. Protesters carried artwork and statues depicting the Virgin Mary and other saints, carried posters demanding a nonviolent transition of power, and prayed the rosary aloud in the streets. When the military ordered the protesters to disperse, they refused to obey. Sociologist Sharon Erikson Nepstad describes what happened next: A protest leader

> spoke to the soldiers through a megaphone, stating that the people were nonviolent and there was no need for bloodshed. Many demonstrators carried pocket radios, listening closely to [the Catholic radio station] for instructions. They were told, "Pray to God that you will not have to follow these instructions, but just in case, they are important. [If] the tanks … start firing, lie down and roll to the side out of the path … Keep as low as you can, and keep praying." When the tanks stopped in front of the

---

[21]Ibid., 36.

[22]Ibid., 34.

[23]For a succinct description of Marcos's corruption and Filipino response, see Sharon Erikson Nepstad, *Nonviolent Revolutions: Civil Resistance in the Late Twentieth Century* (New York: Oxford University Press, 2011), chap. 7.

> human barricade, a commander told [protesters] that they had 30 minutes to disband ... When the allotted time passed and the people still stood their ground, the tension was almost unbearable. At that moment, a group of nuns dropped to their knees in front of the armored vehicles and began praying the rosary. Someone else hung a rosary on a tank's gun barrel ... As the tanks' engines started up again, the nuns continued to pray. Then an 81-year old woman in a wheelchair held up a crucifix and stated: "Stop! I am an old woman. You can kill me but don't kill the young people here." Unwilling to harm her, one soldier climbed down out of the tank and embraced the handicapped grandmother. The crowd cheered ... "You are one of us! You belong to the people. Come back to those to whom you belong." Someone even placed a three-year-old girl on top of the armored personnel carrier; the girl kissed the driver, causing him to turn the engine off ... Finally, an officer announced that they would not kill anyone.[24]

Over the course of two days, 80 percent of Marcos's military had defected, and Marcos himself retreated to exile in Hawaii, where he died a few years later. The Filipino people had ousted their dictatorial leader, and won the right to a new, more just government.

The Black Lives Matter (BLM) movement began when a community organizer named Alicia Garza wrote an impassioned social media post after hearing that the killer of 17-year-old high school student Trayvon Martin had been acquitted of all wrongdoing. At the end of her post she wrote, "black lives matter." Her friend and fellow activist Patrisse Cullors added a hashtag to the phrase, and BLM went viral.

BLM is intentionally not affiliated with any specific religious tradition, and includes people of all faiths, or no faith at all, who participate in and ally themselves with struggles for racial justice. At the same time, BLM has inherited a rich tradition of Black resistance to racial injustice that has often been specifically Christian. According to Dr. Mika Edmonson:

> The Black Lives Matter movement is best understood as one modern expression of a 350-year-old struggle to affirm the dignity of black life in a society that has systematically and historically denied it. This struggle has taken a variety of forms. However, the black church has been its most consistent champion, providing the theological foundation and often the only platform for the full affirmation of the humanity and dignity of African Americans.[25]

While not, like the Civil Rights Movement was, explicitly Christian, BLM counts among its members many who are motivated by their faith in Jesus the Disruptor.

The Movement for Black Lives uses tactics like rallies, marches, and civil disobedience to demonstrate the dignity and inherent worth of Black life in a nation that has a history of denying that worth. In response to their corrupt police department, BLM activists in Ferguson, Missouri, shut down highways and participated in "die-ins" at the St. Louis Galleria shopping mall. In New York City, after a grand jury declined to bring charges against the police officer who choked Eric Garner to death, BLM protesters made an effort to shut down the Rockefeller tree lighting ceremony. In 2015, just a few days after a white supremacist who had posted online photos of himself draped in the Confederate flag murdered nine Black Americans as they prayed together in Mother Emanuel AME

---

[24]Nepstad, *Nonviolent Revolutions*, 120.

[25]Mika Edmonson, *The Power of Unearned Suffering: The Roots and Implications of Martin Luther King, Jr.'s Theodicy* (Lanham: Lexington, 2017).

Church, BLM activist Bree Newsome climbed the flagpole outside the South Carolina Statehouse. As though speaking to the Confederate flag itself, she declared, "You come against me in the name of hatred, repression, and violence. I come against you in the name of God. This flag comes down today." As police officers surrounded the base of the flag pole, she removed flag and began to descend the pole. She declared herself "prepared to be arrested" and prayed the psalms aloud as she was handcuffed and led to a patrol car.

CONCLUSION

The four sources of Christian ethics—scripture, tradition, reason, and experience—reveal the importance for Christian faith and practice of political resistance against injustice. Christian political activism is motivated by the biblical vision of *shalom* and the example of Jesus the Disruptor. It takes its place in a long tradition of working toward the common good and risking injury and death for the sake of freedom and justice. Christian political activism is supported by the social sciences, which point to its effectiveness. Together these three sources culminate in Christian experience of political resistance, whether as individuals, like Bree Newsome, or as organizations like SACC. Generations of Christians have followed the lead of Jesus in holy disobedience, disrupting the false peace and contributing to true peace.

SUGGESTED READINGS

Chenowith, Erica, and Maria Stephan. *Why Civil Resistance Works: The Strategic Logic of Nonviolent Conflict*. New York: Columbia University Press, 2011.

Clark, Meghan J. *The Vision of Catholic Social Thought: The Virtue of Solidarity and the Praxis of Human Rights*. Minneapolis: Fortress, 2014.

Hollenbach, David. *The Global Face of Public Faith: Politics, Human Rights, and Christian Ethics*. Washington, DC: Georgetown University Press, 2003.

Nepstad, Sharon Erikson. *Nonviolent Revolutions: Civil Resistance in the Late Twentieth Century*. New York: Oxford University Press, 2011.

Issues, Applications, and Twenty-First-Century Agenda for Christian Ethics

Section C: Criminal Justice

CHAPTER TWENTY-THREE

Crime and Punishment

MICHELLE A. CLIFTON-SODERSTROM

Matthew 25 is a favorite scripture passage of Christian ethicists and has relevance for the topic of crime and punishment in the twenty-first century. Jesus's parable of the sheep and the goats identifies those affected by the most serious social issues—poverty, sickness, migration, and incarceration. Christians agree that these are dire problems and that the gospel calls upon the community of faith to address them. Yet, instead of care and advocacy, these groups of people make up the majority of those the United States criminalizes.

The United States has and continues to incarcerate those Matthew's gospel names in disproportionate numbers.[1] James Kilgore writes, "During the past three decades, the urge to punish and incapacitate the most vulnerable sectors of the population has replaced the desire to nurture and develop. … Jail embodies our failure to care."[2] Not only does the United States incarcerate vulnerable people groups at the highest rates in the world, these vulnerable groups are also most affected by crime.[3] While care for vulnerable populations is central to the gospel, Christians have not led the work of breaking cycles of crime and addressing the real sources of conflict. In fact, the problematic ways the United States defines and punishes crime find some justification in the Christian tradition.

This chapter backgrounds the criminal justice entries that follow by addressing crime and punishment in the US context. It focuses specifically on their relation to the prison industrial complex defined as (1) the primary response to social problems that involve poverty, immigration, and race, and (2) the web of institutions and people groups who benefit politically, economically, and socially from mass incarceration.[4] This chapter also analyzes key theological and biblical themes that reinforce punishment as an end rather than a means. Conversely, it offers potential areas for Christian ethics to enliven pathways for liberation.

---

[1]The United States locks up more people numerically and per capita than any other country in the world, incarcerating at a rate five to ten times that of Western Europe and other liberal democracies. National Research Council, *The Growth of Incarceration in the United States: Exploring Causes and Consequences* (Washington, DC: National Academies, 2014), 13.

[2]James Kilgore, *Understanding Mass Incarceration: A People's Guide to the Key Civil Rights Struggle of our Time* (New York: New Press, 2015), 1.

[3]Those who are incarcerated are disproportionately people of color, come from economically distressed neighborhoods, suffer from mental illness, are victims of sexual assault or domestic violence, and are less educated than the general population. National Research Council, *Growth of Incarceration*, 13–14, 56–64.

[4]The annual labor connected with the prison industrial complex is approximately $100 billion according to James Samuel Logan, *Good Punishment? Christian Moral Practice and US Imprisonment* (Grand Rapids: Eerdmans, 2008), 2.

REASON

The complexity of crime and punishment requires Christian ethicists to make use of research and sources outside the field. In particular, scholarship in philosophy, political science, law, psychology, and history grounds the intersectional analysis that is essential for moral inquiry on the topic and especially moral inquiry that seeks to account for the experience of human beings in the context of their communities. The literature is extensive, and this entry cannot exhaust the work that has been done in this area. That said, key texts outside the field of Christian ethics include Michel Foucault's *Discipline and Punish: The Birth of the Prison*, Michelle Alexander's *The New Jim Crow*, Baz Dreisinger's *Incarceration Nations*, Lawrence Friedman's *Crime and Punishment in American History*, Marc Mauer's *Race to Incarcerate*, and the writings of Frederick Douglass, Mary Church Terrell, W. E. B. Du Bois, Cornell West, Angela Davis, and James Kilgore.[5] Each of these areas and thinkers contributes to the moral reasoning necessary for an in-depth analysis of crime and punishment.

Angela Davis, in particular, has done significant work in the area of prison abolition.[6] She argues that prisons are a way of disappearing people in the false hopes of disappearing the social problems they represent.[7] Approximately 2.3 million people are currently incarcerated in the United States. Those in prison are disproportionately people of color, come from economically disadvantaged backgrounds, were either unemployed or in a low-skilled job at the time of arrest, and are less educated than people in the free population. Over 80 percent of women who are locked up are sexual assault survivors.[8] One in four persons in prison suffers from a serious mental illness, and close to four hundred thousand have psychological disorders that are exacerbated by the criminal justice system.[9] It is increasingly easier to detain non-US citizens, even though studies show that targeting immigrants does not reduce rates of crime or terrorism.[10]

States protect established forms of punishment. A new prison opened on average every ten days in the United States between 1990 and 2005, despite the fact that there is no evidence that prisons deter crime according to criminologist Baz Dreisinger.[11] Michelle Alexander writes that "the American penal system has emerged as a system of social control unparalleled in world history."[12] Ethicist James Samuel Logan names four primary factors that account for the increase in prisons arguing that the United States has "an ever-increasing social policy commitment to prison incarceration as a control solution

[5]Michel Foucault, *Discipline and Punish: The Birth of the Prison*, trans. by Alan Sheridan (New York: Vintage Books, 1977); Michelle Alexander, *The New Jim Crow* (New York: New Press, 2012); Baz Dreisinger, *Incarceration Nations: A Journey to Justice in Prisons around the World* (New York: Other Press, 2016); Lawrence M. Friedman, *Crime and Punishment in American History* (New York: Basic Books, 1994); Marc Mauer, *Race to Incarcerate* (New York: New Press, 2006).

[6]See Angela Davis, *Are Prisons Obsolete?* (New York: Seven Stories, 2003).

[7]Angela Y. Davis, *Abolition Democracy: Beyond Empire, Prisons, and Torture* (New York: Seven Stories, 2011), 41.

[8]Kilgore, *Understanding Mass Incarceration*, 14, 78, 155, 157; National Research Council, *Growth of Incarceration*, 64–7; Elizabeth Swavola et al., "Overlooked: Women and Jails in an Era of Reform" (Vera Institute of Justice, 2016), 10, https://www.vera.org/publications/overlooked-women-and-jails-report.

[9]Matt Ford, "America's Largest Mental Hospital is a Jail," *The Atlantic*, June 8, 2015, https://www.theatlantic.com/politics/archive/2015/06/americas-largest-mental-hospital-is-a-jail/395012/.

[10]Dominique Gilliard, *Rethinking Incarceration: Advocating for a Justice That Restores* (Downers Grove: InterVarsity, 2018), 65.

[11]Dreisinger, *Incarceration Nations*, 14, 17.

[12]Alexander, *The New Jim Crow*, 8.

geared toward containing and regulating the frustrations of the nation's most exploited residents, those who must perpetually confront society's most entrenched social ills."[13]

Understanding mass incarceration in the United States and its Christian underpinnings is impossible without looking to its origins in slavery and the ongoing racial control in the United States. Much scholarship examines the progression from slavery to the criminalization of Black men. In the words of political scientist Joy James, even the Thirteenth Amendment "ensnares as it emancipates. In fact [the Thirteenth Amendment] functions as an enslaving antienslavement narrative."[14] The United States, in other words, never abolished slavery. Theologian Dominique DuBois Gilliard's book, *Rethinking Mass Incarceration*, traces the historical links between mass incarceration and slavery, sharecropping, lynching, Black codes, and convict leasing.[15]

Further, scholarship, especially in the field of psychology, examines the ongoing effects of slavery on individuals in Black communities—many of which lead to criminal behavior. Psychologist Na'im Akbar writes, "This shock [of slavery] was so destructive to natural life processes that the current generation of African-Americans, although we are five to six generations removed from the actual experience of slavery, still carry the scars of this experience in both our social and mental lives."[16] In her chapter "Slavery's Children," Joy DeGruy names the weaknesses resulting from three hundred years of oppression that African Americans must confront—drug abuse, crime, and moral decay. She continues, "It would be foolish to argue that every maladaptive manifestation of these ills is a result of Post Traumatic Slave Syndrome. Still, it would serve as well to understand to what degree these and other problems of today directly relate to the slave experience of yesterday."[17]

Definitions of criminality in connection with racism and institutions of punishment as means of social control adapt over time. One of the first critical race theorists, Harvard professor Derrick Bell, shows how these adaptations follow political and social achievements of persons who are Black. He writes, "Black people will never gain full equality in this country. Even those herculean efforts we hail as successful will produce no more than temporary 'peaks of progress,' short-lived victories that slide into irrelevance as racial patterns adapt in ways that maintain white dominance."[18] Legal scholar Ian Haney Lopez interacts with Bell's work in *Dog Whistle Politics*.[19] He uses the phrase "valleys of reversal" to describe that which follows peaks of progress.[20] He cites the example of the 1988 presidential campaign when the National Security Political Action Committee ran an attack ad against Michael Dukakis. The ad featured a Black man they called Willie Horton, though he never went by any name other than "William."

---

[13]Logan, *Good Punishment?*, 4.

[14]Joy James, ed., *The New Abolitionists: (Neo)slave Narratives and Contemporary Prison Writings* (New York: State University of New York Press, 2005), xxii.

[15]Gilliard, *Rethinking Incarceration*. See also David M. Oshinsky, *Worse than Slavery: Parchman Farm and the Ordeal of Jim Crow Justice* (New York: Simon and Schuster, 1996); Theodore Brantner Wilson, *The Black Codes of the South* (University: University of Alabama Press, 1965).

[16]Na'im Akbar, *Breaking the Chains of Psychological Slavery* (Tallahassee: Mind Productions, 1996), 3. Jack E. White, "Bush's Most Valuable Player," *TIME Magazine* 132, no. 20 (1968): 20.

[17]Joy DeGruy, *Post Traumatic Slave Syndrome: America's Legacy of Enduring Injury and Healing* (Portland: Joy DeGruy, 2005), 143.

[18]Derrick Bell, *Faces at the Bottom of the Well: The Permanence of Racism* (New York: Basic Books, 1996), 12.

[19]Ian Haney Lopez, *Dog Whistle Politics: How Coded Racial Appeals Have Reinvented Racism and Wrecked the Middle Class* (Oxford: Oxford University Press, 2015).

[20]Ibid., xii.

The image of Horton became etched in the minds of the American public throughout the '88 election season and has remained infamous for reinforcing the views of the "threatening Black man" in the American public. *Time Magazine* even named Horton "Bush's most valuable player" in the election cycle.[21] Dukakis ran a countercampaign featuring a convicted felon named Angel Medrano.[22] This time, the face that covered the ads was a Hispanic male. These alarming examples of powerful white politicians using images of Black and Brown men to bolster their political agenda expose the pathology of equating Black and Brown bodies with criminality. Far from a phenomenon of the 1980s, the fact remains that criminality is closely connected with race in the United States, and many laws target people of color and those who are poor, noncitizens, and mentally ill.[23]

US history bears the sin of abuse of power by criminalizing and punishing some people groups and this has, at the same time, benefited other groups in social and material ways. Ethicist T. Richard Snyder critiques Christians, among others, for not recognizing the racist ideology in the fact that some crimes, and even different forms of the same drug, are considered "dirtier than others" and therefore are sentenced differently.[24] The example of longer sentences for crack versus cocaine is one that falls along racial lines. Within this history, liberation from such unjust relationships makes the relationship between whites and people of color—especially African Americans—an important crucible to deal with the debilitating effects of crime and punishment on all citizens in the United States. While fields beyond Christian ethics are important and necessary for analyzing crime and punishment, the field has a great deal to offer by way of analysis, confession, and good news.

EXPERIENCE

The environment of the prison and the walls that isolate the carceral world from the free world make clear whose sins confine them to punishment and whose do not. Cement walls, barbed wire, guns, uniformed officers, chains, and gates with locks and large keys serve to remind those inside of the worst thing they have ever done.[25] Whether a person incarcerated was wrongly accused, had poor legal representation, or actually committed the crime they were convicted of, the prison architecture symbolizes the exception within the Thirteenth Amendment.

Foucault argues that around the turn of the nineteenth century, methods of punishment shifted from being a public spectacle to being "the most hidden part of the penal process."[26] While public spectacles clearly are morally problematic, a consequence of a hidden system is that "justice no longer takes public responsibility for the violence that is bound up with its practice."[27] Much about the prison environment is unknown by the

---

[21]Federal law punishes offenses involving crack at a rate of one hundred times more severely than those involving powder cocaine, and the vast majority of those who are charged with crack offenses are Black while crimes involving powder cocaine are majority white offenders. Alexander, *The New Jim Crow*, 112.

[22]Keith Love, "Both Campaigns Launch Ads on Prison Furlough Issue," *Los Angeles Times*, October 22, 1988.

[23]For a close analysis of racial targeting in criminal law, see Alexander, *The New Jim Crow*, 53–8, and Chapter Three "The Color of Justice," 97–139.

[24]T. Richard Snyder, *The Protestant Ethic and the Spirit of Punishment* (Grand Rapids: Eerdmans, 2001), 31.

[25]This language comes from Bryan Stevenson, *Just Mercy: A Story of Justice and Redemption* (New York: Spiegel & Grau, 2015).

[26]Foucault, *Discipline and Punish*, 9.

[27]Ibid.

general public. The reality is that the United States locks up human beings in six-by-nine-foot cells for upward of twenty hours a day. It is the only majority world country that sentences juveniles to life without possibility of parole.[28] Most states do not allow women who give birth to remain with their newborn for more than a few days.[29]

The field of Christian social ethics has potential to move in a liberating direction. While there are a number of important experiential components needed to support such a move, three sources of knowledge are at the forefront informing new and necessary contributions: (1) the voices of those directly affected by incarceration; (2) the voices of activists, allies, and advocates for reform or abolition; and (3) the communal and social role of conflict.

First and foremost is the need for Christian ethicists to incorporate the narrative accounts of those who have been harmed by mass incarceration. Those who are impoverished and people of color are the most significantly impacted by punishment in the US context. Communities of faith cannot begin to interrupt cycles of crime and violence, and the logic underlying these cycles, without understanding those who have experienced punishment by the state. Because the people groups most affected by discipline and punishment in the United States are marginalized groups, and because these groups behind bars have even less access to mainstream culture than marginalized people in general, it remains difficult for free society, including the church outside prison, to connect with the experiences of incarcerated persons. One of the notable exceptions to this is the collection of writings by Native American, African American, Latino, Asian, and women intellectuals who are imprisoned in the United States, *The New Abolitionists*, which includes critical intersectional analyses of captivity that broaden the horizons of the concept of abolition and its current relevance.[30] Another exception is Zeke Caligiuri's memoir *This Is Where I Am*[31] and, of course, the writings of Dietrich Bonhoeffer and Martin Luther King Jr. Other avenues for accessing the accounts of those who have experienced punishment in the United States can happen through families of those most deeply affected by incarceration and through the voices of returning citizens.[32]

The second important set of experiences comes from the voices of activists, allies, and advocates. Those who populate this group include those who have been directly affected and marginalized as well as those who enjoy power and privilege, yet have chosen to stand in solidarity with those affected by incarceration and therefore have access to "primary sources." This group's experiences and partnerships offer avenues for creative problem-solving and form the basis for the kind of communal reflection that is necessary to examine the deep roots of punishment in the United States. Hearing from the work of activists, allies, and advocates serves as a bridge between experience and analysis and solutions.

Contributions in the field of Christian ethics that utilize the above categories of experience to speak to ways the United States criminalizes and punishes include Kelly Brown Douglas's *Stand Your Ground*, James Samuel Logan's *Good Punishment?*,

---

[28]Gilliard, *Rethinking Incarceration*, 92.
[29]Dreisinger, *Incarceration Nations*, 146.
[30]James, *The New Abolitionists*.
[31]Zeke Caligiuri, *This Is Where I Am: A Memoir* (Minneapolis: University of Minnesota Press, 2016).
[32]Examples of good first-hand accounts include Stevenson, *Just Mercy*; Ta-Nahisi Coates, *Between the World and Me* (New York: Spiegel and Grau, 2015); Angela Davis, *Freedom Is a Constant Struggle: Ferguson, Palestine, and the Foundations of a Movement*, with a Foreword by Cornel West (Chicago: Haymarket, 2016).

Jennifer McBride's *Radical Discipleship*, and Amy Levad's *Redeeming a Prison Society*.[33] Additional sources in the field that move in this direction include Jennifer Harvey's *Dear White Christians*, Jennifer Graber's *The Furnace of Affliction*, T. Richard Snyder's *The Protestant Ethic and the Spirit of Punishment*, and Mark Lewis Taylor's *The Executed God*.[34] It is notable that almost all of these contributors have spent significant time inside or have the experience of working in jails or prisons.

The third important area for contribution is sustained reflection on the role of conflict in communities and society. Crime and punishment are both outcomes and sources of conflict. Yet many in the Christian tradition are conflict-avoidant, navigate conflict indirectly, or use power and force to control conflict—all of which are avoidance tactics at root. Creative places to find creative approaches to conflict include hip-hop studies and nonviolent communication studies (NVC). Works in hip-hop studies by Christian writers engage expressions of anger through words as they have power and force to name realities while remaining intentionally nonviolent.[35] NVC moves beyond essentialist ways of defining right and wrong because these definitions are usually determined by those at the top of a system. In other words, power plays a role in these definitions, especially as they function at the social level. The kinds of approaches emerging from NVC can serve as a corrective to a Christian worldview that has at times confined the categories of good and evil, or defined who is good and who is not, too narrowly and not critically enough.

Nils Christie's article "Conflicts as Property" provides a useful framework to analyze conflict and its role in society.[36] While dated, the article offers questions and categories for reflection and analysis by Christian ethicists. His thesis is that conflict is valuable and that most societies, especially those that are highly developed, have too little conflict. Moreover, these societies organize institutions around hiding and selling conflict to those not directly involved: for example, police, lawyers, judges, militaries, penal institutions, and, ultimately, the state. Christie claims that the outcome of giving over conflict is that, in addition to third parties economically benefiting, the parties directly involved in the conflict become disengaged.

Christie claims that the victims suffer most when conflict is taken over by the state. He writes, "Not only has [the victim] suffered, lost materially or become hurt, physically or otherwise. And not only does the state take the compensation. But above all [the victim] has lost participation in his own case."[37] Without direct participation in conflict, reasons for actions may not be discovered, and violence and harm are only punished, rather than addressed by processes of healing and restoration. In addition, the community and broader society suffer a loss of the opportunity for norm clarification and pedagogical possibilities that happen when conflict is examined and discussed. Further work in the

---

[33]Kelly Brown Douglas, *Stand Your Ground: Black Bodies and the Justice of God* (Maryknoll: Orbis, 2015); Jennifer McBride, *Radical Discipleship: A Liturgical Politics of the Gospel* (Minneapolis: Fortress, 2017); Amy Levad, *Redeeming a Prison Society: A Liturgical and Sacramental Response to Mass Incarceration* (Minneapolis: Fortress, 2014).

[34]Jennifer Harvey, *Dear White Christians: For Those Still Longing for Racial Reconciliation* (Grand Rapids: Eerdmans, 2014); Jennifer Graber, *The Furnace of Affliction: Prisons and Religion in Antebellum America* (Chapel Hill: University of North Carolina Press, 2011); Mark Lewis Taylor, *The Executed God: The Way of the Cross in Lockdown America*, 2nd ed. (Minneapolis: Fortress, 2015).

[35]See the work of Daniel White Hodge, *Hip Hop's Hostile Gospel* (Boston: Brill, 2016); Hodge, *Heaven Has a Ghetto: The Missiological Gospel and Theology of Tupac Amaru Shakur* (Saarbrücken: VDM Verlag Dr. Müller, 2010); Hodge, *The Soul of Hip Hop: Rims, Timbs and a Cultural Theology* (Downers Grove: InterVarsity, 2010).

[36]Nils Christie, "Conflicts as Property," *British Journal of Criminology* 17, no. 1 (1977): 1–15.

[37]Ibid., 7.

experience of conflict, especially as is offered in restorative justice studies, offers a fruitful pathway for Christian ethicists.

SCRIPTURE

Scripture makes clear that those in prison matter to God and that punishment is not the purpose of God's justice (Ps. 69:33). The afflicted writer of Ps. 102:1 begins, "Hear my prayer O Lord; let my cry come to you. Do not hide your face from me in the day of my distress. Incline your ear to me; answer me speedily in the day when I call." Later in verse nineteen, God joins the lament of the prisoner by looking down from his holy height, from heaven to earth, to hear the groans of the prisoners and to set free those who were doomed to die.

Messianic expectations in scripture point to liberating those in prison. King David gives praise to a God who sets prisoners free, even while bringing the wicked to ruins (Ps. 146:7, 9). Predicting God's good future, the prophets and others speak more than once of liberation and peace for prisoners (1 Kgs 22:27; Isa. 42:7, 49:8-9, 61:1; Zech. 9:11; Lk. 4:18; 2 Cor. 3:17). Scripture even has examples of divine jail breaks (Acts 5:19, 12:7-10, 16:26). Finally, those who follow Christ are called to a deep identification with those in prison (Mt. 25:31-46; Heb. 10:34, 13:3). This identification is so deep that Matthew's gospel compares it to identification with Christ. Further, the charge to care for God's people on the margins in Matthew 25 is introduced as an inheritance (v. 34), making this text a call beyond charity and into the realm of expectation. God, in other words, shows great love and care for those bound by social ills.

This chapter has named the disproportionate number of people of color incarcerated in the United States and has gestured to work that connects mass incarceration and slavery. The logic of slavery is also linked with abuses of scripture by white Christians.[38] White Christians in US history have found warrant in such stories as the Curse of Ham and the notion that the punishment of Africans, including the Atlantic slave trade, is a just outcome of that curse.[39] White Christians have also found exegetical justification for the divine sanctioning of slavery as a form of punishment.[40] Further, biblical arguments have been used to reinforce other systems of punishment, including the lynching of an estimated five thousand Black men and women between 1880 and 1940. James Cone discusses the connections between white Christianity and lynching in his book *The Cross and the Lynching Tree* and shows the ways lynching mirrors the Roman crucifixion of Jesus.[41] While almost no Christian scholarship today would overtly justify slavery, the criminal justice system and Thirteenth Amendment are based on similar logics. Punishment is used, as noted in the section above, as a form of economic, political, and social control as opposed to a vehicle of the gospel.

Beyond the issues of who gets punished and how criminality has been equated with race in the United States, there is also the question of what constitutes punishment in

---

[38]Mark Noll, *The Civil War as a Theological Crisis* (Chapel Hill: University of North Carolina Press, 2006).

[39]For a strong analysis of the biblical argument used to support the Atlantic slave trade as related to the curse of Ham, see Stephen R. Haynes, *Noah's Curse: The Biblical Justification of American Slavery* (London: Oxford University Press, 2002); David Whitford, *The Curse of Ham in the Early Modern Era: The Bible and Justifications of Slavery* (Burlington: Ashgate, 2009).

[40]See Michael Taylor, "British Proslavery Arguments and the Bible, 1823–1833," *Slavery & Abolition* 37, no. 1 (2016): 139–58.

[41]James Cone, *The Cross and the Lynching Tree* (Maryknoll: Orbis, 2014), 31.

relation to God's justice. The following section will look specifically at the theological framework for God's justice. Scripture has direct things to say about punishment and the use of systems to deal with human conflict and wrongdoing.

Biblical scholar Christopher Marshall shows that the New Testament is full of the idea that retributive forms of punishment are redundant because persons already suffer the consequences on their *being* by the act of wrongdoing itself. The real consequences of crime are a moral and spiritual decay, and because of this, it is neither possible to give out just consequences nor is it possible to cancel the effects of a wrong done. The example he offers is that when Paul says that death is the wages of sin (Rom. 6:23), he means that death is the natural consequence of sin, not that death is the retributive punishment for sin. Retribution sees punishment as the consummation of wrongdoing and the undoing of wrongdoing when in actuality it is neither of these.

Marshall argues that scripture overwhelmingly supports direct mediation of conflict, and social ills are addressed within communities without the cover of the legal system. He offers examples of ways that the New Testament advises against the legal system or political authorities as mediators: Paul makes clear that law can do nothing to make people good (Rom. 5:20, 7:7-12; Gal. 3:19-24), Jesus does not advise the court system for addressing wrongs (Mt. 5:25, 40; Lk. 12:57), and he speaks poorly of oath-taking (Mt. 5:33-37). Courtroom scenes in the New Testament frequently pervert justice (John the Baptist), and Paul makes people aware that Roman judges and juries favor those of a higher class and rank (Lk. 18:1-8; Jas 2:6; 1 Corinthians 6). Those carrying out a police function are not exemplars of virtue in scripture, as seen by the massacre of innocents (Mt. 2:16), the execution of John Baptist (Mt. 14:10), the slaughter of Galileans (Lk. 13:1), the arrest and subsequent crucifixion of Jesus (Mt. 26:50, 27:26, 31), the imprisonment of the Apostles (Acts 12:2-3), James's beheading and Peter's arrest (Acts 12), and the scourging of Paul and Silas without a trial (Acts 16:22, 24). Finally, prisons are horrible places where most in custody die from disease, starvation (Mt. 25:36), torture (Mt. 18:34), execution (Mk 6:14-29), or suicide (Phil. 1:19-24).[42] Marshall refers to biblical scholar Lee Griffith who writes,

> The Bible identifies the prison with the spirit and power of death. As such, the problem with prisons has nothing to do with the utilitarian criteria of deterrence. As such, the problem is not that prisons have failed to forestall violent criminality and murderous rampages; the problem is that prisons are *identical in spirit* to the violence and murder that they pretend to combat ... Whenever we cage people, we are in reality fueling and participating in the same spirit we claim to renounce.[43]

Prisons punish violence, but they do not address the causes of violence. Nor does the penal system move in the direction of healing and reconciliation.

Human punishment is never the end of the story in the scriptural narrative. Rather, a restorative justice model that takes into account human relations and the healing of all parties moves beyond civic models of justice and is at the heart of the New and Old Testaments. God's justice is one that is reconciling and restores people to right relationship with God and one another.

---

[42]Christopher D. Marshall, *Beyond Retribution: A New Testament Vision for Justice, Crime, and Punishment* (Grand Rapids: Eerdmans, 2001), 11–14.

[43]Lee Griffith, *The Fall of the Prison: Biblical Perspectives on Prison Abolition* (Grand Rapids: Eerdmans, 1993), 106, emphasis in original.

TRADITION

Scriptural passages regarding liberating the captive are not simply texts about the relationship of God's people to those in prison. Such passages have theological ramifications for the role of punishment in the enactment of God's justice. Determining the relationship between God's justice and human punishment is no easy task. Is the triune God a truth-in-sentencing kind of God? Three strikes God? Capital punishment God? Does God require time served for sins? Much in the Christian tradition has potential to address crime and punishment. After all, Christianity is a faith that professes that Christ died to save human beings from their sins and eternal damnation. This section narrows the focus by naming some of the theological claims in the Christian tradition that distort God's justice and support forms of punishment such as mass incarceration. The section also contrasts these with themes that tend toward healing and liberation, rather than punishment, as the rightful *telos* of justice.

Many of the aforementioned scholars in this entry have addressed distorted theologies as they support unjust punishment in the civic arena. The work of Mark Lewis Taylor is especially notable. Two other religious scholars are worth mentioning. First, Timothy Gorringe offers a detailed exploration of theologies of atonement in relationship to crime and punishment. Specifically, he argues that the connection between retribution, satisfaction, and penal practices in the West is based on faulty understandings of God's justice. He not only names primary victims of punishment in the Western world between the eleventh and nineteenth centuries, which include persons primarily from the bottom of the social classes. He also argues that satisfaction atonement theories more accurately describe human needs for vengeance than the good news of God's judgment and justice. As does Mark Lewis Taylor and many other nonviolent atonement theorists, Gorringe problematizes the use of the cross to legitimize violence. He concludes his study with compelling theological alternatives to retribution and violence based on strategies of reconciliation that he finds at the center of the Christian faith.[44]

Rima Vesely-Flad is a second scholar who has identified connections between Reformed theology and punitive institutions in the antebellum, postbellum, and post-Civil Rights eras.[45] She argues that Reformed theology rooted in notions of depravity and Calvin's doctrines of moral and civil law especially around idleness and work fed and sustained punitive institutions that discriminated against those of African descent.[46] Further, ideas of honor and order reflected civil rather than divine law, and Reformed Christians conformed to this reality. Such views reinforced the idea that "irredeemable baseness distinguished the person of African descent [and] provided clear justification for harsh practices of punishment, particularly to counter idleness and ensure manual labor for rights."[47] Finally, she recounts the ways that theologians, clergy, and laity in the South frequently recited the biblical proslavery texts, using them to underscore Black inferiority.[48]

---

[44]Timothy Gorringe, *God's Just Vengeance: Crime, Violence and the Rhetoric of Salvation*, Cambridge Studies in *Ideology and Religion*, ed. Duncan Forrester and Alistair Kee (New York: Cambridge University Press, 1996), 251.

[45]Rima Vesely-Flad, "The Social Covenant and Mass Incarceration: Theologies of Race and Punishment," *Anglican Review* 93, no. 4 (2011): 541–62.

[46]Ibid., 541–2.

[47]Ibid., 545.

[48]Vesely-Flad cites the following excellent sources on proslave theology: Larry E. Tise, *Proslavery: A History of the Defense of Slavery in America, 1701–1840* (Athens: University of Georgia Press, 1987); E. Brooks Holifield,

A few additional theological themes embedded in the broad tradition of Christian theology distort God's justice while supporting forms of punishment such as mass incarceration for the most vulnerable populations. *The first theme is the idea that salvation is earned rather than God's gracious gift to all.* This Pelagian heresy was refuted in the fifth century by the Council of Carthage, but views that humans attain salvation continue to find implicit support among Protestant Christians, as for example in its work or puritan ethic. Two problems follow. First, definitions of work and purity are defined by dominant groups. T. Richard Snyder references one of the catechism questions exclusively for slaves:

> What makes you lazy?
> My own wicked heart ...
> What makes you curse and fight?
> My own wicked heart ...
> How do you know your heart is wicked?
> I feel it every day ...
> Who teaches you so many wicked things?
> The Devil.[49]

References to laziness are incongruously relegated to slaves not slaveholders—a caricature that continues into the present shaping who and what kinds of work merit goodness.[50] The second hazard with works-righteousness is that those who have earned wealth and status may be shielded from examining social sins and structures that favor some and disadvantage others. Not only is this individualistic, it all too often leads to conflating privilege with God's blessing. Such a worldview reinforces our criminal justice system by associating lack of wealth and status with negative moral traits linked with those in prison.

The second theme that distorts God's justice is equating salvation and security rather than salvation and the kind of vulnerability that fosters community and solidarity. National security and safety are not central to the gospel. God does not bless America, for example, exclusively. Security as a value can act as a protection of a certain kind of lifestyle that is shielded from the social problems that feed into the propensity to incarcerate. The desire for safer streets, for example, or increased public safety are coded claims whites often make in the face of "inner city problems" and immigration. While safety is understandable, it is not a reward or by-product of faith in Christ.

The third, and most powerful, theme that distorts God's justice is that justice requires punishment rather than repentance, forgiveness, and, ultimately, reconciliation. The view that justice is fulfilled through punishment finds warrant in the tradition of penal substitution—the view of atonement held by the majority of Christians.[51] However, this penal substitutionary view of atonement, including the ways it understands the relationship between punishment, wrath, sacrifice, and substitution, faces significant biblical and theological challenges.[52] Specifically, in linking penalty to the justifying

---

Theology in America: Christian Thought from the Age of the Puritans to the Civil War (New Haven: Yale University Press, 2003).

[49]"A Cathecism for Negroes," *The Southern Episcopalian*, April 1, 1854, 7.

[50]Snyder, *Spirit of Punishment*, 50.

[51]Some more contemporary examples include John Stott, J. I. Packer, and James Denney; although to be fair, these thinkers have offered some critiques of more crude forms of penal substitution. Penal substitution forms much of evangelical and Reformed thinking on the atonement.

[52]Michelle A. Clifton-Soderstrom, "Happily Ever After? Paul Peter Waldenström: Be Ye Reconciled to God," *Ex Auditu* 26 (2010): 91–106.

power of Christ's death, penal substitution leaves Christians with a distorted view of the power of repentance, forgiveness, and the work of reconciliation as defining moments of salvation.[53] In penal substitution, the cross is a mechanism of salvation and demonstration of love rather than, as James Cone argues, a symbol of the spiritual power to resist violence that is misplaced and endured *wrongly*.[54]

God's justice in the Old Testament is always toward restoration and *shalom*, not retribution and punishment. In the New Testament, God's justice moves toward reconciliation that results from acts of truth-telling, repentance, and forgiveness. Miroslav Volf writes that the best condemnation of sin is truth and forgiveness: "In the Christian tradition, condemnation is an element of reconciliation, not an isolated independent judgment, *even when reconciliation cannot be achieved* ... That is how God in Christ condemned all wrongdoing."[55] In other words, punishment does not redeem humanity. The temptation to valorize punishment comes from the belief that Christ suffers in humanity's stead and bears the penalty of sin. While one might think that Christ's taking on the penalty of sin would deter Christians from enacting cruel punishment such as life sentences or the death penalty, it can have the opposite effect of justifying or ignoring suffering—especially when it is another's. If Angela Davis is correct that the United States locks up people in the false hope of disappearing its social problems, a theology that shifts punishment to another (even Christ) accommodates a worldview that shifts blame—a view that comprises the logic of the prison industrial complex.

CONCLUSION

Christian ethics is not only concerned with theory but also practices and transformed communities. For structural changes to occur, those in positions of power, specifically white Christians, have a role in owning the oppression throughout US history for many of the people groups represented on the receiving end of the harshest punishments. Part of owning oppression is hearing the effects that institutionalized violence continues to have on people of color.

Much in this chapter leans toward the provocative. This is in large part because a system of punishment so corrupt requires a prophetic voice and the dismantling of power sources that feed it. The best work in the field to date radically rethinks the ways the state administers punishment. Along these lines, this entry concludes with three frontiers within Christian ethics when it comes to crime and punishment in the United States.

First, the history of punishment in the United States requires that the field of Christian ethics seriously consider the strategy of abolition in its research, rhetoric, and response to mass incarceration. The work of many has connected mass incarceration and slavery, and most Christians today would ally with abolition when it comes to slavery. W. E. B. Du Bois and Angela Davis argue that abolition is not simply about deconstruction and disestablishment.[56] It is about creating new institutions free from racism, classism, and other forms of oppression. In this vein, engaging abolition requires scholarly

[53]Ibid., 93.

[54]Cone, *Cross and the Lynching Tree*, 22.

[55]Miroslav Volf, *The End of Memory: Remembering Rightly in a Violent World* (Grand Rapids: Eerdmans, 2006), 15, emphasis added. Volf's book is a careful analysis of the relationship between truthful witness, repentance, forgiveness, justice, judgment, mutual embrace, and reconciliation.

[56]Davis, *Abolition Democracy*, 69.

collaboration between various subspecialties to think newly about social institutions. These subspecialties within Christian ethics include economics, health care, politics, virtue, natural law, liberation theology, and ethnography. Conceiving a society without prisons and doing so within a confessional context, not simply political one, is a potential area for the field of Christian ethics to lead creatively.

Second, further work in the areas of restorative and transformative justice offers much to the advancing topic of crime and punishment. Restorative justice utilizes communities and relationships to move persons involved in crime or conflict toward reconciliation with the person harmed. It emphasizes practices rooted in the Christian tradition, such as truth-telling, repentance, and forgiveness, and the community owns its role in the conflict. Also, as a response to conflict and violence, transformative justice models look ahead to the future rather than restoring what has been lost. Transformative approaches assume that new systems and ways of relating are necessary for all to flourish. They are committed to individual and communal liberation and critique state responses to violence that perpetuate violence. These areas, especially transformative justice, are relatively new for the field of Christian ethics.

Third, a potential area for scholarship from white Christian ethicists is to analyze and break patterns of white supremacy that exist in all subspecialties of the field. Jennifer Harvey's book *Dear White Christians* is a leading example of such scholarship. She argues that white Christians in the United States ought to consider reparations over reconciliation. Instead of distancing one's self and scholarship from the depths of race and other oppressions, white scholars have potential to break these influences through reflection, analysis, and even lament. If racism is an underlying cause of mass incarceration, then scholarship that deals with racism at all levels and in multiple areas has potential to disrupt the US system of punishment.

Each of the above arenas requires concerted effort—effort that is connected with the scholar's history and even character. Though difficult, such scholarship follows in the way of Christ. Christ came to repair and mend relationships within the human community, and the work of repairing harms around interpersonal and systemic forms of violence is the legacy of scholars who profess faith in Jesus Christ. Scholarship in the field of Christian ethics, in other words, has a role to play in alleviating human suffering and enlivening pathways for liberation.

SUGGESTED READINGS

Davis, Angela. *Freedom Is a Constant Struggle: Ferguson, Palestine, and the Foundations of a Movement*. With a Foreword by Cornel West. Chicago: Haymarket, 2016.

Gilliard, Dominique. *Rethinking Incarceration: Advocating for a Justice That Restores*. Downers Grove: InterVarsity, 2018.

Kilgore, James. *Understanding Mass Incarceration: A People's Guide to the Key Civil Rights Struggle of our Time*. New York: New Press, 2015.

Logan, James Samuel. *Good Punishment? Christian Moral Practice and US Imprisonment*. Grand Rapids: Eerdmans, 2008.

Vesely-Flad, Rima. "The Social Covenant and Mass Incarceration: Theologies of Race and Punishment." *Anglican Review* 93, no. 4 (January 2011): 541–62.

CHAPTER TWENTY-FOUR

Mass Incarceration

JAMES SAMUEL LOGAN

By any world measure, the United States jails, imprisons, and indefinitely detains more human beings than any nation (past or present) on the face of the earth. According to the Prison Policy Initiative, the US criminal justice system holds approximately 2.3 million people (combined) in state prisons, federal prisons, local jails, juvenile correctional facilities, "Indian Country" jails, military prisons, civil commitment centers, state psychiatric hospitals, immigration detention centers, and prisons in the US territories.[1]

Indeed, with approximately 4.4 percent of the world's population, the United States houses some 22 percent of its prisoners.[2] (For more than a decade, many sources have consistently averaged these numbers at around 5 and 25 percent, respectively.[3]) The PEW Charitable Trusts has reported, "The United States incarcerates more people than any country in the world, including the more populous country of China"; PEW also reported (in 2008) that "1 in 100 adults is now locked up in America."[4] According to a Prison Policy Initiative report, *Following the Money of Mass Incarceration*, the cost to incarcerate such an unprecedented number of human beings in the United States is a staggering $182 billion every year.[5] Indeed, the Policy Institute found that "mass incarceration costs state and federal governments and American families $100 billion more each year than previously thought." To get to the $182 billion figure, it has been noted by the Equal Justice Initiative (relying partly on data from the Bureau of Justice Statistics that places the cost of operating prisons, jails, and probation in the United States at $81 billion) that the far greater figure includes "policing and court costs, and costs paid by families

[1]Wendy Sawyer and Peter Wagner, "Mass Incarceration: The Whole Pie," *Prison Policy Initiative*, March 19, 2019, https://www.prisonpolicy.org/reports/pie2019.html.

[2]See Roy Walmsley, "World Prison Population List: Tenth Edition," International Center for Prison Studies, November 2013, https://www.prisonstudies.org/sites/default/files/resources/downloads/wppl_10.pdf. US imprisonment of such a staggering percentage of the world's population, particularly since the 1980s, represents what Steven Donziger called "the largest and most frenetic correctional buildup of any country in the history of the world." Steven R. Donziger, ed., *The Real War on Crime: The National Report of the National Criminal Justice Commission* (New York: HarperPerennial, 1996), 31.

[3]Michelle Ye Hee Lee, "Does the United States Really Have 5 Percent of the World's Population and One Quarter of the World's Prisoners," *Washington Post*, April 30, 2015, https://www.washingtonpost.com/news/fact-checker/wp/2015/04/30/does-the-united-states-really-have-five-percent-of-worlds-population-and-one-quarter-of-the-worlds-prisoners/?noredirect=on.

[4]PEW Center on the States, *One in 100: Behind Bars in America 2008* (Washington, DC: PEW Charitable Trusts, 2008), 5.

[5]Peter Wanger and Bernadette Robuy, "Following the Money of Mass Incarceration," Prison Policy Initiative, January 25, 2017, https://www.prisonpolicy.org/reports/money.html. See also, German Lopez, "Mass Incarceration Doesn't Do Much to Fight Crime. But It Costs an Absurd $182 Billion a Year," *Vox*, January 27, 2017, https://www.vox.com/policy-and-politics/2017/1/27/14388024/mass-incarceration-cost.

to support incarcerated loved ones."[6] In addition to those who are confined by various law enforcement agencies across the nation, another six million or so are on probation or parole; about one in ten born since the turn of the twenty-first century is expected to spend time in jail or prison, with one-third of Black males born in this century projected to be incarcerated sometime during the course of their lives.[7]

Not only might one question the nation's reliance on imprisoning such a large portion of its population relative to the rest of the world, one might also wish to discern the extent to which the world-leading rate of incarceration in the United States constitutes a clarion challenge to a life-affirming Christian ethics of faith and hope, grounded in a rugged and sublime divine love as proclaimed by Jesus Christ: "The Spirit of the Lord is upon me, because [God] has anointed me to bring good news to the poor. [God] has sent me to proclaim release to the captives and the recovery of sight to the blind, to let the oppressed go free, to proclaim the year of the Lord's favor" (Lk. 4:18-21).

Indeed, Christian ethics (as a matter of creedal commitment to the principal Christian virtues of faith, hope, and love) must give formidable attention to the US carceral landscape, which has grown exponentially over the past several decades. The expansion of the nation's carceral regime has deleteriously impacted the moral and material well-being of human associations beyond the lives of individual victims, prisoners, and their families. The social appendages of mass incarceration include the exacerbation of racial divisions, broad-scale class-based economic hardship, and social risk for the most vulnerable of the nation's residents (particularly children, and persons who are homeless, mentally and emotionally ill, jobless, and drug addicted). Further, mass incarceration is also expressed in the silencing of political dissent, and in the harsh control and maintenance of alleged terrorists and certain groups of "foreigners" and immigrants seeking political and economic refuge in the United States.[8] The broad and deep scale that defines mass incarceration in the United States expands far beyond narrower understandings of "criminal justice" as a clearly demarcated system of law enforcement directly involved in the apprehension, prosecution, defense, sentencing, and punishing of those suspected or convicted of criminal offenses. Even more so, one must highlight what Michelle Alexander rightly contends is a permanent order of social exclusion tied to a "larger web of laws, rules, polices, and customs that control those labeled criminals both in and out of prison."[9] Although Alexander is speaking here specifically in this context of "released, former prisoners [who] enter a hidden world of legalized discrimination and permanent social exclusion,"[10] the wider social effects of US incarceration criminalize the bodies, spirits, and yearnings of allegedly dangerous, culturally polluted, and highly vulnerable populations thought to pose an existential threat to American exceptionalism.[11] Indeed,

[6]The Equal Justice Initiative, "Mass Incarceration Costs $182 Billion Every Year, Without Adding Much to Public Safety," February 6, 2017, https://eji.org/news/mass-incarceration-costs-182-billion-annually.

[7]See Bryan Stevenson, *Just Mercy: A Story of Justice and Redemption* (New York: Spiegel & Grau, 2014), 15; PEW Center on the States, *Behind Bars in America 2008*, 3, 34; Keramet A. Reiter, *Mass Incarceration* (New York: Oxford University Press, 2018), xi.

[8]I have in mind as political dissenters persons like the Soledad Brothers (George Jackson, John Clutchette, and Fleeta Drumgo), Ruchell Magee, Assata Shakur, Angela Y. Davis, Lenard Peltier, Attica Brothers (like "Big Black" Smith and L. D. Barkley), the Wilmington Ten, Lolita Lebrón, Mumia Abu-Jamal, and so on.

[9]Michelle Alexander, *The New Jim Crow: Mass Incarceration in the Age of Colorblindness* (New York: New Press, 2010), 13.

[10]Ibid.

[11]For outstanding commentary on the moral relationships between American exceptionalism and the marked criminality of the "transgressive" Black body, see Kelly Brown Douglas, *Stand Your Ground: Black Bodies and the Justice of God* (Maryknoll: Orbis, 2015).

a salient feature of mass incarceration is a criminal othering of (predominately darker-hued) persons, groups, communities, and nations *independent* of any contact with the agents of law enforcement in the United States.

Certainly, the influences and consequences of mass incarceration extend beyond what some may see as its most important characteristics in direct relation to prisoners in the United States, as summarized by Keramet A. Reiter in her book, *Mass Incarceration*: "(1) the systematic constriction of prisoners' constitutional rights, (2) the treatment of the mentally ill in prison and especially in solitary confinement, (3) the long-term consequences of having served time in prison, (4) the problem of prisoner disenfranchisement, and (5) the privatization of multiple aspects of the prison industry."[12]

Beyond any raw empirical data on things like drug sentencing, mandatory minimums, and prison profiteering, the social grammar of mass incarceration signals a robustly insidious cultural and political criminalization of Black, Brown, "Red," and "poor" bodies. Alexander has put this most dangerous (often deadly) distortion plainly:

> The declaration and escalation of the War on Drugs marked a moment in our history when a group of people defined by race and class was defined as the "enemy." A literal war was declared on them, leading to a wave of punitiveness that affected every aspect of our criminal justice system ... Counting heads in prison and jails often obscures that social and political history. It also fails to grasp the significance of the drug war in mobilizing public opinion in support of harsh legislation and penalties for all crimes. The drug war corrupted law enforcement by ramping up an "us v. them" war mentality, transforming local police into domestic militaries ... which wound up diverting energy, resources, and attention away from violent crime.[13]

With the contemporary forging of domestic enemies and the concomitant rise of domestic militaries, mass incarceration features the obsessive surveillance, monetary abuse, and militarized policing of subaltern peoples. Indeed, the mission of the criminal justice system "trains its sights," not only on Black men but also (as accurately observed by Angela Y. Davis and many others) "on black women and other men [and women] of color, as well as on poor white people."[14] These are the very persons, rendered pariahs among us, persons who (in significantly disproportionate numbers) endure rituals of death at the hands of state-sponsored executioners.

Even as some sources suggest an ebbing of the US prison and jail population (as has been true for example in the state of California), it must be made clear that the notion of *mass* in mass incarceration is not only about numbers; mass also refers to the ways which this large-scale process of confinement "massifies" throughout society.[15] According

---

[12]Keramet, *Mass Incarceration*, xvii.

[13]Here Alexander is offering an e-mailed response that is included in Eli Hager and Bill Keller's Marshall Project Review, "Everything You Think You Know about Mass Incarceration Is Wrong," February 9, 2017, https://www.themarshallproject.org/2017/02/09/everything-you-think-you-know-about-mass-incarceration-is-wrong. Hager and Keller's analysis offers a summary of John Pfaff's provocative book, *Locked In: The True Causes of Mass Incarceration and How to Achieve Real Reform*, which forwards the argument (summarized by Hager and Keller) that "the war on drugs was not the main driver of incarceration rates that have grown fivefold since 1972"; nor are "overly long sentences ... the main problem"; nor is "the for-profit 'prison industrial complex' the main problem, either."

[14]Angela Y. Davis, "Race, Gender, and Prison History: From the Convict Lease System to the Supermax Prison," in *Prison Masculinities*, ed. Don Sabo, Terry A. Kupers, and Willie London (Philadelphia: Temple University Press, 2001), 35.

[15]Mark Lewis Taylor, *The Executed God: The Way of the Cross in Lockdown America*, 2nd rev. ed. (Minneapolis: Fortress, 2015), 70.

to Mark Lewis Taylor in the revised and expanded edition of his volume, *The Executed God: The Way of the Cross in Lockdown America*:

> As massifying, hyperincarceration today concentrates particular people's experiences and balkanizes targeted and vulnerable groups. Such concentration destroys the intricate fabric of relations within those groups that keep life human, with a sense of opportunity and flourishing. This is what enables families and individuals to claim and feel that their lives are worth living.[16]

The specter of mass incarceration functions to destroy the best hopes of human associations. Taylor suggests that it undermines the well-being of whole communities by way of a hyperincarceration that targets, and reduces to a controllable mass, members of racialized and poor groups.[17] Ultimately, those massified are subject to immobilization and disintegration, thereby hardening inequality and allowing elites to "take aim at maximizing the numbers they can profit from."[18] And, in particular, it continues be the Black male body which is treated as the most dispensable by "communities in the 'free world' that have forsaken those marked as criminal."[19] So too must it not be overlooked that in recent decades, Black and other women have constituted the most rapidly expanding segment among incarcerated populations. Indeed, as this writer pointed out more than a decade ago, "The proportion of women being incarcerated has risen to unprecedented heights, with Black women increasingly subjected to a rate of criminalization paralleling that of their Black male counterparts."[20]

Certainly, a faithful Christian moral example concerning human association and accompaniment alongside those forsaken and marked as criminal by the free world is plain to see in the tragedy, perplexity, and wonder of the Gospels of Mark (15:27) and Luke (23:33), where Jesus is crucified at a place called the Skull alongside two criminals. Here, the twentieth-century theological giant Karl Barth offers to Christians everywhere a provocative summary of the communal and theo-ethical implications of Jesus's crucifixion alongside those marked as criminals. From his 1957 Good Friday sermon entitled "The Criminals with Him," Barth writes,

> "They crucified him *with the criminals.*" Which is more amazing, to find Jesus in such bad company, or to find criminals in such good company? As a matter of fact, both are true! One thing is certain: here they hang all three, Jesus and the criminals, one at the right and one at the left, all three exposed to the same public abuse, to the same in/term/in/able pain, to the same slow and irrevocable death throes. Like Jesus, these two criminals had been arrested somewhere, locked up and sentenced by some judge in the course of the previous three days. And now they hang on their crosses with him and find themselves in solidarity and fellowship with him. ... It was a point of no return

[16]Ibid. Cf. Dylan Rodriguez, *Forced Passage: Imprisoned Intellectuals and the US Prison Regime* (Minneapolis: University of Minnesota Press, 2006), 69–72.
[17]Taylor, *The Executed God*, 71.
[18]Ibid., 71–2.
[19]Davis, "Race, Gender, and Prison History," 35.
[20]James Samuel Logan, *Good Punishment? Christian Moral Practice and US Imprisonment* (Grand Rapids: Eerdmans, 2008). See also, Davis, "Race, Gender, and Prison History," 36; Meda Chesney-Lind, "Imprisoning Women: The Unintended Victims of Mass Imprisonment," in *Invisible Punishment: The Collateral Consequences of Mass Imprisonment*, ed. Marc Mauer and Meda Chesney-Lind (New York: New Press, 2002), 79–94; The Marshall Project, *Women in Prison: A Curated Collection of Links*, 2019, https://www.themarshallproject.org/records/76-women-in-prison.

> for them as for him. There remained only the shameful, painstricken present and the future of their approaching death. …
> *They crucified him with the criminals.* Do you know what this implies? Don't be too surprised if I tell you that this was the first Christian fellowship, the first certain, indissoluble and indestructible Christian community. … The two criminals were the first certain Christian community.[21]

As Christians confront the social and theo-ethical problem of highly racialized mass incarceration in the United States (looking to the Gospels of Mark and Luke as foundational moral guides), so too must the distinctiveness of trans-terror within the culture and fortresses of hyperincarceration be seen (and confronted) by an unflinching practice of Christian faith, hope, and love. Certainly, as Taylor points out, "in prison, trans-persons [trans-gender, trans-sexual, and other LGBTIQ+ persons] are subject to special stigma and abuse." "More broadly," Taylor employs the term "trans-terror" because "when one becomes incarcerated in the US system, one's body tends to be seen as 'deviant,' and hence vulnerable, unprotected, even deserving of abuse."[22] And of course one cannot ignore in all of this the disproportionate numbers of homeless and mentally ill residents caught up in the carceral massification of the nation right alongside those seeking refuge in the United States from other nations.

With respect to even "legal" immigrants, asylees, and refugees to the United States, Teresa A. Miller has noted, "Many of the same policies that define mass incarceration in the criminal justice system are reconfiguring the contours of the US immigration system—so much so that the immigration system is becoming a replica of the criminal justice system."[23] Such a becoming now finds deleterious expression in a widespread cultural and political demagoguery, which feeds not only the xenophobic confinement of adult women and men seeking opportunity and refuge away from economic, social, and political violence but also in the despicable and violent detention (even caging) of children separated from their families by the thousands. As a replica *turned routine carceral expression* of mass incarceration, today's immigration policies foster punitive sanctions that criminalize immigration law, thus tearing apart family unity and, as pointed out by Miller, "[eliminating] avenues of relief from detention previously available, including waiver, bond, and release on the [immigration or refugee seeker's] own recognizance."[24] As is true of what some "postmodern criminological theorists" began to call the "new penology" during the 1990s, a hallmark of today's state of carceral massification, whether applied to traditional penology or to immigration law, is a retributive emphasis on mass efficiencies and management in the service of controlling certain groups of subaltern peoples, including undocumented immigrants to the United States from non-Anglo European nations.[25]

---

[21]See Karl Barth, *Deliverance to the Captives: Sermons and Prayers by Karl Barth* (New York: Harper and Brothers, 1961), 76–7, emphasis in original.

[22]Taylor, *The Executed God*, 101.

[23]Teresa A. Miller, "The Impact of Mass Incarceration on Immigration Policy," in *Invisible Punishment: The Collateral Consequences of Mass Imprisonment*, ed. Marc Mauer and Meda Chesney-Lind (New York: New Press, 2002), 216.

[24]Ibid., 216–17.

[25]Ibid., 214–38. For a fairly brief history of the criminal justice evolution to a "new penology" of efficacy, management, and control see Christian Parenti, "The 'New' Criminal Justice System: State Repression from 1968 to 2001," in Joy James, ed., *States of Confinement: Policing, Detention, and Prisons* (New York: Palgrave, 2002), 303–11.

With particular respect to racialized caste, the legal apparatuses of the American criminal justice system (legislation, police, courts, jails/prisons, etc.), and prison reform efforts, Michelle Alexander has been right to contend "that criminal justice reform efforts—standing alone—are futile. Gains can be made, yes, but the new caste system will not be overthrown by isolated victories in legislatures or courtrooms."[26] A real and present challenge is that the deleterious impulses of mass incarceration have become a very important driver of economic profit in the United States. Therefore, many powerful efforts will be made to ignore and otherwise resist measures to reduce the size of what many prison activists and abolitionists know as the "industrial complex" dimensions of mass incarceration, no matter the ebb and flow of actual crime rates. When it comes to the prison industrial complex,[27] a reduction in crime rates is (at best) not a central concern, and (at worst) any significant reductions to the jailing and imprisonment of US residents are a serious threat to the prison economy. Too much successful reduction in the numbers of people being incarcerated, resulting in the closing of prisons across the nation, would be "an event" (to use Alexander's words) "that would likely inspire panic in rural communities that have become dependent on prisons for jobs and economic growth. Hundreds of thousands of people—many of them unionized—would lose their jobs."[28] If, in addition to the guards, administrators, service workers, and other prison personnel, one were to count all of the persons employed by the wider prison bureaucracy, the economic losses that come with decarceration could affect millions of people.[29]

Indeed, the profit motives of private-sector investors in the continued expansion and management of prisons would be jeopardized if masses of people start questioning corporate entities interested in "expanding the market," or "increasing the supply of prisoners," or "eliminating the pool of people who can be held captive for profit."[30] A clear (as can be) example of private-sector reliance on the flourishing of the primary profit impulse key to the culture of mass incarceration can be seen in the 2005 annual report of the Tennessee-based Corrections Corporation of America (CCA) (now rebranded under the new corporate name, "CoreCivic"). The 2005 report "explained the vested interests of private prisons matter-of-factly in a filing with the United States Security and Exchange Commission":

> Our growth is generally dependent upon our ability to obtain new contracts to develop and manage new correctional facilities. This possible growth depends on a number of factors we cannot control, including crime rates and sentencing patterns in various jurisdictions and acceptance of privatization. The demand for our facilities and services could be adversely affected by the relaxation of enforcement efforts, leniency in conviction and sentencing practices or through the decriminalization of certain activities that are currently proscribed by our criminal laws. For instance, any changes with respect to drugs and controlled substances or illegal immigration could affect the

---

[26]Alexander, *The New Jim Crow*, 230.

[27]For a summary sense of the definition and social function of the prison industrial complex beyond what appears in this chapter, see, e.g., The Empty Cages Collective, "What Is the Prison Industrial Complex?," http://www.prisonabolition.org/what-is-the-prison-industrial-complex/; Eric Schlosser, "The Prison-Industrial Complex," *The Atlantic*, December 1998, https://www.theatlantic.com/magazine/archive/1998/12/the-prison-industrial-complex/304669/.

[28]Alexander, *The New Jim Crow*, 218.

[29]Ibid.

[30]Ibid.

> number of persons arrested, convicted and sentenced, thereby potentially reducing demand for correctional facilities to house them.[31]

Certainly, from the perspective of the private prison industry, "the market for prisoners has continued to expand ... it is as good as it has ever been."[32] "Beyond private prison companies," Alexander has pointed out the naked opportunism of economic investors and political actors in the current age of mass incarceration, which extends out to fuse mutual collaborations between the prison economy and the military industrial complex:

> There are a whole range of prison profiteers [who] must be reckoned with if mass incarceration is to be undone, including phone companies that gouge families of prisoners by charging them exorbitant rates to communicate with their loved ones; gun manufactures that sell Taser guns, rifles, and pistols to prison guards and police; private health care providers contracted by the state to provide (typically abysmal) health care to prisoners; the US military, which relies on prison labor to provide military gear to soldiers in Iraq; corporations that use prison labor to avoid paying decent wages; and the politicians, lawyers, and bankers who structure deals to build new prisons often in predominately white rural communities—deals that often promise far more to local communities than they deliver. All of these corporate and political interests have a stake in the expansion—not elimination—of the system of mass incarceration.[33]

Articulating the motivations that ground the existence of the "prison industrial complex," Angela Davis, in her 2003 book *Are Prisons Obsolete?*, argues,

> The exploitation of prison labor by corporations is one aspect among an array of relationships linking corporations, government, correctional communities, and media. These relationships constitute what we now call a prison industrial complex. The term "prison industrial complex" was introduced by activists and scholars to contest prevailing beliefs that increased levels of crime were the root cause of mounting prison populations. Instead, [these activist and scholars argued that] prison construction and the attendant drive to fill these new structures with human bodies have been driven by ideologies of racism and the pursuit of profit.[34]

Davis goes on to suggest, regarding the usage history of the term "prison industrial complex," that it was the "social historian Mike Davis [who] first used the term in relation to California's penal system, which, he observed, had already begun in the 1990s to rival agribusiness and land development as a major economic and political force."[35] Indeed, Davis's understanding of a prison industrial complex, grounded in an iron triangle of economic profit, politics, and racial ideologies, tells of the wider transnational expanse of mass incarceration beyond more delimited conceptions of crime and punishment.

> The notion of a prison industrial complex insists on understandings of the punishment process that take into account economic and political structures and ideologies, rather than focusing myopically on individual criminal conduct and efforts to "curb crime."

---

[31]Quoted in Alexander, *The New Jim Crow*, 218–19. Primary source, US Securities and Exchange Commission, Correction Corporation of America, Form 10K for fiscal year ended December 31, 2005. Cf. Logan, *Good Punishment?*, 53–60.
[32]Alexander, *The New Jim Crow*, 219.
[33]Ibid., 219–20.
[34]Angela Y. Davis, *Are Prisons Obsolete?* (New York: Seven Stories, 2003), 84.
[35]Ibid., 84–5.

> The fact, for example, that many corporations with global markets now rely on prisons as an important source of profits helps us to understand the rapidity with which prisons began to proliferate precisely at a time when official studies indicated that the crime rate was falling. The notion of a prison industrial complex also insists that the racialization of prison populations—and this is not only true in the United States, but also in Europe, South America, and Australia as well—is not an incidental feature. Thus, critiques of the prison industrial complex undertaken by abolitionist activists and scholars are very much linked to critiques of the global persistence of racism. Antiracist and other social injustice movements are incomplete with[out] attention to the politics of imprisonment.[36]

Beyond all that has been offered here concerning the contemporary forces that fuel mass incarceration, many progressive prison activists and abolitionists see the bone-deep historical roots of mass incarceration: namely, colonialism, market capitalism, and white supremacy (all with their attendant racisms, ethnocentrisms, xenophobias, heterosexisms, transphobias, hegemonic masculinities, and misogyny). Many prison abolitionists (many of whom are not Christians) would want purveyors of Christians ethics and others to know that underlying mass incarceration is a highly racialized neocolonial capitalistic impulse that, by its very nature, must continuously secure endless, replenishable numbers of expendable human bodies in order to "flourish." Today's "advanced" capitalist society manages the mounting frustrations and anger (but also hopes) of masses of surplus subaltern peoples by underemploying them and/or jailing them in fits and starts, thus turning human bodies into the cheap, raw, and replenishable objects of labor who will produce profits both inside and outside the expansive intersecting domains of mass incarceration.

While it is absolutely true that empirical data concerning the frequency of policing encounters, subaltern surveillance, judicial contacts, privatization of prisons, and other forms of confinement for profit are salient features of mass incarceration, it must again be emphasized that the appearance, influence, and consequences of mass incarceration encompass moral corruptions beyond that which are empirically measurable. The moral corruption of mass incarceration includes forging classes of subaltern enemies and undesirables along lines that are racial, ethnic, transphobic, and xenophobic. Between the empirical measures that constitute mass incarceration and the often-unacknowledged forging of transgressive national enemies, there is a constant and unabated reinforcement of hegemonic retributive normalcy. Such retributive normalcy (grounded in a punishing will to inflict pain, suffering, greed, and neglect soaked in a spirit of persistent civic lovelessness) continuously evolves to shape and maintain a carceral national character to which even some within targeted populations participate and acquiesce.[37] And certainly, mass incarceration lives and survives in concert with, is porously adjacent to, and features within its own sphere of existence, other complexes (e.g., the military–industrial complex) of human violence, degradation, and alienation, which fed massive illusions of singular and muscular American exceptionalism.

---

[36]Ibid., 85.

[37]See and hear, e.g., James Forman Jr., *Locking Up Our Own: Crime and Punishment in Black America* (New York: Farrar, Straus and Giroux, 2017); Alicia Montgomery, "Some Blacks Did Support Bill Clinton's Crime Bill. Here's Why," *National Public Radio: Code Switch, Race and Identity, Remixed*, April 9, 2016; Elizabeth Hinton, Julilly Kohler-Hausmann, and Vesla M. Weaver, "Did Blacks Really Endorse the 1994 Crime Bill?," *New York Times*, April 13, 2016.

Indeed, what is foundationally horrifying about the US ethos of mass incarceration is the quiet and contented immoral ruthlessness to which ordinary everyday people (Christians among them) conform. Mass incarceration is profoundly anchored within the American ethos—it is a deeply rooted and common cultural feature undergirded by anxiety, fear, vindictiveness, cynicism, greed, and sightless proximity to the most vulnerable among us. Mass incarceration feeds (and feeds off) so much of the ruthless indifference of society as a whole. Certainly, mass incarceration is now an abiding feature of the often-punishing American psyche. This is a punishing psyche of brutal societal consequence, the demise of which Christians must positively contribute to by way of persistent, gritty, courageous, faithful, merciful, and audaciously hopeful embodiments of Christian love against the widespread and intersecting tentacles of mass incarceration.

SUGGESTED READINGS

Alexander, Michelle. *The New Jim Crow: Mass Incarceration the Age of Colorblindness.* New York: New Press, 2010.

Davis, Angela Y. *Are Prisons Obsolete?* New York: Seven Stories, 2003.

Douglas, Kelly Brown. *Stand Your Ground: Black Bodies and the Justice of God.* Maryknoll: Orbis, 2015.

Dubler, Joshua, and Vincent Lloyd. *Break Every Yoke: Religion, Justice and the Abolition of Prisons.* New York: Oxford University Press, 2019.

Forman, James, Jr. *Locking Up Our Own: Crime and Punishment in Black America.* New York: Farrar, Straus and Giroux; Reprint Edition, 2018.

Levad, Amy. *Restorative Justice: Theories and Practices of Moral Imagination.* El Paso: LFB Scholarly, 2011.

Reiter, Keramet A. *Mass Incarceration: Keynotes in Criminology and Criminal Justice Series.* New York: Oxford University Press, 2018.

Stevenson, Bryan. *Just Mercy: A Story of Justice and Redemption.* New York: Spiegel & Grau, 2014.

Taylor, Mark Lewis. *The Executed God: The Way of the Cross in Lockdown America*, 2nd ed. Minneapolis: Fortress, 2015.

CHAPTER TWENTY-FIVE

Restorative Justice

AMY LEVAD

Christians from diverse theological perspectives have begun appealing to restorative justice as an alternative to retributivism. Over the past fifty years, retributivism, based in the idea that justice requires the state to violently punish people who commit a crime in proportion to the severity of their offense, has increasingly characterized US criminal justice systems, resulting in mass incarceration.[1] In opposition to this shift, in their 2000 statement on criminal justice, the US Conference of Catholic Bishops wrote, "Restorative justice ... reflects our values and tradition. Our faith calls us to hold people accountable, to forgive, and to heal."[2] A Churchwide Assembly of the Evangelical Lutheran Church in America adopted a similar statement in 2013: "Restorative justice, in its attention to the people involved, provides a fuller account of the nature of justice as well as creative alternatives to incarceration."[3] In 2017, the National Association of Evangelicals partnered with the Ethics and Religious Liberty Coalition of the Southern Baptist Convention, Prison Fellowship, and the Colson Center for Christian Worldview to publish "The Justice Declaration," which states, "The Church has both the unique ability and unparalleled capacity to confront the staggering crisis of crime and incarceration in America and to respond with restorative solutions for communities, victims, and individuals responsible for crime."[4] These quotations from diverse Christian perspectives indicate that many Christians now see their faith as aligning with restorative justice, often in opposition to mass incarceration and retributivism.

"Restorative justice" refers to various collective dialogue processes that aim to do justice among the stakeholders in situations of conflict and harm: people who have caused harm, people who suffered harm, and their respective communities.[5] Stakeholders work together to understand the situation, the harm caused, and who bears responsibility. They aim to

[1]For a history of the development of mass incarceration, see Amy Levad, *Redeeming a Prison Society: A Liturgical and Sacramental Response to Mass Incarceration* (Minneapolis: Fortress, 2014).

[2]US Conference of Catholic Bishops, "Responsibility, Rehabilitation, and Restoration: A Catholic Perspective on Crime and Criminal Justice," November 15, 2000.

[3]Evangelical Lutheran Church in America, "The Church and Criminal Justice: Hearing the Cries," August 17, 2013. Other mainline Protestant churches offer similar statements, including the statement of the Presbyterian Church (USA) approved at its 2002 General Assembly, the Social Principles of the United Methodist Church approved in 2016, and a resolution approved at the 2015 General Synod of the United Church of Christ, among others.

[4]The National Association of Evangelicals, the Ethics and Religious Liberty Coalition of the Southern Baptist Convention, Prison Fellowship, and the Colson Center for Christian Worldview, "The Justice Declaration," June 20, 2017.

[5]For a discussion of the complexities of defining "restorative justice," see Amy Levad, *Restorative Justice: Theories and Practices of Moral Imagination* (El Paso: LFB Scholarly, 2012), 97–107.

reach consensus about how to repair the harm as much as possible, acknowledging that some harms are irrevocable. Restorative justice describes numerous practices, including victim-offender reconciliation programs, truth-and-reconciliation commissions, family group conferencing, neighborhood accountability boards, community conferencing, and circles of support and accountability. These practices respond to diverse contexts of conflict and harm such as political oppression in the case of truth-and-reconciliation commissions and familial conflict in the case of family group conferencing; crime is but one of these contexts.

Most advocates trace the roots of contemporary restorative justice in criminal justice contexts to a case in Elmira, Ontario, in 1974.[6] Two 18-year-old men were charged with over twenty counts of willful damage following a drunken rampage in which they slashed car tires, broke house windows, damaged traffic signals, overturned a boat, and ripped a cross from a church sign. The probation officer assigned to the case, Mark Yantzi, off-handedly mentioned to a group of church volunteers that the young men should meet with the victims of their crimes. A member of the Mennonite Central Committee, Dave Worth, took Yantzi seriously and agreed to help. Under the supervision of Worth and Yantzi, and with approval of the judge, the two young men met with victims, discussing damage they caused, apologizing, and assessing victims' financial costs. Based on these conversations, the young men paid for damages, personally delivering payments to each victim. The process resulted in victims not only being paid but also regaining a sense of safety, seeing the young men as trying to take responsibility for their wrongdoing, and feeling that the situation had been made right. Although the young men avoided jail time, they were still accountable for their crimes, but in ways that ultimately enabled them to return fully to their community without inflicting violent punishment. While restorative justice has developed significantly since 1974, this case exemplifies many key features of these processes: collective dialogue, stakeholder involvement, a focus on repairing harm, and accountability for people who do harm.

Despite commitment to restorative justice among many Christians, restorative justice does not obviously align with Christian ethics. As the Elmira case indicates, restorative justice is an innovation in criminal justice systems. Widespread support among Christians for restorative justice has developed only over the last two decades—a relative blip in the timeline of Christianity and criminal justice systems. Dominant ideologies and practices of criminal justice remain retributive, and Christians often defend retributivism as consonant with our faith. Many Christians cite scripture when describing their attitudes about criminal justice: "an eye for an eye, a tooth for a tooth," a phrase known as the *lex talionis* or law of retaliation (Lev. 24:19-20; also, Exod. 21:23-25 and Deut. 19:21). Aspects of Christian tradition, such as Anselm of Canterbury's satisfaction theory and John Calvin's penal substitution theory of the atonement, depend on retributive interpretations of justice, where violent punishment is deemed necessary for redemption of sinners. That Christian faith aligns with restorative justice, and not retributivism, requires examining scripture and tradition to discern how Christians ought to respond to people who have caused harm to others, especially through criminal acts.

[6]RoscoFilms and Community Justice Initiatives, *The Elmira Case*, DVD, directed by Jonathan Steckley (Toronto: RoscoFilms, 2015).

THE *LEX TALIONIS*, BIBLICAL JUSTICE, AND RESTORATION OF GOD'S REIGN

When looking to scripture for guidance about criminal justice, one temptation may be to focus on biblical law, defining which actions are illicit and how to address them. In biblical law, illicit actions are offenses against God or offenses against other persons, both of which disrupt relationships within the covenant community.[7] The *lex talionis* is an oft-cited phrase of biblical law, used to support the conclusion that scripture demands proportional violence against people who have committed particular offenses; the Bible requires retribution, the theory goes. The analogy to criminal justice today seems straightforward: harm those who harm others in proportion to the degree of harm they caused. This interpretation pits justice against mercy and love, disallowing forgiveness without first inflicting violent punishment upon wrongdoers. Focusing on biblical law in isolation from other parts of scripture or without a more robust understanding of how law functions in the Bible could lead to the conclusion that biblical justice is fundamentally retributive.

Pulling the *lex talionis* out of context to support retributivism, however, is an example of proof-texting. This method is inadequate for using scripture as a source of moral wisdom in two ways. First, it does not engage the insights of historical criticism. Biblical scholars, such as Christopher Marshall and Richard Buck, argue that the *lex talionis* does not permit or require retribution, a common misreading of the texts.[8] Rather, it limits retaliation: take *no more* than an eye or a tooth when an eye or tooth is taken. In addition, the law suggests monetary reparation to victims according to the value of the eye or tooth or whatever else might have been taken, instead of the more gruesome and literal removal of body parts. With historical criticism, the *lex talionis* does not support the inference that biblical justice is retributive.

Second, proof-texting does not attend to the breadth and diversity of scripture. Russell Connors and Patrick McCormick note that scripture is multivocal, and moral guidance may come not only from the voice of specific rules or teachings but also from "the shape or direction of a parable or story, from some theme or lesson deeply embedded in the larger fabric of Scripture's narrative or from the experience of being immersed in the parable of Jesus's life, death, and resurrection."[9] With this approach, we may find less "concrete pieces of advice" and more "distinctive perspectives, loyalties, and affections that one 'learns' from becoming a conscientious and attentive listener to God's word."[10] Regarding questions about how to respond to situations in which people harm one another, the Bible contains a wide variety of genres and texts beyond the *lex talionis* that offer additional perspectives, including, for example, God's restoration of sinful Israel to justice in the prophetic books of Amos and Isaiah;[11] Jesus's parables of the prodigal son

---

[7]Richard Buck, "Restorative Justice in the Hebrew Biblical Tradition," in *Redemption and Restoration: A Catholic Perspective on Restorative Justice*, ed. Trudy D. Conway, David Matzko McCarthy, and Vicki Schieber (Collegeville: Liturgical, 2017), 88–97.

[8]Christopher D. Marshall, *Beyond Retribution: A New Testament Vision for Justice, Crime, and Punishment* (Grand Rapids: Eerdmans, 2001), 79.

[9]Russell B. Connors Jr. and Patrick T. McCormick, *Character, Choices, and Community: The Three Faces of Christian Ethics* (Mahwah: Paulist, 1998), 20.

[10]Ibid.

[11]Ted Grimsrud and Howard Zehr, "Rethinking God, Justice, and Treatment of Offenders," in *Religion, the Community, and the Rehabilitation of Criminal Offenders*, ed. Thomas P. O'Connor (Binghamton: Haworth, 2002), 259–85; Kathryn Getek Soltis, "Mass Incarceration and Theological Images of Justice," *Journal of the Society of Christian Ethics* 31, no. 2 (2011): 113–30.

returned to his father and of the good Samaritan caring for a victim of violent crime in the Gospel of Luke (15:11-32);[12] Jesus's discussion of the call to forgiveness in the Gospel of Matthew (18:15-35);[13] and Paul's exhortation to the Corinthian community to practice a "ministry of reconciliation" (2 Cor. 5:11-21),[14] among others. Jesus's discussion of the *lex talionis* in his Sermon on the Mount (Mt. 5–7) is an especially informative text, particularly because he seems to adopt a method of reading scripture for insight about what our perspectives, loyalties, and affections ought to be in response to people who do great harm and are considered enemies.

The Sermon begins with the beatitudes, lifting up dispositions of people who participate in the kingdom of heaven: meekness, mercy, hungering and thirsting for justice, peacemaking, and so on (Mt. 5:1-12). Those people who possess these characteristics are the "salt of the earth" and "light of the world" (vv. 13-16). After the beatitudes, Jesus states that he has not come to supplant the law and prophets, that is, the scriptures of Jesus's Jewish community, but to fulfill them (vv. 17-20). The next passages follow a pattern that illustrates his meaning. In a series of cases, Jesus begins by citing a legal proscription in the scriptures: "You shall not murder" (v. 21; cf. Exod. 20:13; Deut. 5:17), "You shall not commit adultery" (v. 27; cf. Exod. 20:14; Deut. 5:18), "You shall not swear falsely" (v. 33; cf. Lev. 19:12; Num. 30:2; Deut. 23:21). He then states, "but I say to you …" (Mt. 5:22, 28, 32, 34, 39, 44), a phrase that indicates *not* that he rejects the cited law (after all, Jesus is not indicating by this phrase that his followers can murder, cheat, and lie), but that he invites his listeners to adopt virtues that make it *unnecessary* to consult the law when discerning a moral course of action. Those who listen to Jesus will not murder because they have become people who do not anger and who seek reconciliation amidst conflict (vv. 22-26). They will not commit adultery because they do not objectify other people with lustful stares (vv. 28-30). They will not swear falsely because they always speak plainly and forthrightly (vv. 34-37). Jesus then cites the *lex talionis* (again, in biblical law, a limit on retaliation) and instructs his followers to turn the other cheek, give their coats as well when sued for their cloaks, and go the extra mile (vv. 38-42). If this passage follows the established pattern, then it suggests that followers of Jesus need not be warned by law against exceeding limitations on retribution because they have become people of "excelling love" who nonviolently "diffuse situations of conflict."[15] Indeed, they will love their enemies, endeavoring to embody God's perfection (vv. 43-48).

This reading of the Sermon might reasonably lead to worry about whether Jesus sacrifices justice to mercy and love. If retributivism prioritizes justice over mercy and love, does Jesus do the opposite, forgetting justice for the sake of mercy and love? But Jesus also says that those who hunger and thirst for justice will be filled, so justice must also be important to him (Mt. 5:6). Here, it is helpful to recognize that the larger point of the Sermon is to tell Jesus's followers about the kingdom of heaven (kingdom of God, or God's reign, in other gospels), which is not the otherworldly reality of the afterlife, but the conditions here and now—and to be brought about fully in the future—in which

[12]Christopher D. Marshall, *Compassionate Justice: An Interdisciplinary Dialogue with Two Gospel Parables on Law, Crime, and Restorative Justice* (Eugene: Cascade, 2012).

[13]Thomas Noakes-Duncan, *Communities of Restoration: Ecclesial Ethics and Restorative Justice* (New York: Bloomsbury T&T Clark, 2017).

[14]Ched Myers and Elaine Enns, *Ambassadors of Reconciliation: New Testament Reflections on Restorative Justice and Peacemaking*, vol. I (Maryknoll: Orbis, 2009).

[15]James F. Davis, *Lex Talionis in Early Judaism and the Exhortations of Jesus in Matthew 5:38–42* (London: T&T Clark International, 2005), 296.

"we live with God and with one another in relationships that are just."[16] Jesus fulfills the law and prophets by ushering in God's reign, which realizes completely the Hebrew scriptures' notion of *shalom*, or wholeness, peace, integrity, and unity established in covenant with God. Justice is fully accomplished not through violent punishment, but in *shalom* through God's invitation to us to repent, leading to restoration and reparation of broken relationships with humanity.[17] In keeping with the beatitudes and in accordance with the covenant, justice is conceptualized in God's reign according to a logic that works through mercy and love to restore right relationship—not through retribution.

A reading of the *lex talionis* without the insights of historical criticism and without conversation with the many voices of scripture could lead to the conclusion that biblical justice is retributive. An interpretive method drawing upon historical criticism and examining the breadth and diversity of scripture challenges this inference. A variety of virtues, dispositions, and worldviews surface with attentive listening to God's word in the Sermon on the Mount as well as other biblical passages in both testaments. Mercy and love are as important as justice in response to people who harm others, and these values do not conflict, as they do under retributivism, but complement each other in this vision of God's reign. People who listen to God's word do not seek retaliation against people who have caused harm to others. Rather, they work nonviolently toward just relationships, characterized by *shalom*, which requires repentance, reparation, and ultimately reconciliation in response to harmful behaviors. Our methodological shift away from proof-texting isolated biblical laws without attention to context thus yields a conclusion that biblical justice is fundamentally restorative, not retributive.

ATONEMENT, RETRIBUTION, AND RESTORATION IN CHRISTIAN TRADITION

Retributivism, nevertheless, has shaped Christian tradition, including theologies, dogma, liturgies, practices, ethics, and norms. In turn, Christian tradition has contributed to the development of criminal justice practices and ideologies in the West. The influence of retributivism on Christian tradition can be seen, for example, in dominant theories of the atonement, particularly Anselm of Canterbury's satisfaction theory and its development in John Calvin's penal substitution theory. Anselm holds that human sinfulness creates a debt owed to God that requires satisfaction through perfect obedience; as human beings cannot be perfectly obedient, Jesus Christ—fully human and fully divine—satisfies our debt through his sacrificial death on the cross, thus enabling God to forgive humanity while exacting justice. Calvin builds on Anselm's theory, viewing Jesus's death as a punitive sacrifice in which the violence due to sinful humanity is borne instead by the Son of God, who takes our guilt upon himself. Both of these theories assume, first, that God requires a return of violence as a just response to sin and, second, that sacrifice transfers God's violence to sacrificial victims, thereby redeeming sinners. According to Timothy Gorringe, rather than taking Jesus's death and resurrection as an announcement of the end of punishment, these theories have endorsed the idea that divine order necessitates returning harm upon people who have done harm (whether to satisfy their debt or to

---

[16]Mary Katherine Birge, SSJ, "Jesus, the Kingdom of God, and Restorative Justice," in *Redemption and Restoration: A Catholic Perspective on Restorative Justice*, ed. Trudy D. Conway, David Matzko McCarthy, and Vicki Schieber (Collegeville: Liturgical, 2017), 104.

[17]Buck, "Restorative Justice," 88–97.

enact due punishment upon them), in the spirit of the common misreading of the *lex talionis*.[18] As a result, dominant atonement theories provide a metaphysical justification for criminal justice practices and ideologies forged during the height of Christendom in the West since the mid-eleventh century, resulting in penal systems rooted in retributivism.

The influence of retributivism on Christian tradition, and subsequently on criminal justice practices and ideologies, suggests the need to consider tradition both affirmatively and critically in moral discernment. Just as an adequate method of biblical interpretation requires historical criticism, an adequate method of interpreting Christian tradition requires discerning "the difference between continuing a content that expresses divine revelation and a teaching that merely reflects the sociological and cultural circumstances of a particular time and place."[19] Anselm's theory, for example, mirrors assumptions of medieval European feudalism; Calvin's theory draws upon sixteenth-century jurisprudence. Consideration of tradition and scripture also requires attending to the "correlative" relationship between the two.[20] Inadequacies in Christian tradition are often tied to inadequacies of biblical interpretation, and vice versa. For instance, dominant atonement theories depend upon reading of the *lex talionis* as requiring retaliation as well as upon misunderstandings of how sacrifice functioned in biblical law. Richard Buck explains that, in Hebrew law, sacrifices purify one's soul from the stain of sin caused by unintentional offenses; they are "a cleansing process, through which the sinner can come to understand how he or she can learn to become less careless about the actions he or she performs."[21] Sacrifices function neither as restitution owed to God nor as punishment transferred to sacrificial victims. Christopher Marshall likewise notes, "In ancient Israel, sacrifices were made for a variety of purposes. … None of these entail [*sic*] retributive punishment."[22] In contrast with dominant atonement theories, a historical-critical reading of the meanings and practices of sacrifice in scripture would indicate that Christ's death does "not pacify God's anger through bloody punishment."[23] An additional reason to question these theories is their tension with Jesus's instructions in the Sermon on the Mount regarding the *lex talionis*. If emulating God's perfection involves rejecting retaliation by nonviolently diffusing situations of conflict, then how could atonement theories dependent on retributivism exemplify God's justice in responding to sinful humanity?

Criticism of dominant atonement theories ought to lead Christians to consider alternative interpretations rooted in historical-critical reading of scripture and an understanding of biblical justice as restorative. In light of the dominance of Anselm's and Calvin's theories, much work remains in formulating alternatives. Kimberly Vrudny offers one possible model, rooted in a Trinitarian rather than crucicentric soteriology, in which she traces three restorative moves God makes to reconcile with humanity.[24] First, God establishes a covenant with Israel, expressing "God's desire to be in continued relationship with humankind."[25] Covenantal laws, such as the *lex talionis*, defined what

[18]Timothy Gorringe, *God's Just Vengeance* (Cambridge: Cambridge University Press, 1996).
[19]Charles Curran, *The Catholic Moral Tradition Today: A Synthesis* (Washington, DC: Georgetown University Press, 1999), 53.
[20]Ibid.
[21]Buck, "Restorative Justice," 90.
[22]Marshall, *Beyond Retribution*, 63.
[23]Ibid., 64.
[24]Kimberly Vrudny, *Beauty's Vineyard: A Theological Aesthetic of Anguish and Anticipation* (Collegeville: Liturgical, 2016).
[25]Ibid., 175.

the Israelites understood to be required for the realization of *shalom*, and sacrifices atoned for sin by restoring the covenant through an expiatory process. Second, God becomes incarnate: "By living among us and by calling humankind to reconciliation with God, Jesus expressed God's forgiveness."[26] Reconciliation with God—the goal of covenant—is realized fully through our participation in God's reign (the focus of the Sermon on the Mount) in which mercy, love, and justice coalesce in the perfect accomplishment of *shalom*. As Jesus invites us into the kingdom of heaven, he achieves our salvation through his resistance to evil, particularly the violence and oppression of the Roman Empire, which stands in opposition to God's reign. The Romans, of course, crucify Jesus. For Vrudny, sinful humanity, not God, chose this violent death. God's salvific work lies not in the crucifixion but in Jesus's response to it: "Instead of retaliating, instead of harming another human being, Jesus preferred to die. … In so doing, Christ revealed not God's embrace of execution, but God's preference for nonviolent resistance to crucifixion and torture."[27] The resurrection is God's "no" to the killing of Jesus: "God would have victory by bringing life out of death."[28] Third, the Holy Spirit, "by the power of grace, empowers humans to live like Christ."[29] When we resist evil, love our neighbors, offer forgiveness, strive for reconciliation, choose nonviolence, and advance justice that restores, then we participate in God's reign already present and anticipate its coming in fullness. In Vrudny's view, atonement—full restoration of right relationship through God's mercy, love, and justice—occurs through God's three moves of covenant, incarnation, and empowerment, not through the single move of crucifixion.

With this alternative understanding of atonement, Christian ideas and practices concerning how to respond to people who have caused harm to other people ought to shift from retributivism to restorative justice. Whereas Anselm's and Calvin's theories align with retribution, Vrudny's reading of the atonement in conversation with historical-critical interpretations of scripture aligns with restoration. This theory also better fits interpretations of biblical sacrifice, an understanding of the *lex talionis* as limiting retaliation, and Jesus's Sermon proclaiming God's reign as the fulfillment of *shalom*. Christians who understand the atonement in this way may be less likely to view retribution as necessitated by divine order. Rather they may seek nonviolent means to restore relationships among people who have caused harm, people who have suffered harm, and their communities through processes of repentance, reparation, and, ultimately, reconciliation.

Christian tradition involves much more than atonement theories, and numerous other aspects of Christian tradition bear marks of retributivism. In addition, dominant theories of the atonement have influenced other aspects of Christian tradition, including theologies, dogma, liturgies, practices, ethics, and norms. Rethinking atonement will require also rethinking other aspects of Christian tradition that bear the marks of Anselm's and Calvin's ideas. Nonviolent theories of the atonement, such as Vrundy's, are relatively recent developments in Christian tradition and will continue to need refinement in the coming years and decades.[30] Nevertheless, affirmative and critical consideration of

---

[26]Ibid., 176.
[27]Ibid., 186.
[28]Ibid., 182.
[29]Ibid., 184.
[30]Other nonviolent atonement theories have been developed in J. Denny Weaver, *The Nonviolent Atonement* (Grand Rapids: Eerdmans, 2001); and Christopher D. Marshall, "Atonement, Violence, and the Will of God: A Sympathetic Response to J. Denny Weaver's *The Nonviolent Atonement*," *Mennonite Quarterly Review* 77, no. 1 (2003): 69–92.

Christian tradition, drawing upon historical criticism and in conversation with scripture, yields innovative possibilities for recognizing alignments of Christianity with restorative justice, rather than retributivism.

RESTORATION IN EXPERIENCE AND REASON

Although dominant ideologies and practices of criminal justice remain retributive, and although many Christians defend retributivism as consonant with their faith, historical-critical approaches to scripture and tradition reveal strong foundations for the growing consensus among Christians supporting restorative justice. The other fonts of moral wisdom informing Christian ethics—experience and reason—raise a number of concerns Christians ought to consider in future advocacy of and participation in restorative justice. Rather than delve fully into these concerns here, this chapter concludes by highlighting a couple of these concerns. While many Christians may see their faith aligning with contemporary restorative justice, these ideologies and practices remain the work of human beings, and so will inevitably fall short of the full realization of right relationship to which God calls us. With awareness of various concerns, advocates and participants may continue to develop, enhance, or correct these processes appropriately.

Experience involves knowledge culled from history, from various perspectives about particular questions, and—especially for Christians committed to a preferential option for the poor and oppressed—from the insights of people who have been marginalized.[31] The quotations at the beginning of this chapter indicate that many Christians have found in restorative justice a possible answer to mass incarceration, a reality of twenty-first-century US criminal justice systems that exacerbates and contributes to the impoverishment, oppression, and marginalization of millions of people, particularly people of color. Attending to the experiences of these millions of people raises the question of whether restorative justice alone can dismantle mass incarceration or address related social injustices. A persistent critique of restorative justice in criminal justice contexts has been that it too often "fails to address the social structural dimensions of criminal conflict," because its processes focus primarily on interpersonal harm.[32] Practices can be adapted to attend more fully to structural as well as interpersonal harms, but social injustice and mass incarceration remain peripheral matters in most restorative justice processes.[33] I have argued elsewhere that restorative justice alone is not sufficient for dismantling mass incarceration and related social injustices, although it can offer meaningful and impactful alternatives to prisons and jails while mitigating some collateral consequences of incarceration.[34] Christians who support restorative justice in criminal justice contexts ought to continue to ask: What *else* ought we be doing to repair harms caused by social injustice and mass incarceration? In what ways ought we to work for transformative justice as well as restorative justice?[35]

[31]Connors and McCormick, *Character, Choices, and Community*, 19–20.

[32]David Dyck, "Reaching toward a Structurally Responsive Training and Practice of Restorative Justice," *Contemporary Justice Review* 3, no. 3 (2000): 239.

[33]Kathleen Daly, "Restorative Justice in Diverse and Unequal Societies," *Law in Context* 17, no. 1 (2000): 167–90.

[34]Amy Levad, "Restorative and Transformative Justice in a Land of Mass Incarceration," *Journal of Moral Theology* 5, no. 2 (2016): 22–43.

[35]M. Kay Harris, "Transformative Justice: The Transformation of Restorative Justice," in *Handbook of Restorative Justice: A Global Perspective*, ed. Dennis Sullivan and Larry Tifft (New York: Routledge, 2006), 555–66.

Academic disciplines such as philosophy, criminology, psychology, or political science can also provide moral wisdom based on experience.[36] Criminological evaluations of restorative justice offer important insights: Does restorative justice work? If so, at doing what: reducing reoffending, repairing harm, addressing victims' needs, achieving fairness, empowering communities? With what categories of crimes ought restorative justice be used? Are there instances when we ought *not* to employ restorative justice? Without consultation with criminologists, many people might resist restorative justice as a response to violent crimes or sexually based offenses. The temptation may be to reserve restorative justice for only people who present little risk of reoffending, who seem relatively innocent (such as minors), or who committed nonviolent crimes. Evidence from criminology, however, suggests that restorative justice is often most effective at reducing reoffending among people deemed high risk who committed serious crimes, including violent and sexually based offenses.[37] Christians committed to restorative justice ought to consider: Are there limits to whom we would offer restorative justice? If so, are those limits based upon assumptions about their offenses and their possibilities for restoration, and are those assumptions affirmed or challenged by criminological evidence?

In moral discernment, reason serves "to formulate some sort of specifically Christian moral response to the question or issue at hand ... shaped by the insights ... of experience, scripture, and tradition."[38] Historical criticism of the Bible, with all its breadth and diversity, reveals that Christians are called to resist the temptation to retaliate against people who have harmed other people; retributivism is irreconcilable with scripture. Rather we participate in God's reign through nonviolent works of love, justice, and mercy for the realization of *shalom*, which comes to fruition amid relationships restored to rightness. Reflection upon tradition, especially various interpretations of the atonement, opens possibilities for understanding God's redemptive moves through covenant, incarnation, and empowerment as fundamentally restorative. Affirmative and critical approaches to scripture and tradition offer a foundation to the growing consensus among Christians that our faith aligns with restorative justice. As advocacy of and participation in restorative justice continues in the future, Christians may find their footing for this work in scripture and tradition. In doing so, Christians also ought to call for transformation of unjust social structures, especially mass incarceration, and for opening restorative justice even to people whom many consider irredeemable.

SUGGESTED READINGS

Conway, Trudy D., David Matzko McCarthy, and Vicki Schieber, eds. *Redemption and Restoration: A Catholic Perspective on Restorative Justice*. Collegeville: Liturgical, 2017.

[36]Charles Curran, *The Church and Morality: An Ecumenical and Catholic Approach* (Minneapolis: Augsburg Fortress, 1993), 39.

[37]See Donald A. Andrews and James Bonta, *The Psychology of Criminal Conduct*, 5th ed. (New York: Taylor and Francis, 2010), 69–76; Andrew Bates et al., "Circles South-East: The First Ten Years, 2002–2012," *International Journal of Offender Therapy and Comparative Criminology* 58 (2013): 861–85; Grant Duwe, "Can Circles of Support and Accountability (CoSA) Work in the United States? Preliminary Results from a Randomized Experiment in Minnesota," *Sexual Abuse: A Journal of Research and Treatment* 25, no. 2 (2013): 143–65; Robin J. Wilson, Franca Cortoni, and Andrew J. McWhinnie, "Circles of Support and Accountability: A Canadian National Replication of Outcome Findings," *Sexual Abuse: A Journal of Research and Treatment* 21, no. 4 (2009): 412–30.

[38]Connors and McCormick, *Character, Choices, and Community*, 22.

Johnstone, Gerry. *Restorative Justice: Ideas, Values, Debates*, 2nd ed. New York: Abingdon, 2011.
Marshall, Christopher. *Beyond Retribution: A New Testament Vision for Justice, Crime, and Punishment*. Grand Rapids: Eerdmans, 2001.
Zehr, Howard. *The Little Book of Restorative Justice*. New York: Good Books, 2014.

CHAPTER TWENTY-SIX

The Police

ANDY ALEXIS-BAKER

Jordan Edwards in Dallas and Tamir Rice in Cleveland were gunned down when an officer decided to shoot first and ask questions later. Danny Thomas in Houston and Dontre Hamilton in Milwaukee were killed by police who did not recognize their mental illnesses. In 2018, American police killed at least 992 people. US police killed 995 people in 2015, 963 in 2016, and 987 in 2017. Twenty-five percent of those killed had mental health problems. Police are twice as likely to kill unarmed Black men than unarmed white men.[1] Indictments of police officers are rare; convictions rarer. Even when compelling evidence exists of excessive force—such as when officer Jeronimo Yanez shot and killed Philando Castile at point-blank range—prosecutors seldom bring charges and juries seldom convict police.

US police are massively armed. Under the 1033 Program, the Pentagon has transferred over $4 billion in military equipment—such as semiautomatic handguns, fully automatic rifles, hand grenade launchers, and armored vehicles used in war—to local police.[2] In Illinois, campus police at the College of DuPage received fourteen fully automatic M16 rifles, Wheaton police department acquired sixty-eight M16 and M14 rifles, and the Evanston police received twenty fully automatic M16 rifles.[3] Armed with military weapons and trained in military tactics, police forces across the United States surveil, interrogate, and use violence with near impunity.

Despite the militarization of American police and a steady stream of videos documenting police officers shooting and killing unarmed Black men, public support for American police is the highest it has been in decades. Christians overwhelmingly support police. Christian support, however, shifts along racial lines. Seventy percent of white evangelicals, white mainline Protestants, and white Catholics say the police are doing a good or excellent job. However, 55 percent of Black Protestants view the police as doing a lousy job.[4] Despite lower Black support, however, overall support for police rose nearly 14 percent during the three years that videos began surfacing of officers killing unarmed Black men.[5]

---

[1]For the statistic in this paragraph, see the *Washington Post*'s database on police shootings, collected since 2015: https://www.washingtonpost.com/graphics/2018/national/police-shootings-2018/?utm_term=.f597005afbb9.

[2]See American Civil Liberties Union (ACLU), *War Comes Home: The Excessive Militarization of the Armed Forces and the Police* (New York: ACLU, 2014).

[3]See American Transparency, "Federal Weapons Loaned to Public Bodies," 2019, https://www.openthebooks.com/map/?Map=1&MapType=Pin.

[4]Rich Morin, Kim Parker, Renee Stepler, and Andrew Mercer, *Behind the Badge* (Washington, DC: Pew Research Center, 2017).

[5]See Gallup, "Americans' Respect for Police Surges," October 24, 2016.

Although there are some excellent resources on the American criminal justice system from a Christian ethical perspective, Christian ethicists have not yet published any significant books dealing with police in particular. Most Christian work on police deals with policing as a concept that could challenge modern ideas about war rather than the actual institutions and practices of police.[6] So of the four fonts of Christian moral theology—scripture, tradition, experience, and reason—ethicists have so far explored how tradition relates to policing the most. In what follows, I will first examine Christian scriptures and then move to experience drawn from critical disciplines like history, politics, and more to ground theological ethics in theory and history.

POLICE AND CHRISTIAN SCRIPTURE

Police forces are a recent invention. So, scripture does not explicitly address the modern police institution. The New Testament mentions military units and personnel such as "legions," "centurions," "tribunes," and "guards." If police investigate, deter, and prevent ordinary crime, then the Roman military are not police. Citizens undertook these tasks. For example, in Acts 21 Paul's presence in the temple caused some people to shout, "Men of Israel, help." Customarily, when someone called for help like this everyone nearby gathered to aid the person. An angry crowd then dragged Paul from the temple. Seeing an apparent riot, the Roman military intervened, took possession of Paul, and nearly tortured him.

Here we see the Roman military's primary function. They suppressed riots and rebellions. They did not care about crime. Wilfried Nippel even argues, "We do not even know to what degree (if at all) the Roman authorities undertook prosecution of murder."[7] Most scholars claim that Jesus was so threatening and disruptive, particularly with his actions at the temple, that wealthy Jewish and Roman authorities colluded to stop him. They did not execute Jesus because of crime but because he was seen as a rebel leader.

If police are understood merely as a particular institution that prevents, investigates, and arrests criminal activities, then scripture does not speak directly to the modern situation. However, the primary function of modern police is not crime prevention, but the creation and maintenance of a particular order, which ties them to the oppressive structures that arrested, tortured, and executed Jesus.

POLICING RACE AND POVERTY

American police arose from such oppressive structures. Before the Civil War, slave patrols in the southern states guarded roads to verify slaves had travel passes, searched slave quarters for signs of revolt, and helped regulate behavior. After the war, these patrols morphed into the first police departments. Created in 1874, the Atlanta police exemplifies

[6]E.g., see Gerald Schlabach, ed., *Just Policing, Not War* (Collegeville: Liturgical, 2007). An exception is Tobias Winright who has published numerous articles on policing and use of force and its relationship to just war theory. See, e.g., Winright, "What Might a Policing Approach Contribute to the Pacifist/Just-War Debate on Dealing with Terrorism?," in *Conflict and Conciliation: Faith and Politics in an Age of Global Dissonance*, ed. Jason Daverth (Dublin: Columba, 2007), 39–69; Winright, "Community Policing as a Paradigm for International Relations," in *Just Policing, Not War*, ed. Gerald Schlabach (Collegeville: Liturgical, 2007), 130–52. For a collection of several of his essays between 1995 and 2018, see Winright, *Serve and Protect: Selected Essays on Just Policing* (Eugene: Cascade, 2020).

[7]Wilfried Nippel, *Public Order in Ancient Rome* (New York: Cambridge University Press, 1995), 2.

southern police forces. The leading causes of arrest were disorderly conduct, public intoxication, loitering, arrest "on suspicion," "on warrant," larceny, and prostitution.[8] These arrests helped control newly freed Black people. For example, the Atlanta police arrested a Black man on suspicion because he sold a mule too cheaply.[9] In 1877, the *Atlanta Constitution* reported that the police were "determined to break up riotous negro dances."[10] Atlanta police chief, John Ball, stated that Atlanta was a law-abiding city except for the "many petty offenses resultant from a large negro population."[11] In 1903, an Atlanta newspaper called for police to strictly enforce vagrancy laws aimed at "idle shiftless negros—for the majority of the crimes punished in the city court are committed by this class."[12] White people believed that Black people left plantations to avoid work and to attack white people. So police, morphed from slave patrols, arrested Black people on trumped-up, petty charges so that Black people could be forced to work for free again while incarcerated. The entire criminal justice system in the South was predicated on the re-enslavement of Black people.[13] Southern police forces, therefore, represented a white response to the emancipation of Black slaves.

Black people saw police differently than whites. In 1881, a Black-owned Atlanta newspaper stated, "We have lived in Atlanta twenty-seven years, and we have heard the lash sounding from the cabins of slaves, poured on by their masters, but we have never seen a meaner set of low-down cut throats, scrapes, and murderers than the city of Atlanta has to protect the peace."[14] Former slaves indicted the police as crueler than slavery. Police harassment and violence sometimes prompted Black people to resist police by fighting cops, rescuing prisoners, and other actions. In 1866, the *Richmond Dispatch* warned: "The negroes seem determined to try resistance to the police, but whenever they do so, they will find that they have begun a most unwise course. The laws of the State and city must be enforced, disorder and crime must be put down, if it takes every white man in the city to do it."[15]

Neither were northern police departments designed to curb crime but the "dangerous class," meaning the idle poor. From 1820 to 1860, five million immigrants entered American cities. Threatened by immigrant poverty and behaviors, cities created police forces to control them. The 1834 Boston Marshal's report listed police activities such as enforcing traffic and building regulations and curbing vices such as drinking and vagrancy without mentioning crime or criminals.[16] In 1861, the New York governor described the newly formed police departments' main duties—to inspect factories and businesses for health reasons, suppress liquor sales and theater on Sundays, and tackling other vices—christening the police as "guardians of the public morals, health and order."[17] After St. Louis instituted a police force, the 1874 arrest records show 42 total arrests in a city of 300,000 people for murder, robbery, and rape, and 16 arrests for burglary. By contrast,

[8]Eugene J. Watts, "The Police in Atlanta, 1890–1905," *Journal of Southern History* 39, no. 2 (1973): 171.
[9]*Atlanta Constitution*, July 29, 1885.
[10]*Atlanta Constitution*, August 26, 1877.
[11]Quoted in Watts, "The Police in Atlanta," 172.
[12]Ibid.
[13]See Douglas Blackmon, *Slavery by Another Name: The Re-Enslavement of Black People in America from the Civil War to World War II* (New York: Doubleday, 2008).
[14]Watts, "The Police in Atlanta," 172.
[15]*Richmond Dispatch*, July 31, 1866.
[16] Roger Lane, *Policing the City: Boston 1822–1885* (Cambridge: Harvard University Press, 1967), 19–20.
[17]Edwin D. Morgan, "The Governor's Message," *Jamestown Journal*, January 11, 1861. Available at https://nyshistoricnewspapers.org/lccn/sn83031315/1861-01-11/ed-1/seq-1.pdf.

the police arrested over 2,500 for vagrancy, nearly 8,000 for drunkenness, 1,600 for profane language, and 3,300 for disturbing the peace. Most arrestees were immigrants or Black. Of the 24,000 arrests that the entirely Protestant Boston police made in 1860, 20,000 were Irish Catholic immigrants.[18] In city after city, newly created police forces combated vices of the poor, not violent dangerous criminals.

Order meant white order. Politicians used white fears to consolidate state power, whose police activities ensured the moneyed regime's power. This history demonstrates that "order" is not a given, natural phenomenon. Order is a disciplinary regime. However, these first American police carried on an older function of controlling the poor and at establishing and maintaining ruling-class order. The "law and order" rhetoric of American policing is part of a broader shift in the concept of order.

THE QUEST FOR ORDER

The medieval concept of a divinely sanctioned order, in which all beings and all social relations fit within a larger divine order, began to shift as the old feudal order crumbled when peasants revolted across Europe and church authorities lost their power around the time of the Reformation. Inflation and burgeoning wealth among merchants cracked the social hierarchy where people began to look to kings rather than feudal lords for protection. Many farmers and other agricultural laborers were uprooted from their rural environment and moved to cities because of population increases, cycles of inflation and scarcity, increased production and trade, and shifts in landholding. This mass migration resulted in a dramatic increase of urban poor, including so-called masterless men who regularly migrated.

The emerging political and economic powers developed techniques to bring order in new circumstances where landless peasants were increasingly pushed into cities and rulers began to rule "states." English rulers, for example, enacted various police laws to control the new poor. The Vagabonds Act of 1531 forbade all nonstate-licensed begging, allowing only the "deserving poor" to beg. The Act for Punishment of Sturdy Vagabonds and Beggars (1536) mandated public flogging for beggar vagabonds (first offense), ear cutting (second offense), and execution (third offense). In 1555, Queen Mary I mandated that poor people on relief wear badges. Without a badge, beggars could be flogged, mutilated, or executed. These "grotesquely terroristic laws," according to Karl Marx, were meant to form a population of wage laborers and were created "by the forcible expropriation of the people from the soil."[19]

> This free and rightless proletariat could not possibly be absorbed by the nascent manufacturers as fast as it was thrown upon the world. ... These men, suddenly dragged from their accustomed mode of life, could not immediately adapt themselves to the discipline of their new condition. They were turned in massive quantities into beggars, robbers and vagabonds, partly from inclination, in most cases under the force of circumstances. Hence at the end of the fifteenth and during the whole of the sixteenth centuries, a bloody legislation against vagabondage was enforced throughout

---

[18]Charles Tilly, *How Policing Affects the Visibility of Crime in Nineteenth Century Europe and America* (Ann Arbor: University of Michigan Center for Research on Social Organization, 1987), 52.
[19]Karl Marx, *Capital*, vol. 1 (New York: Penguin, 1990), 899.

> Western Europe. The fathers of the present working class were chastised for their enforced transformation into vagabonds and paupers.[20]

Policing managed this flux of poverty. People should work; stay in their social, economic, and geographical place; and obey the state. In seventeenth-century Russia, Peter the Great claimed, "The Police begets good order and sound morality."[21] Disorder meant living at variance with emerging markets and a disciplined labor force. Thus, the ruling classes experimented with policing. In 1521, the Normandy government decreed an ordinance for a *police des pauvres* in Rouen and later created a *bureau des pauvres* that not only collected alms for the needy but also forced people to work.[22] The early police regulated nearly every aspect of life so that bodies would be disciplined into the emerging political and economic order. Creating a particular order is what police have been about since their earliest times.

THE QUEST FOR SECURITY

While police manufacture order, they also bring security. Once upon a time, security was a negative thing. *Securitas* comes from *sine* (without) *cura* (care, troubles, office, or duty). So *securitas* can mean freedom from danger or having no duties or office, which meant being reckless. John Calvin illustrates the theological concern with security. For Calvin, the only reliable experience concerning salvation is the experience of one's unworthiness. Any security arising from the belief one is elect is self-righteous and does not rely on God's righteousness. Calvin said,

> When we say that faith must be certain and secure, we certainly speak not of an assurance which is never affected by doubt, nor a security which anxiety never assails, we rather maintain that believers have a perpetual struggle with their own distrust, and are thus far from thinking that their own consciences possess a placid quiet, uninterrupted by perturbation.[23]

A secure person does not have proper cares and concerns. Security is sinful confidence in human ability.

As new political and economic theories developed apart from theology, security became a positive goal because it was the modern state's reason for being. John Locke claimed, "Government has no other end but the preservation of property."[24] Adam Smith agreed: "Civil government so far as it is instituted for the security of property, is in reality instituted for the defense of the rich against the poor, or those who have some property against those who have none at all."[25] Jeremy Bentham argued that "what men want principally of government is ... security, which is the work of the protection afforded by government in respect of the different possessions, in respect of which security is

[20]Ibid., 896.

[21]Quoted in Mark Neocleous, *The Fabrication of Social Order: A Critical Theory of Police Power* (London: Pluto, 2000), 122, n. 12.

[22]See Mitchell Dean, *The Constitution of Poverty: Toward a Genealogy of Liberal Governance* (New York: Routledge, 1990), 58.

[23]John Calvin, *Institutes of the Christian Religion*, trans. Henry Beveridge (Grand Rapids: Eerdmans, 1989), 84, III.2.17.

[24]John Locke, *Two Treatises of Government* (New Haven: Yale University Press, 2003), 141.

[25]Adam Smith, *The Wealth of Nations* (New York: Bantam, 2003), 907.

exposed to defalcations and shocks."[26] The French *Declaration of the Rights of Man* (1793) proclaimed the natural human rights as "equality, liberty, security, property."[27]

Liberty and security become almost interchangeable in the liberal tradition. Politics is about security. Freedom begins when politics has cleared the terrain and established order for the activities that liberalism defines as freedom, namely the freedom to enjoy private property. Government exists, liberal theorists claim, "for the security of property." This "egoism," Marx argued, presupposes atomistic individuals each of whom is "withdrawn into himself, his private interest and his private desires and separated from the community."[28] This is why Marx claimed that within liberalism "*security* is the supreme social concept of civil society, the concept of *police*, the concept that the whole of society is there only to guarantee each of its members the conservation of his person, his rights and his property."[29] Liberal government protects individuals from their neighbors, so they can enjoy the supposedly natural freedom of property. However, the security the modern state provides entails police because individuals threaten one another's property rights, and the state will police each individual.

As Marx intimates, connecting security, freedom, and property has profound consequences concerning police. The police became necessary because of the poor's disorderly behaviors: begging, gambling, and drinking threaten the security of property, since they make the poor, according to French law, "become addicted to idleness, commit robberies and fall unfortunately into many other crimes."[30] The principal threat to property was unemployed people. Vagrants and homeless people were classified as a vast field of disorder. The new security police that emerged were designed to manage the consequences of creating a vast urban wage-labor force without the traditional social protections of the medieval system.

DISCRETION AND SOVEREIGNTY

Pursuing security means liberal theory has no bulwark against authoritarianism since police invoke security reasons for any action, claiming a particular action was "necessary." Then, an action otherwise considered a crime (e.g., shooting an unarmed person) becomes justified. Claims to necessity create "states of exception" suspending law. Police then operate as a sovereign power above the law.

While attempting to secure property, Locke sought to replace monarchical whim with law. For Locke, "settled and standing rules" should circumscribe discretion, due process should prioritize rights over police powers, and law should protect citizens from arbitrary arrest and ensure fair treatment while in custody. No magistrate or constable should act beyond the law, "for exceeding the bounds of authority is no more a right in a great, than in a petty officer; no more justifiable in a king than a constable." A magistrate who uses discretion and enters somebody's house to execute a warrant should be "opposed as a thief and a robber." For "wherever law ends," Locke proclaimed, "tyranny begins."[31]

[26]Jeremey Bentham, "Institute of Political Economy," in *Jeremy Bentham's Economic Writings*, vol. 3, ed. W. Stark (London: Allen & Unwin, 1954), 310.
[27]As quoted in Marx, "The Jewish Question," in *Early Writings* (New York: Penguin, 1992), 229.
[28]Ibid., 230.
[29]Ibid., emphasis in original.
[30]Quoted in Robert Schwartz, *Policing the Poor in Eighteenth-Century France* (Chapel Hill: University of North Carolina Press, 1988), 19.
[31]Locke, *Two Treatises of Government*, 189, 190.

Police discretion, however, looks like sovereign whim. Echoing Locke, Jeffrey Reiman argues, "Police discretion begins where the rule of law ends: police discretion is precisely the subjection of law to a human decision beyond the law."[32] In the United States, police belong to the executive branch and therefore should not act like judges. If the police believe someone has committed a crime, they must investigate it. If the police discover a crime, they must bring the accused to court. The police cannot ignore crime or free suspects. However, police operate in "low-visibility" settings where the only people likely to know that the police officer decided not to invoke the law are the police officer and the suspect. Hence, police discretion is unreviewable and risks becoming arbitrary and prejudiced. In using discretion, the police usurp both the legislative role by failing to enforce enacted laws and the judiciary by adjudicating and dispensing consequences. Discretion transforms the police into a sovereign power by creating a buffer between the police and the law where police stand apart from and above the law.

Although Locke subjected sovereignty to law, he also allowed for discretion in national emergencies. He promoted executive "prerogative" to allow the sovereign "to act according to discretion for the public good, without the prescription of the law, and sometimes even against it."[33] Sovereign prerogative applies when an emergency threatens the "safety of the people, in a case where the uncertainty and variableness of human affairs could not bear a steady fixed route."[34] While Locke limits discretion to states of emergency, police use discretion daily, normalizing the state of exception and revealing the police as a sovereign power in constant states of exception. Rather than being a limited practice, sovereignty becomes routine through police. This is why police rarely face consequences for actions like shooting unarmed men. The entire liberal state is predicated on sovereign police power.

THE ETHICAL TASK

These issues suggest that efforts to reform police will not produce a better police force. To stop a sovereign power that manufactures order and secures the wealthy's property, operating in a state of exception requires more than police body cameras, teaching continuum of force and de-escalation, civilian oversight, hiring more people of color, and whitewashing the force's oppressive nature by relabeling their work as "community policing." Attempts to reform police without addressing police origins in governing class and race inequalities as sovereign powers—regardless of good intentions—will fail.[35] Technical reforms do not substantively address policing but make for a gentler war on the poor and oppressed.

The moral theologian's first task is to demythologize the police. Myths are deep stories that structure worldviews and give meaning to life's chaos. The myth of the thin blue line—that police are a "thin blue line" of order holding back total chaos and destruction to society—has caused policing to proliferate. We ask officers to police school problems, the mentally ill, the homeless, immigration, drugs, unemployed youth, sex workers, and

---

[32]Jeffrey Reiman, "Is Police Discretion Justified in a Free Society?," in *Handled with Discretion: Ethical Issues in Police Decision Making*, ed. John Kleinig (Lanham: Rowman & Littlefield, 1996), 74.

[33]Locke, *Two Treatises of Government*, 172.

[34]Ibid., 169.

[35]I have focused on the United States. For origins of police in Germany, France, and England, which comes to similar conclusions about police institutions as a tool for class oppression, see Neocleous, *Fabrication of Social Order*; Marc Raeff, *The Well-Ordered Police State: Social and Institutional Change through Law in the Germanies and Russia, 1600–1800* (New Haven: Yale University Press, 1983).

much more. African American communities have a long tradition of demythologizing police. W. E. B. Du Bois described police as historically being

> primarily designed to control slaves. ... For, as I have said, the police system of the South was originally designed to keep track of all Negroes, not simply of criminals; and when the Negroes were freed and the whole South was convinced of the impossibility of free Negro labor, the first and almost universal device was to use the courts as a means of re-enslaving the Blacks. It was not then a question of crime, but rather one of color, that settled a man's conviction on almost any charge. Thus, Negroes came to look upon courts as instruments of injustice and oppression, and upon those convicted in them as martyrs and victims.[36]

The tradition of demythologizing police arose from experiences of police oppression and brutality. The brutality and oppression began immediately as US police arose from slave patrols and labor management. James Cone has examined the "the obvious similarities between Jesus' death on a cross and the death of thousands of Black men and women strung up to die on a lamppost or tree."[37] White theologians were almost entirely silent about the lynchings just as they have been about the police shootings of Black men. One notable exception to this silence, however, is a 2014 statement signed by 456 American Catholic theologians calling for police reforms while at the same time noting the deeply rooted racism involved with American policing, and announcing support for the protests that had swelled at the time against police brutality often equated with the Black Lives Matter movement.[38] The experience of the oppressed, those gunned down by police, mirrors the execution of Jesus and is the first starting point for moral theology when thinking about police. Given the massive support for police among white Christians of every kind, it is reasonable for moral theologians, particularly white ones, to give far more attention to the experiences of the poor and of people of color at the hands of police and to give far more attention to the deeply intertwined problems of police as a tool for oppression in the past and present. Telling history rightly involves reason and paying attention to the experience of the oppressed, and not just a litany of deeds by the "great men." It is an ethical task. That is why tradition is one of the fonts of moral theology. We have to know what has been the case to see why something is the case presently. This chapter is a start in that direction.

SUGGESTED READINGS

Blackmon, Douglas. *Slavery by Another Name: The Re-Enslavement of Black People in America from the Civil War to World War II*. New York: Doubleday, 2008.

Neocleous, Mark. *The Fabrication of Social Order: A Critical Theory of Police Power*. London: Pluto, 2000.

Raeff, Marc. *The Well-Ordered Police State: Social and Institutional Change through Law in the Germanies and Russia, 1600–1800*. New Haven: Yale University Press, 1983.

Schlabach, Gerald, ed., *Just Policing, Not War*. Collegeville: Liturgical, 2007.

---

[36]W. E. B. Du Bois, *Souls of Black Folk* (New York: Penguin, 1989), 124, 125.

[37]James Cone, *The Cross and the Lynching Tree* (Maryknoll: Orbis, 2011), xiii.

[38]Lead author was Tobias Winright, with contributions by Alex Mikulich, Vincent Miller, Bryan N. Massingale, and M. Shawn Copeland. See David Cloutier, "Catholic Theologians for Police Reform and Racial Justice," December 8, 2014, http://catholicmoraltheology.com/statement-of-catholic-theologians-on-racial-justice/.

CHAPTER TWENTY-SEVEN

Capital Punishment

DAVID CLOUTIER

Near—or perhaps at—the center of Christianity is the call to put away vengeance. Vengeance is not the whole of sin, but it may be the primordial sin afflicting human community. If humanity's prideful pretensions to rule the universe as "gods" is the root of the fallen world (Gen. 3:5), vengeance is what happens when we view other humans as rivals to this pretentious rule. If the "original sin" involves our belief that God is a rival to us, the "original sin" of human communal life is a vengeance that sees a fellow human being as a rival, a competitor. If my life is to flourish, we think, something must be done to make my rival's life *not* flourish.

This rivalry is fundamentally contrary to belief in the unity of the human race, which is the foundation for Christian social action aimed at solidarity. It is no accident that the pope of solidarity, St. John Paul II, uses the story of the first murder as his set piece for explaining the Gospel's commitment to life.[1] In the story of Cain and Abel (Gen. 4:1-16), Cain's murder of his brother is not meaningless violence. He has a motive: he feels slighted because his brother's sacrifice is deemed better than his. The text says he "greatly resented this," and instead of heeding God's call to "do well" in the future, he instead lures his brother to the field and kills his rival.[2]

Jesus as the *divine* Son who reveals the face of God decisively reverses our view of God as a competitive rival, instead enacting a relationship with the Father of humble love and obedience. But Jesus's *humanity*, fully united with this divinity, reverses the competitive view of relationship among humans in both his words and deeds—chiefly and ultimately by utterly forswearing vengeance.

Why talk about vengeance in an essay about capital punishment? Because the question of rejecting vengeance—and the tricky relationship of vengeance to justice—is really the core issue in Christian discussion of the morality of capital punishment. First, I outline briefly how Christians have understood and argued over capital punishment, following this book's template of looking at scripture, tradition, experience, and reason. In considering "reason," I then return to the underlying question of vengeance, showing how the logic of the scriptural story is a rejection of human vengeance supremely in Jesus's crucifixion and resurrection.

[1]Pope John Paul II, *Evangelium Vitae* (Vatican City: Libreria Editrice Vaticana, 1995), § 7–9.

[2]All scripture quotations in this chapter are from the New American Bible, revised edition, © 2010, 1991, 1986, 1970 Confraternity of Christian Doctrine, Washington, DC. All rights reserved.

CAPITAL PUNISHMENT: SCRIPTURE AND TRADITION

Many Christian discussions of the death penalty begin with the obvious recognition that the Law of the Old Testament often prescribes it. Its prescriptions presume it as a matter of justice, following the *lex talionis* (an eye for an eye) principle found in many other law codes of other early civilizations. While God, in his mercy, seeks the conversion of the sinner, and not his death (Ezek. 33:11), the death penalty was not seen to contradict this. Jesus, though explicitly challenging the *lex talionis* in the Sermon on the Mount (Mt. 5:38-39), does not speak directly about the institution of capital punishment. Traditional readings of St. Paul's letters have understood his call for Christians to be obedient to lawful authorities, who have proper use of "the sword" (Rom. 13:4), as allowing for civil authorities' use of violence. It is worth noting that David Bentley Hart convincingly argues that the word translated "sword" here refers not to an executioner's sword, but to a small dagger carried by soldiers and other public officers.[3]

The history of the Christian tradition's approach to capital punishment has three phases.[4] The first phase, in the early church, saw some voices at least prudentially criticize the use of the death penalty. While the church fathers of this Patristic Period take for granted the authority of the state to execute, early writers also presume that Christians ought not to participate in such action. Athenagoras, in the second century, notes that Christians "contract guilt and pollution" simply from watching the spectacle of executions, and Tertullian goes further by forbidding participation in offices where one cannot avoid "taking part in sacrifices or capital punishments."[5] Especially before the adoption of Christianity by the emperor Constantine, Christians were most often the victims of capital punishment, not the executioners. While this position is softened slightly after Constantine, there is still significant reservation about the actual practice. The later church father St. Ambrose counsels a magistrate on the issue: "Authority ... has its rights, but compassion has its policy. You will be excused if you do it; but you will be admired if you refrain when you might have done it."[6]

A second phase, through the Middle Ages and early modern period, saw the church become more accepting of the use of violence, including execution, even (infamously) for enforcing religious doctrine. Certain notes of reserve remained—for example, it was ordinarily stipulated that such violence must be applied "not out of hatred, but judiciously," and the church could not, according to canon law, apply the violence itself.[7] St. Thomas Aquinas accepted the death penalty on grounds of justice and protection of the community,[8] but also cautioned that "in this life penalties should rather be remedial than retributive."[9] Indeed, Aquinas sternly suggested that even in the matter of lawful

---

[3]David Bentley Hart, "Further Reflections on Capital Punishment (and on Edward Feser)," *Church Life Journal*, December 19, 2017, http://churchlife.nd.edu/2017/12/19/further-reflections-on-capital-punishment-and-on-edward-feser/.

[4]For detailed historical information, see Donald Campion, SJ, Edward Dillon, James J. Megivern, and Robert L. Fastiggi, "Capital Punishment," *New Catholic Encyclopedia Supplement 2012–13: Ethics and Philosophy*, vol. 1 (2013): 202–8, and the definitive recent history, E. Christian Brugger, *Capital Punishment and Roman Catholic Moral Tradition*, 2nd ed. (Notre Dame: University of Notre Dame Press, 2014).

[5]As quoted in Brugger, *Capital Punishment*, 76–7.

[6]Ibid., 87.

[7]Campion et al., "Capital Punishment," 204.

[8]Thomas Aquinas, *Summa Theologiae*, trans. Fathers of the English Dominican Province (Westminster: Christian Classics, 1981), II–II, 64, 2.

[9]Ibid., II–II, 66, 6. Another translation of "remedial" is "medicinal." For more on this approach, see Peter Karl Koritansky, *Thomas Aquinas and the Philosophy of Punishment* (Washington, DC: Catholic University of America Press, 2012), 157–69.

punishment, "the mind of the avenger" must *not* be "directed chiefly to the evil of the person on whom he takes vengeance and rests there ... because to take pleasure in another's evil belongs to hatred, which is contrary to the charity whereby we are bound to love all men."[10]

Such cautions were not always observed. Moreover, magisterial voices of the Protestant Reformation fashioned a newly stark version of the teaching, skeptical of anything that might hint at Christian perfectionism. Luther famously defended the role of the hangman in doing God's work of keeping order in society, and even offers what one writer calls "a celebrity endorsement for the profession" in commending the role when one sees a need for such services.[11] Strongly differentiating the order of creation and order of redemption, Luther's doctrine of worldly vocation meant any legitimate worldly profession could be carried out by Christians. Calvin similarly assumed its legitimacy, arguing, for example, against Anabaptist claims that capital punishment cuts off the possibility of repentance by citing the thief on the cross with Christ (Lk. 23:42).[12] The communities of the radical reformation renounced the death penalty, as they renounced all other forms of violence, but this was an exceptional position.

However, a third phase, responding to modern Enlightenment visions of the dignity of the human person and the limited power of the state, increasingly restricted and sought to abolish capital punishment. Opponents in the mid-to-late eighteenth century, led by Cesare Beccaria, stressed not only pragmatic arguments that the death penalty did not deter crime and was intolerable if a person was later proven innocent but also the more principled argument that further violence by the state was not a correct response to violence. Over time, the arguments drove a steady reduction in the offenses subject to the penalty.[13]

Although many of these voices were not religious ones, both Catholic and Protestant authorities eventually began to speak against the death penalty. In the Catholic tradition, the decisive move was made by St. John Paul II, in the previously mentioned context of defending an overall "culture of life" against the "culture of death" promoted by abortion and euthanasia. In this context, the pope wrote that the death penalty "must be viewed in the context of a system of penal justice ever more in line with human dignity." Such punishment must primarily "redress the disorder caused by the offense," both in terms of ensuring "public order" and "offering an incentive and help" to the offender "to change his or her behavior and be rehabilitated." Thus, penal justice "ought not to go to the extreme of executing the offender except in cases of absolute necessity: in other words, when it would not be possible otherwise to defend society."[14] Thus, the pope brought this teaching in line with the overall teaching about "legitimate self-defense" in which the death of another is never intended, but only accepted as a side effect of legitimately protecting oneself or those in one's charge. The *Catechism of the Catholic Church* was accordingly revised in the wake of the encyclical, *removing* prior language indicating that certain crimes might be so grave as to "deserve" death as a response of justice. Put

---

[10]Aquinas, *Summa Theologiae*, II–II.108.1.

[11]Joel F. Harrington, *The Faithful Executioner: Life and Death, Honor and Shame in the Turbulent Sixteenth Century* (New York: Farrar Straus and Giroux, 2013), 33.

[12]John Calvin, *Harmony of the Gospels* (1555), commentary on Mt. 13:24-30, 36-43; http://www.ccel.org/ccel/calvin/calcom32.ii.xx.html.

[13]See J. Gordon Melton, "Introductory Essay: The Crusade against Capital Punishment," in *The Churches Speak on Capital Punishment*, ed. J. Gordon Melton (Detroit: Gale Research, 1989), xii–xxiv.

[14]John Paul II, *Evangelium Vitae*, § 56.

simply, no one ever "deserves" to die based on their crimes. In 2018, Pope Francis further stiffened the *Catechism*'s language, stating several factors that now made the death penalty "inadmissible" and committing the church to "its abolition worldwide."[15]

Many mainline Protestant churches also developed their teaching, and taught authoritatively against capital punishment. In the United States, among the earliest were statements by the Methodist (1956) and American Baptist (1958) churches.[16] Both statements assembled multiple reasons for their position, placing special emphasis on "the sacredness of life and the obligation to overcome evil with good" (American Baptist) and the "redemptive principle" of punishment (Methodist).[17] In a later statement, the Methodist church reiterates that it "cannot accept retribution or social vengeance as a reason for taking human life."[18]

Not all share the belief that the Christian tradition has properly developed in opposition to the death penalty. The development is resisted by many more conservative groups, not least because of a commitment to a narrowly literal reading of scriptural texts, especially the aforementioned Rom. 13:4 about "the sword." Beyond biblical references, the National Association of Evangelicals notes that "if no crime is serious enough to warrant capital punishment, then the gravity of the most atrocious crime is diminished accordingly."[19] Most interesting, in this regard, is a lengthy and careful statement by the Christian Reformed Church in North America, which justifies the death penalty by going beyond detailed biblical exegesis, explaining that appropriate punishment properly "symbolizes the offense" and "leads to social healing."[20] Further, a small number of Catholics have suggested that John Paul II's teaching can be understood in a way that is more in continuity with the tradition's previous support of the death penalty. Stephen A. Long claims that John Paul's "defense of society" can be interpreted more broadly than mere self-defense, but also as a "moral defense" of society that emphasizes Aquinas's traditional claim that punishment should "manifest a transcendent order of justice." Long writes that punishment of particularly heinous crimes "purifies society, lifts the social conscience higher," and "bathes the wound" inflicted on the social body by the criminal.[21] Long follows Aquinas's claim that, while punishment by civil authorities should have "more of a medicinal character" than retributive, part of this "medicine" involves removing scandal by marking particular crimes "which conduce to the grave undoing of others."[22]

---

[15]Congregation for the Doctrine of the Faith, *Letter to the Bishops Regarding the New Revision of Number 2267 of the Catechism of the Catholic Church on the Death Penalty* (Vatican City: Libreria Editrice Vaticana, 2018).

[16]Note that historic peace churches, like the Quakers, have always opposed capital punishment.

[17]See American Baptist Churches in the US "Resolution on Capital Punishment," in *The Churches Speak on Capital Punishment*, ed. J. Gordon Melton (Detroit: Gale Research, 1989), 53–4; and United Methodist Church, "Social Creed," in *The Churches Speak on Capital Punishment*, ed. J. Gordon Melton (Detroit: Gale Research, 1989), 135–6.

[18]United Methodist Church, "Statement on Capital Punishment (1980)," in *The Churches Speak on Capital Punishment*, ed. J. Gordon Melton (Detroit: Gale Research, 1989), 139.

[19]National Association of Evangelicals, "Statement on Capital Punishment (1972)," in *The Churches Speak on Capital Punishment*, ed. J. Gordon Melton (Detroit: Gale Research, 1989), 120.

[20]Christian Reformed Church in America, "Statement on Capital Punishment (1981)," in *The Churches Speak on Capital Punishment*, ed. J. Gordon Melton (Detroit: Gale Research, 1989), 89.

[21]Stephen A. Long, "*Evangelium Vitae*, St. Thomas Aquinas, and the Death Penalty," *The Thomist* 63, no. 4 (1999): 523, cited in Koritansky, *Thomas Aquinas*, 178–9.

[22]Aquinas, *Summa Theologiae*, II–II.108.3, ad 2. For more on Long and Aquinas, see Koritansky, *Thomas Aquinas*, 162–7, 177–82.

Yet even these voices often express caution in regards to the use of the death penalty. For example, the Reformed Church, while defending its existence, argues it should be "exercised only with utmost restraint" and urges its members "to renounce all motives of revenge."[23] And Long concludes that the context John Paul II stresses—a "culture of death"—makes the death penalty inadvisable: such a culture does not acknowledge the transcendent order the death penalty is supposed to manifest, and so (presumably) will pursue it out of baser motivations, ones that (as noted) Aquinas would have rejected.

CAPITAL PUNISHMENT: EXPERIENCE AND REASON

The role of experience in evaluating capital punishment is a challenging one. Perhaps the most well-known opponent of the death penalty in the United States, Sr. Helen Prejean, regularly speaks on the issue, and invariably appeals to the "flesh-and-blood" human beings whom she accompanies on death row. The film of her story, *Dead Man Walking* (1995), remains a powerful testimony to the genuine personhood and possibilities of even the worst criminal. In an impassioned response to John Paul II's *Evangelium Vitae*, Prejean notes that his unwillingness to go "all the way" on abolishing the death penalty may be because he "has never visited people on death row." She says that "his heart would dissolve in grief if he ever came anywhere near the real execution of human beings," noting his direct forgiveness of the man who tried to assassinate him.[24] Similarly powerful testimony is given by family members of murder victims who insist that the death penalty is no proper "compensation." Vicki Scheiber's daughter, Shannon, a graduate student who was serving as a volunteer teacher in a poor area of Philadelphia, was brutally raped and murdered. But, in grieving their loss, Scheiber and her husband found that "pursuing the death penalty would not be the way we would want to honor our daughter's life, nor would the decision have helped us deal with the painful remainders of her unfulfilled hopes and dream."[25]

Yet of course, many others feel differently. Polls still indicate a majority of Americans support the death penalty, although this has declined from historic highs in the 1990s back to a level of ambivalence last seen in the early 1970s.[26] Fred Romano's sister and her husband were killed in their home; he believes that the death of their killer is "justice" and not "revenge." His wife agrees: "Revenge would be going out and killing one of [the murderer's] family members."[27] Moreover, the Romanos note that they are not expecting some sort of "closure" from the death penalty; they simply believe that this is the just response to the multiple murders committed. This sentiment is not unusual. At the very least, consideration of diverse experiences should help us avoid broad and unjustified generalizations about people's feelings. Moreover, we ought to recognize that one's experience is always filtered and understood through some kind of interpretive lens, and it may be that different experiences are due to differences in the interpretive lens used.

---

[23] Christian Reformed Church, "Statement," 96.

[24] Helen Prejean, CSJ, "A Response to John Langan's Essay," in *Choosing Life: A Dialogue on Evangelium Vitae*, ed. Kevin Wildes, SJ, and Alan Mitchell (Washington, DC: Georgetown University Press, 1997), 231–5.

[25] Vicki Scheiber, "Conclusion," in *Where Justice and Mercy Meet*, ed. Trudy Conway, David McCarthy, and Vicki Scheiber (Collegeville: Liturgical, 2012), 224.

[26] See Mark Berman, "American Support for the Death Penalty Inches Up, Poll Finds," *Washington Post*, June 11, 2018.

[27] Gregory Kane, "To Murder Victims' Families, Executing Killers Is Justice," *Baltimore Sun*, February 5, 2003.

The varied testimonies about the experience of capital punishment, as well as the various positions taken on the issue in appealing to scripture and tradition, may leave a reader puzzled. It is at this point where one must turn to reason. "Reason" properly understood is not a separate "source" for Christian ethics. Rather than generating a distinct set of "data," "reason" names the systematic task of reflection called for in relation to the "data" from the other sources. For example, "reason" can name that *interpretive* logic used in reading scripture that recognizes statements in the Old Testament must be read in light of the revelation of Jesus Christ in the New. It can also name the practice of establishing a logical development of the tradition, as John Paul II did by *reframing* capital punishment in terms of the traditional understanding of legitimate self-defense, instead of in terms of a sense of just punishment. In general, the use of reason in Christian ethics—and by extension, in any ethics—involves clarifying interpretation of sacred texts, traditions, and experience by articulating a logic by which the issue at hand can be better understood. Also, importantly, reason in ethics connects particular issues to more and more *fundamental principles* in order that we may see what commitments are really at stake.

In the case of capital punishment, reason can distinguish three levels of argumentation. Too often, arguments about capital punishment deploy the different levels willy-nilly in making their case—and it is certainly a good use of clarifying reason to sort out and distinguish the different appeals. But it is also the case that the different levels—pragmatic, principled, and narrative—have different value. Scripture, as the "norming norm" for Christian ethics, employs the logic of narrative to convey God's will, and so I will argue that it is at this most *fundamental*, deepest level where the decisive understanding of the issue of capital punishment is achieved.

A first level of argument over capital punishment is *pragmatic*. Pragmatic arguments simply seek to use data, marshaling statistics and histories, to argue for the "effectiveness" (or lack thereof) of a particular action. They are the familiar currency of political argument in our society: such and such policy is the right thing to do, because the data show that it is effective. In any moral argument, one ought to ask first, "effective for what?" In the case of capital punishment, the primary argument centers on its effectiveness for public safety. The debate is about whether capital punishment is an effective deterrent to crime. Given the extremely complex causation involved in criminal behavior, it is unlikely that one could answer this question with any kind of conclusiveness.[28] But forms of pragmatic argument also buttress the case of death penalty *opponents* in a different form. Many argue that, in its current form, the death penalty is applied in a discriminatory way, and also leads to the execution of people who are later discovered to be innocent. The evidence for these claims is more straightforward, and seems more persuasive.[29]

Note that, for pragmatic arguments on either side of the issue, any moral principles involved in the state killing of criminals need not be in play. In theory, one could make a strong pragmatic argument against the death penalty in its current form based on its

---

[28]For references to many studies suggesting a deterrence effect, see David Mulhausen, "The Death Penalty Deters Crime and Saves Lives," *Heritage Foundation*, June 27, 2007, https://www.heritage.org/testimony/the-death-penalty-deters-crime-and-saves-lives; Robert Tanner, "Studies Say Death Penalty Deters Crime," *Washington Post*, June 11, 2007. Opponents cite the "natural experiment" going on in the United States, where non-death-penalty states have consistently lower murder rates: "Murder Rate of Death Penalty States Compared to Non-Death Penalty States," Death Penalty Information Center, https://deathpenaltyinfo.org/deterrence-states-without-death-penalty-have-had-consistently-lower-murder-rates.

[29]For example, see the history chronicled in Lincoln Kaplan, "Racial Discrimination and Capital Punishment," *New Yorker*, April 20, 2016.

unjust application, but then argue for reform in the system, so that it is applied equally to all. Conversely, one could accept that the death penalty may have a deterrent effect, and nevertheless maintain that it is wrong.

Thus, pragmatic arguments ultimately must defer to certain arguments about *principles*. To simplify, an argument from principle is a claim that a particular action is good or bad because it fulfills or violates some fundamental moral ideal that is of the essence of human goodness. Despite fears and rhetoric about moral "relativism," almost no one lives their lives apart from some such overall sense of claims about morality—even if there is serious disagreement about what they are, how they apply, and whether we actually follow our own principles in all our actions.

The core debate here is about human rights and human dignity. Does the state have a right, and perhaps even a responsibility, to execute certain criminals? Historically, the answer has been "yes." Ordinarily, such an argument begins by acknowledging two things nearly everyone agrees on: that the state is not justified in taking life *arbitrarily*, and that the state has a right and responsibility to *punish* those who violate the shared rules of the social order. Certain crimes are so heinous, such an affront to society, such a grave injustice, that the proper way to punish such crimes is by death—thus, such a decision is not a matter of *arbitrary* killing by the state.

Death penalty opponents may find this illogical: if killing is so wrong, how can more killing in response be right? But this objection neglects the second point above: the response of the state is different in kind from the action of the murderer, because of its special responsibility for protecting the common good. For example, if a person kidnaps someone and holds them against their will for a long time, the state is likely to respond with a prison sentence: that is, taking someone and holding them against their will for a long time! The state may be justified in taking certain actions that are not justifiable for individual citizens.

A more adequate response has to engage the question of the *source* of our rights and dignity. For some, the important claim is that the right to life is not granted by the state. The state can punish someone by curtailing *civil* rights—ones granted by the state—but there are limits on its ability to deprive a person of certain *human* rights. This is the argument used to reject the possibility of bodily torture, even in instances where it might seem pragmatically effective. But these rights claims seem to rest on a deeper account of human *dignity*, which features much more prominently in the Christian tradition. In *Evangelium Vitae*, John Paul II argues that human dignity is rooted in God, and therefore this dignity can never be entirely lost. The dignity is intrinsic; it does not come from our actions, we do not earn it, and therefore we cannot entirely lose it by our actions, either.[30] Thus, the space John Paul leaves for the death penalty is not about an "exceptional" case where a person really does lose all their dignity, but instead about cases where the intention for social self-defense makes capital punishment a regrettable (not deserved) outcome.

CAPITAL PUNISHMENT: JESUS, THE STATE, AND SALVATION FROM VENGEANCE

While this argument based on human dignity seems clear, it has been resisted—even by those who claim to share John Paul II's theologically based view of the intrinsic dignity of

[30]John Paul II, *Evangelium Vitae*, § 53.

all persons. Why? To resolve this requires moving to a third level of reason, "narrative" reason. This is the kind of logic we find in a story or a picture; not simply calculating or deductive, it involves a deeper sense of symbolic or imaginative logic. This is the level on which scripture ultimately operates, and it is here where we must find ultimate resolution on the issue.

As Paul Griffiths notes, capital punishment "produces many fewer corpses than does any other kind of state killing," such as war. Even estimating for executions in China, which refuses to report its use, the number is "unlikely to exceed three or four thousand for the year." And "in the U.S., the yearly mean number of judicial executions over the last few decades tracks closely with the yearly mean number of deaths by lightning strikes." Why, he asks, does this issue provoke such attention? It is because "judicial execution, unlike any other state action ... dramatizes, always with theatricality, the question of sovereignty."[31] The power of the action is much more than a matter of taking a single life. John Langan further describes what he calls the "symbolic" defense of capital punishment. In a highly saturated media environment, certain crimes receive "concentrated public attention" and "become crucial for working out the complex of emotional reactions and reasonable concerns that members of the ordinary public have about crime."[32] These typically involve victims or perpetrators who also have symbolic significance: the killing of a police officer, for instance, or the connection of the perpetrator to terrorist organizations. Or perhaps the crime suggests unexpected social chaos: compare our public attention to suburban school shootings as opposed to our sad neglect of daily murders of children in inner-city neighborhoods.

Langan's description here helps put Griffiths's point about sovereignty in perspective. The symbolic point of public execution in such cases is to engage in an act that curtails the possibility of social chaos suggested by the disturbing action by recourse to the superior power of state order. We know that the execution of, say, an individual terrorist guilty of an attack cannot have any "deterrent" effect on whether another terrorist incident occurs: those involved in such attacks are perfectly willing to give up their lives! The real work of keeping such incidents from happening again falls on things like heightened security measures, intelligence work, and addressing social conditions that generate terrorists.

The "safety from chaos" suggested by the execution is more like a sanitation exercise. It is telling that the ancient Roman writer Seneca relied on a medical analogy for such punishment as a kind of expelling of disease from the community.[33] Recall that Thomas Aquinas used a similar metaphor, comparing certain criminals to diseased limbs needing amputation to save the body.[34] Thus, we should understand the "work" done by such an execution as twofold in purpose. On the one hand, it serves to single out particularly gross and egregious evil for all to see. It sends the message to everyone else that *this* is a horrible, horrible thing. The "deterrence," one might say, is (in the case of terrorism) a vaccination against the presumed "moral disease" that somehow attracts individuals to certain doctrines of violence, such as radicalized forms of Islam. But even apart from

[31]Paul Griffiths, "Against Capital Punishment," *First Things* 278 (2017): 58.

[32]John Langan, "Situating the Teaching of John Paul II on Capital Punishment," in *Choosing Life: A Dialogue on Evangelium Vitae*, ed. Kevin Wildes, SJ, and Alan Mitchell (Washington, DC: Georgetown University Press, 1997), 214.

[33]Brugger, *Capital Punishment*, 74–5.

[34]Cf. fn. 7.

this inoculation, it gives assurance to the rest of the community that this really is just an exceptionally terrible act, far outside the norms of "decent" society.

On the other hand, capital punishment serves to vindicate public authority as the power equipped to secure the population against such incursions of evil. If this evil is a kind of disease, it is the state that plays the role of heroic doctor. When we say "justice has been served," what we really mean is that the evil has been expunged from our midst. The execution is a kind of social cleansing ritual—and importantly, the power conducting the ritual is the state. To the criminal, the state displays wrath, but perhaps even more importantly, the state stands in for the rest of the population as a noble savior and protector of society. The state, in a certain sense, saves us from sin, delivers us from evil.

It is at this deepest level where several arguments come together to suggest the fundamentally problematic character of capital punishment within the Christian worldview. First, even at a purely secular level, the imaginative, symbolic understanding of "state as savior" is (or should be) chastened in light of the emergence of the notion of liberal, constitutionally limited nation-states. Far from seeing the state as the embodiment of good, limited government is a matter of recognizing the fallibility of government; thus, a criminal justice system must protect the common good, but also make room for its own error and correction. The American constitutional restriction against "cruel and unusual punishments" is precisely such an idea of limiting government's reach, and it is likely to be the eventual secular justification for an end to the death penalty in the United States.

Second, from within the Christian perspective, the symbolic ritual of "purifying" the diseased state by dismissing a "scapegoat" has an unusual resonance. It is just such a ritual that God prescribes for the ancient Israelites in Leviticus (16:20-28): the community is commanded to pile its sins on an actual goat that is sent out into the wilderness. As I have written elsewhere, the philosopher René Girard has suggested that this scapegoating mechanism is the way all communities resolve conflicts. Members of a community, instead of facing up to real conflicts, find a third party (usually a despised person or group, not a goat!) and make them responsible for the problems in the community. This scapegoating then justifies collective violence against this person or group. For Girard, a convert to Catholicism, it is Christ's crucifixion that exposes this scapegoat mechanism for what it is. By making himself, the totally innocent one, the carrier of sin, Jesus institutes salvation from sin (at least in part) by exposing this mechanism as the wrong road to resolving social conflict.[35] The right road is, of course, Jesus's teachings about forgiveness, forbearance, inclusion, and humility. This understanding calls his followers to "take up [one's] cross and follow me" (Mt. 16:24)—sometimes becoming innocent scapegoats themselves, but at least rejecting the scapegoat mechanisms in our midst. And, as we have seen, the medical-like justifications for the penalty do in fact work this way: the execution itself does not somehow fix the underlying social conflict, but may even intensify it, by giving us a common enemy on which to focus. This approach, from a Christian perspective, is simply false.

Finally, even beyond Girard's interpretation of the crucifixion of Christ as an exposure of the futile scapegoating mechanism, we can return to the story of Cain and Abel. This is a story about fratricide, a crime always understood as among the most heinous. Even Cain, in his sense that he will be vulnerable once his crime is known, seems to acknowledge

[35]David Cloutier, "Jesus Christ and Sacrifice," in *Where Justice and Mercy Meet*, ed. Trudy Conway, David McCarthy, and Vicki Scheiber (Collegeville: Liturgical, 2012), 72–81.

this. And yet God spares his life, even over the "cries" of his dead brother's blood (Gen. 4:10). As John Paul II notes,

> God, who is always merciful even when he punishes, ... gave him a distinctive sign, not to condemn him to the hatred of others, but to protect and defend him from those wishing to kill him, *even out of a desire to avenge Abel's death*. Not even a murderer loses his personal dignity, and God himself pledges to guarantee this.[36]

Even at this earliest stage in the biblical story, the God of Israel shows restraint, a mercy relative to other commonplace practices of social violence surrounding Israel. While there is constant warning about God's wrath, there is also constant restraint and constant hope. The tension is dramatic: how will God resolve the relationship with the sinful world?

The Christian tradition identifies Jesus as the (penultimate) resolution, a resolution that is surely about as far from a wrathful wiping out of the people and the land as one can imagine. Instead, God appears without vengeance, urges his followers to the same mercy, and eventually sacrifices himself into the violence of virtually every social grouping, including abandonment and betrayal by his own followers. And his response? "Peace be with you," he says to the frightened disciples (Jn 20:19). Insofar as the apostle Paul allots "the sword" to civil authorities, in the same letter his headline message to the Christians at Rome is to "offer your bodies as a living sacrifice, holy and pleasing to God," and to "not conform yourself to this age but be transformed by the renewing of your mind, that you may discern what is the will of God, what is good and pleasing and perfect" (Rom. 12:1-2).

This turn to mercy is a hallmark of Pope Francis's papacy, and his strong rejection of the death penalty:

> No man, "not even a murderer, loses his personal dignity" (*Letter to the President of the International Commission against the Death Penalty*, 20 March 2015), because God is a Father who always awaits the return of his children who, knowing that they have made mistakes, ask for forgiveness and begin a new life. No one ought to be deprived not only of life, but also of the chance for a moral and existential redemption that in turn can benefit the community.[37]

This understanding that the repentance and redemption of the sinner—rather than his or her execution—is what purifies the community is striking. God heals the world by waiting with endurance. Society should be healed from its conflicts by following the same path of rectifying wrongs, patiently enduring and giving as much time as possible for conversion.

Of course, the backdrop for all of this argument, from the Christian tradition, is the resurrection and a final judgment in which all wrongs are addressed and redressed. The tricky relationship between vengeance and justice—which was referenced at the beginning of the chapter, and was prominent in the earlier story of the family of murder victims—is ultimately resolved for Christian theology eschatologically, in the conviction that final judgment is the backdrop for proper action. In Paul's letter to the Romans, soon after mentioning "the sword," he writes, "Beloved, do not look for revenge but leave room for the wrath; for it is written, 'Vengeance is mine, I will repay, says the Lord.' Rather, 'if your enemy is hungry, feed him; if he is thirsty, give him something to drink; for by so doing

[36]John Paul II, *Evangelium Vitae*, § 9, emphasis added.

[37]Pope Francis, "Address to Participants in the Meeting Promoted by the Pontifical Council for Promoting the New Evangelization" (Vatican City: Libreria Editrice Vaticana, 2017).

you will heap burning coals upon his head.' Do not be conquered by evil but conquer evil with good" (Rom. 12:19-21). This Pauline passage, uncomfortable as it may sound in part, nevertheless leaves no doubt that Christians are called to give up the attempt to conquer evil with violence. Instead, the weapons Christians are to use are the traditional "works of mercy," cited here by Paul, but also prominently featured in the Gospel of Matthew's depiction of the criteria for the final judgment of the nations (Mt. 25:31-46). To feed the hungry, visit the imprisoned, pray for those who persecute you—these are what God wants. These are the actions that *actually* save a diseased world from sin. Those who think otherwise will eventually reap what they sow.

SUGGESTED READINGS

Brugger, E. Christian. *Capital Punishment and the Roman Catholic Moral Tradition*, 2nd ed. Notre Dame: University of Notre Dame Press, 2014.

Conway, Trudy, David McCarthy, and Vicki Scheiber, eds. *Where Justice and Mercy Meet*. Collegeville: Liturgical, 2012.

Melton, J. Gordon, ed. *The Churches Speak on Capital Punishment*. Detroit: Gale Research, 1989.

Prejean, Helen. *Dead Man Walking: An Eyewitness Account of the Death Penalty in the United States*. New York: Vintage, 1993.

CHAPTER TWENTY-EIGHT

Deescalating the War on Drugs: A Christian Social Ethic for the Legalization of Marijuana in the United States

JERMAINE M. MCDONALD

In a 1971 presidential address, Richard Nixon vowed to "take every step necessary" to deal with the national emergency of drug abuse.[1] His stated intention was to attack the problem both from the supply side with increased enforcement efforts against "drug peddlers" as well as from the demand side with increased resources for rehabilitation. Yet, the Nixon administration retained the preliminary classification of marijuana as a Schedule I drug, defined as a drug with "no currently accepted medical use and a high potential for abuse." He made this decision against the advice of his own 1972 National Commission on Marihuana and Drug Abuse, chaired by Raymond P. Shafer, which found that marijuana was as safe as alcohol and recommended ending its prohibition and treating marijuana as a public health issue.[2] Nixon's motives for this classification were political, ideological, and racist. Making marijuana illegal and linking its use and abuse to anti-war "hippies" and Blacks would serve to publicly vilify outspoken anti-Nixon political constituencies and pave the way for federal authorities to more aggressively engage them, potentially curtailing their political influence.[3] In other words, Nixon sought to put his political opponents on the wrong side of the law. Thus, from day one,

[1]Richard Nixon, "Special Message to the Congress on Drug Abuse Prevention and Control," June 17, 1971, https://citybase-cms-prod.s3.amazonaws.com/e28b11927e8e48fe874a00ac3f9a978c.pdf.

[2]See "The Report of the National Commission on Marihuana and Drug Abuse: Marihuana—A Signal of Misunderstanding," commissioned by President Richard M. Nixon, March 1972, http://www.druglibrary.org/schaffer/Library/studies/nc/ncmenu.htm.

[3]In a 1994 interview with writer Dan Baum, John Ehrlichman, President Nixon's chief domestic policy advisor and convicted Watergate conspirator, confessed to "lying about the drugs" and intentionally linking marijuana and drug use to hippies and Blacks to disrupt the political impact of those communities. Dan Baum, "Legalize It

the "War on Drugs" had ulterior motives and implications beyond fighting the growing drug abuse problem.

A 2018 Pew Research Center survey found that 62 percent of people in the United States believe marijuana should be legalized, a 100-percent increase from 2000.[4] Despite this growing majority view, the federal government still considers marijuana a dangerous and illicit drug, refusing to change its designation of the drug from Schedule I (no accepted medical use), and has not relinquished the idea of a federal crackdown in states that have legalized the drug.[5] Nevertheless, the laws regulating the use of marijuana vary from state to state. As of August 2019, thirty-three states and the District of Columbia have approved marijuana for medicinal purposes.[6] Of those, eleven have fully legalized marijuana, while another sixteen have only decriminalized the recreational use of marijuana. The distinction between legalization and decriminalization is subtle but important. In decriminalization states, possession of small amounts of marijuana remains illegal, but jail time and a criminal record have been eliminated as possible penalties. Additionally, the sale and distribution of marijuana remains illegal. Thus, decriminalization-only states cannot set up a legalized market for the production and distribution of marijuana and cannabis goods, missing out on potentially millions of dollars in tax revenue, as well as the ability to provide appropriate oversight of the marijuana market. Further, citizens are still subject to marijuana-related stops by police officers. These encounters with police officers for low-level possession offenses happen disproportionately in poor, Black and Brown communities.

There are (at least) five aspects of the US ambiguity on the legality of marijuana that ought to be of concern for Christian-based social ethics. First is whether the personal use or possession of marijuana, a substance that more than likely has the same social effect as alcohol and tobacco, should be an incarceration-worthy offense. The impetus behind *decriminalization* is that possessing small amounts of marijuana should not result in one's incarceration or extended engagement with the criminal justice system. Additionally, the social and financial cost of criminalization to US society is exorbitant. Those who argue for maintaining prohibition worry about the risk of increased usage, the impact of marijuana addiction, and the potential of marijuana use to lead to abuse of other, more dangerous drugs. While these concerns ought to be taken seriously, four decades of marijuana criminalization featuring penalties such as heavy fines, incarceration, and property seizure have failed to achieve the goals of prohibitionists and have imposed significant costs on those arrested, their families and communities, the criminal justice system, and society at large.

The second aspect of the marijuana issue that ought to be of concern for Christian-based social ethics is the systemic racism that undergirds the enforcement of marijuana laws.

All: How to Win the War on Drugs," *Harper's Magazine* (2016): 22–32. See also Radley Balko, *Rise of the Warrior Cop: The Militarization of America's Police Forces* (New York: PublicAffairs, 2013), 87.

[4]Hannah Hartig and Abigail Geiger, "About Six-in-Ten Americans Support Marijuana Legalization," Pew Research Center, October 8, 2018, http://www.pewresearch.org/fact-tank/2018/10/08/americans-support-marijuana-legalization/. The analysis is based on telephone interviews of 1,754 adults living in all 50 states and DC.

[5]See Matt Zapaotsky et al., "Use of Legalized Marijuana Threatened as Sessions Rescinds Obama-Era Directive That Ceased Federal Enforcement," *Washington Post*, January 4, 2018.

[6]See "Map of Marijuana Legality by State," DISA, August 2019, https://disa.com/map-of-marijuana-legality-by-state. Even this aspect of marijuana legalization differs as some states put regulations on the types of illnesses and ailments eligible for marijuana treatment, while others allow for home cultivation or medical marijuana dispensaries. See also "31 Legal Medical Marijuana States and DC: Laws, Fees, and Possession Limits," *ProCon.org*, September 25, 2018, https://medicalmarijuana.procon.org/view.resource.php?resourceID=000881.

According to a 2016 national survey on drug use, whites, Blacks, and Hispanics use illicit drugs at comparable rates.[7] Yet, the marijuana arrest rate for Blacks is 3.72 times more than for whites.[8] Such a significant discrepancy cannot solely be attributed to the individual biases of police officers. Black and Latino neighborhoods, often disproportionately poor with higher rates of crime, are subject to increased policing due to "broken windows" policies. These policies concentrate on low-level, quality-of-life offenses under the theory that cracking down on minor offenses and indicators of neighborhood decay will increase public safety and reduce serious crime attracted to such visual cues of social disorder.[9] "Broken windows" policing morphed into an "arrest-first" approach to low-level crimes, drastically increasing the number of stops, frisks, searches, and other adversarial encounters between police and individuals in these poorer, minority communities. In New York City alone, marijuana arrests went from almost 800 in 1991 to over 59,000 in 2010. The marijuana arrest rate of whites in Brooklyn was 161 arrests per 100,000 people while the arrest rate of Blacks was 1,554 arrests per 100,000 people. Similar discrepancies existed for Manhattan and the Bronx.[10] There is a long-standing tradition within historically Black churches (I am an ordained Black Baptist minister) to resist and oppose institutional and systemic racism. The first Black churches and denominations were formed by Black clergy seeking to worship free from racism. Richard Allen and Absalom Jones cofounded the Free African Society in 1787 to provide aid to Blacks transitioning from slavery to freedom. Both men would become disillusioned with the racist policies of their congregation, which would allow Black parishioners to sit only in the balcony during worship service and would permit Allen and Jones to preach only to all-Black audiences. The two men would individually become pillars of social and religious life in Philadelphia, leading their own churches and participating in organizations and movements dedicated to assisting freed Blacks. Richard Allen would later organize the African Methodist Episcopal Church in 1816. Thus, advocating for the decriminalization or legalization of marijuana because of the way marijuana prohibition disenfranchises and oppresses Blacks fits within the Black church tradition of resisting systemic racism.

The third aspect of the marijuana issue that ought to be of concern to Christian-based social ethics is the question of whether marijuana might have positive medicinal benefits, as well as the lack of robust scientific studies to prove or refute such claims. In Genesis, God explains to the first humans that they have been given "every plant yielding seed that is upon the face of the earth" and that everything God has made is very good.[11] The

[7]See Tables 1.29B and 1.30B in "Results from the 2016 National Survey on Drug Use and Health: Detailed Tables," Substance Abuse and Mental Health Services Administration, Center for Behavioral Health Statistics and Quality, September 7, 2017, https://www.samhsa.gov/data/sites/default/files/NSDUH-DetTabs-2016/NSDUH-DetTabs-2016.pdf. In 2016, 18.7 percent of adult whites had used illicit drugs within the past year, compared to 20.4 percent of adult Blacks and 16.1 percent of adult Hispanics.

[8]American Civil Liberties Union, *The War on Marijuana in Black and White: Billions of Dollars Wasted on Racially Biased Arrests* (New York: ACLU Foundation, 2013), 4, https://www.aclu.org/sites/default/files/field_document/1114413-mj-report-rfs-rel1.pdf. This study tracked arrest data from 2001 to 2010. The data for Hispanics is inconclusive because many jurisdictions did not categorize Hispanic arrests in this time period. For more information on this, see the chapter on "The Latino Data Problem" in the same report.

[9]Ibid., 91.

[10]Ibid., 94.

[11]Gen. 1:29-30. This does not remove our social obligation to investigate the potential good of plants and restrict the use and access of those that can be abused and lead to death. By this standard, if there were ever a legitimate use of a dangerous, highly addictive, potentially fatal drug that also grows from the ground, such as heroin, it too should be reclassified on the drug Schedule.

premise behind medical marijuana is that it has value as a treatment for certain conditions (such as chronic pain or an appetite inducer for patients on chemotherapy), making it a green plant that has the potential for good use. Yet, the US federal government continues to classify marijuana as a Schedule I drug: one with "no currently accepted medical use and a high potential for abuse,"[12] despite these well-known physician-approved uses. Examples of other Schedule I drugs include heroin, ecstasy, and peyote. In comparison, drugs such as oxycodone, fentanyl, cocaine, and methamphetamine are classified as Schedule II: "drugs with a high potential for abuse, with use potentially leading to severe psychological or physical dependence."[13] Drug scheduling is not a function of a drug's inherent danger (almost no one believes marijuana is as dangerous as heroin); it is a consideration of two factors: whether the drug can be abused and the medicinal value of the drug. Thus, criminal laws treat individual drugs differently, regardless of the drug's Schedule classification. For example, marijuana possession is not punished at the same levels as heroin possession. The main difference between Schedule I and II drugs is that the latter are considered to have some medicinal value (backed by scientific data and large-scale clinical studies) and can be obtained with a physician's prescription. In 2017, the National Academies of Science, Engineering, and Medicine, after reviewing over ten thousand studies on the potential benefits and harms of marijuana, concluded that marijuana is a viable treatment for chronic pain, multiple sclerosis-related muscle spasms, and chemotherapy-induced nausea and vomiting.[14] Unfortunately, none of these studies meet the large-scale, controlled clinical trial threshold required by the federal government to demonstrate medicinal value. In a bit of a "Catch-22," the reason such a study does not exist is because the federal government heavily restricts the amount of marijuana available for medical research because of marijuana's Schedule I drug classification.[15] A temporary ease of these restrictions for the purposes of accurately determining the medicinal value of marijuana would be advantageous for US society. It could provide conclusive evidence that marijuana may be the balm in Gilead that addresses the opioid epidemic. If marijuana is an effective painkiller for acute and chronic pain, it can be used as a substitute for opioids that are highly addictive and potentially deadly if abused. In 2016, over forty-two thousand people died from an opioid overdose, seventeen thousand of which can be attributed to opioid prescriptions.[16] If large-scale clinical trials prove conclusive that marijuana is a good, effective drug for managing chronic pain, then this issue alone justifies marijuana being, at the very least, reclassified as a Schedule II drug, available legally for medicinal purposes by the federal government, via prescription.

The fourth aspect of the marijuana issue that ought to be of concern to Christian-based social ethics is the extensive financial resources used to enforce marijuana prohibition, fitting it within the larger need to end the failed US "War on Drugs." Since President

---

[12]"Drug Scheduling," United States Drug Enforcement Agency, 2019, https://www.dea.gov/drug-scheduling.

[13]Ibid.

[14]"Nearly 100 Conclusions on the Health Effects of Marijuana and Cannabis-Derived Products Presented in New Report; One of the Most Comprehensive Studies of Recent Research on Health Effects of Recreational and Therapeutic Use of Cannabis and Cannabis-Derived Products," National Academies of Sciences, Engineering, and Medicine, January 12, 2017, http://www8.nationalacademies.org/onpinews/newsitem.aspx?RecordID=24625.

[15]German Lopez, "The Federal Drug Scheduling System, Explained," *Vox*, August 2016, https://www.vox.com/2014/9/25/6842187/drug-schedule-list-marijuana. Only the University of Mississippi is legally permitted by the federal government to grow marijuana (and only for research purposes), though there are plans to increase the amount available for research.

[16]"What Is the U.S. Opioid Epidemic?," US Department of Health and Human Services, https://www.hhs.gov/opioids/about-the-epidemic/index.html.

Nixon declared it in 1971, the "War on Drugs" has cost the United States an estimated $1 trillion.[17] That money has helped create a system that punishes Black and Brown offenders more often and more harshly than white ones, contributes to a mass incarceration problem in which over two million people in the United States are incarcerated (450,000 for drug offenses), and has barely made a dent in our drug abuse problem as the United States has the highest rate of illegal drug use of any nation in the world.[18] A 2010 report estimated that marijuana legalization would save nearly $14 billion per year in government expenditures on the enforcement of marijuana prohibition and generate as much as $6.4 billion in tax revenue if marijuana was taxed comparably to alcohol and tobacco.[19] The expenditures eliminated by legalization include those related to arrests, prosecutions, judicial hearings, and incarceration of marijuana offenses.[20] Not only must the overall cost of prohibition enforcement to the state be a consideration, but the costs to recreational users who are otherwise functioning, law-abiding citizens also must be factored in. The state of Alabama has some of the harshest marijuana criminalization laws and outcomes in the United States. Someone caught with only a few grams of marijuana could face incarceration, thousands of dollars in fines and court costs, and potentially lose their driver's license and financial aid for college.[21] The experience of Nick Gibson should give anyone pause about marijuana criminalization. In 2013, police conducted a drug raid at the University of Alabama, arresting Gibson and sixty other students for marijuana possession. The officers used Alabama's civil asset forfeiture rule to seize $1,250 from Gibson and charged him with felony first-degree possession of marijuana at the discretion of the prosecutor. Gibson entered a diversionary program, but after he was caught with marijuana again later in the same year, he earned a felony conviction. Gibson never graduated college and the ordeal cost his family $40,000 in fees and court costs.[22] The punishment for marijuana use and possession should not rob someone of their future well-being.

Finally, the fifth aspect for which Christian-based social ethics should be concerned is the potential social impact of marijuana legalization, both for harm and for good. It is not inconsistent to hold the positions that marijuana possession should be legal and that people should abstain from using it recreationally or, at the very least, from using it to the point of dependency. In this view, marijuana should be treated in the same manner as alcohol and tobacco. Just as with alcohol, society must consider the social risks of consumption, particularly the potential costs of addiction treatment, enforcement of Driving While Impaired offenses, the effects of secondhand smoke and other negative health outcomes, and the like. Some experts estimate that binge marijuana users account for 80 percent of consumption.[23] The relatively cheap cost of marijuana (it is less expensive

---

[17]Betsy Pearl, "Ending the War on Drugs: By the Numbers," Center for American Progress, June 27, 2018, https://www.americanprogress.org/issues/criminal-justice/reports/2018/06/27/452819/ending-war-drugs-numbers/.

[18]Glen Olives Thompson, "Slowly Learning the Hard Way: U.S. America's War on Drugs and Implications for Mexico," *Norteamérica* 9, no. 2 (2014): 65.

[19]Jeffrey A. Miron, "The Budgetary Implications of Drug Prohibition," *Criminal Justice Policy Foundation*, February 2010, 1, http://citeseerx.ist.psu.edu/viewdoc/download?doi=10.1.1.481.6226&rep=rep1&type=pdf.

[20]Ibid., 6. Miron's estimates do not factor in potential changes in prevention, education, or treatment expenses, but presumably state-subsidized expenses would decline as courts would no longer be in position to refer people to treatment programs for possession offenses.

[21]Cierra Brinson and Russell Estes, "Alabama's War on Marijuana," Southern Poverty Law Center, October 2018, https://www.splcenter.org/20181018/alabamas-war-marijuana.

[22]Ibid.

[23]Reihan Salam, "Is It Too Late to Stop the Rise of Marijuana, Inc.?" *The Atlantic*, April 19, 2018, https://www.theatlantic.com/politics/archive/2018/04/legal-marijuana-gardner/558416/.

than beer) suggests that if marijuana were legalized, more people would use it as a form of self-medication or escape. The marijuana-based industry that arises out of legalization would most likely try to cater to and increase the number of these kinds of users, many of them from poor or vulnerable communities. This is a legitimate concern that must be taken seriously. It should (but often does not) go without saying that marijuana addiction "exists, is important, and causes harm."[24] Scripture teaches us that our bodies are temples of the Holy Spirit and that we should glorify God in our bodies.[25] Developing a marijuana dependency absent a legitimate medical need is certainly contrary to treating our bodies as such. Therefore, Christians must demand that marijuana legalization come with a plan and resources to effectively address addiction, regulate the market in a way that protects consumers and the public at large, and transparently articulate the harms, benefits, and effects of marijuana usage.

A Christian ethical reflection on the marijuana issue through the prism of scripture, reason, tradition, and experience leads me to endorse the full legalization of marijuana, with a strong state regulation of the marijuana market. The details of marijuana legalization and the regulation of the nascent marijuana market should be a matter of public debate, fused with medical and scientific insight in the form of robust, large-scale clinical studies and sociological analysis of the impact of marijuana use and criminalization in US society. As with alcohol and tobacco, its regulation will most likely differ across state lines.[26] At minimum, the federal government should loosen its Schedule I restrictions of marijuana enough to scientifically determine the viability of marijuana as a medicine for chronic pain, nausea, and so on. This could be as simple as working with states that have already legalized marijuana to cultivate suitable marijuana strands and guidelines for scientific research. Given the tide of public opinion, adding marijuana to the alcohol and tobacco exclusions in the Controlled Substances Act may be the only viable way to get state laws and federal laws in sync. Given the effect of marijuana use on the body and the potential for abuse and addiction, legalization should not occur haphazardly. Churches would do well to discourage the recreational use and abuse of marijuana, encourage societal investment in addiction treatment, and support the sick and infirm in their midst who rely on marijuana to manage their chronic pain or persevere through another round of chemotherapy.

In the end, the Gospel, as understood by Black liberation theology and rooted in the tradition of historically Black churches, issues a clarion call to resist the very systemic, institutional sins produced by the criminalization of marijuana. Jesus declared, after his experience of temptation in the wilderness, "The Spirit of the Lord is upon me, because he has anointed me to bring good news to the poor. He has sent me to proclaim release to the captives and recovery of sight to the blind, to let the oppressed go free, to proclaim the year of the Lord's favor" (Lk. 4:18-19). Marijuana criminalization, in practice, works to create the very social conditions Jesus stands against. Marijuana could be effective for medicinal purposes ("recovery of sight to the blind"), should not be used as a basis to over-police poor, minority communities ("let the oppressed go free"), and is not

---

[24]Alan J. Budney et al., "Marijuana Dependence and Its Treatment," *Addiction Science & Clinical Practice* 4, no. 1 (2007): 4–16.

[25]1 Cor. 6:19-20.

[26]I am assuming that marijuana should be treated similarly to alcohol and tobacco. The federal government establishes some parameters such as an age limit, but the states regulate the market as they see fit. For example, some states prohibit the sale of alcohol on Sundays, others treat the sale of hard liquor differently than wine and beer.

dangerous enough for simple possession to be penalized by incarceration and/or felony convictions ("release to the captives"). The good news of marijuana legalization would be that US society would no longer waste its time, treasure, and talent treating this plant and the people who possess it, particularly those from poor and minority communities, as the scourge of the earth.

SUGGESTED READINGS

Alexander, Michelle. *The New Jim Crow: Mass Incarceration the Age of Colorblindness*. New York: New Press, 2010.

Balko, Radley. *Rise of the Warrior Cop: The Militarization of America's Police Forces*. New York: PublicAffairs, 2013.

Provine, Doris Marie. *Unequal under Law: Race in the War on Drugs*. Chicago: University of Chicago Press, 2007.

Issues, Applications, and Twenty-First-Century Agenda for Christian Ethics

Section D: Medicine and Health Care

CHAPTER TWENTY-NINE

Medicine, Bioethics, and Health Care

CONOR M. KELLY

Although the connections are not always obvious today, Christian ethics has had a profound impact on medicine, bioethics, and health care as a result of two historical realities. First, the earliest Christians identified care for the human well-being of their neighbor as a direct outgrowth of their faith. Consequently, the practice of medicine and the provision of health care touched on the Christian community's understanding of its ethical obligations, allowing the four sources of Christian ethics—most especially scripture and tradition—to influence the development of both medicine and health care over the years. Second, the modern discipline of bioethics began with the work of Christian ethicists, who brought the four sources of Christian ethics—in this case, especially experience and reason—to this burgeoning field, creating a lasting legacy in bioethics as well. By attending to these historical realities, one can appreciate the ways in which scripture, tradition, experience, and reason have all helped to form the practices and practitioners of medicine, bioethics, and health care, and one can therefore identify the most helpful ways in which Christian ethics can contribute to the work of each of these spheres today. In pursuit of these goals, this chapter unfolds in three parts: the first discusses the impact of scripture and tradition on the practice of medicine and the delivery of health care; the second outlines the influence of experience and reason in the field of bioethics; and the third offers a vision for a distinctively Christian approach to medicine, bioethics, and health care that builds on the historical interactions between the four sources of Christian ethics in connections with each of these three spheres.

Before delving into the particular details of these histories, though, a brief note of terminological clarification is in order. Obviously, medicine, bioethics, and health care are all interrelated, but they are nonetheless distinct. Medicine can be defined narrowly as the practice of medicine, that is, the discipline taught in medical schools that traces its roots to Hippocrates and focuses on the improvement of health through a scientific process of diagnosis and treatment. Bioethics, meanwhile, is the practical field dedicated to adjudicating right and wrong in the realms of medicine, health care, and medical research. Health care, finally, refers to the constellation of professionals and approaches that interact in the promotion of a human person's holistic well-being. Health care calls attention to the multifaceted nature of human health and highlights the way in which healing care is delivered through a system and not just via the personal interactions of individual agents. By preserving the distinctions between all three of these interrelated domains, the influence of Christian ethics on all of them is easier to see and to analyze, because the four sources do not necessarily connect to each one in the same way. With these differences in mind, it is possible to turn to the first part of this chapter, which examines the impact of Christian ethics on medicine and health care.

THE PRACTICE OF MEDICINE AND THE DELIVERY OF HEALTH CARE: THE IMPACT OF SCRIPTURE AND TRADITION

In a certain sense, Christianity has a natural affinity with medicine and health care. Scripture attests that Jesus was sought out by his contemporaries as a healer (Mt. 4:23-25; Mk 1:32-34; Lk. 6:17-19; Jn 4:46-54), and his disciples clearly joined in his healing mission (Mt. 10:8; Acts 3:1-10, 5:12-16). The early church was shaped by this history, although there was hardly an expectation that all Christians could heal miraculously in the same way that the disciples did. Instead, Christians embraced the traditional (and eventually scriptural) accounts of Jesus's healing ministry as a summons to care for the health and well-being of their neighbor in a manner that witnessed to the love and compassion of God. In the immediate context of the Greco-Roman world, this meant that Christians identified the practice of medicine—such as it was—as an opportunity for living out their faith, although this congruity required a serious process of theological negotiation as Christians sought to define the proper place of physical healing in relation to their tradition's prioritization of spiritual goods.[1]

In essence, Christianity's early attentiveness to medicine reflected two theological commitments. First, Christians' willingness to care for the bodily well-being of others can be seen as an extension of their belief in the resurrection, since the hope for a corporeal, and not merely spiritual, afterlife elevates the significance of embodiment as a central aspect of the human person. In scriptural terms, this appreciation of embodiment can be seen in St. Paul's reminder to the Corinthians "that your bodies are temples of the Holy Spirit, who is in you, whom you have received from God ... Therefore, honor God with your bodies" (1 Cor. 6:19-20[2]). Through faith in the resurrection and confidence in the sanctifying work of the Spirit, Christians came to acknowledge a concern for physical well-being as an essential extension of their spiritual beliefs. As a result, Christianity's distinct view of the body's purpose in life and ultimate destiny after death justified a respect for and attentiveness to the human person's bodily needs, from food and water to medical care.[3]

Second, the Christian sympathy for medical care also derived from the scriptural understanding of a God who is love (1 Jn 4:8). In the early Christian interpretation, this claim obligated not merely a theoretical assent to the concept that God is love but also a practical effort to imitate the divine nature in this life by loving others. As the author of 1 John explained, affirming the belief that God is love yields the necessary conclusion that every Christian "also ought to love one another" (1 Jn 4:11). The sociologist and religion scholar Rodney Stark notes that this was a revolutionary idea in the pagan world of the early church, and it led Christians to act on behalf of their neighbors in surprising ways,

[1]Gary B. Ferngren, *Medicine and Health Care in Early Christianity* (Baltimore: Johns Hopkins University Press, 2009), 13, 25–41.

[2]Scripture quotation taken from New International Version, NIV, Copyright © 2011 Biblica, Inc.

[3]Daniel J. Harrington and James F. Keenan, *Jesus and Virtue Ethics: Building Bridges between New Testament Studies and Moral Theology* (Lanham: Rowman & Littlefield, 2002), 136–7.

perhaps the most significant of which was a willingness to provide care to the sick and dying when no one else would.[4] Together with the Christian belief in the resurrection, this theological conviction about the nature of God prompted the earliest Christians to see the provision of medical care as a moral obligation. In terms of the four sources of Christian ethics, this theological background means that medicine entered into the realm of Christian ethics initially through the lens of scripture. This was not, however, the only source affecting the Christian understanding of medicine.

By casting medical care as a moral obligation and placing medicine within the realm of Christian ethics, early Christian communities not only sought to fulfill a scriptural summons but also developed a new set of practices that in turn became solidified as part of the tradition. This tradition then informed subsequent interpretations of a Christian's ethical responsibilities to care for the sick and dying, and this in turn allowed a second source in Christian ethics to shape the evolution of medicine. At the level of tradition, the most important contribution of Christian ethics was the expansion of medicine toward health care, which occurred in two interconnected ways.

First, the scriptural framing of medical care as an outgrowth of both faith in the resurrection and the command to "love one another" (Jn 13:34) oriented the practice of medicine toward more holistic ends. Yes, Christians could care for the bodily well-being of the sick because their scriptural attestation to the resurrection led them to believe that the body had an innate connection with the soul, but as the tradition developed, they also began to see that this anthropological link ought to move in both directions. In other words, Christianity's care for the body was an extension of a more fundamental concern for the soul. As the late fourth-century bishop Augustine of Hippo explained, "all things are to be loved for God's sake, and other people are capable of enjoying God together with us," which meant that care for others was motivated by a desire to see them achieve their ultimate end in God.[5] Later in the Christian tradition, Thomas Aquinas would make a similar point, insisting that Christians ought to love their neighbor's spiritual welfare ahead of their own bodily well-being and ahead of the neighbor's bodily well-being.[6] In the tradition of Christian practice, then, medical care could not be divorced from a larger vision for the nature and purpose of a human life, so Christianity came to recast medicine as one part of a larger project. Not coincidentally, this is precisely what the concept of health care does as well by expanding the sphere of care for the sick to include more than just the practice of medicine.

Second, beyond the introduction of a holistic vision, Christian ethics also facilitated a shift toward health care by creating a structural context for the practice of medicine. Since Christians believed that they had an obligation to care for all of their neighbors, and not just their fellow coreligionists, Christians relied on a formalized process for the provision of charity and care for the sick that "created 'a miniature welfare state in an empire which for the most part lacked social services.'"[7] The formalization first began with a local church structure that included deacons, whose chief ministry was to use the pooled resources of the community for the care of the poor. The result was "an organization, unique in the classical world, that effectively and systematically cared for its sick."[8]

[4]Rodney Stark, "Epidemics, Networks, and the Rise of Christianity," *Semeia* 56 (1991): 166–70.

[5]Augustine, *Teaching Christianity*, trans. Edmund Hill, ed. John E. Rotelle (Hyde Park: New City, 1996), I.xxviii.28.

[6]Thomas Aquinas, *Summa Theologiae*, trans. Fathers of the English Dominican Province (New York: Benziger Brothers, 1947), II–II.26.5, c, ad 1, ad 3.

[7]Stark, "Epidemics," 167, quoting Paul Johnson, *A History of Christianity* (New York: Atheneum, 1976), 75.

[8]Ferngren, *Medicine and Health Care*, 114.

This traditional practice quickly reshaped medicine itself, for deacons sometimes used these resources to create dedicated spaces for the care of the sick.[9] Once Christianity gained the support of the Roman Empire in the fourth century, these dedicated spaces took on a more public role as hospitals, providing medical care for the general population in what would today be called an inpatient setting.

Although the earliest hospitals were limited in the care they could provide—most focused exclusively on easing suffering at the end of life rather than curing diseases—these permanent institutions spread throughout the empire and transformed the notion of how medicine should be practiced.[10] Specifically, this systematization of health care laid the groundwork for the professionalization of medicine and the eventual development of the modern hospital as a locus of medical knowledge and medical care.[11] It is this history that has continued to lead Christian communities to sponsor and sustain hospitals to this day, often providing the only means of access to health care for the poor and marginalized in a given area. The contemporary understanding of Western medicine therefore owes its existence to the early Christian tradition of caring for the sick, meaning that Christian ethics has shaped medicine through both scripture and tradition.

CHRISTIAN BIOETHICS: THE ROLE OF EXPERIENCE AND REASON

Given the ways scripture and tradition have shaped medicine and health care, it is not surprising that Christian ethics has also had a profound impact on bioethics. After all, specific bioethical questions take on varying degrees of significance depending on how one defines the nature and purpose of health and medicine. Since Christian ethics has informed this larger teleological question, it has an implicit effect on all bioethical issues. At the same time, Christian ethics has also had an explicit influence on the field of bioethics because a number of Christian ethicists played a formative role in the birth of the discipline in the United States.

Scholars frequently point to the 1974 creation of the National Commission for the Protection of Human Subjects of Biomedical and Behavioral Research as the origin of modern bioethics.[12] Theologians from a variety of religious perspectives, but especially Christianity, served on this commission and shaped its conclusions, including those contained in the 1979 *Belmont Report*, which set the trajectory for biomedical ethics in the Western world.[13] Although the National Commission presented its vision for bioethics in intentionally secular terms, the resources of Christian ethics had a profound impact on the group's deliberations. Specifically, the two sources of experience and reason, which are

---

[9]Gary B. Ferngren and Ekaterina N. Lomperis, *Essential Readings in Medicine and Religion* (Baltimore: Johns Hopkins University Press, 2017), 117–18.

[10]Ferngren, *Medicine and Health Care*, 124, 128–30. See also Andrew T. Crislip, *From Monastery to Hospital: Christian Monasticism and the Transformation of Health Care in Late Antiquity* (Ann Arbor: University of Michigan Press, 2005), 103–20, 138–42.

[11]For a thorough history of these developments, see Geunter B. Risse, *Mending Bodies, Saving Souls: A History of Hospitals* (New York: Oxford University Press, 1999).

[12]See, for instance, Albert R. Jonsen, *The Birth of Bioethics* (Oxford: Oxford University Press, 1998), 99–106, cf. 3; David J. Rothman, *Strangers at the Bedside: A History of How Law and Bioethics Transformed Medical Decision Making* (New York: Aldine de Gruyter, 2003), 188–9.

[13]Robert Baker, *Before Bioethics: A History of American Medical Ethics from the Colonial Period to the Bioethics Revolution* (Oxford: Oxford University Press, 2013), 287.

more amenable to non-Christian interlocutors, allowed Christian theologians contributing to *The Belmont Report* to present a theologically informed yet pluralistically accessible defense of the ethical obligation to protect the human subjects of medical research and procedures, based on common experiences shared by medical professionals and an appeal to the inherent reasonableness of this position as a corrective to contemporaneous ethical crises.[14] The result was a set of principles promoting respect for persons, beneficence, and justice, all of which accorded with the impulses—if not the language—of Christian ethics.[15] These principles were then carried forward, albeit in modified fashion, in the seminal work of Tom Beauchamp and James Childress, whose *Principles of Biomedical Ethics* created "the lingua franca of bioethics."[16] By influencing *The Belmont Report* and thus Beauchamp and Childress's work, Christian ethics had a pivotal role to play in the birth of Western bioethics.

To the extent that Christian ethicists relied on experience and reason as their entrée into the burgeoning field of bioethics, though, they may have inadvertently limited the influence of the more explicitly theological sources (i.e., scripture and tradition) in public bioethics discourse. M. Therese Lysaught has suggested that the erosion of Christian principles in bioethics began with Beauchamp and Childress's work, whose principle of respect for autonomy contrasted quite negatively with the more theologically rich vision of respect for *persons* found in Paul Ramsey's earlier book, *The Patient as Person*.[17] Others date the turning point a little later, but few dispute the claim that theological voices were less likely to enter the bioethics conversation in a theological fashion in the 1980s and 1990s, once bioethics became more of an independent field of study.[18] This is not, however, to say that Christian ethics has had no role in the ongoing development of bioethics. A number of Christian ethicists have brought their theological convictions to bear on the field through a continued reliance on experience and reason as a means of translating their tradition-based assessments into a more readily accessible form of "public reason."[19] Among many possible examples, Daniel Callahan's more recent work is indicative, for his arguments for restricting technology and increasing access to basic care are presented in secular terms that highlight the rational coherence of these positions more than their roots in scripture or tradition. His positions are nevertheless informed by and ultimately faithful to the conception of the common good found in the Catholic theological tradition.[20] At the same time, other Christian ethicists have embraced a different tactic, doubling down on intentionally Christian sources to provide an analysis

---

[14]Stephen E. Lammers, "The Marginalization of Religious Voices in Bioethics," in *Religion and Medical Ethics: Looking Back, Looking Forward*, ed. Allen Verhey (Grand Rapids: Eerdmans, 1996), 21; Baker, *Before Bioethics*, 287–95.

[15]National Commission for the Protection of Human Subjects of Biomedical and Behavioral Research, *The Belmont Report: Ethical Principles and Guidelines for the Protection of Human Subjects of Research* (Washington, DC: US Government Printing Office, 1979).

[16]Baker, *Before Bioethics*, 299.

[17]M. Therese Lysaught, "Respect: Or, How Respect for Persons Became Respect for Autonomy," *Journal of Medicine and Philosophy* 29, no. 6 (2004): 671–3, 675–6. For a more critical appraisal of the theological contributions of Ramsey's book, see Stanley Hauerwas, "How Christian Ethics Became Medical Ethics: The Case of Paul Ramsey," *Christian Bioethics* 1, no. 1 (1995): 11–28.

[18]Lisa Sowle Cahill, *Theological Bioethics: Participation, Justice, Change* (Washington, DC: Georgetown University Press, 2005), 17.

[19]On these distinctions, see John Rawls, *Political Liberalism*, exp. ed. (New York: Columbia University Press, 2005), 212–54, 435–90.

[20]See Daniel Callahan, *Taming the Beloved Beast: How Medical Technology Costs are Destroying our Health Care System* (Princeton: Princeton University Press, 2009), 171–200.

of bioethical issues intended to appeal to the Christian community first and the broader public mainly by extension. In many ways, the work of Allen Verhey exemplifies this, as he applied a scriptural ethic to all manner of bioethics issues, from abortion and assisted reproductive technologies to assisted suicide and euthanasia.[21]

These two different approaches represent two different strategies, and arguably both are necessary, but given the ways in which the pendulum has swung away from theology and toward more secular forms of reasoning in the field of bioethics, it is particularly important for Christian ethics to reassert its particularly Christian voice; otherwise, it risks at the very least a tacit approval of a public bioethics discourse that "is governed by the values of individualism, science, technology, the market, and profits."[22] Since those values are in opposition to the Christian understanding of the purpose of medicine and of the need for health care as outlined above, some reclamation of the distinctive insights of Christian ethics ought to be a bigger part of the Christian engagement with bioethics. Of course, how this should occur is a complex question, but fortunately the long history of Christian ethics in medicine, bioethics, and health care offers a number of resources for a constructive way forward. The final section of this chapter, then, builds on this history to articulate substantive contributions that Christian ethics can make to the ongoing development of medicine, bioethics, and health care without sacrificing the value of any of its four sources.

THE DISTINCTIVE VISION OF CHRISTIAN ETHICS FOR MEDICINE, BIOETHICS, AND HEALTH CARE TODAY

In thinking about the distinctive contributions of Christian ethics for medicine, bioethics, and health care today, there are a number of viable options. Other chapters in this section of the book illustrate some of these options for specific bioethics issues, so I want to focus here instead on the unique contributions of Christian ethics for medicine, bioethics, and health care more broadly. This is quite appropriate since it is Christianity's general vision for what medicine and health care should be that has historically incorporated the most explicitly theological sources by relying more directly on scripture and tradition. When using these sources and this vision, Christian ethics has three important contributions to make, two through the work of Christian health care institutions in particular and one in secular health care contexts more generally.

To begin, Christian ethics has perhaps its greatest opportunity to shape the general understanding of medicine, bioethics, and health care through health care institutions with Christian affiliations. These institutions are numerous. To focus on just one denomination, the Catholic Health Association estimates that one out of every six hospital patients receives care in a Catholic hospital in the United States, and it describes Catholic health care more generally as "the largest group of nonprofit health care providers in the nation."[23] Given this footprint, the reclamation of Christian ethics' unique vision for medicine and health care could indeed have a significant impact through Christian health care institutions. In fairness, many if not most Christian health care institutions already embody this vision, especially through their commitment to care for the poor.

---

[21]See, e.g., Allen Verhey, *Reading the Bible in the Strange World of Medicine* (Grand Rapids: Eerdmans, 2003).
[22]Cahill, *Theological Bioethics*, 18.
[23]Catholic Health Association of the United States, "U.S. Catholic Health Care—2018," last modified January 2018, https://www.chausa.org/about/about/facts-statistics.

Nevertheless, they face constant pressures to conform to the same standards of business efficiency that govern bioethics and medicine—especially in the United States—which means that there will be real struggles to preserve this mission in a shifting health care landscape. To give just one example, a number of Catholic hospitals have found it necessary to merge with some of their non-Catholic counterparts, accepting the complex ethical entanglements that this arrangement creates in order to continue serving the marginalized communities that would otherwise be left unserved.[24]

In order to continue successfully integrating theological values in the face of sometimes contradictory market demands, Christian health care institutions will need to find ways to challenge and transform the prevailing assumptions of the market itself. This will require working to make medicine more affordable, not merely by offering discounts to individual patients who might not be able to cover the cost of care, but also by fighting for structural reforms that could lower the cost of health care across the board. Consider, for instance, what Christian health care institutions might accomplish if they all united to utilize their collective bargaining power to chip away at the hegemony pharmaceutical companies currently enjoy over the price of their drugs.[25] In these and other efforts, Christian health care institutions would be able to reassert the work of the Christian tradition, which cast health care as a form of neighborly love rightfully offered to everyone in need, regardless of their ability to pay.[26] This renewed concern for the poor, then, represents the first theological contribution of Christian ethics for medicine and health care today.

Christian health care institutions can also make a second theological contribution by using the care they provide to promote the particular understanding of medicine found in Christian ethics. Specifically, Christian health care institutions can re-embrace the links between the role of medicine and the power of the resurrection by pursuing healing in a way that reaffirms this life's orientation to the next. One way to do this is to emphasize accompaniment, especially for those who need end-of-life care, so that Christian health care institutions can treat the existential needs of their patients alongside their physical ones.[27] Again, this is something that many patients already find in Christian health care institutions, but it is nonetheless essential for all Christian health care institutions to reaffirm their commitment to this priority at a structural level. Through these and other changes, Christian health care institutions will be able to provide a unique approach to health care that embodies the theological insights into the nature and purpose of medicine found in the resources of Christian ethics.

Finally, the work of Christian ethics can also make a third contribution to medicine, bioethics, and health care today by participating in secular contexts without sacrificing its theological roots. Certainly, this can happen through the work of individual Christians who choose to embrace an alternative vision for the practice of medicine that avoids the tendency to idolize medicine as the sole solution to human limitation. As Stanley Hauerwas

---

[24]For more details, see Thomas Kopfensteiner, "Responsibility and Cooperation: Evaluating Partnerships among Health Care Providers," *Health Progress* 83, no. 6 (2002): 40–2, 59.

[25]The most infamous recent example is Gilead Science's hepatitis C drug, Sovaldi. Margot Sanger-Katz, "$1,000 Hepatitis Pill Shows Why Fixing Health Costs Is So Hard," *New York Times*, August 2, 2014, http://www.nytimes.com/2014/08/03/upshot/is-a-1000-pill-really-too-much.html?abt=0002&abg=0.

[26]Again, care for the poor was an essential element of the earliest hospitals founded by Christian communities ready to offer care free of charge. Ferngren, *Medicine and Health Care*, 124–5.

[27]For more details on what this might look like and how it can be theologically justified, see Conor M. Kelly, "Christology and the Essence of Catholic Health Care," in *Incarnate Grace: Perspectives on the Ministry of Catholic Health Care*, ed. Charles Bouchard (St. Louis: Catholic Health Association of the United States, 2017), 47–52.

explains, this is best achieved "if we remember that the physician's basic pledge is not to cure, but to care through being present to the one in pain," since such an approach allows the Christian physician to live out the mission of the Christian community as "a people called out by a God who is always present to us."[28] In this way, Christian health care professionals can witness to the same hope that Christian health care institutions manifest in an institutional commitment to accompaniment as the end of medicine, but they can do it even in non-Christian settings for explicitly (but not explicitly *stated*) Christian reasons.

Other Christians, especially Christian ethicists, can work to influence secular approaches to medicine, bioethics, and health care in similar ways, and they will be most successful if they focus on matters that effect everyone in a fashion that might elicit broad consensus. Hence, Christians might use their tradition's understanding of medicine as a good to be provided to everyone in need as the basis for touting a more socially conscious approach to the use of health care resources. This could, for instance, include encouragement for individuals to reject the use of what Daniel Daly calls "unreasonable means," that is, "when the burdens to the patient *and community* far outpace the benefits to the patient ... and when the use of these ... means directly or indirectly limits another patient's access to ordinary means."[29] Likewise, Christianity's traditional emphasis on care for all could justify a focus on preventative medicine and self-care on the basis that these actions lower the burden one places on the health care system as a whole. Defending these sorts of choices would align with more secular commitments to social justice and equality, but they would not have to sacrifice Christian convictions in order to do so. As a result, a judicious picking of one's battles would allow the theological resources of Christian ethics to contribute to the development of medicine, bioethics, and health care in a pluralistic context, preserving the insights of scripture and tradition alongside those of experience and reason in the contemporary environment.

CONCLUSION

Overall, Christian ethics has much to say about medicine, bioethics, and health care. As this chapter has shown, all three of these spheres have constituted major concerns for Christian communities, and interactions with the four sources of Christian ethics have shaped each one. In light of the historical trajectory as the whole, the theological commitments of Christian ethics have had the most direct and profound influences on medicine and health care, whereas they have had less explicitly theological, though no less significant, impacts on bioethics. In large part, this reflects a shift from a reliance on scripture and tradition for the former to a reliance on experience and reason for the latter. While not necessarily a problem *in se*, this movement potentially puts some of the distinctiveness of Christian ethics at risk. Nevertheless, this reality does not mean that Christian ethics has nothing unique to offer medicine, bioethics, and health care today. In fact, as the final section of this chapter articulated, by re-embracing the early Christian vision for medicine and health care—which was directly derived from scripture and tradition—Christian ethics has the opportunity to continue shaping medicine, bioethics, and health care for years to come, most profoundly by stressing its special attention to

[28]Stanley Hauerwas, "Salvation and Health: Why Medicine Needs the Church," in *The Hauerwas Reader*, ed. John Berkman and Michael Cartwright (Durham: Duke University Press, 2001), 551, 553.
[29]Daniel J. Daly, "Unreasonable Means: Proposing a New Category for Catholic End-of-Life Ethics," *Christian Bioethics* 19, no. 1 (2013): 52–3, emphasis added.

care for the poor, its prioritization of accompaniment in Christian health care contexts, and its insistence on the social responsibilities of everyone who comes into contact with the health care system. While this influence would certainly be good for the place of Christian ethics in the contemporary world, it would also be a boon for everyone who needs medicine, bioethics, and health care—which is to say, for all of us.

SUGGESTED READINGS

Cahill, Lisa Sowle. *Theological Bioethics: Participation, Justice, Change.* Washington, DC: Georgetown University Press, 2005.

Hauerwas, Stanley. *Naming the Silences: God, Medicine, and the Problem of Suffering.* London: T&T Clark, 2001.

Lysaught, M. Therese, and Joseph Kotva, with Stephen E. Lammers and Allen Verhey, eds. *On Moral Medicine: Theological Perspectives on Medical Ethics*, 3rd ed. Grand Rapids: Eerdmans, 2012.

Lysaught, M. Therese, and Michael McCarthy. *Catholic Bioethics and Social Justice: The Praxis of U.S. Health Care in a Globalized World.* Collegeville: Liturgical, 2019.

Messer, Neil. *Flourishing: Health, Disease, and Bioethics in Theological Perspective.* Grand Rapids: Eerdmans, 2013.

CHAPTER THIRTY

Mental Health and Trauma

WARREN KINGHORN

Psychological trauma shatters the myth that the world as we live in it is orderly and just. It shatters the myth that others—including those in authority, or those in one's family—can be trusted to nurture and not to harm. It shatters the myth that the house of the wicked is destroyed and that the tent of the upright flourishes in the world as we experience it (Prov. 14:11). Though trauma can lead to growth and wisdom, it is first a site of destruction and pain.

There is no Christian faith nor practice, and no Christian ethics, that does not find its place in the landscape of trauma. The entire world as we know it *post lapsum* is a landscape of traumatic events, defined broadly as "events [that] overwhelm the ordinary systems of care that give people a sense of control, connection, and meaning."[1] In the United States, 19.1 percent of women have experienced completed or attempted rape (including 7 percent of women who report experiencing completed or attempted rape prior to age 18), and nearly one in three women and one in six men have experienced some form of sexual violence involving physical touch.[2] One in four women and one in seven men report severe physical violence in intimate relationships.[3] In another context of trauma, war affects not only combatants but also entire populations who live in or flee war zones. Though not all of these experiences will result in prolonged psychological suffering, many will: the rates of post-traumatic stress disorder (PTSD), the psychological syndrome most closely associated with traumatic experiences, are 23 percent among US combat veterans of the wars in Iraq and Afghanistan,[4] 20 percent among sexual assault survivors,[5] and 7 percent among the US population as a whole.[6]

The ubiquity of trauma requires that it not be relegated within Christian ethics to a specialized "ethics of trauma." At best, Christian ethical engagement with trauma sheds important light on how all work in Christian ethics is done and how it is received. Many if not most of the central topics of modern Christian ethics—racism, war, sexual

---

[1]Judith Herman, *Trauma and Recovery: The Aftermath of Violence—from Domestic Abuse to Political Terror* (New York: Basic Books, 1997), 33.

[2]S. G. Smith et al., *The National Intimate Partner and Sexual Violence Survey (NISVS): 2010–2012 State Report* (Atlanta: National Center for Injury Prevention and Control, Centers for Disease Control and Prevention, 2017).

[3]Ibid.

[4]Jessica J. Fulton et al., "The Prevalence of Posttraumatic Stress Disorder in Operation Enduring Freedom/Operation Iraqi Freedom (OEF/OIF) Veterans: A Meta-Analysis," *Journal of Anxiety Disorders* 31 (2015): 98–107.

[5]K. M. Scott et al., "Post-Traumatic Stress Disorder Associated with Sexual Assault among Women in the WHO World Mental Health Surveys," *Psychological Medicine* 48, no. 1 (2018): 155–67.

[6]Ronald C. Kessler et al., "Lifetime Prevalence and Age-of-Onset Distributions of DSM-IV Disorders in the National Comorbidity Survey Replication," *Archives of General Psychiatry* 62 (2005): 593–602.

violence, abortion, environmental harm, and family relationships—are permeated with and inextricably tied to trauma. Trauma informs what questions are taken up by Christian ethicists, how these questions are framed, and how the work of Christian ethics is received by trauma survivors and others who are touched by trauma. A classroom discussion about the relative merits of just war theory and pacifism may be received very differently by a class of combat veterans or refugees from war zones (or both) than by a class of students who have never been touched personally by war. A church discussion group about contraception or abortion may be received very differently by survivors of sexual assault than by those who have never been closely affected by sexual assault or intimate partner violence. Christian ethics is always done in the context of trauma, often *by* trauma survivors, and often *for* and *with* trauma survivors.

But it is not only trauma *survivors* who perform and receive the work of Christian ethics. In recent years, the field of Christian ethics has been forced to grapple with the reality that Christian ethicists have also been *perpetrators* of trauma, forcing difficult but necessary conversations about whether and how to engage their work in the light of their conduct. The more complete reckoning of the abuse perpetrated on female students and colleagues by the eminent Mennonite pacifist ethicist John Howard Yoder has led to painful self-examination among Christian ethicists who knew something of the abuse but did not sufficiently confront it, and has left a subsequent generation of Christian ethicists grappling with how to receive and to teach Yoder's and others' "tainted legacies."[7]

In this chapter I will explore particular ways that the insights of trauma studies and the psychology of trauma can helpfully inform the work of Christian ethics, and will also explore ways that Christian ethics can helpfully inform broader conversations about trauma and appropriate responses to trauma survivors. I will conclude with recommendations of how Christian ethics might be performed in the light of trauma.

It is important, at the outset, to note the relationship between mental health and trauma, as I engage both in this chapter. Mental health problems (defined here as the persistent presence of unwanted experience and behavior socially judged to merit clinical attention) and traumatic experiences are related, though in an imperfect and complex relationship. They are not synonymous. Though many mental health problems such as borderline personality disorder, dissociative identity disorder, somatoform disorders, and (by definition) PTSD are often correlated with traumatic experiences, many who live with mental health problems are not survivors of trauma. Relationships of cause and effect can be complex: though traumatic experiences can give rise to mental health problems, it is also the case that mental health problems often place people at increased risk for traumatic experiences—for instance, when a person with schizophrenia becomes unhoused and therefore at higher risk for being a victim of physical and sexual assault. Furthermore, not all survivors of trauma experience subsequent mental health problems, even though these experiences may continue to be painful. And many people, even amid the pain of traumatic experiences, find in them significant opportunities for growth and development of habits and practices that lead to flourishing. In this chapter, recognizing this complexity, I will focus on traumatic experience rather than on mental health *per*

[7]David Cramer et al., "Scandalizing John Howard Yoder," *The Other Journal*, July 7, 2014, https://theotherjournal.com/2014/07/07/scandalizing-john-howard-yoder/; Karen V. Guth, "Moral Injury, Feminist and Womanist Ethics, and Tainted Legacies," *Journal of the Society of Christian Ethics* 38, no. 1 (2018): 167–86; Karen V. Guth, "Moral Injury and the Ethics of Teaching Tainted Legacies," *Teaching Theology and Religion* 21, no. 3 (2018): 197–209; Tobias Winright, "I Was John Howard Yoder's Graduate Assistant. Should I Still Use His Work?," *Sojourners*, October 23, 2015, https://sojo.net/articles/i-was-john-howard-yoders-graduate-assistant-should-i-still-use-his-work.

se and will allude to mental health problems insofar as they are directly related to the experience of trauma.

HOW MIGHT WORK ON TRAUMA INFORM THE WORK OF CHRISTIAN ETHICS?

Current work on trauma can and should inform the work of Christian ethics in four dimensions: by highlighting and foregrounding subjects for urgent ethical inquiry, by contributing important insights into human experience and human agency, by challenging commonplace ethical and theological assumptions, and by unlocking interpretations of scripture and important Christian texts.

First, current work on trauma can highlight and foreground subjects for urgent ethical inquiry. Psychiatrist Judith Herman, in her seminal work on trauma, states that "the study of psychological trauma has a curious history—one of episodic amnesia."[8] Since the mid-nineteenth century, she claims, investigation of particular contexts of trauma have generated intense attention—but because the study of trauma "has repeatedly led into realms of the unthinkable," challenging "fundamental questions of belief," these investigations have often been anathematized and forgotten, only to be rediscovered by a later generation.[9]

Christian ethicists have not been immune to this episodic amnesia. Some of the more urgent ethical problems of the past century have been contexts of trauma that could not be—but are—true. The scope of racial terror lynchings in the American south in the early twentieth century, the systematic cover up of clerical sexual abuse by Catholic bishops (and similar offenses by Protestant leaders), the hidden-in-plain-sight reality that a leading pacifist thinker was engaging in inappropriate relationships with women—all of these *could not be*, but are, true. They came into public consciousness only when courageous people—some within the field of Christian ethics but mostly outside of it—dared to bring them to light, leading to significant *post hoc* grappling among Christian ethicists. But understanding the dynamics of trauma, and particularly the way that trauma hides its reality in plain sight because it too deeply challenges our settled conceptions of the world, can point the way for Christian ethicists to respond proactively rather than reactively to urgent topics.

Second, current work on trauma contributes to Christian ethics important insight into human experience and human agency. The psychology of trauma is deeply concerned not just with what trauma survivors have experienced but also with how trauma informs survivors' ways of being in the world. While trauma varies widely in context and the experience of survivors is highly variable, an appreciation of the psychological effects of trauma is critical for pastoral and ethical engagement with survivors. It is common, for example, for survivors of trauma to exhibit various degrees of dissociation, moments of disconnection from one's body or one's social space. Though dissociation may be adaptive as an immediate response to trauma—enabling a survivor to retreat from an unbearable and overwhelming experience—it may impair future relationships, future engagement in community life, and the ability to heal. Trauma survivors are often understandably vigilant when exposed to situations that bear resemblance to their trauma and may react in ways

---

[8]Herman, *Trauma and Recovery*, 7.
[9]Ibid.

that appear to unaware observers as "paranoid" or hostile. Survivors often exhibit some degree of alexithymia, an inability to name and to recognize emotion, that may threaten survivors' ability to thrive in Christian communities that associate particular emotional experiences with spiritual authenticity. Though the precise pathways are still unknown, developing work in epigenetics suggests that trauma-induced stress may affect gene expression in children of trauma survivors, leading to transgenerational vulnerability to mental health problems.[10] These psychological reflections are all important for Christian ethicists who write about, or for, survivors.

Third, psychological work on trauma can also be helpful insofar as it challenges ethical and theological assumptions that are deeply ingrained in Christian thought and practice. Jennifer Beste, for example, appreciatively summarizes Karl Rahner's account of human freedom to effect a fundamental option for or against God's offer of Godself but argues that Rahner's account does not sufficiently attend to the way that human agency can be limited and fragmented by interpersonal trauma. Juxtaposing Rahner's thought with the feminist philosophy of Judith Butler and Diana Meyers, Beste uses trauma as a lens to critique Rahner but also to foreground more pastoral writings in which Rahner argues that grace may be mediated socially and intersubjectively. For Beste, this provides a Rahnerian way to affirm that the human reception of grace may be limited by profound interpersonal trauma.[11]

Similarly, appreciation of trauma can unsettle pervasive assumptions about civil religion and the relationship of state practices to Christian faith. In a pioneering work written soon after the Vietnam war, former US Army chaplain William Mahedy reflects on the way that many US service members were profoundly alienated from church and Christian faith as a result of their service in Vietnam, moving from earnest religious commitment to the apparent nihilism of "it don't mean nothin'." Mahedy argues, however, that these disillusioned veterans gave voice to "the most significant spiritual journey of our time," testifying to the idolatry inherent in their post-Second World War childhood religious formation that so equated Christianity with American interests that it was unthinkable that the United States could be on the wrong side of an armed conflict.[12]

Fourth, in recent years theologians and biblical scholars have employed trauma theory to engage particular biblical texts with results that are striking and illuminating for the work of Christian ethics. Kathleen O'Connor, for example, suggests that the very characteristics of the book of Jeremiah that render it unpalatable and unattractive to modern Christians—the violence of its language, its cacophonous intermingling of voices, its narrative indeterminacy—vividly display the experiences of a people grappling with the social, political, and military trauma of exile. The tears of Jeremiah and anguish of the book, she suggests, "[promise] to awaken hearts turned to stone by brutality."[13] Similarly, Anathea Portier-Young describes Jewish apocalyptic texts, including the book of Daniel, as modes of engagement with and resistance to Seleucid state terror.[14] Serene

[10]Rachel Yehuda and Amy Lehrner, "Intergenerational Transmission of Trauma Effects: Putative Role of Epigenetic Mechanisms," *World Psychiatry* 17, no. 3 (2018): 243–57.

[11]Jennifer Beste, *God and the Victim: Traumatic Intrusions on Grace and Freedom* (New York: Oxford University Press, 2007).

[12]William Mahedy, *Out of the Night: The Spiritual Journey of Vietnam Vets* (Knoxville: Radix, 2004), 12.

[13]Kathleen O'Connor, *Jeremiah: Pain and Promise* (Minneapolis: Fortress, 2011), x.

[14]Anathea Portier-Young, *Apocalypse against Empire: Theologies of Resistance in Early Judaism* (Grand Rapids: Eerdmans, 2011).

Jones brings John Calvin's commentary on the Psalms into direct conversation with trauma theory to argue that the reading and communal performance of the Psalms may—but also may not—be a powerful resource for trauma healing.[15] Shelly Rambo closely engages the garden and upper room narratives of John 20, unseating settled readings of the disciples' post-resurrection joy and Thomas's doubt and expression of belief, and instead highlighting the way that the Easter disciples *didn't* see the empty tomb clearly, *didn't* believe the women who were the earliest witnesses, huddled in fear in the upper room, and *didn't* engage Jesus's wounds even when beckoned to do so.[16] The work of these scholars, and more, points to scripture as a text that vividly witnesses to the complex realities of trauma, and that must therefore be an essential resource for any Christian ethical engagement with trauma.

HOW MIGHT CHRISTIAN ETHICS HELPFULLY INFORM BROADER CONVERSATIONS ABOUT TRAUMA?

I have discussed ways that work in trauma theory and the psychology of trauma might vitally inform the work of Christian ethics. But the relationship, I argue, is bidirectional: Christian ethics has a vital role to play in shaping broader work on trauma. Specifically, Christian ethics can and must attend to the contexts in which trauma is described, resisting any limitation to medical or psychological language, modeling interpretations of trauma that incorporate sociopolitical, historical, and theological perspectives, and pointing toward constructive models of recovery and healing.

Reflecting on the way that trauma has been framed over the past century, journalist David Morris writes,

> How people respond to horrific events has always been determined by a complex web of social, political, and technological forces. For most of human history, interpreting trauma has been the preserve of artists, poets, and shamans. ... Today, for better or worse, we deal with trauma and horror almost exclusively through a complex, seemingly arbitrary cluster of symptoms known as post-traumatic stress disorder. ... This fact alone is worthy of further exploration: most of us no longer turn to poetry, our families, or the clergy for solace post-horror. Instead, we turn to psychiatrists.[17]

Though there is nothing about the nature or experience of traumatic events that mandates their framing as medical or psychological problems, the discourses of psychiatry, psychology, and associated clinical disciplines have dominated the way that trauma has been narrated over the last two centuries.[18] To be sure, as noted above, this clinical reflection on trauma has yielded wisdom that is productive for the work of Christian ethics. But the reverse is also true: Christian ethics done well can help to rescue trauma

---

[15]Serene Jones, *Trauma and Grace: Theology in a Ruptured World* (Louisville: Westminster John Knox, 2009), 43–67.

[16]Shelly Rambo, *Spirit and Trauma: A Theology of Remaining* (Louisville: Westminster John Knox, 2010); Rambo, *Resurrecting Wounds: Living in the Afterlife of Trauma* (Waco: Baylor University Press, 2017).

[17]David Morris, *The Evil Hours: A Biography of Post-Traumatic Stress Disorder* (New York: Houghton Mifflin Harcourt, 2015), 3.

[18]Allan Young, *The Harmony of Illusions: Inventing Post-Traumatic Stress Disorder* (Princeton: Princeton University Press, 1995); Didier Fassin and Richard Rechtman, *The Empire of Trauma: An Inquiry into the Condition of Victimhood* (Princeton: Princeton University Press, 2009).

studies from the biological reductionism and excessive focus on symptom relief that haunts the clinical mental health disciplines.

Modern trauma clinicians usually care deeply about trauma survivors and are very aware of the moral, social, and political contexts of trauma. But the *methods* of modern psychology and psychiatry often promote the conceptual abstraction of trauma (e.g., by gathering the experiences of survivors of different traumatic contexts under the generic category of "PTSD") and elucidation of empirically supported, standardized, scalable psychological interventions for trauma. Because these interventions (such as Cognitive Processing Therapy [CPT] and Eye Movement Desensitization and Reprocessing [EMDR]) are intended to help people with widely ranging experiences of trauma and are focused on the experience of individual survivors in a clinical context, it is important that psychological work on trauma not distract attention from the moral, social, and political contexts from which trauma emerges, including war, poverty, political violence, and particular expressions of patriarchy. Christian ethics, already attuned to these contexts as central subjects of engagement, offers nuance and context to these psychological conversations.

The recent rediscovery of "moral injury," particularly in veterans of war, vividly displays how clinical conversations on trauma can be sharpened in conversation with Christian ethics.[19] Moral injury, broadly conceived as traumatic experience that results from actions *done* or *witnessed* in a context such as war rather than only what *was done to* a survivor, often characterized by shame and guilt in the survivor rather than primarily fear and anxiety, has been broadly discussed in clinical trauma work since the publication of a research report by a group of prominent empirical trauma researchers in 2009.[20] It is hardly a new discovery, though. Early observers of the experience of US veterans of the Vietnam War were keenly attentive to the way that veterans often suffered from the memory of what they did and witnessed in Vietnam and Southeast Asia, with attendant shame and guilt.[21] In a prime example of Herman's concept of episodic amnesia, however, the diagnosis of PTSD, when it was first introduced in 1980, largely ignored trauma that resulted from actions done or witnessed, and scientific research on trauma largely ignored this dimension of trauma for the next quarter-century.

The introduction of the term "moral injury" did not actually originate with new empirical findings about combat trauma. Empirical research, after all, can only answer questions that are asked. Rather, it came when psychiatrist Jonathan Shay, placing the combat narratives of Vietnam veterans alongside Homer's *Iliad*, used the Homeric narrative to highlight obvious but underappreciated moral dimensions of combat trauma, proclaiming that "moral injury is an essential part of any combat trauma that leads to lifelong psychological injury."[22] More recently, Christian ethicist Joseph Wiinikka-Lydon, reflecting on the narratives of veterans of the wars in Iraq and Afghanistan and drawing on anthropologist Veena Das's account of "poisonous knowledge," has proposed that

---

[19]Warren Kinghorn, "Combat Trauma and Moral Fragmentation: A Theological Account of Moral Injury," *Journal of the Society of Christian Ethics* 32, no. 2 (2012): 57–74.

[20]Brett T. Litz et al., "Moral Injury and Moral Repair in War Veterans: A Preliminary Model and Intervention Strategy," *Clinical Psychology Review* 29, no. 8 (2009): 695–706.

[21]Robert Jay Lifton, *Home from the War: Vietnam Veterans: Neither Victims nor Executioners* (New York: Simon and Schuster, 1973); Chaim Shatan, "The Grief of Soldiers: Vietnam Combat Veterans' Self-Help Movement," *American Journal of Orthopsychiatry* 43 (1973): 640–53.

[22]Jonathan Shay, *Achilles in Vietnam: Combat Trauma and the Undoing of Character* (New York: Scribner, 1994), 20.

moral injury be framed not as "betrayal of what's right by someone who holds legitimate authority in a high-stakes situation" (Shay's formulation) or as "perpetrating, failing to prevent, or bearing witness to acts that transgress deeply held moral beliefs and expectations" (the 2009 definition of Litz et al.), but rather as "burdensome knowledge embodied that concerns one's self and one's culture and society."[23] Wiinikka-Lydon's political reframing of moral injury is intriguing because it suggests that the experience of moral injury may not only result from particular actions done (or not done) by warriors but may also relate to simply being present in a war zone and finding one's moral ground split open.

As the phenomenon of moral injury—however defined—makes clear, trauma can never be reduced to neuroscience or to stimulus-response psychology because it is often the interpretation that survivors ascribe to traumatic events that makes them traumatic. Trauma can never be separated from the meaning that a survivor ascribes to his or her trauma—and this meaning can only be understood when trauma theorists consider human life in its thick, lived complexity. Insofar as Christian faith and practice has shaped not only the experience of trauma for many survivors but also the just-world assumptions that are deeply threatened by trauma, then understanding trauma requires theological nuance and depth—precisely the nuance and depth that Christian ethics, at its best, can offer to trauma studies.

IDENTIFYING CONSTRUCTIVE MODELS FOR TRAUMA RECOVERY AND HEALING

In a popular overview of his expansive and sometimes unorthodox research and clinical career, trauma studies pioneer Bessel van der Kolk comments that "clinicians have only one obligation: to do whatever they can to help their patients get better."[24] Given his openness to exploring novel approaches to trauma healing, it is notable that even van der Kolk largely ignores the role of religious practices and faith communities in trauma healing. Van der Kolk is not alone in his neglect of faith-based trauma healing resources: because trauma research is largely funded in the United States through government agencies such as the National Institutes of Health and the Department of Veterans Affairs, trauma-healing programs rooted in particular religious traditions are often excluded from research funding and, hence, from the attention of researchers and policy makers. But even a cursory internet search reveals a complex and constantly shifting web of nonprofit ministries, church-based outreach programs, denominational programs, faith-based clinics and inpatient institutions, and professional organizations that market themselves as trauma healing resources. Many of these organizations are fragile, driven by the vision of one or two leaders, and connected in complex ways to one or more religious traditions: Shelly Rambo, for example, offers a detailed account of the "healing circles" sponsored by Warriors Journey Home, a church-based nonprofit in Ohio that draws on principles of Christian spirituality and Native American "earth medicine."[25]

---

[23]Joseph Wiinikka-Lydon, "Moral Injury as Inherent Political Critique: The Prophetic Possibilities of a New Term," *Political Theology* 18, no. 3 (2017): 219–32.

[24]Bessel van der Kolk, *The Body Keeps the Score: Brain, Mind, and Body in the Healing of Trauma* (New York: Viking, 2014), 262.

[25]Rambo, *Resurrecting Wounds*, 109–43.

Faith-based trauma healing programs, with their powerful and volatile mix of theology, ritual practices, prayer, trauma therapy, and connection to religious institutions, are capable of good but also capable of harm if they highlight theologies and practices that exploit the vulnerability of trauma survivors.[26] Standard clinical methods of program evaluation can evaluate these programs in part—for instance, by ensuring compliance with regulations for health care facilities and by evaluating the degree to which they adhere to empirically validated treatment models—but they cannot evaluate or often even name the theological and religious commitments that motivate and inform these programs. That is the responsibility for those who are trained in the internal discourses and practices of religious traditions, and points to a critical and needed voice for Christian ethics within the larger world of trauma studies.

PERFORMING CHRISTIAN ETHICS IN THE LIGHT OF TRAUMA

As stated above, trauma pervades every corner of human life and culture, including the culture of churches and religious organizations. Engaging trauma—listening closely and attentively to the stories of survivors, feeling with survivors the vulnerability and pain of trauma—is deeply hard. Honestly engaging the way that long-held theological commitments, long-admired theological authorities, and long-inhabited religious and theological institutions might promote and perpetuate trauma is also hard, requiring deep commitments to justice and to self-implicating vulnerability. But both are necessary, not just for the integrity of a Christian ethics of trauma, but for Christian ethics as a whole.

Performing Christian ethics in the light of trauma foremost requires a robust theology of sin. Though trauma survivors must never be blamed or scapegoated for their experiences—survivors have most often been sinned *against* in profound ways—trauma is one way that sin manifests, insidiously and powerfully, in lived reality. Engaging trauma requires naming the reality of sin and the pervasive possibility of sin, not only in others, but also and especially in our institutions, in our formative assumptions, and in ourselves. Christian ethicists, as noted above, can just as easily *perpetuate* trauma as address trauma—and yet unless we are deeply committed to humility, transparency, and close engagement with trauma survivors, we can often be painfully blind to the way that trauma implicates our own work. It is always important, then, to preach, teach, write, and act with the experiences of trauma survivors in mind. For this, several key practices are required.

First, Christian ethicists must name the ways that trauma connects to the subjects of their teaching, writing, and other work, even if they are not engaging trauma specifically. Not to do so is to silence the experiences and voices of survivors, and to be complicit with the "episodic amnesia" that Herman describes. No article or book on the ethics of war, for example, is complete unless it acknowledges the traumatic effects of war upon both soldiers and civilians.[27] No article or book on race and racism is complete unless it acknowledges the way that trauma has been used to enforce racialization and racial

[26]Jennifer Miller, "The Mercy Girls," *Slate*, April 24, 2016, http://www.slate.com/articles/life/cover_story/2016/04/at_mercy_multiplied_troubled_young_women_come_to_believe_their_mental_health.html.

[27]See, e.g., Tobias Winright and E. Ann Jeschke, "Combat and Confession: Just War and Moral Injury," in *Can War Be Just in the 21st Century? Ethicists Engage the Tradition*, ed. Tobias Winright and Laurie Johnston (Maryknoll: Orbis, 2015), 169–87. Their essay also devotes attention to a theology of sin.

privilege. No article or book on Christian approaches to parenting or educating children is complete unless it is written with awareness of the prevalence of childhood physical and sexual abuse. Such work might challenge the way that trauma is understood and defined—it should not simply channel the perspective of trauma psychology, which itself stands in need of historical and conceptual refinement, but it must name the uncomfortable, lived human realities to which trauma points.

Second, Christian ethicists must speak, write, and teach with the understanding that Christian ethics is never just *about* trauma but rather is performed *with* and *by* trauma survivors. Virtually every course in Christian ethics in every institution will include trauma survivors, most of whom will be students and some of whom will be instructors. When Christian ethicists write syllabi, teach courses, select and teach texts, engage public audiences, and write articles and books, this must be done with the expectation that trauma survivors will be among every primary audience.

Finally, Christian ethicists must engage the resources of Christian faith and practice not only for ways to name trauma's reality but also to point toward healing. A religious movement whose most prominent early interpreter told an early audience that "I decided to know nothing among you except Jesus Christ, and him crucified" (1 Cor. 2:2), and whose scriptures offer piercing displays of the reality and anguish of trauma, should hardly be surprised by anything emerging from modern attention to trauma. Attention to trauma sweeps away not Christian faith itself, but the polite, moralistic pretensions that have so often passed for Christian faith and that need to die if the good news of Jesus is to be proclaimed in a twenty-first-century world. Engaging trauma is deeply hard. But it is only by engaging trauma that Christians can know what it means to be "afflicted in every way, but not crushed; perplexed, but not driven to despair; persecuted, but not forsaken; struck down, but not destroyed; always carrying in the body the death of Jesus, so that the life of Jesus may also be made visible in our bodies" (2 Cor. 4:8-10). In a trauma-riddled world, trauma survivors just might know something about the life of Jesus that the church and the rest of the world need to learn.

SUGGESTED READINGS

Beste, Jennifer. *God and the Victim: Traumatic Intrusions on Grace and Freedom*. New York: Oxford University Press, 2007.

Herman, Judith. *Trauma and Recovery: The Aftermath of Violence—from Domestic Abuse to Political Terror*. New York: Basic Books, 1997.

Jones, Serene. *Trauma and Grace: Theology in a Ruptured World*. Louisville: Westminster John Knox, 2009.

Rambo, Shelly. *Spirit and Trauma: A Theology of Remaining*. Louisville: Westminster John Knox, 2010.

Shay, Jonathan. *Achilles in Vietnam: Combat Trauma and the Undoing of Character*. New York: Scribner, 1994.

CHAPTER THIRTY-ONE

Death and Dying

CHRISTOPHER P. VOGT

At least one thing is true for every person alive in the world today: one day we will die. If Christian ethics is about how to live in a Christian way, and if dying is an inevitable part of the story of how we live our lives, then no account of Christian ethics could be complete without careful consideration of death and dying. This topic is also critical because the belief that Jesus Christ has been raised from the dead—thereby overcoming the power of death itself—is fundamental for Christianity. Given its importance, it will not come as a surprise that all four sources of the Wesleyan Quadrilateral (scripture, tradition, experience, and reason) have something essential to contribute to our analysis of death and dying.

This chapter begins with experience, examining how death is understood and what it is like to die in the context of advanced twenty-first-century medicine. This examination allows us to develop an implicit secular theology of death that can be compared to one that is more deeply rooted in a worldview shaped by Christian scripture and tradition. A significant portion of the scholarship written on death and dying in Christian ethics over the last fifty years centered on whether specific treatment decisions are right or wrong.[1] We will take up some of these treatment questions in order to illustrate the ethical framework that is typically used to analyze these cases from a Christian perspective, and also to highlight the inescapable role of prudence in these matters. Finally, the chapter concludes by turning to the Christian tradition to retrieve the idea that dying might be approached as an art that must be learned.

Any theology is undertaken from a particular point of view and with attention to a specific context. This chapter is written from a North American perspective and will address the topic as it arises in the context of Europe and the United States. This Northern and Western focus is specific and by no means universal. A perspective emerging from the Global South likely would be more attentive to epidemiology or how inequality in wealth and access to health care affect mortality rates.[2] Rather than exploring a number of different cultural and geographic contexts, this chapter finds its breadth in the variety of dimensions of death and dying it takes up; limitations of space make it impossible to offer a survey that is broad in both respects.

---

[1]Lisa Sowle Cahill, *Theological Bioethics: Participation, Justice, and Change* (Washington, DC: Georgetown University Press, 2005), 16–18.

[2]Allan Kellehear, "The Nature of Contemporary Dying: Obsessions, Distortions, Challenges," *Studies in Christian Ethics* 29, no. 3 (2016): 273–4.

DEATH AND DYING IN THE TWENTY-FIRST CENTURY

For many people in Europe and North America today, not only is dying traumatic, but it also is unintelligible.[3] We struggle to find a place in the narrative of our lives for death; we live as if we are immortal without giving much thought to how our living eventually will converge with our dying.[4] There is no place for death in our lives in the literal sense either; death occurs in spaces set apart from the ordinary—not in homes but in hospitals, nursing homes, and occasionally in hospices.[5] Dying and disability have been removed from view as much as possible in order to help us maintain an illusion of absolute autonomy and invulnerability.[6] The scope of modern medicine is also complicit in erasing death in that it is often unclear whether someone should be considered to be dying.[7] There is always "just one more treatment" that can be tried; as a result, people sometimes die before we acknowledge the fact that they have been dying. Medical science exerts a disproportionate influence over the ways we understand death and the way that we die—so much so that these typical contemporary attitudes and patterns might be called "medicalized dying."[8]

In the context of medicalized dying, we conceive of death as a fearsome, menacing, antihuman force from which we need protection. We are conditioned to see modern medicine as a hero of sorts, which protects us against the threat of personal extinction.[9] The metaphor of an absolute "war" against death predominates in the popular imagination as the way of explaining what the practice of medicine is about. This leaves the dying person in a passive role.

Before the advent of modern medicine, the dying person played an instrumental role in the rituals surrounding their own death. They reconciled with people they had wronged, made provisions for the loved ones they would leave behind, and attempted to grow in faith and hope in the face of death. In a medicalized context, the dying person is not an agent or actor in the unfolding of their own death. Instead, they often feel helpless or invisible. The focus is not on them or their feelings and experiences as persons but rather on their body as the site of another battle in the war between death and modern medicine. They typically feel objectified and experience a sense of distance between their body and their "self"; they feel that medical professionals treat them like an "it" rather than as a person and may even see their own body as "it" rather than as "me."[10]

---

[3]David Elliot, "The Theological Virtue of Hope and the Art of Dying Well," *Studies in Christian Ethics* 29, no. 3 (2016): 304.

[4]Philippe Ariès, *Western Attitudes toward Death: From the Middle Ages to the Present* (Baltimore: Johns Hopkins University Press, 1974), 106.

[5]In the UK and the United States, approximately 80 percent of people die in a health care facility. From 1974 to 2003, the percentage of people who die at home fell from 31 percent to 18 percent. If current trends continue as few as one in ten deaths will take place at home. Only 4.3 percent of deaths occurred at an in-patient hospice. See Barbara Gomes and Irene J. Higginson, "Where People Die (1974–2030): Past Trends, Future Projections and Implications for Care," *Palliative Medicine* 22 (2008): 37. For comparative information, see J. B. Broad et al., "Where Do People Die? An International Comparison of the Percentage of Deaths Occurring in Hospital and Residential Aged Care Settings in 45 Populations, Using Published and Available Statistics," *International Journal of Public Health* 58, no. 2 (2013): 257–67.

[6]S. Kay Toombs, "Vulnerability and the Meaning of Illness: Reflections on Lived Experience," in *Health and Human Flourishing*, ed. Carol R. Taylor and Roberto Dell'oro (Washington, DC: Georgetown University Press, 2006), 120.

[7]Allen Verhey, *The Christian Art of Dying: Learning from Jesus* (Grand Rapids: Eerdmans, 2011), 14.

[8]Ibid., 9–75.

[9]William May, *The Physician's Covenant: Images of the Healer in Medical Ethics* (Philadelphia: Westminster, 1983): 64–6.

[10]Verhey, *Christian Art of Dying*, 16.

In a medicalized context, any sense of hope a person might experience is always drawn against an underlying background of despair. Medical science provides the hope that by its power, death can be fought back for now.[11] However, despite the many advances of modern science, the fact that we will die eventually remains. Our fixation with science and its power comes with a price: the eclipse of any transcendent dimension of human experience or what Therese Lysaught has called "the loss of an eschatological horizon."[12] In other words, the process of dying is experienced entirely within the realm of the physical and empirical, leaving no room for the metaphysical. As such, realities such as self and God, and any hope that extends beyond biological survival are lost.

THE MEANING AND SIGNIFICANCE OF DEATH IN A CHRISTIAN CONTEXT

Medicalized dying portrays death as a mortal enemy that can only be defeated through its elimination by the power of science. In truth, many Christians have adopted that point of view as well. The theological task of the moment is not to observe how Christians understand death differently but rather to articulate a Christian alternative to the dominant, secular, medicalized paradigm of death and dying and to find ways to support that alternative in practice. For this task the scriptural component of the Wesleyan Quadrilateral is very helpful.

In the Old Testament, a long life was a sign of blessing from God; an early or violent death at the hands of one's enemies was a curse.[13] Death was not understood to be a supernatural force but rather a tragic part of life—one that separated us from family, community, and life itself. Life after death is rarely addressed in the Old Testament. When resurrection imagery is used (e.g., Ezekiel 37), it is typically a metaphor for the restoration of Israel as a people, not a reference to whether individual persons might find life after death. The concept of an "immortal soul" is alien to the Old Testament; rather, hope depends upon God's faithfulness to the covenant with Israel along with God's love and mercy.

Some activists for improving end-of-life care have suggested that we should see death as a natural part of life. Both scripture and Christian tradition call for a different point of view. In the book of Wisdom we read that God "created us for incorruption" (2:23). Death is not natural; it was only by sin that death entered into the world. For Christians, death is a not a neutral fact of life but rather a tragic consequence of the fall of humanity.[14] It causes real pain: physically, emotionally, and existentially. Death is something of real consequence and irretrievably part of the reality of being human.

Medical science attempts to defeat death by extending our lives indefinitely and eliminating the physical reality of death. A Christian approach to overcoming death is different. Christians believe that God has defeated death through the life, death, and

---

[11]Daniel Callahan, *The Troubled Dream of Life: In Search of a Peaceful Death* (New York: Simon & Schuster, 1993), 128.

[12]M. Therese Lysaught, "Love Your Enemies: Toward a Christoform Bioethic," in *On Moral Medicine: Theological Perspectives on Medical Ethics*, ed. M. Therese Lysaught and Joseph J. Kotva Jr. (Grand Rapids: Eerdmans, 2012), 1155.

[13]Verhey, *Christian Art of Dying*, 180.

[14]Vigen Guroian, "Learning How to Die Well: Lessons from the Ancient Church," in *On Moral Medicine: Theological Perspectives on Medical Ethics*, ed. M. Therese Lysaught and Joseph J. Kotva Jr. (Grand Rapids: Eerdmans, 2012), 1072.

resurrection of Jesus Christ. It is worth noting that when Jesus returns to his disciples after he has been raised from the dead, his body retains the marks of his violent death (Lk. 24:39; Jn 20:27). The reality of death is not removed but overcome eschatologically. Our own individual deaths remain painful and even tragic, but they are set in a new context in which Christians hope for definitive union with God beyond death. Christian hope is for a new heaven and a new earth (2 Pet. 3:13) in which we (and all of creation) will be united with God. It is a cosmic hope for a new future in which we experience the redemption made possible for us by Christ. Because the reality of death remains part of our world, and because our redemption is eschatological, Christian hope remains always intermingled with mourning. Each of us must still pass through death, and we recognize the distance between our present reality and the future for which we hope.[15]

The fact that the defeat of death takes place at the metaphysical level allows Christians to see the purpose of medicine in a new light. Medicine no longer carries the burden of being our only hope to escape death; God has accomplished that for us. Instead, medicine has the more limited purpose of supporting bodily health and flourishing.[16] Recognizing that the purpose of medicine is not to save us from death also allows room for accepting the inevitability of death and making treatment decisions that reflect the fact that dying is not something that must always be avoided at all costs.

TREATMENT DECISIONS AT THE END OF LIFE

In contexts where there is a highly developed health care infrastructure, many people face questions about whether to accept or decline life-prolonging treatments and procedures. On the one hand, Christians should recognize that their lives are gifts from God that should be cherished. Therefore, Christians have at least some moral obligation to preserve their own lives. On the other hand, Christians should recognize that it is not this mortal life but eternal life with God that is their ultimate destiny.[17] Lutheran theologian Gilbert Meilaender captured this tension well when he wrote, "Life is not our god, but a gift of God; death is a great evil, but not the ultimate evil. There may come a time, then, when it is proper to acknowledge death and cease to oppose it."[18]

These broad guidelines might be clear, but it remains difficult to prescribe precise rules about when to accept and when to refuse potentially lifesaving treatment. We can derive some guidelines from the Christian tradition, but these require application to specific patients and circumstances. In the sixteenth century, Francisco de Vitoria and his contemporaries developed a framework for making treatment decisions that remains important for Roman Catholics even today: the principles of ordinary versus extraordinary means of treatment.[19] Although typically only Catholics use this language,

---

[15]Verhey, *Christian Art of Dying*, 269.

[16]Guroian, "Learning How to Die Well," 1074.

[17]H. Tristram Engelhardt, "End of Life: The Traditional Christian View," *Lancet* 366, no. 9490 (2005): 1045.

[18]Gilbert Meilaender, *Bioethics: A Primer for Christians*, 3rd ed. (Grand Rapids: Eerdmans, 2013), 71.

[19]Kevin D. O'Rourke, "The Catholic Tradition on Forgoing Life Support," in *On Moral Medicine: Theological Perspectives on Medical Ethics*, ed. M. Therese Lysaught and Joseph J. Kotva Jr. (Grand Rapids: Eerdmans, 2012), 1118. See also Daniel Cronin, "The Moral Law in Regard to the Ordinary and Extraordinary Means of Conserving Life," in *Conserving Human Life*, ed. Russell E. Smith (Braintree: Pope John XXIII Medical-Moral Research and Educational Center, 1989); Francisco de Vitoria, OP, *On Homicide and Commentary on Summa Theologiae IIe–IIae Q. 64*, trans. John Doyle (Milwaukee: Marquette University Press, 1997).

the approach to making decisions about treatment that stands behind it is embraced more widely across the spectrum of contemporary Christianity.[20]

The fundamental insight here is that Christians should use all fitting means to maintain and preserve their lives while remaining free to refuse treatments that are not fitting or that impose an excessive burden. Treatments that are fitting and not excessively burdensome are labeled "ordinary"; those that are unfitting or excessively burdensome are labeled "extraordinary."[21] Of course, this raises the question of what is "fitting" and what constitutes an "excessive burden." Any treatment that would fail to bring meaningful benefit or hope thereof to the patient may be refused. For treatments that offer at least some benefit, consideration must be given to whether the expected benefit is outweighed by the anticipated burdens of treatment. Both the potential benefits and burdens of treatment should be considered holistically. It is likely that most treatments would bring some degree of physical benefit, but the real question is whether the treatment will facilitate a person's ability to pursue the physical, psychological, social, and spiritual goods of life.[22] Similarly, we must conceive of burdens broadly. We must take into account not only the physical burdens of treatment but also the economic, psychological, physiological, social, and spiritual costs incurred by the patient and his or her family and society.

Consideration of burdens and benefits of treatment are specific to the individual patient. For example, the benefits and burdens of dialysis would be different for someone who is also suffering from stage IV metastatic cancer than it would be for someone who is healthy apart from suffering from renal failure. Hence, decisions about treatment require the use of practical reasoning and the virtue of prudence. Prudence is suited to complex situations that call for deep discernment. A prudent person is able to situate consideration of a specific action within the context of his or her own flourishing and that of society.[23] Only with prudence can a person take into account the goods at stake as well as the contingent details of the situation and arrive at a conclusion about whether a particular treatment is "fitting" and not excessively burdensome.

ARTIFICIAL NUTRITION AND HYDRATION: A SPECIAL CASE?

For centuries, the framework of ordinary and extraordinary means has been applied to virtually all treatment decisions and has become widely used and noncontroversial in Christian circles. However, there has been some ongoing disagreement about whether these categories can be applied to decisions about the administration of artificial nutrition and hydration. Although total parenteral nutrition or "tube feedings" is relatively new, moral reflection on nutrition and hydration predates modern medicine. In the sixteenth century, theologians affirmed that food can sometimes be considered to be a form of medical care. For example, when particular foods are prescribed to restore strength and health, the tradition held that those foods could be refused if they were too burdensome

---

[20]Meilaender, *Bioethics*, 72.

[21]In more recent years, Roman Catholic magisterial documents (e.g., the 1980 *Declaration on Euthanasia*) have introduced the terms "proportionate" and "disproportionate" because the term "ordinary" was being confused with "typical" or "routine"; however, the traditional terms remain in widespread use. See O'Rourke, "Catholic Tradition on Forgoing Life Support," 1121.

[22]Ibid., 1122.

[23]Celia Deane-Drummond, "The Ethics of Assisted Dying: A Case for the Recovery of Prudence Among the Virtues," *Studies in Christian Ethics* 24, no. 4 (2011): 452–3.

to obtain or consume.[24] Despite that clear precedent in the tradition, the question of whether the administration of artificial nutrition and hydration is morally obligatory has remained controversial, particularly among Roman Catholics.

Christians affirm that human beings have intrinsic worth and must always be treated in a manner that respects their dignity as persons. Regardless of a patient's prognosis, they must be provided with "basic care" (kept clean, comfortably warm, and provided with appropriate food, water, accommodation, etc.). Some Christians have taken the moral imperative to provide basic care to mean that food and water must *always* be administered, even when a patient can no longer take water or nourishment orally. This point of view received a boost in 2004 when Pope John Paul II said that "the administration of water and food, even when provided by artificial means, always represents a *natural means* of preserving life, not a *medical act*. Its use furthermore, should be considered, in principle, *ordinary* and *proportionate*, and as such morally obligatory."[25] The extent to which this statement should be regarded as authoritative and morally binding for Catholics was a matter of considerable debate.[26] Despite the fact that it did not receive any additional papal support, the statement has proven influential, particularly when the United States Conference of Catholic Bishops incorporated some of the pope's language into the sixth edition of the *Ethical and Religious Directives for Catholic Health Care Services*, which guides operational policy for Catholic health care systems.[27]

Emerging theological consensus indicates that the position that artificial nutrition and hydration is "in principle" obligatory while acknowledging legitimate cases in which the treatment can be refused effectively means it should be judged under the same ordinary/extraordinary rubric that is used for any other treatment.[28] Providing nourishment is a form of basic care and can carry connotations of hospitality, love, and fellowship that far exceed the physical sustenance food provides. This may make it more emotionally challenging to accept a patient's wishes to discontinue nutrition and hydration, but in the end the same considerations discussed above that are applied to all treatments are appropriate. We may worry that lack of food and water might add to the suffering of the dying. However, from a clinical point of view, it is worth noting that there is no correlation between thirst and fluid intake for patients near the end of life, and offering ice chips or other comfort measures can alleviate any experience of thirst.[29]

PHYSICIAN-ASSISTED SUICIDE AND EUTHANASIA

Advances in medical science and successful public health initiatives have pushed the average lifespan higher and higher across Europe and North America. Although a longer

[24]Julia Fleming, "When Meats are like Medicines: Vitoria and Lessius on the Role of Food in the Duty to Preserve Life," *Theological Studies* 69, no. 1 (2008): 99–115.

[25]Pope John Paul II, "Address of Pope John Paul II to the Participants in the International Congress on 'Life-Sustaining Treatments and Vegetative State: Scientific Advances and Ethical Dilemmas'" (Vatican City: Libreria Editrice Vaticana, 2004), § 4, emphasis in original.

[26]Thomas A. Shannon and James J. Walter, "Assisted Nutrition and Hydration and the Catholic Church," *Theological Studies* 66, no. 3 (2005): 651–62. John J. Paris, James F. Keenan, and Kenneth R. Himes, "Quaestio Disputata: Did John Paul II's Allocution on Life-Sustaining Treatments Revise Tradition," *Theological Studies* 67, no. 1 (2006): 163–8.

[27]United States Conference of Catholic Bishops, *Ethical and Religious Directives for Catholic Health Care Services*, 6th ed. (Washington, DC: USCCB, 2018).

[28]O'Rourke, "Catholic Tradition on Forgoing Life Support," 1120.

[29]Anna Nowaska, "Clinically Assisted Hydration and the Liverpool Care Pathway: Catholic Ethics and Clinical Evidence," *Journal of Medical Ethics* 41, no. 8 (2015): 647.

life should be regarded generally to be a good thing, some people find themselves living for many years with seriously compromised physical and mental capacities. Some people experience this decline to be a great burden to bear, particularly when they require physical care or assistance carrying out the tasks of everyday life. They find their dependence on others for care to be an assault on their dignity.[30] The frustrations inherent in the loss of physical and/or mental capability are amplified by cultural factors in these regions, where autonomy is often valued very highly and where independence, accomplishment, and achievement are the criteria by which a person's worth is measured.[31] A combination of all of these factors lead some people to conclude that they would prefer to end their lives "on their own terms" by committing suicide. Euthanasia or physician-assisted suicide is already a legal option in Canada, the Netherlands, Belgium, Luxembourg, Switzerland, and some states in the United States, and there is significant public support to expand this option in the United States and Western Europe.[32]

Roman Catholic theologian Hans Küng, Reformed theologian Harry Kuitert, and others have argued that physician-assisted suicide is morally legitimate in some circumstances (e.g., when the dying person initiates the request and regards their suffering as intolerable).[33] Echoing secular proponents of physician-assisted suicide and euthanasia who stress the importance of autonomy, Küng argues that the person dying must play a central role in making decisions about their own care even to the point of choosing to put an end to their own lives. He writes, "If God makes the whole of human life a human responsibility, then this responsibility also applies to the last phase of our lives."[34] Here Küng alludes to the impossibility of "letting God decide" or allowing people to die "on God's time," because human beings are already always so intimately involved in the treatment and care of dying persons. Not acting is not necessarily more in accord with God's will than acting, and we must not conceive of God's activity exclusively in the form of supernatural interventions. For example, we would not refrain from treating pneumonia with antibiotics in order to "let God decide" whether the person should recover. Likewise, Küng might claim that when we or someone we love is facing intolerable, incurable suffering at the end of life we must act to end it; doing nothing is a failure to take responsibility for the situation, not a way of yielding to God's will or Providence or "letting God decide."

Perhaps the most forceful objections to Küng's view can be found in the *Declaration on Euthanasia*. In this document, the Roman Catholic Church's Sacred Congregation for the Doctrine of the Faith maintained that intentionally taking an innocent human life is always wrong regardless of whether it is one's own life or that of another person.[35] Furthermore, the document argued that suicide is contrary to the natural law in that it contradicts our natural instinct to live. Protestant theologian Stanley Hauerwas comes to a similar conclusion about the impermissibility of suicide and euthanasia, but by way of a different line of reasoning. He maintains that Christians must see their lives as gifts from God that we never fully possess and therefore not something over which we can exercise

[30]Timothy E. Quill, *Death and Dignity: Making Choices and Taking Charge* (New York: W. W. Norton, 1993).

[31]Toombs, "Vulnerability and the Meaning of Illness," 127.

[32]E. J. Emanuel et al., "Attitudes and Practices of Euthanasia and Physician-Assisted Suicide in the United States, Canada, and Europe," *JAMA* 316, no. 1 (2016): 79–90.

[33]Hans Küng, "A Dignified Dying," in *On Moral Medicine: Theological Perspectives on Medical Ethics*, ed. M. Therese Lysaught and Joseph J. Kotva Jr. (Grand Rapids: Eerdmans, 2012), 1093–4.

[34]Ibid., 1096.

[35]Sacred Congregation for the Doctrine of the Faith, *Declaration on Euthanasia* (Vatican City: Libreria Editrice Vaticana, 1980).

absolute control. Ending one's own life would violate our obligation to care for God's gift of life and would cause injury to our family, friends, and fellow Christians. Hauerwas envisions the church as a community of those who care for one another and who learn to accept that care in return. By caring and accepting care, people give witness to the way to be Christians in the world.[36]

Other theologians might allow that euthanasia or assisted suicide might be morally acceptable in rare cases but nevertheless maintain that the practice should remain illegal. Making assisted suicide or euthanasia an option changes the conditions under which people must navigate disability and terminal illness. Suddenly they must give reasons as to why they want to carry on living—whereas before the only question was how best to face whatever life had dealt them.[37] For those suffering from chronic, debilitating diseases that might not prove fatal for many years, assisted suicide could be more convenient and less costly than the provision of long-term care. This can exert pressure on the dying and disabled (particularly those of modest means) to choose to end their lives. Hence, many theologians reject the legalization of physician-assisted suicide on the grounds that it exposes the most vulnerable to social pressure to end their lives.

THE *ARS MORIENDI* TRADITION

In recent decades there has been a revival of interest among theologians and some medical practitioners in a more holistic approach to death and dying known as the *Ars Moriendi* or "Art of Dying" tradition. This approach has a long history in Christian tradition and practice, and it takes account of existential, social, and medical challenges that confront people at the end of life while framing dying well as a sort of art that people must learn with the support of their families, communities, and health care professionals. This source is notable because it draws deeply upon three elements of the Wesleyan Quadrilateral: experience, tradition, and scripture.

The Christian *Ars Moriendi* tradition dates back to two anonymously written texts: the *Tractatus artis bene moriendi*, which appeared in 1415, and a shorter, later work, which consisted primarily of a series of illustrations and some brief excerpts from the *Tractatus* that addressed how a dying person might face the difficulties and temptations of the deathbed.[38] These materials emerged in the wake of the Black Death when people were dying so quickly and in such large numbers that many passed away without the support of clergy.[39] They became enormously popular in the fifteenth century and were translated widely into a variety of language across Europe.

The tradition became considerably more sophisticated when some of the leading theologians of the sixteenth and seventeenth centuries wrote their own accounts of how to die well.[40] Whereas the medieval *ars moriendi* texts focused almost entirely on the

---

[36]Stanley Hauerwas, "Rational Suicide and Reasons for Living," in *On Moral Medicine: Theological Perspectives on Medical Ethics*, ed. M. Therese Lysaught and Joseph J. Kotva Jr. (Grand Rapids: Eerdmans, 2012), 1100.

[37]Allen Verhey, "Assisted Suicide and Euthanasia: A Biblical and Reformed Perspective," in *Must We Suffer Our Way to Death*, ed. Ronald P. Hamel and Edwin R. DuBose (Dallas: Southern Methodist University Press, 1996), 258.

[38]Mary Catherine O'Connor, *The Art of Dying Well: The Development of the* Ars Moriendi (New York: Columbia University Press, 1942).

[39]Lydia Dugdale, "Dying, A Lost Art," in *Dying in the Twenty-First Century: Toward a New Ethical Framework for the Art of Dying Well*, ed. Lydia Dugdale (Cambridge: MIT, 2015), 6–7.

[40]Christopher P. Vogt, *Patience, Compassion, Hope, and the Christian Art of Dying Well* (Lanham: Rowman & Littlefield, 2004), 15–51.

deathbed, offering tips to the dying about how to avoid losing faith or hope in one's final moments and giving suggestions for how those at the bedside might support the dying, the later tradition set dying into the context of a person's entire life of faith. Erasmus was among the first theologians to make this shift in his 1533 work, *Preparing for Death*, in which he maintained that the best remedy for fear of death is to seek to know and love God ever more deeply and to have faith in the promises of mercy and salvation made by God to us through Christ.[41] Various versions of the *ars moriendi* were written by theologians from virtually every Christian denomination. Among the most notable and popular Protestant works were those by Thomas Becon and William Perkins, while Robert Bellarmine authored one of the most popular and influential Roman Catholic essays.[42]

The Anglican theologian Jeremy Taylor's work, *The Rule and Exercises of Holy Dying*, is widely seen to be the most important work in this tradition and is counted among the classic texts of Western Christian spirituality.[43] Taylor's main point is that it is necessary to prepare throughout life if one is to hope to die well. A person must consciously endeavor to learn to endure suffering well and to trust in God's love and mercy. Much of his book consists of meditations and spiritual practices that are meant to help a person grow in patience, faith, hope, and other virtues. Two of the most important practices Taylor proposed were *memento mori* (remembering death) and attending to the dying. Taylor believed that a conscious awareness of one's own mortality helped keep a person focused on what is most important in life and made it easier to face death because it would never come unexpectedly. Being at the bedside of the dying was itself a practice of *memento mori* and it served the further purposes of providing support for people facing death while allowing witnesses to learn to die well by the example of friends and family who passed away before them.

LEARNING THE ART OF DYING WELL TODAY

The *ars moriendi* texts from centuries ago remain helpful and interesting, but they were written at such a historical distance that they cannot speak directly to challenges of today. They were written at a time when life after death was taken for granted, and many of them have a problematic understanding of death and human suffering as things willed by God that people must learn to accept gladly.[44] Furthermore, some theologians take issue with the fact that they were at times more influenced by the Stoics and platonic philosophy than the scriptures.[45] Nevertheless, many theologians and medical practitioners agree that an updated version of the *ars moriendi* is a promising approach to death and dying for the twenty-first century.

---

[41]Desiderius Erasmus, *Preparing for Death* (*De praeparatione ad mortem*), trans. John N. Grant, in *Spiritualia and Pastoralia*, *Collected Works of Erasmus* v. 70, ed. John W. O'Malley (Toronto: University of Toronto Press, 1998), 389–450.

[42]Thomas Becon, "The Sicke Man's Salve," and William Perkins, "A Salve for a Sicke Man," in *The English Ars Moriendi*, ed. David W. Atkinson (New York: Lang, 1992), 87–163. Robert Bellarmine, *The Art of Dying Well*, in *Robert Bellarmine: Spiritual Writings*, trans. and ed. John Patrick Donnelly and Roland J. Teske (New York: Paulist, 1989).

[43]Jeremy Taylor, *Holy Living and Holy Dying*, vol. 2: *Holy Dying*, ed. P. G. Stanwood (Oxford: Clarendon, 1989).

[44]Vogt, *Patience, Compassion, Hope*, 39–42.

[45]Verhey, *Christian Art of Dying*, 91–9. Vogt offers a more sympathetic reading in *Patience, Compassion, Hope*, 15–39.

Lydia Dugdale is a leading advocate for a new, secular *ars moriendi* that is grounded in bioethics. She argues that an exclusively Christian *ars moriendi* is inadequate for today given the wide diversity of religious identities and the growing percentage of people with no religious affiliation at all. She highlights two primary dimensions of the contemporary task of dying well: coming to terms with human finitude (a task with different dimensions for individuals, medical practitioners, and society) and connecting patients to communities of support so that they can be accompanied in their dying.[46] Lysaught echoes those goals of connecting patients to communities and coming to terms with finitude, but she questions whether they can be achieved within the framework of contemporary bioethics. Any practices that might be developed to help people face the ordeals of dying cannot exist apart from a broader set of rituals, beliefs, virtues, and practices that are cultivated across a person's lifetime.[47]

Allen Verhey attempted to provide a twenty-first-century version of the *ars moriendi* in his 2011 book, *The Christian Art of Dying: Learning from Jesus*. Verhey combined a rich, biblically based theology of death with a critique and retrieval of the *ars moriendi* tradition. He describes some of the virtues (faith, hope, love, patience, humility, courage) that must be developed during one's lifetime if one is to hope to die well, and names some of the practices that help a person grow in those virtues (prayer, scriptural reflection, worship, etc.), but the book remains more of a work about how to develop an *ars moriendi* than an actual handbook for dying persons. Furthermore, his approach does not adequately take into account the many people who fade away over time rather than passing through a defined dying process. How to meet the difficult challenges of Alzheimer's disease or other forms of loss of mental capacity, for example, is not addressed.[48] Hence, the challenge to develop a comprehensive, holistic, Christian approach to dying well remains a task for the current generation and those that follow to take up.

SUGGESTED READINGS

Dugdale, Lydia, ed. *Dying in the Twenty-First Century: Toward a New Ethical Framework for the Art of Dying Well.* Cambridge: MIT, 2015.

Evans, Abigail Rian. *Is God Still at the Bedside? The Medical, Ethical, and Pastoral Issues of Death and Dying.* Grand Rapids: Eerdmans, 2011.

Lysaught, M. Therese, and Joseph J. Kotva Jr., eds. *On Moral Medicine: Theological Perspectives on Medical Ethics.* Grand Rapids: Eerdmans, 2012.

Verhey, Allen. *The Christian Art of Dying: Learning from Jesus.* Grand Rapids: Eerdmans, 2011.

Vogt, Christopher P. *Patience, Compassion, Hope, and the Christian Art of Dying Well.* Lanham: Rowman & Littlefield, 2004.

[46]Lydia S. Dugdale, "Conclusion: Toward a New Ethical Framework for the Art of Dying Well," in *Dying in the Twenty-First Century: Toward a New Ethical Framework for the Art of Dying Well*, ed. Lydia Dugdale (Cambridge: MIT, 2015), 178–87.

[47]M. Therese Lysaught, "Ritual and Practice," in *Dying in the Twenty-First Century: Toward a New Ethical Framework for the Art of Dying Well*, ed. Lydia Dugdale (Cambridge: MIT, 2015), 69.

[48]Michael Banner, "Scripts for Modern Dying: The Death before Death We Have Invented, the Death before Death We Fear and Some Take Too Literally, and the Death before Death Christians Believe in," *Studies in Christian Ethics* 29, no. 3 (2016): 249–55.

CHAPTER THIRTY-TWO

Assisted Reproductive Technologies and Genetics

KARA N. SLADE

As an Episcopal priest active in parish ministry, I have been asked many times what my church teaches about assisted reproductive technology and genetic testing. Often the question comes from couples who are struggling with infertility or worried about a high-risk pregnancy. While official Catholic teaching on assisted reproduction and genetic testing is clear, mainline Protestants and evangelicals are often left wondering how to navigate these questions, with little or no guidance coming from their own ecclesial contexts until they find themselves in a moral dilemma. But this is much too late and too far downstream from the theological, moral, and cultural questions that technological interventions at the beginning of life pose. It is not sufficient to parse the hypothetical and decontextualized acceptability of *in vitro* fertilization or of prenatal genetic testing. Rather, moral formation around these topics should take place much further upstream, as a regular part of the church's proclamation and teaching, such that parishioners are already habituated to take the right things for granted. An interrogation of reproductive technologies must start further upstream as well, considering the cultural "smoke in the room" that forms the default moral environment within which the church is called to witness to the gospel of Christ. Karl Barth explains this in his *Church Dogmatics*:

> It is one of the consolations of the coming kingdom and expiring time that this anxiety about posterity, that the burden of the postulate that we should and must bear children, heirs of our blood and name and honour and wealth, that the pressure and bitterness and tension of this question, if not the question itself, is removed from us all by the fact that the Son on whose birth alone everything seriously and ultimately depended has now been born and has now become our Brother. No one now has to be conceived and born. We need not expect any other than the One of whose coming we are certain because He is already come. Parenthood is now only to be understood as a free and in some sense optional gift of the goodness of God.[1]

Two examples may be illustrative as we further interrogate these questions.

The first is an advertisement that appeared, among other places, in the concourse of the Newark airport, where it brought me to a stop in the middle of a bustling crowd. In the large poster, a blond-haired girl is standing against the door frame for her obviously

[1]Karl Barth, *Church Dogmatics*, vol. 3, pt. 4, *The Doctrine of Creation* (Edinburgh: T&T Clark, 1969), 266.

adoring young father to mark her height. I vividly recall my own father doing the same thing in my childhood home. The caption read, "You can measure hope: Learn more about our 72% IVF delivery rate." The clinic sponsoring the advertisement, a regional reproductive medicine practice, bills itself as "The source for new beginnings."[2] It takes little imagination to read the theological valences of advertisements such as this one. In what is our hope placed, and how did that hope become something to be quantified, measured, packaged, and marketed for its success rate? And what sort of "new beginning" is being marketed?

The second example comes from the burgeoning market for commercial genetic testing. One advertisement for a popular consumer testing service, AncestryDNA, featured the story of "Kyle," an American who was raised to believe that his family came to the United States from Germany. As an enthusiastic German-American, Kyle wore lederhosen and participated in a German dance group. With the help of AncestryDNA, however, Kyle discovered that his DNA made him Scottish, so he replaced his lederhosen with a kilt—and, one assumes, a new constellation of cultural practices. Kyle's story is a figment of the advertiser's imagination, but the same conflation of genetics and culture can be found in a new collaboration between the streaming music service Spotify and AncestryDNA. As the website states, Spotify can generate a Spotify playlist based on your genetic results:

> With an AncestryDNA test you can discover more about yourself—from learning your ethnicity to connecting with distant relatives. And now your AncestryDNA results can play a unique Spotify mix of music, inspired by your origins.[3]

This conflation of genetics and culture is but the most egregious example of a broader phenomenon in which genetic information is presumed to be determinative for what it means to be human. DNA promises to unlock the human past, present, and future. It purports to explain where we come from, to shape our lives in the present, and to determine our future.

Underlying both examples is a deep optimism in the human capacity to improve our own lot and a faith in progress to perfect the vulnerabilities and frailties of human life. My aim in this brief chapter is not only to review the state of moral conversations around assisted reproductive technologies and genetics. Rather, I intend as well to invite Christian readers to ask deeper questions about the quality and source of the hope promised by these technologies.

GENETIC TESTING AS A TECHNOLOGY OF VISION

The casual reader engaging the subject of genetics and ethics for the first time may be first drawn to the most familiar, and most contentious, medical application for genetic information: prenatal genetic testing for fetal abnormality. At once, the technology raises the question of providing information in the absence of guidance toward a response, information that creates a social apparatus that can tend toward intervention, up to and including termination of the pregnancy. In other words, visible and invisible structures of power interact so that a particular end is favored and may seem to be an inevitable matter

---

[2]Although an online version of this advertisement may no longer be available, see this blog for something similar from said clinic: https://rmanetwork.com/blog/coping-infertility-and-the-holidays/.

[3]"If You Could Listen to Your DNA, What Would It Sound Like?," Ancestry.com, https://www.ancestry.com/cs/spotify.

of common sense.[4] It invites an intervention for suffering that is intended to eliminate the sufferer. The question of genetics has been captured by that of prenatal genetic testing and particularly around selective termination in cases of disability. Certainly, this is an important moral problem, even as it has been enfolded in the American culture wars around abortion to the extent that the deeper issues posed by the ready availability of genetic information can be obscured.

For Catholic, Orthodox, or conservative evangelical Christians, the impermissibility of abortion may mark prenatal testing impermissible but leaves much unsaid about other applications of genetic information. For mainline Protestants in churches like my own, the entire question of genetics tends to exist inside a faith in knowledge, expertise, and progress, coupled with a reticence to make morally normative statements on this issue. For example, the General Convention of the Episcopal Church passed a resolution on abortion that describes human life as "sacred from its inception until death" and that states "we emphatically oppose abortion as a means of birth control, family planning, sex selection, or any reason of mere convenience."[5] And yet, when discussing prenatal testing, Episcopal ethicists have sometimes been noncommittal, arguing that "individuals need to be free to make their own decisions—and their own mistakes," even as they admit that advocacy for genetic testing comes from a subset of the population, "people who value knowledge, who have worked hard for their achievements and delayed having children, and who are ambitious in the sense of having hopes and aspirations for their children."[6] Unfortunately, this argument speaks directly to the aspirations of middle- to upper-middle-class populations from which the Episcopal Church draws many of its adherents. The notion of the well-planned family, and of meticulously controlled reproduction, all too easily becomes enmeshed with that of the financially and socially mobile family.

Rather than directly approach the question of genetic testing and intervention from the standpoint of autonomous decision making or the permissibility of particular tests or interventions, such as germ-line treatment, this chapter addresses at first instance the knowledge promised by these technologies as well as the anthropology that is constructed by such knowledge. Who is the human being revealed through genetic information? And what is the nature of that revelation? Here, the work of Michel Foucault can be helpful in unpacking the situation. Writing in *Birth of the Clinic*, Foucault traces the historical development of medical knowledge of the human in terms of vision, of the "visible invisible."[7] The history of the medical gaze is the history of seeing ever deeper into the body, and in so doing to know its death as well as its life: "The Gaze that envelops, caresses, details, atomizes, the most individual flesh and enumerates its secret bites is that fixed, attentive, rather dilated gaze which, from the height of death, has already condemned life."[8] And it is death that is "constitutive of singularity," that constitutes the individual in his or her uniqueness.[9] As Foucault writes,

[4]Giorgio Agamben, "What Is an Apparatus?," in *What Is an Apparatus? And Other Essays*, trans. David Kishik and Stefan Pedatella (Stanford: Stanford University Press, 2009), 2.
[5]General Convention of the Episcopal Church, "Resolution C047," *Journal of the General Convention of the Episcopal Church, Indianapolis, 1994* (New York: General Convention, 1995), 323–5, https://www.episcopalarchives.org/cgi-bin/acts/acts_resolution.pl?resolution=1994-A054.
[6]Mary T. White, "The Many Facets of Genetic Testing," in *A Christian Response to the New Genetics: Religious, Ethical, and Social Issues*, ed. David Smith and Cynthia Cohen (Oxford: Rowman & Littlefield, 2003), 41.
[7]Michel Foucault, *The Birth of the Clinic*, trans. A. M. Sheridan Smith (New York: Vintage, 1994), 170.
[8]Ibid., 171.
[9]Ibid.

> It is in the perception of death that the individual finds himself escaping from a monotonous, average life; in the slow, half-subterranean, but already invisible approach of death, the dull, common life becomes an individuality at last; a black border isolates it and gives it the style of its own truth.[10]

The promise posed by genetic information is the ultimate instantiation of the process of making disease visible and thus discovering the truth of the body. Moreover, it is in this knowledge that the self is constituted *as a self*. What does it mean, for example, that the direct-to-consumer genetic testing service 23andMe offers two categories of testing: one to assess the risk of disease and carrier status, and one for ancestry? Genetic testing promises the past as well as the future. It promises the past, to give its customers a story of genetically determined ancestry and thus a culture. And it promises the future, as an assessment of propensity for disease and in anticipation of the corpse that we all one day will become. It promises control through knowledge and technological progress. It promises to give us ourselves.

And yet the givens upon which these promises are based are not givens at all. It is instead a part of what Gerald McKenny calls the "Baconian project" to "relieve the human condition" of "misery and necessity" through technological means.[11] The Baconian project promises to minimize human suffering, if not to provide a means of liberation from human limitation itself:

> This project of technological control over nature (including the human body) and a moral commitment to relieve suffering by preventing the harms and eliminating all the conditions and limitations that threaten bodily life accounts for a large part of the nature and task of medicine in the modern era.[12]

In McKenny's account, modernity encompasses not only this attack on suffering in all its forms but also includes the effort of the self to constitute itself as a self, to narrate our own stories as autonomous individuals and thus to create our own fulfillment through that individuality. As he explains,

> A second aspect of the modern moral framework is what [Charles] Taylor calls inwardness. Inwardness has deep Augustinian and Cartesian roots, but during the Romantic period it surfaced in the inner conviction of the importance of one's own natural fulfillment. The idea is not only that each individual is unique and original but that this uniqueness and originality determines how he or she ought to live. There is an obligation (more aesthetic than moral) for each person to live up to his or her originality.[13]

Under late capitalism, both medicine and the project of self-generated meaning have been captured and monetized. The knowledge of what makes us unique, and thus the raw material of self-created meaning, is what is often for sale along with our genetic information.

---

[10]Ibid.
[11]Gerald McKenny, *To Relieve the Human Condition* (New York: State University of New York Press, 1997), 19.
[12]Ibid.
[13]Ibid., 19–20. See Charles Taylor, *The Sources of the Self: The Making of the Modern Identity* (Cambridge: Cambridge University Press, 1989), 370–6.

ANXIETY AND POSTERITY

If genetic testing offers us knowledge of our past and future, and indirect control by means of that knowledge, then assisted reproductive technologies offer a vision of direct control of the human future. As seen in the airport advertisement, it offers a quantifiable and measurable sort of hope. Most moral-theological thinking around assisted reproductive technologies has focused on two issues: the severing of the sexual act from conception and thus procreation, as well as the creation of excess embryos in the process of *in vitro* fertilization.

Addressing the first instance, Sidney Callahan notes that the conservative analysis that focuses on the integrity of "lovemaking and babymaking," the unity of the sexual act and procreation, is mirrored by a liberal analysis that also focuses on acts. In the liberal framework, this moral calculus focuses on "a person's desire for a child and the individual acts a person might perform in carrying out private arrangements for reproduction."[14] In both instances, the individual act is the focus of moral deliberation and as such may be severed from its social and cultural contexts—both in the sense of occurring within a community and tradition and in the sense of existing within a particular cultural matrix. For Christians, the ecclesial community is called to remind its members that even the most intimate of decisions are not individual, autonomous decisions. Rather, they are made in community. For example, a couple's discernment around in vitro fertilization (IVF), foster parenting, or adoption occurs in the context of the church's promise at baptism to support a child in their life in Christ, and indeed to be family to them through sacramental, Christological kinship.

At the same time, cultural and structural factors, especially those that surround the status of women, also play a role in how assisted reproduction is perceived, developed, and marketed as the locus of hope. As Allen Verhey notes, "Patriarchy always risks reducing women to their reproductive capacities." But, as he continues, "the 'power of God' will make itself felt when the relations of men and women are not governed by patriarchal marriage laws nor by a man's need to secure for himself a name and an heir but by the mutuality and equality that belongs to God's good future."[15] In other words, a Christian account of reproduction involves both partners equally. It is not incumbent on women to provide for men a secure future through heredity, and women are not defined by their capacity to bear children. As the next section will discuss, the future for men and women alike is grounded elsewhere.

LIVING FROM THE MIDDLE

Matters of family are in a deep sense matters of time. Part of thinking *otherwise* about the moral challenges posed by genetics and assisted reproductive technology is thinking otherwise about time—about past and future alike, and particularly about our modern human anxiety around the question of origins. Yet Christian thinking around time seems inextricably enmeshed with our thinking of, around, and before our own beginnings in both the philosophical and biological sense. Where else can we begin but the beginning,

---

[14]Sidney Callahan, "The Ethical Challenge of the New Reproductive Technology," in *Medical Ethics: A Guide for Health Professionals*, ed. John F. Monagle and David C. Thomasma (Rockville: Aspen, 1988), 26–37.

[15]Allen Verhey, "A.R.T., Ethics, and the Bible," in *Reading the Bible in the Strange World of Medicine* (Grand Rapids: Eerdmans, 2003), 253–404.

even as it constantly tempts us to secure our own position by thinking behind it? Where else can our story begin, if not in our genetic origins? And how else can our story continue in the future, if not through biological heredity?

As Dietrich Bonhoeffer noted in his exegesis of Genesis 1, human thought "pounds itself to pieces" on a beginning that it both "wants and cannot want power to attain."[16] Yet he continues by explaining that the Christian life in time is not a matter of securing the beginning but of living from the middle. In that temporal middle, we receive both our beginning and our end from the crucified and risen Christ, and only from Christ, in the Paschal event.

A similar form of argument can be found in the work of Karl Barth. While *Church Dogmatics* III/2 is concerned with the doctrine of creation, Barth's consideration of human existence in time proceeds from not from Genesis 1 but from the time of God through and in Jesus Christ. The exegetical hinge of § 47 is Heb. 13:8, "Jesus Christ is the same yesterday, today, and forever." As Barth explains, both this verse and his theological reflection on creaturely existence in time hinges on cross and resurrection, in which "Jesus Christ belongs not only to yesterday, or to-day, or an indefinite future" but rather "belongs to all times simultaneously." As a result, he "is the same Christ in all of them," and "there is no time which does not belong to him." Jesus Christ "really is the Lord of time."[17]

At the beginning the next section (§ 48, "Given Time"), Barth explains that a theological consideration of our time as human beings can only proceed from this basis:

> The subject of our enquiry is the being of man in his time. In order to see man in his time correctly, we have investigated the being of the man Jesus in his time. To do this, we had to start with the revelation of the being of this man in His resurrection from the dead. This enabled us to see His being as that of the Lord of time, and His time as the fulfillment of all time, which, as His own time, extends backwards and embraces all prior time as its beginning, the beginning of all time, and extends forwards and embraces all subsequent time as its end, the end of all time.[18]

As this fullness of time in Jesus Christ embraces our time, it gives our time back to us again, no longer as a possession to be grasped but as a gift.

Then, in the next subsection of § 47, Barth expands on this notion as he describes time in terms of gift. While discussions of time as gift are fairly common in theological discourse, Barth is distinguished by making this gift completely determined in and by Christ, rather than in or by the creative act of God in itself. As he writes, "The existence of the man Jesus in time is our guarantee that time as the form of human existence is in any case willed and created by God, is given by God to man, and is therefore real."[19] Human existence in time is, for Barth, a continuous positive act of divine preservation:

> Surprising as it is, it is to the free grace of God in Jesus Christ that we owe the fact that the nature in which we were created, and from which we have fallen by falling away from God, is not taken away from us, but is maintained and preserved; that in spite

[16]Dietrich Bonhoeffer, *Creation and Fall (Dietrich Bonhoeffer Works Vol. 3)*, trans. Douglas Stephen Bax (Minneapolis: Fortress, 1997), 26.

[17]Karl Barth, *Church Dogmatics*, vol. 3, pt. 2, *The Doctrine of Creation* (Peabody: Hendrickson, 2010), 466.

[18]Ibid., 511–12.

[19]Ibid., 520.

> of the falsehood in which we have become involved we may be genuinely in time and have true and genuine time.[20]

Determined by and in Christ, the time which is given to human beings takes on a new and different significance as the form of human existence.[21] To be human is to be in time, but to be a human being in Christ is to live in time but not as a captive to time. As the Lord of time, Jesus "stands at the beginning of all our attempted thinking about time, ruling and establishing, illuminating and proving."[22] At this beginning stands the end of all "false and cheerless conceptions of time."[23]

As Christians, we receive both our past and future, our identity and our posterity, from Christ in baptism. Moral discernment around genetics and assisted reproduction, of the direction of the biological past and future, is too often posed as a matter of casuistry alone. Yet these questions also involve our beginnings and our endings, our attempts to grasp our time and turn it toward some end. Seen from this perspective, perhaps we can begin to more fully interrogate the questions behind the question of whether or not a particular technology may faithfully be used. Who benefits from the provision of self-generated subjectivity in a capitalist society? Who profits from the packaging of hope? In what, or in whom, does our hope lie? This point, the fixed point of Jesus Christ in whom our hope truly rests and our time is truly made hopeful, is where our discernment begins.

SUGGESTED READINGS

Hall, Amy Laura. *Conceiving Parenthood: American Protestantism and the Spirit of Reproduction*. Grand Rapids: Eerdmans, 2016.

McKenny, Gerald. *Biotechnology, Human Nature, and Christian Ethics*. Cambridge: Cambridge University Press, 2018.

McKenny, Gerald. *To Relieve the Human Condition: Bioethics, Technology, and the Body*. New York: State University of New York Press, 1997.

O'Donovan, Oliver. *Begotten or Made? Human Procreation and Medical Technique*. Oxford: Clarendon, 1984.

[20]Ibid.

[21]Ibid., 552.

[22]Ibid.

[23]Ibid.

CHAPTER THIRTY-THREE

Health Inequities Are Killing Us: Christians Better Show Up

AANA MARIE VIGEN

Does the phrase "medical ethics" bring to mind topics like CRISPR, artificial reproduction, physician-assisted suicide, and abortion? If so, it's not surprising given how many headlines in medicine and bioethics (especially before, but also in the era of Covid-19) focus on moral questions related to emerging medical technologies, innovations in diagnosis and treatment, the sanctity of life, and human autonomy. For me, what consistently stands out is inequality—pervasive, unjust, ugly. I picture faces of people, disproportionately Black and Brown, who too often receive too little and/or anemic care. Entrenched racial-ethnic and socioeconomic disparities pose a strong rebuke to any celebrated successes in medical performance or innovation. Indeed, I argue that pursuing excellence without an equal passion for equity is a moral catastrophe. And it is one with which far too few ethicists, people of faith, health care professionals, and policy makers have reckoned. On too many tables of contents of medical ethics texts, "health disparities" constitutes one chapter or a relatively small section of a much larger volume. That needs to change. Health and health care inequity are *not* simply a topic among others in medicine and ethics; rather, it is *a central theme* that runs through most (if not all) of them.

Moreover, too often we discuss medical topics in a vacuum—divorcing them from integral and particular social, economic, racial-ethnic, gendered, cultural, and religious contexts. To be sure, many of the technologies that improve the care of some also serve as yet another line in the divide between those with sufficient access to them and those without. In short, we need to rethink *how* we think about bioethics. Thankfully, incisive recent works such as *Catholic Bioethics & Social Justice* are beginning to contribute exactly this kind of analysis.[1]

When I confront the depth and breadth of health inequities, I often feel forlorn. In such moments, I try to remember to pray and voice my distress. Prayers and practices of lament are integral to both Jewish and Christian traditions. Over sixty of the 150 biblical psalms—composed and first sung and prayed by Jews—are laments. These Psalms have become central to the spiritual and moral lives of generations of diverse

---

[1]M. Therese Lysaught and Michael McCarthy, eds., *Catholic Bioethics and Social Justice: The Praxis of US Health Care in a Globalized World* (Collegeville: Liturgical, 2018).

Christians—persecuted, monastic, enslaved, and myriad others—who feel gutted by all that overwhelms them. When I pray, I take a cue from Anne Lamott, who distills the essence of prayer to three words: *Help, Thanks, Wow*[2] (often leaning on the first one). And in moments of acute worry, I listen to music that evokes lament, such as "Calling All Angels" by Jane Siberry.[3]

Here is a snapshot of what troubles me: Regardless of education attained, socioeconomic class, or profession, "a black woman is 22 percent more likely to die from heart disease than a white woman, 71 percent more likely to perish from cervical cancer, but 243 percent more likely to die from pregnancy- or childbirth-related causes."[4] Hispanic, Native American, Alaskan Native, and/or Black people in the United States are at a disproportionately higher risk of being uninsured and they suffer from poorer health and health care outcomes than their white counterparts.[5] Nationally, patients of color experience less positive patient-provider relations than non-Hispanic white patients.[6] On average, Black people live 3.5 fewer years than white people.[7]

Moreover, in resource-stressed contexts—*both* in parts of the United States and around the world—millions of people struggle to access high-quality medical care. Far too many lack access to clean water and affordable, nutritious food. Most urgently, millions (again predominately Black and Brown peoples)—those that have contributed the least to climate change—are already living on its front lines. They disproportionately confront the loss of their homes, livelihoods, sources of food, and increases in climate-related diseases, such as cholera and malaria.

To be sure, thanks to the tireless efforts of professionals in primary care, public and global health, and so on, progress has been made in several important arenas. There are positive trends in several infectious diseases, especially diarrheal disease, TB, and HIV-AIDS.[8] Globally, the average life expectancy has gone up. Yet, systemic inequalities deeply undercut so many efforts and good intentions.

In what follows, I wish to do three things: unpack some of the most alarming and pernicious inequities; explain why climate change is, *by far*, the most pressing human health crisis we face; and briefly offer a few thoughts on how Christian ethics might help us to move through lament to creative action. We must not shrink from the daunting challenges before us. We need to build resilient moral sinews. The dire times in which we now live demand that we cultivate tangible, vibrant, and tenacious ways to show up with grit and vision.

---

[2]Anne Lamott, *Help, Thanks, Wow: The Three Essential Prayers* (London: Hodder & Stoughton, 2001).

[3]Jane Siberry, "Calling All Angels" (Burbank: Reprise Records, 1991).

[4]Nina Martin and Renee Montagne, "Nothing Prevents Black Women from Dying in Pregnancy and Childbirth," *ProPublica*, December 7, 2017.

[5]Kendal Orgera and Samantha Artiga, "Disparities in Health and Health Care: Five Key Questions and Answers," KFF, August 8, 2018, https://www.kff.org/disparities-policy/issue-brief/disparities-in-health-and-health-care-five-key-questions-and-answers/. See also Samantha Artiga et al., "Key Facts on Health and Health Care by Race and Ethnicity," Kaiser Family Foundation, June 7, 2016.

[6]Nynikka R. A. Palmer et al., "Racial and Ethnic Disparities in Patient-Provider Communication, Quality of Care Ratings, and Patient Activation among Long-Term Cancer Survivors," *Journal of Clinical Oncology* 32, no. 36 (2014): 4087–94.

[7]Elizabeth Arias, Melonie Heron, and Jiaquan Xu, "United States Life Tables, 2014," *National Vital Statistics Reports* 66, no. 4 (2017): 4.

[8]"The Top 10 Causes of Death," World Health Organization, May 24, 2018, http://www.who.int/news-room/fact-sheets/detail/the-top-10-causes-of-death. See also 2016 data: "Life Expectancy Data," World Health Organization, https://www.who.int/gho/mortality_burden_disease/life_tables/situation_trends_text/en/.

EXAMPLES OF EGREGIOUS INEQUITIES

I find it helpful to describe health and health care in high-income contexts versus low- or middle-income contexts rather than frame the distinction solely as one between United States versus global realities. There are, of course, critical differences between many aspects of US health care when compared with any other nation, each with its own specific health care systems and challenges. Yet, it is also true that there are significant pockets within the United States where particular communities suffer from similar anemic health care as someone living in a less affluent country. And in some pockets of the two-thirds world, certain people are increasingly able to access high-quality care that results in good outcomes when they live close to well-developed medical services and have the requisite social and economic capital.

In short, the specific social, economic, racial contexts in which a given person or community lives, works, grows, learns, and plays—*the social determinants of health*—strongly influence how healthy they are, how long they live, and what health problems they face.[9] For example, in the United States, one's zip code can often predict life expectancy. The difference can be as much as twenty years.[10] The harsh irony is that we in the United Sates have both a system in which some may enjoy excessive access to nearly everything that money/insurance can buy (even when it does not improve health outcomes), while others—living in the same city or just a zip code away—have far too little access to both effective preventive and therapeutic interventions.[11]

Again, overall, human beings are living longer than in prior decades.[12] However, the mortality picture changes significantly when we specifically compare high income to low income contexts.[13] Indeed, while we will all die, some of us, depending on specific social locations, are at a much higher risk of dying from infectious, transmissible diseases than others—diseases that are both highly preventable and treatable as long as effective health infrastructures are in place. Consider maternal health: the World Health Organization (WHO) reports that "only 51% of women in low-income countries benefit from skilled care during childbirth" and that over three hundred thousand women die every year due to complications from childbirth.[14] These maternal deaths occur disproportionately in resource-stressed contexts. For decades, physician Paul Farmer and others have termed the high rates of premature (meaning preventable) death as "stupid deaths" because we have both the know-how and resources to prevent them.[15]

---

[9]"Social Determinants of Health: Know What Affects Health," Centers for Disease Control and Prevention, Social Determinants of Health, https://www.cdc.gov/socialdeterminants/ (accessed January 29, 2018).

[10]For overall data on life expectancy, see Arias, Heron, and Xu, "United States Life Tables, 2014," 1–63. More specifically, see Laura Dwyer-Lindgren et al., "Inequalities in Life Expectancy among US Counties, 1980 to 2014: Temporal Trends and Key Drivers," *JAMA Internal Medicine* 177, no. 7 (2017): 1003–11. Discussed on NPR's All Things Considered: "Life Expectancy Can Vary by Twenty Years Based on Where You Live," *NPR*, May 8, 2017. See also this interactive tool: "Could Where You Live Influence How Long You Live," Robert Wood Johnson Foundation, https://www.rwjf.org/en/library/interactives/whereyouliveaffectshowlongyoulive.html#.

[11]Aana Marie Vigen, "Loving God and the Neighbor," in *Prevention vs. Treatment: What's the Right Balance?*, ed. Halley S. Faust and Paul T. Menzel (Oxford: Oxford University Press, 2012), 321–8.

[12]Global Health Estimates 2016: Deaths by Cause, Age, Sex, by Country and by Region, 2000–2016 (Geneva: World Health Organization, 2018), http://www.who.int/news-room/fact-sheets/detail/the-top-10-causes-of-death.

[13]See World Health Organization, "The Top 10 Causes of Death." See also Neil Emery, "How the World Gets Sick and Dies," *The Atlantic*, January 24, 2013.

[14]"10 Facts on Maternal Health," World Health Organization, November 2015, https://www.who.int/features/factfiles/maternal_health/en/.

[15]Paul Farmer, *Pathologies of Power: Health, Human Rights, and the New War on the Poor* (Berkeley: University of California Press, 2003), 144.

Furthermore, the problem is *not only* insufficient access to care but also poor-*quality* care. In 2018, *The Lancet* published findings from a major two-year international study[16] that estimates that "5 million people die every year because of poor-quality health care in low- and middle-income countries. That's significantly more than the 3.6 million people in those countries who die from not having access to care."[17] Why do these additional deaths occur? Even when people do see a doctor or other health care professional, the provider too often fails or is otherwise unable to follow up on recommended clinical actions and/or take sufficient time with patients to assess the problem. There can also be long delays between the time patients initially seek help and when they receive a diagnosis, let alone treatment. In sum, *both equity in access* and *consistently high-quality care* must be provided.

How do we define quality? In an interview, Margaret Kruk, a co-commissioner of the 2018 *Lancet* study, elucidates:

> Quality is about three things. One is effective care that can improve or maintain health. The second is about earning the trust of people. The third is that systems have to adapt and adjust. That means a quick adjustment when there's an outbreak but also the ability to change over time ... About 1 in 3 patients consistently has a poor experience of care. Disrespectful care, extremely short visits, poor communication, long wait times. Many parents—40 to 50 percent—leave the clinic without knowing the child's diagnosis.[18]

Can you imagine receiving consistently disappointing care but not having other options? Have you ever left a medical appointment unsure of a diagnosis or what the providers meant? Millions routinely negotiate such hurdles. These facts ought to sting. Particularly for Christians who place a high premium on notions of intrinsic human dignity and the love of God and neighbor, honest grappling with health care inequity is *not* an elective. Such work is at the very center of Christian responsibility.

Before turning to the health effects of climate change, I want to unpack three interrelated, root causes of inequity that manifest in distinct ways in the United States. First is insurance. Even after the passage of the Affordable Care Act (ACA/Obamacare), whose future remains precarious,[19] significant numbers of people remain uninsured.[20] US communities of color "make up 42% of the *overall* nonelderly US population but account for over half [55 percent] of the total nonelderly *uninsured* population [32.3 million]."[21]

---

[16]Margaret E. Kruk et al., "Mortality Due to Low-Quality Health Systems in the Universal Health Coverage Area: A Systematic Analysis of Amenable Deaths in 137 Countries," *Lancet* 392, no. 10160 (2018): 2203–12.
[17]Melody Schreiber, "What Kills 5 Million People a Year? It's Not Just a Disease," *NPR*, September 5, 2018.
[18]Ibid.
[19]There are ongoing efforts to resume limits or denials of coverage for people with preexisting conditions. See Sabrina Corlette, Maanasa Kona, and Justin Giovannelli, "Lawsuit Threatens Affordable Care Act Preexisting Condition But Impact Will Depend on Where You Live," The Commonwealth Fund, August 29, 2018; Rachel Fehr et al., "Mapping Pre-existing Conditions Across the U.S.," Kaiser Family Foundation, August 28, 2018.
[20]Rachel Garfield, Kendal Orgera, and Anthony Damico, "The Uninsured and the ACA: A Primer—Key Facts about Health Insurance and the Uninsured amidst Changes to the Affordable Care Act," Kaiser Family Foundation, January 25, 2019. It is important to note that even those with insurance are still shocked by the costs of their medical care, e.g.: Alison Kodjak, "Surprised by A Medical Bill? Join the Club. Most Americans Say They Have Been," *NPR*, September 2, 2018.
[21]Emphasis added. Artiga et al., "Key Facts on Health." Moreover, "Hispanics and Blacks have significantly higher nonelderly uninsured rates (17% and 12%, respectively) than Whites (8%)." "Differences in coverage by race/ethnicity likely reflect a combination of factors, including language and immigration barriers, income and work status, and state of residence." Garfield, Orgera, and Damico, "Uninsured and the ACA."

Living without insurance has tangible, deleterious effects: delaying seeking care, going without needed medications, not having a regular health care provider, defaulting to the Emergency Department for care and at a later stage of disease.[22] Latinos, Blacks, Native Americans, and Alaska Natives are all more likely to delay seeking care or simply go without it than their white counterparts.[23]

Second, while there are both gaps in the data and also mixed data for Hispanics and Asians, it is fair to say that some communities—especially Black, Native American, and certain Asian and Hispanic populations—suffer from poorer health and worse outcomes when treating chronic disease than white and other select Asian populations.[24] To illustrate the scope, according to the Kaiser Family Foundation, 17 percent of Black children have asthma as compared with 10 percent of whites. Hispanic, Native American/Alaska Native, and Black individuals all have higher rates of diabetes than whites. Black people have higher rates of cancer and heart disease than whites. Twice as many Native Americans/ Alaska Natives have had a heart attack or have heart disease as compared with whites. The HIV death rate for Black people is eight times higher than for white people.[25] While many US inhabitants suffer from inadequate mental health services, Black and Brown people are at a particularly high risk of receiving no or poor quality care.[26] Racial-ethnic disparities persist to end-of-life care.[27]

Third is the complicated reality of racial privilege and stereotypes. Implicit biases and stereotypes are woven into the fabric of US society. Many white Americans struggle to accept this unflattering portrait because we profess to be egalitarian-minded and claim to be "color-blind." Health care providers take, and take very seriously, an oath to treat all patients equally. Yet, it is quite possible to be both well-intentioned and to act, often unwittingly, in ways that reflect bias and apply generalized stereotypes to discrete individuals.

As Ijeoma Oluo and Jennifer Harvey, respectively, explain, white people—across educational and vocational lines—too often fail to understand both our own racial advantages *and also* how deep-seated racial-ethnic assumptions poison relationships.[28] In health care settings, these misfires lead to worse health outcomes for Black and Brown peoples. Doctors and nurses are often altruistic and dedicated professionals; they are also human. Stereotypes and biases are most potent when they are unconscious and they thrive in time- and resource-stressed environments. Especially when people are under pressure, they are less able to step back and reflect critically. Moreover, people are less able to acknowledge bias and/or stereotypes (in themselves or in coworkers) when they are in defensive postures (e.g., worried about being blamed for poor outcomes).

Certainly, *everyone*—across racial-ethnic, socioeconomic, cultural differences—can and does act based on implicit biases and unspoken assumptions. Assumptions are "cognitive shortcuts" that people use to assess situations and make decisions about what

---

[22]See Artiga et al., "Key Facts on Health."

[23]Ibid.

[24]Ibid. "Among the nonelderly population, Asians, Hispanics, Blacks, and American Indians and Alaska Natives generally fare worse than Whites across measures of access to and utilization of care."

[25]Ibid.

[26]Regina Bussing et al., "Eliminating Mental Health Disparities by 2020: Everyone's Actions Matter," *Journal of the American Academy of Child & Adolescent Psychiatry* 51, no. 7 (2012): 663–6.

[27]See J. Rizzuto and M. D. Aldridge, "Racial Disparities in Hospice Outcomes: A Race or Hospice-Level Effect?," *Journal of American Geriatric Society* 66, no. 2 (2018): 407–13.

[28]Ijeoma Oluo, *So You Want to Talk about Race?* (New York: Hachette Book Group, 2018); Jennifer Harvey, *Raising White Kids: Bringing Up Children in a Racially Unjust America* (Nashville: Abingdon, 2017).

to do, how to act, and so on. Sometimes, they can save lives by sizing up a situation quickly in the Emergency Department, for example.

Nonetheless, *it is also true* that assumptions and unconscious/automatic reliance on stereotypes can cause providers to misread a person or situation, which can lead to misdiagnosis, a lack of time/empathy, and inadequate trust and rapport. Stereotypes are even written into medical texts.[29] Consider pain management. Research has well established that Black patients are undertreated for pain as compared with white patients.[30] To illustrate: A 2016 University of Virginia study found that half of the 418 medical students and residents they tested believed at least one biological/racial myth related to how different race-ethnicities respond to pain, thinking, for example, that Black patients have a "thicker skin" and/or are more tolerant of pain than white patients.[31] Even after completing medical training, "14 percent of medical residents agreed with the mysterious statement that 'blacks age more slowly than whites.'"[32] Such mythologies can be refuted with facts. Yet, racial myths—along with stereotypes—are prevalent and toxic. They live under the surface most of the time. Even the medical textbooks that do address racial-ethnic disparities often focus primarily on "cultural competence" without sufficiently offering critical analysis of medical cultures. The predominant US medical culture shapes health care providers in ways that leave erroneous beliefs and simplistic generalizations about diverse racial-ethnic groups intact and unchallenged.

Furthermore, while everyone—including patients—may well express implicit biases or fall back on stereotypes, power dynamics matter. A patient's stereotyping of a doctor may well be irritating and stressful, but when physicians act uncritically on the basis of stereotypes/bias, the stakes are generally much higher. Doctors write prescriptions and make referrals. They can appeal an insurance company's decision. They can try to get a patient on a drug trial. They have a lot of weight in deciding on care plans. And they are in a position where they can choose to either advocate for, refer, or drop any given patient.

Disparities in US maternal care bring together much of the preceding analysis and illumine the profound costs to Black lives. The statistics are downright shocking to some and shameful for the United States as a nation: US Black women are three to four times more likely to die from complications from childbirth than white women.[33] Every year, twice as many Black infants born in the United States die before their first birthday than white infants.[34] Being pregnant is quite literally life-threatening for Black women. And being affluent and well insured—even a celebrity—does not fully insulate one from these

---

[29]Scott Jaschik, "Anger over Stereotypes in Textbook," Inside Higher Ed, October 23, 2017.

[30]Brian B. Drwecki, "Education to Identify and Combat Racial Bias in Pain Treatment," *AMA Journal of Ethics* 17, no. 3 (2015): 221–8.

[31]Kelly M. Hoffman et al., "Racial Bias in Pain Assessment and Treatment Recommendations, and False Beliefs about Biological Differences between Blacks and Whites," *Proceedings of the National Academy of Sciences* 113, no. 16 (2016): 4296–301.

[32]Alice Robb, "Too Many Doctors Still Believe Dangerous Racial Stereotypes," *The Cut*, November 2, 2017.

[33]From 2011 to 2013, the US Centers for Disease Control and Prevention (CDC) reports that pregnancy-related morality rate for Black women was 43.5 vs. 12.7 for white women: "Pregnancy Mortality Surveillance System," Centers for Disease Control and Prevention, June 4, 2019, https://www.cdc.gov/reproductivehealth/maternalinfanthealth/pmss.html.

[34]The 2015 infant mortality rate for non-Hispanic white infants was 4.82, 5.20 for infants identified as Hispanic, and 11.73 for Black, non-Hispanic infants: Sherry L. Murphy et al., "Deaths: Final Data for 2015," *National Vital Statistics Reports* 66, no. 6 (2017): 14.

numbers. In 2018, Serena Williams recounted how she nearly died after giving birth, in part, because her providers did not listen to her in crucial moments.[35]

Williams is far from alone. ProPublica and NPR collected over two hundred stories from Black mothers in 2017. A recurring theme is how provider biases make these women feel disrespected:

> The young Florida mother-to-be whose breathing problems were blamed on obesity when in fact her lungs were filling with fluid and her heart was failing. The Arizona mother whose anesthesiologist assumed she smoked marijuana because of the way she did her hair. The Chicago-area businesswoman with a high-risk pregnancy who was so upset at her doctor's attitude that she changed OB-GYNs in her seventh month, only to suffer a fatal postpartum stroke. Over and over, black women told of medical providers who equated being African American with being poor, uneducated, noncompliant and unworthy.[36]

What we consciously or unconsciously believe about others—especially those different from us in significant ways—shapes how we see them, how we interact with them and assess the situation. Stereotypes can *and do* affect everything from treatment plans to stress levels to outcomes.[37]

In sum, dogged, systemic US health care inequities problematize and silence any simplistic boast that "all people are treated equally." Neither lofty platitudes referencing human dignity nor vague, aspirational mission statements suffice. It is time to act resolutely and, especially as we consider climate change, time is excruciatingly short.

CLIMATE CHANGE: *THE* HUMAN HEALTH CRISIS OF THE TWENTY-FIRST CENTURY

Even as the scope of medicine should focus more specifically on social, economic, and racial-ethnic inequities, it simultaneously needs to expand to address the impending, disastrous health effects of climate change. For too long, climate change was viewed as an environmental threat, not primarily as a threat to human health. That was a critical mistake in messaging. *Climate change exacerbates and intensifies every other social ill*, including health care and health inequities. National and international research centers demonstrate these connections.[38] Indeed, the United Nations,[39] the WHO,[40] the US Centers for Disease Control and Prevention (CDC),[41] and the American Public Health Association[42] all identify climate change as a game-changing threat to public health.

---

[35]Rob Haskell, "Serena Williams on Motherhood, Marriage, and Making Her Comeback," *Vogue*, January 10, 2018.

[36]Martin, "Nothing Prevents Black Women."

[37]Louis A. Penner et al., "Reducing Racial Health Care Disparities: A Social Psychological Analysis," *Policy Insights from the Behavioral and Brain Sciences* 1, no. 1 (2014): 204–12.

[38]See, for example, online resources from The Harvard Center for Climate, Health, and the Global Environment, https://www.hsph.harvard.edu/c-change/, and The Center for Climate Change and Health, http://climatehealthconnect.org.

[39]"Climate Change Impacts Human Health," United Nations, April 12, 2017.

[40]"Climate Change and Health," World Health Organization, February 1, 2018.

[41]"Public Health Response to a Changing Climate," Centers for Disease Control and Prevention, last modified July 18, 2018, https://www.cdc.gov/features/changingclimate/index.html.

[42]Linda Rudolph et al., *Climate Change, Health, and Equity: A Guide for Local Health Departments* (Oakland: American Public Health Association, 2018), https://www.apha.org/-/media/files/pdf/topics/climate/climate_health_equity.ashx?la=en&hash=14D2F64530F1505EAE7AB16A9F9827250EAD6C79.

Since the 1970s, internationally respected scientists have unequivocally warned the US government and the world of the varied and dire implications—sea-level rises, extinctions, biodiversity losses. In October 2018, the Intergovernmental Panel on Climate Change (IPCC), the most authoritative collection of international scientists, issued its most stark report to date.[43] Specifically, it warned that human activity has already increased the global average temperature by 1 degree Celsius and that raising it to 2 degree Celsius would have far more devastating and far-reaching effects than previously thought. Even more, the IPCC gives world leaders only twelve years to take the massive, coordination actions needed to keep the rise to 1.5 degree Celsius.[44] While a 1.5 degree increase will still create tremendous hardship, half a degree would exponentially intensify varied forms of planetary instability. Such statements may sound like apocalyptic science fiction, but they are not hyperbole. If we have been guilty of irresponsible speech, it is that we have been far too optimistic in stating the risks and timeline available to make needed changes to our industries and ways of life.

In fact, given the intensity of storms and droughts, the rapid melting of ancient glaciers and dramatically changing landscapes, we are already watching the climate chickens coming home to roost. Texans, New Yorkers, Alaskans, Floridians, New Jerseyans, North Carolinians, Puerto Ricans, and those living in Gulf Coast states are all among the first-hand witnesses. In August 2016, after a two-week long rainstorm, Jayden Foytlin, 13 years old, woke up to a flooded bedroom. Most of her home, even though it was *not* built along a flood plain, was destroyed by the water and sewage that seeped throughout.[45] Jayden observed, "They called it a thousand-year flood, meaning it should only happen every thousand years or so. But in my state—Louisiana—we have had that 1,000-year flood and eight 500-year floods in less than two years. A few weeks ago, I literally stepped out of my bed and was up to my ankles in climate change."[46] Levi Draheim from Satellite Beach, Florida, was just 11 years old when he explained, "I have personally had to evacuate my home because of hurricanes … I've seen fish kills on my beach and I have seen changing weather and more and more hot days."[47] These are not isolated, random events. Unprecedented heat waves, floods, and droughts are taking a grave toll across the United States and around the world. They are changing maps—islands are disappearing, coasts are changing, and numerous areas—from Bangladesh[48] to Haiti; from Alaskan villages to New Orleans; from Chennai[49] to Houston—where tens of thousands, even millions, of people live are rapidly becoming either too hot and parched or too wet and too submerged to live.

And there are steep costs to agriculture and industry. For example, historic flooding in 2019 dealt major blows to farms, ranches, businesses, and homes in Nebraska, Missouri,

[43]"Global Warming of 1.5 °C: Summary for Policy Makers," The Intergovernmental Panel on Climate Change, October 6, 2018.

[44]Jonathan Watts, "We Have 12 Years to Limit Climate Change Catastrophe, Warns UN," *Guardian*, October 8, 2018.

[45]Laura Parker, "'Biggest Case on the Planet' Pits Kids vs. Climate Change," *National Geographic*, November 9, 2018.

[46]"Jayden F.," Our Children's Trust, https://www.ourchildrenstrust.org/jayden/.

[47]Jacob Pinter, "Young Activists Can Sue Government Over Climate Change, Supreme Court Says," *NPR*, November 3, 2018.

[48]Robert Glennon, "The Unfolding Tragedy of Climate Change in Bangladesh," *Scientific America*, April 21, 2017.

[49]Somini Sengupta, "Chennai, an Indian City of Nearly 5 Million, Is Running Out of Water," *New York Times*, June 21, 2019.

South Dakota, and Iowa—large swaths of the "bread basket" of the United States. Small towns are ill-prepared for the increasing storms.[50]

> Warren Preston, deputy chief economist for the Department of Agriculture, said extraordinarily wet conditions across the Corn Belt, combined with a cool spring, have shortened the planting season and the number of growing degree days. The floods have also taken roughly 3 million acres of corn production out of the economy [in 2019]. That translates into a 4% reduction in income to farmers, or $4.5 billion in corn receipts, he said.[51]

In 2018, Hurricane Florence killed over 3 million chickens and 5,500 hogs.[52] In all, North Carolinian agriculture lost an estimated $2.4 billion dollars to Florence.[53] Indeed, the most immediate link to human health is that the droughts, floods, sea-level rises, and changes in ocean chemistry (which kill off fish and other sea life) already create food and freshwater shortages for the majority of the world's inhabitants.

Yet, the health implications of climate change extend beyond hunger and thirst.[54] Per the WHO: "The direct damage costs to health (i.e. excluding costs in health-determining sectors such as agriculture and water and sanitation), is estimated to be between USD 2–4 billion/year by 2030."[55] And that may be a gross underestimate. The WHO also conservatively estimates, "Between 2030 and 2050, climate change is expected to cause approximately 250,000 additional deaths per year, from malnutrition, malaria, diarrhoea and heat stress."[56] Lyme disease-carrying ticks are becoming more prevalent. Cholera thrives in warmer waters. Longer, hotter summers produce more smog and pollens, which in turn trigger more asthma and allergies.[57] This quick list leaves out many serious vector borne diseases and other health concerns, such as serious strains on mental health.[58] In June 2019, seventy medical and public health organizations, including the American Medical Association, American Academy of Pediatrics, and American Heart Association, came together to issue a public call to action directed to US government and business sectors: "The health, safety and wellbeing of millions of people in the US have already been harmed by human-caused climate change, and health risks in the future are dire without urgent action to fight climate change."[59]

Bluntly put, climate change is not simply hazardous to our collective health; it is lethal. And the most despicable irony and injustice is that those who contribute the least to climate change—disproportionately Black and Brown peoples in the United States and

---

[50]Rebecca Hersher, "Small Towns Fear They Are Unprepared for Future Climate-Driven Flooding," *NPR*, July 25, 2019.

[51]Daniel Cusick, "No End in Sight for Record Midwest Flood Crisis," *Scientific American*, June 26, 2019.

[52]Michael Graff, "Millions of Dead Chickens and Pigs Found in Hurricane Floods," *Guardian*, September 22, 2018.

[53]Chuck Abbott, "North Carolina AG Losses from Florence Soar to $2.4 Billion," *Successful Farming*, October 11, 2018.

[54]For an eye-opening, comprehensive overview of the various facets, see Allison Crimmins et al., "USGCRP, 2016: The Impacts of Climate Change on Human Health in the United States: A Scientific Assessment," US Global Change Research Program, April 2016.

[55]World Health Organization, "Climate Change and Health."

[56]Ibid.

[57]Martha Bebinger, "Has Your Doctor Talked to You about Climate Change?," *NPR*, July 13, 2019.

[58]"Asthma and Climate Change," Yale Climate Connections, 2017, https://www.yaleclimateconnections.org/2017/11/asthma-climate-change/.

[59]"US Call to Action on Climate, Health, and Equity: A Policy Action Agenda," Climate Health Action, June 2019, https://climatehealthaction.org/media/cta_docs/US_Call_to_Action.pdf.

elsewhere—are paying the highest prices. Vulnerable constituencies—communities of color, children,[60] indigenous populations, the working classes, those living in poverty—bear more than their share of the weighty consequences. They are already losing homes, opportunities, livelihoods, health—*futures*.

Given the mind-boggling pace of some of these changes combined with having very few options, increasing numbers of people are on the move. It is a matter of survival. According to the Internal Displacement Monitoring Centre, between 2008 and 2015, 203.4 million people were displaced by disasters, with the likelihood of being displaced by disasters doubling since the 1970s.[61] Climate change is also a threat multiplier, likely exacerbating conflict, for example, over depleted resources.[62] When whole communities are disrupted and displaced, tensions rise. Indeed, even as the misguided Trump administration denies climate change, the US military is actively preparing for it.[63]

The Syrian Civil War (which began in 2011) is just one example. It was immediately preceded by the worst drought (lasting four years) in the country's history and was met by a government unable and/or unwilling to help people in crisis—who were losing their livelihoods and also their ability to procure sufficient food.[64] Similarly, one of the root causes of the humanitarian crisis that began in 2015 in Yemen is water scarcity.[65] To date, over three million people have had to flee their homes in Yemen and over twenty-two million are in need of food, water, and adequate shelter.[66]

Thus, despite any border walls or changes to immigration policies, changes in the climate will increasingly force unprecedented levels of migration. People who have no good options will sacrifice every coin and asset they have for a slim chance to cross the Mediterranean in leaky boats or to walk or swim across the border into the United States. As of 2019, there is no legal framework to protect climate refugees.[67]

Like any species, humans will either adapt or perish. If we do not act quickly—on an international scale of collaboration unknown since the Second World War or perhaps ever, the future for health and well-being looks truly bleak. The problem is not so much a lack of knowledge, technologies, or resources. Rather, it is a question of moral courage and grit.

---

[60]See Rebecca Pass Philipsborn and Kevin Chan, "Climate Change and Global Child Health," *Pediatrics* 141, no. 6 (2018): 1–5; "Climate Change and Global Child Health," American Public Health Association, https://www.apha.org/~/media/files/pdf/topics/climate/childrens_health.ashx.

[61]Internal Displacement Monitoring Centre (IDMC), "Global Estimates 2015: People Displaced by Disasters," July 2015, https://www.internal-displacement.org/publications/global-estimates-2015-people-displaced-by-disasters.

[62]Ellen Hansen et al., eds., "Climate Change and Disaster Displacement: An Overview of UNHCR'S Role," UNHCR, 2017, http://www.unhcr.org/en-us/protection/environment/5975e6cf7/climate-change-disaster-displacement-overview-unhcrs-role.html.

[63]Juliet Eilperin, Brady Dennis, and Missy Ryan, "As White House Questions Climate Change, US Military Is Planning for It," *Washington Post*, April 8, 2019.

[64]See Mark Fischetti, "Climate Change Hastened Syria's Civil War," *Scientific America*, March 2, 2015; Thomas L. Friedman, "Without Water, Revolution," *New York Times*, May 18, 2013.

[65]Colin Douglas, "A Storm without Rain: Yemen, Water, Climate Change, and Conflict," The Center for Climate and Security, August 3, 2018.

[66]"Yemen War: No End in Sight," Amnesty International, updated March 14, 2019, https://www.amnesty.org/en/latest/news/2015/09/yemen-the-forgotten-war/.

[67]Matus Kalisky, "Climate Change 'Will Create World's Biggest Refugee Crisis'," *Guardian*, November 2, 2017.

WHAT CHRISTIAN ETHICS MIGHT CONTRIBUTE TO THIS URGENT MOMENT

Everyone from theologians, philosophers, anthropologists, cultural critics, to postmodern theorists, to even some biologists and physicians have long debated what or whether there is anything essential or common to all human beings. To be sure, it is very hard to say that any particular experience is common to all peoples across time, geography, culture, religion, and so on. Some quip that "death and taxes" are the only two unavoidable dimensions of human living. For my part, I keep coming back this notion: human beings are born and we die—and in between—how much we flourish or struggle—is greatly influenced by the degrees to which we are able to receive and give authentic love, care, and a sense of fundamental worth.

The fact that we are mortal—and knowing that we all one day will die—could be a way to bind us to one another, to help shoulder the heavy weight of also knowing that all we love about our own lives and that all those whom we love are fleeting, temporary, transient. I contend that at its best, Christian ethics lays bare the paradoxes inherent in what it means to be human—both fragile and powerful; broken and beloved; violent and healing. And through it all, accountable to God, to one another, and to creation.

In large measure, I won life's lottery. I have had access to, and could afford, as much education as I could ever want. I have job security. I am white and so strangers—health care professionals, store clerks, law enforcement officers—regularly treat me with respect and give me the benefit of the doubt. At present, I am healthy and I have comprehensive insurance for when I am not. I can change health care providers if I choose. US laws recognize my marriage. I own my apartment. I can take vacations and can afford to eat well and to exercise. I know climate change is all around me, but in many ways I can still (for a bit longer) insulate myself from its most visible effects. So, I could ignore the inequalities spelled out above. But the pricking of my conscience and dull heartache are relentless. My understanding of Christian vocation and responsibility tell me I must "do" something about the things I lament.

I am heartsick because I am both a scholar and a parent, as well as an aunt and a Sunday school teacher. I worry for my son and for others—especially Black and Brown children who are particularly and acutely at risk. In order to do ethics well, I contend that we must allow our hearts to be broken—to let others' suffering enter in and affect us in visceral ways. Otherwise, genuine empathy is not possible.

Furthermore, to do ethics well, we cannot simply apply abstract moral principles to these conundrums. At its best, Christian ethics helps us ask, and ask again, what are the goals of medicine and health care? What ought they to be? To what do we aspire? How can health care make us more human, rather than seek to transcend our humanity? Christian traditions and scripture are most alive when they help us remember who we are and to whom we belong. When we know these deep truths about ourselves, we can see more clearly our responsibilities to one another.

When I witness the passive neglect and disinterested complacency of the well-intentioned and too comfortable, I find myself both weary and angry. How is it that in the twenty-first century, with the immense technological advances in medicine, the natural sciences and health care, we as a species allow wholly solvable problems to remain unsolved and, in many cases, to intensify? It is hard to fathom by rational intellect alone. *Help.*

White Christian ethicist Beverly Wildung Harrison's essay, "The Power of Anger in the Work of Love," helps me remember that these feelings are not misplaced:

> Anger is not the opposite of love. It is better understood as a feeling-signal that all is not well in our relation to other person or groups to the world around us. Anger is a mode of connectedness to others and it is always a vivid form of caring ... Where anger rises, there the energy to act is present.[68]

The adrenaline that runs in my veins is a visceral reminder that I am connected to—and accountable to—others (human and not), that our well-being and futures are bound up with one another—no matter how proximate or distant they may be to me. Anger can function like an alarm that all is not right among us. Harrison reminds us that human-embodied intuition and sensuality are powerful and needed resources for our moral lives. As we are able to reflect on and listen to them, our emotions and embodied knowledge can help wake us up and discern what we must do.

For Christians, an authoritative measure by which we are to measure our actions is the person, life, and witness of Jesus. One of the most paradigmatic dimensions of his life and ministry was healing. He cast out demons; he brought the dead back to life; he cured lepers; and he restored people to their communities. He did not check people's nationalities or ask for payment or insurance. He sought out the hurting—the lost, the diseased, the outcast, the outsider—again and again. He reminded anyone with ears that when care for those in greatest need or peril or dire straits, we are showing love to the divine (Mt. 25:40). An analogy to emergency medicine may be helpful. Jesus practiced a kind of "theo-ethical triage"—attending to those most hurting and in need of healing. Liberation theology's explication of the "preferential option for the poor" is a modern expression of this same ethos.

And while this ethic cannot be summed up neatly into a motto or bumper sticker, and while we cannot simply pour ourselves out for one another to the point of utter depletion, we cannot let ourselves off the hook too easily either. Indeed, again and again, Jesus calls out whoever is unconcerned for the needs of the suffering or overly proud or confident that they are "good people" or "insiders." He continuously pulls stunning reversals—the last shall be first, those who are disparaged by those with status are the invited ones—whether children, tax collectors, women, foreigners, lepers, religious outsiders, and so on. The Gospel "good news" is supposed to comfort the afflicted and, to a degree at least, afflict those who are too comfortable or self-satisfied.

Many Christians ponder "what would Jesus do?" as they navigate their lives. Back in 1980, Harrison prophetically answered this question for us living in the twenty-first century:

> Like Jesus, we are called to a radical activity of love, to a way of being in the world that deepens relations, embodies and extends community, passes on the gift of life. Like Jesus, we must live out this calling in a place and time where the distortions of loveless power stand in conflict with the power of love. We are called to confront, as Jesus did, that which thwarts the power of human personal and communal becoming, that which

[68]Beverly Wildung Harrison, "The Power of Anger in the Work of Love: Christian Ethics for Women and Other Strangers," in *Making the Connections: Essays in Feminist Social Ethics*, ed. Carol S. Robb (Boston: Beacon, 1985), 14.

twists relationship, which denies human well-being, community and human solidarity to so many in our world.[69]

While the problems before us are monstrous, we have power to act. And our choices matter a great deal. Not all choices are as good as others. So, we need to own this responsibility, attune all of our moral antennae, and discern wisely with our whole beings. We can either choose to act in ways that heal the wounds within our reach and make amends for the harms we have caused or contributed to, or we can foment the alienation and suffering of others. When we choose the latter, we distort our own humanity. Health care disparities and the death-dealing effects of climate change do not just infect the well-being of those who suffer most directly at their hands. When those of us who are not their most immediate targets refuse to reflect on the pain, or augment it, or deny its existence, our own moral and spiritual characters suffer.

The present moment is stressful, heartbreaking, and urgent. It calls for fewer abstracted discussions of ethics and more concrete, strategic policy interventions. Reorienting medical ethics in this way can help us see more clearly the demands of the times in which we live and who we are called to be in them. There are reasons to hope that we can create positive change. Recall Jayden from Louisiana and Levi from Florida mentioned above. They are two of the twenty-one youths suing the federal government for its failure to act responsibly to counteract climate change. First filed in 2015, *Juliana v. United States* surpassed many hurdles, surprising many naysayers and legal experts. It was dismissed in early 2020.[70] Other exemplary, prophetic people abound, from Catholic nuns to Black preachers such as the Rev. William Barber, and more.

When feeling forlorn or weak of heart, try to remember that lament is central to Christian practice and spirituality. And remember that the purpose of lament is *not* to wallow or get stuck in the paralysis of grief, but to experience *catharsis*—express and share burdens, to cry out for help, and then to move to concrete, creative, renewed action. Increasingly, I understand *hope* as a verb—*actions to do, to create*, rather than wait for its cavalry to save the day.

Take heart. Make most of your transient life to be an agent of healing, especially to those bearing the burdens of inequity in their very bodies, while you have breath, energy, and resources to do so. Perhaps doing so will help you remember and reconnect with the deepest parts of your own being and with the most profound senses of who you feel called to be—as academics, students, professionals, and as human beings. Together, we can move from lament to protest and even further to creating new, more just ways of living on this beautiful, struggling planet. May the angels be with us.

SUGGESTED READINGS

Dahill, Lisa E., and James B. Martin-Schramm, eds. *Eco-Reformation: Grace and Hope for a Planet in Peril*. Eugene: Wipf and Stock, 2016.

Farmer, Paul et al., eds. *Reimagining Global Health: An Introduction*. Berkeley: University of California Press, 2013.

---

[69]Ibid., 18–19.

[70]Parker, "'Biggest Case on the Planet'." For more about the lawsuit, see https://www.ourchildrenstrust.org/; https://www.washingtonpost.com/news/powerpost/paloma/the-energy-202/2020/01/21/the-energy-202-youth-climate-lawsuit-dismissal-shows-challenge-of-using-courts-to-tackle-climate-change/5e25e86388e0fa6ea99d0d4d/.

Harvey, Jennifer. *Raising White Kids: Bringing Up Children in a Racially Unjust America.* Nashville: Abingdon, 2017.

Lysaught, M. Therese, and Michael McCarthy, eds. *Catholic Bioethics & Social Justice: The Praxis of US Health Care in a Globalized World.* Collegeville: Liturgical, 2018.

O'Brien, Kevin. *Violence of Climate Change: Lessons of Resistance from Nonviolent Activists.* Washington, DC: Georgetown University Press, 2017.

Oluo, Ijeoma. *So You Want to Talk about Race?* New York: Hachette Book Group, 2018.

Roberts, Dorothy. *Killing the Black Body: Race, Reproduction, and the Meaning of Liberty.* New York: Random House, 2016.

Washington, Harriet. *Medical Apartheid: The Dark History of Medical Experimentation on Black Americans from Colonial Times to the Present.* New York: Random House, 2006.

CHAPTER THIRTY-FOUR

Neuroethics

NEIL MESSER

Neuroethics is concerned with the whole range of theoretical and practical ethical questions raised by neuroscience and its clinical applications. As a defined field, it is quite a recent arrival on the ethical scene (the term was first coined around 2002), though some of its questions and concerns have engaged philosophers and theologians for much longer. One major stimulus for its emergence has been the remarkable growth of neuroscience since the 1990s, made possible in part by brain imaging techniques such as functional magnetic resonance imaging (fMRI). Advances in neuroscience are said to generate new insights and raise perplexing questions about what it is to be human. Another stimulus comes from the expanding range of current and anticipated applications of this knowledge. Developments in neuroscience promise great advances in understanding brain diseases and disorders, new approaches to their treatment, and (it is said) unprecedented power to modify the functioning of our brains in all kinds of ways. This new knowledge, and the uses to which it may be put, generate a distinctive set of ethical concerns. In the words of Adina Roskies, one of the founders of the field, "The intimate connection between our brains and our behaviors, as well as the peculiar relationship between our brains and our selves, generate distinctive questions that beg for the interplay between ethical and neuroscientific thinking."[1]

These questions are of various kinds. Roskies divides the field into two parts, the "ethics of neuroscience" and the "neuroscience of ethics."[2] The *ethics of neuroscience* includes some fairly familiar questions about the ethical conduct of neuroscientific research: informed consent, confidentiality, storage and use of data, risks and harms, and so on. These issues have particular salience in neuroscientific research, because many of the disorders of brain and mind studied by neuroscientists may have an impact on patients' identity, personality, or capacity for decision-making. Also included in the ethics of neuroscience are ethical issues raised by neuroscientific findings and their applications. One example, the issues raised by brain imaging studies of disorders of consciousness (DoCs), will be discussed later. Another is the modification of brain functions using drugs and other technologies: technological enhancements of cognition, mood, and morality are all discussed in the literature, along with more far-reaching speculations about enhancing ourselves to the point where we are no longer human, but posthuman.[3] A third example

---

[1]Adina Roskies, "Neuroethics for the New Millennium," *Neuron* 35, no. 1 (2002): 21.

[2]Ibid., 21–3.

[3]See Neil Messer, *Theological Neuroethics: Christian Ethics Meets the Science of the Human Brain* (London: T&T Clark, 2017), 144–9.

is "brain reading": attempting to use functional brain imaging to gain information about mental states or activities for various purposes, such as lie detection.

By the *neuroscience of ethics*, Roskies means such things as the study of moral agency, deliberation, and action from the perspective of neuroscience. One example would be the contribution of neuroscience to long-standing debates about determinism, free will, and moral responsibility. Another, discussed more fully below, is the neuroscientific investigation of moral cognition and judgment.

Although the ethics of neuroscience and the neuroscience of ethics can be distinguished, it is clear that they are closely interconnected. For example, neuroscientific perspectives on agency, determinism, and free will might suggest that freedom and moral agency are impaired in certain individuals or underdeveloped at some stages of life. This could raise questions about how we understand the moral responsibility of such individuals and might have practical implications in areas such as the criminal law. Indeed, some authors go so far as to suggest that in light of neuroscience, the meaning of legal responsibility for everyone, not just certain individuals, needs radical revision—though this claim has not yet found general acceptance.[4]

NEUROETHICS AND CHRISTIAN ETHICS

Neuroethics is a highly interdisciplinary field, involving (among others) neuroscientists, psychologists, clinicians, philosophers, and lawyers. However, it is surprisingly rare for theologians to be included in this interdisciplinary dialogue, and theology is largely absent from major texts in the field.[5] For their part, theological ethicists have engaged surprisingly little with neuroethics as a field until recently, although some of the issues that it includes (such as the care of patients with DoCs and the ethics of human enhancement and transhumanism) have long attracted much theological attention. Engagement with neuroethics as a whole is a timely and important task for theological ethicists, if they do not wish to see this fast-growing field dominated by purely secular, and often quite reductive, approaches.

If it is important for Christian ethicists to engage with neuroethics, how should they go about it? Different theological traditions will, of course, hold diverse views of the parts played by *scripture* and *tradition* in shaping a Christian ethical engagement with neuroscience. But neuroethics also raises the question of how scientific *reason* should interact with scripture and tradition to shape a Christian moral vision and guide moral deliberation and action. For example, if neuroscientific findings question time-honored assumptions about moral agency, how much weight should be given to those findings—and what kind of work should they do—in forming a Christian theological and moral self-understanding? Or again, what kind of role should scientific information play in Christian ethical reasoning about practical questions such as the care of patients with DoCs? Finally, neuroscientific research may offer new insights or make new claims about human *experience*, including moral and religious experience. What bearing might such claims and insights have on the contribution that experience is thought to make to Christian ethics?

---

[4]Joshua Greene and Jonathan Cohen, "For the Law, Neuroscience Changes Nothing and Everything," in *Neuroethics: An Introduction with Readings*, ed. Martha J. Farah (Cambridge: MIT, 2010), 232–58.

[5]E.g., Judy Illes and Barbara J. Sahakian, eds., *The Oxford Handbook of Neuroethics* (Oxford: Oxford University Press, 2011).

To be more specific about these questions and learn more about the various shapes that Christian neuroethical reasoning might take, it will be helpful to explore particular examples. In the remainder of this chapter, two representative neuroethical issues will be discussed.

THE NEUROSCIENCE OF MORAL JUDGMENT

Since the early 2000s, neuroscientists have been investigating moral judgment and decision-making. Some of the best-known (and most controversial) studies have been conducted by Joshua Greene and his colleagues, who studied the brain activity of subjects responding to scenarios such as the so-called trolley problems.[6] According to Greene et al., when subjects considered "impersonal" scenarios (e.g., should one divert a runaway trolley from the main line to a siding so that it will avoid five workers on the main line but will collide fatally with one in the siding?), there was greater activity in parts of the brain associated with reason. When they considered "personal" scenarios (e.g., should one push a bystander into the path of a trolley to stop it hitting five workers?), there was greater activity associated with emotion. The majority of subjects answered "yes" to the first kind of question and "no" to the second, but a minority answered "yes" to both. This minority took longer to respond to the second kind.

Greene argues that these findings are explained by a dual system of moral reasoning in the brain.[7] He maintains that humans have evolved a fast, intuitive system that generates emotionally powerful moral judgments about situations that would have been relevant to our evolutionary ancestors (e.g., it is wrong to kill innocent bystanders). Our ancestors' survival depended on living together in social groups, and the intuitive system was efficient at generating the rough-and-ready rules that enabled this social coexistence. We also have a slower system of conscious reason, which is sometimes used to justify our intuitive judgments post hoc. But it can also be used to perform utilitarian ethical calculations; according to Greene, all subjects considering the first kind of trolley scenario and the minority who answered "yes" to the second kind were using their rational system to perform such utilitarian calculations. He believes that this research supports utilitarian ethics against Kantian and other deontological approaches, which might prohibit certain kinds of action universally; he maintains that his findings expose such deontological claims as elaborate rationalizations of our moral intuitions, which are themselves contingent products of our evolutionary history.[8]

The conceptualization, design, analysis, and interpretation of these studies have been robustly criticized in various ways (and, needless to say, robustly defended by Greene).[9] What should theologians make of this work and these disputes? Some might choose to reject such studies altogether, agreeing with those philosophical critics who consider them irrelevant at best and misleading at worst. Others might respond more positively—though still cautiously and critically—arguing that if the studies prove robust and stand the test

---

[6]Joshua D. Greene et al., "An fMRI Investigation of Emotional Engagement in Moral Judgment," *Science* 293, no. 5537 (2001): 2105–8.

[7]Joshua D. Greene, *Moral Tribes: Emotion, Reason, and the Gap between Us and Them* (London: Atlantic, 2014).

[8]Joshua D. Greene, "The Secret Joke of Kant's Soul," in *Moral Psychology, Vol. 3*, ed. Walter Sinnott-Armstrong (Cambridge: MIT, 2008), 36–79. See also Peter Singer, "Ethics and Intuitions," *Journal of Ethics* 9, nos. 3–4 (2005): 331–52.

[9]For a survey of these debates, see Messer, *Theological Neuroethics*, 44–55.

of time, Christian ethics may have important things to learn from them.[10] But different theological and ethical traditions will suggest varying views of *what* Christian ethics should learn.

Some natural law theorists, for example, might see parallels between the intuitive moral judgments described by Greene and the Thomist claim that the primary precepts of the natural law are known to all.[11] On such a view these intuitive judgments might be seen, not merely as products of evolution with no necessary moral salience, but as genuine (though partial) insights into the good of human creatures. In that case, the use of reason to justify, reflect on, and refine these intuitive judgments need not be debunked as after-the-act rationalization. Rather, it could be seen as the exercise of practical wisdom, drawing more detailed and specific conclusions about the good and the right from the intuitively known first principles.

For example, the doctrine of double effect makes a moral distinction between the intended outcomes of an agent's actions and those that are foreseen but unintended by the agent. This doctrine would draw a morally significant difference between the two kinds of scenario studied by Greene. In the first kind (diverting the trolley onto the siding), the death of one person is a foreseen but unintended consequence of the action that saves the lives of five others. In the second (pushing the bystander into the path of the trolley), it is intended as the *means* of saving the five others' lives. The majority of subjects intuitively made this kind of moral distinction between intended and unintended outcomes of their actions: they believed it would be justified to divert the trolley, but wrong to push the bystander into its path. Greene maintains that this intuitive distinction is a contingent product of our evolutionary history, and the doctrine of double effect is simply a post hoc rationalization of it, which is debunked by the neuroscientific evidence and evolutionary explanation. Christians adopting a natural law perspective could in principle accept Greene's evolutionary narrative about the origins of the moral intuitions. However, they need not agree with him that this narrative debunks either the moral intuitions or the doctrine of double effect which codifies them.

In contrast to such a natural law-based approach, a Christian ethic informed by theologians like Barth and Bonhoeffer might begin with a theologically motivated *suspicion* of the human knowledge of good and evil.[12] One fragment of Bonhoeffer's unfinished *Ethics* begins: "The knowledge of good and evil appears to be the goal of all ethical reflection. The first task of Christian ethics is to supersede that knowledge."[13] This claim is motivated by Bonhoeffer's theological reading of Genesis 3, in which the knowledge of good and evil is at the heart of the humans' disastrous attempt to become "like God" (*sicut deus*). Likewise, Barth sees the human pretension to knowledge of good and evil as an aspect of the sin of pride, which leads us to rely on our own resources and so alienate ourselves from God.[14]

From this standpoint, the critical perspective on human moral judgment offered by authors such as Greene should be untroubling and perhaps even helpful. If many of what

---

[10]E.g., John Perry, "Jesus and Hume among the Neuroscientists: Haidt, Greene, and the Unwitting Return of Moral Sense Theory," *Journal of the Society of Christian Ethics* 36, no. 1 (2016): 69–85.

[11]Thomas Aquinas, *Summa Theologiae*, trans. Fathers of the English Dominican Province (New York: Benziger Brothers, 1948), I–II.94.6.

[12]For a fuller elaboration of this perspective, see Messer, *Theological Neuroethics*, 56–69.

[13]Dietrich Bonhoeffer, *Ethics*, trans. Reinhard Krauss et al., ed. Ilse Tödt et al. (Minneapolis: Fortress, 2005), 299.

[14]Karl Barth, *Church Dogmatics*, vol. 4.1, ed. Geoffrey W. Bromiley and Thomas F. Torrance (Edinburgh: T&T Clark, 1956–75), 448.

we take to be reasoned moral judgments are in fact rationalizations of intuitions that are contingent products of our evolutionary history, this should not seem surprising from a theological perspective that emphasizes the limited, fallible, and fallen character of our moral reason. If, as Greene suggests, our moral intuitions are often a source of division and conflict in the modern world, this also should not surprise theologians who have learned from Bonhoeffer that the attempt to be "like God, knowing good and evil" (Gen. 3:5) alienates us from God and one another.[15] Thus, to the extent that his findings prove scientifically robust, Greene could prove an unexpected ally in the theological critique of ethics-as-human-project informed by Barth and Bonhoeffer. Neuroscientific findings such as these could also have a valuable critical role to play in the theological *reconstruction* of ethics that must follow the critique. For example, they could offer an ongoing warning and check on the self-deception, bias, and distortion to which Christians—like everyone else—are still prone in their moral discernment and action.

These contrasting theological responses to Greene are of course just two among various possible ones. The choice between them will be motivated by a set of interrelated theological commitments and decisions about questions such as the weight given to scripture relative to the other fonts of Christian ethics, the ways in which scripture can inform Christian moral reasoning, the capacity of natural human reason to discern the good, and the extent to which our moral reason is compromised by human sinfulness.

The neuroscience of moral judgment is one of those topics categorized by Roskies as "the neuroscience of ethics," and it may appear quite abstract and theoretical—though Greene certainly intends his work to have practical implications for ethical debate and decision-making in morally plural societies. Our second example of a neuroethical issue is more obviously practical, though it touches on some deep theoretical questions along the way. It is also one of those issues that was familiar in bioethics, and attracted the attention of Christian ethicists, even before the appearance of neuroethics as a discrete field.

FUNCTIONAL NEUROIMAGING AND DISORDERS OF CONSCIOUSNESS

Brain damage caused by traumatic injury, stroke, or other events may result in brain death or various *DoCs*. One of these is the *vegetative state* (VS), in which patients have periods of sleep and wakefulness but show no behavioral signs of conscious awareness. (Recently the alternative name of *unresponsive wakefulness syndrome*, UWS, has been proposed for this condition.[16]) Patients who have sleep/wake cycles and show limited signs of conscious awareness are said to be in a *minimally conscious state* (MCS). Patients may progress through VS and MCS on the way to recovering higher levels of consciousness, but some remain in one or other condition chronically. If VS persists for long enough, recovery of consciousness is judged extremely unlikely and the state is described as *permanent* (PVS).

Since these disorders were first characterized they have been diagnosed behaviorally, by observing patients' responsiveness to instructions or stimuli. However, in recent years functional brain imaging studies have suggested that a proportion of patients with a PVS diagnosis may have some level of conscious awareness, even though they

---

[15]Cf. Dietrich Bonhoeffer, *Creation and Fall: A Theological Exposition of Genesis 1–3*, trans. Douglas Stephen Bax, ed. Martin Rüter et al. (Minneapolis: Fortress, 2004), 131–6.

[16]Steven Laureys et al., "Unresponsive Wakefulness Syndrome: A New Name for the Vegetative State or Apallic Syndrome," *BMC Medicine* 8, no. 1 (2010): 68.

show no behavioral signs of it. In some studies, for example, patients were asked yes/no questions and instructed to perform different mental tasks for "yes" and "no"; the mental tasks corresponded to different patterns of brain activity distinguishable by fMRI. Some patients studied in this way generated patterns of activity corresponding to verifiably correct answers to the questions they had been asked.[17] This research has proved controversial, with some critics expressing skepticism that the results can be taken as evidence of conscious awareness.[18] However, ongoing work in this area has provided increasing support for the conclusion that conscious awareness is present in some patients with DoCs and is detectable by neuroimaging. Moreover, these techniques have been used to ask questions about patients' preferences and to elicit clinically relevant information (e.g., "Are you in any pain?").[19]

These findings have far-reaching implications for the care of such patients. They suggest that a proportion of patients diagnosed with PVS or MCS have a higher level of conscious awareness than indicated by their diagnoses, which are based on behavioral signs. The research also opens up the possibility of using these techniques to communicate with such patients and involve them in decisions about their care. But probably the most ethically fraught issue raised by the research is the withdrawal of the artificial nutrition and hydration (ANH) needed to sustain these patients' lives.

In a number of countries, ANH is regarded in law as medical treatment that may be withdrawn from patients in PVS. Ethically, this is often justified by arguments about personhood. In contemporary bioethics, a distinction is commonly made between "human beings" and "persons," and it is the latter who are entitled to the moral regard we typically show to one another. On this view, not all human beings qualify as persons: to be a person one requires various capacities or abilities, and some capacity for conscious awareness is generally included among these. Patients who have permanently lost all capacity for conscious awareness are no longer persons (so the argument goes). Bringing about their deaths by withdrawing ANH may therefore be permissible, even if it would be wrong to bring about the death of a *person* in this way.

The neuroimaging research just described raises the possibility that some patients whose lives have been ended by the withdrawal of ANH were in fact persons according to this view. Furthermore, in the nature of the case, ANH would have been withdrawn without their consent. On the face of it, this seems highly disturbing. If one takes this view of personhood, the research raises serious questions about the legitimacy of deciding, on the basis of behavioral tests, that patients have permanently lost the capacity for conscious awareness and ANH may therefore be withdrawn.[20]

This view, however, has been contested. For example, Julian Savulescu and his colleagues have drawn on philosophical theories of consciousness to argue that it has different aspects, and an individual could conceivably possess some aspects of consciousness without

---

[17]Davinia Fernández-Espejo and Adrian M. Owen, "Detecting Awareness after Severe Brain Injury," *Nature Reviews Neuroscience* 14, no. 11 (2013): 801–9.

[18]Daniel J. Miklin and Robin N. Fiore, "fMRI Imaging and Decision Making in Vegetative Patients: Ethics, Technology and Welfare," *AJOB Neuroscience* 6, no. 2 (2015): 49–51.

[19]Laura E. González-Lara and Adrian M. Owen, "Identifying Covert Cognition in Disorders of Consciousness," in *Coma and Disorders of Consciousness*, ed. Caroline Schnakers and Steven Laureys (London: Springer, 2018), 77–96.

[20]It also raises the question whether these techniques could be used to communicate with patients and ask *them* whether they wish ANH to be withdrawn—though in that case there would be further significant ethical and practical issues to be addressed.

others. They question whether the aspects of consciousness detectable by neuroimaging are sufficient for these patients to be recognized as persons. Moreover, if some of these patients did have the kind of consciousness that qualified for personhood, they would be aware of their surroundings but totally unable to communicate, and therefore incapable of any interaction or two-way relationship with other people. Savulescu and his colleagues claim this may be such an awful situation that it could turn out to be a moral *obligation* to end these patients' lives.[21]

How might Christian ethicists respond to these issues and arguments? While some might hold a similar view of personhood to the one outlined above, others strongly oppose such a view. For example, in magisterial Catholic teaching, what makes a human person is the presence of a human soul, which is not dependent on consciousness or any other capacity.[22] PVS patients are persons with the same moral standing and entitlements as any other. Moreover, magisterial teaching regards ANH as basic care to which any person is in principle entitled, not as medical treatment that may be withdrawn if it is judged futile or excessively burdensome.[23]

In debates such as this one, it is striking how the protagonists can define the concept of the person in such widely differing ways, and their different definitions lead to diametrically opposite practical conclusions. In view of this, some Christian ethicists question whether arguments about personhood really offer a promising approach to difficult life-and-death decisions in health care. Some have proposed Jesus's parable of the Good Samaritan (Lk. 10:25-37) as the starting point for an alternative approach, in the following way.[24] In the dialogue between Jesus and a lawyer about the greatest commandment of the Law, the lawyer's question, "Who is my neighbor?" seems to function as a way of drawing boundaries around those whom he is commanded to love. Jesus's parable does not answer his question, but turns it back on him, inviting him to consider instead how he is called to *be* a neighbor to anyone who needs his love and compassion. By analogy, perhaps Jesus's refusal and reframing of the lawyer's question should prompt Christians to refuse and reframe the modern bioethicist's question, "Who is a person?" Christians reflecting on difficult questions, such as the care of patients with DoCs, might do better to begin by asking: What does it mean to be a neighbor, acting with love and compassion, to such patients?

Those whom God calls us to love as neighbors are not a uniform category, but have particular histories, circumstances, and networks of relationships. Therefore, one implication of this approach is that much of what it requires must be worked out in each particular situation. However, some generalizations can be made. Among other things, those who take this approach will be very wary of judgments by third parties that the lives of patients with DoCs are not worth living. They will also be unpersuaded by the familiar personhood-based arguments in favor of withdrawing ANH. However, it is conceivable that in some situations the means necessary to deliver it would be futile, disproportionately burdensome, and not an appropriate expression of care for some

[21]Guy Kahane and Julian Savulescu, "Brain Damage and the Moral Significance of Consciousness," *Journal of Medicine and Philosophy* 34, no. 1 (2009): 6–26; Neil Levy and Julian Savulescu, "Moral Significance of Phenomenal Consciousness," *Progress in Brain Research* 177 (2009): 361–70.

[22]Pope John Paul II, *Evangelium Vitae* (Vatican City: Libreria Editrice Vaticana, 1995), § 60.

[23]Congregation for the Doctrine of the Faith, "Responses to Certain Questions of the United States Conference of Catholic Bishops Concerning Artificial Nutrition and Hydration," August 1, 2007.

[24]E.g., Ian McFarland, "Who Is My Neighbor? The Good Samaritan as a Source for Theological Anthropology," *Modern Theology* 17, no. 1 (2001): 57–66; Messer, *Theological Neuroethics*, 128–42.

particular patients. Therefore (among its other implications), this approach suggests a strong, but perhaps not absolute, presumption against withdrawal of ANH.[25]

CONCLUSION

As suggested earlier, Christian engagement with neuroethics as a field is only just beginning. The two examples discussed in the later sections of the chapter illustrate something of the range of resources that a Christian ethical tradition can bring to neuroethical reasoning and debate. However, there are many further possibilities for Christian ethical engagement with these questions, and many more neuroethical debates in which these rich resources are badly needed. This range of issues can only grow as research in neuroscience progresses, and their urgency and importance will increase as the results of this research are applied more widely in health care and other areas of life.

SUGGESTED READINGS

Beauregard, James. *Personalist Neuroethics, Volume 1: Fundamental Neuroethics*. Wilmington: Vernon, 2018.

Glannon, Walter. *Brain, Body and Mind: Neuroethics with a Human Face*. Oxford: Oxford University Press, 2011.

Illes, Judy, ed. *Neuroethics: Anticipating the Future*. Oxford: Oxford University Press, 2017.

Illes, Judy, and Barbara J. Sahakian, eds. *The Oxford Handbook of Neuroethics*. Oxford: Oxford University Press, 2011.

Messer, Neil. *Theological Neuroethics: Christian Ethics Meets the Science of the Human Brain*. London: T&T Clark, 2017.

---

[25]See Messer, *Theological Neuroethics*, 138–41.

Issues, Applications, and Twenty-First-Century Agenda for Christian Ethics

Section E: Economics

CHAPTER THIRTY-FIVE

Property, Capitalism, and Economics[1]

CHRISTINA MCRORIE

This chapter surveys key historical sources of ethical reflection on property in the Christian tradition. It then introduces the development of social ethics and individual economic ethics in modern capitalism, arguing that the range of perspectives on the morality of capitalism itself reflects the ambivalent moral analysis of ownership and wealth at the heart of Christian thought. This chapter concludes by discussing disagreements over the use of economics in Christian ethics and by proposing considerations for ethicists using economic theory and research as a source of insight into human experience.

PROPERTY

Along with its parent tradition Judaism, Christianity has historically claimed that God is the only true owner of all property (Lev. 25:23; Ps. 24:1; the focus in the Hebrew Bible is especially upon God's ownership of the land, the most important form of property in premodern economies). However, God has entrusted the earth to humanity's care, and charged them to be fruitful and multiply by possessing and using its resources well. In doing so, humans imitate God's example by exercising dominion; Christians understand this analogy between human and divine *dominium* to legitimate human ownership of the goods of creation as property. At the same time, the necessary *dis*analogy between human and divine ownership logically in light of divine transcendence also limits human claims of ownership.

This is especially the case with regard to the ownership of private property, which, as its linguistic root in *privatus* (the past participle of the word, meaning "to separate, bereave, or deprive") implies, is always in some sense a good *withdrawn* from the community. In the Christian theological imagination, property's withdrawnness is intrinsically related to our fallen condition: the institution of private property is a concession to, and in turn a restraint upon, fallen humanity's tendency to sin. Like state-sanctioned violence, theoretically, private property would not have been necessary had humanity persisted in its original state of innocence.[2] This theological formulation thus simultaneously justifies

[1]For helpful comments on earlier drafts of this chapter, the author is grateful to Dan Finn and David Cloutier.
[2]E.g., see Thomas Aquinas, *Summa Theologiae*, trans. Fathers of the English Dominican Province (New York: Benziger Brothers, 1948), II–II.66.2; I.98.1.

private property and identifies it as an object of moral suspicion. In our current state, private ownership may be socially efficient, but its very necessity makes it also a sign of living in "the world."[3]

An important source of this moral suspicion of private property—and, above all, of property in the form of wealth—is found in Christ's earthly example of voluntary simplicity and his instructions to his disciples to sell all they have, embrace a life of material simplicity, and not place their trust in earthly possessions. Alongside the testimony that the church in Jerusalem shared "all things in common" (Acts 2:45, 4:32),[4] such passages can be read as indicating that communal ownership is morally superior to private property, and that the renunciation of wealth and possessions altogether may even be required in order to follow Christ. Christian communities have attempted to embody this scriptural ideal in different ways over the centuries. An anti-property impulse is particularly visible in monastic and ascetic literature, such as the writings of the Desert Fathers and, more recently, of Dorothy Day, but can also be seen in Mennonite, Amish, and other communities that practice voluntary simplicity and simple living.[5]

In general, however, the ideal of radical renunciation has rarely been taken as a concrete moral norm, and the ownership of private property is widely accepted. Even so, in light of its inverse moral justification, in the Christian worldview it has remained an artifact of human, or positive (as opposed to natural) law, and therefore to a certain extent unnatural, at least theoretically.[6] Moreover, it is intrinsically spiritually dangerous, and the wealthy must be especially on guard against being "possessed" by their possessions, and forgetting their spiritual dependence upon God (Prov. 30:8-9). The proper attitudinal and subjective handling of property has thus been a perennial and important theme in Christian theology and preaching. One of the most enduring accounts of how to cope with this danger is found in Augustine of Hippo's distinction between enjoyment, *frui*, and use, *uti*. Material goods, he maintained, are not to be desired either inordinately or enjoyed for their own sake, but rather *used* as a means to enjoy the only truly intrinsic good: God.[7] In an Augustinian view, moral agents must cultivate appropriately virtuous dispositions in order to be able to own and use property correctly.

While much of Christian ethical reflection on property focuses on this inner, or subjective, treatment of wealth and goods, the external and objective treatment of goods is at least as important a topic. How much wealth and property can Christians own, and what should they do with it? In answering such questions, Christians often return to the foundational claim that only God truly owns the earth and all that is in it, properly speaking, including human life—humanity has merely been entrusted with its temporary stewardship. We can discern the responsibilities of this position by considering God's original intentions for creation in light of scriptural commands. Thomas Aquinas's articulation of the import of this for the ethics of ownership has been particularly influential. As he put it, because

---

[3]On the significance of this trope in Christian thought, see Adrian Hastings, Alistair Mason, and Hugh S. Pyper, eds., *The Oxford Companion to Christian Thought: Intellectual, Spiritual, and Moral Horizons of Christianity* (New York: Oxford University Press, 2000).

[4]See Justo González, *Faith and Wealth: A History of Early Christian Ideas on the Origin, Significance, and Use of Money* (Eugene: Wipf and Stock, 1990), 71–91.

[5]See Peter Brown, *Through the Eye of a Needle: Wealth, the Fall of Rome, and the Making of Christianity in the West, 350–550 AD* (Princeton: Princeton University Press, 2012) on the role of this ideal of radical renunciation in the "two tier" ethic of the late antique and early medieval world.

[6]E.g., Aquinas, *Summa Theologiae*, II–II.66.2.

[7]Augustine, *De Doctrina Christiana*, trans. R. P. H. Green (Oxford: Clarendon, 1996), 1.4.

created goods are "ordained for the purpose of succoring man's needs by their means ... Whatever certain people have in superabundance is due, by natural law, to the purpose of succoring the poor."[8] That is, while the individual accumulation of private property itself is legally and morally lawful, it must be bounded by the needs of others; we are not entitled to enjoy in excess when others are suffering from need. Indeed, a central claim throughout the entire tradition has been that withholding what we own in the face of urgent need is morally equivalent to theft, and even to murder. As John Chrysostom reasoned, "This also is theft, not to share one's possessions. ... Not to share our own wealth with the poor is theft from the poor and deprivation of their means of life; we do not possess our own wealth but theirs."[9]

In premodern centuries, Christian moral analysis of property in light of these norms focused primarily upon individual character and action, and in particular upon the ethical responsibilities of those blessed with abundant resources. However, this analysis has broadened considerably as the contingency of social life has become apparent. Contemporary Christian ethics now also addresses what sort of goods ought and ought not be treated as property, what legal rights and responsibilities ownership ought to confer, and the cultural, political, and economic institutions structuring the distribution and accumulation of resources in the first place.

CAPITALISM

This expanded analysis of property has been shaped by a number of significant cultural and structural transformations during the past centuries. One of the most fundamental of these occurred during the transition from the largely feudal order of premodern Europe to the global capitalism of today, as wealth replaced honor and social status as the most important currency of social power. During this shift the division of labor and commerce expanded dramatically, as more and more of the goods of everyday life were provided through industrial production and extended networks of market exchange, rather than through subsistence agriculture. This has enabled a historically unprecedented rise in material living standards across the globe, although this rise is by no means uniformly distributed.

An important conceptual development brought about by, and in turn fueling, this expansion of markets was the recognition that economic interactions can be "positive sum" in nature: that value and wealth can be created through trade, and not merely exchanged or transferred. In the subsistence economies of antiquity, it was taken for granted that the amount of wealth in the world was fixed, and that therefore profit in trade was necessarily gained at the expense of another.[10] The insight that this is no longer the case had significant implications for Christian economic ethics. Among other things, it enabled a gradual awareness of the important social role played by merchants and bankers, and acceptance of trade and finance as callings appropriate for the Christian life (a development that was further cemented by the increased moral and spiritual

---

[8]Aquinas, *Summa Theologiae*, II–II.66.7.

[9]John Chrysostom, *On Wealth and Poverty*, trans. Catherine Roth (New York: St. Vladimir's Seminary Press, 1984), 49–55.

[10]For more on the zero-sum nature of what has been called the "limited good" view of wealth, see Bruce Malina, *The New Testament World: Insights from Cultural Anthropology*, 3rd ed. (Louisville: Westminster John Knox, 2001).

appreciation of everyday life initiated by the Protestant Reformation). This acceptance signaled a remarkable development in Christian thought and practice, which had earlier been characterized by a vague moral suspicion of these professions inherited in part from Greek philosophy.

At the same time that it became clear that economic interactions were no longer necessarily zero-sum, early modern canonists and theologians also had begun to notice that money was not as sterile as Aristotle had famously assumed, an assumption that had seemed commonplace, even as recently as Aquinas. Through a centuries-long process of using casuistry to ask whether emerging lending and insuring practices were usurious, in fact, these jurists slowly developed the modern theory of money as capital, in which money has a productive capacity of its own in addition to its use as a means of exchange. Recognition of this was achieved through, and in turn legitimized, the fundamental transformation of the usury prohibition, at the end of which the moral permissibility of receiving interest on a loan was widely accepted.

Another historical development that bears especial mention is the Enlightenment belief that all individuals possess an inalienable dignity that has political and social dimensions. This can be seen in the emergence of rights discourse, and in the conviction that each individual deserves an equal opportunity to pursue "the good life," now defined in no small part by material well-being. (Although this latter view has now thoroughly permeated modern Christian thought, it is worth noting that it would not have been taken as axiomatic a millennium or more ago, despite Christianity's historical commitment to care for the poor.) The economic consequences of the diffusion of this conviction have included the abolishment of legal property rights over humans, or slavery, and the extension of property rights to women.

As a socioeconomic order, global capitalism thus developed alongside and through significant conversation with the evolution of Christianity in Europe. As Weber famously argued, in fact, Protestant ethics was a particularly important source from which the "spirit of capitalism" emerged, at least originally.[11] Despite such mutual historical influences, however, Christian ethical reflection generally does not take capitalism overall to express Christian values straightforwardly, or to be perfectly compatible with them.

Two exceptions to this are worth noting. The first is academic: against critiques of capitalism raised by liberation theologians in the mid-to-late twentieth century, some American theologians constructed an enthusiastic theological defense of capitalism in an attempt to vindicate it against its socialist and communist competitors.[12] The second is the remarkable global growth of the prosperity gospel movement. The controversial theology undergirding this movement centers on the belief that Christ's atonement offers physical and material well-being to believers alongside justification, and God rewards

---

[11]Specifically, Weber noticed what he called an "elective affinity" between capitalism and the work ethic that emerged in Protestant, and particularly Calvinist, parts of Europe after the Reformation. As he identified it, this ethic centered on the Protestant affirmation that all believers (and not merely the priestly class) have a calling, and the sense that the diligence with which one attends to one's vocation in the world may be a sign of election. As proof of this "worldly asceticism," profit was thus viewed within this ethic as a potential sign of grace. Max Weber, *The Protestant Ethic and Spirit of Capitalism*, rev. 1920 ed., trans. Stephen Kalberg (New York: Oxford University Press, 2011).

[12]Michael Novak has argued that capitalism expresses Catholic social teaching better than other modes of organizing economic life. Michael Novak, *Will It Liberate?* (New York: Paulist, 1986); Novak, *The Spirit of Democratic Capitalism* (New York: Simon and Schuster, 1982). Max Stackhouse had similarly argued that capitalism is grounded in and can be made consonant with Protestant covenant theology. Max Stackhouse, *Public Theology and Political Economy: Christian Stewardship in Modern Society* (Grand Rapids: Eerdmans, 1987).

faithfulness and godly behavior with prosperity.[13] As such, the theological worldview of the movement tends to embrace market-based societies as functionally congruent with the demands of Christian discipleship.

While such an unequivocal endorsement of capitalism is rare within Christian theology and ethics, the polar opposite view, of total critique, is not quite as rare. Nineteenth-century proponents of Christian socialism such as Walter Rauschenbusch comprised an early example of this (although it is interesting to note that they often advocated a kind of economic democracy and/or democratic socialism that is not entirely foreign to what today is called the "Nordic model" of capitalism).[14] In the twentieth century, a number of Latin American liberation theologians in conversation with Marxist ideology critically argued that capitalist power relations are fundamentally unjust and at odds with the preferential option for the poor found in the gospel.[15] And, from a somewhat different angle, John Milbank and other radical orthodox theologians claim that capitalist political economy implicitly participates in the agonism and nihilism at the core of liberal modernity. Theologians writing in this vein accordingly construe the task of Christian ethics vis-à-vis capitalism as one of genealogical excavation of its idolatrous crypto-theologies, although they may also advocate forms of Christian socialism.[16]

Stridently pro- and anti-capitalist arguments in Christian thought thus employ a variety of theological loci and methods to address a range of practical and theoretical issues. Underneath this, however, it is possible to read such arguments as a fundamental disagreement over the morality of private property, with each side focusing on one particular aspect of the multivalent analysis found in both scripture and the history of the tradition—defenders emphasizing its legitimacy, and critics its spiritual dangers. In interesting ways these Christian conversations thus present theological analogues to the secular disagreements between inheritors of Marxist thought and economic liberalism, which propose quite different narrations of capitalism as a moral context based precisely on divergent assessments of property as a form of power. Indeed, conversation between those gripped by these two views, whether within Christian ethics or without, handily illustrates why "capitalism" defies easy definition, and arguably qualifies as what philosopher W. B. Gallie has called an "essentially contested concept."[17]

---

[13]Kate Bowler, *Blessed: A History of the American Prosperity Gospel* (New York: Oxford University Press, 2013). See also Simon Coleman, *The Globalisation of Charismatic Christianity: Spreading the Gospel of Prosperity* (New York: Cambridge University Press, 2000); Philip Jenkins, *The New Faces of Christianity: Believing the Bible in the Global South* (New York: Oxford University Press, 2006).

[14]See W. D. P. Bliss, *What Is Christian Socialism* (Boston: Society of Christian Socialists, 1890). See also Alan Wilkinson, *Christian Socialism: Scott Holland to Tony Blair* (London: SCM Press, 1998).

[15]Of course, it should be noted that the extent to which liberation theologians embraced Marxist social analysis, and/or practically advocated non- or postcapitalist politics, varied widely. Examples of those that are more clearly opposed to capitalism include Leonardo Boff, *Cry of the Earth, Cry of the Poor* (Maryknoll: Orbis, 1997); Boff, *The Lord's Prayer* (Maryknoll: Orbis, 1983); Ulrich Duchrow and Franz Hinkelammert, *Property for People, Not for Profit: Alternatives to the Global Tyranny of Capital* (London: Zed, 2004); Jon Sobrino, *No Salvation outside the Poor: Prophetic-Utopian Essays* (Maryknoll: Orbis, 2008). Duchrow and Hinkelammert and Sobrino especially and explicitly connect this rejection of capitalism with its foundation in private property rights.

[16]See Daniel M. Bell Jr., *Liberation Theology after the End of History: The Refusal to Cease Suffering* (New York: Routledge, 2001); Bell, *The Economy of Desire: Christianity and Capitalism in a Postmodern World* (Grand Rapids: Baker Academic, 2012); John Milbank, *Theology and Social Theory: Beyond Secular Reason*, 2nd ed. (New York: Wiley-Blackwell, 2006); Philip Goodchild, *Capitalism and Religion: The Price of Piety* 2009 (New York: Routledge, 2002); D. Stephen Long, *Divine Economy: Theology and the Market* (New York: Routledge, 2000).

[17]Which is to say that, much like "art" or "justice," its very meaning remains a matter of dispute. W. B. Gallie, "Essentially Contested Concepts," *Proceedings of the Aristotelian Society* 56 (1956): 167–98.

Despite the visibility of dialogue between such polar views in the field of Christian ethics, in both practice and academic literature the far more common approach blends criticism with appreciation. In this view, a market-based society is by no means congruent with the coming kingdom of God, and can never become so. Nonetheless, Christians should provisionally appreciate the advantages and partial approximations of justice that capitalist institutions do enable (which are considerable when seen against the backdrop of socialism and communism in recent history). Further, Christians are called to lend what aid they can in improving the conditions of economic life in light of the mandate of biblical justice. Capitalism arguably thus presents Christians with the same challenges and opportunities that life in the *saeculum*, or "the world," always does: while the world cannot be our ultimate home—and indeed, we must avoid becoming worldly while we endure trials—we nonetheless are called to transform it by participating with God's own redeeming action in its very midst.

This theological perspective has practical implications for both individual and social ethics. A robust body of academic and pastoral literature examines the implications for Christians in their personal lives—as parents, parishioners, and homeowners.[18] A growing conversation attends in particular to the distinct spiritual challenges (and occasional opportunities) presented by consumerism, and consumer culture.[19] A related body of scholarship speaks to Christians whose vocational calling is to work in management, finance, and the business corporation.[20] This literature particularly emphasizes that faith must inform one's entire life, and the responsibility that Christians have to work for the common good, even and especially when pursuing profit. While many of the specific topics the literature addresses are new, they extend conversations on how individuals ought to approach trade, wealth, and charity that stretch back through the thought of figures such as Martin Luther, Thomas Aquinas, and Clement of Alexandria to the Hebrew Bible.

In contrast, Christian social ethics takes society as a whole, rather than individual character and action, as its subject. Although a commitment to social justice has been central to Christian thought since the writings of the Hebrew prophets, systematic ethical attention to society itself only emerged in the late nineteenth century in response to new issues presented by urbanization, industrialization, and globalization. As these increasingly revealed the fundamental contingency of all social institutions, theologians and ecclesial leaders began extending the earlier insights of the tradition to speak to political, economic, and social structures for the first time. Statements and resolutions

---

[18]E.g., Doug Hicks, *Money Enough: Everyday Practices for Living Faithfully in the Global Economy* (San Francisco: Jossey-Bass, 2010); David Matzko McCarthy, *The Good Life: Genuine Christianity for the Middle Class* (Eugene: Wipf and Stock, 2006); David Cloutier, *The Vice of Luxury: Economic Excess in a Consumer Age* (Washington, DC: Georgetown University Press, 2015).

[19]E.g., Vincent Miller, *Consuming Religion: Christian Faith and Practice in a Consumer Age* (New York: Continuum, 2003); John Kavanaugh, *Following Christ in a Consumer Society* (Maryknoll: Orbis, 2006), William T. Cavanaugh, *Being Consumed: Economics and Christian Desire* (Grand Rapids: Eerdmans, 2008); Paul Louis Metzger, *Consuming Jesus: Beyond Race and Class in a Consumer Church* (Grand Rapids: Eerdmans, 2007).

[20]E.g., Pontifical Council, *Vocation of a Business Leader*, XXIV UNIAPAC World Congress in Lyon, France, March 30, 2012; Michael Naughton, *The Logic of Gift: Rethinking Business as a Community of Persons* (Milwaukee: Marquette University Press, 2012); Helen Alford and Michael Naughton, *Managing as If Faith Mattered: Christian Social Principles in the Modern Organization* (Notre Dame: University of Notre Dame Press, 2001); David Miller, *God at Work: The History and Promise of the Faith at Work Movement* (New York: Oxford University Press, 2007); Scott B. Rae and Kenman L. Wong, *Business for the Common Good: A Christian Vision for the Marketplace* (Downers Grove: IVP Academic, 2011); Alejo José G. Sison, Ignacio Ferrero, and Gregorio Guitán, eds., *Business Ethics: A Virtue Ethics and Common Good Approach* (New York: Routledge, 2018).

on economic concerns issued by Christian groups in recent decades illustrate the wide range of ways that Christian commitments can be used to morally interpret the specific sociopolitical and cultural challenges that capitalism presents, and the duties of churches, states, and other institutions vis-à-vis these challenges.[21]

In the United States, the development of social ethics in Protestant thought has its roots in the Social Gospel movement. Leaders such as Walter Rauschenbusch argued that the overly individualistic and spiritualized theology of their time had failed to attend to structural sin and the fundamentally social vision of salvation found within the gospel. Drawing upon the resources of then-emerging social sciences such as sociology, they advocated for social welfare programs and improved labor and housing conditions.[22] As noted above, Rauschenbusch himself condemned capitalism overall as sinful, and contemporary inheritors of this tradition have continued this legacy of critical engagement with capitalist institutions and culture (although Protestant ethicists today do not necessarily or uniformly reject capitalism, per se). In recent decades Protestant scholars have also increasingly focused on the importance of grounding all social and economic analysis within a particular context, and have pushed Christian economic ethics to attend to race, gender, class, and power.[23]

Arguably the most well-developed conversation on the economy within Christian social ethics can be found in the field of modern Catholic social thought. The 1891 papal encyclical *Rerum Novarum* set the tone for later Catholic analyses of capitalism by using a natural law framework to affirm the legitimacy of private property while also condemning any ideology that subordinates the common good and the dignity of the worker to property rights.[24] Subsequent encyclicals, pastoral letters, and theological scholarship have built on this foundation of Thomistic property ethics by articulating the principle of the "universal destination of goods," which claims that a "social mortgage" exists on all property—that is, that "the right of private property is subordinate to the right of common usage, the destination of goods for all."[25] In this view, the property rights on which capitalist institutions are founded necessarily entail positive responsibilities to the common good, and in particular to those in need. These responsibilities are, in the first instance, incumbent upon private individuals and institutions, and are moral before they are political. However, Catholic social thought also asserts that it is the duty of

---

[21]For a typological analysis of some of the theological themes and approaches structuring ecclesial statements in the latter half of the twentieth century, see Aart van den Berg, *God and the Economy: Analysis and Typology of Roman Catholic, Protestant, Orthodox, Ecumenical and Evangelical Theological Documents on the Economy* (Delft: Eburon, 1998).

[22]For more on this history, see Gary Dorrien, *Social Ethics in the Making: Interpreting an American Tradition* (New York: Wiley-Blackwell, 2010), 60–125.

[23]For recent examples of work on and within this field, see C. Melissa Snarr, *All You That Labor: Religion and Ethics in the Living Wage Movement* (New York: New York University Press, 2011); Keri Day, *Religious Resistance to Neoliberalism: Womanist and Black Feminist Perspectives* (New York: Palgrave Macmillan, 2015); Gary Dorrien, *Economy, Difference, Empire: Social Ethics for Social Justice* (New York: Columbia University Press, 2010); Joerg Rieger, *No Rising Tide: Theology, Economics, and the Future* (Minneapolis: Fortress, 2009).

[24]See Kenneth Himes, ed., *Modern Catholic Social Teaching: Commentaries and Interpretations*, 2nd ed. (Washington, DC: Georgetown University Press, 2018), for an introduction to the magisterial teaching at the heart of this tradition of social analysis.

[25]Pope John Paul II, *Laborem exercens* (Vatican City: Libreria Editrice Vaticana, 1981), § 14. See also Pope Paul VI, *Gaudium et spes* (Vatican City: Libreria Editrice Vaticana, 1965), § 69; and John Paul II, *Sollicitudo rei socialis* (Vatican City: Libreria Editrice Vaticana, 1987), § 42, for early uses of these terms in encyclicals, respectively, and the *Catechism of the Catholic Church* (Vatican City: Libreria Editrice Vaticana, 2000), § 2402–6, for a summary of their current use in the field.

government to ensure that economic freedom not be used to harm the common good, and therefore assumes that states have an essential role to play in structuring market activity. Other principles central to Catholic economic analysis include solidarity, subsidiarity, human dignity, and a preferential option for the poor. The last of these originated within the field of liberation theology and ethics, which is in significant ways deeply consistent and in sustained conversation with the broader field of Catholic social thought.[26] While liberation ethicists frequently critique capitalism overall as an intellectual, social, and economic system of power, Catholic social thought has tended to focus on specific institutions, policies, and even practices that are unjust and in need of reform.[27] However, Pope Francis's articulation of this tradition illustrates a more recent and developing emphasis in the field on the affective roots and consequences of economic injustice, as well, and a growing engagement with the cultural dimensions of capitalism.[28]

ECONOMICS

As this volume emphasizes, the task of Christian ethics requires critical reflection on human experience, an important resource for moral reflection. As a category, this includes insight available from academic disciplines that study the natural and human world, such as biology, history, and sociology. In the area of economic ethics, the most immediately relevant such discipline is economics.

Although systematic reflection on economic themes traces at least as far back as Aristotle, the modern science of economics is generally considered to have begun with the Scottish moral philosopher Adam Smith. In the twentieth century, the field underwent a positivist revolution, after which the mainstream of the discipline focused primarily on explaining prices and choices using a rational choice framework.[29] Microeconomics studies the behavior and interaction of individuals, households, and firms that make up markets. Macroeconomics studies the behavior of entire economies and addresses topics such as growth, inflation, unemployment, and the effect of monetary and fiscal policy.

There is some disagreement within Christian ethics over whether and what sort of resources for moral reflection can be found within economics, and over how to engage those it does offer. Some of this reflects the different analyses of capitalism already mentioned, and centers on the question of whether economics presents an ideological defense of the status quo that must be demystified. The most vocal in this regard are radical orthodox theologians who contend that economics is essentially an apology for secular reason's separation of facts from values and presumption of agonistic relations,

---

[26]For a discussion on the relation of these literatures and approaches to Christian economic ethics, see Michael Kirwan, SJ, "Liberation Theology and Catholic Social Teaching," *New Blackfriars* 93, no. 1044 (2012): 246–58.
[27]For recent examples of scholarship on and within this field, see Albino Barrera, *Modern Catholic Social Documents and Political Economy* (Washington, DC: Georgetown University Press, 2001); Barrera, *Globalization and Economic Ethics: Distributive Justice in the Knowledge Economy* (New York: Palgrave Macmillan, 2007); Daniel Finn, ed., *The Moral Dynamics of Economic Life: An Extension and Critique of Caritas in Veritate* (New York: Oxford University Press, 2012); Finn, ed., *The True Wealth of Nations: Catholic Social Thought and Economic Life* (New York: Oxford University Press, 2010).
[28]See especially Pope Francis, *Evangelii gaudium* (Vatican City: Libreria Editrice Vaticana, 2013), § 52–60. For more on this turn to engage affectivity in Catholic social thought, see Bernard Brady, "From Catholic Social Thought to Catholic Social Living: A Narrative of the Tradition," *Journal of Catholic Social Thought* 15, no. 2 (2018): 318.
[29]For more on the history of the field see Ben Fine and Dmitris Milonakis, *From Political Economy to Economics: Method, the Social and the Historical in the Evolution of Economic Theory* (New York: Routledge, 2008).

and insinuates a heretical theology that undermines Christian discipleship.[30] From such a perspective, the only moral insight that economics offers is into the self-description of a fallen and idolatrous social order.

Other critiques focus on the field's individualistic assumptions. Along with other scholars, theologians have pointed out the shortcomings of the *homo economicus* model, given that humans are not—and should not aspire to become—the rationally individualistic agents it describes. Indeed, such critics allege, the discipline overall is based upon a functional endorsement of self-interest (and perhaps selfishness) that is antithetical to the gospel.[31] Finally, others worry that its methodological individualism denies the existence of a common good at all; within the confines of economic theory, it is only possible to imagine unconnected individuals flourishing alongside each other—and for that matter, to define flourishing in material terms and/or as the maximization of unconstrained choice.

While there is some truth to these critiques, there is also much that they miss. For one thing, the models and theories structuring economic inquiry are intended neither as normative ideals nor as plausible descriptions of why economic agents act as they do. Ideally, these simply enable economists to describe and predict how forces causally interact in markets; the "explanations" to which economic inquiry aspires are therefore somewhat more modest than is the case in related fields such as sociology and psychology.[32] It is therefore a mistake to charge economists with normatively endorsing selfishness solely on the basis of the assumptions undergirding *homo economicus*.

For another, there is much within the methodological framework of economics that may be useful to social ethicists. Among other things, the "economic way of thinking" prompts one to consider the untended consequences of all political and institutional decisions in light of the incentives they create for individuals. It also encourages an awareness of how spontaneous and undirected orders emerge and function, a focus on opportunity costs and trade-offs (and on externalities, which are costs imposed upon other parties), and attention to the unique challenges that the provision of different kinds of goods (private, public, club, and common) presents.[33]

In addition to this particular way of thinking, the field also offers ethicists a body of empirical insight into what types of policies are likely to promote the common good in the future, in light of experience gleaned from both history and laboratory research. And for most mainstream economists, this is in fact precisely the *raison d'etre* of their science: to be useful to those in charge of promoting what Adam Smith had called the "wealth of nations." Theoretically, the resources that economics offers toward this end are themselves value-neutral, in much the way that knowledge developed in biology, physics,

[30]E.g., Long, *Divine Economy*, 4. See his critique of the concept of opportunity costs and his allegation that this "contains a complex metaphysics" that leads to "death, violence, and antagonism."

[31]Seen above all in Smith's famous observation that we receive our dinner not from the benevolence of the butcher, brewer, or baker, "but from their regard for their own interest." Adam Smith, *An Inquiry into the Nature and Causes of the Wealth of Nations*, ed. R. H. Campbell and Andrew S. Skinner (Indianapolis: Liberty Classics, 1979), I.ii.2.

[32]For the classic articulation of this methodological approach, see Milton Friedman's 1953 essay, "The Methodology of Positive Economics," in *The Philosophy of Economics: An Anthology*, 3rd ed., ed. Daniel M. Hausman (New York: Cambridge University Press, 2007), 145–78.

[33]See, e.g., Andrew Yuengert, "What Can Economists Contribute to the Common Good Tradition?," in *Empirical Foundations of the Common Good: What Theology Can Learn from Social Science*, ed. Daniel Finn (New York: Oxford University Press, 2017), 36–63; Daniel Finn, "What We Should and Should Not Learn from Economics," in *Christian Economic Ethics: History and Implications* (Minneapolis: Fortress, 2013), 217–36.

or other natural sciences is thought to be empirical rather than normative. Consider the contested political issue of a living wage: while economic theory itself does not contain a moral account of wage justice or a philosophical argument for or against minimum wage legislation, it can be used to forecast the likely consequences of enacting such legislation. Others may then use this information to decide whether to support a given law in light of their (externally decided-upon) values and priorities. On this reading of the field, economics itself does not offer moral insight per se, but it does offer theories, methods, and data that ethicists may find useful when making prudential judgments.

But alas, this is too simple; while this tidy account of economics as a source for Christian ethics is not entirely untrue, neither is it true without remainder. For one thing, economics is a *social* science, a fact that should prevent any easy comparison between the use of economics with appeals to physics or biology in Christian ethics.[34] As a social science, economics reflects and participates in the human world it observes. As Marx pointed out, for example, classical economics took for granted a historically contingent view of land, labor, and capital as salable commodities. While there is nothing intrinsically unethical in this view, there is much that it leaves out; therefore, when inhabiting this perspective it may be difficult to discuss—and perhaps even to notice—much that matters about land, labor, and capital. As an analytical gaze, economics thus brings some aspects of social issues into focus while obscuring others.

Moreover, a growing body of research indicates how powerfully metaphors organize human perception and cognition.[35] In light of this, it should not be surprising that economic tools of social analysis may in turn shape those who wield them: research indicates that exposure to mainstream economic theory is associated with more individualistic, and sometimes more selfish, behavior.[36] What is more, the social influence of economics extends beyond academia. An emerging body of research on the "performativity" of economics finds that economic theory regularly shapes, enacts, and influences market activity and economies as much as it observes them from a distance.[37]

It is difficult to gain conceptual traction on these ineliminably social dimensions of economics from within the analytical framework of the current mainstream of the discipline. However, a number of heterodox branches now exist that depart from the positivism and/or methodological commitments of the mainstream to varying degrees. Behavioral economics, for example, employs insights from the cognitive and behavioral sciences to examine the cognitive biases and heuristics that shape economic decision-making, and that

[34]It is easy to lose sight of this in light of the use of metaphors and language from the hard sciences, and from physics in particular, in economic discourse. On the importation of physics into economics, see Philip Mirowski, *More Heat than Light: Economics as Social Physics, Physics as Nature's Economics* (New York: Cambridge University Press, 1989).

[35]E.g., consider Paul H. Thibodeau and Lera Boroditsky, "Metaphors We Think With: The Role of Metaphor in Reasoning," *PLoS ONE* 6, no. 2 (2011): e16782, 3; see also George Lakoff and Mark Johnson, *Metaphors We Live By* (Chicago: University of Chicago Press, 1980).

[36]This has been called a "debasing effect." For an overview of this literature, see Amitai Etzioni, "The Moral Effects of Economic Teaching," *Sociological Forum* 30, no. 1 (March 2015): 228–33; also Yoram Bauman and Elaina Rose, "Selection or Indoctrination: Why Do Economics Students Donate Less than the Rest?," *Journal of Economic Behavior and Organization* 79, no. 3 (2011): 318–27. It is worth noting that scholars disagree over the implications of this research. Nonetheless, it presents important food for thought for Christian ethicists seeking to make use of economic theory.

[37]See Michel Callon, ed., *The Laws of the Markets* (Malden: Blackwell, 1998); Donald MacKenzie and Fabian Muniesa, *Do Economists Make Markets? On the Performativity of Economics* (Princeton: Princeton University Press, 2008); Ivan Boldyrev and Ekaterina Svetlova, eds., *Enacting Dismal Science: New Perspectives on the Performativity of Economics* (New York: Palgrave Macmillan, 2016).

lead agents to act in ways that deviate from the utility-maximizing rationality classically expected of *homo economicus*. The field of feminist economics seeks to correct masculinist biases in the methods and foci of the discipline by uncovering the links between the social construction of gender and the social construction of their discipline. Other heterodox branches likewise seeking to amend mainstream analysis include ecological, institutional, and Austrian economics.[38] Each of these provides a distinct analytical lens with which to consider the moral issues that arise in markets.

Broad engagement with heterodox economic scholarship thus offers ethicists an opportunity to gain critical insight into the perspectival limitations of all economic theory, and therefore resources with which to engage the field advisedly. Especially helpful is the way that heterodox discourses often reject the naturalistic and mechanistic metaphors and models of the mainstream. These can subtly suggest a reified picture of capitalism, as if "the economy" were in fact a self-contained and entirely asocial arena governed by its own immutable laws and forces. Such a depiction is not only empirically inaccurate but also morally problematic, insofar as it implies that market processes and outcomes are not properly the subject of moral analysis. (This picture of markets has political implications as well, given that it rhetorically casts political action as necessarily "intervening" into preexisting phenomena.) With this in mind, it is useful for ethicists considering economic questions that heterodox fields focus in different ways on the institutional and cultural determinants of economic behavior, processes, and outcomes. As such, they offer helpful reminders of the fundamentally social nature of the lessons to be learned from economic experience.

SUGGESTED READINGS

Barrera, Albino. *Biblical Economic Ethics: Sacred Scripture's Teachings on Economic Life*. Lanham: Lexington, 2013.

Finn, Daniel. *Christian Economic Ethics: History and Implications*. Minneapolis: Fortress, 2013.

Finn, Daniel. *The Moral Ecology of Markets: Assessing Claims about Markets and Justice*. New York: Cambridge University Press, 2006.

González, Justo. *Faith and Wealth: A History of Early Christian Ideas on the Origin, Significance, and Use of Money*. Eugene: Wipf and Stock, 2002.

Hirschfeld, Mary. *Aquinas and the Market: Toward a Humane Economy*. Cambridge: Harvard University Press, 2018.

Oslington, Paul, ed. *The Oxford Handbook of Christianity and Economics*. New York: Oxford University Press, 2014.

Schweiker, William, and Charles Mathewes, eds. *Having: Property and Possession in Religious and Social Life*. Grand Rapids: Eerdmans, 2004.

van den Berg, Aart. *God and the Economy: Analysis and Typology of Roman Catholic, Protestant, Orthodox, Ecumenical and Evangelical Theological Documents on the Economy*. Delft: Eburon, 1998.

[38]For a more substantial introduction to these fields and to their use for religious ethicists, see Christina McRorie, "Heterodox Economics, Social Ethics, and Inequality: New Tools for Thinking Critically about Markets and Economic Injustices," *Journal of Religious Ethics* 47, no. 2 (2019): 232–58.

CHAPTER THIRTY-SIX

Wealth, Poverty, and Personal Holiness

KATE WARD

Christian ethics provides believers with a training guide for personal holiness, otherwise described as imitating Christ, growing in virtue, or leading a life of discipleship. Every believer is called to personal holiness, which may be viewed as linked to one's hope of salvation. Despite its personal, even apparently individualistic focus, holiness is not a private project. Christians pursue holiness in community, through their ordinary lives, and the ordinary circumstances of these lives matter for Christian ethics. Christian ethics reflects on how life circumstances affect personal holiness particularly through its multiple strands of thought dealing with wealth and poverty. Starting with the Hebrew Bible, and with renewed focus in every age, the sources of Christian ethics examine how wealth and poverty affect the pursuit of holiness.

Two consistently influential ways of regarding the role of wealth and poverty in the life of holiness might be called spiritualized and materialist views. Those who spiritualize wealth and poverty believe one's attitude to their concrete situation to be morally determinative. They think we can possess riches without being possessed by them, as Augustine says; maintaining material wealth with an attitude of detachment can be morally praiseworthy.[1] Spiritualized views of poverty tend to de-emphasize the suffering of the poor and promote their hoped-for spiritual reward. In contrast, what I am calling materialist views of wealth and poverty hold that material reality functions morally. Without fully determining the personal holiness of wealthy people, material wealth does function to interfere in their relationships with God. Actual divestment, not simply spiritual detachment, may be required of wealthy people who wish to pursue holiness. Poverty, too, influences the quest for holiness, with some materialists holding that even involuntary poverty encourages a praiseworthy dependence on God. Others view poverty as unjust, against God's design, and believe privation can morally damage the believer. Proponents of each of these views can point to material within the sources of Christian ethical tradition in support of their claims.

---

[1]Augustine, *Letters, Volume III (131–164)*, trans. Wilfrid Parsons, SND (Washington, DC: Catholic University of America Press, 1953), 348.

SCRIPTURE

There is no univocal scriptural tradition on the implications of wealth and poverty for personal holiness, but multiple voices that sing not in dissonance, but in harmony. What cannot be said is that the Bible regards wealth as merely spiritualized, in the sense that its material use is irrelevant to the life of holiness. Indeed, rituals of cultic purity and redistributive practices to alleviate poverty are interwoven and mutually reliant throughout the Hebrew Bible's covenant and law books.[2] According to Sondra Ely Wheeler, the Hebrew Bible presents four streams of tradition on wealth. Wealth is depicted variously as a potential temptation to idolatry, replacing the focus and trust properly directed to God alone; as the "fruit of injustice," accumulated through violation of the dictates of charity and duty to others; as a blessing with which God justly rewards the faithful; and as the "reward of labor."[3]

We can see that at least some of these views of wealth in the Hebrew Bible presume analogous views of poverty. If wealth is the reward of labor, poverty must be the result of blameworthy idleness (as it is depicted in the Wisdom literature); if wealth is God's blessing, perhaps the poor are divinely cursed. On the other hand, if wealth is the fruit of injustice, clearly the poor suffer through no fault of their own, and if wealth tempts to idolatry, perhaps only the poor truly know how to depend on God.[4] Albino Barrera finds "an impressive convergence" of scripture scholars who say that a central biblical theme demands the poor be assisted.[5] Such assistance takes the form of restoration to independence in the Hebrew Bible, and of an ethics of fellowship, urged against patronage relationships between rich and poor, in the New Testament.[6] Such detailed insistence on what concern for the poor looks like belies interpretations that assign poverty to the failings of those who are poor and, in so doing, place them beyond the bounds of believers' concern.

These varying voices from the Hebrew Bible continue to inform Christian views of wealth, poverty, and personal holiness down to the present day. However, Wheeler shows that the account of the New Testament, while itself internally varied, is less contradictory in one important way. The New Testament depicts wealth multifariously: as a "stumbling block" to following Jesus in discipleship; as a potential competitor to devotion to God, consistent with Hebrew Bible warnings against idolatry; and, again following the Hebrew Bible, as the result of economic injustice. With the repeated exhortations that believers share possessions in Acts and the Pauline letters, wealth is also depicted as a resource for meeting human needs.[7]

Wheeler points out that New Testament traditions on wealth sideline Hebrew Bible understandings of wealth as just reward and divine blessing. Foregrounded, rather, are concerns about idolatry, skepticism about wealth's provenance, and calls to use goods to help the needy. However, as Wheeler says, there is no hint of denying the goodness of material reality, or of failure to recall that all creation is God's gift.

---

[2]Albino Barrera, *Biblical Economic Ethics: Sacred Scripture's Teachings on Economic Life* (Lanham: Lexington, 2013), chap. 3.

[3]Sondra Ely Wheeler, *Wealth as Peril and Obligation: The New Testament on Possessions* (Grand Rapids: Eerdmans, 1995), 123–7.

[4]Ibid.

[5]Barrera, *Biblical Economic Ethics*, 253.

[6]Ibid., chap. 13.

[7]Wheeler, *Wealth as Peril*, 127–33.

Does the biblical tradition enable Christian ethicists to say anything about the implications of wealth and poverty for personal holiness, given the tradition's multivalence and even internal contradiction? It seems difficult to discount the insistent voice, throughout the tradition, that warns that wealth can replace God as the proper object of trust, dependence, and even veneration. Biblical injunctions to share with the needy thus help those in want while allowing those with means to practice the detachment necessary for their spiritual lives. Barrera concludes that scriptural promises of material sufficiency are both general and conditional. That is, we should understand that God offers sufficiency to all humanity, not to isolated individuals, and that this sufficiency is contingent both on continued moral rectitude and on human ability to divide the goods of the earth according to the needs of all—an action that itself embodies moral rectitude.[8] While wealth can feel like a sure sign of God's providence and blessing, it is also a potential moral threat. Nor is the source of wealth immaterial; wealth created through injustice comes in for biblical censure. Those who have means should take care that their material abundance does not distract their focus from God, and they should act to provide for the needs of the poor and to restore their independence.

TRADITION

The early Church Fathers, including Origen (*c.* 184–253), Clement of Alexandria (*c.* 150–215) and Augustine (354–430), warned of the moral and spiritual dangers of wealth. Wealth could enable the practice of vice; become an idol, replacing proper veneration of God; and inspire misplaced trust, rather than the dependence on God necessary for a Christian believer. Almsgiving was heavily enjoined, not only for the good of those in need, but as reflecting the proper posture toward goods on the part of the rich: holding them with a light hand, ready to give them away. Giving was a useful tool for salvation, as the poor who received could, in Augustine's memorable phrase, serve as a "catapult" to bear goods to heaven.[9] This sometimes led to a depiction of poor people that seems frankly utilitarian from today's perspective—as Helen Rhee writes, one where "the visibility and portrayal of the poor are always attached to their instrumentality in the salvation of the rich."[10]

At times the work of various Church Fathers betrays a tendency to spiritualize wealth, admitting the possibility of remaining wealthy without being viciously attached to one's riches. However, a more materialistic strand in their thought insists that simply owning wealth invited vicious attachment and that divestment was morally safer. A strict reading of the universal purpose of the goods of creation led to patristic insistence that any surplus is a necessity denied to those in need—for example, the extra coat hanging in one's closet is stolen from a person without one.[11] The tension between spiritualized and materialist understandings of poverty is also found in varying views of the spiritual or moral benefits associated with poverty. Those who are poor against their own will might be credited

---

[8]Barrera, *Biblical Economic Ethics*, chap. 11.

[9]Kate Ward, "Porters to Heaven: Wealth, the Poor, and Moral Agency in Augustine," *Journal of Religious Ethics* 42, no. 2 (2014): 216–42.

[10]Helen Rhee, *Loving the Poor, Saving the Rich: Wealth, Poverty, and Early Christian Formation* (Grand Rapids: Baker Academic, 2012), 86.

[11]See, e.g., St. Basil's homily, "Will I Pull Down My Barns?," in *The Sunday Sermons of the Great Fathers*, vol. 1, ed. M. F. Toal (San Francisco: Ignatius Press, 2000), 325–32; and Augustine's Exposition on Psalm 147, https://www.newadvent.org/fathers/1801147.htm.

with praiseworthy dependence on God, or the benefits of holiness might be reserved for practitioners of voluntary poverty.

Monastic movements formalized the link between poverty and personal holiness traceable back to the New Testament in ways that continue to influence Christian life and theology today. However, these movements differed significantly from one another in their views regarding the necessity of voluntary poverty to achieve holiness, which Christians ought to pursue voluntary poverty, and the degree of poverty necessary to achieve the goals of holiness. The widely influential Rule of St. Benedict (*c.* 480–547) prescribed that monks and nuns hold all property in common, own nothing of their own, distribute goods and money to the poor, and practice moderation in food and drink.[12] More demanding in his interpretation of holy poverty, St. Francis of Assisi (*c.* 1181–1226) forbade members of his order from accepting money, even to redirect it to the poor, or owning dwellings, and desired them to obtain through begging those basic needs they could not attain through work.[13] While these extreme measures were prescribed only to vowed members of Francis's religious order, his preaching to ordinary Christians similarly emphasized giving up material possessions in order to avoid sin and increase one's dependence on God.[14]

The practice of voluntary poverty pursued by vowed religious is perhaps the most consistently visible and historically long-standing witness of the Christian tradition with respect to the relationship of wealth and personal holiness. For the majority of Christian history, voluntarily poor vowed religious women and men have served as living signs casting suspicion on purely spiritualized views of wealth that deny it any impact on the pursuit of holiness.

Thomas Aquinas (*c.* 1225–1274) is widely cited for his view that it is not vicious to spend what one needs to maintain a decent life in keeping with one's social position.[15] However, Thomas coupled this apparently spiritualized insight with challenging views about the impact of wealth on the life of virtue. He was concerned enough about the impact of wealth on his own virtuous life that he joined a mendicant religious order, the Dominicans, instead of pursuing a more comfortable religious life, and strongly defended the mendicant lifestyle in his writings.

Aquinas clearly hews to the materialist view that wealth inexorably acts on the moral impulses of its owner—not for him the equivocal "possessing wealth without being possessed by it." Wealth tempts to pride and threatens virtue—"the hope of gaining, or keeping, material wealth, is the poison of charity."[16] So, Thomas says, "those who wish to live virtuously need to avoid abundance of riches."[17] Possessing goods causes us to "despise" the goods we have and pushes us to seek other goods to satisfy our disordered desires.[18] There is a clear materialist understanding here: material comforts act on the

---

[12]Leonard J. Doyle OblSB, trans., *The Rule of St. Benedict* (Collegeville: Liturgical, 2001). Also see https://www.osb.org/our-roots/the-rule/.

[13]"The Rule of St. Francis" (Ordo Fratrum Minorum, Franciscan Friars), https://ofm.org/about/rule/.

[14]Kenneth Baxter Wolf, *The Poverty of Riches: St. Francis of Assisi Reconsidered* (New York: Oxford University Press, 2003), chap. 8.

[15]Thomas Aquinas, *Summa Theologiae*, trans. Dominican Fathers of the English Province (London: Burns Oates & Washbourne, 1921), II–II.118.1.

[16]Ibid., II–II, 162.3; Thomas Aquinas, "Liber de Perfectione Spiritualis Vitae [The Perfection of the Spiritual Life]," trans. John Procter, OP (Westminster: Newman, 1950), chap. 6, http://dhspriory.org/thomas/PerfectVitaeSpir.htm.

[17]Aquinas, *Summa Theologiae*, III.40.3.

[18]Ibid., I–II.2.1 ad 3.

moral tendencies of the wealthy, their attitudes notwithstanding. The moral dangers of wealth could be addressed through almsgiving, including giving from one's substance rather than simply from one's surplus; Thomas believed most of us give ourselves a generous margin when budgeting to maintain our current lifestyle.[19]

Influential leaders of the Protestant Reformation are too often read backward through the lens of Max Weber's "Protestant work ethic," suggesting that the reformers assigned moral goodness to the pursuit and accumulation of wealth. The reality is far more complex. Reformers did focus on the goodness of work. Mostly married men who lived in ordinary working communities, rather than celibate, cloistered religious, they daily encountered the financial burdens of working families and reflected that in their theological ethics. However, it is wrong to say that reformers uncritically legitimized the possession of wealth or forgot the historic Christian suspicion of wealth's role in the moral life.

While Martin Luther (1483–1546) famously rejected the selling of indulgences, he maintained a connection between the use of money and personal holiness, treating poverty as a virtue and criticizing the attachment of Catholic clergy to "accursed wealth."[20] John Calvin (1509–1564) frequently spoke of the rich as "stewards" of God's goods, charged with distributing them to meet the needs of the poor, and insisted that this duty could even demand reducing one's standard of living. His best-known contribution to Christian thought on economic life is permitting certain Christians to charge and receive interest on loans, a practice until his time regarded as the sin of usury.[21] The Reformation's return to scripture inspired some Christians to make more radical connections between wealth, poverty, and personal holiness; for example, many Anabaptists practiced (and continue to practice) communal sharing of possessions.

John Wesley (1703–1791) famously urged his followers to "gain all you can [albeit with significant reservations that the labor not hurt self or others]; save all you can; give all you can."[22] This injunction, often cited in support of the Protestant work ethic, comes in the context of a sermon in which wealth is equated with "temptations and snares," more wealth enabling the pursuit of vices such as vanity. The Protestant Reformation drew new theological attention to the concrete realities of work and financial markets while continuing to warn Christians of the dangers wealth could pose to the relationship with God.

Several overlapping factors combined to decrease interest in reflection on wealth and poverty in light of personal holiness following the Enlightenment. A greater interest in the use of scientific methods to understand society's workings shifted religious leaders' focus to economic systems, which they analyzed in light of God's intent for humanity. The body of Catholic social thought, beginning with Pope Leo XIII's encyclical letter *Rerum novarum* (*On the Condition of Labor*) in 1891, analyzed social systems and

---

[19]Ibid., II–II, 32.6.

[20]Martin Luther, "On the Freedom of a Christian," in *Modern Internet History Sourcebook*, ed. Paul Halsall, from Henry Wace and C. A. Buchheim, *First Principles of the Reformation* (London: John Murray, 1883), https://sourcebooks.fordham.edu/mod/luther-freedomchristian.asp; Martin Luther, "Address to the Nobility of the German Nation," in *Modern Internet History Sourcebook*, ed. Paul Halsall, trans. C. A. Buchheim, from C. W. Eliot, ed., *Harvard Classics 36* (New York: P.F. Collier, c1910), https://sourcebooks.fordham.edu/mod/luther-nobility.asp.

[21]Daniel K. Finn, *Christian Economic Ethics: History and Implications* (Minneapolis: Fortress, 2013), 165–76.

[22]John Wesley, "Sermon 50: The Use of Money," ed. Jennette Descalzo and George Lyons, The Wesley Center for Applied Theology, Nampa, ID, 1872/1999, https://www.whdl.org/sites/default/files/publications/EN_John_Wesley_050_use_of_money.htm.

employer–worker relationships in light of God's intent that all humans flourish, enjoy work and family, and attain self-sufficiency. The Social Gospel tradition in Protestant theology continued this focus on the injustice of economic systems, even as leading figures like Walter Rauschenbusch (1861–1918) envisioned personal conversion as the key to social change. As struggling working people were addressed directly, the need to warn of wealth's moral danger may have seemed less urgent. Poverty continued to be depicted as contrary to God's intent. Another factor in this shift may have been an increased interest in privatized spirituality and piety, catalyzed by the Enlightenment's focus on the person as individual. However, to complicate this picture, a flowering of active religious orders of women and men who vowed poverty showed that Christian communities continued to realize the dangers wealth posed to personal holiness.

If the post-Enlightenment period turned theological attention to the experience of ordinary members of the working classes, the postcolonial era significantly changed theology with what liberation theologian Gustavo Gutiérrez (1928–) calls "the irruption of the poor."[23] Living with, and studying scripture with, people living in desperate poverty in Latin America, liberation theologians told the world that poverty is contrary to God's intent and exposed the systemic complicity of the well-off in the systems that keep people in poverty. Just as earlier generations had largely rejected a spiritualized understanding of wealth in which one could have wealth without having it, liberation theologians rejected a romanticized vision of poverty in which the struggle for survival was explained away as deserving of a reward in heaven. They found God's preferential love for the poor reverberating throughout the scriptures, and called those with wealth and power to "make a preferential option for the poor" and work to enable God's intent that all humans have sufficient resources to live and thrive. This is not to say that universal wealth was envisioned as the goal. The Medellín conference encouraged the church in Latin America to pursue both material poverty and spiritual detachment in solidarity with the poor and as a path to holiness.[24]

EXPERIENCE

Reflection on everyday experience makes clear that wealth and poverty invite different moral perils and, perhaps, convey different moral benefits. Wealth makes it easier to care for self and others, to give generously without depriving loved ones of needed resources. Wealthy people also worry about losing satisfaction in meaningful work, focusing on consumption to the exclusion of personal relationships, and raising children who take their prosperity for granted. Poverty is frequently said to provide clarity about the things that really matter in life, but the experiences of poor people testify that the struggle to survive can distract from these goods and that being treated by society as disposable takes an immense personal toll.

While holiness is certainly beyond the scope of secular disciplines, a vast array of social science literature explores links between wealth or poverty and the types of moral virtues that Christians associate with holiness. Psychologists examine these connections in laboratory settings, investigating actual wealth and poverty on the basis of self-report and

---

[23]Gustavo Gutiérrez, "The Option for the Poor Arises from Faith in Christ," *Theological Studies* 70, no. 2 (2009): 319.

[24]CELAM, General Conference of the Bishops of Latin America and the Caribbean, "Medellín Document: Poverty of the Church," September 6, 1968.

also inducing fictive states of wealth or poverty relative to others. Sociologists conduct interviews with persons who are wealthy or poor, and economists and scientists of behavioral health work to discern trends in large sets of data.

"Affluenza" is a widely used term of pop psychology describing a broad range of moral and psychological harms thought to be caused by wealth and privilege, from selfishness to discontent with empty consumerism to the inability to understand the consequences of one's harmful actions. Psychological research suggests that this folk understanding that wealth harms moral capacity has basis in fact: wealthier people are more likely to act selfishly and break rules than those worse off.[25]

The emerging science of scarcity demonstrates how the stress of poverty burdens cognitive load, inhibiting patience, long-range planning, and commitment, several qualities linked to the Christian virtue of prudence and necessary for acquiring other virtues.[26] Ethicists are growing in understanding of the important role of positive self-regard, which might be described by virtues such as self-care or humility, properly called. In situations of scarcity, it is clearly more difficult to practice acts of self-care such as eating a healthy diet or going to the doctor. But the impact of poverty on the moral life is not limited to simply material privation. In most societies, to be poor is to be despised. The experience of those who are or who have been poor, reported in memoir, journalism, and sociology, movingly reflects that such societal disregard can become internalized, leading those who are poor to regard themselves as deserving of less than full human dignity.[27] Author Jesmyn Ward wrote about her experience growing up Black and poor in the United States: "Sometimes we caught ourselves repeating what history said, mumbling along, brainwashed: *I am nothing*."[28]

Those who reflect on the lived experience of poverty frequently note a result that is morally positive from a Christian perspective. Solidarity in Christian theological understanding is the recognition of our communal human nature: that my personhood, my flourishing, is bound up with that of others. Poverty frequently invites a lived understanding and practice of solidarity because of the practical reality that those in poverty will struggle to survive without depending on others and allowing others to depend on them. One of the inventive, indigent off-the-books workers interviewed in Chicago by sociologist Sudhir Venkatesh put it this way: "The ones who ain't got nothing, not even a roof over their head, we're the ones who are caring for each other ... We have to know how to live with each other or else we couldn't get by."[29] Christian ethics demands all people recognize and live into our shared communal nature, to "know how to live with each other." The lived experience of poverty seems to aid some persons in developing this important moral understanding. Those throughout the Christian tradition who upheld the relationship of poverty to personal holiness intuited this important truth.

---

[25]See Paul K. Piff et al., "Higher Social Class Predicts Increased Unethical Behavior," *Proceedings of the National Academy of Sciences of the United States of America* 109, no. 11 (2012): 4086–91.

[26]Sendhil Mullainathan and Eldar Shafir, *Scarcity: Why Having Too Little Means So Much* (New York: Times Books, Henry Holt, 2013).

[27]See Jesmyn Ward, *Men We Reaped: A Memoir* (New York: Bloomsbury, 2013); Linda Tirado, *Hand to Mouth: Living in Bootstrap America* (New York: Putnam Adult, 2014); Rick Bragg, *All over but the Shoutin'* (New York: Pantheon, 1997); Sarah Halpern-Meekin et al., *It's Not Like I'm Poor: How Working Families Make Ends Meet in a Post-Welfare World* (Oakland: University of California Press, 2015); Kathryn Edin and Timothy Jon Nelson, *Doing the Best I Can: Fatherhood in the Inner City* (Berkeley: University of California Press, 2013).

[28]Ward, *Men We Reaped*, 249, emphasis in original.

[29]Sudhir Alladi Venkatesh, *Off the Books: The Underground Economy of the Urban Poor* (Cambridge: Harvard University Press, 2006), 187–8.

REASON: CONTEMPORARY PERSPECTIVES

The depth of scientific inquiry into the moral and behavioral impacts of wealth and poverty shows that interest in the topic is not limited to religious ethicists. A remaining question is how to understand "wealth" and "poverty," these recurring themes throughout the Christian tradition, as they apply to persons in today's globalized world, marked by extreme inequality within and among nations. Some Christian ethicists broaden the category of "poor," understanding the preferential care for the poor demonstrated by God and enjoined upon Christians throughout the tradition to apply to several categories of excluded, despised, or marginalized persons. I have argued that the terms "wealth" and "poverty" as used in the Christian tradition should be interpreted through a materialist lens—where "poor" refers to those truly struggling to survive, and "wealthy" denotes those who have more than they need, with no middle ground. This admittedly broad definition of wealth, in my view, accurately captures the material and moral distinctions between wealth and poverty throughout the Christian tradition.

Many more Christian ethicists are at work complicating or broadening the category of "the wealthy." Scholars such as David Cloutier, Miguel De La Torre, and Julie Hanlon Rubio question the easy assumptions often made by middle-class persons in wealthy countries that the warnings of scripture and Christian tradition about wealth's moral danger do not apply to them.[30] Cloutier warns of the vice of luxury even among middle-class consumers, and Rubio notes how rarely contemporary families practice tithing, which the New Testament depicts as the minimum level of financial sacrifice for Christians. These and other perspectives embody the Christian tradition's materialist view of wealth's role in morality. Wealth, no more than any other factor, is not fully determinative of moral goodness; it does not have the power to take away human agency. However, wealth *is* an obstacle on the moral journey. Possessions do not determine, but they do shape, our moral lives. Despite this renewed insight, spiritualized understandings of wealth that insist it is possible to possess goods without becoming attached to them, or that view the poor instrumentally in the salvation of the rich, continue to arise. Popular "Prosperity Gospel" preachers in Africa, Latin America, the United States, and elsewhere retrieve the Hebrew Bible view of wealth as blessing and its implicit corollary that poverty is earned through moral failure.

In North America and Europe, reflections on the moral impacts of poverty have been few in recent years, perhaps motivated by fears of blaming the victim that emerge in analogous conversations in social science. One group of theologians who do not demur from addressing the moral impacts of poverty on the poor is theologians of liberation. Far from romanticizing unchosen poverty as salvific, liberation theologians unflinchingly address the psychological, social, and moral harms of being systematically treated as a "non-person."[31] Pope Francis rejects instrumental views of the poor in God's plan with his continued insistence that salvation is found in genuine encounters with those on the margins.

---

[30]David Cloutier, *The Vice of Luxury: Economic Excess in a Consumer Age* (Washington, DC: Georgetown University Press, 2015); Miguel A. De La Torre, *Doing Christian Ethics from the Margins*, 2nd rev. ed. (Maryknoll: Orbis, 2014); Julie Hanlon Rubio, *Family Ethics: Practices for Christians* (Washington, DC: Georgetown University Press, 2010).

[31]For example, Brazilian theologian Ivone Gebara addresses the impact of multiple systematic oppressions on poor women's senses of self-worth in *Out of the Depths: Women's Experience of Evil and Salvation* (Minneapolis: Fortress, 2002).

CONCLUSION

Christian holiness entails imitating Jesus, the Incarnate Word. It is no surprise that the actions of our incarnate bodies, in the everyday circumstances of our lives, are of critical interest to Christian ethics. Contrary to what is sometimes asserted, economic life is not separate from Christian ethics but of deep concern to believers, particularly since the tradition so strongly and consistently insists that wealth and poverty matter for personal holiness. While the tradition is not univocal, and continues to grow and change, the strong materialist emphasis—which insists that wealth and poverty do affect the pursuit of holiness, notwithstanding personal attitude toward them—cannot be ignored. These insights from scripture and tradition find ready confirmation in practical experience, social science, and contemporary theological reflection. Any Christian, wealthy or poor, committed to pursuing a life of holiness should take them seriously.

SUGGESTED READINGS

Farmer, Paul, and Gustavo Gutiérrez. *In the Company of the Poor: Conversations with Dr. Paul Farmer and Fr. Gustavo Gutiérrez*, ed. Michael Griffin and Jennie Weiss Block. Maryknoll: Orbis, 2013.

Finn, Daniel K. *Christian Economic Ethics: History and Implications*. Minneapolis: Fortress, 2013.

Johnson, Kelly S. *The Fear of Beggars: Stewardship and Poverty in Christian Ethics*. Grand Rapids: Eerdmans, 2007.

Ward, Kate. "Porters to Heaven: Wealth, the Poor, and Moral Agency in Augustine." *Journal of Religious Ethics* 42, no. 2 (2014): 216–42.

Wheeler, Sondra Ely. *Wealth as Peril and Obligation: The New Testament on Possessions*. Grand Rapids: Eerdmans, 1995.

CHAPTER THIRTY-SEVEN

Work and Vocation

ELISABETH RAIN KINCAID

Work, as defined by Thomas Aquinas, is not simply physical labor but "all those human occupations whereby man can lawfully gain a livelihood, whether by using his hands, his feet, or his tongue."[1] Work consumes our time, fills our lives, burdens our souls, and can become the source of our greatest worldly success or our greatest failure. The average employed American in 2018 could expect to spend one-third of her life at work. The all-consuming nature of work is often cited as a major cause of stress in an individual's life, especially as new communication technologies make it more difficult to "switch off," extending work into every sphere of human existence. The necessity of work for providing the resources needed to meet one's own and one's dependents' needs also makes the workplace an arena of life prone to exploitation and harassment. Growing awareness of the effects of globalization and environmental degradation have also resulted in a greater awareness that each person's work, while bringing individual benefits, may also tax the broader community.

However, sociologies and psychologies of work have confirmed that under- and unemployment can be just as stressful than overemployment, if not more. New physiological research confirms that some form of constructive work is beneficial for human physical and psychological flourishing.[2] This is especially true for jobs that the worker finds to be fulfilling or clearly connected to a greater cause.[3] The sense of having a vocation—a specific call to a specific job—and seeing that one's work produces meaningful and significant results can make large differences in life satisfaction. Of course, all of these options—between over- and underemployment and between fulfilling and non-fulfilling work—are typical only of recent opportunities in developed nations. For much of human history, work simply meant the difference between survival and starvation.

These negative and positive aspects of work, drawn from the experience of contemporary workers, must be integrated into any Christian ethic of work and vocation. A contemporary theology of work will also need to respond to new challenges arising from

---

[1]Thomas Aquinas, *Summa Theologiae*, trans. Fathers of the English Dominican Province (New York: Benziger Brothers, 1948), II–II.187.

[2]See Brent Rosso, Kathryn Dekas, and Amy Wrzesniewski, "On the Meaning of Work: A Theoretical Integration and Review," *Research in Organizational Behavior* 30 (2010): 91–127, for an overview of literature on this question.

[3]Kirsten Weir, "More than Job Satisfaction," *Monitor on Psychology* 44 (December 2013): 11–39. In 2018, Gallup found that only four in ten employees could claim that "the mission or purpose of my company makes me feel my job is important." This lack of fulfilment and personal engagement with one's work has substantive costs. The Gallup findings indicate that "by moving that ratio to eight in 10 employees, organizations could realize a 41% reduction in absenteeism, a 50% drop in patient safety incidents and a 33% improvement in quality."

both technological and economic development. In the rest of this chapter, I will present a theological framework—drawing upon scripture, tradition, reason, and experience—to address these challenges.

SCRIPTURE

Christian scripture begins by presenting the basic dichotomy between work as a source of fulfilment and work as a burden. Genesis 1 describes how God first makes humans in God's own image and then gives them dominion over all of creation and instructs them to subdue the earth.[4] A link is immediately established between human nature—a creature in God's image—and the task which that nature makes possible—the work of caring for creation. God explicitly gives this work of dominion to men and women together, not to men alone. In Genesis 2, the relationship between human nature and work is made even more explicit. Immediately after creation, "the LORD God took the man and put him in the garden of Eden to till and keep it" (Gen. 2:15). The requirement to "till and keep" carries with it a responsibility for being good caretakers of God's creation, but caretakers who engage in creative cultivation. God does not place humans in an already perfectly complete creation but rather involves them in the work of creation itself. Genesis 2 also contains the first reference to the Sabbath. Human work is located between God's action of creation and God's rest. From the very beginning of scripture, therefore, a connection is made between humanity's created nature in the image of God, the responsibility to work, and the relationship between humans, who are called to this task together. Human work, by giving the human community the opportunity to participate in God's creative act, draws them into deeper relationships with nature, with each other, and with God.

However, Genesis also presents the negative aspects of work. After the fall, work becomes punishment, characterized by sadness, brokenness, and sin (Gen. 3:16-20). Work is no longer an act of sharing in God's image and creativity but rather a necessity for survival, and can even be painful, humiliating, and frustrating. Work now places humans in opposition to nature rather than making them cooperative partners with God in care for nature. Work now also divides men and women, who no longer share in the same type of work as partners, but toil alone. Men work the soil by the sweat of their brow; women labor and bear children with pain. The alienating effects of work without God quickly become clear. In the story of the Tower of Babel, human work and creativity, perverted by the attempt to replace God's power and establish autonomous dominion, results in the further separations of humans from God, from each other, and from the rest of creation (Gen. 11:1-9).

The scriptural engagement with work does not end with Genesis. Rather, in the story of Israel and of the church, God redeems human work and incorporates it within God's plan for the redemption of the world. This new redemptive aspect of work first becomes apparent in the Mosaic law, where work becomes an important element in the creation of a holy community, set apart for the worship and praise of God. First, the importance of work for human dignity is affirmed by provisions ensuring that everybody has the opportunity to work. Gleaning provisions allow even the poor the chance to engage as part of the community working in the fields (Lev. 33:22). Likewise, the redistribution

[4]See chapters in the ecology section of this present volume for further discussion of these terms.

of land in the Jubilee Years ensures that nobody possesses a disproportionate amount of land, thereby excluding others from the means of productive work (Lev. 25:13-19). These provisions also call the holy community to the care of the poor and the vulnerable. Additional provisions ensure that the proceeds of work support not only oneself and family but also those who are not able to work: the poor, the widow, and the orphans (Exod. 22:22-27). In addition, because of the way in which the circumstances of work can provide opportunities for domination, the Mosaic law seeks to ensure that all are provided with fair conditions to carry out their own work (Deut. 24:14-15).

The story of Ruth provides an allegory for how work can contribute to the formation of the holy community of Israel. Ruth, a foreigner, engages in both women's work (caring for her mother-in-law) and men's work in the fields (Ruth 2:2-3). Boaz recognizes her character through her work and takes steps to make the working conditions easier and more humane for her (Ruth 2:14-16). However, although he eases her labor, he does not take away her work but rather acknowledges how the work contributes to her dignity. Ruth is empowered through her work to seek out Boaz as her kinsman/redeemer. Their union, which leads to the line of King David, foreshadows the eschatological union of foreigner and Jew.

The connection between work and a specific calling from God, a vocation, also begins to develop in the Old Testament. As part of God's work of redemption, God calls specific people to specific work. David, Samuel, and Moses all receive direct calls from God to serve as leaders. However, God also calls people to other work than the traditional leadership roles of prophet, priest, and king. For example, God "calls by name Bezalel the son of Uri ... and Aholiab the son of Ahisamach" as "gifted artisans," responsible for building the tabernacle (Exod. 31:1-6). Mordecai reminds Esther that God has placed her in the position of queen consort "for such a time as this" in order to save the Jewish people (Est. 4:14). At times, this calling occurs through a direct word from God to the person. At other times, it occurs through a series of signs and circumstances.

The understanding of human work as utilized in God's project of redemption is developed through the story of the church in the New Testament as well. One part of human life that Jesus Christ takes on through his incarnation is human work, inasmuch as he spends the years up until the beginning of his ministry working as a carpenter (Mk 6:3). When Jesus calls the disciples to leave their careers (as fishermen and tax collectors), he does not call them to give up work but rather calls them to a different form of work: to be fishers of people (Mt. 4:19). However, work is never presented as an ultimate end or good. When Jesus urges Martha to follow Mary's example of being with him rather than being "busy about many things," he reminds her that even good human work of caring for others can become a distraction to one's relationship with God (Lk. 10:41).

Work binds together the church in Acts in the same way it did the nation of Israel. The Christians in Jerusalem share their resources, the results of their work, meaning that the work of each one benefits all, especially those in need (widows, orphans) and those called to ministries of preaching (Acts 4:32-35). The curse, which mandates that men work for food, has been reversed in this new divine economy. While the apostle Paul does emphasize that those who are able to should work for their food, and that his own work as a tentmaker is an important part of his witness as an apostle, he places work within a new theological horizon as well: the building up of the body of Christ (2 Thess. 3:10). Christians have different gifts, which means they are called to different work. But all of this work serves the same end: strengthening the body of Christ present in the world for the world's eventual redemption (1 Cor. 12:4-11).

In conclusion, the scriptural narrative provides certain key concepts to inform a theological understanding of work. First, work is God-ordained and integral to human nature and human dignity. Second, through work, humans are given the opportunity to engage in Christ's redemption of the world, which is work's proper end. Third, work is properly integrated into the human community and human life when it advances proper worship of God and care for the poor, and when it is properly balanced with appropriate leisure and rest (entering into God's Sabbath).

TRADITION AND EXPERIENCE

Christian theologians have drawn upon these three aspects of work—as part of created human nature, as a curse, and as an activity of the redeemed community—to engage with theories and experiences of work within their own context. In the early church, Christians were challenged by the philosophical tradition that the contemplative life was more noble than the active life, which effectively minimized the value of human work.[5]

In response, Christian theologians argued that human work has its own intrinsic good, when placed within the proper context of worshipping God. Augustine synthesized the Christian and the philosophical approaches by arguing that both active and contemplative approaches are necessary to live a life motivated by love. Love calls a person to the contemplation of God, and love calls that same person to labor for the good of others. "No man has a right to lead such a life of contemplation as to forgo in his own ease the service due to his neighbor; nor has any man a right to be so immersed in active life as to neglect the contemplation of God."[6] Simeon the New Theologian articulated this stance by claiming that "there is in us a natural bent for work, the movement towards good."[7] However, love only motivates labor for the good of others in this life. Christians must always remember that, just as the work of each week leads to the Sabbath, so human work will ultimately be replaced by the ultimate Sabbath rest in God. This eschatological Sabbath will not be free of work, but it will be the joyful and fulfilling work of praising God.[8] Aquinas, like Augustine, reckoned the appropriate balance between the active and contemplative life through considering the mandates of love. While the contemplative life per se advances a higher good, the active life may at times be the more virtuous choice in a fallen world. "For instance through excess of Divine love a man may now and then suffer separation from the sweetness of Divine contemplation for the time being, that God's will may be done and for His glory's sake."[9]

The rule of St. Benedict provides a living example of this synthesis of the active and contemplative by requiring monks to engage in the spiritual work of worship and the physical work required for everyday provision. On the one hand, the work of the Lord—the seven daily offices of prayer—enjoys priority.[10] On the other hand, regular engagement in manual labor remains an important part of the monastic life and growth in holiness, "for idleness is the enemy of the soul."[11] Work also serves to bring the brothers

---

[5]See, e.g., Thomas Bénatouil and Mauro Bonazzi, eds., *Theoria, Praxis and the Contemplative Life after Plato and Aristotle* (Boston: Brill, 2012).

[6]Augustine, *The City of God*, trans. Marcus Dodds (Peabody: Hendrickson, 2009), XIX.19.

[7]Andrew Louth, ed., *Genesis 1–11* (Downers Grove: Intervarsity, 2001), 60–1.

[8]Augustine, *The City of God*, XXII.30.

[9]Aquinas, *Summa Theologiae*, II–II.182.2.

[10]Leonard J. Doyle, trans., *St. Benedict's Rule for Monasteries* (Collegeville: Liturgical, 1950), chap. 16.

[11]Ibid., chap. 48.

together in love. Each monk has a responsibility to serve others. And each, no matter how weak, receives the opportunity and responsibility to use his labor to care for his brothers, "for this service brings increase of reward and of charity."[12]

However, this theology of work—which prioritized worshiping God without losing sight of work as care for others—was challenged during the early modern period. Reformation theologians argued that the spiritual priority given to monasticism had devalued the work and vocation of each Christian. In his commentary on Psalm 111, Luther observed that "a servant, maid, son, daughter, man, woman, lord, subject, or whoever else may belong to a station ordained by God, as long as he fills his station, is as beautiful and glorious in the sight of God as a bride arrayed for her husband."[13] Calvin, in his own commentary on Genesis, claimed that God's plan for each person is to engage in diligent work, in which each person "regard[s] himself as the steward of God in all things which he possesses."[14] In response, Catholic reformers as well emphasized this greater range of vocations. For example, in the section of the *Spiritual Exercises* on discerning states of life, Ignatius of Loyola also emphasized that people may properly discern a call to the married life, as long as this is understood as a means to the end of serving God.[15]

The reformers were able to recover a scriptural emphasis on the value of ordinary work and ordinary life. In the following centuries, these theological approaches, impacted by numerous other social and political factors, often resulted in a cultural separation of the goodness of work from the goodness of relationship with God and work's place in God's plan of redemption. When describing this culture shift, Charles Taylor writes, "The transition I am talking about here is one which upsets these hierarchies, which displaces the locus of the good life from some special range of higher activities and places it within 'life' itself. The full human life is now defined in terms of labor and production, on one hand, and marriage and family life, on the other."[16]

On the one hand, the development of technological and material advancement from this valorization of ordinary life resulted in a great many tools and opportunities that "relieve and benefit the condition of man."[17] On the other hand, these new technologies, developing up to and beyond the industrial revolution, negatively transformed much of the understanding of work itself. Theories of work no longer described it as an important human contribution in serving God, caring for others, and advancing God's redemptive work in the world. Rather than bringing people closer together within a redeemed community, these theories of work stressed how work caused alienation and served as a tool of domination, echoing the original curse. Karl Marx analyzed the plight of the modern worker in tones reminiscent of the curse in Genesis 3:

> Labor is exterior to the worker, that is, it does not belong to his essence. Therefore, he does not confirm himself in his work, he denies himself, feels miserable instead of happy, he deploys no free physical and intellectual energy, but mortifies his body and

[12]Ibid., chap. 35.

[13]Cited in Ian Hart, "The Teaching of Luther and Calvin about Ordinary Work. 1: Martin Luther," *Evangelical Quarterly* 67, no. 1 (1995): 37.

[14]John Calvin, *Commentary on Genesis*, trans. John King (Edinburgh: Calvin Translation Society, 1847), https://www.ccel.org/ccel/calvin/calcom01.html.

[15]Ignatius of Loyola, "Making a Choice of a Way of Life," in *The Spiritual Exercises*, trans. Luis J. Puhl, SJ, http://spex.ignatianspirituality.com/SpiritualExercises/Puhl#c15-1234.

[16]Charles Taylor, *Sources of the Self* (Boston: Harvard University, 1989), 213.

[17]Ibid.

> ruins his mind. Thus the worker only feels at home outside his work and in his work he feels a stranger ... Finally, the external character of labor for the worker shows itself in the fact that it is not his own but someone else's, that it does not belong to him, that he does not belong to himself in his labor but to someone else.[18]

Rather than becoming part of a way in which a worker can be engaged in God's work in the world, work becomes "a sacrifice of his life. It is a commodity which he has made over to another."[19] Max Weber used sociological analysis to point to the same degradation, contrasting the approach of the earlier Puritans to specific vocation with the experience of work by his contemporaries: "The Puritan wanted to work in calling; we are forced to do so ... In Baxter's view the care for external goods should only lie on the shoulders of the 'saint like a light cloak, which can be thrown aside at any moment.' But fate decreed that the cloak should become an iron cage."[20]

In response to these critiques, Protestant and Catholic theologies of work in the twentieth century focused on retrieving the connection between work and God as articulated in scripture and tradition. Karl Barth countered the Marxist critique that work consumes the worker's life by arguing that the Sabbath must be understood first before any doctrine of human work can be formulated, placing all human work back in the context of radical dependence upon God. "Can he value and do justice to his work except in the light of its boundary, its solemn interruption? Is not this interruption the true time from which alone he can have other time? Is not the paradoxical 'activity' of the holy day the origin of all other activity which seems to have better reason for this designation?"[21] In addition, he argues for a return to seeing all aspects of human life, including work, as marked by radical dependence on God. In his claim, he develops the Calvinist perspective that humans are not cocreators but merely stewards. "There neither is nor can be issued a corresponding summons to the week's work as a supplementary and imitative participation by man in God's creative work."[22] However, work is still good and special because it is the place of human responsibility, a response to God's specific call to each individual.[23]

In his encyclical *Laborem exercens*, published in 1991, John Paul II directly engages the Marxist critique that early capitalism treated humans as mere "instruments of production," arguing for a higher view of work that takes seriously both the "true dignity" of work and, most importantly, of the worker. Through his own commentary on Genesis, John Paul II argues that, while work in itself can add value to human life, "in the first place work is 'for man' and not man 'for work.'"[24] This insistence that work is for humans carries with it an expectation that work should be accompanied by justice, respect human dignity, and foster solidarity with those for whom work brings suffering and toil. In addition, through an analysis of the importance of work in the gospels and Genesis, John

[18]Karl Marx, "1844 Manuscripts," in *The Thought of Karl Marx: An Introduction*, ed. David McLellan (London: Macmillan, 1980), 167–8.
[19]Ibid.
[20]Max Weber, *The Protestant Ethic and the Spirit of Capitalism* (New York: Scribner, 1953), 181.
[21]Karl Barth, *Church Dogmatics: The Doctrine of Creation* III/4, trans. A. T. MacKay et al. (London: T&T Clark, 2004), 51.
[22]Ibid., 52.
[23]Ibid., 274.
[24]Pope John Paul II, *Laborem exercens*, in *Catholic Social Thought: Encyclicals and Documents from Leo XIII to Francis*, 3rd rev. ed., ed. David J. O'Brien and Thomas A. Shannon (New York: Orbis, 2016), § 6.

Paul II reclaims the view that work participates, on a lesser, human scale, in God's creative and redemptive work in the world.

> The Christian finds in human work a small part of the Cross of Christ and accepts it in the same spirit of redemption in which Christ accepted his Cross for us. In work, thanks to the light that penetrates us from the Resurrection of Christ, we always find a *glimmer* of new life, of the *new good,* as if it were an announcement of "the new heavens and the new earth" in which man and the world participate precisely through the toil that goes with work.[25]

Perhaps the most significant addition to theologies of work and vocation in the last several decades has been the inclusion of voices from the margins, who have developed and expanded Christian theologies of work based on their own experiences of exclusion, poverty, sexism, or racism. These voices provide important reminders that work can be exploitative and oppressive—in short, that all the provisions of the curse from Genesis 3 still apply, often as the result of systemic sin. However, along with these critiques, these same voices can also offer compelling visions of how human work can become a part of God's redemption of the world. For example, Martin Luther King Jr. explicitly linked struggles against racism and segregation to struggles to reclaim the value of all work. Just like all humans, all forms of work have dignity. It is important for "the well-being of the total community" that all work should therefore be properly respected and compensated.[26] Liberation theologians have argued for the spiritually and physically liberatory value of the work of the poor. Gustavo Gutiérrez describes the work of the poor and the oppressed as belonging especially, even preferentially, to God's plan of salvation. "To work, to transform this world, is to become a man and to build the human community; it is also to save."[27] Feminist theologians have focused on the importance of work carried out by women: either domestic labor—traditionally understood as "women's work"—or work done by women in the broader workplace or in the church. Like King, they emphasize that if the work of all participants in the community is not properly valued and appreciated, the ability of the whole community to pursue flourishing is limited, and the value of all is diminished. All three perspectives emphasize the personal and communal loss that occurs when societal limitations hinder a person's ability to respond to God's call.

In addition to critiques from experience, contemporary theologies of work also have access to entire fields of scientific study and philosophical reflections on work, which provide insights from reason into how work affects people's lives. Many of these studies uphold scripture and tradition's claim that work is important to advance human dignity and human flourishing, while also recognizing reason and experience's claim that context and societal limitations do place important limits on how people can actively engage in fruitful work, without harming the larger community.

[25]Ibid., § 27, emphasis in original.

[26]Martin Luther King Jr., "All Labor Has Dignity," in *All Labor Has Dignity*, ed. Michael K. Honey (Boston: Beacon, 2011), 172. See also, "Facing the Challenge of a New Age," December 3, 1956, http://okra.stanford.edu/transcription/document_images/Vol03Scans/451_3-Dec-1956_Facing%20the%20Challenge%20of%20a%20New%20Age.pdf.

[27]Gustavo Gutiérrez, *A Theology of Liberation*, trans. Caridad Inda and John Eagelson (Maryknoll: Orbis, 1988), 91.

CONCLUSION

All of these resources provide the broad parameters for how Christians can confront new questions related to work, including automation and job reduction, environmental degradation, poverty and income polarization, and limited opportunities for work among the global poor. Remembering the aspect of work that is oriented toward stewardship places a high responsibility on Christians to ensure that their work is truly stewarding creation, rather than abusing it . In a similar way, the relationship of work to human dignity makes it important that Christians should seek to provide others with meaningful opportunities for fulfilling work, even when technology and economic challenges make this difficult. Echoing God's work at creation, they should seek to emphasize work's creative aspects. Christians need to take seriously critiques from sociology and experience that point out the limits that societal structures may place upon the ability to participate in this meaningful work. They should seek to provide people with opportunities to pursue the vocations God has for them. Finally, Christians should view work as appropriately related to God's Sabbath and God's love. Since work culminates in God's Sabbath rest, work should be understood as conditioned and limited by that Sabbath rest, even here before the eschaton. This connection to Sabbath means that work must always be bounded by and subservient to the worship of God. In a similar way, remembering that human work is part of the redemption of the world means that all work must always be measured and directed by love. This implies work must be motivated by love for others and must appropriately express that love, both for the workers and those affected by the work. Most importantly, work should never distract from love for and contemplation of God but should rather be a tangible sign of that love to a hurting and broken world.

SUGGESTED READINGS

Cosden, Darrell. *A Theology of Work: Work and the New Creation*. Eugene: Wipf and Stock, 2006.

John Paul II. *Laborem exercens*. In *Catholic Social Thought: Encyclicals and Documents from Leo XIII to Francis*, 3rd rev. ed., ed. David J. O'Brien and Thomas A. Shannon. New York: Orbis, 2016.

Volf, Miroslav. *Work in the Spirit: Toward a Theology of Work*. Eugene: Wipf and Stock, 2001.

Witherington III, Ben. *Work: A Kingdom Perspective on Labor*. Grand Rapids: Eerdmans, 2011.

CHAPTER THIRTY-EIGHT

Orthodox Christianity and Poverty

PHILIP LEMASTERS

Orthodox Christianity views tradition as that which the Holy Spirit has revealed through the experience of the Orthodox Church. The scriptures, worship, example and teaching of the saints, creeds, canons, icons, chant, ascetical practices, and church architecture represent various manifestations of God's truth as handed down in and through the common life of the Body of Christ—and that is not an exhaustive list of sources. They all exist "within Tradition" and do not stand over against it.[1] Consequently, a Quadrilateral that stems from the theology of Christian communities with very different understandings of tradition in relation to scripture, reason, and experience does not provide an appropriate hermeneutical structure for presenting Orthodox teaching on poverty. This discussion integrates those four sources within the larger context of Orthodox Christianity's understanding of the manifold ways in which the church has experienced and responded to God's truth in relation to the economic, social, and political challenges presented by the unmet needs of the poor.

Consonant with the centrality of worship for the knowledge of God in Eastern Christianity, the celebration of the Eucharist in the Divine Liturgy provides an illuminating context for understanding Orthodoxy's perspective on poverty. Eucharistic worship makes present mystically the church's entrance into the kingdom of heaven, in which God will heal and overcome all corruption and deprivation. The celebration of the Eucharist functions as a prophetic act that highlights the grave tension between the agony of a world in which so many are poor and the joy of the messianic banquet. Persons commune with Christ in a fashion that makes them participants already in the heavenly reign, in the coming fullness of the Hebrew prophets' hope being accomplished for meeting every human need (e.g., Isa. 2:3-4; Amos 9:13-15). The Eucharist is a meal in which common food and drink become the body and blood of Christ in a fashion beyond human understanding; those who receive them truly commune with the Son of God.[2] In this light, the lack of sustenance, clothing, shelter, and other necessities of life stands as a paradigmatic sign of how human beings have become alienated from participation in

[1]Timothy (Kallistos) Ware, *The Orthodox Church* (London: Penguin, 1997), 197.

[2]Alexander Schmemann's *For the Life of the World* (Crestwood: St. Vladimir's Seminary Press, 1998) and his *The Eucharist* (Crestwood: St. Vladimir's Seminary Press, 1988) provide lucid accounts of the relevance of the Eucharist for engaging the challenges of life in the world. See also Vigen Guroian, *Ethics after Christendom: Toward an Ecclesial Christian Ethic* (Grand Rapids: Eerdmans, 1994), 39–43.

the fulfillment of God's gracious purposes for them. Such deprivation is an affront to the dignity of each person, as all bear the image and likeness of God.

Orthodox Christianity understands every human being as a living icon. Jesus Christ, as the New Adam, has set right humanity's corruption of the divine image and fulfilled the primal vocation for people to become like God in holiness. They become "partakers of the divine nature" (2 Pet. 1:4) as they participate personally in the gracious divine energies and grow in union with God.[3] Such an entrance into holiness is not a mystical escape from the harsh realities of life in a world enslaved to corruption, but a transformative communion with Christ such that his selfless love becomes characteristic of every dimension of one's existence as a human being. Hence, to receive the sacred gifts of the holy mystery of the Eucharist demands sharing the mundane gifts of creation with other living icons of God who are in need of the physical sustenance necessary for a decent human life. The Eucharist calls those who receive the philanthropic bounty of God to manifest the divine mercy toward their hungry and wretched neighbors. To refuse to do so is not only to fall short of embracing fully the implications of receiving the sacrament; it is to fail to serve Christ himself as he is present in "the least of these my brethren."[4]

On the penultimate Sunday before Great Lent, the parable of the Last Judgment in Mt. 25:31-46 serves as the gospel reading in the Divine Liturgy of Eastern Orthodox churches. The liturgical placement of the text puts the Lenten discipline of almsgiving in a context of profound spiritual seriousness. In giving or withholding resources from impoverished and suffering people, congregants show their love or lack thereof for Christ.[5] How they treat their needy neighbors reveals the health of their souls and whether they are in the process of uniting themselves with the Lord in holiness. To accept Christ's gracious invitation to dine at the heavenly banquet of the Eucharist while disregarding him in his living icons is to place oneself in the spiritually and morally false position of wanting succor from God while refusing to manifest that same mercy to others. Such actions reflect a distorted understanding of what it means to participate personally in the gracious divine energies. God's grace is transformative and participatory, uniting human beings to God in a fashion that enables them to manifest holiness. A common Orthodox image for a person's participation in the divine energies is an iron poker left in a roaring fire and taking on some of the qualities of the fire (i.e., heat and light) while remaining iron. The view that grace is a mere commodity or legal decree that may be possessed or applied to a person without attendant personal transformation stands in severe tension with the most basic Orthodox theological commitments. To experience grace is truly to experience God, who calls the recipients to become holy.[6]

The patristic teachers for whom the two most commonly celebrated liturgies of the Orthodox Church are named, St. Basil of Caesarea and St. John Chrysostom, were both bold proponents of justice for the poor and hungry.[7] Together with other luminaries of

[3]See John Meyendorff, "Introduction," in *The Triads*, ed. Gregory Palamas (Mahwah: Paulist, 1983), 20–2, where he explains the distinction between the essence and energies of God in Orthodox theology.

[4]See Vigen Guroian, *Incarnate Love: Essays in Orthodox Ethics* (Notre Dame: University of Notre Dame Press, 2002), 97; Pantelis Kalaitzidis, *Orthodoxy and Political Theology* (Geneva: World Council of Churches, 2012), 120–1; Christos Yannaras, *The Freedom of Morality* (Crestwood: SVS Press, 1996), 93–4.

[5]His All Holiness Ecumenical Patriarch Bartholomew, *Encountering the Mystery: Understanding Orthodox Christianity Today* (New York: Doubleday, 2008), 148.

[6]See Kallistos Ware, *The Orthodox Way* (Crestwood: St. Vladimir's Seminary Press, 1995), 68.

[7]See C. Paul Schroder, trans., *On Social Justice: St. Basil the Great* (Crestwood: St. Vladimir's Seminary Press, 2009); and Catherine P. Roth, trans., *On Wealth and Poverty: St. John Chrysostom* (Crestwood: St. Vladimir's Seminary Press, 1999), for collections of their homilies on poverty.

the early church, such as Gregory the Theologian and Gregory of Nyssa, they taught that all possessions beyond those necessary to meet one's basic needs belong to the poor as a matter of justice. Basil, who was from an extremely wealthy family, gave away massive amounts of wealth to create orphanages, hospitals, and other philanthropic institutions that integrated prayer and social service. Chrysostom also gave generously to the poor and, like Basil, could preach with integrity on these matters because of his own example. Through their teaching and practical ministries, these and other patristic figures elevated the common masses of poor people from a virtually subhuman status to the exalted identity of the Body of Christ. They made clear that the Lord is present not only in churches and liturgies but also in the starving, sick, and ill-clad bodies of people in profound need. Their orthodoxy called for orthopraxy that served as a socially embodied icon of the divine mercy celebrated in the Eucharist. Liturgy was not an escape for them from thorny social problems but a lens through which they saw Christ in their wretched neighbors.[8]

Basil and Chrysostom did not limit their critique of disregard for the poor to moralistic exhortations but criticized social structures and practices that led to the exploitation of the needy. They appealed to those with political and economic power to use it to ameliorate the suffering of people in their society in particular ways. Throughout the history of the Byzantium, emperors engaged personally in philanthropic efforts and promoted reforms to protect the weak from abuse. For example, in the sixth century, Justinian and Theodora established "institutions to care for the sick, the elderly, orphans, the homeless and poor travelers," and they along with other rulers established laws "to remedy social injustices and change structures in society which victimized the disadvantaged."[9] A tradition of similar endeavors was also characteristic of Russian rulers after the conversion of their lands to Orthodox Christianity.

From the perspective of most contemporary sensibilities, these initiatives fell short of meeting the needs of the poor or establishing an acceptable level of social justice. Nonetheless, they reflect the prophetic core of Orthodoxy's vision of poverty as a fundamentally unjust reality that calls for a response that coheres with God's philanthropy. In this light, participation in the divine love entails manifesting that love to the living icons in whom Christ is present. The transformative and unitive dimensions of *theosis* or union with God are infinite, as there are no upward limits to the holiness entailed by sharing in the life of God by grace. In a world that has not yet entered into the fullness of the heavenly kingdom, there are inevitably practical limits to how well a social order will become an icon of any dimension of eschatological blessedness, including the relief of the poor. Consequently, the Orthodox critique of the conditions and actions leading to poverty should be constant, as should be the appeal for philanthropic efforts that manifest God's gracious intentions for suffering persons.

In the many petitions of the Divine Liturgy, the church prays for the peace of the world, a life free of danger and distress, and the salvation of all. Specific pleas for God's blessing upon the sick, the suffering, captives, and those in various forms of need and deprivation occur regularly throughout the liturgical services of the Orthodox Church. In

[8]Helpful accounts of patristic responses to poverty include: Peter Brown, *Poverty and Leadership in the Later Roman Empire* (Hanover: Brandeis University Press, 2002); Justo González, *Faith and Wealth: A History of Early Christian Ideas on the Origin, Significance, and Use of Money* (San Francisco: Harper & Row, 1990); Susan Holman, *The Hungry Are Dying: Beggars and Bishops in Roman Cappadocia* (Oxford: Oxford University Press, 2001); Holman, ed., *Wealth and Poverty in Early Church and Society* (Grand Rapids: Baker Academic, 2008); James Thornton, *Wealth & Poverty in the Teachings of the Church Fathers* (Berkeley: St. John Chrysostom, 1993).

[9]Verna Harrison, "Poverty in Orthodox Tradition," *Saint Vladimir's Theological Quarterly* 34, no. 1 (1990): 22–5.

cooperation with God's grace, those who pray these petitions have an obligation to act personally for their fulfillment in relation to their neighbors. To invoke a divine solution without offering one's own resources to address such needs would be to fall short of accepting the responsibility that persons have to work together with God for the salvation of the world and all its inhabitants. To celebrate with integrity Christ's self-offering on the cross, and especially to commune in his body and blood, requires offering tangible dimensions of one's life for the sake of those in whom he is present. Characteristic Orthodox prayers warn against the dangers of receiving the Eucharist unworthily and incurring the judgment of God. A concomitant awareness of the importance of living worthily after communing is also in order, especially in the sense of cooperating with God's philanthropy in blessing the poor. To commune sacramentally with the Lord while disregarding him in the living icons of the impoverished is to separate liturgy and life in a fashion contradictory to the spiritual vision of Orthodoxy.[10]

Such offerings on behalf of others serve as signs of the restoration of the use of the resources of creation for their intended purposes. Basil, for example, stressed the universal destination of the goods of creation toward a decent life for all who bear God's image and likeness. Those who keep more than enough for themselves while others lack basic necessities are guilty, not simply of insufficient charity, but of theft.[11] Philanthropic generosity that distributes excess possessions to those in want is not a supererogatory work but a basic requirement of the Christian life. Though the practical details will vary, monks, nuns, married people, and others who live in the world are called to the same praxis of generosity. When faced with the needs of those more impoverished than themselves, even poor people have an obligation to share their resources with others.[12]

There is an ascetical dimension to such responses to poverty that demonstrates the integration of the spiritual life with social action in Orthodox Christianity. The passions of pride and greed tempt people to cling to their wealth and attendant social status in a way that shows how the diseases of one's soul harm one's neighbors. Passions are misdirected powers of the soul that give rise to thoughts, words, and deeds that disorient persons from using their abilities and possessions in accordance with God's purposes for them.[13] The problems at stake in social situations characterized by poverty and social injustice do not amount simply to the characteristics of material reality but root in disordered desires that lead to the exploitation and disregard of others. Even those with few possessions and little social standing or cultural capital may be enslaved to self-centered desires that make it very hard for them to give to those more destitute than themselves. Consequently, the struggle to share with others, and to gain the strength to look critically at the social structure in which one participates, is part of the battle for the healing of the soul. Since humans are created in God's image with the calling to become ever more like God in holiness, those progressing in *theosis* will advance in their ability to manifest the divine philanthropy in their use of their wealth and possessions. They will become icons of

---

[10]Philip LeMasters, "*Philanthropia* in Liturgy and Life: The Anaphora of Basil the Great and Eastern Orthodox Social Ethics," *St Vladimir's Theological Quarterly* 59, no. 2 (2015) 187–211.

[11]Basil the Great, "I Will Tear Down My Barns," in *On Social Justice*: *St. Basil the Great* (Crestwood: St. Vladimir's Seminary Press, 2009), 69–70.

[12]Emmanuel Clapsis, "Wealth and Poverty in Christian Tradition," *Greek Orthodox Theological Review* 54, nos. 1–4 (2009): 178–9; Samantha L. Miller, "Chrysostom's Monks as Living Exhortations to Poverty and the Rich Life," *Greek Orthodox Theological Review* 58, nos. 1–4 (2013): 84.

[13]Theophan the Recluse, *The Spiritual Life and How to be Attuned to It* (Platina: St Herman of Alaska Brotherhood, 1995), 227.

Christ's sacrificial love as they deny themselves in order to bless their neighbors. The path to growth in holiness requires the ascetical praxis of putting the needs of others before one's own desires, comfort, or social standing.[14]

The prominence of icons in Orthodox Christianity reflects the faith's strongly incarnational orientation. Wood and paint, for example, may be fashioned into a tangible reminder that the Son of God became a human being with a body, even while remaining divine. The celebration of Christ's baptism at Theophany (or Epiphany) commemorates the revelation of the Holy Trinity when he entered into the water of the Jordan River in order to make it, and the entire creation, holy. In ways appropriate to their particular celebrations, each of the holy mysteries or sacraments fulfills the place of bread, wine, water, and oil in accordance with God's purposes for the creation. The relics of the saints have become holy through the divine energies and remain conduits of blessing and healing. This incarnational context of physical reality permeated with God's grace highlights the spiritual significance of embodied gestures on behalf of the poor, such as limiting one's self-indulgence in order to have resources for economic sharing with needy persons. Actions involving "worldly" matters such as wealth are in no way denigrated due to their physical, mundane characteristics. Indeed, they fit coherently within the incarnational theology of Orthodoxy as enacted icons of divine mercy focused on meeting the bodily needs of those with whom Christ identified himself.[15]

Basil, Chrysostom, and other patristic teachers proclaimed that those who give to the poor receive more than they offer.[16] By serving Christ in their neighbors, they receive forgiveness for their sins and open themselves to eternal blessedness. Such statements do not reflect a commercial or mechanistic understanding of the work of God's grace, but instead the belief that those who selflessly love the poor are actually selflessly loving Christ. By repenting of pride and greed, they advance in the healing for their souls as they offer themselves tangibly to the Lord in their neighbors and thus grow in union with him. They must perform such acts with humility before God and *kenotic* or self-emptying love for their recipients in order to grow in holiness, as otherwise pride blocks their participation in the gracious divine energies. Eastern Christianity stresses the constant dependence of all persons on the Lord's mercy, as in the frequently repeated Jesus Prayer, "Lord Jesus Christ, Son of God, have mercy on me, a sinner." Philanthropic actions manifest one's cooperation with God's grace, and even the most generous donor remains in constant need of ever-greater participation in the divine energies for the healing of the soul. Since the human vocation is to become like God in holiness, none may claim to have fulfilled it perfectly.[17]

Orthodox Christianity confesses God to be Father, Son, and Holy Spirit. Human persons created in God's image and likeness, then, are not isolated individuals meant to find fulfillment in serving only themselves. Instead, they are persons in communion who will flourish by embracing their common life with one another. Their unique identities find fulfillment through loving relationships with others that serve as channels for the accomplishment of God's purposes for them.[18] Their common life must be characterized

---

[14]Aristotle Papanikolaou, *The Mystical as Political Democracy and Non-Radical Orthodoxy* (Notre Dame: University of Notre Dame Press, 2012), 196–7.

[15]Hilarion Alfeyev, *The Mystery of Faith* (London: Darton, Longman, and Todd, 2002), 112–16.

[16]Basil the Great, "In Time of Famine and Drought," in *On Social Justice*: *St. Basil the Great* (Crestwood: St. Vladimir's Seminary Press, 2009), 86; Harrison, "Poverty in the Orthodox Tradition," 21–2.

[17]Ware, *The Orthodox Way*, 138.

[18]Alfeyev, *The Mystery of Faith*, 59; Ware, *The Orthodox Way*, 27.

by meeting the economic necessities of a decent standard of living in which distinct persons are free from deprivation. Those who do not limit their acquisitiveness for the sake of their neighbors fall short of the demands of true personhood.

This understanding of human beings as persons in communion provides a basis for criticizing self-centered and individualistic approaches to the proper use of financial and material resources. It also grounds the priority of philanthropic acts in which the donor and the recipient relate to one another as persons. Activism for social justice that obscures the uniqueness of each person or treats him or her as an anonymous statistic falls short of the unitive trajectory of love. Even as *theosis* refers to the process of growth in holiness and union with God, philanthropic offerings find their proper place in the context of strengthening relationships between particular persons. The free offering of one's resources, time, and attention on behalf of another in need serves as a means for healing relationships strained by injustices that arise from a lack of love for one in whom Christ is present. Such efforts reflect Orthodoxy's view of human beings as persons in communion; well-intentioned relief efforts that fall short of fostering such relationships fail to embody the fullness of God's philanthropy for particular persons.[19]

At the same time, Orthodox Christianity recognizes that some social orders serve God's purposes for the flourishing of people more than others. In the various liturgical services of the church, there are petitions for governmental leaders, peaceful times, and the succor of those who suffer from deprivations and injustices of the sort that require address by political and social institutions that extend beyond the visible boundaries of the church. Since the well-being of the poor and hungry is at stake in many of the policies of governments and economic institutions, Orthodox social concern legitimately extends beyond personal philanthropy to include larger questions of public order. However, conventional political activism may not replace the primary obligation of members of the Eucharistic community to offer their resources for the sake of the particular needy persons in whom they encounter the Lord. Self-denial for the sake of others remains a venerable path for the healing of the soul from passions and may open the eyes of both giver and recipient to a new relationship in which they see Christ in one another as unique persons.

Orthodox engagement with public questions of political and economic policies concerning poverty is underdeveloped. From the fall of the Byzantine Empire to the Ottoman Turks in 1453 CE to the rule of Communism in Russia and Eastern Europe in the twentieth century, the experience of the vast majority of Orthodox churches was one of persecution and marginalization from the dominant forces of the larger social order. Simply maintaining the liturgical life of their communities was a great challenge in such circumstances; addressing matters of economic justice in the public sphere was a practical impossibility. In the Soviet Union, the Orthodox Church was forbidden from undertaking any form of social ministry, let alone to advocate for policy positions.[20]

Since the fall of Communism, other factors have deterred a strong focus on public policy in relation to poverty. For example, the association of Latin American liberation theology with Marxism has hindered some Orthodox voices in Eastern Europe and the West from supporting agendas perceived to align with stances antithetical to traditional Christianity.[21]

---

[19]Harrison, "Poverty in the Orthodox Tradition," 44.

[20]Ibid., 44–6.

[21]Peter C. Bouteneff, "Liberation: Challenges to Modern Orthodox Theology from the Contextual Theologies," *Union Seminary Quarterly Review* 63, nos. 3–4 (2012); LeMasters, "Latin American Liberation Theology and Eastern Orthodox Social Ethics: Is a Conversation Possible?," *The Wheel* 3 (2015): 13.

In some traditionally Orthodox lands, various nationalistic agendas have taken precedence over efforts to ameliorate conditions that give rise to and perpetuate poverty. In the West, Orthodox Christians comprise a miniscule percentage of the population and do not have the cultural or political influence necessary to engage effectively questions of public policy. Despite the growing number of converts to Orthodoxy in the West, the Orthodox Church is often perceived as a religious institution for ethnic groups oriented at least as much toward the preservation of the cultures of their nations of origin as to engagement with current social realities in the countries to which they have immigrated. Apart from occasional statements by church leaders, academicians, and activist groups, Orthodox Christians engage in little distinctive advocacy on questions of social justice.

In this light, Orthodox teaching and praxis concerning poverty focuses more on inspiring the actions of particular people than on critically engaging the structure or function of larger institutions, such as government, business, and organized labor. Ecclesiastical jurisdictions and parishes promote involvement in charitable efforts on behalf of the poor, especially during the season of Lent with its focus on almsgiving. The Antiochian Orthodox Christian Archdiocese of North America, for example, makes frequent appeals for donations in support of refugees, internally displaced persons, and other victims of the war in Syria. In the current climate of increased religious intolerance, it is notable that the Orthodox Church in Syria and Lebanon established philanthropic efforts by the middle of the nineteenth century that provided services to those in need, regardless of religious identity.[22] The Coptic Church also has a history of providing relief to both Muslims and Christians in Egypt.[23] Orthodox philanthropic organizations such as International Orthodox Christian Charities (IOCC) perform remarkable work in facilitating efforts to address the unmet needs of marginalized persons and communities around the world, irrespective of the religious affiliation of the recipients. The organization sponsors programs ranging from disaster relief to microloans, education, water purification, and agricultural support.[24]

From its origins in the Egyptian desert to the present day, Orthodox monasticism presents powerful examples of ministry to the poor, including the unusual prophetic witness of "fools for Christ."[25] In the *basiliad* of Basil the Great in the fourth century, monks and nuns provided a variety of health and social services to the poor.[26] St. Elizabeth the New Martyr, a member of the Russian royal family who became a nun after the assassination of her husband in 1905, founded the Convent of Sts. Mary and Martha in Moscow. Its work focused on caring for the poor and hungry, as well as for soldiers wounded in the First World War. She was martyred by the Bolsheviks in 1918.[27] The witness of St. Maria of Paris, also known as Mother Maria Skobtsova, provides another notable expression of ministry to the destitute. A Russian émigré in France after the

[22]Metropolitan George Khodr, "The Social Action and Thought among Arab Orthodox Christians (1800–1920)," in *Separation Without Hope?: Essays on the Relation between the Church and the Poor during the Industrial Revolution and the Western Colonial Expansion*, ed. Julio de Santa Ana (Maryknoll: Orbis, 1980), 120.

[23]Bishop Youannes, "Orthodox Diakonia & Development Witness in a Multi-Faith Context," Coptic Orthodox Church, May 2004, https://docplayer.net/15267465-Orthodox-diakonia-development-witness-in-a-multi-faith-context-by-his-grace-bishop-youannes-may-2004.html.

[24]"International Orthodox Christian Charities," https://www.iocc.org.

[25]Harrison, "Poverty in the Orthodox Tradition," 36.

[26]Demetrios J. Constantelos, "Basil the Great's Social Thought and Involvement," *Greek Orthodox Theological Review* 26, nos. 1–2 (1981): 81.

[27]Antiochian Orthodox Christian Archdiocese of North America, "Saint Elizabeth the New Martyr of Russia," http://ww1.antiochian.org/node/18906.

rise of Communism, she embraced a monastic vocation of hospitality for the poor. She aggressively sought out those needing assistance and shared her home and life with them. St. Maria established a network of houses and other philanthropic institutions for the destitute of Paris in the 1930s, especially Russian émigrés who suffered from poverty, alcoholism, and other maladies that put them on the street. After the German invasion of France in 1940, she worked with other Orthodox to hide Jews from the Nazi persecution. St. Maria, along with others engaged in this lifesaving work, were eventually arrested by the German authorities. She died in a concentration camp before the end of the war, by some accounts taking the place of another prisoner in the gas chamber on Good Friday, 1945.[28]

In view of the rich liturgical, ascetical, and philanthropic context in which Orthodox Christianity addresses ministry to the poor, there is a need for enhanced critical engagement with the economic ideologies and practices that produce and perpetuate poverty in the contemporary world. At the same time that the Church calls upon its members to perform acts of generosity, its clergy and teachers should draw on the resources of the tradition to form members to discern which public policies are most in keeping with God's purposes for the collective life of humanity and to advocate for them. Such engagement must not replace the struggle to turn away from greed and pride such that one is able to share generously with the needy. It must not fall down to the level of partisan rhetoric and serve only the self-interest of certain factions or political ideologies. Instead, it should enable those shaped by the ascetical, philanthropic practices of the church to participate in the debates of the public square toward the end of directing social institutions to serve God's purposes for the flourishing of the poor more than they currently do. In light of the prayers of the Divine Liturgy for the accomplishment of God's gracious intentions for the collective life of suffering humanity, the Orthodox must provide greater attention to such matters in order to fulfill their vocation of offering the world to God for blessing as an icon of the heavenly reign. Those who commune at the messianic banquet must make every dimension of their life in the world, including their engagement in the public square, a sign of its fulfillment in God.

SUGGESTED READINGS

Brown, Peter. *Poverty and Leadership in the Later Roman Empire*. Hanover: Brandeis University Press, 2002.

González, Justo. *Faith and Wealth: A History of Early Christian Ideas on the Origin, Significance, and Use of Money*. San Francisco: Harper & Row, 1990.

Holman, Susan. *The Hungry Are Dying: Beggars and Bishops in Roman Cappadocia*. Oxford: Oxford University Press, 2001.

Holman, Susan, ed. *Wealth and Poverty in Early Church and Society*. Grand Rapids: Baker Academic, 2008.

Skobtsova, Maria. *Mother Maria Skobtsova: Essential Writings*. Maryknoll: Orbis, 2003.

[28]See Sergei Hackel, *Pearl of Great Price: The Life of Mother Maria Skobtsova 1891–1945* (Crestwood: St. Vladimir's Seminary Press, 1982); Maria Skobtsova, *Mother Maria Skobtsova: Essential Writings* (Maryknoll: Orbis, 2003); Helene Arjakovsky-Klepinine, *Dimitri's Cross: The Life & Letters of St. Dimitri Klepinin, Martyred during the Holocaust* (Ben Lomond: Conciliar Press Ministries, 2008).

Issues, Applications, and Twenty-First-Century Agenda for Christian Ethics

Section F: Ecology

CHAPTER THIRTY-NINE

Land and Ecosystems

DANIEL SCHEID

The various sets of interrelated concerns that constitute the ecological crisis have confronted Christians, and indeed all humanity, with the realization that we must adopt new ethical principles in our relationship to the planet. A central focus of Christian ecological ethics in the twenty-first century is the adoption of a moral vision that places human beings and human interests in a wider web, which sees the value not only of individual creatures and of various species but also of the interrelationships between them. Thus, Christian ecological ethics focuses not only on water and biodiversity, climate change and environmental racism, but it also adopts an ecosystemic vantage point that is alert to the ways in which these issues impact each other.

The concern of a holistic ecological ethics is a contemporary one, but it has extensive roots in Christian theology through an affirmation of the goodness of creation and in an ethical responsibility for the land. Within Christian scripture and tradition, we learn that humans are responsible to God the Creator for how we use the land and that there is an intimate connection between doing justice to the land and to the poor, the widow, and the orphan. Christians endeavor to recover these core theological insights and to orient them to the concerns of the twenty-first century.

This chapter will trace out three ethical principles and their roots in scripture, tradition, reason, and experience before addressing the trajectories of Christian ecological ethics in thinking of land and ecosystems. The principles are:

1. *The dignity of the land and a corresponding ethic of respect.* The land provides humans and human communities with an identity and a sense of belonging in creation. In turn, it also gives humans a role and a corresponding ethical responsibility. Indeed, human dignity is discovered, in part, through our taking care of the land.
2. *The centrality of the whole and of the order of creatures.* This is ecosystemic thinking, attentive to the ways in which creatures are connected to each other, and intent on supporting creatures in filling their roles in creation. Christian ethics begins not from the good of individual creatures alone but is oriented to the common good, which in this case can be described as a planetary common good, and even a cosmic common good.
3. *The inextricable call to do justice to the land and to the marginalized.* Christians are called to respect the land and to foster its fecundity, and this call is conjoined to the summons to work for the liberation of the poor and the restoration of their dignity.

SCRIPTURE

In the first (though not earliest) account of creation in the book of Genesis (1–2:4), we witness God bringing forth creation, and at the end of each day God calls what has been created "good." While there has been much discussion of whether these are six literal days, or days that are to be interpreted figuratively, less attention has been paid to the structure of these days. In the first three days of creation, God brings forth light and darkness, waters and land, that provide the context for the creatures called forth on days four through six. For example, on the first day God separates light from darkness, and on the fourth day God creates the sun and the moon. On the second day God separates waters from the sky, and on the fifth day God creates the fish of the seas and the birds of the air. Days one through three create the habitat for the creatures who emerge in days four through six. In this way, Genesis displays an implicit form of ecosystemic thinking, depicting creatures as belonging to a particular habitat. Creatures are not only good because God has created them, but they are good because they fit into an allotted place within creation. This account establishes the dignity and goodness of all creatures, as well as the relationships that govern the lives of creatures.

Only at the end of day six, following the creation of human beings, does God declare that these creatures all together are "very good." Just prior to this, when God creates human beings, God blesses humanity and calls them to be fruitful and multiply and to "subdue" the Earth and have "dominion" over it. This is a much-contested passage, questioning the scriptural vision of humanity's role in creation. For some, the call to "subdue" nature demonstrates that only human beings have intrinsic value, while others assert a modified version of "dominion." Yet this passage must be understood in the overriding context of the dignity of all creation. The common good of the universe takes precedence over the dignity of any individual creature, because it includes and fulfills the various individual species. The book of Genesis establishes the bedrock theological reality that only all creatures operating in harmony with each other can be understood, finally, as "very good."

In the second (which is actually older) account of creation (Gen. 2:4-25), God creates the human being from the Earth: humans from *humus*. This causal relationship linked the Israelites to the land, and indeed it posits an essential continuity between human beings and the land that forms their very bodies. Later God places this human in the garden and bestows upon the human a moral obligation "to till it and keep it" (Gen. 2:15). In the Hebrew, these terms (*avad* and *shamar*) indicate a more encompassing ethic than interpretations that encourage a simplistic dominion. Humans are called to work (*avad*) and to till the land, but work here also means to work for, to serve. The land has its own limits and proper activities, and humans work in line with these capacities. Similarly, to "keep it" (*shamar*) has the language of legal observance. Humans are called to study the land, to learn its patterns, and from there to protect it. Together, these two accounts of creation affirm the goodness of all creatures and humanity's ethical responsibility to learn its own place within the order of creation and to protect the land.[1]

Another important idea in scripture that has contributed to Christian ecological ethics begins in the book of Exodus and extends though the prophetic texts. The central salvation experience for the Israelites was their rescue from slavery in Egypt and God's bringing them

[1]Ellen Davis, *Scripture, Culture, and Agriculture: An Agrarian Reading of the Bible* (New York: Cambridge University Press, 2009).

to the Promised Land. The later prophets—including Isaiah, Jeremiah, and Micah—never lost the essential connection between the God who liberated the Israelites and blessed them with a land of their own and the God who created the universe and established the place of every creature within it. When the Israelites lost sight of their responsibilities to the poor, this injustice was reflected in the vitality of the land. For example, the prophet Hosea depicts Israel as an unfaithful spouse: "There is no faithfulness or loyalty, and no knowledge of God in the land," the prophet declares, "Therefore the land mourns, and all who live in it languish; together with the wild animals and the birds of the air, even the fish of the sea are perishing" (Hos. 4:1, 3). There is thus an intimate connection between justice done to the land and justice to people: when both are treated with respect, there is health and flourishing in the land. When injustice is done to the poor, the land suffers. The world's first climate refugees, for example, demonstrate this connection. Though island nations like the Maldives and Seychelles, or the indigenous peoples of the Arctic, produced only a miniscule portion of greenhouse gases, they bear the brunt of rising oceans and intensifying storms, and they shoulder the burden and cost for relocating to safer lands.

While the New Testament does not display the same extensive concern for the land, there is a holistic and cosmic dimension to Christ's salvific work that displays a kind of ecosystemic viewpoint. In the letter to the Romans, Paul suggests that all creation desires the redemption initiated by Christ and "waits with eager longing for the revealing of the children of God" (Rom. 8:19). In the book of Revelation, John recovers the eschatological vision of Isaiah and beholds a "new heaven and a new earth" (Rev. 21:1). In addition to the many parables of Jesus that draw on agricultural themes and evince respect for nonhumans, the New Testament continues the Old Testament concern for the land and for human responsibility to watch and care for it.

TRADITION

The leading thinkers of the early Christian churches, now known as the Church Fathers, continued the basic theological conviction of the goodness of creation. They argued against those who thought the world was evil or wholly corrupted, and they traced the order of the universe back to God the Creator. While they did not share the same communal relationship to the land that the Old Testament writers had, these thinkers did more than just affirm of the goodness of the world. They exhibited a religious respect for the roles that creatures played in their various habitats and for the common good of the entire universe. Augustine, for example, affirmed that there are different grades or degrees of goodness in creatures but that each is necessary for the harmonious order of the universe. Drawing on Wis. 11:20, Augustine described how a Trinitarian God ordains every creature to its place in the universe through measure, number, and weight. Measure (associated with the Father) points to each creature's finitude, its limitations within the scope of the universe. Number (the role of the Son) expresses the form that creatures have, and Augustine celebrates the variety of creatures in the universe, evidenced in creation's splendor, abundance, variation, and power. Weight (the work of the Spirit) describes how creatures are led or drawn to occupy their place, to fulfill their role within cosmic order. Augustine's Trinitarian formulation provides a further theological justification for the dignity of creatures and for the way they are ordered to each other.[2]

[2]Augustine, *The Literal Meaning of Genesis*, trans. John Hammond Taylor, SJ (New York: Paulist, 1982), 4.3–4.4.

Medieval theologians extended and elaborated this tradition. For Thomas Aquinas, the importance of the common good was a central organizing principle in his theology of creation. Aquinas confirmed God as the ultimate common good of the entire universe, and he also asserted the superior dignity of the human person within creation above other earthly creatures. Yet he also insisted on the goodness of each creature pursuing its own natural inclinations. He further taught that a diversity of creatures was essential to the perfection of the universe: "For goodness, which in God is simple and uniform, in creatures is manifold and divided; and hence the whole universe together participates the divine goodness more perfectly, and represents it better than any single creature whatever."[3] Even more so, Aquinas argued that the greatest perfection of the universe was not just a diversity of creatures but the way in which they are ordered to each other. "Now the best among all things caused is the order of the universe, wherein the good of the universe consists, even as in human affairs the good of *the nation is more God-like than the good of the individual.*"[4] Just as the individual finds her good through participating in and contributing to the common good of society, so too human beings are called to contribute to the good of the order of the universe. By living temperately and restraining their use of Earth's goods, by promoting justice for the poor and the land, and by knowing and loving God through God's creation, human beings fulfill their earthly role to cultivate and care for the land.

The beginning of Christian ecological ethics proper emerged in the twentieth century as a theological response to the burgeoning environmental consciousness. In the Catholic tradition, concern for the land and for a planetary common good was expressed in many papal documents and through multiple bishops' conferences, and indeed Vatican City was the first carbon-neutral country in the world. The most sophisticated Catholic statement on ecology is the papal encyclical, *Laudato Si': On Care for Our Common Home*.[5] Throughout the document Pope Francis expresses deep concern for the land and he articulates a profoundly ecosystemic, holistic moral framework. The scriptures, Francis contends, emphasize a threefold relationship with God, our neighbor, and the Earth.[6] Sin has ruptured each of these relationships, so that when we fail to do justice to our neighbor or to the Earth, it will impact all our relationships: "Disregard for the duty to cultivate and maintain a proper relationship with my neighbour, for whose care and custody I am responsible, ruins my relationship with my own self, with others, with God and with the earth."[7] Commenting on Gen. 2:15 and the human vocation to till and keep the land, Francis asserts that this passage implies "a relationship of mutual responsibility between human beings and nature."[8] Francis forcefully connects justice for the Earth with justice for the poor, linking the degradation of our wetlands, oceans, and forests with the struggles of millions of the poor to survive. A true ecological ethic, he argues, must also be a social ethic, and vice versa. Ecological ethics must "integrate questions of

[3]Thomas Aquinas, *Summa Theologiae*, trans. Fathers of the English Dominican Province (Chicago: Benziger Brothers, 1948), I.47.1.

[4]Thomas Aquinas, *Summa Contra Gentiles*, trans. Fathers of the English Dominican Province (Chicago: Benziger Brothers, 1924), II.42.3, emphasis in original.

[5]Pope Francis, *Laudato Si'*: *Praise Be to You*: *On Care for Our Common Home* (Vatican City: Libreria Editrice Vaticana, 2015).

[6]Ibid., § 66.

[7]Ibid., § 70.

[8]Ibid., § 67.

justice in debates on the environment, so as to hear *both the cry of the earth and the cry of the poor.*"[9]

Numerous theologians and churches within the Reformed and Protestant traditions have developed extensive ecological statements. In the 1970s, the World Council of Churches (WCC) began to perceive that environmental problems were not simply a subset of social justice issues but indeed constituted their own set of ethical concerns. Initially they articulated this by advocating for a "Just, Participatory, and Sustainable Society," thus adding "sustainability" to their already well-established aims of justice and peace. As the language of sustainability began to be championed by myriad groups and on behalf of multiple social goals, some good and some ambiguous, the WCC substituted their language of "sustainability" with the "integrity of creation." Since then, multiple Christian groups have focused on the threefold goal of justice, peace, and the integrity of creation. Justice for the poor is bound up with a theological affirmation of the dignity and oneness of creation.

Patriarch Bartholomew has similarly articulated an Orthodox concern for the land and for the health of ecosystems. Invoking the classical language of sin, Bartholomew voices a commitment to justice for the land and for the poor: "For human beings ... to destroy the biological diversity of God's creation; for human beings to degrade the integrity of the earth by causing changes in its climate, by stripping the earth of its natural forests or destroying its wetlands; for human beings to contaminate the earth's waters, its land, its air, and its life—these are sins."[10] In 1994, Bartholomew established the *Religious and Scientific Committee*, which has since held multiple interreligious symposia on various ecosystems under threat, such as the Baltic Sea, the Amazon, and the Arctic, highlighting the importance of addressing ecological pressures with a holistic framework. Thus, it is evident that the Christian tradition, including its many trajectories and denominations, overwhelmingly affirms the principles stated at the beginning of this chapter: the dignity of creatures, the centrality of the common good, the link between justice for the land and for the poor, and humanity's responsibility to contribute to this just and sustainable planetary common good.

REASON

While Christianity possesses a rich heritage in its scripture and traditions that address the planetary common good, it was the efforts of the secular sciences that truly awakened a Christian ecological ethic. The field of ecology as a separate science emerged in the nineteenth century. Stemming from the Greek word "oikos," or household, ecology examined how various animals and plants coexisted to form stable ecosystems. In its early decades the field absorbed the prevailing mathematical approach to its research and was intent on developing metrics and quantitative measures to assess the stability of an ecosystem. Later figures developed a more qualitative approach, beginning not with the habits of separate species but with a holistic overview that emphasizes their relationships (i.e., ecosystems).[11] Aldo Leopold, for example, was a leading figure in American ecology, and he is famous for his articulation of a "land ethic." Ethics, he suggested, has traditionally

---

[9] Ibid., § 49, emphasis in original.

[10] John Chryssavgis, *On Earth as in Heaven: Ecological Vision and Initiatives of Ecumenical Patriarch Bartholomew* (New York: Fordham University Press, 2012).

[11] John Grim and Mary Evelyn Tucker, *Ecology and Religion* (Washington, DC: Island Press, 2014), 62–84.

been focused on only one of two realms: relations between individuals, and later between individuals and societies. The early conservation movement, he surmised, represented the beginning of a third form of ethics, between humans and the land. He summarized his land ethic: "A thing is right when it tends to preserve the integrity, stability, and beauty of the biotic community. It is wrong when it tends otherwise."[12]

Since the 1960s, a new environmental consciousness has deepened and permeated global culture. This new ecological awareness stresses the rate and extent of human-caused destruction. In 1968, Rachel Carson published *Silent Spring*, which brought attention to how human use of pesticides such as dichlorodiphenyltrichloroethane (DDT) causes unintentional havoc in ecosystems. Since then, the scientific consensus on ecosystemic threats has grown. Some scientists have proposed a new name for our current geological era. They suggest that the Holocene, which spans from the end of the last ice age to now, has functionally ended, and we now live in the Anthropocene, an age in which great planetary systems are defined and shaped by human activity.[13] Other scientists have proposed new standards and limits for planetary fields such as freshwater use and ozone depletion. Delineating "planetary boundaries" is their attempt to define a safe operating space in which human beings may continue to survive. Currently two of these thresholds have been transgressed, and others are in imminent danger.[14] Nobel Peace Prize winner, the United Nations (UN) Intergovernmental Panel on Climate Change (IPCC), has published multiple global assessments of the Earth's changing and warming climate, as well as special reports on the land and oceans.[15] The voice of the natural sciences clearly indicates that humanity must recover or fashion anew an ethic to the land (and other ecosystemic homes like oceans, rivers, and jungles that support a multiplicity of creatures) that prioritizes the common good of the whole and emphasizes respect for the inherent dignity of various kinds of beings.

The social sciences have also stressed the connection between justice to the land and justice to the marginalized. In the context of climate change, the UN refugee agency acknowledges the presence of "nexus dynamics," in which conflict or violence, natural disasters, and environmental degradation come into increasing contact and lead to internal displacement or refugees crossing national boundaries. Those already displaced by political instability, or drought-induced famine, wind up in "climate hot-spots" and are more likely to be displaced a second time.[16] Oxfam reports that the carbon footprint of the world's poorest billion people amounts to just 3 percent, but poor communities bear the brunt of climate change.[17] Positively, the UN has promulgated a list of global social and ecological goals, known as the sustainable development goals (SDGs) or "Global Goals." They represent "a universal call to action to end poverty, protect the planet and ensure that all people enjoy peace and prosperity by 2030."[18] These goals are integrated, meaning that advancement in one will benefit all the other areas, and true development

[12]Aldo Leopold, *A Sand County Almanac* (New York: Oxford University Press, 1949), 224–5.

[13]Will Steffen, P. J. Crutzen, and J. R. McNeill, "The Anthropocene: Are Humans Now Overwhelming the Great Forces of Nature?," *Ambio* 36, no. 8 (2007): 614–21.

[14]Stockholm Resilience Center, "Nine Planetary Boundaries," Stockholm Resilience Center, https://www.stockholmresilience.org/research/planetary-boundaries/planetary-boundaries/about-the-research/the-nine-planetary-boundaries.html.

[15]International Panel on Climate Change, https://www.ipcc.ch/.

[16]UNHCR, "Climate Change and Disasters," https://www.unhcr.org/climate-change-and-disasters.html.

[17]Oxfam, "Climate Change," Oxfam, https://www.oxfamamerica.org/explore/stories/climate-change/.

[18]United Nations Development Programme, "Sustainable Development Goals," United Nations Development Programme, https://www.undp.org/content/undp/en/home/sustainable-development-goals.html.

must balance social, economic, and ecological well-being.[19] Like the Hebrew prophets, these organizations recognize that when planetary boundaries are exceeded and the land, waters, and air are not treated with respect, it is the poor who suffer. Similarly, when justice is advanced in one area, the common good of the whole improves.

EXPERIENCE

Finally, there is a wealth of experience, both personal and communal, that attests to the importance of the land and valuing the planetary common good. Many are well familiar with St. Francis of Assisi, the patron saint of ecology for Catholics. Francis not only loved nature, interacting lovingly with birds, fish, and flowers, but also he also committed himself and his friars to the poor and to peace. He embodied the Christian mission to work for justice, peace, and the integrity of creation, as the WCC expressed centuries later. Countless Christians today affirm Francis's intuition that a more intimate relationship to nature deepens our love of God the Creator whose Spirit gives life to all things. Coupled with a keen awareness of how the planet's health and well-being are at risk, and in grief for the myriad ecosystems, habitats, and species we are losing, Christians experience the beauty and goodness of the Earth as a summons to protect it and to foster its fecundity for the good of future generations.

Many Christians working at the margins of tradition express even more forcefully the need for continued exploration of the planetary common good. Ecofeminist authors, for example, underscore the intersectional nature of race, class, and gender. Melanie Harris contends that the logic of domination that led predominantly white, European peoples to colonize much of the Earth and to exploit its resources, is the same logic that seeks control over Black women's bodies.[20] Indigenous authors, such as American Indian George Tinker, also emphasize the connection between justice for the land and its people. Tinker, a theologian and citizen of the Osage nation, reflects on the long history of suffering of Native Americans and offers their worldview as a corrective for others. For Tinker, Native Americans view the world primarily in terms of space rather than time, and as a result they privilege the community over the individual and stress the interrelatedness of all living creatures and of all the created world. They articulate an ethic of filial responsibility to the land and an ecological ethic that stresses balance and reciprocity.[21] Kenyan theologian Teresia Hinga reflects on the floods and droughts that impacted Kenya's agriculture in the early 2000s. While Hinga acknowledges the benefits of Western science, she also criticizes the a priori dismissal of indigenous knowledge systems and instead calls for local control of seeds and food.[22]

NEW DIRECTIONS

Christian ecological ethics continues to draw out insights from scripture and tradition regarding the ethical responsibility to care for the land and to privilege an ecosystemic

---

[19]Ibid.

[20]Melanie Harris, *Ecowomanism: African-American Women and Earth-Honoring Faiths* (Maryknoll: Orbis, 2017).

[21]George Tinker, *American Indian Liberation: A Theology of Sovereignty* (Maryknoll: Orbis, 2008).

[22]Teresia Hinga, "Of Empty Granaries, Stolen Harvests, and the Weapon of Grain: Applied Ethics in Search of Sustainable Food Security," in *Just Sustainability: Ecology, Technology, and Resource Extraction*, ed. Christiana Peppard and Andrea Vicini, SJ (Maryknoll: Orbis, 2015): 94–104.

viewpoint of the planetary common good. Future research then will develop ecologically sensitive biblical hermeneutics, retrieving key insights into the nexus of justice for the land and for the poor, while also reformulating or revising outdated themes of human superiority over and against the land. Theologians will continue to explore the ecological dimensions of core systematic categories, such as eschatology, incarnation, pneumatology, and ecclesiology, and to articulate their ethical implications in terms of the sacred entanglement with all creatures in creation. In particular within ethics, scholars need to develop more robust standards for ecological virtues, including virtues for organizations and systems, which can assist agents in perceiving their vital participation in the common good. Given the dire predictions of scientists and activists, Christian ethics must also generate resources for cultivating and sustaining hope, and hence also for generating action. And in light of intensifying economic inequality, and the likelihood of increasing political disruption from climate change and other environmental degradation, ethicists must continue to deepen the connections between sustainability for the land and justice for the poor, retrieving the inextricable connection between them in scripture. Christian ethicists will highlight the links between systemic racism and sexism and ecological degradation, and will amplify the voices of indigenous traditions, and the voices of all those who bear the greatest impact of environmental stressors. In all of this work, though, Christian ethicists can draw on a rich variety of moral guidance in their scriptures, their theological traditions, the experiences of the faithful and continuing dialogue with all sources of truth.

SUGGESTED READINGS

Bouma-Prediger, Stephen. *For the Beauty of the Earth: A Christian Vision for Creation Care*, 2nd ed. Grand Rapids: Baker, 2010.

Peppard, Christiana, and Andrea Vicini, SJ, eds. *Just Sustainability: Ecology, Technology, and Resource Extraction*. Maryknoll: Orbis, 2015.

Pope Francis. *Laudato Si': Praise Be to You: On Care for Our Common Home*. Vatican City: Libreria Editrice Vaticana, 2015.

Scheid, Daniel P. *The Cosmic Common Good: Religious Grounds for Ecological Ethics*. Oxford: Oxford University Press, 2016.

CHAPTER FORTY

Climate Change

JEREMY KIDWELL

Climate change is no longer a hazard far off into the future—the effects are all around us. This can be seen in the increased number and intensity of forest fires, floods and hurricanes, wider variability in temperatures, which is most evident in the form of heat waves, and coastal erosion driven by sea-level rise. As of the writing of this chapter in late 2018, human activities have already caused an overall warming of the earth's climate system of 1 degree centigrade[1] above preindustrial levels and this is more extreme in some regions, such as the Arctic, which has experienced two to three times that level of warming. Projections suggest that without significant interventions to mitigate climate change, this is likely to increase to 2 degrees or more. These suggestions are all represented in a scholarly consensus among climate scientists that this climate change is anthropogenic (caused by human activities). Theologians have been reflecting on the theological ethics of climate change since the 1970s, with nearly a dozen volumes having been produced.[2] At the same time, Christian leaders and laypeople have been increasingly visible in social mobilization on the issue of climate change.

Christian theological engagement with the issue of climate change has been modest but sustained, both in scholarly and lay contexts, but it is important to note at the outset that the scholarly conversation is still in flux. Climate change is an issue, which has the tendency to reconfigure the existing frames that are brought to it, and this is shown in a range of new approaches to ethics and critical studies in environmental history, eco-criticism, and eco-theology. Facing climate change does not simply challenge *us*, it changes us and our ways of seeing the world. With this in mind, in this chapter, I briefly explore some of the key characteristics of climate change as an issue, in order to reflect at greater length on the ways that climate change might reconfigure and bring new challenges to Christian ethics.

WHAT SORT OF ETHICAL ISSUE IS CLIMATE CHANGE?

At a time when nationalism seems to be on the rise, climate change is persistent and increasingly unique in its character as (1) a *global* phenomenon. Carbon emissions circulate through one of the most irrevocably common and constantly circulating terrestrial resources: the air we breathe. Given the way that pollution from China can circulate over to Portland, Oregon, in just over a week, climate change presents a true

---

[1]Intergovernmental Panel on Climate Change (IPCC), 2018.

[2]Jeremy Kidwell, Franklin Ginn, Michael Northcott, Elizabeth Bomberg, and Alice Hague, "Christian Climate Care: Slow Change, Modesty and Eco-Theo-Citizenship," *Geo: Geography and Environment* 5, no. 2 (2018).

test of cosmopolitan ethical systems that are based on the politics of maximal global consensus. While this global aspect has given rise to an impressive mobilization in the form of an ongoing conference process that has resulted in a series of United Nations Intergovernmental Panel on Climate Change (IPCC) reports, it has also revealed the struggles of the whole project of global governance. Philosopher Stephen Gardiner suggests that these features, especially "dispersion of causes and effects, fragmentation of agency, and institutional inadequacy," make climate change the "perfect moral storm."[3] Though climate change is intensely global and dispersed, it is important to note that neither carbon contributions nor consequences are distributed evenly. Economists, such as Lucas Chancel and Thomas Piketty, have increasingly pointed to the disparities between accumulated carbon emissions of wealthy developed nations and the two-thirds world, and also to the acute disparity *within* developed nations between those persons who rank in the top 5 percent of wealth and the remaining 95 percent.[4] Climate change forces us to examine the contemporary capacities of cosmopolitan agreement, while it also compels an examination of local culpabilities.

Climate change is also a problem that focuses our thinking toward the presence and problem of (2) *systems*. Picking further up on this theme of dispersal, climate change as a phenomenon troubles classic (neoliberal) accounts of agency and the moral agent. Who is acting? Who is being acted upon? While it can sometimes be portrayed simplistically, as Gardiner hints, climate change involves an array of complex entanglings of different creatures and here we find that non-sentient creatures (like volcanoes) or even interactions across fields of agents (in the form of "feedbacks") can also have significant "agency" in ways that are not predictable. Climate change is a moral problem that forces us to take an ecological view. There is also a knock-on implication for a political theology of climate change. In seeking to replace unsatisfactory neoliberal accounts of justice and action, environmentally oriented ethicists, especially eco-feminists and Christian anarchists, have sought to bypass the binary that pits neoliberalism against hegemonic Marxist critique toward a more positive, open-ended, or eudaemonistic ethic.[5]

Climate change is also a problem that (3) *entangles* our systems and defies tidy classification. On the face of things, climate change is simply a matter of atmospheric concentrations of CO_2 and other greenhouse gases. However, as soon as we begin to probe the sources of greenhouse gas emissions, we quickly find that most domains of environmental concern are drawn in: land use and deforestation, extinction, industrial horticulture, pollution, and many others can each be said to play a part in contributing to climate change. It is important to bear this in mind, especially when examining the subject of climate change through an interdisciplinary lens like theological ethics. The ethical issues at play are necessarily wide-ranging. In a similar way, while it can be tempting to think of climate change as a matter of environmental and other physical sciences, climate change is also the result of a range of political and cultural elements and scholars are increasingly drawing attention to the fact that mitigation will require an analysis that gets at the deep roots of those cultural frames (including theological ones)

---

[3]Stephen M. Gardiner, *A Perfect Moral Storm: The Ethical Tragedy of Climate Change* (New York: Oxford University Press, 2011), 24.

[4]Unpublished report by Chancel and Piketty, *Carbon and Inequality: from Kyoto to Paris: Trends in the Global Inequality of Carbon Emissions (1998–2013) & Prospects for an Equitable Adaptation Fund*, Paris School of Economics, November 3, 2015, http://piketty.pse.ens.fr/files/ChancelPiketty2015.pdf.

[5]Rosi Braidotti, "In Spite of the Times: The Postsecular Turn in Feminism Explorations in Critical Social Science," *Theory, Culture & Society* 25, no. 6 (2008): 1–24.

that support and inhibit sustainable lives. Toward this end, environmental scientist and contributor to the IPCC process Mike Hulme has suggested, "Science has universalised and materialised climate change; we must now particularise and spiritualise it."[6] So let us now turn to explore what exactly this kind of work might look like in the context of Christian ethics.

CHRISTIAN ETHICS AND CLIMATE CHANGE

Having discussed above some key demands that the phenomenon of climate change poses to ethical reflection, the next and main task of this chapter is to explore the ways that Christian ethics might respond to these demands. I do not want to advance a generic programmatic proposal at this juncture, as has been done famously by H. R. Niebuhr with his Christ-and-culture typologies. Instead I will explore, as other authors have done, how we might confront the issue of climate change through the Quadrilateral. I want to emphasize at this juncture how my use of this frame is not meant to mirror a set of epistemological claims. Indeed, I would hold that such an approach would be seriously problematic. As Scharen and Vigen rightly note in their book *Ethnography as Christian Theology and Ethics*, "Experience is not simply a source for theology and ethics—it is the primary lens through which human beings access any and all scientific, moral, or theological knowledge."[7] In particular, theological engagements with science must be cautious about subordinating the category of "experience" and by extension suggesting that other sources of theological reflection might be somehow unmediated by experience. This is because at the core, a coherent exposition of the doctrine of creation that serves as a crucial corollary to discussion of science ought to involve a meaningful consideration of God's good world as being full of purposive divine action. As many of my coauthors in this volume have suggested, we can treat this Quadrilateral framing as a kind of reflective heuristic, and with this in mind, I will consider each heading in turn.

EXPERIENCE

One of the ways we can foreground experience in a theological ethics of climate change is to conduct an experiment in grassroots theology. To provide one example, in my own research, I sought to engage more systematic doctrinal reflection in a proximate context through observations and interviews with Scottish Christians (2015–18) involved in the Eco-Congregation movement.[8] What we found is that among these many Christians who were focusing their ministry on climate change mitigation, reasons for concern were rarely packaged in ways that might easily map onto systematic theological categories. Their concerns were constituted around more domestic and intuitive themes: concern to secure a safe future for their children, anxieties about their own household finance, and a prophetic burden for the well-being of more distant neighbors who might be suffering most acutely from the effects of climate change. While one reaction to this finding might

[6]Mike Hulme, *Why We Disagree about Climate Change: Understanding Controversy, Inaction, and Opportunity* (Cambridge: Cambridge University Press, 2009), 330.
[7]Christian Scharen and Aana Marie Vigen, *Ethnography as Christian Theology and Ethics* (New York: Continuum, 2011), 63.
[8]Kidwell et al., "Christian Climate Care."

be to suggest that climate change is not a "theological" issue, I would prefer to take this as an opportunity to widen the scope of what gets called "theological." A number of Christian ethicists have begun to emphasize the validity of reflection, which is first grounded in the messy everyday life of Christians working through these issues. This leads to a kind of Christian ethics that starts with lay knowledge and foregrounds lay concerns as a subject for ethical analysis.[9]

Building on this suggestion, a theology of climate change ought also to be *liberative*, that is focused on the most acute suffering felt by those on the margins of our global economy. Some of the most prophetic calls to action on climate change have come from Pacific Island communities for whom the threat of climate change through sea level rise is imminent. It is important to avoid "armchair" liberation theology, for example, when developed-world theologians advocate benevolently on behalf of (but not alongside) peoples and lands that are on the margins of these debates. Rather, I want to suggest that Christian carbon polluters (i.e., in the United States, Australia, and Europe) should pay attention to the unique inflection that Christian theology takes in those places where the impacts of climate change are most severe. Jesus's preaching came across as shocking and counterintuitive to a number of his fellow Jewish contemporaries, just as the apostle Paul brought "foolishness" to the Greeks. By appropriating the voices of others, Christian ethics can too often implicitly smuggle forms of white privilege into reflection on contemporary issues. Climate change is a perfect context for countermovements where theological reflection is structured as listening. To provide just one example of what I mean, Hannah Fair provides an example of the ways that Christians in the Pacific Islands are framing climate change as an issue. She shares a range of ways that islanders foregrounded different aspects of the text of the biblical flood in Genesis 6–9, in light of the very real threat of climate change-related flooding of their homes.[10] Some islanders found a tension with the rainbow covenant promise that floods would never be an instrument of divine judgment. Others saw Noah as an "aspirational figure," that is, an icon of faithful response in preparing for impending trouble. Finally, yet another set of respondents presented a liberative reading—drawing attention to the often-ignored cries of those who remained outside the ark: "Those outside the ark need to be liberated and I think God is with those who are outside the ark. God is struggling with them, trying to alleviate them while Noah he is enjoying the luxury life, you know."[11]

My point here is that, particularly in the multiple failures by scientific and political bodies to galvanize public concern, climate change is an issue for ethical deliberation that encourages the ethicist to begin not with prophetic proclamation (though that may well be due) but with listening to the groans of creation (more on this below) and those persons who are on the front lines of climate change impacts, and who are also the victims of racialized marginalization and injustice. Such theology-from-below can foreground new theological resources and provide more robust contexts in which to invite reflection on more abstract and academic framings of climate change as an issue.

---

[9]In addition to Scharen and Vigen, cited above, see Luke Bretherton, *Hospitality as Holiness: Christian Witness amid Moral Diversity* (Aldershot: Ashgate, 2006).
[10]Hannah Fair, "Three Stories of Noah: Navigating Religious Climate Change Narratives in the Pacific Island Region," *Geo: Geography and Environment* 5, no. 2 (2018), DOI: 10.1002/geo2.68.
[11]Ibid., 11.

SCRIPTURE

I have briefly noted the utter novelty of climate change and, turning to scripture, this might be taken to be problematic—given such novelty, none of the texts of the Bible can be said to address anthropogenic climate change directly. Given my suggestion above that reflection on climate change can often telescope outward to cover a much broader environmental concern, it may be useful to zoom out a bit and consider what sort of biblical texts speak to and frame the issue of climate change for Christian ethics. I have already pointed to the possible value of liberative readings, but it is also worth noting that ecological concerns have already been the sustained preoccupation of a range of scholars working in the field of ecological hermeneutics. This project has matured from an early focus on a limited range of texts that might be taken to be about creation (particularly Genesis 1–2) toward a more canonically encompassing view, from Genesis through to Revelation.

Biblical scholarship has struggled to shake off a suspicion that Christianity, and by extension, biblical theology, has been the cause of the environmental crisis. While there are good reasons to dispute this claim, it is important to appreciate the impact this attitude has had on contemporary ecological readings of the Bible.[12] This takes shape particularly in the Ecological Hermeneutics and Earth Bible projects in the form of a hermeneutics of suspicion.[13] In my view, a proper ecological hermeneutic must accept and embrace canonical polyphony. There are, in Christian scripture, a range of human voices speaking of ecology in different ways, and also a range of other-than-human voices that are presented by human writers in some quite counterintuitive and important ways. I cannot possibly summarize the range of relevant texts in this brief chapter, but can provide a few examples to demonstrate what I mean.

The Hebrew Bible has an extensive catalogue of the speech of nature and the prophetic significance of geological activity and terrestrial weather patterns. The earth is often portrayed as resonating with divine anger and disappointment, as in 2 Sam. 22:8, where we read that the "earth reeled and rocked and the foundations of the earth trembled and quaked, because he was angry" (see parallel in Ps. 18:7). This parallels regular use of "rocks" and "mountains" across both the Hebrew Bible and the New Testament as a metaphor for a steadfast creator God (as in 2 Sam. 22:2 and Ps. 18:2). On one level, this metaphor rests on the edge of becoming literal as we see the consequences of hydraulic fracking and other recent efforts at unconventional fossil fuel extraction in the increasing occurrence of earthquakes that threaten human life and well-being. On another level, though, these texts convey a symmetry between divine and terrestrial communication, that is, divine anger at human unrighteousness is mirrored in groans, cries, and shaking in nature (Ps. 114; Mt. 27:51-54), while divine pleasure is shown in dancing and singing by nature (Ps. 69:34, 98:4).

One implication of these texts, which has been taken up over the centuries in Christian natural theology, is that the creation can serve, in an albeit mitigated way, to convey God's intentions and frustrations. This is certainly the attitude conveyed by the Psalmist. By extension, I want to ask whether we might consider the empirical scientific work that seeks to measure anthropogenic environmental impacts as a form of listening for divine

---

[12]Jeremy Kidwell, "The Historical Roots of the Ecological Crisis," in *Oxford Handbook of Ecology and Bible*, ed. Hilary Marlow and Mark Harris (Oxford: Oxford University Press, 2020).

[13]See Jeremy Kidwell, review of *Exploring Ecological Hermeneutics*, ed. Norman C. Habel and Peter Trudinger, *Expository Times* 122, no. 11 (2011): 563.

communication. Ignoring the signs of climate change also has a spiritual significance—it portrays a hardening of hearts when (some) humans have agendas for development and wealth, which they prefer not to have impeded by practical considerations or anthropogenic harms. This is a straightforward reading of the text of Job 31:38-40, where he gives the land a prophetic voice: "If my land has cried out against me and its furrows have wept together, if I have eaten its yield without payment and made its owners breathe their last, let thorns grow instead of wheat and foul weeds instead of barley" (ESV). The parallels between prophetic apocalyptic imagery and present consequences of human ecological devastation (particularly in airborne pollution, desertification, and geological activity) can be breathtaking, as in Jer. 4:27ff where the writer describes the consequences of human foolishness and evil as resulting in the land becoming a "desolation"—a reversing of God's creative activity, which organized chaos into lively forms: "I looked on the earth, and behold, it was without form and void ... all the hills moved to and fro. I looked, and behold, there was no man." There are good divine purposes at work in sustaining, renewing, and preserving the whole created order, including its vulnerable human inhabitants, and (I would argue) this divine work is perceptible to the careful observer. However, they may be obscured by the scale of impacts like climate change. There is an abiding sense conveyed particularly in the Hebrew Bible that humans are left to feel some of the ecological consequences of misbehavior, particularly in the face of stubborn resistance so clearly evident in human response to four decades of climate science.

REASON

As we have learned more in recent decades about the surprising liveliness of the created order, it has become increasingly difficult to sustain the enlightenment-era notion of the rational self. To take just one example, research into bacteriology and the human microbiome has exposed ways in which microscopic life is intrinsically related, indeed coevolved, within human life in the form of tiny creatures that dwell in the human gut (and elsewhere). The microbiome within each human body contains up to one hundred times the total genetic material that can be found elsewhere in the body, and researchers have found that the creatures in your gut can have meaningful impacts on our well-being and cognition.[14] This represents a serious and possibly fatal challenge to Enlightenment model of each human working as an epistemologically autonomous reasoner, what Charles Taylor has called the "buffered self." Taylor's model holds that "the things beyond [our personal epistemological boundary] don't need to 'get to me' ... This self can see itself as invulnerable, as master of the meanings of things for it."[15] These microbiological insights that commend a more complex model of agency are matched by a range of other new fields that go by a range of names: post-humanism, object-oriented ontology, new materialism, actor-network theory, and so on.[16] In one way, this is simply a rehearsal of

[14]Readers interested in more on bidirectional communication between the brain and the gut microbiota can read more in Andrew P. Allen, Timothy G. Dinan, Gerard Clarke, and John F. Cryan, "A Psychology of the Human Brain-Gut-Microbiome Axis," *Social and Personality Psychology Compass* 11, no. 4 (April 2017).

[15]Charles Taylor, *Sources of the Self: The Making of the Modern Identity* (Cambridge: Harvard University Press, 1989), 38.

[16]See, e.g., Karen Barad, *Meeting the Universe Halfway: Quantum Physics and the Entanglement of Matter and Meaning* (Durham: Duke University Press, 2007); Ian Bogost, *Alien Phenomenology, or What's It Like to Be a Thing* (Minneapolis: University of Minnesota Press, 2012); Tim Ingold, *Being Alive: Essays on Movement, Knowledge and Description* (London: Routledge, 2011).

what liberal and anarchistic political theologians have been insisting for decades: that we can only meaningfully think "together" and that our modes of "reasoning" are inextricably entangled with the influence and thoughts of others. But few political theologians have yet integrated the notion of "thinking with" other-than-human forms of life.

A similarly fatal challenge has been issued to the Cartesian reduction of other-than-human life to automatons. To note just a few of the hundreds of different vectors that come together here from across biological and botanical science, Frans de Waal (and the ethologists who have followed that research) has observed the politics embedded in social behavior of chimpanzees; recent research has observed the ways that trees communicate and collaborate in response to threats; and birds and mammals have surprising abilities in problem-solving and urban adaptation.[17] Climate change has certainly not displaced the anthropocentric hierarchies evident in late-medieval chains of being—we are clearly the most impactful species on earth. However, it is now quite radically unclear whether human distinctiveness can be affirmed in terms of our ability to perceive and reason about the world, even with all of our impressive instrumentation. If we are to reason out a full account of what biospheric thriving looks like, it will have to be in collaboration with a much wider host of God's creatures.[18]

TRADITION

I have emphasized the contemporary aspect of climate change above: it is a novel problem that provokes creative responses in a range of fields including theology. Undergirding this characterization, however, is another important one, which is that the features of contemporary theological thought which I want to resist (e.g., the "buffered self" or the sense that other-than-human forms of life lack agency or sentience) are only slightly less recent innovations with respect to the broader cloth of Christian historical theology. There is much about our present framings that I want to disrupt: our assumptions that "progress" and "development" are moral goods or necessities, instrumentalized notions of other-than-human creatures, and hermeneutics of suspicion regarding the "communication" of nature. To be fair, versions of each of these views have a provenance in premodern Christian theology. However, it is disingenuous to suggest that they have always been mainstream within the Christian tradition, or that they are theologically necessary ways of conceiving human relationships to the created order.

To give just one example of what I mean here, we can look to the notion of creation as "communicative." A number of scholars in science and theology have noted Galileo's 1615 metaphor of the two books, in which he describes the "book" of Nature and the Book of Scripture and his suggestion that we should "read" them both.[19] This was appreciated by Galileo's contemporaries such as Tommaso Campanella. These suggestions regarding

---

[17]Frans de Waal, *Chimpanzee Politics: Power and Sex among Apes* (Baltimore: Johns Hopkins University Press, 2007); Peter Wohlleben, *The Hidden Life of Trees* (Vancouver: Greystone, 2016); Robert W. Shumaker, Kristina R. Walkup, and Benjamin B. Beck, *Animal Tool Behavior: The Use and Manufacture of Tools by Animals* (Baltimore: Johns Hopkins University Press, 2011).

[18]Space does not permit a sustained treatment here, but philosophers have provided some examples of what this might look like in practice. See Michelle Bastian et al., eds., *Participatory Research in More-than-Human Worlds* (London: Routledge, 2016); S. Eben Kirksey and Stefan Helmreich, "The Emergence of Multispecies Ethnography," *Cultural Anthropology* 25, no. 4 (2010): 545–76.

[19]See Klaas van Berkel and Arjo Vanderjagt, eds., *The Book of Nature in Early Modern and Modern History* (Leuven: Peeters, 2006).

the importance of the created world are carried forward into Protestant theology as recounted in work by Belden Lane, Mark Stoll, and Evan Berry.[20] Indeed, many historians of science go so far as to argue that modern Western science arose not in spite of or against Christian theology, but because it cultivated attentive study of the natural world and its creatures. We need not stop our work of retrieval in the sixteenth century, however. There are a number of precursors to these medieval scientists: the Franciscan tradition of animal stories and awareness of the "voice" of creatures much earlier in monastic literature arising from Desert spirituality and reflection by Patristic voices such as John of Chrysostom or Augustine of Hippo.[21]

There is a theology of history that this confrontation with climate change seems to press us toward. This is a historical theology that might inform a prophetic renewal of a vision of the good life and the horizon of future human inhabitation of the earth. The new field of environmental history has offered a similar challenge to the broader discipline of history and archaeology. Stories we have told about the past in the modern telling of history have excluded and marginalized environmental factors. New insights from paleobiology have begun the work of reasserting the tight integration of human life with other forms of life on earth. Ultimately, what I am pressing for is a historical theology that can aid this work of retrieval. We might look toward the work of *nouvelle theologie* in attempting a *ressourcement* or to Orthodox theologians such as Georges Florovsky and John Zizioulas who argued for a Neo-Patristic synthesis. These recent traditions offer models of the kind of double-perspectived rehabilitation, which looks both forward and backward. Ultimately, there is significant range here for an eco-theological rehabilitation of the theology of history, and I would argue that such a rehabilitation must be attempted if we are to carry forward an ecologically coherent theological ethics.

CONCLUSION

I am convinced that the failure of the developed world to mobilize in response to four decades of climate science and the clear and present signs of climate change represents not just a moral failure in terms of apathy or a lack of action, but there are underlying problems with the ways that we frame human action and creaturely interrelation, and Christian theology has been captive to these problems as much as many secular critical frames. To respond to climate change we must not just "rally the troops," though there are many encouraging signs that there is now a new groundswell of Christian action and mobilization in response to climate change. We must also prophetically bring forward the resources of the Christian tradition. This involves modes of praxis, particularly the spiritual disciplines of meditation (listening) and asceticism (fasting). This also involves reconsiderations of a range of theological conceptions including the nature of grace: of ourselves as graced bodies dwelling sometimes awkwardly on this earth and of our relationships with others as being "graced" toward hope for our terrestrial future. Only when we inhabit the fullness of the Christian tradition, and take up all the spiritual

[20]Belden C. Lane, *Ravished by Beauty: The Surprising Legacy of Reformed Spirituality* (Oxford: Oxford University Press, 2011); Mark Stoll, *Protestantism, Capitalism, and Nature in America* (Albuquerque: University of New Mexico Press, 1997); Evan Berry, *Devoted to Nature: The Religious Roots of American Environmentalism* (Oakland: University of California Press, 2015).
[21]David Clough, *On Animals* (New York: T&T Clark, 2012).

resources available, will we be able to coherently and robustly respond to an issue like climate change.

SUGGESTED READINGS

McFague, Sallie. *A New Climate for Theology: God, the World, and Global Warming*. Minneapolis: Fortress, 2008.

Northcott, Michael S. *Moral Climate: The Ethics of Global Warming*. Maryknoll: Orbis, 2007.

Northcott, Michael S. *A Political Theology of Climate Change*. Grand Rapids: Eerdmans, 2013.

Northcott, Michael S., and Peter M. Scott, eds. *Systematic Theology and Climate Change: Ecumenical Perspectives*. London: Routledge, 2014.

Schaefer, Jame. *Confronting the Climate Crisis: Catholic Theological Perspectives*. Milwaukee: Marquette University Press, 2011.

CHAPTER FORTY-ONE

Nonhuman Creatures

DAVID L. CLOUGH

If the words in this book were divided according to the relative mass of human and nonhuman creatures in the universe, not one would be allocated to humans. If we made the book longer, say equal to the combined length of all the books that have ever been published, we still could not allocate a single word to humans on this basis. We would need to increase the number of books by seven octillion times—seven followed by twenty-seven zeroes, or six orders of magnitude more than all the grains of sand on earth—before the human fraction of the universe justified a single word.[1] If we restricted our interest to living creatures, things would be very different: on the basis of comparing human biomass with that of all living creatures on earth, humans would be entitled to twenty-two of the roughly two hundred thousand words in this book. If we were interested only in Christian ethics in relation to animals, we would be justified in allocating to humans a short six-thousand-word chapter.[2]

The reason human creatures are the focus of all but one or two chapters of this book is that Christian theologians and ethicists have judged that the ethical ordering of our relationships toward other humans is much more important than those we have toward nonhuman creatures. As we shall see, there are influential accounts of theological ethics that go further to imply there should be no space at all given to nonhuman creatures in this book, because they are entirely outside the boundaries of Christian ethical concern. In this chapter I argue that this exclusion of nonhuman creatures from Christian ethics should be rejected. There are good reasons to begin with humans when we reflect on our responsibilities toward other creatures, but there are no good reasons to end with them. Most of this chapter focuses on the implications of widening the circle of Christian concern to our next-nearest neighbors, fellow animal creatures, but I also raise the possibility that Christian ethics should include other living and even nonliving creatures within its sphere of concern. The chapter considers Christian ethical responsibility toward nonhuman creatures under the headings of scripture, tradition, and reason.

---

[1]Estimate based on: 8 billion humans of average mass 70 kilograms; mass of universe 10^{53} kilograms; length of book two hundred thousand words; books ever published: 130 million; grains of sand on earth 5×10^{21}.

[2]Biomass of all life on earth: 550 gigatonnes of carbon; human biomass 0.06 gigatonnes of carbon. Estimates from Yinon M. Bar-On, Rob Phillips, and Ron Milo, "The Biomass Distribution on Earth," *Proceedings of the National Academy of Sciences USA* 115 (2018): 6506–11.

SCRIPTURE

The fundamental scriptural insight for a Christian ethics of nonhuman creatures is that they are creatures of God and common recipients with humans of God's grace. In Genesis 1–2, the great psalms of creation such as Psalm 104, the closing chapters of Job, in the teaching of Jesus (e.g., Mt. 10:29), and the prologue to John's Gospel, we find affirmations that all creatures were made by God, declared good by God, and are sustained by God's providential care. All creatures respond to God with praise and thanksgiving (Ps. 65, 66:1-4, 98:7-8, 145:7, 10; Isa. 42:10-12, 43:20); all creatures are gathered up and reconciled in the work of Jesus Christ (Eph. 1:8b-10; Col. 1:15-20) as a result of God's love for the world of creatures (Jn 3:16); all creatures will be liberated from their groaning bondage into the freedom of the children of God (Rom. 8:18-23) so that God may be all in all (1 Cor. 15:28). Nonhuman animal creatures have even more in common with humans: they are fleshy creatures made of dust and inspired by the breath of life (Genesis 2); they are given a common table with humans (Gen. 1:29-30); they are covenant partners with God alongside human beings (Gen. 9:8-17; Hos. 1:18); they experience the fragility of life as the common recipient of God's blessing and judgment (e.g., Jer. 7:20; Ezek. 14:13-21; Joel 1:4, 10, 18, 20); they will live in peace with each other and humans when the Messiah comes (Isa. 11:6-9); and they are part of the chorus of praise around the throne in the new creation (Rev. 4:6-11, 5:11-14). These are strong biblical affirmations of the place of all creatures in God's great works of creation, reconciliation, and redemption.[3]

Biblical texts also set out particular ethical responsibilities of humans toward other creatures. In the Old Testament they are included under the obligations of the Israelite law. It is repeatedly emphasized that domesticated animals should share in the Sabbath rest (Exod. 20:8-11, 23:12; Deut. 5:14), and it is recognized that the septennial Sabbath for the land benefits wild animals (Lev. 25:6-7). First-born male livestock should remain with their mothers for seven days before sacrifices (Exod. 22:30), cows and ewes may not be slaughtered with their young (Lev. 22:28), even the donkeys of enemies must be set free from burdens trapping them (Exod. 23:4-5; Deut. 22:1-4), kids must not be boiled in their mothers' milk (Exod. 23:19; Deut. 14:21), mother birds must not be taken with fledglings or eggs (Deut. 22:6-7), oxen must not be muzzled when treading grain (Deut. 25:4), different species of livestock must not be yoked together or cross-bred (Deut. 22:10; Lev. 19:19), and Jesus discusses emergencies in caring for domesticated animals as obvious exceptions to law in relation to the Sabbath (Mt. 12:11; Lk. 14:5). The rationale for the prohibition on consuming the blood of animals is that "the life of every creature is its blood" (Lev. 17:14), suggesting a further profound commonality between humans and other animals.

The permissibility of the human use of other animals for food is a live question at several points within the biblical texts. The first chapter of Genesis specifies a plant-based diet for humans and other animals (1:29-30) and God gives explicit permission for humans to kill animals for food only after the flood (Gen. 9:3). When God miraculously provides manna to sustain the people of Israel, they are ungrateful and crave meat, a lust that is punished with a plague "while the meat was still between their teeth" (Numbers 11). The prophetic accounts of peace between humans and other animals noted above suggest that the permission given for meat-eating in Genesis 9 is an interim measure that

[3]For further discussion of biblical perspectives on nonhuman animals in relation to the doctrines of creation, reconciliation, and redemption, see David L. Clough, *On Animals: Vol. 1. Systematic Theology* (London: T&T Clark/Continuum, 2012), esp. chap. 2.

falls short of the full expression of God's will for relationships between creatures. In the New Testament, Paul's letter to the Romans indicates that divisions have arisen between those who have adopted a vegetarian diet and those who eat meat (Rom. 14:1-4). The stringent regulations for the sacrifice of animals (e.g., Leviticus 1, 3–5, 6–9, 14–16, 22–23) make clear that the taking of the lives of nonhuman animals is a morally weighty matter that must be done with very great care, and the killing of animals outside the sacrificial system was prohibited. The practice of animal sacrifice is later criticized by the prophets as undesirable to God with an uncomfortable resemblance to the killing of humans and idolatry (Isa. 1:11, 66:3). John's account of the crucifixion describes it in terms of an animal sacrifice, suggesting both a commonality between the Jesus Christ and nonhuman animals and the ending of the need of animal sacrifices for the followers of Christ.[4]

Some biblical texts have frequently been cited to justify human use or even abuse of animals. Foremost among these is God's granting of human dominion over other animals in Genesis 1 (vv. 26-28), repeated in Ps. 8:6-8. Martin Luther called Gen. 9:3 the license establishing butchers' shops.[5] Jesus's teaching comparing the value of human and nonhuman life has been used to discount the value of animals (Mt. 6:26, 10:31, 12:11-12; Lk. 12:6-7, 24), as has Paul's rhetorical question in 1 Corinthians asking whether God is concerned for oxen in relation to the law against muzzling them (v. 9). Peter receives a vision of all kinds of animals and is told to "kill and eat" (Acts 10:11-13). None of these texts, however, provides good grounds for excluding animals or other nonhuman creatures from ethical consideration. The granting of human dominion over other creatures attributes a particular role to humans, but it is followed by the stipulation of a vegan diet for both humans and other animals, so does not seem to include the right for humans to kill animals for food. The close association between dominion and imaging God in Gen. 1:26-8 suggests that humans should understand their divinely mandated role as being exercised for the benefit of all God's creatures, rather than merely to advance human interests. The specification of the human task as tilling and keeping the garden of Eden (Gen. 2:15) further supports the idea that humans are divinely appointed to care for the lives of other creatures. Luther was keen to combat Roman Catholic rules about dietary practice through his affirmation of the Genesis 9 permission to eat meat, but he understood meat-eating as a second best to God's original plan and believed a plant-based diet would be much healthier.[6] Jesus's teaching suggests any flat equivalence between human and nonhuman creaturely life is inappropriate, but his aim of reassuring his listeners that God cares for them is realized through an argument that takes as its premise a shared understanding that God cares for even the humblest of creatures. This shared understanding of God's concern for all creatures means that reading Paul's question about oxen as denying that God cares for oxen is highly implausible. Instead, we should understand him to be making a technical point that God provided the law for those who can read it. Peter's animal vision is explicitly interpreted metaphorically twice in Acts: God's message is not that he should kill animals but that he should welcome gentiles into the church (Acts 10:28, 11:12).[7]

---

[4]See discussion in ibid., 127–9.

[5]Martin Luther, *Luther's Works*, vol. 2, ed. Helmut T. Lehmann and Jaroslav Pelikan (Philadelphia: Muhlenberg, 1958–67), 133.

[6]Martin Luther, *Luther's Works*, vol. 1, ed. Jaroslav Pelikan (Saint Louis: Concordia, 1958), 36.

[7]For further discussion of these texts, see the Introduction to David L. Clough, *On Animals: Vol. 2. Theological Ethics* (London: T&T Clark/Bloomsbury, 2019), esp. xvi–xvii and xxii.

Biblical texts therefore provide a strong basis for affirming both the value of nonhuman creatures to God and the importance of human responsibilities to care for other creatures. Attempts to use the Bible to posit a divine mandate for the unlimited exploitation of other creatures by humans are implausible if the texts cited for this purpose are read in a wider biblical context.

TRADITION

Given the biblical affirmation of God's delight in and providential care for a diverse array of creaturely life, it is striking that early Christian theologians came quickly to the view that God made everything for human beings. The Jewish thinker Philo of Alexandria (*c.* 20 BCE–*c.* 50 CE) compared the account of creation in Plato's *Timaeus* with that of Genesis 1, and felt the need to explain the anomaly that whereas humans had a place of honor in being created first in Plato's account, Genesis seemed to consider humans less important by leaving them until last. Philo presented a number of arguments to explain why Genesis affirmed human preeminence, including seeing God's creation of all nonhuman creatures as merely making preparations for the arrival of humans, much as a host giving a banquet would get everything ready before the arrival of honored guests.[8] Among the early Christian theologians who provide very similar arguments of creation are Lactantius, Gregory of Nyssa, and John of Chrysostom, and later thinkers as diverse as Bonaventure, Martin Luther, John Calvin, and William Kirkby adopt similar positions.[9] Origen, Justin Martyr, and Irenaeus of Lyons affirm the broader conclusion that God made everything for the sake of humans.[10] The explanation for this endorsement of anthropocentrism is various, but it often seems driven by a desire to affirm God's special providential care for human beings in the face of competing worldviews that deny it. In relation to ongoing disputes between Greek and Roman philosophical traditions, Christian thinkers often saw advantage in endorsing Stoic positions that defended such special providence, and with them took on other Stoic tenets such as human superiority over other animals on the basis of their possession of the divine attribute of reason.

The idea that humans were uniquely rational was quickly deployed in relation to Christian ethical responsibility in relation to nonhuman creatures. In *The City of God*, Augustine notes that some have argued that the Decalogue prohibition of killing should apply "even unto beasts and cattle, and would have it unlawful to kill any of them." He argues against this on the basis that it could equally well be applied to plants as well, and this leads to the "foul error of the Manichees." Instead, Augustine contends, the commandment "You shall not kill" does not apply to plants because they are not sensitive, and it does not apply to nonhuman animals because "they have no society with us in reason."[11] Thomas Aquinas cites Augustine's view with approval, and adds to it Aristotle's position in the *Politics* that plants were made for the sake of animals and nonhuman animals for the sake of humans.[12] Aquinas goes on to deny that humans have duties toward other animals in relation to justice or charity, on the basis that humans were given

[8]Philo of Alexandria, *On the Creation of the Cosmos According to Moses*, ed. D. T. Runia (Leiden: Brill, 2001), chap. 14, § 77–84.
[9]See Clough, *On Animals: Vol. 1*, 6–9.
[10]Ibid., 10–13.
[11]Augustine, *The City of God*, trans. John Healey, ed. R. V. G. Tasker (London: Dent & Sons, 1945), I.19.
[12]Thomas Aquinas, *Summa Theologica*, trans. Fathers of the English Dominican Province (London: Blackfriars, 1963–75), II–II.64.1, citing Aristotle, *Politics*, trans. C. D. C. Reeve (Indianapolis: Hackett, 1998), I.8, 1256b.

dominion over them, and that we cannot will good things for nonhuman animals because they are irrational and cannot possess them.[13]

The arguments of Augustine and Aquinas have been influential in providing reasons to discount the inclusion of nonhuman creatures within the boundaries of Christian ethics, but do not withstand critical scrutiny. Augustine's disavowal of positions associated with his previous Manichaeism makes him overly hasty in ruling out concern for nonhuman animals. Elsewhere he is alert to the cognitive capacities of animals, such as his observation that the ability of fish in the Bulla Regia fountain to anticipate being fed by humans demonstrates that Basil of Caesarea was wrong to judge that fish do not have memory.[14] Contrary to Augustine's position, rationality is not a plausible basis for determining who counts morally. We do not exclude nonrational humans—such as newborn infants, or those with severe learning disabilities, or persons with dementia—from moral consideration, and, as discussed in the next section, rationality is complex and graduated and, therefore, cannot function as the clear boundary marker Augustine's argument needs. Aquinas's appeal to Aristotle's view of natural hierarchies between creatures is also problematic: in the same passage Aristotle defends slavery on the basis that some peoples are "intended by nature" to be enslaved. The idea of a hierarchy between creatures is subverted in biblical wisdom literature, such as the closing chapters of Job or the view expressed by the author of Ecclesiastes of fundamental similarities between humans and other animals (Eccl. 3:18-21). It is also rejected by Basil of Caesarea and Gregory of Nyssa, who argue that there are no orders of being and that every creature has the same ontological status.[15] It is convenient for humans to ground a right of unlimited exploitation of nonhuman animals theologically, just as it was convenient for slave owners to justify slavery on an ideological basis, but neither rationality nor supposed creaturely hierarchies are convincing grounds for doing so.

The early-fifteenth-century English commentary on the Ten Commandments, *Dives and Pauper*, a dialogue between the eponymous characters, presents a very different understanding of the commandment "Thou shalt not kill" as it pertains to animals. Dives—consistently on the wrong side of every dispute—argues with Augustine's opponents that the commandment must prohibit the killing of nonhuman animals. Pauper cites Gen. 9:3 to defend the human killing of other animals for food when necessary, but goes on to state that cruelty toward animals is prohibited: "For God that made all has care of all, and he shall take vengeance on all that misuse his creatures." Pauper concludes that humans "should have compassion on beast and bird and not harm them without cause and have regard for the fact that they are God's creatures," and he adds that those who torment beasts or birds for cruelty or vanity "sin very grievously."[16] This recognition that Christian compassion extends beyond human neighbors is also frequently evident in the lives of the saints, such as St. Macarius's healing of a hyena's pup; St. Jerome's hospitality to a lion; St. Kevin's care for blackbird making a nest in his outstretched praying hand; or St. Werburgh's resurrection of a goose killed by her steward, to name but a small sample.[17]

---

[13]Aquinas, *Summa Theologica*, II–II.102.6; II–II.25.3.

[14]Discussed in Clough, *On Animals: Vol. 1*, 55–6, n. 34.

[15]See discussion in Colin E. Gunton, *The Triune Creator: A Historical and Systematic Study* (Edinburgh: Edinburgh University Press, 1998), 71–2; Robert W. Jenson, *God after God: The God of the Past and the God of the Future, Seen in the Work of Karl Barth* (Philadelphia: Fortress, 2010), 20.

[16]Priscilla Heath Barnum, ed., *Dives and Pauper*, vol. 1 (Oxford: Early English Text Society/Oxford University Press, 1976), pt. 2, chap. 15, 33–6, English modernized.

[17]For a valuable collection of such stories, see Helen Waddell and Robert Gibbings, *Beasts and Saints* (London: Darton, Longman & Todd, 1995).

The *Dives and Pauper* commentary and such stories seem more successful than Augustine or Aquinas in grounding an animal ethics responsive to the appreciation of the value of the lives of nonhuman creatures evident in the biblical texts discussed in the previous section, and suggest that the positions of Augustine and Aquinas were not representative of Christian understandings of how other animals should be treated. The explicitly Christian basis of the campaigns for legislation against animal cruelty, and against vivisection, in Britain in the nineteenth century, drew on the same recognition of a Christian obligation to treat other animals with respect for their creator.[18]

REASON

New scientific knowledge both concerning the commonality between human and nonhuman creatures and the capabilities of the latter has the potential to destabilize the kind of neat divisions between human and nonhuman creatures that have frequently characterized Christian theological discussions. Genetics provides one striking starting point for reflecting on our commonality with other creatures: we share a fifth of our genes with all other life forms, over half with all eukaryotes—including protozoa, algae, fungi, and plants—three-quarters with all animals, 97 percent with orangutans, 98.5 percent with gorillas, and 98.9 percent with chimpanzees.[19] About 8 percent of human DNA is made up of around one hundred thousand sequences originating in invasive retroviruses.[20] Our bodies are also more than human: they are sites of coexistence of multiple organisms including thousands of species of bacteria, archaea, viruses, and various eukaryotes such as fungi and protists, without which we would be unable to survive.[21]

We have also exaggerated the distinction between humans and other creatures in our estimation of the capabilities of nonhuman animals. We now know that chimpanzees perform better than humans in computer games involving the retention and recall of numerical sequences, and exhibit empathy, morality, and politics; that sheep are capable of remembering hundreds of faces; that dolphins can parse grammar; that crows are able to fashion tools innovatively to solve problems; that parrots can comment on the abstract properties of objects such as color and shape; and that different groups of sperm whales—like very many other species—have culturally specific modes of life and communication.[22] This new knowledge has the potential to subvert a wide range of criteria previously believed to distinguish between humans and nonhumans, but a historical example demonstrates that whether we allow it do so depends on our prior commitments. Three-quarters of Philo of Alexandria's work, *On Animals* (*c.* 50 CE) is taken up with examples of surprising animal behavior, such as a dolphin who fell in love with a human boy and grieved after his death, but the final part of the book attributes every single example to instinctive behavior rather than demonstrating intelligence or

---

[18]See Chien-hui Li, "A Union of Christianity, Humanity, and Philanthropy: The Christian Tradition and the Prevention of Cruelty to Animals in Nineteenth-Century England," *Society & Animals* 8, no. 3 (2000): 265–85; Chien-hui Li, "Mobilizing Christianity in the Antivivisection Movement in Victorian Britain," *Journal of Animal Ethics* 2, no. 2 (2012): 141–61.

[19]Mark Ridley, *Evolution*, 3rd ed. (Malden: Blackwell, 2004), 558.

[20]Carl Zimmer, "We Are Viral from the Beginning," National Geographic, June 14, 2014, https://www.nationalgeographic.com/science/phenomena/2012/06/14/we-are-viral-from-the-beginning/.

[21]Jason Lloyd-Price, Galeb Abu-Ali, and Curtis Huttenhower, "The Healthy Human Microbiome," *Genome Medicine* 8, no. 1 (2016): 51.

[22]See Clough, *On Animals: Vol. 1*, 30.

virtue, which are judged to be unique to humans.[23] Those committed to maintaining a strict unitary human/nonhuman boundary wall will no doubt continue Philo's project of seeking to establish an absolute difference between humans and other animals.

The deep connections between human and all other creaturely life revealed in scientific accounts of genetics and animal behavior are consonant with the commonality between creatures affirmed both in the biblical and theological texts discussed in the previous sections, and provide additional support for a Christian ethics that takes nonhuman creatures seriously.

CONCLUSION

By the year 1900, humans had expanded their keeping of domesticated animals to such an extent that the biomass of domesticated animals exceeded that of all wild land mammals by 3.5 times. During the century that followed, the numbers of domesticated animals quadrupled, which contributed to a halving of the numbers of wild animals. As a result, by the year 2000, the biomass of domesticated animals exceeded that of wild land mammals by twenty-four times.[24] During the same period industrial fishing has led to the depletion of marine populations of fish and other species by 90 percent.[25] These statistics demonstrate a dramatic expansion of human influence at very great cost to nonhuman creatures. The decline in wild land animal numbers is largely due to their being deprived of habitat: displaced as forests are cut down and land taken to graze livestock. The rapid growth in livestock numbers also impacts other creatures indirectly: it is a major contributor to the anthropogenic climate change that now threatens a significant proportion of living species on earth, and contributes to local and regional pollution of the environment. These are not the only ways in which humans harm fellow animal creatures: the uses we make of them for clothing and textiles, labor, research experimentation, sport and entertainment, as pets and companions, and our treatment of wild animals also merit attention. On grounds of scale, intensity, and impact, however, the use humans make of other animals for food should be a priority concern. Reducing human consumption of animal products alongside seeking to improve the welfare of farmed animals are two obvious policy responses that should be broadly and rapidly adopted by Christian ethicists and Christian churches at large.[26]

While the status of animal creatures as our nearest creaturely neighbors justifies attending to them first among nonhuman creatures, we should also consider whether the concerns of Christian ethics should extend to other nonhuman creatures. Karl Barth cites with approval Albert Schweitzer's account of reverence for life, in which even the thoughtless plucking of a leaf or pulling of a flower can be seen as a failure of respect.[27] Pope Francis's encyclical *Laudato Si'* laments the abandonment and maltreatment of our

[23]Philo of Alexandria, *Philonis Alexandrini De Animalibus*, Studies in Hellenistic Judaism, trans. and ed. Abraham Terian (Chico: Scholars, 1981).

[24]Vaclav Smil, "Harvesting the Biosphere: The Human Impact," *Population and Development Review* 37, no. 4 (2011): 619.

[25]Heike K. Lotze and Boris Worm, "Historical Baselines for Large Marine Animals," *Trends in Ecology and Evolution* 24, no. 5 (2009): 254–62.

[26]For an extensive survey of how humans use other animals and discussion of how such use should be evaluated ethically by Christians, see Clough, *On Animals: Vol. 2*.

[27]Karl Barth, *Church Dogmatics*, vol. III/4, trans. A. T. MacKay et al., ed. Thomas F. Torrance and Geoffrey W. Bromiley (Edinburgh: T&T Clark, 1961), 349.

sister earth as a wrong in itself, and not merely because of the impacts of such maltreatment on humans and other animals.[28] Extensive work has been done at the interface between theology and environmental ethics, but few authors consider the ways in which Christian ethics might bear on human treatment of particular nonanimal creatures.[29] While most humans could thrive without consuming other animals, they could not survive without consuming plants. This does not mean, however, that we could not do wrong in our treatment of an oak tree, such as by its willful and needless destruction. Perhaps even nonliving creatures need to be within the purview of Christian ethics so that we could understand a failure in our respect for a mountain, for example, if we use our power to destroy it in order to extract minerals. Such questions are ripe for investigation as Christian ethics seeks to engage adequately with human responsibilities in relation to nonhuman creatures.

SUGGESTED READINGS

Bauckham, Richard. *Living with Other Creatures: Green Exegesis and Theology*. Waco: Baylor University Press, 2011.

Boff, Leonardo. *Cry of the Earth, Cry of the Poor. Ecology and Justice*, trans. Philip Berryman. Maryknoll: Orbis, 1997.

Clough, David. *On Animals: Vol. 1. Systematic Theology*. London: T&T Clark/Continuum, 2012.

Clough, David. *On Animals: Vol. 2. Theological Ethics*. London: T&T Clark/Bloomsbury, 2018.

Deane-Drummond, Celia. *A Primer in Ecotheology*. Eugene: Wipf and Stock, 2017.

[28]Pope Francis, *Laudato Si': On Care for Our Common Home* (Vatican City: Libreria Editrice Vaticana, 2015).

[29]For a survey of the field of eco-theology, see Celia Deane-Drummond, *A Primer in Ecotheology* (Eugene: Wipf and Stock, 2017).

CHAPTER FORTY-TWO

Just Eating? Bodies, Gifts, and Daily Bread

DEBRA DEAN MURPHY

There is nothing to eat,
seek it where you will,
but the body of the Lord.
The blessed plants
and the sea, yield it
to the imagination
intact.[1]

We must eat to live. This is an elemental truth of our creaturehood. Whether from privilege or poverty, each of us daily must see to the nourishment of hungry bodies—our own and those in our care. And the nourishment we seek is determined profoundly by our privilege or our poverty, by the social, cultural, and economic conditions that govern the kinds of food we can afford and have been socialized to eat. For the privileged, eating habits often signal social status, excess leisure, a preoccupation with novelty; for those conscious of body-image, food can also be an enemy. For the impoverished, basic nutrition can be an elusive luxury as systems conspire to rob persons and whole communities of the enjoyment of affordable, healthy, delicious food. In these and other ways, all eating is fraught with ethical considerations.

We must eat to live. This is an elemental truth of the church's life together in God. Through bread and wine—blessed, broken, and shared—a body is constituted and provisioned for flourishing. This body exists not for its own sake but that it might bear Christ, be Christ in a fractured, unjust world. This body is fed so that it might see to the nourishing of other bodies, especially the abused, broken, hungry bodies in its midst and beyond its borders. Rightly understood and practiced, the holy yet thoroughly mundane meal that Christians share is always justice in the midst of injustice and partiality, generosity in the midst of accumulation and greed, communal conviviality in the midst of private pain and loneliness. For Christians, therefore, the Eucharist implicates all our eating and informs the food-related moral questions of this and every age.

[1]William Carlos Williams, "The Host," in *The Collected Poems of William Carlos Williams, Vol. 2: 1939–1962* (New York: New Directions Books, 1991), 259. Reprinted by permission of New Directions Publishing Corp. Reproduced in the British Commonwealth by permission of Carcanet Press Limited, https://www.carcanet.co.uk/cgi-bin/indexer?product=9781857545234.

That we must eat to live—as vulnerable, finite creatures and as Christ's body the church—is to acknowledge the gift-character of all our eating. Food is not, first of all, product or commodity; quick, convenient, and cheap are not its prime virtues. Food, first of all, is grace and mystery: sustenance from the earth that, from seed to shoot to bounteous harvest, is both ordinary and miraculous. And whether it is the Lord's Supper on Sunday or dinner at home on a Tuesday night, such gifts are best received—as all good gifts ought to be—with delight and gratitude: "A deep enjoyment of food and its preparation is evidence of the love of the creativity of God that is both wildly expansive and precise."[2]

What follows is an exploration of a theological ethic of eating that holds together contingency and providence—human finiteness and God's infinite love for all that God has made—and that acknowledges the gift-character of all our eating. Within this framework, we will reflect on three things: First, how the elemental act of eating reveals our shared vulnerability with all creatures, human and other-than-human, who must eat to live. Second, the truth that our complicity in an industrial food economy means we are never "just eating." And, finally, how the Eucharist is not only a meal but also a story, and one that reveals the ways we regularly betray Christ's body even as it makes possible "a material world for all ... without borders, without frontiers. A common table, with broad linens, a table for everybody."[3]

EATING AND VULNERABILITY

To eat—and thus to exist—is to be always in a posture of dependence. Self-sufficiency when it comes to food is a fiction, even for the most accomplished gardener or well-stocked homesteader. The gifts of sun, soil, seed, and rain must conspire in an array of fortuitous configurations for edible goodness to emerge from the earth. Those who do not grow any of their own food—the majority of people in the industrialized world—are dependent in additional ways, relying upon a complex economic system of food production and distribution rarely ordered to the well-being of all creation. In short, we are all dependent eaters.

Yet to acknowledge dependence, for the affluent especially, is a difficult thing. Americans are schooled routinely in the doctrine of independence—our forebears declared it, after all, and waged war for it. The stories of frontier expansionists in the seventeenth and eighteenth centuries and "self-made men" in the twentieth and twenty-first both reflect and fund mythologies that undergird the lies we tell ourselves and our children: "you must make your own way in the world"; "the only person you can depend on is yourself." Proud individualism has long colonized our collective imagination; dependence of any kind, even if we sympathize with those in situations of chronic need, is thought to be a kind of weakness, if not a moral failing.

Yet to be is to be-in-relationship. We are social creatures "all the way down," dependent from the beginning of life until its end on others who make our thriving possible. Scripture, too, from beginning to end, is a story of the formation of a *people*—a covenant community that flourishes when each of its members flourishes, and that suffers

[2]Deborah Madison's Introduction to *The Supper of the Lamb*, by Robert Farrar Capon (New York: Random House, 2002), xiii.

[3]Rutilio Grande, SJ, quoted in Jon Sobrino, *Jesus in Latin America*, trans. Robert R. Barr (Maryknoll: Orbis, 1987), 96–7.

when a member suffers. St. Paul expresses this conviction when he speaks of the church as a body with many constitutive members. The creation accounts in Genesis are stories of dependence and interdependence, summoning us to see our full humanity not in terms of self-actualization (which may be one way to name the temptation yielded to in the Garden) but as a gift we receive when we live in the communion we were made for—with God, one another, and all of creation.

Vulnerability is likewise both condition and gift. The state of uncertainty and risk that comes with our finitude is also that by which we know ourselves to be most fully alive. There is freedom in acknowledging this, especially when we recognize the view of the human person that undergirds it: we are made for belonging. We may resist this truth materially, practically, even as we consent to it intellectually, so seductive are the competitive and contractual models of human identity and interaction. But the being-in-relationship that characterizes our identity as persons created in the image of a triune God is at heart a belonging-to-one-another. This makes concern for the most vulnerable among us a matter of our own well-being as much as theirs.

What does this have to do with food? Our very need for food is the first kind of vulnerability: the reality noted earlier that we must eat to live. But the giftedness of vulnerability is more complex. It can be presumptuous for the privileged to speak of vulnerability as a gift when the daily lives of so many are an exhausting, demoralizing struggle for food and shelter, dignity and acceptance, health of mind, body, and spirit. Pronouncements of a shared vulnerability can easily exempt the privileged from their own complicity in systems that create and sustain these unwelcome burdens. As we will note in the next section, there are painful, dehumanizing vulnerabilities we should commit ourselves to ending.

If we do indeed belong to each other, and if the food that sustains us day by day is a gift, then perhaps the food-secure can discover or recover vulnerability as another of God's good gifts through which self-sufficiency and entitlement are exposed as the falsehoods they are. For when we break bread with neighbors, especially with those whose food struggles are acute (eating *with* them, not just preparing meals *for* them), we meet at the most basic level of our humanness. And if we are willing to rest in, rather than resist or deny, that shared vulnerability, we may discover that food can make us friends, and that friendship is the preeminent way of living into our belongingness.

The gift-character of food and the vulnerability we share with all finite creatures also has implications for the ethics of eating animals. It is notable, yet not often noted, that when the ancient Israelites composed the origin stories that would be central to their identity as God's covenant people, their vision of the flourishing of all creation precluded the consumption of animals by humans and other animals (Gen. 1:29-30). As these stories were being written, redacted, and authorized as normative texts more than a thousand years into Israel's history as a people, the communities of both the north and south were meat-eaters and the sacrifice of animals in religious rituals was a long-standing practice. Some of the most well-known stories of both the Old and New Testaments involve eating meat and sacrificing animals: the thicket-caught ram offered by Abraham; the venison stew Jacob prepared for his father when stealing his brother's blessing; lamb's blood on door lintels at Passover; the fatted calf of the prodigal's feast; the feeding of the five thousand; and Jesus eating fish on the beach with his fishermen disciples.

But the full flourishing of God's good creation, as envisioned in the opening lines of Genesis, assumes that animals were not originally meant for food or sacrifice. One can imagine the priestly writer accommodating Israel's well-established omnivorous eating habits into the text, justifying, even if obliquely, the consumption of animal flesh for human thriving and the sacrifice of animals as a cultic necessity. That the writer(s) did not do this is suggestive of how they imagined (and perhaps aspired to) fullness of life in the *shalom* of God. As a liturgical poem, Genesis 1 gives form to a certain way of seeing the world, and accurate perception, notes Ellen Davis, "provides an entrée to active participation in the order of creation."[4] In other words, the literary structure of the text itself, with its order and harmonies (what Wendell Berry calls its "formal integrity"[5]), affords a way of participating in *this* world. Words create a world (God *speaks* creation into being, after all) and poetic form alludes to other "harmonies by which we live."[6] Genesis 1 issues an invitation to bear witness to the original vision of a harmonious relationship between humans and (other) animals.

Along these lines Alicia Ostriker notes that in Hebrew anthropology, both humans and animals possess "soul" (*nafshi*). At the beginning of the familiar, beloved Psalm 23, the poet declares: "The Lord is my shepherd, I shall not want." Ostriker observes that "the psalmist does not declare 'I am a sheep' or 'I am like a sheep,' but speaks directly as from the animal soul, the *nefesh*, itself."[7] Likewise, Ps. 42:1 ("As a deer longs for flowing streams, so my soul longs for you, O God") communicates this intimate creaturely connection. "What a melancholy yet sweet image of the desire for God," says Ostriker, "the desire of a thirsting animal."[8] The same breath (*ruach* in Hebrew, *pneuma* in Greek) described in the Creation poem of Genesis 1 as giving life to human beings also ensouls "living things both small and great" (Ps. 104:25).

Such sensibilities about all animal beings ought at least to problematize the consumption of meat for contemporary Christians. Although there is no biblical mandate for vegetarianism, there is the original peace and plenitude at the book's beginning by which all creatures live free from the threat of harm from other creatures. While evil soon enough disrupts this primordial vision, the Christian tradition has refused to ontologize the tragedy of human sin. "The Fall" names not inevitability but the contingency through which rivalry and violence operate as perversions of God's good creation. The fact that Israel's prophetic literature also imagined an eschatological peaceableness within the animal kingdom, one where wolf and lamb lie down together and lions are herbivores (Isa. 11:6-7), suggests that refusing to eat animals in our own day may be one modest way of bearing witness to a different kind of relationship among God's creatures, one that resists the claim that the flourishing of some necessitates the killing of others.

EATING AND BROKENNESS

In the 1930s the green revolution began with the promise to feed a hungry world. Championed by agronomist Norman Borlaug, who was awarded the Nobel Peace Prize in 1970 for his work, the movement advocated the use of chemical fertilizers, insecticides, fungicides, and herbicides for the purpose of dramatically increasing crop yields. It sought the speedy commercialization of agriculture, promoted massive systems of global

[4]Ellen Davis, *Scripture, Culture, and Agriculture: An Agrarian Reading of the Bible* (New York: Cambridge University Press, 2008), 43.
[5]Wendell Berry, *What Are People For? Collected Essays*, 2nd ed. (Berkeley: Counterpoint, 2010), 89.
[6]Ibid.
[7]Alicia Ostriker, *For the Love of God: The Bible as an Open Book* (New Brunswick: Rutgers University Press, 2009), 56.
[8]Ibid., 58.

transport, and in later decades advanced biotechnological innovations like genetically modified foods. The green revolution did help to reduce starvation in many impoverished places—a feat that should not be gainsaid. But it was also costly in ways we are now reckoning with—both in terms of environmental degradation (soil infertility, aquifer depletion, etc.) and the loss of whole realms of food once eaten but eradicated by Borlaug's enterprise. The mass production of genetically engineered golden rice, for example, which was designed to treat blindness caused by vitamin A deficiency, "ignored the fact that one of the reasons for the decline in Vitamin A consumption was that nutritious vegetables and weeds traditionally grown or harvested with rice were no longer available."[9]

As a direct result of the green revolution, the food economies of most modern industrialized countries today are fueled by complex operations dedicated to the large-scale production and consumption of beef, chicken, pork, and, increasingly, factory-farmed fish. Books like *The Omnivore's Dilemma* and *Eating Animals* and documentary films like *Super Size Me*, *Food, Inc.*, and *Fresh* have chronicled in disturbing detail how modern industrial eaters have been habituated to a system in which animal protein is deceptively inexpensive and fruits and vegetables unnecessarily cost-prohibitive.[10] For decades this distorted economic model, which depends on the systematic mistreatment of animals, land, and workers, was largely unquestioned; in some sectors it still is.

A cheap, fast-food burger, for instance—the go-to meal for cash-strapped college students and overscheduled young families—comes at great cost. The price is artificially low because of government assistance all along the chain of production: from subsidies for the corn fed to the cattle (a grain that wreaks havoc on a ruminant's digestive system) to tax breaks for the corporate monoliths that have long dominated the market. On a "factory farm" (an oxymoron both funny and tragic), the cattle rarely see sunlight. They spend their short lives deeply stressed and are susceptible to diseases that threaten both animal and human health. Workers in such facilities are forced to do crippling, repetitive tasks for low wages often for ten or twelve hours a day. Many are undocumented and do not feel free or safe enough to complain about dangerous conditions. In large-scale poultry operations where many of these exploited laborers live and work, the chickens and turkeys they process are engineered for the big-breasted meatiness consumers have been conditioned to expect for their family feasts. The birds are overfed corn (not good for their stomachs either) to dramatically and painfully accelerate the growing process and are kept in cramped, dark "houses" where, under the stress of their own grotesque body weight, their small legs often collapse and they spend their brief lives squirming in their own excrement.[11]

These and other truths of the industrial food system are well-known and have helped to galvanize a revolution aimed at reimagining our relationship with food and encouraging patterns of eating that are more holistic and just. Localization, in response to the corruptions of a globalized food economy, has become a welcome watchword.

[9]Sharon Astyk, "How Much Did the Green Revolution Matter? Or Can We Feed the World without Industrial Agriculture?," *Resilience*, January 29, 2007, https://www.resilience.org/stories/2007-01-29/how-much-did-green-revolution-matter-or-can-we-feed-world-without-industrial-agri/.

[10]Michael Pollan, *The Omnivore's Dilemma: A Natural History of Four Meals* (New York: Penguin Books, 2007); Jonathan Safran Foer, *Eating Animals* (New York: Little, Brown, 2009); Morgan Spurlock, *Super Size Me*, Samuel Goldwyn Films, 2010; Robert Kenner, *Food, Inc.*, Magnolia Pictures, 2009; Ana Sofia Joanes, *Fresh*, Cinedigm, 2009.

[11]These conditions have been widely documented in texts and films already cited: Foer, Joanes, Kenner, and Pollan.

Families and whole communities have initiated creative, sustainable ways to eat as responsibly as possible while also supporting farmers, farmworkers, and practices dedicated to the well-being of land and livestock. The locavore and slow food movements, community-supported agriculture, farmers' markets, neighborhood food cooperatives, and community gardens are some of the many ways that eating well—with integrity, joy, and shared purpose—has been recovered or discovered for the first time. These practices also constitute movements of moral and economic resistance to industrial agriculture and the executives and lobbyists who profit from it.

But ethical concerns remain. Three interconnected ones can be named only briefly.

First, much of the food revolution has left behind vulnerable populations. Eating locally and sustainably has largely been ethics for elites—those who can afford the artificially high cost of organic meats, fruits, and vegetables and who have the leisure to prepare healthy meals for themselves and their families. Children are always among the vulnerable and while many are part of families and communities committed to eating well and growing good food (family farms and edible schoolyards, for instance), millions more are not. Increasingly, vulnerable children learn poor eating habits early, suffer from food insecurity during their formative years and often beyond, and develop risk factors and chronic health conditions previously unknown in their demographic group. Type 2 diabetes and high blood pressure, linked to the consumption of fast food and sugary drinks, have risen at alarming rates in children of rich and poor countries alike.

Second is the geography of nutrition: how it is that where one lives and eats determines how well one lives and eats. In the developed world, the term "food desert" describes an area with low availability or high cost of healthy foods. Conventional wisdom has been that supplying these regions with affordable, healthy fare (luring grocery stores into neighborhoods with tax incentives; initiating programs that get fresh fruits and vegetables to children) will substantially improve the chronic health conditions and raise life expectancies of the residents of these communities. But evidence derived from several scientific studies, including a monumental effort undertaken by Stanford University researchers, does not support the claim that eliminating food deserts has material effects on the diets of the poor. The data show in fact that people who live in these areas do buy most of their food from well-stocked grocery stores, though they travel long distances to do so. The differences between affluent and impoverished communities in terms of access to supermarkets offering healthy options do not appear to explain why the wealthy eat more healthfully than the poor.[12]

What does, then? Most research on health disparities suggests that people who live in poverty are sicker and die earlier than their counterparts in more affluent areas because of the stress of poverty itself. While they do of course have to choose what and how much to eat, those living in poverty are also preoccupied with other decisions: electric bill or water bill this month? Rent or prescription medication? The science of stress on the human body over time indicates what seems intuitively, anecdotally obvious: physiological and neurological responses to constant stress and uncertainty (floods of adrenaline or cortisol, for instance) exert adverse effects that can lead to lasting damage in the body and the brain. One major adverse effect, the body's inability to regulate inflammation, underlies

[12]Hunt Allcott, Rebecca Diamond, and Jean-Pierre Dubé, "The Geography of Poverty and Nutrition: Food Deserts and Food Choices across the United States," National Bureau of Economic Research, Working Paper No. 3631, January 2, 2018, https://www.gsb.stanford.edu/faculty-research/working-papers/geography-poverty-nutrition-food-deserts-food-choices-across-united.

all illnesses, the most common of which among the poor are depression, heart disease, hypertension, and diabetes.[13]

Still, a theology of eating is driven less by statistical data on poverty and more by scripture's summons to "seek the peace of the city" (Jer. 29:7). Responses to this call look different in different food-insecure regions. It might mean risking vulnerability by moving into a poor urban neighborhood to live with and learn from those who are poorly fed—to "build houses and settle down, plant gardens and eat what they produce" (Jer. 29:6).

A third ethical challenge of our broken food system is how to frame the complex issue of obesity. The epidemiology is sobering: in just a generation, countries around the world, rich and poor, have experienced skyrocketing rates of obesity in all age groups. The rising prevalence of childhood obesity alone portends staggering burdens on individuals, families, and health care systems in the decades to come.[14] The causes are many and multilayered. The increased consumption of processed foods, for one, has been driven in large part by mechanized transport systems and clever marketing strategies. Genetics, socialization, and socioeconomics are other factors in the epidemiology of obesity. A theologically informed ethic of eating must consider these and other causes of obesity in populations, especially vulnerable ones, since the ready availability and seductive marketing and advertising of all the wrong foods demand systemic redress.

But while obesity is a public health problem it is also a neighbor-love problem (as are all the problems briefly outlined here). It has to do with how we are taught, overtly and subtly, over the course of our lives to regard human bodies, including our own: whose bodies are beautiful, worthy of respect and love, worthy of safety and justice, and whose are not. Socialization about bodies is of a piece with bias, discrimination, and forms of oppression based on markers like gender, race, social class, sexual orientation, ethnic origins, disability, and size. In cultures that commodify and objectify bodies, there is astounding pressure to conform to certain standards of bodily health that are almost never healthy, rooted as they are in impossible, unsustainable ideals of form and fitness. In such contexts and perhaps especially within the industrial food economy and its built-in exploitations and injustices, obese persons are neighbors to love (and sometimes the self we need to love)—not objects of pity or scorn, not projects or problems to fix. That our love for these neighbors is complicated is also true since knowing how to love well is not always easy. And because "the grace that is the health of creatures can only be held in common,"[15] their flourishing is bound up with our own.

EATING AND STORIES

Eating and storytelling are inseparable. The meals we most remember are less about the food we ate than the company we kept. They are about stories shared by friends or family that made us laugh or weep or both, that made us feel the joy of being alive. Good stories savored around a table are as nourishing as the food on the plate and often leave us hungering for more. Meals are also central to the stories of our lives. In every

[13]Achim Peters, Bruce S. McEwen, and Karl Friston, "Uncertainty and Stress: Why It Causes Diseases and How It Is Mastered by the Brain," *Progress in Neurobiology* 156 (2017): 164–88.
[14]Adela Hruby and Frank B. Hu, "The Epidemiology of Obesity: A Big Picture," *Pharmacoeconomics* 33, no. 7 (2015): 673–89.
[15]Berry, *What Are People For?*, 9.

known culture, significant events within the narrative arc of a human life or community of people are accompanied by ritual eating.

The story of scripture, too, cannot be told apart from food, from the garden of abundance in Genesis to the marriage supper of the Lamb in Revelation. The Torah's dietary laws reveal a God who desires to be present in the most domestic, quotidian ways. For the hungry Israelites, manna in the wilderness kept their bodies and their hopes alive. Jesus was born in the "house of Bread" (*Beth-lehem*), slept in a feeding trough, and, in his first public sign, saved a wedding feast from disaster by keeping the good wine flowing. Feeding hungry bodies and eating with all the wrong people were at the heart of his way in the world. His last meal before being executed was a reworking of Israel's signature feast in which he offered himself as food for his heartbroken companions.

In the Eucharist, supper and story merge. Through the liturgy of word and sacrament we are invited to narrate our lives according to the story of God's forgiving, restoring, reconciling ways with us. We perform the story of scripture's original vision of peace and plenitude, rehearsing its plot and subplots: how sin disrupts this vision but never gets the last word; how in Jesus God's infinite mercy and goodness became incarnate and we are offered, even now, hope and newness of life. In the action of grace at the table (*eu-charis*) we enact a story of divine superabundance, the cosmic drama of our belovedness, our belongingness, and the truth that the whole of creation lives from the inexhaustible goodness of God. This story joins us to all of creation, human and nonhuman, in kinship and mutual care.

The bread and wine we take into our bodies in the Eucharist, fruit of the earth and work of human hands, is also a reminder of other stories that would claim us: stories of scarcity and fear, of bodies broken by despair, of the misuse of the gifts of creation:

> Think of the domination, exploitation, and pollution of man and nature that goes with bread, all the bitterness of competition and class struggle ... all the wicked oddity of a world distribution [system] that brings plenty to some and malnutrition to others ... And wine too ... the source of some of the most tragic forms of human degradation: drunkenness, broken homes, sensuality, debt. What Christ bodies himself into is bread and wine like this, and he manages to make sense of it, to humanize it. Nothing human is alien to him. If we bring bread and wine to the Lord's Table, we are implicating ourselves in bringing to God, for him to make sense of, all which is broken and unlovely.[16]

When we fail to live the Eucharist as a story of resistance to all forms of oppression that would rob all creatures of their dignity, when we "eat and drink without discerning the body of Christ," as St. Paul says, the meal becomes a form of judgment (1 Cor. 11:29). We scandalize the church's witness in the world when our lives individually and corporately do not reflect the Eucharist's "circle of never-ending provision."[17] If we do not see to the nourishment of the weakest members of the body (1 Cor. 12:22-23), we betray Christ when we meet him in the meal, for those who suffer are identified with his suffering. When we resist the truth of our own vulnerability and our shared humanity with those with whom we eat—even as we partake of one loaf and a common cup—we discredit the witness of unity that ought to flow from the table. We come to the Eucharist

---

[16]Geoffrey Preston, "God's Way to Be Man," in Timothy Radcliffe's *Why Go to Church? The Drama of the Eucharist* (London: Continuum, 2008), 103.

[17]Samuel Wells, *God's Companions: Reimagining Christian Ethics* (Oxford: Blackwell, 2006), 212.

week after week with our palms open to receive the bread of life, yet often live by stories of hoarding, stinginess, and close-fisted self-sufficiency, failing to trust God's provisioning in all things. When food itself is narrated as commodity rather than gift and severed from the practices of a shared table, it becomes a problem to be solved—calories, scarcity, distribution, obesity. This is the poverty of our moral imagination and a repudiation of the divine gratuity at the heart of the sacrament.

It turns out the Eucharist is a story we can swallow, a love story, in fact, and one that orients us to the truth that "all the food of this world is divine love made edible."[18] Christ's own body consumed at the table is sustenance for the pressing, joyful work of being Christ's body for underfed and overfed and poorly fed neighbors everywhere.

CONCLUSION

We are never just eating. This awareness is not a burden but a gift, for it frees us from illusions of independence and self-preservation. Our complicity in the industrial food economy makes all our food choices matters of deep scrutiny and much repentance. Hence we do not just eat when we come to the communion table. The sacrament we share with the transglobal body of Christ, a simple meal that makes us this very thing, bears revolutionary witness to the health and well-being—the *shalom* of God—that is Creation's true end.

SUGGESTED READINGS

Adler, Tamar. *An Everlasting Meal: Cooking with Economy and Grace*. New York: Scribner, 2011.

McCormick, Patrick T. *A Banqueter's Guide to the All-Night Soup Kitchen of the Kingdom of God*. Collegeville, MN: Liturgical, 2004.

Miles, Sara. *Take This Bread: A Radical Conversion*. New York: Ballentine Books, 2007.

Wirzba, Norman. *Food and Faith: A Theology of Eating*. Cambridge: Cambridge University Press, 2011.

[18]Anthony Bloom, *Beginning to Pray* (New York: Paulist, 1970), 41.

Issues, Applications, and Twenty-First-Century Agenda for Christian Ethics

Section G: Sex, Gender, Marriage, and Family

CHAPTER FORTY-THREE

Sex and Sexuality

KAREN PETERSON-IYER

Sexual ethics is an unmistakably challenging field of Christian thought in a twenty-first-century context. The social and moral norms that were thought to find universal purchase, even as recently as a century ago, most decidedly do not do so today. It is increasingly apparent that the expression of human sexuality takes breathtakingly diverse forms, making it difficult to generalize meaningfully about what counts as genuine sexual flourishing. Christian ethics has, of course, sought to do so—and too often has arrived at prescriptive norms that function to block rather than foster human well-being.

An examination of the history of Christian sexual ethics reveals remarkable shifts over time. Hierarchies once understood to be written into the character of intimate relationships are increasingly challenged as unjust and oppressive. Procreation is decreasingly employed as the primary justification for sex. And a profound distrust of sexual pleasure that has sometimes characterized the tradition has given way to an active affirmation of pleasure as reflective of divine goodness. Underneath these shifts, human nature, once assumed to be largely static and ahistorical, is now recognized as deeply interrelated with history and context.

The present chapter will track some of these shifts as they are reflected in the thought of various Christian theologians through the course of history. Especially noteworthy is the moral source of *experience* as it intersects with ethical conclusions; that is, experience is a useful lens with which to consider the changes in Christian understandings of sex and sexuality. On the whole, a history of Christian sexual ethics reveals a gradual expansion of the category of experience beyond that of elite males to encompass all human persons. This expansion has fostered a progressively egalitarian and justice-oriented ethic, as well as one focused less on procreation and more on the nuances of gender, race, class, and sexual diversity within the human community.

THE FOUR SOURCES AND CHRISTIAN (SEXUAL) ETHICS

Each of the four sources of Christian ethics has at times been clarifying and instructive—and at other times problematic and limiting. Individually, each has the capacity to contribute valuable insight about what it means for human persons to flourish, sexually speaking. Taken together, they also correct and refine each other, such that none alone should be taken as decisive for the construction of sexual norms.

Historically speaking, an emphasis on the use of *scripture* as a normative source has been especially characteristic of Protestant theological ethics, though over the past half-century, Roman Catholicism, too, has increasingly affirmed the Bible as a central source of Christian wisdom. The Bible is not a self-interpreting document, however, and perhaps nowhere is this truer than in the realm of sex. Sex plays very little explicit role in the Hebrew Scriptures, with the notable exceptions of the creation (and union) of Adam and Eve in the book of Genesis, and the erotic poetry and celebration of desire found in the Song of Songs. In the New Testament, love of God and neighbor arguably provides an overarching normative framework for human sexual life. Yet patriarchal context and a historical emphasis on fertility and procreation together function to impede easy or direct interpretation of biblical guidance.[1] Moreover, a dual emphasis on *purity* and *property* as organizing principles problematically shapes the New Testament witness in matters of sex.[2] Still these ancient texts do contain hints of more democratic sexual concepts—such as the parity of men and women in the first Genesis creation story; or marriage understood as a partnership of equals rather than merely a patriarchal social arrangement, in Paul's first letter to the Corinthians. Thus, the Bible, which has arguably been used too often in the service of sexual inequality and even oppression, also contains the seeds of a more liberating ethic.

Revelation of divine truth is of course much larger than scripture alone; a second source for Christian ethics is constituted by insights stemming from the Christian *tradition*. Tradition must be understood both as what has been taught over the course of Christian history and as a work in progress. That is, in any moral realm—and most certainly in the realm of sex and sexuality—we bring the wisdom of tradition to new questions, plumbing its guidance for deep insight but also recognizing that it must be revised as representative of a lived faith through time. This source has played a notably weighty role in Catholic sexual ethics, centered on magisterial teaching as a conduit of moral wisdom. Theologians Todd Salzman and Michael Lawler describe a progression over time from an essentially classicist worldview—including a somewhat fixed understanding of nature—to a more historically conscious and fluid worldview, one that affirms a subjective and flexible understanding of sexual nature and maintains a greater focus on the empirical and relational human person, *qua* sexual actor.[3] Many modern Protestant theologies, too, have moved toward this more historical and malleable understanding of the human person.

The third source of Christian ethics, *reason*, is broadly interpreted as rational reflection that seeks to integrate the other sources. Some theologians, however, include in the category of reason the insights gained into the nature of reality from contemporary secular disciplines—philosophy, natural sciences, psychology, or literature, for example.[4] However one defines it, reason cannot be considered a "pure" source; while a genuine basis of insight, reason also has genuine limitations. Perspective and social location impact human reason, often causing the one who employs it to value certain modes of analysis or knowledge (logical discernment, for example) over others (such as emotional or intuitive powers). We must, therefore, employ reason cautiously and knowingly, recognizing that it is easily manipulated.

Finally, the category of *experience* until recently perhaps qualified as the most under-recognized of the four sources in Christian sexual ethics. The tendency to universalize

---

[1]Margaret A. Farley, *Just Love: A Framework for Christian Sexual Ethics* (New York: Continuum, 2006), 184.
[2]L. William Countryman, *Dirt, Greed, and Sex: Sexual Ethics in the New Testament and Their Implications for Today* (Philadelphia: Fortress, 1988).
[3]Todd A. Salzman and Michael G. Lawler, *The Sexual Person: Toward a Renewed Catholic Anthropology* (Washington, DC: Georgetown University Press, 2008), esp. prologue and chap. 1.
[4]Others, including many authors in the present volume, include such insights under the category of experience.

one particular type of sexual experience—often white, male, heterosexual, cisgender experience—has arguably characterized the bulk of Christian sexual ethics. Yet the category of experience (understood here as personal and communal lived reality, past and present) has broadened over the past half-century explicitly to include the experience of socially marginalized groups. Accordingly, Christian understandings of sex and sexuality have also diversified to include the sexual experience not only of women (of all races and ethnicities) but also of persons who identify as lesbian, gay, bisexual, transgender, queer, and intersex. So understood, experience functions both to inform and critique how Christian thought characterizes human sexual flourishing. Like the other sources, experience should not be considered to be self-interpreting; rather, diverse experiences must be construed with a measure of epistemic humility, even as they are placed into conversation with one another.

These four sources of course show up differently throughout the history of the Christian tradition, and much could be debated about their relative importance. Yet a brief examination of that history reveals not only the expanding role of experience in the shaping of Christian sexual understanding but also the way in which that expansion opens into the questions characteristic of twenty-first-century Christianity.

THE EARLY TRADITION AND THE SOFTENING OF THE PROCREATIVE ETHIC

Most Christian theological ethicists would identify Augustine of Hippo as a pivotal figure in the development of sexual ethics. Before Augustine, Christian sexual ethics could not rightly be called systematic. With thought borrowed in part from the Stoics and characterized by a deep distrust of sexual passion, Augustine articulated the contours of an essentially procreative ethic based in creation, Fall, and redemption—one that carried on for centuries. Thomas Aquinas later refined this procreative ethic under his careful delineation of natural law reasoning. Indeed, it was arguably not until the Magisterial Reformation that the procreative ethic was fundamentally challenged in the work of Martin Luther. Yet even so, the emphasis on procreation as a defining norm of what makes for good, right, and ethical sex persists in some quarters, right up to the present.

Augustine himself was neither anti-body nor anti-marriage, but his negative legacy vis-à-vis these realities is noteworthy. He viewed the body and its desires not as fundamentally corrupt but rather as limiting. The prominent role that original sin played in his thinking, along with the framing of his theology over and against competing worldviews, meant that Augustine possessed a rather complicated approach to sexuality. He argued that sex and marriage were created by God and thus fundamentally good—even if heavily impacted by sin. Sexual passion was not intrinsically evil, but rather the ready *bearer* of evil.[5] In clear contradistinction to Pelagian optimism about the perfectibility of human nature, Augustine held that original sin left human sexual appetites in total disorder, as evidenced by sexual concupiscence. Passion and desire should rightly be subordinated to

[5]Augustine, *On Marriage and Concupiscence*, trans. Peter Holmes and Robert Ernest Wallis, rev. Benjamin B. Warfield, in *Nicene and Post-Nicene Fathers, First Series*, vol. 5, ed. Philip Schaff (Buffalo: Christian Literature, 1887), Book I, chaps. 3, 5, 32, and Book II, chap. 14. See also Augustine, *Of the Good of Marriage*, trans. C. L. Cornish from *Nicene and Post-Nicene Fathers, First Series*, vol. 3, ed. Philip Schaff. (Buffalo: Christian Literature, 1887).

the influence of reason and will, which, in his view, characterized original human nature before the disordering impact of sin.[6] In this way, sex should be rationally integrated into a larger love of God and neighbor. Augustine thus understood sex as fundamentally justified only by rational purposing—that is, for the reason of procreation, within the context of heterosexual marriage. Marriage, like sex, is here fundamentally good; but its goodness is expressed by way of fidelity, indissolubility, and, above all, procreation. Indeed, without procreative intent, Augustine deemed the sexual act to have at least "venial fault," even within a faithful marriage.[7]

While sex and sexuality do not figure as conspicuously into the work of Thomas Aquinas, his prominence in the tradition merits at least cursory examination of the theme. Thomas, following Aristotle, affirmed a tight connection between the human body and spirit; yet he tended to focus more squarely on the former when it came to matters of sex. Like Augustine, Thomas understood sexual passion and desire not as intrinsically evil but rather as needing to be brought into line with human reason by way of the justifying purpose of procreation. He organized his views on human sexuality using principles of reason reflecting upon the "natural order" of things—a natural law perspective with a clear emphasis that biological and physical nature indicate the ultimate purposes of sex.[8] According to this view, procreation remains the primary purpose of sexual expression and thus the primary end of marriage. The goal of fostering love between spouses is present within Thomas's thought, particularly as he understands marriage as a form of friendship that confers grace upon the spouses.[9] Yet the procreative norm holds sway, driven by a strong emphasis on the role of human reason to discern the physical/biological ends of sex. Indeed, it is this physicalist character of Thomas's natural law reasoning about sex that ultimately paved the way for controversy centuries later about whether the tradition needs to be re-centered less on the biological and more on the psychological and affective dimensions of sex.

A turn toward those affective dimensions is traceable, at least in part, to the sea changes associated with the Reformation, and especially the thinking of Martin Luther. Luther, too, saw sexuality as essentially part of God's good creation but damaged by original sin. And like Augustine and Aquinas before him, Luther argued that only in marriage can human sexuality be expressed nondestructively; marriage represented a "necessary remedy for disordered [sexual] desire."[10] Yet later in his writings, Luther also described marriage as a school for character and the context of our forgiveness by God, thereby introducing a distinctly more positive purpose. It is not that Luther discarded the

[6]See, e.g., St. Augustine, *The City of God*, trans. Henry Bettenson (New York: Penguin, 1984), XIV.16–24. See also Augustine, *On Marriage and Concupiscence*.

[7]Augustine, *Of the Good of Marriage*, 6, 32. See also Salzman and Lawler, *The Sexual Person*, 30–1. For a helpful understanding of how Augustine's views about human sexuality intersect with gendered hierarchical relations, see Rosemary Radford Ruether, "Misogynism and Virginal Feminism in the Fathers of the Church," in *Religion and Sexism*, ed. R. Ruether (Eugene: Wipf and Stock, 1998), 150–83; Kari Elisabeth Borreson, *Subordination and Equivalence: The Nature and Role of Women in Augustine and Thomas Aquinas* (Kampen: Kok Pharos, 1996). For an alternative feminist understanding of Augustine's views, see Maryanne Cline Horowitz, "The Image of God in Man—Is Woman Included?," *Harvard Theological Review* 72, nos. 3–4 (1979): 201–4.

[8]Vincent J. Genovesi, *In Pursuit of Love: Catholic Morality and Human Sexuality* (Collegeville: Liturgical, 1996), 118–21.

[9]Thomas Aquinas, *Summa Contra Gentiles*, trans. Joseph Rickaby, SJ (The Catholic Primer, 2005), III.123, III.124, and IV.78, https://d2y1pz2y630308.cloudfront.net/15471/documents/2016/10/St.%20Thomas%20Aquinas-The%20Summa%20Contra%20Gentiles.pdf; Aquinas, *Summa Theologiae*, trans. Fathers of the English Dominican Province (New York: Benziger Brothers, 1948), II–II.26.11. See also Farley, *Just Love*, 44.

[10]Farley, *Just Love*, 45.

procreative norm for sex; in fact, he referred to offspring within marriage as the world's "noblest and most precious work."[11] But he accentuated several additional aims: the mutual affection/cherishing of the spouses, a remedy for fornication, and the stability that marriage confers upon society more generally. Turning away from the prevailing monastic ideal, Luther described the bond between spouses with great affection and urged husband and wife to "live together in love and harmony, that one may cherish the other from the heart and with entire fidelity."[12] He embraced a hierarchical family structure and opposed premarital and extramarital sex, as well as same-sex sexual relations.[13] But he also allowed for divorce, under certain limited circumstances, representing a departure from his predecessors.

Taken as a whole and understood within the context of marriage, Luther's thought represents a de-emphasis on the procreative norm as a justification for sexual activity, relative to both Augustine and Aquinas. His descriptions of spousal relations undoubtedly reflect the patriarchal and heteronormative expectations of the time. Yet female subservience in Luther's thought was based more squarely in social practice (i.e., the patriarchal family structure) than in religious understanding. That is, socially speaking, women were to be subservient to men. But theologically speaking, Luther affirmed the divinely created goodness of both female and male images and bodies; moreover, in the kingdom of Christ, all people "are one and equal before God."[14]

The relaxing of the procreative norm—still pursued, however, through a reasoned interpretation of human nature—took center stage centuries later, during the time of the Second Vatican Council (1962–5). Certainly even before then, conjugal love and intimacy within marriage surfaced not just in Protestant sources but also in Roman Catholic teachings, even when these teachings prioritized a procreative ethic—for example, in Pius XI's *Casti connubii*.[15] Controversy ensued in the Catholic tradition about the relative weight of the procreative and the unitive ends of marriage, leading ultimately to a nonhierarchical elevation of both in *Gaudium et spes* in 1965.[16] Yet a few years later, Paul VI's 1968 encyclical letter *Humanae vitae* called for openness to procreation in *each and every* act of marital sexual intercourse, rather than within the marriage more broadly—effectively (though not explicitly) muffling incipient stress on interpersonal union as the hallmark of marital sexuality.[17] Although the resulting prohibition on artificial contraception far from defines contemporary Catholic sexual ethics—and indeed is itself rejected by vast numbers of Catholics today—it does function as a very real backdrop to sexual ethical thought in present-day Catholic tradition.

By comparison, twentieth-century Protestantism has diverged from a strictly procreative ethic and has accepted artificial contraception for many decades. Instead, the Protestant tradition in more recent times has wrestled with how to affirm and explicate a genuinely positive role for sexual desire, both within and outside of marriage. This is particularly

[11]Martin Luther, "The Estate of Marriage (1522)," in *Luther's Works*, vol. 45, ed. Walther I. Brandt (Philadelphia: Muhlenberg, 1962), 46.

[12]Martin Luther, *The Large Catechism*, trans. F. Bente and W. H. T. Dau (St. Louis: Concordia, 1921), http://www.iclnet.org/pub/resources/text/wittenberg/luther/catechism/web/cat-07.html. Luther himself had a long and apparently happy marriage to Katharina von Bora, and perhaps this influenced his thinking in these regards.

[13]Farley, *Just Love*, 47.

[14]Luther, "The Estate of Marriage," 17–8; Paul Althaus, *The Ethics of Martin Luther* (Philadelphia: Fortress, 1972), 57.

[15]Pope Pius XI, *Casti connubii* (Vatican City: Libreria Editrice Vaticana, 1930), § 53–6, 59.

[16]Second Vatican Council, *Gaudium et spes* (Vatican City: Libreria Editrice Vaticana, 1965), § 48–50.

[17]Pope Paul VI, *Humanae vitae* (Vatican City: Libreria Editrice Vaticana, 1968), see esp. § 11.

challenging in the context of patriarchal and heteronormative social practices that (some argue) effectively discount the full dignity of women and sexual minorities, explicitly or implicitly. Moreover, postmodern intersectional awareness—recognizing the overlapping experiences of sex, race, class, sexual orientation, and gender identity, for instance—has risen to the fore in both Catholic and Protestant thought, setting the context for much recent reflection in the field of sex and sexuality.

"TRADITIONALIST" MODERN APPROACHES TO SEXUAL ETHICS

It is impossible to examine in any depth here what might count as a modern-day "traditionalist" approach to sexual ethics, Catholic or Protestant. Therefore, I shall offer only the briefest snapshot of two views that might be described this way—first, the normative guidance developed by Pope John Paul II; and, second, the views of Protestant ethicist Helmut Thielicke.

Over the course of several years (1979–84), John Paul II gave a series of lectures during his general audiences, forming the basis of what has become known as the "Theology of the Body." Here, the pope developed an understanding of human sexuality characterized by an emphasis on the basic goodness of the body as revelatory of God's will. Working from a sexual anthropology based heavily in the Genesis creation stories, John Paul II developed a position wherein men and women, in heterosexual marriage, "complete" each other, such that the two "become one flesh" in "natural complementarity."[18] This complementarity is characterized at once as both biological and personal—although some have pointed out that biological (and, especially, heterogenital) complementarity functions here as the sine qua non for normative sexual activity, thus expressly prohibiting homosexual acts.[19] Indeed, for John Paul II, heterosexual marriage is the correct context for sexual intercourse, which should be understood as the truthful "language of the body."[20] Sexual intercourse includes both procreative and unitive meanings, and marriage realizes these meanings in the context of the "natural" complementarity of men and women.[21]

While John Paul II's views have been influential in modern Catholic thought, they also have been the subject of substantial criticism, worth noting here. In spite of the pope's emphasis on human relationships, encoded within these views is a prioritizing of the "natural" (understood as ahistorical) instead of what might be seen as a more relational, cultural, and historical understanding of the human person. The theology here simplifies the complexity of gender roles and identity, as they are embedded in and influence human behavior and sexual self-understanding. One glaring example is the depiction of motherhood as fundamentally constitutive of women's sexual identity[22]—a portrayal that

---

[18]Pope John Paul II, *General Audience*, November 21, 1979; John Paul II, *Familiaris consortio* (Vatican City: Libreria Editrice Vaticana, 1981), § 19.

[19]See Salzman and Lawler, *The Sexual Person*, 87.

[20]Pope John Paul II, *The Theology of the Body: Human Love in the Divine Plan* (Boston: Pauline Books & Media, 1997), 357–65.

[21]Salzman and Lawler, *The Sexual Person*, 88.

[22]Pope John Paul II, "Mystery of Woman Revealed in Motherhood," *General Audience*, March 12, 1980; John Paul II, *Familiaris consortio*, § 23; John Paul II, *Mulieris dignitatem* (Vatican City: Libreria Editrice Vaticana, 1988), § 18. On this point, see Lisa Sowle Cahill, "Catholic Sexual Ethics and the Dignity of the Person: A Double Message," *Theological Studies* 50, no. 1 (1989): 145–6.

is, at best, reductionistic. Further, in the Theology of the Body, the bodies and experiences of LGBTQ+ persons—lacking an idealized version of complementarity—are treated as nonnormative. Even the complex lived sexual experience of married heterosexual couples—including the "messy, clumsy, awkward, charming, casual, and yes, silly aspects of love in the flesh"—is obscured behind an essentially abstract definition of the sexual person.[23]

Standing in some contrast to John Paul II's sexual ethics are the views of Lutheran theologian Helmut Thielicke, who devoted the third volume of his monumental work in theological ethics to the "ethics of sex."[24] In an effort to move beyond the valorization and static characterization of nature, Thielicke drew upon Luther's "orders of creation," which are linked to, yet transcend, the order of nature. While God's original intent is expressed in such orders, the fallen quality of human experience and the saving work of Jesus Christ together mandate that we not cling to the "natural" order of things as if it were law. The body is in no way inferior to human rationality. But, for Thielicke, we must move beyond the biological aspect of nature to a more holistic, historical, and contextualized understanding of what it means to be human.[25] Thus a sexual ethic must address the total person, in historical context, even as it works not to contradict God's original intent for humanity.

Thielicke's specific ethical teachings are marked by a distinct awareness of historical, cultural, and social forces, as well as by a notably pastoral emphasis. In the context of a fallen world, it is incumbent upon us to examine persons in their *situatedness* and, finally, to adapt to the exigencies of our broken existence. A prime example of this approach is male/female sexual relationships. Like the traditional Catholic position, Thielicke affirms a sexual complementarity between males and females. Yet he describes the Genesis creation story as affirming a basic theological equality before God; patriarchal superiority here stems from humanity's fallen state.[26] Within this context, marriage is grounded in a primeval relationship between the sexes, a partnership corresponding to God's will. Divorce is contrary to this will; yet Thielicke did allow for it pastorally.[27] Similarly, sociohistorical circumstances justify the use of artificial contraception. Thielicke understood same-sex sexual activity to be contrary to God's original intent (a "distortion or depravation" of the created order); yet he recognized the disposition itself (as well as society's discriminatory posture toward it) as genuine. He argued that "homosexual" persons should seek sexual self-realization from within their "questionable" constitution and be urged to discover the charism inherent in their particular existence.[28]

To modern ears striving to take seriously lived, diverse human sexual experiences, Thielicke's approach can seem tone deaf and damaging at times. Yet his effort to maintain an uneasy relationship between the will of God and a fallen world invites an increased level of serious historical engagement. Moreover, his sexual ethics—patriarchal, heteronormative, and cisgendered as they are—nevertheless foreshadow escalating attentiveness toward a diversity of human sexual experience.

[23]Luke Timothy Johnson, "The Way Not Taken: A Disembodied Theology of the Body," chapter 1 in *The Revelatory Body: Theology as Inductive Art* (Grand Rapids: Eerdmans, 2015), 24–5.

[24]Helmut Thielicke, *The Ethics of Sex*, trans. John W. Doberstein (Cambridge: James Clarke, 1964).

[25]Ibid., 17.

[26]Ibid., 7–8.

[27]Ibid., 163–76.

[28]Ibid., 283–8.

PROGRESSIVE APPROACHES OF THE TWENTIETH AND TWENTY-FIRST CENTURIES

The late twentieth century engendered sociocultural shifts that resulted in an explosion of fresh perspectives onto the theological scene. Foremost among these was women's entry into positions of greater leadership, both in churches and academic institutions, as well as in civic life more generally. As women began to speak and write more publicly on matters of human sexuality, perhaps the most noticeable development was attention to the ways traditional Christian sexual ethics has failed to take genuine account of *women's* experiences and has thus ignored or even undermined women's well-being.

On the Catholic side of this development, Lisa Sowle Cahill and Margaret A. Farley are emblematic of a revisioning of the sexual ethics tradition. Cahill, whose writings span a wide range of theological and social topics, works from within a squarely Roman Catholic and Aristotelian-Thomistic natural law tradition; yet she also powerfully challenges that tradition from a feminist angle. Cahill forges a path that avoids reductionistic Enlightenment "universals" while nevertheless affirming certain common values and aspects of human flourishing. She proposes to reach these commonalties inductively and dialogically, by way of our shared (albeit socially shaped) human experience. Working from this approach, Cahill affirms—as constitutive of human flourishing—the equality of men and women as well as the "bodily meaning" of sex as realized in the values of reproduction, pleasure, and intimacy.[29] She rejects traditionalist views that emphasize the preeminence of motherhood for women and fail to take serious account of harmful gender roles; but she also rebuffs an overly individualistic approach to sex that disregards its embodied nature and procreative potential, as well as the social context of sexual actions. These values lead Cahill to nuanced treatment of specific topics. To take but one example, she affirms, with the Catholic tradition, that procreation constitutes an important meaning of human sexuality; yet she rejects the tradition's posture toward artificial contraception, arguing instead that contraception must be contextualized within larger, critically important questions of economic and political justice for women.[30]

Farley, a Roman Catholic Sister of Mercy, shares many of Cahill's allegiances and concerns but proposes her sexual ethics more explicitly from a framework of justice, based in a feminist anthropological understanding of human personhood. For Farley, the primary ethical question in matters of sex is whether particular actions and practices are *justly* loving in ways that honor and affirm human nature, understood as fundamentally autonomous and relational. From this framework, she elaborates seven key norms (do no unjust harm, free consent, mutuality, equality, commitment, fruitfulness, and social justice) to inform concrete moral deliberation.[31] To name just a few examples, Farley embraces the possibility of ethical same-sex sexual relationships (justified by the same ethic as heterosexual relationships), and the possibility of divorce where the framework of marriage no longer serves authentic love and human well-being.[32] But hers is not an "anything-goes" ethic; in every case, she relies upon norms of justice to frame what genuinely conduces to human well-being, and what does not.

---

[29]Lisa Sowle Cahill, *Sex, Gender, and Christian Ethics* (New York: Cambridge University Press, 1996), 110.
[30]Ibid., 213.
[31]Farley, *Just Love*, chap. 6, esp. 208–32.
[32]Ibid., 271–96 (see esp. 295), and 304–7.

While both of these moral theologians place great stress on women's experience as a source for sexual ethics, the clearest example of that emphasis belongs to Protestant social ethicist Beverly Wildung Harrison. Harrison reenvisioned Christian sexual ethics from a feminist and socialist posture, maintaining a relentless focus on gender justice and attention to women's well-being in concrete societal context. Women's moral agency, argued Harrison, is of central moral significance; and, in the context of unequal social power, this necessarily yields an emphasis on bodily integrity and women's control over their own sexuality. She rejected any conception of human nature that relies either upon "natural" differences between men and women or upon a dualism that privileges disembodied reason over embodied sensuality. For her, justice, understood as "right relationship," translates into postures and policies honoring women's full and equal embodied moral agency. She thus rejected procreative reductionism as well as the idea that heterosexuality is in any way a paradigmatic expression of sex—embracing instead norms of justice, mutual respect, and radical equality.[33]

Theological ethicists such as these, drawing heavily upon gendered experience as a moral category, have paved the way for radical postmodern critique in the twenty-first century. In the ethical context, such a critique includes a focus on the intersecting realities of race and ethnicity, class, sexual orientation, and gender identity as fundamental descriptors of moral experience and sources of normative understanding. These patterns of thought are among the most iconoclastic directions in which Christian understandings of sex are presently aimed.

Representative of this category of thinkers is womanist theologian Kelly Brown Douglas. Utilizing a power analysis in the tradition of Michel Foucault, Douglas highlights how Black sexuality specifically has been exploited in the service of white social power, ultimately used to justify white patriarchal and heterosexist hegemony. Douglas urges a "sexual discourse of resistance" in the face of such dehumanizing and oppressive trends.[34] For her, it is key to recognize that God's radical embodied revelation in Jesus confirms the goodness of the body and divine presence in loving relationships, including sexual relationships. This emphasis on radical embodiment, read through the daily struggle of oppressed people, yields a sexual ethic that accentuates justice, liberation, healing, and empowerment, and condemns sexism, racism, homophobia, and heterosexism. Douglas forcefully and explicitly resists the toxic impacts of white exploitation, "affirms the goodness of human sexuality in all of its complexity," and calls for Black self-acceptance as a necessary precursor to loving others and to loving God.[35]

Another contemporary author whose analysis shares affinities with that of Douglas is Miguel De La Torre. A Latino Christian ethicist, De La Torre weaves together biblical interpretation—read explicitly "from the margins"—with social analysis and an emphasis on the experience of sexually marginalized persons. He promotes an ethic of embodiment, liberation, and justice (understood as "the fostering of non-oppressive structures").[36] De La Torre endorses "orthoeros" as a justice-based norm for sex, one characterized by mutually giving, vulnerable, faithful, consensual, loving, committed,

---

[33]Beverley Wildung Harrison, *Making the Connections: Essays in Feminist Social Ethics*, ed. Carol S. Robb (Boston: Beacon, 1985). See also Harrison, *Our Right to Choose: Toward a New Ethic of Abortion* (Boston: Beacon, 1983).

[34]Kelly Brown Douglas, *Sexuality and the Black Church: A Womanist Perspective* (Maryknoll: Orbis, 1999), 7.

[35]Ibid., 122–3.

[36]Miguel A. De La Torre, *A Lily among the Thorns: Imagining a New Christian Sexuality* (San Francisco: John Wiley & Sons, 2007), xiii.

intimate relationships. Drawing upon these norms, he, too, squarely rejects a procreative, strictly marital, or heteronormative ethic.

Finally, Christian sexual ethics in the twenty-first century has notably expanded in a postcolonial direction with the work of Marcella Althaus-Reid, a liberationist and queer theologian who radically challenged the sexual status quo to promote "indecency" as a descriptor for the doing of theology.[37] Queer theology, for Althaus-Reid, challenges all forms of oppression and colonization, including those related to gender, race, class, and sexuality. Experience—found in the form of the sexual stories of oppressed persons—is where we encounter God. Althaus-Reid called for a theological celebration of sexual desire and rejected a binary system that reified masculine/feminine categories and compulsory heterosexuality—instead seeking to welcome a God who "queers" ordinary identities and boundaries. Although Althaus-Reid's relatively early demise surely cut short her contributions to Christian sexual ethics, she inspired a generation of queer theologians to follow—paving the way for greater emphasis on the experience of sexually oppressed persons as indicative of the holy.

CONCLUSION: A NORMATIVE POSTURE FOR CHRISTIAN SEXUAL ETHICS TODAY

If anything can be gleaned from this brief overview of the variety of Christian approaches to sex and sexuality, it is that the picture has grown increasingly complex over time—in large part due to the radical expansion of the normative value of human experience. Over the past century, the incorporation of women's voices into theological reflection has forced the tradition to reckon with the ways sexual ethics has falsely universalized the experience of (some) men. This move has exposed how a lopsided emphasis on procreativity and gender complementarity within marriage has harmed women—and some men—devaluing both their freedom and their well-being.

In fact, the turn to human experience as a moral norm means that we must face the nuance of that very experience. That means not simply taking account of "women's" concrete realities as we reenvision Christian sexual ethics, but rather acknowledging the false universals that Christian feminist ethics itself has sometimes employed, as it has sought to articulate norms and virtues. In this vein, liberationist ethicists have rightly called white feminism to take greater and more accurate account of the breadth of human experience.

In truth, human experience is far more complex than a simple gender-binary model indicates. Experiences of asexuality, gender dysphoria, and intersexuality challenge Christian ethics to rethink and expand its understanding of human sexual flourishing in the twenty-first century. The work of Cahill, Farley, Harrison, Douglas, De La Torre, and Althaus-Reid points toward the need for broad and deep reflection about what that flourishing entails. No longer is it enough to consider only the topics of marriage and divorce, artificial contraception, or gender hierarchies. While these remain important, they are joined by issues that are pressing to a still broader range of persons—for example, marriage equality, transgenderism, polyamory, and the prevalence of sexual power dynamics in an age of #MeToo awareness.

[37]See Marcella Althaus-Reid, *Indecent Theology: Theological Perversions in Sex, Gender, and Politics* (New York: Routledge, 2000); Althaus-Reid, *The Queer God* (New York: Routledge, 2003).

How Christian sexual ethics responds to these new questions will reflect how seriously it takes the moral category of human experience, and the way in which that experience impacts an historically and culturally sensitive understanding of personhood. We have learned that a static understanding of human nature harmfully excludes huge swaths of real persons. Yet to relinquish any meaningful articulation of human nature leaves us precious little normative ground upon which to base our descriptions of sexual justice, healthy relationality, or other pathways to human flourishing. Ultimately, the question comes down to the following: How can we bring postmodern sensibilities to the ethical task, while also finding enough moral footing to stake normative claims that defend genuine human well-being? This is the question that Christian sexual ethics must face if it is to speak meaningfully into the multifaceted twenty-first-century world in which it finds itself.

SUGGESTED READINGS

Farley, Margaret A. *Just Love: A Framework for Christian Sexual Ethics*. New York: Continuum, 2006.

Jordan, Mark D. *The Ethics of Sex*. Malden: Blackwell, 2002.

Salzman, Todd A., and Michael G. Lawler. *Sexual Ethics: A Theological Introduction*. Washington, DC: Georgetown University Press, 2012.

Talvacchia, Kathleen T., Michael F. Pettinger, and Mark Larrimore, eds. *Queer Christianities: Lived Religion in Transgressive Forms*. New York: New York University Press, 2015.

CHAPTER FORTY-FOUR

Marriage and Family

MARCUS MESCHER

Marriage and family life are home to the most primal relationships, potent formation, soaring expectations, and painful wounds. Marriage and family involve profoundly intimate bonds and influential social institutions. It is difficult to imagine any ethical issue that does not overlap with the sphere of family life. Today the norms associated with marriage and family are experiencing significant change, which raises new questions about what Christians are required to do and empowered to become within the interdependent links of love and responsibility. This chapter proceeds in three steps: first, to describe some of the key biblical perspectives as they relate to marriage and family; second, to highlight relevant church teaching in Protestant and Catholic traditions; third, to address several contemporary ethical issues related to loving and doing justice in marriage and family life.

BIBLICAL PERSPECTIVES

Scripture begins with a vision of spouses as coequal partners who are united in becoming "one body" (Gen. 2:23-24, 5:2). Their bodies, their sexuality, and their fertility are all "very good" (Gen. 1:31) as part of a divine plan for creating order out of chaos. Their equality and unity are derived from their complementarity as whole persons, which includes but cannot be reduced to their genitalia.[1] The love and loyalty between spouses point to God's steadfast fidelity to Israel (Deut. 6:5, 23:18; cf. Jer. 31:3 and Hos. 3:1). Respect shown to one's family and genealogy honors Yahweh's covenant with Israel, which is carried forward as families share their faith and customs with each new generation. Love in the Hebrew Scriptures is less about affection than it is an expression of loyalty, obedience, and service. God's love for Israel serves as the template for human marriage (Mal. 2:16). Israelite identity is rooted in allegiance to one's kin and tribe. However, the command to "love your neighbor as yourself" (Lev. 19:18) is eclipsed by the duty to those outside one's family ties and others nearby; partiality is owed to the stranger, the widow, and the orphan (an obligation repeated more than thirty-five times; see, e.g., Exod. 22:21-22; Lev. 19:34; Deut. 10:19; Ps. 10:14, 82:3).

The biblical narrative is rife with stories of God's people failing to live up to these ideals as marriages and families are ravaged by immorality. For example, Lot offers his daughters to be raped by a mob of men from Sodom and, later, Lot's daughters get him

[1]Complementarity is a complex issue that cannot be adequately addressed here, especially as it relates to gender "essentialism." Many theologians and ethicists are critical of this kind of language because it is often used to promote inequality and male dominance, as well as to exclude LGBTQ+ individuals and relationships.

drunk and are impregnated by him (Gen. 19:8, 19:32-36). Conflicts between Abram and Lot (Gen. 13:5-7), Sarah and Hagar (Gen. 16:1-12), Jacob and Essau (Gen. 25:19-34, 27:41-45), Laban and Jacob (Gen. 29:16-30, 30:25-43), Leah and Rachel (Gen. 30:1-15), and Joseph and his brothers (Gen. 37:4-28) poignantly illustrate how relationships between spouses, in-laws, siblings, as well as parents and children are susceptible to lust and infidelity, deception and greed, envy and abuse. The Hebrew Scriptures include stories of religious leaders who fail miserably in their parental duties. For example, Aaron's sons defy him and are burned alive, while Aaron watches in silence (Lev. 10:1-3); Jephthah sacrifices his daughter to keep his vow to God (Judg. 11:30-39); the sons of Eli and Samuel are depraved and corrupt (1 Sam. 2:22-25, 8:1-5); several of David's sons are unruly, violent, and his firstborn is a rapist (2 Sam. 13:1-22, 18:9-20; 1 Kgs 2:1-34); Solomon loses his faith and his sons become inept successors (1 Kgs 11:4, 14:21-24); and kings Ahaz and Manasseh sacrifice their children by immolation (2 Kgs 16:3, 21:6). These failures in family relationships yield sorrow and violence; they test Israel's covenantal fidelity to Yahweh.

Alternatively, the Hebrew Scriptures also provide inspiring examples of spouses and parents who are faithful, selfless, and strong like Jochebed the mother of Moses (Exod. 2:1-10), Rachel the mother of Joseph and Benjamin (Gen. 30:22-24), Hannah the mother of Samuel (1 Samuel 1), Deborah the prophet and judge (Judges 4 and 5), and Job who is described as a perfect father (Job 1:1-5). There are even exemplary figures who do not fit cleanly into the traditional views of marriage and family, such as Esther who was an orphan (Est. 2:7) and Ruth, who, after being widowed, committed her life to her mother-in-law Naomi (Ruth 1:4-18). Numerous proverbs extol the blessings of a spouse and children (Prov. 15:20, 18:22, 19:14, 20:6-7, 31:10). Likewise, several psalms commemorate these intimate bonds as gifts from God (Ps. 127:3, 128:3, 139:13-16). In a most compelling way, the Song of Songs celebrates the ecstasy of erotic intimacy between lovers, which also serves as an allegory of God's love. Verses that sanctify sexuality (some in a female voice, no less) offer new possibilities to restore and transform embodied love and intimate relationships in the face of widespread personal and social sin—via patriarchy, misogyny, and abuse—in the biblical narrative.

Whereas the Hebrew Scriptures consider marriage to represent the mutual covenant relationship between Yahweh and Israel, in the Christian Scriptures marriage also functions as a symbol for the bond between Christ and the church. The author of the letter to the Ephesians critiques the cultural norm for marital relationships (the wife's subservience to her husband) by arguing for the mutual subordination of the spouses (Eph. 5:21-33). This, in turn, fosters availability, attentiveness, and responsiveness; the strength of their unity is measured by the mutuality of their obedience, service, and loyalty. Love between spouses is marked by an inclination to yield to the other, compassion for the other, and a willingness to meet the needs of the other. Marital love should reflect the teaching and healing ministry of Jesus, who "did not come to be served but to serve" (Mk 10:45).

However, there are also mixed messages about marriage and family in the Christian Scriptures. Paul assumes equality between the spouses in his first letter to the Corinthians (1 Cor. 7:3-4), but the authors of 1 Timothy and 1 Peter expect the wife to be submissive to her husband (1 Tim. 2:8-15 and 1 Pet. 3:1-6). When questioned about divorce, Jesus teaches that it is wrong to sever the marital bond, but he does not say it is never acceptable in Matthew's gospel (5:31-32 and 19:3-12), as compared to the total prohibition on divorce in Mark (10:1-12). It is important to note that Jesus's objections to divorce would prevent his followers from arbitrarily leaving their wives, protecting wives from exploitation. This subversive teaching resisted the cultural norm of patriarchal control over women and insisted on ensuring the protection of women and children through maintaining the integrity of the family.

Jesus did not often discuss family life, but his statements are surprising and sometimes perplexing. He celebrates children and calls his followers to be more like them, even though his contemporaries viewed children more as property than as precious persons. He affirms the respect owed parents and elders (Mt. 15:4) and also minimizes the importance of blood ties by saying, "Whoever does the will of God is my brother, sister, and mother" (Mk 3:35; Mt. 12:50; Lk. 8:21). Going even further, Jesus asserts that the demands of discipleship supersede family obligations (Mk 10:29-30; Mt. 10:34-37, 19:29; Lk. 12:51-53, 18:29-30). He warns, "If anyone comes to me without hating his father and mother, wife and children, brothers and sisters, and even his own life, he cannot be my disciple" (Lk. 14:25-26). While this can sound rather harsh to modern ears, it is a prophetic admonition intended to keep family bonds from orbiting around security and status. Jesus also expands his followers' conception of family so that it is no longer defined by blood; his instruction to pray to *Abba* (Daddy) makes everyone part of a family of believers (Lk. 11:2). The Christian moral life is profoundly shaped by marriage and family, but its scope reaches far beyond these intimate bonds.

The gospels present a countercultural vision of family that includes a more egalitarian pattern of relationships among kin as well as a new, more inclusive kinship produced by disciples' moral obligations in community. Insofar as following Jesus implies conversion (Lk. 5:32) and costliness (Mk 8:34), this can rupture preexisting relationships. When the first converts to Christianity were rejected by their families, they discovered a sense of belonging in the *koinōnia* (fellowship) of the family of the faithful. The Christian Scriptures also indicate that duties to others based on need outweigh responsibilities to one's proximate relationships; Jesus explicitly teaches that salvation relies on actions marked by courage, mercy, generosity, and boundary-breaking solidarity to the neediest among us (Lk. 10:25-37; Mt. 25:31-46). Informed by scripture, the Christian ethics of marriage and family life seek to find a proper balance between honoring one's commitments to a spouse, children, siblings, parents, and other family members without becoming so consumed by these obligations that one becomes unaware or unresponsive to their moral obligations outside the home. Scripture affirms the central role of marriage and family in human experience while also recasting these intimate bonds relative to the expectation that God's people work to heal a wounded world (Isa. 58:12) as ambassadors of reconciliation (2 Cor. 5:17-20).

CHRISTIAN TRADITION

The *ordo amoris* or "ordering of love" is the task of each moral agent to find the proper balance in honoring the demands of both proximate relationships and the needs of others. Christian tradition is filled with debates about the function of sexuality and the role of the family in striving to be faithful to the demands of discipleship. Monasticism viewed celibacy and leaving one's family as a higher calling, a safer route to avoid being distracted or contaminated by a sinful world. Bishops like Chrysostom of Constantinople (349–407) and Augustine of Hippo (354–430) maintained a perspective that sought to integrate love, mercy, and justice in and outside the home.

Chrysostom described the embodied union of a married couple as a parallel to Christ's union with the church and parental love as a reflection of God's providence. Chrysostom also taught that the family unit (father–mother–children) incarnates a triune communion of love.[2] At the same time, Chrysostom prophetically called on Christian families to reconsider their comfortable lifestyles that prevented them from loving and serving their neighbors in need. Chrysostom is among the first to link the vocation to family as a service to the gospel by claiming that "the household is a little church."[3]

Augustine focused more on the temptations involved with sexual desire than friendship between spouses or the dynamics of the parent–child relationship. Augustine's own experiences of sexuality, marriage, and family made it easier for him to recognize the risks than the gifts of these dimensions of personal formation and moral development. He was suspicious of sexual desire, even within marriage. For those who cannot maintain a chaste lifestyle, marriage is an acceptable alternative because of its three goods: sexual fidelity, procreation, and the sacramental bond of the spouses that reflects Christ's indissoluble union with the church.[4] Whereas Augustine concentrated more on lust and political order, Chrysostom focused on the promise for social change within and among families who embraced self-sacrifice and generosity with the poor. Chrysostom saw parents as shapers of social norms: if parents could instill in their children modesty and mutuality, respect and responsibility, then the Christian household could make a new social order possible.[5] When spouses are united as friends and lovers and children are raised to be hospitable and compassionate, then a new, more inclusive and egalitarian social solidarity is possible.

By the time Thomas Aquinas (c. 1225–1274) developed his theological framework, church teaching on marriage and family life had long been shaped by a hierarchical structure composed of celibate priests and bishops. Patriarchal support for the status quo blunted the prophetic edge of the early church's vision of the family as the nucleus of a more egalitarian and inclusive community. In his support for Augustine's three goods of marriage, Aquinas placed greater emphasis on friendship between spouses. Although friendship implies a degree of equality, Aquinas also viewed women as dependent on men, less capable of reason, and less reliable moral authorities.[6] Aquinas accounted for the finitude of a moral agent, the natural limitations that keep any person from loving all others equally. Thomas defined a clear *ordo amoris* (or *ordo caritatis*) oriented toward cooperation with God by loving others in descending priority: first God, and next self, followed by spouse, children, parents, siblings, relatives, friends, and then others based on proximity before need.[7] Aquinas trusted institutions (like marriage and families, law, and the state) to help promote the good of the individual and society as a whole. If everyone looks after to those nearest to them, Aquinas presumes that this *ordo amoris* will provide the rules and goals for personal and communal flourishing.

[2]John Chrysostom, "Homily on Ephesians," in *Marriage in the Early Church*, trans. and ed. David G. Hunter (Minneapolis: Fortress, 1992), 83.

[3]Ibid., 87.

[4]Augustine, "On the Goods of Marriage," in *Marriage in the Early Church*, ed. David G. Hunter (Minneapolis: Fortress, 1992), 102.

[5]Peter Brown states that "John elevated the Christian household so as to eclipse the ancient city." See Brown, *The Body and Society: Men, Women, and Sexual Renunciation in Early Christianity* (New York: Columbia University Press, 1988), 313.

[6]Thomas Aquinas, *Summa Theologiae*, trans. Fathers of the English Dominican Province (New York: Benziger Brothers, 1948), I.92.1 ad 2.

[7]Ibid., II–II.26.6, 31.3, 32.9, 32.5.

It was not until 1563—at the Council of Trent—that the Roman Catholic Church formally defined marriage as a sacrament. Long before this, however, the Catholic Church ruled over the pastoral and legal dimensions of marriage. Martin Luther (1483–1546) argued that marriage and family life are part of God's command to bring order to creation, not confined to God's covenant with Israel, making them issues that are more civic than ecclesiastical. After his marriage to Katherine von Bora, Luther's writing on marriage shifted from concerns about sexual temptations like lust and fornication to the gifts and tasks of spousal love and co-parenting. Luther described this as a "noble and great" vocation, as Christians form a school of virtue in caring for the physical and spiritual well-being of children.[8] Luther maintained a patriarchal position of husbands ruling over wives, even though he affirmed that women and men were created equal. He called on spouses to be faithful and forgiving but also allowed for divorce in the case of infidelity. Luther upheld the authority of parents over children except in the case of arranged marriage. He proposed that parents are responsible for raising their children in the faith, shielding them from the sins of the world, and learning the practice of loving and serving their neighbors. In his "Lectures on Genesis," Luther called on Christians to follow the example provided by Adam and Eve in their sinless state before the Fall. Because he believed that celibacy is a special calling reserved for only a few and should not be uniformly expected of all the church's ministers, Luther rejected the idea (which gained prominence with the rise of the monastic tradition) that marriage and family life are a secondary vocation for those who cannot remain chaste. Instead, Luther viewed marriage and family as an interdependent calling from God to bring unity and order to the world, a way to honor the kingdom of God.

In the Catholic tradition, marriage and family life regained prominence along with some of the key reforms in the Second Vatican Council (1962–5). For example, the council's final document, *Gaudium et spes*, lists marriage and family first among "problems of special urgency," distinguished by their "superlative value" to the church and world for fostering human dignity and promoting the unity of the human family.[9] The document describes God calling a couple to marry for a number of benefits and purposes, all of which "have a very decisive bearing on the continuation of the human race, on the personal development and eternal destiny of the individual members of a family, and on the dignity, stability, peace and prosperity of the family itself and of human society as a whole." The "unbreakable oneness" of the spouses, through their marital love, incarnates Christ's presence and power in the world. Their love is connected to the "saving activity" of the church, part of what sanctifies the world and glorifies God.[10] As spouses practice equality and mutuality, their love for each other and their children builds a family that forms a "school of deeper humanity," bringing harmony to the home and society as a whole.[11]

This soaring vision of marriage and family life avoids the dark and painful experiences of abandonment, betrayal, and abuse that sometimes mark domestic life. Instead, it focuses on the power of love, "merging the human with the divine" to be "indissoluble," unbreakable, profaned neither by adultery nor divorce.[12] It is also a love ordered to the

---

[8]Martin Luther, "The Estate of Marriage," in *Luther's Works*, XLV, ed. Walter Brandt (Philadelphia: Muhlenberg, 1962), 46.

[9]Second Vatican Council, *Gaudium et spes* (Vatican City: Libreria Editrice Vaticana, 1965), § 46–52.

[10]Ibid., § 48.

[11]Ibid., § 52.

[12]Ibid., § 49–50.

transmission of life, as *Gaudium et spes* rejects artificial contraception and abortion.[13] Birth control was revisited in Pope Paul VI's encyclical *Humanae vitae*, released in 1968. While this document reiterated the prohibition on any method to separate the unitive and procreative dimensions to conjugal love, except for "therapeutic means,"[14] this ban opposed the counsel provided by a special commission (including lay couples) that studied family planning decisions for several years. The church's condemnation of contraception remains a teaching that is not well-received by the lay faithful, as some studies indicate that over 90 percent of US Catholic couples still use artificial contraception to guide the timing and number of their pregnancies. While bishops' conferences subsequently affirmed the anti-contraceptive teaching of *Humanae vitae*, they also provided pastoral instruction on the freedom of inquiry and licit dissent. The subsequent years have seen plenty of inquiry and dissent on this teaching.

In 1981, Pope John Paul II published his apostolic exhortation, *Familiaris consortio*, addressing marriage and family life "as an interplay of light and darkness." The pope emphasized families as places of education and evangelization: parents pass on their faith to children, promote love and the transmission of life, and work to combat a "contraceptive mentality" that warps the world.[15] He lamented the rise in divorce and prevalence of abortion, and he briefly addressed some of the most difficult problems families face.[16] In light of these challenges to freedom and responsibility, the pope called for "a continuous, permanent conversion" to the gifts and demands of God's love.[17] After rehearsing familiar images of marriage as a communion of love with God, covenant, and sacrament, the pope stated that spouses serve as "the permanent reminder to the Church of what happened on the Cross; they are for one another and for the children witnesses to the salvation in which the sacrament makes them sharers."[18] Linking love to the Cross underscores the redemptive possibilities of self-sacrifice and suffering, and yet it also might leave some spouses and children with the mistaken impression that they should endure abuse at the hands of their own family (abuse is never mentioned much less denounced in the document). John Paul II summoned couples to "mutual sanctification"[19] by leading their families to "become what you are," an "intimate community of life and love." The pope outlined four central roles for the family: forming a community of persons, serving life, participating in the development of society, and sharing in the life and mission of the church.[20] Presenting marriage and family as a "domestic church" and foundational cell for society, *Familiaris consortio* marked a return to the early views of family (from the gospels and early church fathers like Chrysostom) where family life is oriented both to supporting its members and defending their rights[21] as well as serving the common good in the spirit of inclusive solidarity.[22]

Familiaris consortio highlighted the personal and social dimensions of marriage and family life, bringing attention to the ways that family units exercise agency in shaping

[13]Ibid., § 51.
[14]Pope Paul VI, *Humanae vitae* (Vatican City: Libreria Editrice Vaticana, 1968), § 15.
[15]Pope John Paul II, *Familiaris consortio* (Vatican City: Libreria Editrice Vaticana, 1981), § 6.
[16]Ibid., § 77.
[17]Ibid., § 9.
[18]Ibid., § 13.
[19]Ibid., § 56.
[20]Ibid., § 17.
[21]Ibid., § 46.
[22]Ibid., § 72.

culture at the same time that they are shaped by culture. But it seems to exhort more than support families, especially in comparison to Pope Francis's 2016 apostolic exhortation, *Amoris laetitia*. Whereas mercy appears only in one section referencing the sacrament of reconciliation in *Familiaris consortio*, the central theme of *Amoris laetitia* is mercy: it is who God is and what God wants for and from God's people. *Amoris laetitia* is the result of two synodal gatherings of bishops on the topic of marriage and family life in 2014 and 2015. It also speaks to and from the responses to forty-six questions about the lay faithful's experience of the context and challenges of marriage and family life, a reflection of Francis's desire to cultivate a "listening church," a church "without frontiers" and a "mother to all," a church that is like a "field hospital," going out to care for the sick and wounded.[23]

Amoris laetitia breaks new ground as an ecclesial document that engages the lived experience of the lay faithful. The process of collecting feedback also unearthed a lot of displeasure among the lay faithful, who reported finding the church to be more focused on following rules than discerning what is best for people in their own circumstances. The laity voiced lament that their home parish is out of touch with their needs and desires and that churches have been reduced to places where sacraments are dispensed. They wish to belong to a vibrant and inclusive faith community that offers support to families preoccupied with navigating all that life brings. They want a church that can imagine new possibilities for building right relationship with God and one another in light of the "signs of the times."

Amoris laetitia grapples with addressing couples and families across the globe who experience marriage and family in a diverse array of sociocultural, political, and economic contexts. *Amoris laetitia* calls the church to be oriented by mercy and encourages "everyone to be a sign of mercy and closeness wherever family life remains imperfect or lacks peace and joy."[24] The lived experience of marriage and family life reveals a host of serious cultural challenges: decreasing support from social structures and institutions,[25] rising individualism,[26] a lack of commitment,[27] loneliness and powerlessness,[28] "excessive idealization" of marriage and family,[29] a "culture of the ephemeral,"[30] and various personal and social sins including sexual exploitation like pornography, prostitution, and sex trafficking,[31] lack of affordable housing and dignified employment,[32] sexual abuse of children,[33] hardships faced by migrants, refugees, and those living in extreme poverty,[34] the isolation of the elderly,[35] drug use and domestic violence,[36] and patriarchy and abuse of women.[37]

[23]Pope Francis, "A Listening Church," *America*, October 17, 2015, https://www.americamagazine.org/content/all-things/pope-calls-listening-church. For Pope Francis's interview see Antonio Spadaro, SJ, "A Big Heart Open to God," *America*, September 30, 2013, http://www.americamagazine.org/pope-interview. See also Pope Francis, *Evangelii gaudium* (Vatican City: Libreria Editrice Vaticana, 2013), § 210.
[24]Pope Francis, *Amoris laetitia* (Vatican City: Libreria Editrice Vaticana, 2016), § 5.
[25]Ibid., § 32.
[26]Ibid., § 33.
[27]Ibid., § 34.
[28]Ibid., § 43.
[29]Ibid., § 36.
[30]Ibid., § 39.
[31]Ibid., § 41.
[32]Ibid., § 44.
[33]Ibid., § 45.
[34]Ibid., § 46.
[35]Ibid., § 48.
[36]Ibid., § 51.
[37]Ibid., § 54.

All of these examples are listed without ever using the phrase "social sin," which is problematic because it misses an important opportunity to identify how and why families suffer because of vicious social values, practices, and structures. Couples and families endure hardships not only because of the failures of individuals but also at the hands of corrupt institutions and harmful policies. Instead of denouncing these sinful social structures, Francis appeals to the tender embrace of God[38] and the need to reclaim the vocation of the family, which is to incarnate God's infinite love and tenderness in the world.[39] The document proceeds by reaffirming the church's vision of family life where love is an experience of the common good,[40] the family is the "sanctuary of life,"[41] and the church is a "family of families"[42] charged with supporting its members, especially those in greatest need.[43] Francis writes, "The Gospel of the family responds to the deepest expectations of the human person: a response to each one's dignity and fulfillment in reciprocity, communion and fruitfulness. This consists not merely in presenting a set of rules, but in proposing values that are clearly needed today, even in the most secularized of countries."[44] Parishes are called to be more than places where sacraments are dispensed; they are tasked with being on the front lines of caring for families: "The main contribution to the pastoral care of families is offered by the parish, which is the family of families, where small communities, ecclesial movements and associations live in harmony."[45] Francis anticipates this will require a more robust commitment to pastoral outreach and a "more adequate formation" of priests, deacons, women religious, catechists, and parish staff.[46]

Amoris laetitia also offers families advice on facing crises,[47] acclaims the practice of accompaniment,[48] and emphasizes the importance of the ethical formation of children in freedom, virtue, and conscience formation,[49] especially the virtues of faith, hope, and love.[50] In addressing the church as a whole, Pope Francis calls for gradualness in working for change,[51] discernment in being attentive and responsive to the presence and power of the Holy Spirit,[52] and a commitment to adopting a praxis of mercy.[53] Francis also acknowledges the special challenge tied to the "teaching of moral theology,"[54] which ought to be shaped by "pastoral discernment" that aspires to "open our hearts to those living on the outermost fringes of society."[55] The document concludes with the claim that "all family life is 'shepherding' in mercy."[56] In this way, Pope Francis elevates the family

---

[38]Ibid., § 28.
[39]Ibid., § 59.
[40]Ibid., § 70.
[41]Ibid., § 83.
[42]Ibid., § 87.
[43]Ibid., § 197.
[44]Ibid., § 201.
[45]Ibid., § 202.
[46]Ibid.
[47]Ibid., § 232–8.
[48]Ibid., § 241–6.
[49]Ibid., § 263–7.
[50]Ibid., § 274–9.
[51]Ibid., § 295.
[52]Ibid., § 296–300.
[53]Ibid., § 309–10.
[54]Ibid., § 311.
[55]Ibid., § 312.
[56]Ibid., § 322.

and the local church as essential loci for carrying forward the "revolution of tenderness" announced in his 2013 apostolic exhortation, *Evangelii gaudium*.[57]

CONTEMPORARY ISSUES

It is hard to fathom any ethical issue standing apart from marriage and family life, since each person is a product of and participant in these intimate relationships. This means there is no shortage of issues to address. In the West, marriage rates are declining, as individuals express deep concerns about finding a lifelong partner and being capable of abiding by the church's teaching on the "indissolubility" of this commitment. Family dynamics are experiencing a profound cultural shift as the traditional "nuclear family" structure is being eclipsed by the number of families shaped by divorce and remarriage, cohabitation, and blending previous relationships. At the same time, many of those who are married report low levels of satisfaction in their relationship and rather high rates of stress, anxiety, as well as infidelity. In the Global South, marriage is less common for a number of reasons, ranging from cultural trends (including changing gender roles), financial challenges, and a shortage of priests and parishes to make a union official. Future theological and ethical analysis will have to explore how to navigate the significant differences between what the church teaches about marriage and family life and what people actually experience in the world today.

For example, the claim that marriages should live up to the unity of Adam and Eve as "bone of my bones and flesh of my flesh" (Gen. 2:23) raises important questions about whether this prelapsarian standard is tenable in a sinful world. Discussion of marriage as a lifelong covenant, sacrament, and "indissoluble" union ought to be less idealistic and more aspirational. This is also true for theological and ethical discourse about sex. For instance, when *Humanae vitae* refers to conjugal love as "the marital act,"[58] this raises questions about whether and how the entirety of the sacrament of marriage can be expressed in this single action. It also invites inquiry about what this means for couples who are unhappy or unfaithful, abstain from sex, experience sex as part of a power struggle, have endured physical, emotional, or sexual abuse, or suffer from painful intercourse. There are also critical issues to explore about gender roles in marriage and family life. Church teaching about essential qualities of "maleness" and "femaleness" and their complementarity does not always cohere with what we learn about gender identity from human experience and the social sciences. This is an increasingly important matter, given how sexuality is portrayed—and often objectified—by digital media and rampant pornography, patriarchy, and misogyny. Some of the most important ethical questions pivot around the treatment of LGBTQ+ individuals, especially given the wide range of respect and freedoms they experience across the world: in some countries, LGBTQ+ couples are welcomed and their unions blessed but in far too many other places, they endure hatred, violence, and exclusion; there are even some places where it is illegal to identify as anything other than heterosexual. It is a great shame and scandal that many Christian communities demonize and exclude LGBTQ+ individuals, exacerbating discrimination and vulnerability with tragic results: some estimates indicate that 40 percent of homeless teens are LGBTQ+,

[57] Francis, *Evangelii gaudium*, § 88.
[58] Paul VI, *Humanae vitae*, § 11.

more than half of whom have been rejected by and abused in their families;[59] one in five LGBTQ+ youth attempted suicide in the past year, another result of internalized degradation and isolation.[60] Far too many individuals, families, and communities fail to treat those who identify as LGBTQ+ so that they are "accepted with respect, compassion, and sensitivity" as required by the *Catechism of the Catholic Church*.[61] While the church has long focused on the unitive and procreative dimension of human sexuality, more work needs to be done to analyze and apply the moral norms that ensure the integrity of love and justice, like consent, mutuality, and a vision of fruitfulness that expands beyond biological procreation.[62]

This is just the tip of the iceberg. Racism and xenophobia unjustly harm couples and families that increasingly cross racial and ethnic lines. The well-being of marriages and families relies on improved access to health care for mental and physical needs, treatment for substance abuse and addiction, a living wage, paid parental leave, childcare, protection from violence and corruption, as well as debt relief and astute financial planning. Climate change will negatively impact more and more families, especially those who are poor, who are routinely subject to these adverse conditions first and worst. Ecological degradation, species loss, flooding, and other changes to our habitat (exacerbated by the destructive effects of irresponsible industry, overconsumption, conflict, and war) will result in even more persons on the move—some estimates predict as many as a billion people by 2050—making the moral obligation to welcome migrants and refugees among the most pressing concerns for the unity and stability of marriage and family life. Given economic uncertainty, social instability, and political dysfunction, many families are tempted to turn inward and put the good of their own unit ahead of others. This is what Edward Banfield warned against years ago, an "amoral familism" that maximizes the self-interest of one's own family and assumes that other families do the same.[63] This trend makes it harder for couples and families to be aware of and responsive to the needs of others, resulting in a shrinking sense of our shared interdependence and mutual accountability. In the face of these and other challenges, the church calls on couples and families all over the globe to keep striving to cultivate faith, hope, and love in their beliefs, actions, and relationships within and beyond the family unit.

CONCLUSION

Marriage and family are essential to the divine ordering of human life; they are home to formative lessons about faith and love, failure and suffering, forgiveness and healing. The ethical task is to employ careful discernment to discover and share the virtues and practices that foster right relationship with God, self, and one another just as much as it is to avoid the personal and social sins that undermine relationships that ought to be marked

---

[59]Adam P. Romero, Shoshana K. Goldberg, and Luis A. Vasquez, "LGBT People and Housing Affordability, Discrimination, and Homelessness" (Los Angeles: Williams Institute, 2020), https://williamsinstitute.law.ucla.edu/wp-content/uploads/LGBT-Housing-Apr-2020.pdf.

[60]"The Trevor Project National Survey on LGBTQ Youth Mental Health" (2019), https://www.thetrevorproject.org/wp-content/uploads/2019/06/The-Trevor-Project-National-Survey-Results-2019.pdf.

[61]United States Conference of Catholic Bishops, *Catechism of the Catholic Church* (Washington, DC: USCCB, 2000), § 2358.

[62]See Margaret Farley, *Just Love: A Framework for Christian Sexual Ethics* (New York: Continuum, 2008), 216–32.

[63]Edward C. Banfield, *The Moral Basis of a Backward Society* (Glencoe: Free Press, 1958), 85.

by mutual respect, love, and responsibility. Scripture and tradition can offer couples and families insight and encouragement for prudent moral deliberation. Embracing the lived experience of couples and families today can help accentuate their embodied wisdom, tenderness, and resilience. This can also help ministers, pastors, bishops, and theologians more effectively articulate theological insights, ethical principles, and pastoral approaches. Describing marriage and family as covenants, sacraments, and communions of life and love can give the impression that these institutions arrive at holiness at their inception like the flip of a switch rather than a lifelong process in becoming ever more faithful and loving in the face of many challenges. As couples and families reciprocally practice virtues like mercy, honesty, humility, patience, and loyalty, their intimate bonds deepen. As couples and families practice hospitality, courage, generosity, hope, and boundary-breaking kinship, they fortify the kinds of relationships and organizations that will bring people together across differences of gender and sexual orientation, ethnicity and race, class, religion, and nationality. As they grow in virtue, couples and families aspirationally become the "structures of grace," "schools of solidarity," and "factories of hope" the church and world need.[64]

SUGGESTED READINGS

Cahill, Lisa Sowle. *Family: A Christian Social Perspective*. Minneapolis: Fortress, 2000.

Gaillardetz, Richard. *A Daring Promise: A Spirituality of Christian Marriage*. Liguori: Liguori/Triumph, 2007.

King, Jason, and Julie Hanlon Rubio, eds. *Love, Sex, and Family: Catholic Perspectives*. Collegeville: Liturgical, 2020.

Massey, Julie Donovan, and Bridget Burke Revizza, eds. *Project Holiness: Marriage as a Workshop for Everyday Saints*. Collegeville: Liturgical, 2015.

McCarthy, David Matzko. *Sex & Love in the Home: A Theology of the Household*. Eugene: Wipf and Stock, 2001.

Post, Stephen. *More Lasting Unions: Christianity, the Family, and Society*. Grand Rapids: Eerdmans, 2000.Rubio, Julie Hanlon. *Family Ethics: Practices for Christians*. Washington, DC: Georgetown University Press, 2010.

Roche, Mary M. Doyle. *Schools of Solidarity: Families and Catholic Social Teaching*. Collegeville: Liturgical, 2015.

Rubio, Julie Hanlon. *Family Ethics: Practices for Christians*. Washington, DC: Georgetown University Press, 2010 .

[64]John Rogerson refers to families among several "structures of grace" in the Hebrew Bible in his chapter, "The Family and Structures of Grace in the Old Testament," in *The Family in Theological Perspective*, ed. Stephen C. Barton (Edinburgh: T&T Clark, 1996), 36. Pope Francis used the phrase "schools of solidarity" in an address on December 29, 2014. See also, Mary M. Doyle Roche, *Schools of Solidarity: Families and Catholic Social Teaching* (Collegeville: Liturgical, 2015). The phrase "factories of hope" comes from an unscripted address at the Festival of Families in Philadelphia; the official version released by the Vatican uses the phrase "workshop of hope." Pope Francis, "Prayer Vigil for the Festival of Families," September 26, 2015, http://w2.vatican.va/content/francesco/en/speeches/2015/september/documents/papa-francesco_20150926_usa-festa-famiglie.html.

CHAPTER FORTY-FIVE

Adoptive Families

DARLENE FOZARD WEAVER

Adoptive families are clearly a very small portion of the overall population. Why, then, devote an entire chapter to adoptive families in this volume? Some 5 million Americans are adoptees, about 1.8 million of whom are children under the age of 18, representing about 2 percent of the population. Adoptive families likewise comprise about 2 percent of families in the United States.[1] Surely, adoption and adoptive families are a minor issue in Christian ethics, applying to and of interest to only a few students of ethics.

This chapter mounts a contrary argument. Adoption and adoptive families concern a range of ethical issues that are morally significant for all persons. Moreover, adoption and adoptive families are also a lens or microcosm for significant aspects of Christian ethics, including key theological and moral commitments, deeply personal moral experiences, and urgent issues in social ethics. This chapter first considers adoption and adoptive families in light of the sources of Christian ethics. It then discusses ethical issues that adoption involves. The scope of these issues shows that ethical analysis of adoption and adoptive families cannot be limited to the fields of sexual ethics. A broad social ethical approach is needed. From there the chapter explores adoption and adoptive families as a microcosm for Christian ethics. Finally, the chapter draws several moral conclusions about obligations each of us has toward other human beings, particularly the most vulnerable children.

ADOPTION AND ADOPTIVE FAMILIES: SOURCES OF CHRISTIAN ETHICS

Scripture provides resources for moral reflection on kinship as well as a theology of adoption that can orient adoption ethics. Scriptural resources on these two themes point both to moral support for adoption and to the broader theological significance of adoption for Christians. Scriptural sources on families are ambivalent. At many points scripture posits the foundational importance of the family as a social unit and utilizes familial imagery to describe God's active solicitude for human beings (Lk. 15:11-24). At other times scripture includes manifestly anti-family passages, often attributed to Jesus (Mt. 10:21, 34-36; Mk 14:12; Lk. 14:25-26). As Lisa Sowle Cahill observes, "Jesus dichotomizes discipleship and family by seeming to demand that family relations be completely repudiated and abandoned."[2] By opposing discipleship and kinship, Christian scripture provides a critical

[1]Jo Jones and Paul Placek, "Adoption: By the Numbers," *National Council for Adoption*, February 15, 2017, http://www.adoptioncouncil.org/publications/2017/02/adoption-by-the-numbers.
[2]Lisa Sowle Cahill, *Family: A Christian Social Perspective* (Minneapolis: Fortress, 2000), 29.

perspective on prevailing power relations within kinship networks and realign familial loyalties. "Loyalty to one's own group and dedication to the status of that group over all others and at the expense of whoever stands in its way are incompatible with a life of mercy, service, and compassion for the neighbor in need or for the social outcasts and the poor existing on the margins of society."[3] Taken together, the varied treatments of kinship in scripture indicate that biological kinship ties are valuable and a locus of moral obligations but that they must also be transcended as Christians join a new family of discipleship in which God, not biology, provides the source of one's identity.

Scripture also provides a theology of adoption in the letters of St. Paul. The term "adoption" appears only a handful of times in Paul's epistles but it encapsulates core elements of Pauline theology. Paul describes all Christians as adopted children of God. We become adopted sons and daughters of God when we receive God's Spirit (Rom. 8:15). In the "spirit of adoption" we receive a new manner of life, which Paul describes by contrasting spirit and flesh. Our adoption by God is not an external fiction, whereby God chooses to regard us "as if" we were God's own children, but an internal transformation. God's steadfast love for us *makes us* God's children, and makes us truly siblings of one another. Indeed, Paul identifies our adoption by God as God's intention in sending Jesus to become human for our redemption (Gal. 4:4-5). Put differently, our adoption is the *goal of salvation history* as well as the *form our redemption takes*. Adoption, then, is a key Christian term. It has implications for Christian ethical reflection on human adoption, and human adoption can illuminate our understanding of our divine adoption. More significantly, adoption captures and conveys the central character of Christian life.

A second source for Christian ethics is tradition. Christian tradition offers a mixed record on adoption. On the one hand, Christian teaching explicitly supports adoption throughout history. On the other hand, Christian tradition reinforces the notion that adoption is a "second choice" by discussing it almost exclusively in the context of sympathy for infertile couples, or by presenting it as an exemplary act of service, or as a matter of mission or evangelization.[4] Many Christian denominations offer little explicit and sustained attention to adoption. Christian discussion of adoption and adoptive families is fairly quiet and remains stuck in a rhetorical framework of altruism. Framing adoption and adoptive families through the rhetoric of altruism emphasizes the sacrifice—even heroism—of adoptive parents. This has unfortunate implications. It plays into stigmas that orphans and adoptees are somehow fundamentally unwanted, defective, or potentially problem children because their genetic origins are unknown or their social histories are marked by trauma. An altruistic framework eclipses the overwhelming experience of adoptive parents, who welcome and experience their children as gifts who enrich their lives immeasurably, rather than as opportunities to practice sacrificial love for neighbors. An altruistic framework also effaces the experience of birthparents, largely through a near-total neglect of their experience. This inadvertently contributes to the cultural stigmatization of birthparents. Finally, an altruistic framework presents adoption as a supererogatory practice—morally praiseworthy but not obligatory. Not everyone can or should adopt, but, as this chapter argues below, adults (especially Christian adults[5])

---

[3]Ibid.

[4]Darlene Fozard Weaver, "Adoption, Social Justice, and Catholic Tradition," *Journal of Catholic Social Thought* 13, no. 2 (2016): 197–213.

[5]I do not claim that Christians are better suited to adopt. My point here is that Christian faith convictions have normative implications that suggest all Christian adults should ponder whether they can welcome and parent children in need of families.

should discern whether adoption or foster care is a commitment they can undertake. Furthermore, Christian communities should deliberately cultivate ways of speaking about adoption that are informed by the experience of persons directly affected by adoption and by adoption providers. Unfortunately, recent Catholic statements point to adoption in the context of religious liberty, treating it more as a battle line in culture wars regarding same-sex relationships.[6] Some Catholic-affiliated adoption agencies have closed rather than comply with legislation requiring them to treat same-sex prospective parents equally in adoption placement processes.[7] When Christian teaching about adoption, which is already so limited, utilizes adoption as a knee-jerk appeal in arguments against abortion, or focuses mostly on arguments against same-sex adoption, churches forfeit important opportunities to advocate for adoption and to develop their theologies of adoption. As we will see in a moment, Christian tradition frames and shapes adoption in important ways through teachings on sexual morality.

A third source for Christian ethics is experience, where the record on adoption is even more mixed. Christian communities have significant adoption-related experience on which to draw. Catholic religious orders, hospitals, and charitable organizations have cared for foundlings and orphans and facilitated adoptions for millennia.[8] A number of large Protestant organizations exist to facilitate domestic and intercountry adoptions.[9] Moreover, in some contemporary Protestant communities the practice of adoption is promoted to such an extent that social networks of adoptive families support and encourage families who are considering adopting a child.[10] Despite some positive and ethically appropriate promotion and facilitation of adoption by Christian organizations, it is important to note that Christian churches have also supported and participated in the forced separation of children and their parents in a number of contexts, and have also been responsible for the abusive treatment of mothers and children.[11] Traditional Christian teaching on sexual ethics and Christianity's long-standing normative preference for intact biological family units contributed to environments in which forced separation appeared to some Catholic leaders to be the charitable thing to do. Granted, these convictions were—and still are—part of larger, gendered cultural landscapes that included laws regarding "illegitimate" children and limited options for women's economic independence.[12] Attending to

[6]See United States Conference of Catholic Bishops, "Discrimination against Catholic Adoption Services," 2018, http://www.usccb.org/issues-and-action/religious-liberty/discrimination-against-catholic-adoption-services.cfm.

[7]Ibid. Pope Francis has made several public comments against same-sex adoption. For one example see his remarks for a General Audience on February 4, 2015, http://www.bbc.com/news/magazine-18585020. See also Congregation for the Doctrine of the Faith, *Considerations Regarding Proposals to Give Legal Recognition to Unions between Homosexual Persons*, § 7, http://www.vatican.va/roman_curia/congregations/cfaith/documents/rc_con_cfaith_doc_20030731_homosexual-unions_en.html.

[8]Lisa Sowle Cahill, "Adoption: A Roman Catholic Perspective," in *The Morality of Adoption*, ed. Timothy P. Jackson (Grand Rapids: Eerdmans, 2005).

[9]Kathryn Joyce, *The Child Catchers: Rescue, Trafficking, and the New Gospel of Adoption* (New York: Public Affairs, 2013).

[10]Tony Merida, *Orphanology: Awakening to Gospel-Centered Adoption and Orphan Care* (Birmingham: New Hope, 2011).

[11]Paul Jude Redmond, *The Adoption Machine: The Dark History of Ireland's Mother and Baby Homes and the Inside Story of How 'Tuam800' Became a Global Scandal* (Newbridge: Irish Academic, 2018); Anne Fessler, *The Girls Who Went Away: The Hidden History of Women Who Surrendered Children for Adoption in the Decades before Roe v. Wade* (New York: Penguin, 2006); Marylin Irvin Holt, *Orphan Trains* (Lincoln: University of Nebraska Press, 1992).

[12]John Witte, *The Sins of the Fathers: The Law and Theology of Illegitimacy Reconsidered* (Cambridge: Cambridge University Press, 2009).

Christian tradition means acknowledging Christian complicity in specific practices of adoption and in contributing to broader cultural stigmas surrounding adoption. Because Christian tradition has a mixed record spanning ethical adoption practices to involvement in forced separation of parents and children, Christian theological and ethical attention to adoption, and Christian involvement in adoption practices must prioritize listening to and learning from the experiences of adoptees, birthparents, and adoptive families. Listening to the experiences of women whose children were taken from them has been an important, though still insufficiently addressed, step toward more ethical adoption practices and more accurate, sensitive cultural scripts around adoption.

Scripture, tradition, and experience should inform moral reasoning about adoption. In my judgment these sources yield several normative commitments that obligate all adults but are particularly significant for Christians given the relative subordination of biological kinship and the central dynamic of divine adoption in Christian life. I share these obligations at the end of this chapter. Although other sources inform moral reasoning about adoption, reason itself is crucial for the critical examination and use of these sources. Yet, we must also admit that reason is influenced and shaped by historical and cultural factors that can distort ethical reasoning. Reason must be tutored through critical thinking, and exercised in conversation with other sources that can mutually inform, challenge, and correct each other.

ADOPTION, SEXUAL ETHICS, AND SOCIAL ETHICS

Adoption is a morally complex enterprise and therefore entails many ethical issues. As we have already begun to see, adoption is also an issue within and a reflection of larger convictions in sexual ethics. This section argues that adoption is properly examined within the realm of social ethics.

Whether an adoption involves extended biological family, domestic nonrelative ("stranger") adoptions, intercountry adoptions, or so-called embryo adoption, any adoption involves competing rights and interests among members of the adoption triad: child, birthparents, and adoptive parents. These rights and interests include procedures for informed consent, access to information (such as original birth certificates, medical histories for biological family members, identifying information for birth or adoptive families), and standards for determining the "best interests" of the child.

Domestic adoptions (in which the biological parents and adoptive parents live in the same country) have trended from "closed" adoptions, in which the biological and adoptive parents had no identifying information, and adoptees themselves were often unaware of their adoptive status, to "open" adoptions. In open adoptions, which involve the exchange of some identifying information between birthparents and adoptive parents, there is also the issue that original agreements regarding contact between birth and adoptive families do not enjoy the legal enforceability of contracts. Legal processes for relinquishing or terminating parental rights are also ethically significant. Adoptions involve requirements and preferences for certain characteristics in children, adoptive parents, and prospective birthparents. Demand is highest for Caucasian infants, and the costs associated with adopting white infants tend to be higher than costs associated with other children. Older children, African American children, children with disabilities, and sibling sets are more difficult to place with families. Moreover, adoptions, be they closed or open, involve a variety of expenses. Fees for social workers and attorneys, differential fee structures for Caucasian infants versus infants of color, the payment of birthparent living expenses, financial support for foster parents, and financial incentives for adoption "facilitators" who may coerce women into relinquishing children for their own profit are all important moral issues. Adoptions that involve parents and children of different racial, ethnic, or cultural backgrounds raise additional issues. For example, in the United States the Indian Child Welfare Act (1978) requires that children descended from indigenous tribes must be placed with documented members of those tribes, or at least members of other tribes.[13] The law is intended to stop practices of forced separation and to protect indigenous American cultures that have been devastated by white populations. All of these policies have moral dimensions, as well as legal and economic implications, and import for birthparents, adoptees, and adoptive parents. Interracial adoptions raise ethical issues regarding their impact on racial communities, on children's identities and outcomes, and on parental responsibilities regarding children's familiarity with and relation to their culture of origin.

In intercountry adoptions children are placed with parents who reside outside the child's country of origin. Intercountry adoptions have grown since the 1990s.[14] Intercountry adoptions include some distinctive ethical issues. They are less likely to include identifying information between birthparents and adoptive families. The availability of children for adoption and prospective adoptive parents' demand for them reflect economic, legal, and cultural issues. Some countries are more likely to be countries of origin, countries from which children are adopted by adults in destination countries, especially the United States.[15] For example, China's One Child policy, in conjunction with cultural preferences for boys, contributed to large numbers of Chinese girls being relinquished for adoption in other countries.[16] Unsurprisingly, supply and demand relationships can foster fraudulent or even coercive practices to obtain children for comparatively affluent adults to adopt. One response to rising rates of intercountry adoptions was the Hague Convention on Protection of Children and Co-operation in Respect of Intercountry Adoption (the Hague Adoption Convention). Since 1995 the Convention has limited corruption and exploitation associated with intercountry adoption.

Adoption and adoptive families lie at the intersection of broader issues in sexual ethics and family ethics. Adoption often figures in moral arguments about abortion and reproductive technologies. Pro-life arguments sometimes appeal to adoption as an alternative to abortion for women who do not want or are not able to parent their children. As noted above, adoption increasingly appears as an issue within arguments about religious liberty and same-sex couples. Court cases in a number of states have prompted some Catholic-affiliated adoption organizations to cease operation rather than place children with same-sex families.[17] In the wake of Supreme Court decisions like

---

[13]Lila J. George, "Why the Need for the Indian Child Welfare Act?," *Journal of Multicultural Social Work* 5, nos. 3–4 (1997): 165–75.

[14]Department of Economic and Social Affairs of the United Nations Secretariat, *Child Adoption: Trends and Policies* (New York: United Nations, 2009), xviii.

[15]Ibid., 75–7.

[16]Avraham Ebenstein, "The 'Missing Girls' of China and the Unintended Consequences of the One Child Policy," *Journal of Human Resources* 45, no. 1 (2010): 87–115.

[17]Stephen T. Watson and Harold McNeil, "Catholic Charities Ending Foster, Adoption Programs over Same-Sex Marriage Rule," *The Buffalo News*, August 23, 2018, https://buffalonews.com/2018/08/23/catholic-charities-ending-foster-care-adoption-program-over-states-same-sex-marriage-rule/.

Masterpiece Cakeshop v. Colorado Civil Rights Commission, however, such organizations may find legal support for their refusal.

Given the availability of reproductive technologies, adoption often figures as a "second choice" to having a "child of one's own." Elizabeth Bartholet has coined the term "biologism" to refer to the enshrinement of biological kinship.[18] It is worth noting that many forms of reproductive technologies involve the use of donor eggs or sperm, or a surrogate who may or may not also contribute the egg. In so-called heterologous forms of assisted reproduction (methods involving donors), the pursuit of a "child of one's own" depends on devaluing this same genetic connection between the donor and one's offspring. Discourse regarding reproductive technologies and adoption also reflects the commodification of children, just as adoption fees reflect a hierarchy of desirable children. Consider that egg donors can fetch thousands of dollars, with higher rates having been offered to donor women who are Ivy League students, athletes, and so on. The high cost of most reproductive technologies also leads to international surrogacy programs between similar-origin and destination countries discernible in intercountry adoption. Reproductive technologies have also created moral issues involving excess embryos. Approximately four hundred thousand cryopreserved embryos are indefinitely stored. Some Christians consider this a violation of the human dignity of embryos and seek to "adopt" them, gestating them to parent themselves or to relinquish for traditional adoption.[19]

Adoption also figures in sexual ethics with regard to men's reproductive responsibility.[20] Some men avoid either consenting to or actively opposing a prospective birthmother's adoption plan. They simply choose not to act. In the United States, most states have developed putative father registries, ostensibly to protect men's rights to oppose an adoption plan in order to parent their biological child.[21] The registries are designed to allow men to notify the states of their female sexual partners so that if one of them initiated adoption proceedings the putative father of her child would be notified. In practice putative father registries may in fact facilitate the "involuntary" termination of paternal rights so that women can move forward with their adoption plans. Most men are unaware the registries exist, and failure to register, particularly along with failures to support the mother during her pregnancy, can be interpreted legally as abandonment and therefore grounds for terminating his rights.

Adoption certainly touches on sexual and reproductive ethics, but it would be a mistake to confine moral analysis of adoption to these subfields in ethics. Adoption is better understood as an issue in social ethics. Historically, adoption has functioned both as a mechanism of financial sustainability and social mobility within economic systems (for instance, in cultures and historical periods where children were placed with other families for apprenticeships).[22]

---

[18]Elizabeth Bartholet, *Family Bonds: Adoption, Infertility, and the New World of Child Production* (Boston: Beacon, 1999).

[19]Sarah-Vaughan Brakman and Darlene Fozard Weaver, eds. *The Ethics of Embryo Adoption and the Catholic Tradition: Moral Arguments, Economic Reality and Social Analysis* (Dordrecht: Springer, 2008).

[20]Laura Oren, "Thwarted Fathers or Pop-Up Pops? How to Determine When Putative Fathers Can Block the Adoption of Their Newborn Children," *Family Law Quarterly* 40, no. 2 (2006): 153–90.

[21]Mary Beck and Lindsay Biesterfeld, "A National Putative Father Registry-With Appendix Survey of Putative Registries by State," *Capital University of Law Review* 36 (2007): 295.

[22]Peter Conn, *Adoption: A Brief Social and Cultural History* (New York: Palgrave Macmillan, 2013).

Reproductive technologies are about making babies for people who want them (and can afford assisted reproduction), but adoption is about finding families for children who need them. The simple fact that approximately 112,000 children in the foster care system are waiting to be adopted, not to mention hundreds of thousands of children worldwide who require families, is morally telling.[23] The particular vulnerability of children calls for socially coordinated responses to disruptions in their caregiving. Children need temporary or permanent family placements for a variety of reasons. While the fact that some children will need foster care or adoption is perennial—illness, accident, and violence can orphan anyone—trends in children's need for temporary or permanent care are also symptomatic of larger social pressures. Consider the current opioid addiction crisis afflicting communities across the United States, which is increasing the need for foster and adoptive parents. Because children are distinctively vulnerable human beings given their significant and long-term dependence on adult caregivers, and because there will always be cases in which their caregiving networks are disrupted and alternative arrangements need to be made, Christian ethics should invest more energy and attention into understanding and promoting adequate and ethical social systems to assist children in need.

Beyond the fact that children require and deserve well-coordinated, compassionate, and ethical social responses to their need for alternative familial care, adoption is better approached within the realm of social ethics than sexual ethics because many of the most significant moral issues connected with adoption concern social systems and forces that unjustly *exacerbate* the need for foster and adoptive placements. Indeed, perhaps the most urgent moral issues concern broader social structures surrounding adoption, though they seldom receive significant attention in Christian ethics. Importantly, although the topic of adoption may conjure images of a teenager confronting an unplanned pregnancy or a nonfertile couple adopting an infant, the vast majority of domestic adoptions are by stepparents or extended biological family members. Adoption, whether by stepparents, extended family, or by strangers, is a reparative response to the breakdown of the original biological family. Many birthparents are already parenting children and may consider adoption as a resolution for an unplanned pregnancy in order to continue to care for their prior children as best they can.[24] These demographic features of adoption show that adoption reflects more basic economic and social realities.

What kind of economy do we live within where parents must relinquish their children in order to survive economically? What kind of culture do we live within where parents lack access to the social support systems that would provide sufficient health care (including mental health services), affordable childcare, and social services to enable them to parent their children? Adoption is not only a matter of finding families for children in need of them. It is also, unfortunately, about policing poor families and families of color. Even a cursory study of practices within family services programs in the United States shows significant disparities between the treatment of white families and families of color.[25]

[23]The number of children in foster care is substantially larger. Roughly 428,000 children are in the foster system who may be reunited with their biological parents. US Department of Health and Human Services, Administration for Children and Families, Administration on Children, Youth and Families, Children's Bureau, "The AFCARS Report: Preliminary FY 2015 Estimates as of June 2016," no. 23 (Adoption and Foster Care Analysis and Reporting System), https://www.acf.hhs.gov/sites/default/files/cb/afcarsreport23.pdf.

[24]Lee Hipple and Barb Haflich, "Adoption's Forgotten Clients: Birth Siblings," *Child and Adolescent Social Work Journal* 10, no. 1 (1993): 53–65.

[25]Tanya Asim Cooper, "Racial Bias in American Foster Care; the National Debate," *Marquette Law Review* 97, no. 2 (2013): 243.

Moreover, although specific financial issues involving adoption fees and facilitators were noted above, it is important to attend to larger economic pressures that make it difficult for women to parent their children and which can induce women to relinquish children for adoption.

Adoption is best approached within the realm of social ethics not only because it is a response to children's needs that has social implications, and not only because social forces contribute to unjust family separations, but because the mere fact that so many children must wait for, and so many never receive, permanent families is itself a moral scandal. Children in the foster system face significant odds against being adopted based on age, membership in a sibling group that would ideally be adopted into the same family, or health needs. They are heartbreakingly known as "waiting children." What kind of culture do we live within, where children in need of stable, permanent homes wait for years, and age out of foster care into legal adulthood, while adults with the means to provide homes for them do not welcome these children?

ADOPTION AND ADOPTIVE FAMILIES AS A MICROCOSM FOR CHRISTIAN ETHICS

Adoption and adoptive families are more than a niche issue within Christian ethics. They illuminate key theological and moral commitments in Christian ethics, basic human moral experiences, and urgent moral issues. Adoption and adoptive families concern a range of ethical issues that are morally significant for all persons.

Adoption and adoptive families manifest key themes and convictions in Christian faith. To be a Christian is to be an adoptee. In baptism one's family of origin is superseded by one's new ecclesial family. Baptism is an adoption ceremony that reconfigures a Christian's primary loyalty. These claims may seem odd. Contemporary Christian culture in the United States often seems to link faith and family (not to mention patriotism) in a manner that implies there is no tension between them whatsoever. As our discussion of sources showed, however, Christian thinking about kinship is deeply informed by an appreciation of the subversive power of discipleship. Following Jesus Christ means becoming part of a new family.

All this is to say that adoption and the experiences of adoptive families can teach us a great deal about the ways we negotiate identity and construct other people *as* "other" or as "one of us," "my own," or as "family." To whom do we belong? What grounds our identity? What do we owe others? How should we distribute our resources, energy, and concern among those we identify as "ours" and those who fall outside our special relationships of family, friends, and preferred social circles? The supreme moral command in Christian ethics is to love God with all one's heart, mind, and soul, and to love one's neighbor as oneself (Mk 12:30-31). Biblical sources and Christian tradition further teach us that the category of neighbor is to be defined in a radically inclusive manner. All fellow human beings are our neighbors, and all deserve to be loved as we love ourselves. To be sure, Christian moral life includes ongoing judgments about how to adjudicate our limited amounts of time and resources, but given human tendencies to make these judgments under the influence of sinful forms of self-interest, Christian moral development involves an ongoing commitment to enlarge the scope of our moral concern for others in ever more inclusive directions, and to make care for vulnerable neighbors our priority. Adoption and adoptive families teach us that we are capable of *choosing* to make an "other" our "own."

Like any ethics, Christian ethics evaluates not only social structures but also people's choices, behaviors, and character traits. Moreover, like any ethics, Christian ethics can exercise this evaluative work in ways that range from rigid to lax and punitive to merciful. The moral evaluation of one's own and others' choices should be undertaken with a commitment to truthful moral insight, just consideration of others, and compassion.

Adoption and adoptive families can teach us several things about evaluating others' choices. Adoption always involves the interplay of deeply personal decisions situated within social structures and "choice architectures" that affect the real or apparent choices available to us and the ways we make them. Adoption teaches us that the practice of making moral judgments about other's choices needs to be mindful of the complexity of our moral lives as well as the weighty consequences of our choices.

WHAT YOU ARE NOW OBLIGATED TO DO

This chapter has argued that the ethics of adoption and adoptive families should concern every person, not only members of the adoption triad, and that adoption and adoptive families provide a microcosm for Christian ethics. It ends with several moral obligations, obligations that can be grounded in appeals to human dignity or human rights without any explicit reference to religious faith. However, Christian convictions sharpen these obligations for followers of Jesus Christ.

To begin, every adult should carefully discern whether they are able to adopt or foster children in need. Consider in particular whether you can welcome children who are harder to place with permanent families. Second, help to reframe adoption and members of the adoptive triad. Resist the presentation of adoption as a second choice to be considered only by infertile couples or morally heroic persons. Monitor the ways you speak about adoption and members of the adoptive triad and call out others when they make disparaging remarks, including seemingly benign jokes about placing one's children for adoption or teasing a family member that they might be adopted. Stop referring to biological children as children of "one's own." Third, advocate for children and families, particularly for meaningful social safety nets and for transparent and ethical practices related to family welfare and adoption. Speak to your political representatives about the importance of quality social services. Educate yourself about and fight against the insidious presence of racism in departments of children and family services. Support access to quality prenatal care, quality childcare, and generous family leave policies, things that make it easier for birthparents to parent their children, and that might make it easier for would-be adoptive parents to make a commitment to a child who needs a family. Learn the signs of human trafficking, report suspicious circumstances, and support organizations that combat trafficking. Fourth, take responsibility for your own procreative potential. Inform yourselves about laws regarding parental rights and child relinquishment, particularly putative father registries. Fifth, cultivate virtues that are essential for caring about other people's children—empathy, compassion, justice, and solidarity—as well as cultural competencies necessary to do so. Evaluate your choices in terms of how they contribute to or detract from the social conditions other families require if they are to stay intact and flourish. Hundreds of thousands of children need stable families *right now* and we fail them miserably if we adults do not each ask ourselves what we can do to meet their needs.

SUGGESTED READINGS

Freundlich, Madelyn. *Adoption and Ethics*, vols. 1–4. Washington, DC: Child Welfare League of America, 2000.

Jackson, Timothy P. *The Morality of Adoption: Social-Psychological, Theological, and Legal Perspectives*. Grand Rapids: Eerdmans, 2005.

Meilaender, Gilbert. *Not by Nature but by Grace: Forming Families through Adoption*. Notre Dame: University of Notre Dame Press, 2016.

CHAPTER FORTY-SIX

Nondiscrimination Legislation and Sexual Orientation and Gender: A Critical Analysis of the Catholic Position[1]

TODD A. SALZMAN AND MICHAEL G. LAWLER

By common theological agreement, the data to which Christian ethicists attend—on which they reflect, about which they seek to understand, on the basis of which they make ethical judgments and decide to act on them—are mined from what is referred to as the Wesleyan Quadrilateral, four established sources of ethical knowledge in the Christian perspective: scripture, tradition, reason, and human experience. Because they are more pertinent to the question at hand, in this chapter we draw especially from Catholic tradition, reason, and experience to analyze and evaluate the United States Conference of Catholic Bishops' (USCCB's) response to the Employment Nondiscrimination Act (ENDA), which prohibits discrimination on the basis of sexual orientation and gender identity.[2]

In 2016, Georgia and North Carolina were embroiled in controversy over ENDA-like legislation and claims to religious liberty. The governor of Georgia vetoed legislation that would have permitted discrimination against the LGBT community; the governor of North Carolina supported similar legislation. A 2016 survey reveals overwhelming support for

---

[1] An earlier attempt at addressing this topic may be found at Todd A. Salzman and Michael G. Lawler, "Religious Liberty and Gender and Sexual Orientation Nondiscrimination Legislation: A Critical Analysis of the Catholic Perspective," *Journal of Religion and Society Supplement* 14 (2017): 105–32.

[2] United States Conference of Catholic Bishops, "Questions and Answers about the Employment Non-Discrimination Act" (2013) [hereinafter *Backgrounder*], http://www.usccb.org/issues-and-action/human-life-and-dignity/labor-employment/upload/enda-backgrounder-2013.pdf. In 2019, the United States House of Representatives passed the Equality Act, which expands the protections of ENDA. The legislation has stalled in the Senate. The USCCB issued a document critiquing the Equality Act, with many of the same arguments that it used to critique ENDA legislation ("Questions and Answers about the Equality Act of 2019: Sexual Orientation, Gender Identity, and Religious Liberty Issues," http://www.usccb.org/issues-and-action/marriage-and-family/marriage/promotion-and-defense-of-marriage/upload/Equality-Act-Backgrounder.pdf). Our critical-analysis of the USCCB's response to ENDA applies to the similar arguments in its response to the Equality Act.

ENDA laws among the public (71 percent) and Catholic populations (73 percent).[3] Many states have already passed ENDA laws, but there is an ongoing resistance to those laws from Catholic bishops who argue they are a violation of religious freedom.

In April 2015, an urgent communication was issued by the Nebraska Catholic Conference (NCC) regarding a proposed state legislative bill prohibiting all discrimination on the basis of sexual orientation and gender identity. Among other things, it warned the bill "would prevent a Catholic school from reprimanding a transgender male coach who insists on using the girls' shower and restroom facilities" and "would require employers, including Catholic schools, to engage in employment practices that would affirm sexual behavior contrary to Church teaching."[4] These statements are drawn from the USCCB's *Backgrounder*, which argues against ENDA legislation.

In the *Backgrounder*, there is a brief nod to the Catholic teaching that "all people ... possess an innate human dignity that must be acknowledged and respected by other persons and by the law," but this is quickly qualified by fear-mongering language that claims ENDA-like legislation promotes unethical sexual behavior and threatens religious liberty. The fundamental question surrounding the issue of religious freedom and ENDA is how to balance one person's civil right to religious freedom with the civil rights of others when the two rights conflict. The claims for religious freedom in both the USCCB and NCC statements have evolved from seeking to protect the *ad intra* practice of religious institutions to seeking to protect also its *ad extra* practice in a pluralist society. The bishops seek to move beyond a religious exemption from a *just* law to advocate for the repeal of nondiscrimination law they regard as *unjust*. How, we ask, did we get to this point?

USCCB ON RELIGIOUS FREEDOM AND ENDA: A CRITICAL ANALYSIS

In April 2012, the USCCB issued *A Statement on Religious Liberty* that contains alarmist language that freedoms in the United States are "threatened" and that "religious liberty is under attack."[5] There are two issues in the text that have a bearing on the USCCB's stance against ENDA legislation: the common good and just and unjust laws. We consider each in turn and conclude that ENDA legislation is a civil rights imperative that the Catholic Church is obligated to support in a pluralist American society.

The USCCB *Statement* proclaims that "what is at stake is whether America will continue to have a free, creative, and robust civil society—or whether the state alone will determine who gets to contribute to the common good, and how they get to do it."[6] This claim, of course, requires definitions of the common good, the role of the church in relation to the common good, and whether and how ENDA legislation threatens the common good. The Second Vatican Council describes the common good as "the sum of

---

[3]Betsy Cooper et al., "Beyond Same-Sex Marriage: Attitudes on LGBT Nondiscrimination Laws and Religious Exemptions from the 2015 American Values Atlas," Public Religion Research Institute, February 18, 2016, https://www.prri.org/research/poll-same-sex-gay-marriage-lgbt-nondiscrimination-religious-liberty/.

[4]Nebraska Catholic Conference, "LB 586 Information," February 27, 2015, https://creightonprep.creighton.edu/cf_news/view.cfm?newsid=1073.

[5]United States Conference of Catholic Bishops, *Our First, Most Cherished Liberty: Statement on Religious Liberty* (2012) [hereafter, *Statement*], http://www.usccb.org/issues-and-action/religious-liberty/our-first-most-cherished-liberty.cfm.

[6]Ibid.

those conditions of social life which allow social groups and their individual members relatively thorough and ready access to their own fulfillment."[7] What facilitates this social and personal fulfillment is good, ethical, and to be supported; what frustrates it is evil, unethical, and to be opposed. Sociological surveys reveal a pluralism within the church with respect to sexual norms and this pluralism has implications for, first, defining and, then, realizing the common good.[8]

How, we ask, are we to realize the common good in the public realm given the pluralism both inside and outside the Catholic Church? On the one hand, the USCCB emphasizes that every person's human rights must be protected; on the other hand, this "should be done without sacrificing the bedrock of society that is marriage and the family and without violating the religious liberty of persons and institutions."[9] ENDA legislation presents a conflict of values between protecting human rights and protecting religious freedom, marriage, and family as these are defined by the bishops. David Hollenbach and Thomas Shannon raise the question: "When and how is civil legislation an appropriate means for the promotion of the ethical norms taught by the Church's Magisterium?"[10] They respond by arguing, correctly in our opinion, that there needs to be a reevaluation of both the church's role in defining and realizing the common good and how this definition and realization should influence the church's involvement in the political realm.

With its opposition to ENDA legislation, the USCCB has shifted its religious liberty claims from exemptions from a just law on the basis of conscience to repeal of an unjust law. They explain in the *Statement*: "Conscientious objection permits some relief to those who object to a just law for reasons of conscience. ... An unjust law is 'no law at all.' It cannot be obeyed, and therefore one does not seek relief from it, but rather its repeal."[11] ENDA legislation, the bishops maintain, is an unjust law and should be repealed. The justification for their claim is in reality a bias against people with a homosexual orientation, and distorted notions of gender, religious liberty, and conscience. We consider each in turn.

THE USCCB ON SEXUAL ORIENTATION AND GENDER

The USCCB's *Backgrounder* focuses on ENDA's definition of sexual orientation and the problems that definition poses. ENDA fails, the bishops argue, to distinguish between "sexual inclination" and "sexual conduct," and since that distinction has not been made, "courts have construed a term such as 'homosexuality' to protect both same-sex attraction and same-sex conduct."[12] Catholic teaching distinguishes between homosexual acts, judged to be intrinsically unethical, and homosexual inclination, judged to be "objectively disordered" but not unethical.[13] Since ENDA makes no distinction between

[7]Second Vatican Council, *Gaudium et spes*, in *The Documents of Vatican II*, ed. Walter M. Abbott, SJ (Piscataway: New Century, 1966), § 26.

[8]See, e.g., Robert P. Jones and Daniel Cox, "Catholic Attitudes on Gay and Lesbian Issues," Public Religion Research Institute, March 2011, http://friendsandfamilyplan.org/wp-content/uploads/2012/10/Public-Religion-Catholics-and-LGBT-Issues-Survey-Report.pdf.

[9]United States Conference of Catholic Bishops, "Marriage: Love and Life in the Divine Plan," November 17, 2009, http://www.usccb.org/upload/marriage-love-life-divine-plan-2009.pdf.

[10]David Hollenbach, SJ, and Thomas Shannon, "A Balancing Act: Catholic Teaching on the Church's Rights—and the Rights of All," *America*, March 5, 2012, http://americamagazine.org/issue/5131/article/balancing-act.

[11]USCCB, *Statement*.

[12]USCCB, *Backgrounder*.

[13]*Catechism of the Catholic Church* (New Jersey: Paulist, 1994), § 2358.

sexual inclination and sexual conduct, and it *might* happen that some homosexuals will engage in homosexual acts (though many are celibate), it is just and ethical to discriminate against them since the church "teaches that all sexual acts outside of the marriage of one man and one woman are ethically wrong and do not serve the good of the person or society."[14] On this basis, all employers, religious and nonreligious alike, can exercise their religious freedom by claiming an exemption from an already approved law or by repealing proposed ENDA legislation.

There are several possible responses to the USCCB's argument. First, its *Backgrounder* asserts the Catholic teaching that all sexual acts outside of heterosexual marriage and all sexual acts within marriage not open to procreation are unethical. A religious exemption from ENDA is based in part on the concern that the failure to distinguish between sexual orientation and sexual act would force employers to promote unethical sexual activity. If this is really the USCCB's argument, it should argue that there should also be a religious exemption to discriminate against both married heterosexuals who *might* use artificial contraceptives or have oral or anal sex and unmarried heterosexuals who also *might* engage in any of these unethical actions. Heterosexuals *might* engage in unethical sexual acts that would "not serve the good of the person or society" every bit as much as homosexuals *might* engage in unethical homosexual acts. The USCCB has not made this logical argument, which would indicate that its objection is not to unethical sexual acts but simply to homosexual orientation and acts. By rejecting ENDA legislation, the USCCB is violating the common good and the protection of individual human dignity by promoting both a generalization that homosexuals *might* engage in unethical sexual acts and unjust discrimination against even celibate homosexuals performing no homosexual acts.

There is a more fundamental response to the USCCB's concern with homosexual activity, one that challenges the very claim that homosexual activity is intrinsically unethical and destructive of human dignity. The Catholic Church has consistently taught that homosexual acts are intrinsically unethical, but that teaching is now seriously challenged and surveys show that the majority of contemporary Catholics do not accept it.[15] The fact that the majority of Catholics do not accept Catholic teaching on the ethics of homosexual acts is not, of course, a compelling argument that they are ethical. Ethics is not determined by majority consensus. The burden of proof, however, is on the church to make a compelling argument that convinces both Catholic and non-Catholic citizens that its teaching in this case is true. Hollenbach and Shannon advise, and we agree, that "the church should not ask the State to do what it has not been able to convince its own members to do."[16] The burden of proof is on the church to demonstrate that homosexual acts are destructive of human dignity and cannot serve "the good of the person or society," and so far it has not offered any argument that has been found to be compelling. An unproven assertion should not be advanced as the basis for an abuse of religious freedom aimed at repealing ENDA legislation and imposing on the broader society the church's ethically questionable and broadly questioned teaching on the immorality of homosexual acts.

---

[14]USCCB, *Backgrounder*.

[15]Michael J. O'Loughlin, "Poll Finds Many U.S. Catholics Breaking with Church over Contraception, Abortion, and L.G.B.T. Rights," *America*, September 28, 2016, reports that only 32 percent of the Catholics believe that homosexual acts are wrong and only 13 percent believe that contraceptive acts are wrong.

[16]Hollenbach and Shannon, "A Balancing Act."

The bishops argue that ENDA uses law to support a misperception of gender as "nothing more than a social construct or psychosocial reality that can be chosen at variance from one's biological sex."[17] According to Catholic views on gender, humans are born with not only female or male *sex* but also female or male *gender* designed to serve the complementarity of spouses in the sexual relationship between a man and a woman in a monogamous marriage. Reducing gender to a social construct or to a psychological reality would allow for a continuum between the physical sex of a person and the perceived psychological and/or social perception of gender that would, in turn, allow for gender transformation that violates the gender identity assigned by God.

The distinction between biological sex (male/female) and socially construed gender (masculine/feminine) is frequently absent in magisterial discussions of gender.[18] There are also gender stereotypes in magisterial documents where femaleness is defined primarily in terms of motherhood, receptivity, and nurturing, and maleness is defined primarily in terms of fatherhood, initiation, and activity.[19] This claim of ontological gendered psychological traits does not recognize the culturally construed nature of gender, and does not adequately reflect the complexity of the human person and her/his relationships. Within individuals and relationships, psychoaffective, social, and spiritual traits are not "natural" to one gender but may be found in both genders.[20] The masculinity and femininity of nonbiological elements are construed by culture and are not essential components of male and female human nature.[21] The church's view of gender as a biological given is blind to its different construals across the world's various cultures.

The bishops also assert that ENDA's definition of gender identity "would adversely affect the privacy and associational rights of others."[22] It "would prevent a Catholic school from reprimanding a transgender male coach who insists on using the girls' shower and restroom facilities."[23] We have two responses to these assertions. First, if experientially reliable evidence is a source of ethical knowledge and a basis in assisting in the construction of an ethical argument, and we believe it is,[24] then there is no reliable evidence of transgendered male coaches or teachers who insist on using female facilities of any kind. There is, however, ample experience in America of workplace discrimination based on sexual orientation and gender identity.[25] Second, federal law and many state laws include the categories of gender and sexual orientation as bases for hate crimes

[17]USCCB, *Backgrounder*.

[18]Susan A. Ross, "The Bridegroom and the Bride: The Theological Anthropology of John Paul II and Its Relation to the Bible and Homosexuality," in *Sexual Diversity and Catholicism: Toward the Development of Ethical Theology*, ed. Patricia Beattie Jung with Joseph A. Coray (Collegeville: Liturgical, 2001), 56, n. 5.

[19]See Pope John Paul II, *Familiaris consortio* (Vatican City: Libreria Editrice Vaticana, 1981), § 23; "Letter to Women," June 29, 1995, § 9, https://w2.vatican.va/content/john-paul-ii/en/letters/1995/documents/hf_jp-ii_let_29061995_women.html.

[20]Christina Traina, "Papal Ideals, Marital Realities: One View from the Ground," in *Sexual Diversity and Catholicism: Toward the Development of Ethical Theology*, ed. Patricia Beattie Jung with Joseph A. Coray (Collegeville: Liturgical, 2001), 280–2.

[21]Elaine L. Graham, *Making the Difference: Gender, Personhood, and Theology* (Minneapolis: Fortress, 1996).

[22]USCCB, *Backgrounder*.

[23]Nebraska Catholic Conference, "LB 586 Information."

[24]Michael G. Lawler and Todd A. Salzman, "Human Experience and Catholic Moral Theology," *Irish Theological Quarterly* 76 (2011): 35–56.

[25]Brad Sears and Christy Mallory, "Documented Evidence of Employment Discrimination & Its Effects on LGBT People," The Williams Institute, July 2011, http://williamsinstitute.law.ucla.edu/wp-content/uploads/Sears-Mallory-Discrimination-July-2011.pdf.

and for increasing the penalties for such crimes.[26] The multiplicity of lawsuits charging discrimination in housing and employment on the basis of sexual orientation and sexual identity and of hate crimes rooted in the same issues disproves any claim that, since proponents of ENDA legislation cannot produce experiential evidence of "widespread" employment discrimination based on sexual orientation and gender identity, it is not a legal or ethical concern.

The USCCB also cites religious liberty to argue for exemption from or repeal of ENDA legislation. Douglas Laycock notes that "reliance on a distinction between just laws that violate the tenets of a particular faith, for which the solution is an exemption, and unjust laws for which the only solution is repeal" is the most problematic aspect of the bishops' *Statement* on religious liberty.[27] Seeking an exemption or repeal on the basis of religious liberty is to confuse the arguments about ethical issues and religious liberty.[28]

The USCCB cites Pope Benedict in his defense of religious liberty: "Many of you have pointed out that concerted efforts have been made to deny the right of conscientious objection on the part of Catholic individuals and institutions with regard to cooperation in intrinsically evil practices."[29] Among those intrinsically evil practices are homosexual acts and contraception. As Hollenbach and Shannon note, however, again correctly, "Catholic ethical tradition has long stressed that civil law should be founded on ethical values but need not seek to abolish all unethical activities in society."[30] The bishops are free to assert that governments should exclude homosexuals from employment and from becoming foster or adoptive parents. That, however, is an ethical assertion seeking to regulate life in the public society, and we can ask if such an ethical argument should be codified in legislation? It is one thing for a religious institution to claim an exemption from a just law based on conscientious objection to the ethical contents of the law, it is quite another to seek repeal of a law based on that objection. The bishops have not made this distinction in their resistance to ENDA legislation and seek to make Catholic ethical doctrines on sexuality the law of the nation. They claim that ENDA laws are "unjust laws" because they promote unethical sexual conduct. They note that it is essential to understand the distinction between conscientious objection and law. Conscientious objection seeks a religious exemption from a just law. "An unjust law is 'no law at all.' It cannot be obeyed, and therefore one does not seek relief from it, but rather its repeal."[31] Laycock notes correctly, "The difference between exemption and repeal is the difference between seeking religious liberty for Catholic institutions and seeking to impose Catholic ethical teaching on the nation."[32]

In their *Statement*, borrowing Martin Luther King's phrase, the bishops want to be the "conscience of the state." They seek to extend Catholic ethical teaching beyond a religious exemption from a just law to the repeal of what they view as an unjust law. Although the Catholic Church teaches that same-sex relationships, abortion, and contraception are ethically wrong, a majority of Americans consider them basic human rights. As William

[26]Ibid. The Matthew Shepard and James Byrd Jr. Hate Crimes Prevention Act expands a federal hate-crimes law to include crimes committed against people based on gender identity or sexual orientation.
[27]Douglas Laycock, in William Galston, "The Bishops & Religious Liberty," *Commonweal*, May 30, 2012, https://www.commonwealmagazine.org/bishops-religious-liberty.
[28]Ibid.
[29]USCCB, *Statement*.
[30]Hollenbach and Shannon, "A Balancing Act."
[31]USCCB, *Statement*.
[32]Laycock, in Galston, "Bishops & Religious Liberty."

Galston notes, "The bishops make no effort to understand why their antagonists think that justice requires what the Catholic hierarchy thinks it forbids."[33] The bishops have every right to teach an ethical position and to seek to protect religious institutions from participating in what they perceive as unethical activity, but they have no right to seek to impose their ethical teachings legislatively on a pluralistic society. To do so would be an ultimate act of proselytizing and could lead to prohibited violation of well-informed consciences.

CONSCIENCE AND ITS ROLE IN ENDA LEGISLATION

Already in the thirteenth century, Thomas Aquinas established the authority and inviolability of conscience.[34] Seven hundred years after Aquinas, the Second Vatican Council taught in *Gaudium et spes* that "conscience is the most secret core and sanctuary of man. There he is alone with God whose voice echoes in his depth. In a wonderful manner conscience reveals that law which is fulfilled by love of God and neighbor."[35] In *Dignitatis Humanae* the Council went further to assert the inviolability of conscience:

> In all his activity a man is bound to follow his conscience faithfully, in order that he may come to God for whom he was created. It follows that he is not to be forced to act contrary to his conscience. Nor, on the other hand, is he to be restrained from acting in accordance with his conscience, especially in matters religious.[36]

Several points are evident from these conciliar statements on the nature and inviolability of conscience. First, conscience is sacred; it is a gift from God.[37] Second, it is an intrinsic faculty of the human person.[38] Third, following one's conscience on ethical issues facilitates human dignity; violating one's conscience on ethical issues frustrates human dignity.[39] Fourth, no one is ever to be forced to act against her or his conscience; such force is a fundamental violation of conscience and of human dignity.[40] Fifth, the authority granted to conscience presumes that one's conscience is well-formed.[41]

While the freedom, authority, and inviolability of personal conscience are all affirmed in Catholic tradition, in the public realm they must all be assessed against the competing freedom, authority, and inviolability of the consciences of others, and in particular against the responsibility to promote the common good in a pluralistic society. In their statements, the bishops seem to be unaware of any competing rights and responsibilities and present their particular religious freedom as an absolute. In the final part of the *Statement*, the authors issue an invitation to fellow bishops to "be bold, clear, and insistent in warning against threats to the rights of our people. Let us attempt to be the 'conscience of the state.'"[42] As M. Cathleen Kaveny points out, however, "Vatican II's

---

[33]Galston, "Bishops & Religious Liberty."

[34]Thomas Aquinas, *In IV Sent.*, dist. 38, q. 2, art. 4: "Anyone upon whom the ecclesiastical authorities, in ignorance of the true facts, impose a demand that offends against his clear conscience should perish in excommunication rather than violate his conscience."

[35]*Gaudium et spes*, § 16.

[36]*Dignitatis Humanae*, § 3.

[37]*Gaudium et spes*, § 16.

[38]Ibid.

[39]Ibid., and *Dignitatis Humanae*, § 3.

[40]*Dignitatis Humanae*, § 3.

[41]*Gaudium et spes*, § 16.

[42]USCCB, *Statement*.

Declaration on Religious Freedom recognizes that there are 'due limits' on the exercise of religious freedom, including the need to promote a 'just public order,' and preserve the 'equality of the citizens before the law.'"[43] This equality of citizens before the law in a democratic, pluralistic society, in which one person's or one institution's exercise of conscience and religious liberty can come up against another person's or institution's exercise of conscience and religious liberty raises serious questions of conscience.

Douglas NeJaime and Reva Siegel refer to these conscience questions as "conscience wars" that are manifested in "complicity-based conscience claims." These are "faith claims about how to live in community with others who do not share the claimant's beliefs, and whose lawful conduct the person of faith believes to be sinful."[44] It is one thing to follow one's conscience on religious and ethical matters; it is quite another *to force* one's conscience on religious and ethical matters legislatively onto others who disagree. Such enforcing may be a violation of conscience for, and can cause extensive dignitary harm to, others.

The bishops have taken it upon themselves to become the "conscience of the state" in sexual matters, seeking to impose Catholic sexual ethics on the broader society and moving beyond a mere exemption from a just law to advocating for repeal of what they perceive as an unjust law based on their judgment that the law violates their ethical code. What is most striking about the bishops' strategy in claims to religious liberty is the absolute nature of those claims, the use of their freedom of conscience to justify those claims, and the total ignoring of the equal freedom of conscience of others who disagree with them. "If we are not free in our conscience and our practice of religion," the bishops write, "all other freedoms are fragile. If citizens are not free in their own consciences, how can they be free in relation to others, or to the state?"[45] True, but there is an underlying problem that is ignored: when my conscience conflicts with the consciences of others and I seek to impose my claims of conscience legislatively, the consciences of others will be violated. Kaveny notes correctly that the bishops provide no indication that such claims "must be assessed in a framework of competing rights and duties [and, we add, informed consciences], particularly the duty to promote the common good."[46]

Rights claims and conscience claims must always take into consideration relational responsibilities. Complicity-based conscience claims attempt to impose one person's or one institution's conscience on another person's or institution's conscience under the umbrella of religious freedom and the maintenance of the ethical integrity of individuals or institutions to avoid complicity in sin. It is one thing to make such a claim on undisputed ethical issues such as race and segregation, where there is virtually unanimous social and ethical agreement that they are fundamental violations of the common good. It is quite another to make the claim on disputed sexual ethical issues where the majority of the people in the society, including the majority of Catholics with well-informed consciences, disagree with Catholic sexual teachings.

---

[43] M. Cathleen Kaveny, in Galston, "The Bishops & Religious Liberty."
[44] Douglas NeJaime and Reva B. Siegel, "Conscience Wars: Complicity-Based Conscience Claims in Religion and Politics," *Yale Law Journal* 124, no. 7 (2015): 2519.
[45] USCCB, *Statement*.
[46] Kaveny, in Galston, "Bishops & Religious Liberty."

CONCLUSION

Catholic bishops have every right to advocate for their sexual ethical teachings and for abstention from actions they deem unethical; they do not have the right to impose their ethical teachings legislatively in a society where the majority of citizens conscientiously disagree. That would be the worst kind of proselytism. Neither do they have any right to arrogate to themselves Martin Luther King's claim to be the "conscience of the state." King was, indeed, the genuine "conscience of the state" for civil rights; the bishops' claims trample on the civil rights of LGBT citizens that King fought so hard to validate.

SUGGESTED READINGS

Graham, Elaine L. *Making the Difference: Gender, Personhood, and Theology*. Minneapolis: Fortress, 1996.

Kaveny, M. Cathleen. *A Culture of Engagement: Law, Religion, and Morality*. Washington, DC: Georgetown University Press, 2016.

Salzman, Todd A., and Michael G. Lawler. *The Sexual Person: Toward a Renewed Catholic Anthropology*. Washington, DC: Georgetown University Press, 2008.

Thatcher, Adrian, ed. *Oxford Handbook of Theology, Sexuality, and Gender*. Oxford: Oxford University Press, 2015.

Thatcher, Adrian. *Redeeming Gender*. Oxford: Oxford University Press, 2016.

Conclusion: Christian Ethics: Past, Present, and Future

ANDREA VICINI, SJ

At the end of the engaging and demanding journey that has been reading this volume one might wonder where we, as readers, find ourselves. Are we oriented toward the past, perched on a theological approach that informed the reasoning and the actions of those who, centuries ago, preceded us? Christian ethics was quite a different endeavor then.[1] The moral agents, knowledgeable in moral theology, were few and they belonged to the hierarchical, ecclesial elite. Reflections on moral agency were centered on sins and, at the same time, on how to avoid them and set the apt penances. Finally, the historical context revealed a very highly stratified society, but where the various social strata were not necessarily isolated. Any type of social fluidity that existed was not marked by social mobility, but by the social proximity of the citizens belonging to the multiple social layers that constituted past societies.[2] Such a past is gone, some could say. However, one wonders whether, still, in our present, there are some traces of what we thought was gone, whether these fragments concern the moral agents, or moral agency, or the context.

Today, in the present, the moral agents are many, and generally more empowered, but, sadly, we continue to witness marginalization and exclusion, whether because of one's sex or gender, race, ethnicity (e.g., in the case of indigenous peoples), social or geographical location, lack of education, and disabilities. Agency continues to be curtailed by the increasing racial violence and the intolerant and arrogant nationalist populisms

[1]See John Mahoney, SJ, *The Making of Moral Theology: A Study of the Roman Catholic Tradition*, The Martin D'Arcy Memorial Lectures 1981–2, Clarendon Paperbacks (Oxford: Oxford University Press, 1987); Charles E. Curran, *Moral Theology at the End of the Century*, The Pere Marquette Lecture in Theology 1999 (Milwaukee: Marquette University Press, 1999); James F. Keenan, SJ, *A History of Catholic Moral Theology in the Twentieth Century: From Confessing Sins to Liberating Consciences* (London: Continuum, 2010). See also the following volumes of Marciano Vidal in his series *Historia de la Teología Moral*, published by Editorial Perpetuo Socorro (Madrid): *La Moral en el Cristianismo Antiguo (ss. I–VII)*, 2010; *Moral y Espiritualidad en la Cristiandad Medieval (ss. VIII–XIV)*, 2011; *La Moral en la Edad Moderna (ss. XV–XVI): Vol. 1: Humanismo y Reforma*, 2012; *La Moral en la Edad Moderna (ss. XV–XVI): Vol. 2: América: "Problema Moral,"* 2012; *De Trento al Vaticano II: Vol. 1. Crisis de la Razón y Rigorismo Moral en el Barroco (s. XVII)*, 2015; *De Trento al Vaticano II: Vol. 2. El Siglo de la Ilustración y la Moral Católica (s. XVIII)*, 2017; *De Trento al Vaticano II: Vol. 3: Alfonso de Liguori (1696–1787): El Triunfo de la Benignidad Frente al Rigorismo, Moral y Ética Teológica*, 2019.

[2]See Zygmund Bauman, *Liquid Modernity* (Cambridge: Polity, 2000).

that, from the United States to India and the Philippines—just to name a few countries across the globe—cause an expanding and worrying disempowerment. Climate change, with its dire consequences for all living creatures, is already beginning to affect the poor in the Global South and further deepens the current national and global context marked by sharp and deep inequities. Lack of hope and the difficulty to envision a better future become an unwelcomed but forced refuge for many.

In ways that counter any lack of hope, globally, today Christian ethics offers multiple reasons to hope. This book witnesses the hopeful engagement of many scholars and practitioners who contribute to the articulation of theologically ethical thinking and praxes, joining many more who, on the ground—in cities, towns, from the steppe to the savanna—work for a better present aiming at promoting the common good for the whole planet. Revisiting anew the four foundational sources of Christian ethics, Part 1 nourishes hope. Scripture, tradition, experience, and any reasoned approach to reality continue to provide solid and dynamic foundations to ethical thinking and action, with the wisdom of the past and the openness to the present and to the future. In Part 2, the multiplicity of methodological approaches sharpens the ethicists' critical analysis and provides diversified ways to articulate social and ecclesial engagements.

Equipped with a fresh immersion in the sources of Christian ethics, and empowered by the methodological richness of the discipline, in Part 3 thirty-two Christian ethicists frame the ethical agenda for the present generation, while looking at the future, at those who will follow us. First, these colleagues focus on politics as well as social dynamics and phenomena, for example, from migrations to terrorism and cyber warfare. Examining political and social issues entails a continued attention to specific ethical approaches, from human rights to feminist contributions and particular practices. Second, ethical issues in criminal justice are engaged in depth, by considering many of their dimensions: from the ethical legitimacy of punishing versus restorative justice, to critically examining mass incarceration and capital punishment, from policing to the war on drugs and the legalization of marijuana.

With aging populations and a reduced birth rate in the Global North, and continuing health challenges in the Global South (from the plague of infectious diseases to the needed promotion of health care systems and health care delivery), medicine and health care are enduring ethical challenges. Six colleagues study how bioethical reflection influenced the practice of medicine and the delivery of health care in a context marked by profound inequities; they also examine specific issues: from trauma to reproductive technologies, from mental health to end-of-life issues, from genetics to neuroethics.

Economics and ecology further contribute to framing the issues encountered in the social fabric, and they are also part of their solution. Examining human work, wealth, and poverty enriches the needed attention to economic dynamics and systems. Sustainability demands committed ethical actions that address climate change and its consequences for the land and ecosystems, while human beings reflect on their behaviors (e.g., eating) and, in a not-anthropocentric perspective, how nonhuman creatures are affected.

Christian ethics continues to critically examine sexual orientation and practices, gender, marriage, family life, and adoptive families while aiming at flourishing, well-being, and integration to promote just dynamics that foster the common good.

In this volume, the topics frame a renewed agenda, less influenced by disciplinary divisions (i.e., social ethics, bioethics and health care ethics, sexual and family ethics) and more attentive to clusters of ethical issues that today's citizens are facing and struggle with. This choice suggests, on the one hand, the complexity of each area of ethical inquiry beyond disciplinary divisions and, on the other hand, the need of a focused approach that, while aims at being interdisciplinary, articulates the original insights of Christian ethics.

Scholars and practitioners across the planet are dedicated at implementing this agenda, and they further enrich it with their particular and specific cultural contributions. Moreover, training centers in the Global South are changing the face and the voice of Christian ethicists by allowing their particularity and locality to emerge. In the recent decades, networks of ethicists promoted gatherings and initiatives that allowed the decentralization of ethical reasoning from Europe and North America to Nairobi, Manila, Bangalore, Mexico City, Belo Horizonte, Bogota, Buenos Aires, and Santiago de Chile—just to name a few. Among Catholics, since 2006 the network Catholic Theological Ethics in the World Church (CTEWC) promoted global conferences (at Padua in 2006, Trent in 2010, and Sarajevo in 2018) as well as regional conferences in Africa, Asia, East Europe, and Latin America to foster interactions between colleagues from the South and the North, the East and the West.[3] Moreover, a series of collective CTEWC volumes with contributors from all continents makes available to students and colleagues global scholarship by providing opportunities for expanding one's ethical perspectives.[4] To go beyond conferencing, CTEWC just launched virtual engagement involving groups of colleagues across the continents who gather virtually to discuss challenging topics, share expertise, and plan initiatives. Indeed, many of the contributors to this volume have participated in a number of these initiatives and gatherings.

Looking at the future, many cringe with fear. They doubt the ability of the moral agents to face challenges, manifest the moral agency that will empower them, and transform their contexts. However, there are reasons to hope. The contributors of this volume nourish our hope. Inspired by scripture, rooted in the moral tradition, enriched by global, diverse, and plural experiences, illuminated by the contributions of many disciplines, and with the insights that each contributor shared in these pages, as moral agents we live the present, each in particular contexts, aware that we have the ability to promote the common good in the days and years that will follow.

Seneca, a voice from the past, can still inspire us and reinforce our commitment to examine Christian ethics by relying on its past, engage it in the present, and look at the future with hope: "But those who forget the past, neglect the present, and fear for the future have a life that is very brief and troubled; when they have reached the end of it, the poor wretches perceive too late that for such a long while they have been busied in doing nothing."[5]

---

[3]See Christopher Steck, SJ, "Catholic Ethics as Seen from Padua," *Journal of Religious Ethics* 39, no. 2 (June 2011): 365–90; Linda Hogan and Kristin Heyer, "Beyond a Northern Paradigm: Catholic Theological Ethics in Global Perspective," *Journal of the Society of Christian Ethics* 39, no. 1 (Spring/Summer 2019): 21–38; James F. Keenan, "Pursuing Ethics by Building Bridges beyond the Northern Paradigm," *Religions* 10, no. 8 (2019): 490.

[4]As an example, see Antonio Autiero and Laurenti Magesa, eds., *The Catholic Ethicist in the Local Church*, Catholic Theological Ethics in the World Church series (Maryknoll: Orbis, 2018).

[5]Seneca, *On the Shortness of Life*, trans. John W. Basore (Plano: Vigeo, 2016), XVI, 32.

CONTRIBUTORS

Andy Alexis-Baker (PhD, Marquette University) is Clinical Associate Professor of Theology at Arrupe College of Loyola University Chicago.

Trevor George Hunsberger Bechtel (PhD, Loyola University Chicago) is the student engagement coordinator at Poverty Solutions at the University of Michigan.

Kathryn D. Blanchard (PhD, Duke University) is Charles A. Dana Professor of Religious Studies at Alma College.

Elizabeth Sweeny Block (PhD, University of Chicago) is Assistant Professor of Christian Ethics and Theological Studies at Saint Louis University.

James T. Bretzke, SJ (STD, Pontifical Gregorian University) is Professor of Theology at John Carroll University.

David A. Clairmont (PhD, University of Chicago) is Associate Professor of Theology at the University of Notre Dame.

Michelle A. Clifton-Soderstrom (PhD, Loyola University Chicago) is Professor of Theology and Ethics at North Park Theological Seminary.

David L. Clough (PhD, Yale University) is Professor of Theological Ethics at the University of Chester.

David Cloutier (PhD, Duke University) is Associate Professor of Moral Theology at the Catholic University of America.

Elizabeth Agnew Cochran (PhD, University of Notre Dame) is Professor of Theology at Duquesne University.

Elizabeth Collier (PhD, Loyola University Chicago) is Professor of Business Ethics and Christopher Chair in Business Ethics at Dominican University.

Kathryn Lilla Cox (PhD, Fordham University) is a research associate and visiting scholar in the Department of Theology and Religious Studies at the University of San Diego.

Daniel Daly (PhD, Boston College) is Associate Professor of Moral Theology at Boston College School of Theology and Ministry.

Dallas Gingles (PhD, Southern Methodist University) is Associate Director of the Houston-Galveston Extension Program at Perkins School of Theology at Southern Methodist University.

Demetrios Harper (PhD, University of Winchester) is Assistant Professor of Church History and Moral Theology at Holy Trinity Seminary.

Michael P. Jaycox (PhD, Boston College) is Associate Professor of Christian Ethics at Seattle University.

Laurie Johnston (PhD, Boston College) is Associate Professor of Theology and Religious Studies at Emmanuel College.

Conor M. Kelly (PhD, Boston College) is Assistant Professor of Theology at Marquette University.

Jeremy Kidwell (PhD, University of Edinburgh) is Senior Lecturer in Theological Ethics at the University of Birmingham in Edgbaston.

Elisabeth Rain Kincaid (PhD, University of Notre Dame; JD, University of Texas School of Law) is Assistant Professor of Ethics and Moral Theology at Nashotah House Theological Seminary.

Warren Kinghorn (MD, Harvard Medical School; ThD, Duke University Divinity School) is Esther Colliflower Associate Professor of the Practice of Pastoral and Moral Theology at Duke Divinity School, and Associate Professor of Psychiatry at Duke University Medical Center.

Michael G. Lawler (PhD, Aquinas Institute of Theology) is Amelia and Emil Graff Professor of Catholic Theology, Emeritus, Creighton University.

Philip LeMasters (PhD, Duke University) is Professor of Religion at McMurry University.

Amy Levad (PhD, Emory University) is Associate Professor of Moral Theology at the University of St. Thomas in St. Paul, Minnesota.

James Samuel Logan (PhD, Princeton Seminary) is Associate Academic Dean and Professor of Religion and African and African American Studies, Earlham College, Richmond, Indiana.

D. Stephen Long (PhD, Duke University) is the Cary M. Maguire University Professor of Ethics at Southern Methodist University.

Jermaine M. McDonald (PhD, Emory University) is Part-Time Assistant Professor of Ethics with the Seigel Institute for Leadership, Ethics and Character at Kennesaw State University.

Christina McRorie (PhD, University of Virginia) is Assistant Professor of Theology at Creighton University.

Marcus Mescher (PhD, Boston College) is Associate Professor of Christian Ethics at Xavier University in Cincinnati.

Neil Messer (PhD, University of Cambridge) is Professor of Theology at the University of Winchester.

Sarah Moses (PhD, Boston College) is Associate Professor of Religion in the Department of Philosophy and Religion at the University of Mississippi.

Debra Dean Murphy (PhD, Drew University) is Associate Professor of Religious Studies at West Virginia Wesleyan College.

William O'Neill, SJ (PhD, Yale University) is Professor Emeritus of Social Ethics at the Jesuit School of Theology at Santa Clara University.

Karen Peterson-Iyer (PhD, Yale University) is Assistant Professor of Theological and Social Ethics at Santa Clara University.

Elizabeth Phillips (PhD, University of Cambridge) is research fellow at the Margaret Beaufort Institute of Theology.

Esther D. Reed (PhD, Dunelm) is Professor of Theological Ethics at the University of Exeter.

Todd A. Salzman (PhD, Katholieke Universiteit Leuven) is Professor of Catholic Theology at Creighton University.

Daniel Scheid (PhD, Boston College) is Associate Professor of Theology at Duquesne University.

Anna Floerke Scheid (PhD, Boston College) is Associate Professor of Theology at Duquesne University.

Matthew A. Shadle (PhD, University of Dayton) is Associate Professor of Theology and Religious Studies at Marymount University.

Kara N. Slade (PhD, Duke University) is Canon Theologian of the Episcopal Diocese of New Jersey, Adjunct Professor of Theology at Princeton Theological Seminary, and Associate Rector at Trinity Church, Princeton.

Brian Stiltner (PhD, Yale University) is Professor of Theology and Religious Studies at Sacred Heart University.

Andrea Vicini, SJ (STL, PhD, Boston College; MD, University of Bologna) is Michael P. Walsh Professor of Bioethics and Professor of Moral Theology in the Boston College Theology Department.

Aana Marie Vigen (PhD, Union Theological Seminary in New York City) is Associate Professor of Christian Social Ethics at Loyola University Chicago.

Christopher P. Vogt (PhD, Boston College) is Associate Professor of Theology and Religious Studies at St. John's University (NY).

Kate Ward (PhD, Boston College) is Assistant Professor of Theological Ethics at Marquette University.

Darlene Fozard Weaver (PhD, University of Chicago) is Associate Provost for Academic Affairs and Professor of Theology at Duquesne University.

Stephen B. Wilson (PhD, University of Notre Dame) is Associate Professor of Theology at Spring Hill College.

Tobias Winright (PhD, University of Notre Dame) is Associate Professor of Theological Ethics and Associate Professor of Health Care Ethics at Saint Louis University.

INDEX

CPSIA information can be obtained
at www.ICGtesting.com
Printed in the USA
LVHW051809240223
740359LV00005B/407

9 780567 700261